SPECIMENS

OF THE

PRE-SHAKSPEREAN

DRAMA

This is the silliest stuff that e'er
  I heard!
The best in this kind are but shadows;
  and the worst are no worse, if
  imagination amend them.

107036

SPECIMENS

OF THE

PRE-SHAKSPEREAN

DRAMA

Selected, Edited and with a Preface by

JOHN MATTHEWS MANLY

IN TWO VOLUMES

Volume I

DOVER PUBLICATIONS, INC., NEW YORK

This Dover edition, first published in 1967, is an unabridged and unaltered republication of the work originally published in 1897 by the Athenaeum Press, a division of Ginn and Company.

Library of Congress Catalog Card Number: 67-18096

Manufactured in the United States of America
Dover Publications, Inc.
180 Varick Street
New York, N. Y. 10014

TO

THE MEMORY

OF

Francis James Child

MY

MASTER AND FRIEND

PUBLISHER'S NOTE

IN compiling these plays Dr. Manly originally envisaged a third volume which would have included additional explanatory material and a glossary. This third volume was never published. The two volumes of the present Dover edition therefore constitute the entire work as published in 1897.

PREFACE.

SOME four years ago it became clear that the two volumes originally announced as the scope of this book would not suffice. In the first place, a good many minute but not insignificant facts regarding the history of almost every period of the drama had come to light, making necessary a somewhat longer historical sketch than was originally planned. In the second place, it seemed not merely desirable, but even imperative, to illustrate certain phases of the early drama which had in collections of a similar character either been neglected or not sharply defined against the apparently monotonous background of mediæval dramatic art. Thirdly, a somewhat different kind of annotation from that hitherto provided seemed worth attempting, if these volumes were to serve as an effective introduction to an art as spacious and as hospitable as the mediæval Church, and to render intelligible and vital to the student forms of art so different from ours in aim, in spirit, in method, in conventions, and in material accessories. A plan for a three-volume[1] edition was therefore submitted to the general editors of the series and to the publishers, who readily agreed to any change that would make the book more useful and interesting.

At the suggestion and request of some teachers who wish to use the book, the texts have been put together in two volumes, and the whole of the illustrative and explanatory material reserved for the third. It is hoped that this arrangement will make the volumes more convenient for use.

Preceding the main body of texts will be found certain documents which, though, for one reason or another, not entitled to a place among the main texts, are nevertheless indispensable in a book of this kind. Taken together, they represent various stages of the liturgical drama, without which the inter-relations of the

[1] See Publisher's Note.

Scripture cycles will be altogether misunderstood. The first two of them are dramatic tropes of the office of Easter. The third presents a later form of the same trope, very highly developed within itself, but free from the accretions by which this dramatic office grew into a cyclic drama of the life of Christ. The fourth has a twofold interest : it is, perhaps, the only extant example of a MS. prepared for the use of a single actor and containing only his part and his cues ; and it also affords an interesting glimpse of the vernacular liturgical drama as presented in the churches during the florescence of the craft-plays.

I should have been glad to include in this preliminary section an example of the Latin cycle developed by the combination of such separate plays as the Easter plays just mentioned ; but, although it can hardly be doubted that such cycles existed in England, no text of English origin has yet come to light. I have felt less regret at my inability to include a Latin miracle-play of English origin, because, although miracle-plays, in the strict sense of the term, were common in England from the time of their origin to the sixteenth century, there is a total lack of documents illustrating the stages of development of this species of play, the earliest extant English example being *The Play of the Sacrament*.

In the main body of texts, Part I is devoted entirely to the craft-cycles and their congeners. It will be observed that the arrangement adopted is that of the order of the subjects in cosmical history. For obvious reasons, an arrangement based on the order of composition of the cycles would have been sometimes impossible and sometimes misleading ; and in a book of this kind it seemed more desirable to present materials for giving the student some conception of the nature and effect of the cyclic drama as a whole than to try to illustrate the inter-relations of the cycles, — a line of inquiry which demands, indeed, a more elaborate equipment both of knowledge and of documents than seems to have been suspected even by some serious investigators. My choice of pageants was not, however, entirely determined by the wish to present an artificial cycle. It seemed desirable, in the first place, that all the extant cycles should be represented (the

Newcastle *Noah* play has been omitted on account both of its fragmentary character and its corrupt text), and, secondly, that the representative pageants should each have some specific claim to attention. Thus, the two Norwich pageants afford the only known example of a pageant and the substitute which later took its place. The Towneley *Noah*, with its characteristically English conception of Noah's wife, justifies itself. The Hegge *Noah* is included both as a contrast to this and as containing in the Lamech episode an English example of a farce, in the original sense of the word. Whether the Brome *Abraham and Isaac* belongs to a cycle or is an isolated play, it clearly could not be omitted. The Towneley *Isaac* and *Jacob* pageants are included, not only because, in ten Brink's opinion, they are the most primitive of all the pageants, but also because of their remarkable combination of intensity of conception and phrasing with a simplicity — not to say nakedness — of presentation. The Chester *Balaam* pageant affords, in the version here given, an unparalleled example of the transition stage of the *Processus Prophetarum*, and, although unknown to Sepet when he wrote *Les Prophètes du Christ*, confirms in an interesting manner his theory of the development and influence of the pseudo-Augustinian sermon. The question of the additions and excisions by which this version was reduced to the ordinary form must, of course, be reserved for the Notes. The Hegge *Salutation and Conception* contains the most striking example in English of that debate between the Four Daughters of God which played so commanding a part in mediæval religious thought. The Towneley *Secunda Pastorum* has so long been recognized as the best extant example of individualization of typical characters and of rapid transition from the farcical to the sublime that it is expected in every book of selections. In the Coventry Plays choice was limited to two ; *The Pageant of the Shearmen and Taylors* was selected because it illustrates so admirably the way in which several originally distinct pageants were, by force of circumstances, combined into one. A pageant dealing with the Resurrection seemed to be absolutely demanded by the importance of the Easter play in the development of the cyclic drama : the example here given from the York series will be found to contain reminiscences of the most primitive form of this strangely fated trope. A treble interest attaches to the Chester *Antichrist* pageant, here printed from a hitherto unpublished and practically unknown MS., — a prompt-book antedating by a century the other MSS. of this unique play. No English cycle would be complete without a pageant of the Judgment, that specifically English development ; and no one, I think, can fail to be impressed by the dignity and power of the specimen here presented from the York Plays.

In the artificial cycle thus constructed certain subjects find, of course, no representation ; but, for all that, the student can obtain from it a clear and not wholly inadequate conception of the craft-cycle as a form of the drama. That I have put together pageants from various sources can hardly, in view of the heterogeneous character of the cycles themselves and their complex inter-relations, be a serious objection. And any one who wishes to form an idea of the distinctive characteristics of the various cycles can, with the aid of the table of contents, easily bring together the specimens of each.

Part II contains two religious plays totally unconnected with the Scripture cycles. *The Conversion of St. Paul*, therefore, uninteresting as it is as dramatic literature, can hardly be neglected by the literary historian. *The Play of the Sacrament* not only exhibits the Banes in their real function of a preliminary announcement of the play, but also claims attention by its entirely and doubly unique character.

Part III affords illustrations of important phases of dramatic activity heretofore too little regarded by students. No one who reads the scanty records of dramatic performances in the fifteenth and sixteenth centuries, with their constantly recurring notices of May plays, Robin Hood plays, St. George plays, and sword plays and dances, will fail to welcome the three Robin Hood plays, or, in view of the clearly antique elements which form the basis of the St. George plays and *The Revesby Sword Play*, cavil at the introduction of texts so recently committed to writing.

Of the five Moralities forming Part IV little need be said. I wished to print one of the unpublished Macro plays ; Dr. Furnivall offered me *Mankind*, and I gladly accepted it. *Mundus et Infans* and *Hycke-scorner* complete the representation of this important class of Moralities. *Every-man* has so long and so justly figured as the most impressive play of its kind that its omission may need justification. Here I can only say briefly that, in spite of its enormous influence upon general European literature, this seemed justified by Logeman's proof that it is not of English composition, but a translation from the Dutch, by its accessibility in cheap and convenient form, and by the fact that the type to which it belongs is sufficiently represented by the plays just mentioned. *Wyt and Science* is not only one of the most perfect allegories extant, but also an excellent example of the Morality in the service, not of religious, but of secular education. *Nice Wanton* is, without doubt, the most vividly dramatic of all the Moralities.

Heywood's *Johan-Johan, Tyb and Syr Jhan* I had intended to print, as being the only one of his interludes possessed of real dramatic movement; but instructors will perhaps not regret to see instead their old favorite, *The Foure PP*.

Kynge Johan, Roister Doister, Gammer Gurton's Needle, Cambises, Gorboduc, Alexander and Campaspe, James IV, David and Bethsabe, and *The Spanish Tragedy* need no comment to render their significance clear. Marlowe finds no place here, because he is too important to be represented by anything less than his complete works, and they are now easily accessible.

Most of the texts here published have been either copied or collated anew for this book. Collations of *The Play of the Sacrament* and of *Mundus et Infans* were made under the supervision of Dr. T. K. Abbot, the Librarian of Trinity College, Dublin. The copy of Mr. Wynne's MS. of the *Antichrist* pageant was made by Mrs. Agnes Furnivall and revised by Dr. F. J. Furnivall. All other copies and collations were made by Mrs. Furnivall, whose accuracy has been confirmed by such tests as I have been able to apply.

In printing the texts I have aimed at fidelity to my originals. This ideal, however, did not seem to me impaired by the introduction of modern usage in regard to capitals and punctuation.

Upon the latter a good deal of care has been expended, and,
though I cannot hope to have avoided all errors, I do hope that
it will be found in general an aid to the reader and in ambiguous
passages an indication of the most probable interpretation. Attention has also been devoted to exhibiting the metrical structure of
these poems. The stanza-forms are various and in some cases
confused, but the effort to detach to the eye such parts as possess
definite stanzaic form seemed worth making, if only for the light
thus thrown upon the composite character of certain plays and
the artistic helplessness of the authors of certain others. In these
three matters I have introduced my own system without special
notification and have not recorded variations from it on the part
either of ancient scribes and printers or modern editors. Instances in which a different punctuation from mine indicates a
different interpretation will be discussed in the Notes in vol. III
when they seem of sufficient importance. In regard to the forms
of certain letters, it is perhaps inconsistent that I should strictly
reproduce ancient usage in regard to *i*, *u*, and *v*, and neglect it in
regard to *s*; but I have perhaps often failed to be consistent, and
in this particular matter I may plead precedent as well as the
fact that in textual cruces I have reproduced long *s* in the footnotes. Stage-directions not in the original are printed in brackets.
When I began to print I intended to credit to previous editors
those supplied by them, but the attempt was soon abandoned, as
it became clear that too much space would be required to set
forth that in this instance I had changed the place and in another
the form of a direction supplied by one of my predecessors.
Such a record could, moreover, have scarcely any other interest
than that of curiosity, whereas it is clearly a matter of great importance that the text should not be sophisticated by confusion of
ancient documents with modern conjectures.

With the modifications just noted, I may say in general that I
have made no unindicated alterations in the texts. When the
treatment of a text varies in any particular from that adopted in
general, a distinct account of such difference is given in the headnote preceding the play; and I believe it will always be found
possible for the textual critic to learn from text and footnotes
exactly the appearance of the original. Expanded contractions

are, of course, indicated by italics. It will be observed that in the early plays I have recorded with scrupulous minuteness the readings of other editions. In the later texts this seemed both unnecessary and undesirable; but I have aimed to omit no variant which, the date of the text being considered, could have even the slightest significance. On the earlier texts a large number of conjectural emendations have been printed in various publications. These I have, for the sake of convenience and completeness, attempted to collect and record. The later plays have, fortunately for the editor, not been subjected to so much ingenuity.

A warning must be issued in regard to the footnotes; it is never safe to interpret the symbols attached to variants and emendations without reference to the headnote of the particular play. For instance, in some plays H. means Halliwell, in others Holthausen; but perhaps the greatest danger of confusion resides in the symbol K., which in several plays marks the textual notes of Professor Kölbing, and in one the readings of an edition by the printer John Kyng, but never the emendations of Professor Kittredge, whose suggestions, as being unpublished and communicated directly to me, are always distinguished by his unabbreviated surname.

A word or two in regard to the contents of vol. III seem necessary.[1] It will contain an Introduction, with certain appendices, a body of Notes, and a Glossary. The Introduction will trace the history of the drama on the Continent as well as in England from the beginning of the tenth century to the formation of the Scripture cycles, and then in England alone from that time to the end of the sixteenth century. In the appendices will be given a bibliography and lists of places in England at which performances are known to have occurred before the Age of Elizabeth, and of persons and places possessing companies of players, with the nearest ascertainable dates of recorded performances. A map illustrating the distribution of plays in England will accompany the list of performances.

The Notes will give information as to date, authorship, place and mode of presentation, character of costumes, etc., when such

[1]See Publisher's Note.

information is obtainable. In the case of plays with international affiliations the more important parallels and congeners will be pointed out. Effort will also be made to aid the reader in involved or obscure passages by explanation and paraphrase, and to emphasize the dramatic elements as distinct from the literary. Elaborate linguistic annotation seems inappropriate in a book intended to aid the study of a form of art, and consequently the linguistic notes will be confined to passages of obscure or ambiguous signification. Much of the linguistic information usually given in notes will be found in the Glossary.

The Glossary will aim to meet the needs of the intelligent student who has no training in the older forms of English. It will therefore include all words obsolete as to either form or meaning and words which by their strange spelling are likely to elude the ingenious ; but it will not include words which ought, even in their strange spelling, to be recognizable by any intelligent Englishman.

The material for vol. III has, with the exception of that published recently, been in hand since the summer of 1893. I therefore hope that the appearance of that volume need not be postponed much longer.

The list of persons to whom my thanks are due is a long one. Would that I might give them a pleasure equal to that with which I remember their services and here record their names!

First, as to texts. W. R. M. Wynne, Esq., of Peniarth, Wales, not only allowed me to have copies made of two of his most interesting MSS., but, with a kindness which I cannot adequately acknowledge, himself brought them from Peniarth to London for the use of my copyist, and allowed them to remain in the British Museum for a longer time than it is pleasant to recall. Dr. F. J. Furnivall, of London, with his accustomed liberality, allowed me to have a copy made of his copy of *Mankind*, and sent me advance sheets of the Towneley Plays. Miss Lucy Toulmin Smith, of Oxford, with the generosity of a scholar, was willing that I should make use of the texts so well edited by her, and the Delegates of the Clarendon Press kindly allowed me to reprint two pageants from her edition of the York Plays.

Thanks for the loan of books are due to the Rev. Father Shandelle, S. J., of St. Joseph's School, Providence; to W. E. Foster, Esq., the obliging Librarian of the Public Library, Providence; and, most of all, to T. J. Kiernan, Esq., Superintendent of Circulation in the Harvard College Library, whose unfailing kindness and matchless knowledge of the resources of his library are gratefully remembered by so many scholars.

For helpful answers to inquiries addressed to them I have to thank Dr. John Young, Keeper of the Hunterian Museum, Glasgow, and the Rev. Canon Fowler and the Rev. Canon Wordsworth, of Lincoln.

Professor Barrett Wendell, of Harvard University, nearly ten years ago first awakened my interest in the subject of these volumes. In the Introduction he will doubtless recognize, as his own, ideas which, after the lapse of so long a time, I am unable to credit to their rightful owner. For inspiration, however, I should thank most of all, were he still alive, my lamented teacher and friend, to whom I had hoped to offer these volumes, but whose friendship and aid I can now record only in a dedication to his memory.

To Professor J. F. Jameson, of Brown University, and Professor A. R. Marsh, of Harvard, I am grateful for interest in my work and for notification of interesting materials which would otherwise have escaped me. Professor E. S. Sheldon, of Harvard, has been tireless in answering questions in the field of Old French and in helping me through many a dark and difficult passage. To Professor G. L. Kittredge, of Harvard, I am indebted for aid so various that space fails me not only to record the instances, but even to enumerate the kinds. With him, from the very beginning of my work, I have discussed theories and facts of all degrees of importance; again and again I have received from him notes of books and documents that had escaped my observation; and more recently he has done me the inestimable service of reading with me all the proofs of vol. I and aiding me in the establishment and punctuation of the text. Some of his aid I have been able to point out specifically, but much of it has been such as cannot be recorded.

For such errors as time and criticism may disclose I, of course, am alone responsible. I have striven to make them few.

In conclusion, I express the hope that these volumes may really serve the purpose for which they were planned, — that of helping the student to follow the fortunes of the modern drama through its strange and interesting nonage, to come into sympathy with the aims and methods of the known and nameless artists whose work is here presented, and to form some conception of the vast amount of dramatic activity and the widespread dramatic interest which made possible the career of Shakspere. Such results cannot be attained by him who regards even the poorest of these plays as a mere butt for nineteenth-century ridicule, or who forgets that the old German playwright touched the root of the whole matter when he said in regard to his play : " Das wässen vn̄ das läben diss vnd andren spilen stodt nit alleyn in̄ sprüchen, sonder vyl meer im̄ wässen, würcken vnd gbärden."

JOHN MATTHEWS MANLY.

BARNSTABLE, Aug. 30, 1897.

CONTENTS OF VOL. I.

Part II.

Part III.

Part IV.

Part V.

Part VI.

LITURGICAL TEXTS.

DRAMATIC TROPES.

These two dramatic tropes of the service of Easter are of interest not only because they are among the earliest known texts of the germ from which developed the great mediæval Easter cycle, but also because they show that before the Norman Conquest the development of the drama in England had begun.

The first is printed from the *Regularis Concordia Monachorum*, ascribed to Dunstan or, with more probability, to Ethelwold, and usually assigned to the year 967 (on both these points, see vol. III).[1a] The text is, of course, based upon W. S. Logeman's edition, *Anglia*, XIII, 426-428, in preference to any of the older editions; but the contractions and word-division of the original are not indicated. In this version, it will be observed, the trope occurs in the nocturnal service, immediately after the third responsory.

The second is found in two tropers originally belonging to Winchester Cathedral, the earlier assigned to the years 979-1016 (and probably before Oct. 20, 980), the later to the middle of the eleventh century. In the text I follow " The Winchester Troper," edited by W. H. Frere for the Henry Bradshaw Society, London, 1894; but I have not followed Frere (p. 17) in putting in brackets words found in the earlier version but not in the later. In the earlier MS. this trope precedes the Benedictio cerei, etc., of Easter Eve, but, for all that, it appears to be here, as, in Gautier's opinion, it is in origin, a trope of the Introit of the Mass.

I.

Dum tertia recitatur lectio, quatuor fratres induant se, quorum unus alba[1] indutus ac si ad aliud agendum ingrediatur, atque latenter sepulchri locum adeat, ibique manu tenens palmam, quietus sedeat. Dumque tertium percelebratur responsorium, residui tres succedant, omnes quidem cappis induti, turribula cum incenso[2] manibus gestantes ac pedetemptim ad similitudinem querentium quid, ueniant ante locum sepulchri. Aguntur enim hec ad imitationem angeli sedentis in monumento atque mulierum cum aromatibus uenientium ut ungerent corpus Ihesu. Cum ergo ille residens tres uelut erraneos ac aliquid querentes uiderit sibi adproximare, incipiat mediocri uoce dulcisono cantare :

Quem queritis [in sepulchro, o Christicole] ?[3]

[1] MS. abba.   [2] Logeman, incensu.
[3] *All words in brackets are supplied from other versions of the play.*
[1a] See Publisher's Note.

Quo decantato fine tenus, respondeant hi tres uno ore:

> Ihesu[m] Nazarenum [crucifixum, o celicola].

Quibus ille:

> Non est hic; surrexit, sicut predixerat:
> Ite, nuntiate quia surrexit a mortuis.

Cuius iussionis[1] uoce uertant se illi tres ad chorum dicentes:

> Alleluia! resurrexit Dominus!

Dicto hoc, rursus ille residens, uelut reuocans illos dicat antiphonam:

> Uenite, et uidete locum [ubi positus erat Dominus, alleluia! alleluia!]

Hec uero dicens surgat, et erigat uelum, ostendatque eis locum cruce nudatum, sed tantum linteamina posita quibus crux inuoluta erat. Quo uiso, deponant turribula que gestauerunt in eodem sepulchro, sumantque linteum et extendant contra clerum, ac, ueluti ostendentes quod surrexerit Dominus et iam non sit illo inuolutus, hanc canant antiphonam:

> Surrexit Dominus de sepulchro,
> [Qui pro nobis pependit in ligno].

Superponantque linteum altari. Finita antiphona, Prior congaudens pro triumpho Regis nostri, quod, deuicta morte, surrexit, incipiat hymnum:

> Te, Deum, laudamus.

Quo incepto, una pulsantur omnia signa; post cuius finem dicat sacerdos versum:

> In resurrectione tua, Christe,

uerbo tenus, et initiet matutinas dicens:

> Deus, in adiutorium meum intende!

---

[1] MS. iussimus; Dugdale, *Monasticon Angl.*, missionis.

II.

ANGELICA DE CHRISTI RESURRECTIONE.

Quem queritis in sepulchro, [o] Christicole?

Sanctarum mulierum responsio:

Ihesum Nazarenum crucifixum, o caelicola![1]

Angelice uocis consolatio:

Non est hic, surrexit sicut praedixerat,
Ite, nuntiate quia surrexit, dicentes :

Sanctarum mulierum ad omnem clerum modulatio:

Alleluia ! Resurrexit Dominus hodie,
Leo fortis, Christus filius Dei ! Deo gratias dicite, eia!

Dicat angelus:

Uenite et uidete locum ubi positus erat Dominus, alleluia!
alleluia!

Iterum dicat angelus:

Cito euntes dicite discipulis quia surrexit Dominus, alleluia!
alleluia!

Mulieres[2] una uoce canant iubilantes:

Surrexit Dominus de sepulchro,
Qui pro nobis pependit in ligno, alleluia!

---

[1] *The later MS. has* celicole.   [2] Frere *has* mulieri.

EASTER DRAMATIC OFFICE.

This version of the *Officium Sepulchri* is taken from a fourteenth-century MS. Processional of the Church of St. John the Evangelist, Dublin. The text is based upon the facsimile given by Frere, "The Winchester Troper," plate 26[b]. The four pages reproduced by Frere unfortunately do not contain the very beginning of the office. I have therefore supplied a few lines in brackets, mainly on the basis of a very similar Orléans version óf the thirteenth century (Lange, "Die lateinischen Osterfeiern," München, 1887, pp. 160 ff.). In a few instances I have called attention to deviations from the forms found in other service-books, but in general it seemed best to print the text without change or remark, startling as it sometimes is.

The music of the office is written on the unbarred four-line staff, and is reproduced very clearly in Frere's facsimile. I may add here that plate 26[a] in Frere's book is a facsimile of the later MS. of the Winchester Easter trope given above, the musical notation of which is in neumes.

At the top of the first of the four pages of the facsimile is written, not in the bookhand of the rest, but in cursive script: "Condimentis aromatum vnguentes corpus *sanctissimum* quo *pre*ciosa. This is a part of the hymn, "Heu! pius pastor occiditur," and was probably written here by some one who remembered the hymn as a whole.

[Ad faciendam similitudinem Domini sepulcri primum procedant tres fratres induti dalmaticis][1] sericis [2] capitib*us* uelatis quasi tres Marie querentes *Christu*m, si*n*gule portantes pixidem in manib*us* q*ua*si aromatib*us*, qua*rum* prima ad ingressu*m* chori usque sepulcru*m* procedat et [3] quasi lamentando dicat:

> Heu! pius pastor occiditur,[4]
> Quem nulla culpa infecit:
> O mors lugenda!

[1] *Supplied by me.*
[2] MS. *seems to have* tericis *or* cericis.
[3] MS. p*er*.
[4] *The* Orléans *version has* occidit; *but the musical notation makes it clear that* occiditur *is the right reading here.*

Factoque modico interuallo, intret [1] secunda Maria simili modo et dicat:

> Heu! nequam gens Iudaica,
> Quam dira frendet [2] uesania,
> Plebs execranda!

Deinde iij Maria consimili modo:

> Heu! uerus doctor [3] obijt,
> Qui uitam functis [4] contulit:
> O res plangenda!

Ad huc paululum procedendo prima Maria dicat hoc modo:

> Heu! misere cur contingit
> Uidere mortem Saluatoris?

Deinde secund[a] Maria:

> Heu! Consolacio nostra,
> Ut quid mortem sustinuit!

Deinde tercia Maria:

> Heu! Redempcio nostra,
> Ut quid taliter agere uoluit!

Tunc se coniungant et procedant ad gradum chori ante altare dicentes:

> Iam, iam, ecce,[5] iam properemus ad tumulum
> Ungentes Dilecti corpus sanctissimum!

Tunc secunda Maria dicat per se:

> Nardi uetet commixtio,
> Ne putrescat in tumulo
> Caro beata!

---

[1] MS. intre t (n *erased, but still visible*).
[2] Orléans frendens.
[3] Orléans *has* pastor *here as well as above.*
[4] MS. *clearly has* functis; Orléans *has* sanctis.
[5] MS. effe.

Deinde tercia Maria:

> Sed nequimus hoc patrare [1] sine adiutorio.
> Quisnam saxum hoc reuoluit a monumenti ostio?

Facto interuallo, angelus nixus sepulcrum appariat eis et dicat hoc modo:

> Quem queritis ad sepulcrum,[2] o Cristicole?

Deinde respondeant tres Marie simul:

> Ihesum Nazarenum crucifixum, o celicola!

Tunc angelus dicat sic:

> Surrexit, non est hic, sicut dixit;
> Uenite et uidete locum ubi positus fuerat.

Deinde predicte Marie sepulcrum intrent inclinantes se et prospicientes undique intra sepulcrum, alta uoce quasi gaudendo et admirantes et parum a sepulcro recedentes dicant simul:

> Alleluya! resurrexit Dominus!
> Alleluya! resurrexit Dominus hodie!
> Resurrexit potens, fortis, *Christus*, Filius Dei!

Deinde angelus ad eas dicens:

> Et euntes dicite discipulis eius et Petro quia surrexit.

In qua reuertant ad angelum quasi mandatum suum ad implendum parate dicentes simul:

> Eya! pergamus propere
> Mandatum hoc perficere!

Interim ueniant ad ingressum chori due persone nude pedes sub personis apostolorum Iohannis et Petri indute albis sine paruris cum tunicis, quarum Iohannes amictus tunica alba palmam in manu gestans, Petrus uero rubea tunica indutus claues in

---

[1] *Most other versions of this line have* patere, *but* patrare *seems preferable.*
[2] *Usually* in sepulcro.

manu deferens; *et* predicte mulieres de sepulcro reuertentes *et* quasi de choro simul exeuntes, dicat prima Maria sequenciam:

> Victime paschali laudes
> Immolant *Christ*iani.

Secunda Maria:

> Agnus redemit oues:
> *Christus* innocens Patri
> Reconsiliauit peccatores.

Tercia Maria di*cat*:

> Mors et uita duello
> Confl[i]xere [1] mirando:
> Dux uite mortuus [2]
> Regnat uiuus.

Tunc obuiantes eis in medio chori predicti discipuli, interrogantes simul dicant:

> Dic nobis, Maria,
> Quid uidisti in uia?

Tunc prima Maria respondeat quasi monstrando:

> Sepulcrum *Christ*i uiuentis,
> Et gloriam uidi resurgentis.

Tunc ij Maria respondeat quasi monstrando:

> Angelicos testes,
> Sudarium et uestes.

Tercia Maria respondeat:

> Surrexit *Christus*, spes nostra,
> Precedet uos in Galileam.

Et sic procedant [3] simul ad ostium chori; *et* interim currant duo ad monumentum; uerumptamen ille discipulus quem diligebat Ihesus uenit prior ad monumentum, iuxta euangelium: " Curre-

---

[1] *Every trace of* i *has disappeared.*
[2] MS. mortuis.
[3] MS. precedant.

bant au*tem* duo sim*ul et* ille alius discipulus [1] p*r*ecucurrit cicius Petro *et* uenit p*r*ior ad monume*n*tu*m*, non ta*me*n introiuit." Uidentes discipuli sepulcru*m* uacuu*m et* uerbis Marie credentes reue*rta*n*t se ad chorum dicentes hoc modo :

> Credendum est magis soli Marie ueraci
> Q*uam* Iudeo*rum* turbe fallaci !

Tunc audito *Christ*i resurreccione, chorus p*r*osequat*ur* alta uoce quasi gaude*n*tes *et* exultantes s*ic* dica*n*t :

> Scimus *Christu*m surrexisse
> A mortuis uere.
> Tu nobis, uictor Rex, miserere !

Qua finita,[2] executor officii incipiat :

> Te, Deum, laudamus.

----

[1] MS. discipulis.　　　　　　[2] *Possibly* facta.

FRAGMENTS OF LITURGICAL PLAYS.

The following document was published in *The Academy*, January 11, 1890, pp. 27 ff., by the Rev. Professor W. W. Skeat. The MS., belonging to the library of Shrewsbury School, consists of forty-two leaves — five quires of eight leaves (one leaf cut out) and one quire of three leaves. The first thirty-six leaves contain Latin anthems; the plays begin on leaf 38. Dr. Skeat assigns the MS. to the beginning of the fifteenth century.

The claim of these fragments upon the attention of scholars is even greater than Dr. Skeat declared it to be. We have here, not merely fragments of a hitherto unrepresented set of plays, but the only known example of a class of plays, the existence of which is otherwise established, but the nature of which, and their relations to the craft-cycles, could hardly be set forth with certainty but for the discovery of this document. It is, indeed, a fragment, not, as Dr. Skeat suggests, of the lost Beverley cycle, or any similar collection, but of a series of plays performed in a church on the days and in the service celebrating the events of which the plays treat. This is clearly established by the phraseology of the Latin with which the second and third plays begin, — the beginning of the first is, as will be seen, missing.

Dr. Skeat points out the fact that many of the Latin passages are provided with a musical notation and that some of them are from the Gospels. That they are noted for singing arises from their being in reality parts of the troped service of the Church for the days to which the plays belong. Details as to this will be given in the Notes, in vol. III; here let it suffice to direct attention to this interesting illustration of the manner in which, in the later stages of the liturgical drama, the liturgical texts appear side by side with the vernacular additions.[1]

As Dr. Skeat has shown, we have here a MS. prepared for the use of a single actor, and containing only his part and his cues. In order to make the fragments intelligible, I have, where it seemed worth while, supplied, on the basis of similar plays, information as to the action and speeches omitted.

[1] See Publisher's Note.

I.

[OFFICIUM PASTORUM.]¹

Pastores erant in regione eadem uigilantes et custodientes
gregem suum.   Et ecce angelus Domini astitit iuxta
illos et timuerunt timore magno.²

[*The Star appears and the Angels sing.*]

[II. PASTOR.]³ We, Tib!
III. PASTOR.   Telle on!

[II. PASTOR.] . . . . . . *th*e nyght.

III. PASTOR.   Brether, what may *th*is be,
 *Th*us bright to man *and* best?   7

[II. PASTOR.] . . . . . . at hand.
 III. PASTOR.   Whi say ȝe so?
[II. PASTOR.] . . . . . . warand.   10

III. PASTOR.   Suche siȝt was neu*er* sene
 Before in our*e* Iewery ;
Su*m* merueles wil hit mene
 *Th*at mu*n* be her*e* in hy.   14

[II. PASTOR.] . . . . . . a sang.⁴

---

¹ MS. *contains no heading. In the corresponding* York play, *to the*
relations of which with this Dr. Skeat *has called attention, each of the*
three shepherds speaks a stanza of twelve lines concerning the Messianic
prophecies before the point at which this play begins is reached. Possibly
this play lacks at the beginning, not only a heading similar to those of the
other two plays of this MS., *but also a speech by the Third Shepherd ; but it*
may be that, in view of the nature of the church service, the introductory
speeches were regarded as unnecessary, and that we have the beginning of
the play.   ² *Noted for voices.*

³ *Here and throughout the three plays the speaker's name in brackets is*
supplied by Dr. Skeat. *Whether sometimes the cue word does not belong to*
another actor is an idle question.

⁴ *In* York *the First and Second Shepherds declare that they* " can synge
itt alls wele as he " ; *to which the Third Shepherd's reply is similar to that*
here.

III. PASTOR.   ӡe lye, bothe, by *th*is liӡt,
    And raues as recheles royes![1]
Hit was an angel briӡt
    *Tha*t made *th*is nobull*e* noyes.   19

[II. PASTOR.]   . . . . . .   of p*r*ophecy.

III. PASTOR.   He said a barn schuld be
    In *th*e burgh of Bedlem born ;
And of *th*is, my*n*nes me,
    Our*e* fadres fond be-forn.   24

[II. PASTOR.]   . . . . . .   Iew*us* kyng.

III. PASTOR.   Now may we se *th*e same
    Eue*n* in our*e* pase puruayed ;
*Th*e angel nemed his name, —
    "Crist, Saueo*ur*," he saied.   29

[II. PASTOR.]   . . . . . .   not raue.

III. PASTOR.   ӡone brightnes wil vs bring
    Vnto *tha*t blisful boure ;
For solace schal we syng
    To seke our*e* Saueo*ur*.   34

*Transeam*us *us*que *Bethelem, et uideamus hoc verbu*m *q*uod
    factum est, *q*uod *fecit Dominus* et *ostendit nobis*.[2]

[They follow the Star.]

[II. PASTOR.]   . . . . . .   to knawe.

III. PASTOR.   For no-*th*ing thar vs drede,
    But thank God of all*e* gode ;
*Th*is light eu*er* wil vs lede
    To fynde *tha*t frely fode.   41

[1] *In this part of* York, *which is in a different stanza from the rest of the
play, the resemblances to our fragment extend only to the main course of
the thought and an occasional phrase.*
[2] *Noted for voices.*

[They enter the stable and adore the Child.]

[II. PASTOR.   Now wat ȝe what] [1] I mene.

III. PASTOR.   A! loke to me, my Lord der*e*,[2]
Alle if I put me noght in pr*e*se !
To suche a pr*i*nce wi*th*out[en] [3] per*e*
Haue I no pr*e*sand *tha*t may plese.
But lo! a horn-spone haue I her*e*
   *Tha*t may herbar an hundrith pese :
*Th*is gift I gif *th*e wi*th* gode cher*e*, —
   Suche dayntese wil do no disese.
      Far*e*-wele now, swete swayn,
         God graunt *th*e lifyng lang !
      [I. PASTOR.   And go we hame agayn,
         And mak mirth as we gang !] [4]   54

---

[1] *After reaching Bethlehem the shepherds in* York *adore the Child, each speaking one stanza of twelve lines.   That of the Third Shepherd is identical with his speech here and the speeches of the others are in the same stanza-form.*   Dr. Skeat *is, therefore, right in inferring that the words,* I mene, *which end the speech of the Second Shepherd in both plays, point to a practical identity of those speeches.*

[2] *Before this line in* MS. *there is a star referring to the words:* Salua-torem, Christum, Dominum, infantem pannis inuolutu*m*, secundu*m* sermo-nem angelicam (*sic*).   *These words are in a later hand.   They belong to a dramatic trope (of Christmas) which will be given in full in the discussion of the origins of the drama in the Introduction.*

[3] *Supplied by* Skeat.

[4] Dr. Skeat *says:* "*I supply these two lines from the* York Mysteries, *and assign them to the First Shepherd instead of to the Third, because the* MS. *has here two blank lines, showing that the Third Shepherd did not speak them.*"

II.

[OFFICIUM RESURRECTIONIS.] [1]

Hic incipit Officium Resurreccionis in die Pasche.

[*Enter the three Marys on their way to the Sepulchre.*]

III. MARIA.[2]   *Heu! Redemcio Israel,*
            Ut quid mortem sustinuit! [3]

[II. MARIA.] . . . . . . payne.

III. MARIA.   Allas! he *that* me*n* wend schuld by
        All*e* Israel, bothe knyght *and* knaue,
    Why suffred he so forto dy,
        Sithe he may all*e* sekenes saue?
            Heu! cur ligno fixus clauis
            Fuit doctor tam suauis?
            Heu! cur fuit ille natus
            Qui perfodit eius latus?   11

[II. MARIA.] . . . . . . is oght.

III. MARIA.   Allas, *tha*t we suche bale schuld bide
        *Th*at sodayn sight so forto see,
    *Th*e best techer in world wide
        W*ith* nayles be tacched to a tre!
    Allas, *tha*t eu*er* so schuld be-tyde,
        Or *tha*t so bold mo*n* born schuld be
    For to assay our*e* Saueo*ur* side
        And open hit with-oute pite!   20

---

1 *The corresponding* York play *is printed below,* pp. 153 ff. *It is in a*
different metre. The character of the York play *on the appearance of*
Christ to Magdalen suggests that it was once connected with a play very
similar to this, especially when the nature of the corresponding Towneley
play *is considered.*

2 *In* MS. *the name is written* iij[a] m .

3 *What the others probably said may be seen above,* p. xxiii.

[ALL THREE.][1] *Iam, iam, ecce, iam properemus ad tumu-*
lum,
    Vngentes Dilecti corpus sanctissimum ! [2]

      Et appropiantes sepulcro cantent:

[ALL THREE.]   *O Deus, quis reuoluet nobis lapidem*
    Ab hostio monumenti? [2]   24

[II. MARIA.] . . . . . . him leid.

III. MARIA.   He *th*at *th*us kyndely vs has kend
    Vn-to *th*e hole wher*e* he was hid,
Su*m* socour*e* sone he wil vs send,
    At help to lift away *th*is lid.   29

    [*They find the stone rolled away, and learn from the angels that Christ*
    is risen.]

III. MARIA.   Alleluya schal be our*e* song,
    Sithe*n* C*r*ist, our*e* Lord, by angell*us* steuen,
Schew*us* hi*m* as mon her*e* vs among
    And is Goddis Son, heghest i*n* heue*n*.   33

    [*The Marys return and announce the Resurrection to the disciples.*][3]

[II. MARIA.] . . . . . . was gon.

[CHORUS.   *Dic nobis, Maria,*
             Quid uidisti in uia?
I. MARIA.   *Sepulcrum Christi uiuentis,*
             Et gloriam uidi resurgentis.
II. MARIA.   *Angelicos testes,*
             Sudarium et uestes.
III. MARIA.]   *Surrexit Christus, spes n*ostra,
             *Precedet vos i*n *Galilea*m *!* [4]   42

---

[1] *Cf.* p. xxiii, *above.*
[2] *Noted for voices.*
[3] *A red line here in* MS.
[4] Skeat *assigns these two lines to the angel (he speaks of only one angel)*;
but there is no reason why the words of the angels should appear in this
MS. *I have supplied in brackets all the words from* CHORUS *to* III.
MARIA *to sustain my view that the two lines belong to the Third Mary;*
cf. p. xxv, *above.*

III. MARIA.   Crist is rysen, wittenes we [1]
   By tokenes *tha*t we haue sen *th*is morn!
Our*e* hope, our*e* help, our*e* hele, is he,
   And hase bene best, sithe we wer*e* born!
Yf we wil seke hi*m* for to se,
   Lettes noght *th*is lesson be for-lorn:
"But gose eue*n* vn-to Galilee;
   There schal ȝe fynd hi*m* ȝow beforn!"[2]   50

III.

[OFFICIUM PEREGRINORUM.] [3]

Feria secunda *in ebdo*mada *Pasche discipuli* i*nsimul cante*n*t* :

[CHORUS.] [4] Infidelis incursum populi
           Fugiamus, Ihesu [5] discipuli!
           Suspenderu*n*t Ihesum patibulo;
           Nulli p*ar*cent eius discipulo.[6]   4

[The disciples depart; Luke and Cleophas go together.]

[LUKE.] [7] . . . . . . fast to fle.

[CLEOPHAS.] But if we fle, *th*ai wil vs fang,
   And ful felly *th*ai wil vs flay;[8]
Agayn to Emause wil we gang,
   And fonde to get *th*e gaynest way.

---

[1] *I suppose this speech to have been preceded by similar ones from the other two Marys, but no cue is given in* MS.

[2] *After this a red line in* MS.

[3] Skeat *supplies as the heading:* The Two Disciples going to Emmaus.

[4] *The actor was one of this Chorus, or their words would not appear here.*

[5] MS. ihesum; *corr. by* Skeat.

[6] *Noted for voices. A red line after this verse.*

[7] *This play does not give the name of either speaker.* Skeat *points out that the one who appears later among the apostles is probably Cleophas; the other,* Luke.

[8] *Qy.* slay.

And make i*n* mynd eu*er* vs amang
    Of our*e* gode Maister, as we may,
How he was put to paynes strang, —
    On *th*at he tristed con hi*m* be-tray![1]   13

[Jesus enters and talks with them.][2]

[JESUS.] . . . . . but agayn.

[CLEOPHAS.] By wy*m*men wordis wele wit may **we**
    Christ is risen vp in gode aray;
For to our*e*-self *th*e sothe say[d][3] he,
    Whe*r*e we went in *th*is world away,
*Tha*t he schuld dye *and* doluen be,
    And rise fro *th*e dethe *th*e thrid day.
And *tha*t we my3t *tha*t si3t now se,
    He wisse vs, Lord, as he wele may!   22

[JESUS?] . . . . . resou*n* ri3t.

[CLEOPHAS.][4] *Et quoni*am *t*radideru*n*t eu*m summi sacer-
    dotes* et *principes n*ostri i*n* da*m*p*n*acione[*m*][3] *mortis* et
    *crucifixeru*n*t eu*m.

Right is *tha*t we reherce by raw
    *Th*e maters *tha*t we may on mene,
How p*r*estis *and* princes of our*e* lawe
    Ful tenely toke hi*m* hom be-twen,
And dampned hi*m*, wi*th*-oute*n* awe,
    For to be dede w*ith* dole,[5] be-dene;
*Th*ai crucified him, wele we kñaw,
    At Caluary, w*ith* caris kene.   34

---

[1] *After this verse a red line in* MS. *Probably, as* Skeat *suggests, Jesus enters here.*

[2] *This conversation in all the plays on this subject follows very closely Luke xxiv, 17-21.*   [3] *Supplied by* Skeat.

[4] Skeat *does not assign the Latin to any one; he puts* CLEOPHAS *opposite the first line of the English which follows.*

[5] Skeat *has* dele.

[CLEOPHAS AND LUKE.][1] *Dixerunt eciam se visionem ange-*
lorum vidisse, qui dicunt eum viuere.

[LUKE.] . . . . . . wraist.

[CLEOPHAS.]   The wymmen gret, for he was gon ;
   But ȝet thai told of meruales mo :
Thai saw angellus stondyng on the ston,
   And sayn how he was farne hom fro.
Sithen of oures went ful gode wone
   To se that siȝt, and said right so.
Herfore we murne and makis this mon ;
   Now wot thou wele of alle oure wo.   45

[LUKE?][2] . . . . . . in pese.

[CLEOPHAS AND LUKE.][3] *Mane nobiscum, quoniam ad-*
uesperascit et inclinata est iam dies.   Alleluya![4]

[*They approach Emmaus.*]

[JESUS.] . . . . . . wight.

[CLEOPHAS.][5]   Amend oure mournyng, maister dere,
   And fond oure freylnes for to felle!
Herk, brother ! help to hold him here,
   Ful nobel talis wil he vs telle!   53

[LUKE.] . . . . . . lent
[CLEOPHAS.]   And gode wyne schal vs wont non,
   For ther-to schal I take entent.

---

[1] Skeat *does not indicate the speaker ; the cue following he assigns to
Jesus. It seems unlikely that a speech by Jesus existed between this Latin
and the English in which Cleophas gives the substance of it. I therefore
suppose both disciples to have recited the Latin and then each to have given,
as was usual, the sense of it, each emphasizing different features.*

[2] *It is impossible to decide whether to assign this to Luke or to Jesus.*

[3] *Not indicated by* Skeat.

[4] *Noted for voices.*

[5] *Omitted by* Skeat.

[Jesus breaks the bread, and, after giving it to them, vanishes.]

[LUKE.] . . . . . . he went.   57

[CLEOPHAS.]   Went he is, *and* we ne wot how,
    For her*e* is noght left in his sted! [1]
Allas! wher*e* wer*e* our*e* wittis now?
    With wo now walk we, wil of red!
        [LUKE.] . . . . . . [he brak] [2] our*e* bred.   62

[CLEOPHAS.]   Our*e* bred he brak *and* blessed hit;
    On mold wer*e* neu*er* so mased me*n*,
Whe*n* *tha*t we saw hi*m* by vs sit,
    *Tha*t we couthe noght consayue hi*m* *the*n.   66

[LUKE.] . . . . . . ay.

[Cleophas and Luke return to the other disciples, singing :]

[CLEOPHAS AND LUKE.]   *Quid agam*us *uel dicam*us,
                        *Ignorantes quo eam*us,
                        *Qu*i *Doctorem sciencie*
                        Et patrem consolacionis
                        Amisimus? [3]   72

[LUKE.] . . . . . . gode state

[CLEOPHAS.]   We schal hom tell*e*, w*it*h-oute*n* trayn,
    Bothe word *and* werk, how [that] hit was,
I se hom sitt samyn i*n* a playn.
    Forthe in apert dar I not pas!   77

[They join the other disciples.] [4]

    [LUKE?] . . . . . . *and* wife.
[CLEOPHAS.]   We saw hi*m* holl*e*, hide *and* hewe;
    *Ther*fore be still, *and* stint ʒoure strife!

---

1 MS. stid; *corr. by* Skeat.
2 *Supplied by* Skeat.
3 *Noted for voices.*
4 *A red line here in* MS. Skeat *interprets it as I do.*

*Tha*t hit was Crist ful wele we knewe,
He cutt our*e* bred wit*h*-oute*n* knyfe.   82

[*All the disciples sing* :]

[CHORUS.]   *Gloria tibi, Domine,*
             Qui surrexisti a mortuis,
             *Cu*m *Pat*re et *Sancto Spiritu,*
             In sempiterna secula; Amen! [1]

[*Enter St. Thomas, who refuses to believe until convinced by the appearance of Christ.*] [2]

[CHORUS.]   *Frater Thoma, causa tristicie*
             Nobis tulit summa leticie!

[*Explicit.*]

[1] *Noted for voices.*
[2] Skeat *thinks a new play begins here; but the Incredulity of St. Thomas is not celebrated on Easter Monday.*

PART I.

NORWICH WHITSUN PLAYS.

These two versions of the pageant of the Grocers of Norwich are reprinted from : "Norwich Pageants. The Grocers' Play. From a MS. in the possession of Robt. Fitch, Esq., F.G.S. [Privately printed.] Norwich, 1856." The first of them was composed before June 16, 1533 ; the other, in 1565.

I.

The Story of *the*[1] Creacion[2] of Eve, with *the* Expellyng of Adam *and* Eve out of Paradyce.

PATER. *Ego principiu*m, *Alpha* et ω, *in altissimis habito ;*
  In *the* hevenly empery I am resydent.
Yt ys not semely for man, *sine adjutorio*,
  To be allone, nor very convenyent.
  I have plantyd an orcheyard most congruent
For hym to kepe *and* to tylle, by contemplac*i*on.
Let us make an adjutory of our formac*i*on   7

To hys symylatude, lyke in plasmac*i*on.
  In-to Paradyce I wyll nowe descende
W*ith* my mynysters angelicall of our creac*i*on
  To assyst us in ow*er* worke *tha*t we intende,
  A slepe in-to man be soporac*i*on to sende.
A ribbe out of man*n*ys syde I do here take ;
  Bothe flesche *and* bone I do thys creatur blysse ;
And a woman I fourme, to be his make,
  Semblable to man ; beholde here she ys.   16

[1] F. y^e ; *so below.*
[2] *Perhaps this ought to be expanded as* Creacyon.

ADAM.   O my Lorde God, incomprehensyble, withoute mysse,
   Ys thy hyghe excellent magnyfysens.
Thys creature to me ys *nunc ex ossibus meis*,
   And *virago* I call hyr in thy presens,
   Lyke on-to me in naturall preemynens.
Laude, honor and glory to the I make.
Bothe father and mother man shall for hyr forsake.   23

PATER.   Than my garden[1] of plesure kepe thou suer.
   Of all fruts *and* trees shall thou ete *and* fede,
Except thys tre of connyng, whyle ye bothe indure ;
   Ye shall not touche yt, for that I forbede.
   ADAM.   Thy precept, Lorde, in will, worde and deede
Shall I observe, and thy request fulfyll
As thou hast com*m*andyd, yt ys reason *and* skyll.   30

PATER.   Thys tre ys callyd of connyng good *and* yll ;
   That day that ye ete thereof shall ye dye,
   Morte moriemini, yf that I do you aspye ;   33

Showe thys to thy spowse now by and bye.
   I shall me absent for a time and space ;
A warned man may lyve ; who can it denye ?
   I make the lord therof ; kepe wyll my place ;
   If thou do thys, thou shall have my grace ;
In-to mortalite shall thou ell*es* falle.
Looke thow be obedyent whan I the calle.   40

ADAM.   Omnipotent God and hygh[2] Lord of all,[2]
   I am thy servante, bownde onder thyn obedyens,
And thou my creatour, one God eternall ;
   What thou com*m*andest, I shall do my dylygens.
   PATER.   Here I leve the, to have experyens,
To use thys place in vertuse occupac*i*on,
For nowe I wyll retorne to myn habitac*i*on.   47
ADAM.   O lovely spowse of God*es* creac*i*on,
   I leve the here alone, I shall not tary longe,
For I wyll walke a whyle for my recreac*i*on

---

[1] *A stroke over* n.   [2] *Both the* h *and the* ll *are crossed.*

And se over Paradyce, that ys so stronge.
No-thynge may hurt us, nor do us wronge ;
God ys ower protectour *and* soverayn [1] guyde ;
In thys place no*n* yll thynge may abyde.   54

SERPENS. O gemme of felycyte and femynyne love,
    Why hathe God und*er* precept pr*o*hybyte thys frute,
That ye shuld not ete therof to yo*u*r behofe ?
    Thys tre ys plesant wi*th*outen refute.   58

EVA. *Ne forte* we shuld dye, *and* than be mortall ;
    We may not towche yt, by God*es* com*m*andement.
SERPENS. *Ne-quaq*ua*m*, ye shall not dye perpetuall,
    But ye shuld be as god*es* resydent,
Knowyng good *and* yll spyrytuall ;
No-thyng can dere you *tha*t ys carnall.   64

EVA. For us than now what hold you best,
    That we do not ow*er* God offende ?
SERPENS. Eate of thys apple at my requeste.
    To the, Almyghty God dyd me sende.
      EVA. Nowe wyll I take therof ; *and* I intende,
To plese my spowse, therof to fede,
To know good *and* yll for ow*er* mede.   71

ADAM. I have walkyd abought for my solace ;
    My spowse, how do you? tell me.
EVA. An angell cam from God*es* grace
    And gaffe me an apple of thys tre.
    Part therof I geffe to the ;
Eate therof for thy pleasure,
For thys frute ys God*es* own treasure.   78

PATER. Adam, Adam, wher art thou thys tyde?
    Before my presens why dost thou not appere?

        [A large gap in the MS. here.]
Musick.
Aftyr that Adam and *Eve be drevyn out of Paradyse, they schall speke
thys foloyng :*

      [1] *A stroke over* n.

ADAM.   O, w*ith* dolorows sorowe we may wayle *and* weepe !
    Alas, alas, whye ware we soo bolde ?
Bye ow*er* fowle presumpsyon we ar cast full depe,
    Fro pleasur to payn, w*ith* carys manye-fold.   84

EVA.[1]   W*ith* wonderows woo, alas ! it cane not be told ;
    Fro Paradyse to ponyschment *and* bondage full strong.
O wretchys that we are, so ev*er* we xal be inrollyd ;
    Therfor ow*er* hand*es* we may wrynge w*ith* most dullfull[2]
        song.   88

    *A*n*d so* the*i xall syng, walkyng together abowt the place, wryngyng ther*
    hands :

    Wythe dolorous sorowe we may wayle *and* wepe
    Bothe[3] nyght *and* daye in sorowe,[4] sythys full depe.   90

    [*N.B.   These last 2 lines set to musick twice over and again, for a chorus*
    of 4 pts.][5]

II.

The Storye of *th*e Temptac*i*on of Man in Paradyce,
beyng therin placyd, *and th*e Expellynge of Man
and Woman from thence, newely renuid[6] *and*
accordynge unto *th*e Skrypture, begon thys yere,
A° 1565, A° 7 Eliz.

    ITEM.   *Yt ys to be notyd* that *when the Grocers Pageant is played with-owte*
    eny other goenge befor yt, then doth the Prolocutor say in this *wise :*

[THE FIRST PROLOGUE.]

Lyke as yt chancyd before this season,
    Owte of God*es* Scripture reuealed, in playes
Was dyvers stories sett furth, by reason,
    Of pageants apparellyd in Wittson dayes ;
    And lately be fallen into decayes ;

    [1] F. Eve.   [3] *In* F. *at end of preceding line.*
    [2] F. dull full.   [4] F. sory.
    [5] *This note is apparently added by* F.
    [6] F. renvid.

Which stories dependyd in theyr orders sett
By severall devyces, much knowledge to gett; 7

Begynnyng in Genesis, that story repleate,
    Of God his creacion of eche lyvynge thynge,
Of heaven *and* of erth, of fysh smalle *and* greate,
    Of fowles, herbe *and* tre, *and* of all best*es* crepynge,
    Of angel, of man, w*hi*ch of erth hath beynge,
And of *th*e fall of angell[s], in *th*e Apocalyps to se ;
W*hi*ch stories w*i*th the Skriptures most justly agree. 14

Then followed this ow*er* pageant, w*hi*ch sheweth to be
    *Th*e Garden of Eden, w*hi*ch God dyd plante,
As yn *th*e seconde chapter of Genesis ye se ;
    Wherin of frutes pleasant no kynde therof shulde wante;
    In w*hi*ch God dyd putt man to cherish tre *and* plante,[1]
To dresse *and* kepe *th*e grownde, *and* eate what frute hym lyste,
Except *th*e tre of knowledge, God*es* high wyll[2] to resyste. 21

The story sheweth further, that, after man was blyste,
    The Lord did create woman owte of a ribbe of man ;
W*hi*ch woman was deceyvyd with *th*e Serpent*es* darkned myste ;
    By whose synn ow*er* nature is so weake no good we can ;
    Wherfor they were dejectyd *and* caste from thence than
Unto dolloure *and* myseri[3] *and* to traveyle *and* payne
Untyll God*es* spryght renuid ;[4] and so we ende certayne. 28

*Note that yf ther goeth eny other pageant*es *before yt,* the Prolocutor *sayeth
as ys on* the *other syde* and *leaveth owte this.*

[THE SECOND PROLOGUE.]

THE PROLOCUTOR. As in theyr former pageant*es* is semblably
    declared
    Of God*es* mighty creac*i*on in every lyvyng thynge,
As in *th*e fyrst of Genesis to such it is pr*e*pared [5]

---

  [1] F. [hym] taute.   [4] F. renvid.
  [2] F. wytt.   [5] F. pr*o*pared.
  [3] F. nyseri.

As lust they have to reade to memory to brynge
Of pride *and* fawle of angells that in hell hathe beinge;
In *th*e seconde of Genesis of mankynde hys creacion
Unto this Garden Eden is made full preparacion.   7

And here begynneth ow*er* pageant to make *th*e declaracion,
From *th*e letter C in *th*e chapter before saide,
Howe God putt man in Paradyse to dresse yt in best fassion,
And that no frute therof from hym shuld be denayed,
Butt of *th*e tre of lyffe *tha*t man shuld be afraide
To eat of, least that daye he eate yt he shuld dye ;
And of womans creacion apperinge by *and* bye;   14

And of *th*e Deavills temptacion discouv[r]inge w*ith* a lye
The woman beinge weakest, *tha*t cawsed man to tast.
That[1] God dyd so offende, that even contynentlye
Owte of *th*e place of joye was man *and* woman cast,
And into so great dolloure *and* misery browght at last ;
Butt that by God his spright was comforted ageyne.
This is of this ow*er* pagent *th*e some *and* effect playne.   21

[THE CREATION AND FALL.]

GOD *THE* FATHER.   I am Alpha et Homega, my Apocalyps
        doth testyfye,
    That made all of nothinge for man his sustentacion;
And of this pleasante garden *tha*t I have plante most goodlye
    I wyll hym make *th*e dresser for his good recreacion.
    Therfor, Man, I gyve yt the, to have thy delectacion.
In eatyng thou shalt eate of every growenge tre
Excepte *th*e tre of knowledge, *th*e which I forbydd the;   7

For in what daye soever thou eatest [2] thou shallt be
    Even as the childe of death ; take hede ; *and* thus I saye,
    I wyll the make an helper, to comforte the alwaye.
Beholde, therfore a slepe I bryng this daye on the,

---

1 F. *inserts* [he].   2 F. eaten.

And owte of this thy ribbe, that here I do owte-take,
A creature for thy help behold I do the make.
A-ryse, *and* from thy slepe I wyll the nowe awake,
And take hyr unto the, that you both be as one
To comfort one thother when from you I am gone.   16

And, as I saide before when *that* thou wert alone,
   In eatying thow mayst eate of every tre here is,
Butt of *the* tre of knowledge of good *and* evyll eate non,
   Lest that thou dye the deth by doenge so amysse.
   I wyll dep*ar*te [1] now wher myn habitacion is.
I leave you here.
Se *that* ye have my wordes in most high estimacion.

Then Man and *Woman speke bothe.*

[MAN AND WOMAN.]   We thank the, mighty God, *and* gyve
   the honoracion.   24

Man spekethe.

[MAN.]   Oh bone of my bones *and* flesh of my flesh eke,
   Thou shalt be called Woman, by-caus thou art of me.
Oh gyfte of God most goodlye, *that* has [2] us made so lyke,
   Most lovynge spowse I muche do here rejoyce of the.
   WOMAN.   And I lykewyse, swete lover, do much reioyce of
   the.
God therefore be praised, such comforte have us gyve
That ech of us w*it*h other thus pleasantly do lyve.   31

MAN.   To walke abowt this garden my fantasye me meve;
   I wyll the leave alone tyll that I turne ageyne ;
   Farewell, myn owne swete spouse, I leave *the* to remayne.
   WOMAN.   And farewell, my dere lover, whom my hart
   doth conteyn.   35

The Serpent spekethe.

[THE SERPENT.]   Nowe, nowe, of my purpos I dowght nott
   to attayne ;
   I can yt nott abyde, in theis joyes they shulde be.
Naye ! I wyll attempt them to syn unto theyr payne ;

---

[1] F. dep*ro*te.   [2] F. hast.

By subtylty to catch them the waye I do well se ;
    Unto this, angell of lyght I shew mysylfe to be,
With hyr for to dyscemble ; I fear yt nott at all,
Butt that unto my haight some waye I shall hyr call.   42

Oh lady of felicite, beholde my voice so small !
    Why have God sayde to you, "Eate nott of every tre
    That is within this garden " ?   Therein now answere me. 45

WOMAN. We eate of all the frutte that in the grownde we se,
    Excepte that in the myddest, wherof we may nott taste,
For God hath yt forbydd, therfor yt may nott be,
    Lest that we dye *th*e deth *and* from this place be caste.
    THE SERPENT. Ye shall not dye *th*e deth; he made you
        butt agaste ;
Butt God doth know full well *tha*t when you eate of yt
    Your eys shall then be openyd *and* you shall at *th*e last
As god*es* both good *and* evyll to knowe ye shall be fytt.   53

WOMAN. To be as God [1] indede *and* in his place to sytt,
    Therto for to agre my lust conceyve somewhatt;
Besyd*es* the tre is pleasante to gett wysedome *and* wytt,
    And nothyng is to be comparyd unto that.
    THE SERPENT. Then take at my request, *and* eate,*and*
        fere yt natt.   58

    Here she takyth and *eatyth,* and *Man cumyth in* and *sayeth unto hyr :*

MAN. My love, for my solace I have here walkyd longe.
    Howe ys yt nowe w*ith* you? I pray you do declare.
WOMAN. In-dede, lovely lover, the heavenly kynge most stronge
    To eate of this apple his angell hath prepare ;
Take therof at my hande thother frutes amonge,
    For yt shall make you wyse *and* even as God to fare.   64

    Then Man taketh and *eatyth* and *sayethe :*

[MAN.]   Alack ! alacke ! my spouse, now se I nakid we ar;
    The presence of ow*er* God we can yt nott abyde.

          [1] F. God*es.*

We have broke his precepte, he gave us of to care;
    From God therfor in secrete in some place lett us hide.
  WOMAN. With fygge-leavis lett us cover us, of God we
    be nott spyede.   69

THE FATHER. Adam! I saye, Adam! Wher art thou now
    this tyde,
    That here before my presence thou dost nott now apere?
ADAM. I herde thy voyce, oh Lorde, but yett I dyd me hide.
    For that which I am naked I more greatly dyd feare.   73

THE FATHER. Why art thou then nakyd? Who so hath
    cawsyd the?
MAN. This woman, Lord and God, which thou hast gyven
    to me.
THE FATHER. Hast thou eat of the frute that I forbyd yt the?
    Thow Woman, why hast thou done unto him thys trespace?
  WOMAN. The Serpente diseayvyd me with that his fayer
    face.   78

THE FATHER. Thow Serpente, why dydst thou this wise pre-
    vente my grace,
    My creatures and servantes in this maner to begyle?   80
THE SERPENTE. My kynde is so, thou knowest, and that in
    every case, —
    Clene oute of this place theis persons [1] to exile.[2]

THE FATHER. Cursed art for causynge my commandement to
    defyle,
    Above all cattell and beastes. Remayne thou in the fylde;
Crepe on thy bely and eate duste for this thy subtyll wyle;
    The womans sede shall over-com the, thus yt [3] have I wylde.
    Thou, Woman, bryngyng chyldren with payne shall be
    dystylde,
And be subiect to thy husbonde, and thy lust shall pertayne [4]
To hym. I hav determynyd this ever to remayne.   89

<hr>

1 F. prosons.   3 F. yt.
2 F. excite.   4 F. protayne.

And to the, Man, for *tha*t my voyce thou didst disdayne,
    Cursed is *th*e erth for ever for thy sake ;
Thy lyvyng shall thou gett with swett unto thy payne,
    Tyll thou departe unto the erth [wherof] I dyd the make.
    Beholde, theis letherin aprons unto *you*rselves now take.   94

Lo ! Man as one of us hathe bene, good *and* evyll to knowe;
    Therfor I wyll exempte hym from this place to aslake,
Lest of the tre of lyfe he eate *and* ever growe.
    Myne angell, now cum furth *and* kepe *th*e waye *and* porte,
    Unto *th*e tre of lyfe that they do nott resorte.   99

THE AUNGELL. Departe from hence at onys from this place of
    comforte,
    No more to have axcesse or ells for to apere.
From this place I exile you, that you no more resorte,
    Nor ever do presume ageyne for to come here.   103

Then Man and *Woman departyth to* the *nether parte of* the *pageant,* and *Man
    sayeth :*

[MAN.] Alack ! myn owne sweteharte, how am I stroke w*it*h fear,
    That from God am exiled a*nd* browg*h*t to payne *and* woo.
Oh! what have we lost ! Why dyd we no more care,
    And to what kynd of place thatt we resort *and* goo?
    WOMAN. Indede into *th*e worlde now must we to *and* fro,
And where or how to rest I can nott saye at all.
I am even as ye ar, what-so-ever me be-fall.   110

Then cumeth Dolor and *Myserye* and *taketh Man by both armys* and *Dolor
    sayeth :*

[DOLOR.] Cum furth, O Man, take hold of me !
    Through envy hast lost thy heavenly lyght
By eatynge ; in bondage from hence shall be.
    Now must thou me, Dolor, have always in sight.   114

MYSERYE. And also of me, Myserye, thou must taste *and* byte,
    Of hardenes *and* of colde *and* eke of infirmitie ;

Accordinge to desarte thy portion is, of right,
>To enioye that in me that is withoute certentye.   118

ADAM.   Thus troublyd, nowe I enter into Dolor *and* Miserie.
>Nowe, Woman, must we lerne ow*er* lyvyng*es* to gett
With labor *and* with travell; ther is no remedye,
>Nor eny-thyng therfrom we se that maye us lett.   122

Then cumyth in the *Holy Ghost comforting Man* and *sayeth* :

[THE HOLY GHOST.]   Be of good cheare, Man, *and* sorowe
>   no more ;
>This Dolor *and* Miserie that then thou hast taste
Is nott in respecte, layd up in store,
>   To *th*e joyes for the that ever shall[1] last.
>   Thy God doth not this the away to cast,
But to try the as gold is tryed in *th*e fyer ;
In the end, premonyshed, shalt have thy desire.   129

Take owte of the Gospell *tha*t yt the requyre,
>   Fayth in Chryst Jhesu *and* grace thatt ensewe.
I wylbe thy guyde *and* pay the thy hyer
>   For all thy good dylygence *and* doenge thy dewe.
>   Gyve eare unto me, Man, *and* than yt ys trewe,
Thou shalt kyll affect*es that* by lust in the reygne,
And put Dolor *and* Mysery and Envy to payne.   136

Theis armors ar preparyd, yf thou wylt turne ageyne ;
>   To fyght wyth, take to the, *and* reach Woman the same:
The brest plate of rightousnes Saynte Paule wyll the retayne ;
>   The shylde of faythe to quench, thy fyrye dartes to tame;
>   The hellmett of salvacion the devylls wrath shall lame;
And *th*e sworde of *th*e spright, w*h*ich is *th*e worde of God, —
All theis ar nowe the offred to ease thy payne *and* rodd.   143

ADAM.   Oh ! prayse to the, Most Holye, *tha*t hast w*ith* me
>   abode,
>   In mysery premonyshynge by this thy Holy Spright.

1 F. shalt.

Nowe fele I such great comforte, my syns they be unlode
    And layde on Chrystes back, wh*i*ch is my joye *and* lyght.
This Dolor *and* this Mysery I fele to me no wight ;
    No ! Deth is overcu*m* by fore predestinacion,
    And we attayned wyth Chryst in heavenly consolacion.   150

Therfor, myne owne swett spous, w*it*houten cavylacion
    Together lett us synge, *and* lett o*u*r hart*es* reioyse
    And gloryfye ow*e*r God wyth mynde, powre *and* voyse.   153
        Amen.

      [*Old musick, Triplex, Tenor, Medius, Bass* :][1]

With hart *and* voyce
Let us reioyce
    And prayse the Lord alwaye
    For this o*u*r joyfull daye,
To se of this o*u*r God his maiestie,
Who [2] hath given himsellfe ov*e*r us to rayne *and* to gov*e*rne us.
    Lett all o*u*r harte[s] reioyce together,
    And lett us all lifte up o*u*r voyce, on of us with another. 161

   [1] *Apparently added by* F.
   [2] F. Who the hath. *Perhaps something is lost that is necessary to the regularity of the stanza.*

TOWNELEY PLAYS.

Reprinted from advance sheets of the edition of the Early English Text Society.
I have not reproduced the crosses, tags, and curls usually attached in this MS. to
ll, *th*, *ht*, *t*, *f*, and *r*, for they seem mere flourishes. The MS. dates from the second
half of the fifteenth century. In the footnotes, M. indicates Mätzner's "Alteng-
lische Sprachproben," I, 1, pp. 357 ff.

Processus Noe cu*m* filiis. Wakefield.

NOE. Myghtfull God veray, / maker of all that is,
Thre p*er*sons, withoutten nay, / oone G̦od in endles blis,
Thou maide both nyght & day, / beest, fowle, & fysh ;
All creatures that lif may / wroght thou at thi wish,
   As thou wel myght;
The son, the moyne, verament,
Thou maide; the firmament ;
The sternes also full feruent
    To shyne thou maide ful bright ;   9

Angels thou maide ful euen, / all orders that is,
To haue the blis in heuen : — / this did thou more & les.
ffull mervelus to neuen, / yit was ther vnkyndnes,
More bi fold*is* seuen / then I can well expres;
   ffor why
Of all angels in brightnes
God gaf Lucifer most lightnes,
Yit prowdly he flyt his des,
    And set hym euen hym by.   18

He thoght hymself as worthi / as hym that hym made,
In brightnes, in bewty. / Therfor he hym degrade;
Put hym in a low degre / soyn after, in a brade,
Hym and all his menye, / wher he may be vnglad
      ffor euer.
Shall thay neuer wyn away,
Hence vnto domysday,
Bot burne in bayle for ay ;
      Shall thay neuer dysseuer.   27

Soyne after that gracyous Lord / to his liknes maide man,
That place to be restord / euen as he began,
Of the Trinite bi accord, / Adam, & Eue that woman.
To multiplie without discord / in paradise put he thaym,
      And sithen to both
Gaf in commaundement,
On the tre of life to lay no hend;
Bot yit the fals feynd
      Made hym with man wroth,   36

Entysyd man to glotony, / styrd him to syn in pride ;
Bot in paradise, securly, / myght no syn abide,
And therfor man full hastely / was put out, in that tyde,
In wo & wandreth for to be; / [1] paynes full vnrid
      To knawe, [2]
ffyrst in erth, sythen [3] in hell
With feyndis for to dwell,
Bot he his mercy mell
      To those that will hym trawe.   45

Oyle of mercy he hus hight, / as I haue hard red,
To euery lifyng wight / that wold luf hym and dred ;
Bot now before his sight / euery liffyng leyde
Most party day and nyght / syn in word and dede
      ffull bold;

[1] E. E. T. S. *has* In paynes.
[2] MS. knowe.
[3] E. E. T. S. *has* in sythen in; M. *reads* and sythen.

Som in pride, ire, and enuy,
Som in couetyse [1] & glotyny,
Som in sloth and lechery,
        And other wise many-fold.   **54**

Therfor I drede lest God / on vs will take veniance,
ffor syn is now alod / without any repentance;
Sex hundreth yeris & od / haue I, without distance,
In erth, as any sod, / liffyd with grete grevance
        All-way;
And now I wax old,
Seke, sory, and cold,
As muk apon mold
        I widder away;   **63**

Bot yit will I cry / for mercy and call;
Noe thi seruant am I, / Lord, ouer-all!
Therfor me and my fry, / shal with me fall,
Saue from velany / and bryng to thi hall
        In heuen;
And kepe me from syn
This warld within;
Comly Kyng of mankyn,
        I pray the here my stevyn!   **72**

DEUS.   Syn I haue maide all thyng / that is liffand,
Duke, emperour, and kyng / with myne awne hand,
ffor to haue thare likyng / bi see & bi sand,
Euery man to my bydyng / shuld be bowand
        ffull feruent,
That maide man sich a creatoure,
ffarest of favoure.
Man must luf me paramoure,
        By reson, and repent.   **81**

Me thoght I shewed man luf / when I made hym to be
All angels abuf, / like to the Trynyte;

---

[1] MS. Couetous; *corr. by* M.

And now in grete reprufe / full low lig*is* he,
In erth hy*m*self to stuf / w*ith* syn that displeasse me
      Most of all;
Veniance will I take
In erth for syn sake,
My grame thus will I wake
      Both of grete and small.   90

I repente full sore / that eu*er* maide I man,
Bi me he sett*is* no store / and I am his soferan;
I will distroy therfor / both beest, man, and woman,
All shall p*er*ish, les and more; / that bargan may thay ban
      That ill has done.
In erth I se right noght
Bot syn that is vnsoght;
Of those that well has wroght
      ffynd I bot[1] a fone.   99

Therfor shall I fordo / all this medill-erd
With flood*is* that shall flo / & ryn w*ith* hidous rerd;
I haue good cause therto; / ffor me no man is ferd;
As I say shal I do, / of veniance draw my swerd,
      And make end
Of all that beris life,
Sayf Noe and his wife,
ffor thay wold neu*er* stryfe
      W*ith* me then[2] me offend.   108

Hym to mekill wyn / hastly will I go,
To Noe my s*er*uand, or I blyn, / to warn hy*m* of his wo.
In erth I se bot syn, / reynand to and fro,
Emang both more & myn, / ichon other fo
      W*ith* all thare entent;
All shall I fordo
W*ith* flood*is* that shall floo,
Wirk shall I thaym wo,
      That will not repent.   117

[1] MS. bo^t.   [2] MS. then; E. E. T. S. ne.

[God descends and comes to Noah.][1]

Noe, my freend, I thee commaund, / from cares the to keyle,
A ship that thou ordand / of nayle and bord ful wele.
Thou was alway well wirkand, / to me trew as stele,
To my bydyng obediand; / frendship shal thou fele
   To mede.
Of lennthe thi ship be
Thre hundreth cubett*is*, warn I the,
Of heght euen thirte,[2]
    Of fyfty als in brede.   126

Anoynt thi ship w*ith* pik and tar / w*ith*out & als w*ith*in,
The wat*er* out to spar / this is a noble gyn;
Look no man the mar; / thre chese[3] chambres begyn;
Thou must spend many a spar / this wark or thou wyn
   To end fully.
Make in thi ship also
P*ar*loures oone or two,
And houses of offyce mo
   ffor beest*is* that ther must be.   135

Oone cubite on hight / a wyndo shal thou make;
On the syde a doore w*ith* slyght / be-neyth shal thou take;
W*ith* the shal no man fyght / nor do the no kyn wrake.
When all is doyne thus right, / thi wife, that is thi make,
   Take in to the;
Thi sonnes of good fame,
Sem, Iaphet, and Came,
Take in also [t]hame,[4]
   Thare wif*is* also thre.   144

ffor all shal be fordone / that lif in land bot ye,
W*ith* flood*is* that from abone / shal fall, & that plente;
It shall begyn full sone / to rayn vncessantle,

---

1 *Supplied by* E. E. T. S.   3 MS. chefe.
2 E. E. T. S. thrirte.   4 *Corr. by* M.

After dayes seuen be done, / and induyr dayes fourty,
    Withoutten fayll.
Take to thi ship also
Of ich kynd beestis two,
Mayll & femayll, bot no mo,
    Or thou pull vp thi sayll.   153

ffor thay may the avayll / when al this thyng is wroght;
Stuf thi ship with vitayll, / ffor hungre that ye perish noght,
Of beestis, foull, and catayll, / ffor thaym haue thou in thoght;
ffor thaym is my counsayll / that som socour be soght
    In hast;
Thay must haue corn and hay,
And oder mete alway;
Do now as I the say,
    In the name of the Holy Gast.   162

NOE.   A ! benedicite ! / what art thou that thus
Tellys afore that shall be ? / Thou art full mervelus !
Tell me, for charite, / thi name so gracius.
DEUS.   My name is of dignyte / and also full glorius
    To knawe.[1]
I am God most myghty,
Oone God in Trynyty,
Made the and ich man to be:
    To luf me well thou awe.   171

NOE.   I thank the, Lord so dere, / that wold vowch-sayf
Thus low to appere / to a symple knafe;
Blis vs, Lord, here; / for charite I hit crafe;
The better may we stere / the ship that we shall hafe,
    Certayn.
DEUS.   Noe, to the and to thi fry
My blyssyng graunt I:
Ye shall wax and multiply,
    And fill the erth agane,   180

---

[1] MS. knowe.

When all thise flood*is* ar past/ and fully gone away.
NOE.   Lord, homward will I hast / as fast as that I may;
My [wife]¹ will I frast / what she will say,   [*Exit Deus.*]¹
And I am agast / that we get som fray
      Betwixt vs both;
ffor she is full techee,²
ffor litill oft angre,
If any-thyng wrang be,
      Soyne is she wroth.   189

        Tunc perget ad vxorem.

God spede, dere wife, / how fayre ye?
VXOR.   Now as eu*er* myght I thryfe, / the wars I thee see.
Do tell me belife, / where has thou thus long be?
To dede may we dryfe / or lif for the,
      ffor want.
When we swete or swynk,
Thou dos what thou thynk,
Yit of mete and of drynk
      Haue we veray skant.   198

NOE.   Wife, we ar hard sted / with tythyngis new.
VXOR.   Bot thou were worthi be cled / in Stafford blew;
ffor thou art alway adred, / be it fals or trew.
Bot God knowes I am led, / and that may I rew
      ffull ill;
ffor I dar be thi borow,
ffrom euen vnto morow
Thou spek*is* eu*er* of sorow:
      God send the onys thi fill!   207

We women may wary / all ill husband*is*.
I have oone, bi Mary / that lowsyd me of my band*is* !
If he teyn, I must tary, / how-so-eu*er* it stand*is*,
With seymland full sory, / wryngand both my hand*is*
      ffor drede.

¹ *Supplied by* E. E. T. S.   ² E. E. T. S. tethee.

Bot yit other while,
What with gam & w*ith* gyle,
I shall smyte and smyle,
   And qwite hym his mede.   216

NOE. We ! hold thi tong, ram-skyt, / or I shall the still.
VXOR. By my thryft, if thou smyte, / I shal turne the vntill.
NOE. We shall assay as tyte. / Haue at the, Gill !
Apon the bone shal it byte. /
VXOR.   A, so, Mary ! thou smyt*is* ill !
   Bot I suppose
I shal not in thi det
fflyt of this flett!
Take the ther a langett
   To tye vp thi hose ! [*Striking him.*] 225

NOE. A! wilt thou so ? / Mary, that is myne.
VXOR. Thou shal [have] thre for two, / I swere bi God*is* pyne.
NOE. And I shall qwyte the tho, / in fayth, or syne.
VXOR. Out apon the, ho ! /
NOE.   Thou can both byte and whyne
   W*ith* a rerd!
ffor all if she stryke,
Yit fast will she skryke;
In fayth, I hold none slyke
   In all medill-erd;   234

Bot I will kepe charyte, / ffor I haue at do.
VXOR. Here shal no man tary the; / I pray the go to!
ffull well may we mys the, / as eu*er* haue I ro.
To spyn will I dres me. /
NOE.   We ! fare well, lo;
   Bot, wife,
Pray for me besele,
To eft I com vnto the.
VXOR. Euen as thou prays for me,
   As eu*er* myght I thrife.   243

NOE.   I tary full lang / fro my warke, I traw ;
Now my gere will I fang / and thederward draw.
I may full ill gang, / the soth for to knaw.
Bot if God help amang, / I may sit downe daw
　　　　　To ken ;
Now assay will I
How I can of wrightry,
In nomine Patris, & Filii,
　　　　Et Spiritus Sancti, Amen.　　　　　　　252

To begyn of this tree / my bonys will I bend ;
I traw from the Trynyte / socoure will be send.
It fayres full fayre, thynk me, / this wark to my hend ;
Now blissid be he / that this can amend.
　　　　　Lo, here the lenght,
Thre hundreth cubettis euenly ;
Of breed, lo ! is it fyfty ;
The heght is euen thyrty
　　　　Cubettis full strenght.　　　　　　261

Now my gowne will I cast, / and wyrk in my cote ;
Make will I the mast, / or I flyt oone foote.
A ! my bak, I traw, will brast ! / this is a sory note !
Hit is wonder that I last, / sich an old dote
　　　　　All dold !
To begyn sich a wark,
My bonys ar so stark,
No wonder if thay wark,
　　　　ffor I am full old.　　　　　　270

The top and the sayll / both will I make ;
The helm and the castell / also will I take ;
To drife ich a nayll / will I not forsake ;
This gere may neuer fayll, / that dar I vndertake
　　　　　Onone.
This is a nobull gyn,
Thise nayles so thay ryn
Thoro more and myn,
　　　　Thise bordis ichon ;　　　　　　279

Wyndow and doore, / euen as he saide,
Thre ches-chambre, / thay ar well maide ;
Pyk & tar full sure / ther-apon laide ;
This will eu*er* endure, / therof am I paide ;
        ffor why
It is bett*er* wroght
Then I coude haif thoght.
Hym that maide all of noght
        I thank oonly.   288

Now will I hy me, / and no-thyng be leder,
My wife and my meneye / to bryng euen hed*er*.

           [Goes to find his wife.]

Tent hedir tydely, / wife, and consid*er* ;
Hens must vs fle / all sam togeder
        In hast.
Vxor.   Whi, syr, what alis you?
Who is that asalis you?
To fle it avalis you
        And ye be agast.   297

Noe.   Ther is garn on the reyll / other, my dame.
Vxor.   Tell me that ich a deyll, / els get ye blame.
Noe.   He that cares may keill, — / blissid be his name ! —
He has [spokyn?] [1] for oure seyll, / to sheld vs fro shame,
        And sayd,
All this warld aboute
With flood*is* so stoute,
That shall ryn on a route,
        Shall be oue*r*laide.   306

He saide all shall be slayn / bot oonely we,
Oure barnes, that ar bayn, / and thare wif*is* thre ;
A ship he bad me ordayn / to safe vs & oure fee.
Therfor w*ith* all oure mayn / thank we that fre,
        Beytt*er* of bayll.

        [1] *No word nor gap in* E. E. T. S.

Hy vs fast ; go we thedir !
VXOR.   I wote neu*er* whedir ;
I dase and I dedir
　　　　ffor ferd of that tayll.　　　　　　　　　315

NOE.   Be not aferd ; haue done ; / trus sam oure gere,
That we be ther or none, / w*ith*out more dere.
I [1] FILI*US*.   It shall be done full sone. / Brether, help to bere.
II FILI*US*.   ffull long shall I not hoyne / to do my devere,
　　　　Brether Sam.
III FILIUS.   W*ith*out any yelp,
At my myght shall I help.
VXOR.   Yit for drede of a skelp
　　　　Help well thi dam.　　　　　　　　　324

　　　　[They go to the Ark ; Uxor enters it.]

NOE.   Now ar we there / as we shuld be ;
Do get in oure gere, / oure catall and fe
In-to this vessell here, / my chyld*er* fre.
VXOR.   I was neu*er* bard ere, / as eu*er* myght I the,
　　　　In sich an oostre as this.
In fa[i]th, I can not fynd,
Which is before, which is behynd.
Bot shall we here be pynd,
　　　　Noe, as haue thou blis ?　　*[Exit from Ark.]*　　333

NOE.   Dame, as it is skill, / here must vs abide grace ;
Therfor, wife, w*ith* good will / com into this place.
VXOR.   Sir, for Iak nor for Gill / will I turne my face,
Till I haue on this hill / spon a space
　　　　On my rok.
Well were he, myght get me !
Now will I downe set me ;
Yit reede I no man let me,
　　　　ffor drede of a knok.　　　　　　　　　342

　　[1] *Here and below MS. has the regular contracted forms of the Latin ordinal
numerals.*

NOE.   Behold to the heuen, / the cateractes all,
Thay [1] are open full euen, / grete and small,
And the planett*is* seuen / left has thare stall ;
Thise thoners and levyn / downe gar fall
     ffull stout
Both halles and bowers,
Castels and towres ;
ffull sharp ar thise showers
       That renys aboute ;   351

Therfor, wife, haue done ; / com into ship fast.
VXOR.   Yei, Noe, go cloute thi shone, / the bett*er* will thai last.
I MULIER.   Good mod*er*, com in sone, / for all is ou*er*-cast,
Both the son and the mone. /
II MULIER.   And many wynd blast
    ffull sharp ;
This flood*is* so thay rin,
Therfor, mod*er*, come in.
VXOR.   In fayth, yit will I spyn ;
      All in vayn ye carp.   360

III MULIER.   If ye like ye may spyn, / mod*er*, in the ship.
NOE.   Now is this twyys : com in, / dame, on my frenship.
VXOR.   Whed*er* I lose or I wyn, / in fayth, thi felowship,
Set I not at a pyn. / This spyndill will I slip
     Apon this hill
Or I styr oone fote.
NOE.   Pet*er* ! I traw we [2] dote ;
W*ith*out any more note,
     Come in if ye will.   369

VXOR.   Yei, wat*er* nyghys so nere / that I sit not dry ;
Into ship w*ith* a byr, / therfor, will I hy
ffor drede that I drone here. /   [*Rushes into the ship.*]
NOE.   Dame, securly,
It bees boght full dere, / ye abode so long by
    Out of ship.

[1] E. E. T. S. That.   [2] *Qy.* ye,

VXOR.   I will not, for thi bydyng,
Go from doore to mydyng.
NOE.   In fayth, and for youre long taryyng,
    Ye shall lik on the whip.   378

VXOR.   Spare me not, I pray the, / bot euen as thou thynk,
Thise grete word*is* shall not flay me. /
NOE.   Abide, dame, and drynk,
ffor betyn shall thou be / w*ith* this staf to thou stynk.
Ar strok*is* good ? say me. /   [*Striking her.*]
VXOR.   What say ye, Wat Wynk ?
    NOE.   Speke !
Cry me m*er*cy, I say !
VXOR.   Therto say I nay.
NOE.   Bot thou do, bi this day,
    Thi hede shall I breke.   387

VXOR.   Lord, I were at ese / and hertely full hoylle,
Might I onys haue a measse / of wedows coyll ;
ffor thi saull, w*ith*out lese, / shuld I dele penny doyll ;
So wold mo, no frese, / that I se on this sole
    Of wif*is* that ar here,
ffor the life that thay leyd,
Wold thare husband*is* were dede ;
ffor, as eu*er* ete I brede,
    So wold I oure syre were.   396

NOE.   Yee men that has wif*is*, / whyls they ar yong,
If ye luf youre lif*is*, / chastice thare tong.
Me thynk my hert ryf*is*, / both levyr and long,
To se sich stryf*is* / wedmen emong ;
    Bot I,
As haue I blys,
Shall chastyse this.
VXOR.   Yit may ye mys,
    Nicholl Nedy !   [*Fighting* ad lib.]   405

NOE.   I shall make *th*e still as stone, / begynnar of blunder !
I shall bete the, bak and bone, / and breke all in sonder.

Vxor.   Out, alas, I am gone ! / oute apon the, mans wond*er* !
Noe.   Se how she can grone / and I lig vnd*er* !
   Bot, wife,
In this hast let vs ho,
ffor my bak is nere in two.
Vxor.   And I am bet so blo
   That I may not thryfe.   414

I Filius.   A ! whi fare ye thus, / ffad*er* and mod*er* both ?
II Fili*us*.   Ye shuld not be so spitus, / standyng in sich a
   woth.
III Fili*us*.   Thise [strifis ?]¹ are so hidus, / w*ith* many a cold
   coth.
Noe.   We will do as ye bid vs ; / we will no more be wroth,
   Dere barnes !
Now to the helme will I hent,
And to my ship tent.
Vxor.   I se on the firmament,
   Me thynk, the seven starnes.   423

Noe.   This is a grete flood, / wife, take hede.
Vxor.   So me thoght, as I stode ; / we are in grete drede ;
Thise wawghes ar so wode. /
Noe.   Help, God, in this nede !
As thou art stere-man good, / and best, as I rede,
   Of all,
Thou rewle vs in this rase,
As thou me behete hase.
Vxor.   This is a p*er*lous case :
   Help, God, when we call !   432

Noe.   Wife, tent the stere-tre, / and I shall asay
The depnes of the see / that we bere, if I may.
Vxor.   That shall J do ful wysely ; / now go thi way,
ffor apon this flood haue we / flett many day
   W*ith* pyne.

    ¹ *No word nor gap in* E. E. T. S.

NOE. Now the wat*er* will I sownd :
A ! it is far to the grownd ;
This trauell, I expownd,
   Had I to tyne.   441

Aboue all hillys bedeyn / the wat*er* is rysen late
Cubett*is fyfteyn ;* [1] / bot in a high*er* [2] state
It may not be, I weyn, / for this well I wate,
This forty dayes has rayn beyn ; / it will therfor abate
   Full lele.
This wat*er* in hast
Eft will I tast ;
Now am I agast,
   It is wanyd a grete dele.   450

Now are the weders cest / and cateractes knyt,
Both the most and the leest. /
VXOR.   Me thynk, bi my wit,
The son shynes in the eest ; / lo, is not yond it?
We shuld haue a good feest, / were thise flood*is* flyt,
   So spytus.
NOE. We have been here, all we,
Thre hundreth [3] dayes and fyfty.
VXOR. Yei, now wanys the see ;
   Lord, well is vs !   459

NOE. The thryd tyme will I prufe / what depnes we bere.
VXOR. How [4] long shall thou hufe ? / Lay in thy lyne there.
NOE. I may towch with my lufe / the grownd evyn here.
VXOR. Then begynnys to grufe / to vs mery chere ;
   Bot, husband,
What grownd may this be?
NOE. The hyllys of Armonye.
VXOR. Now blissid be he
   That thus for vs can ordand !   468

---

[1] MS. xv.   [3] MS. ccc.
[2] E. E. T. S. hight*er*.   [4] E. E. T. S. Now; *corr. by* Child.

Noe.   I see the toppys of hyllys he, / many at a syght ;
No thyng to let me, / the wedir is so bright.
Vxor.   Thise ar of mercy / tokyns full right.
Noe.   Dame, thou[1] counsell me / what fowll best myght
          And cowth
With flight of wyng
Bryng, without taryying,
Of mercy som tokynyng
          Ayther bi north or southe ;   477

ffor this is the fyrst day / of the tent moyne.
Vxor.   The ravyn, durst I lay, / will come agane sone ;
As fast as thou may, / cast hym furth ; haue done.
He may happyn to-day / com agane or none
          With grath.
Noe.   I will cast out also
Dowfys oone or two.
Go youre way, go,   [*He sends out the birds.*]
          God send you som wathe !   486

Now ar thise fowles flone / into seyr countre ;
Pray we fast ichon, / kneland on our kne,
To hym that is alone / worthiest of degre,
That he wold send anone / oure fowles som fee
          To glad vs.
Vxor.   Thai may not fayll of land,
The water is so wanand.
Noe.   Thank we God all-weldand,
          That lord that made vs.   495

It is a wonder thyng, / me thynk sothle,
Thai ar so long taryyng, / the fowles that we
Cast out in the mornyng. /
Vxor.   Syr, it may be
Thai tary to thay bryng. /
Noe.   The ravyn is a-hungrye
          All-way ;

---

[1] E. E. T. S. thi ; *corr. by* Kittredge.

He is w*ith*out any reson ;
And he fynd any caryon,
As p*er*aventure may befon,
      He will not away ;   504

The dowfe is more gentill, — / her trust I vntew, —
Like vnto the turtill, / for she is ay trew.
Vxor.   Hence bot a litill / she co*m*mys.   Lew, lew !
She bryng*ys* in her bill / som novels new.
      Behald !
It is of an olif tre
A branch, thynk*ys* me.
Noe.   It is soth, p*er*de,
      Right so is it cald.   513

Doufe, byrd full blist, / ffayre myght the befall !
Thou art trew for to trist / as ston in the wall ;
Full well I it wist, / thou wold com to thi hall.
Vxor.   A trew tokyn ist, / we shall be sauyd all ;
      ffor why
The wat*er*, syn she com,
Of depnes plom
Is fallen a fathom
      And more, hardely.   522

I Filius.   Thise flood*is* ar gone, / fad*er*, behold.
II *Filius*.   Ther is left right none, / and that be ye bold.
III *Filius*.   As still as a stone / oure ship is stold.
Noe.   Apon land here anone / that we were, fayn I wold.
      My child*er* dere,
Sem, Japhet and Cam,
W*ith* gle and w*ith* gam
Com go we all sam,
      We will no long*er* abide here.   531

Vxor.   Here haue we beyn, / Noy, long enogh,
W*ith* tray and w*ith* teyn / and dreed mekill wogh.

NOE.   Behald, on this greyn / nowd*er* cart ne plogh
Is left, as I weyn, / nowd*er* tre then bogh,
     Ne other thyng,
Bot all is away ;
Many castels, I say,
Grete townes of aray,
     fflitt has this flowyng.   540

VXOR.   Thise flood*is* not afright / all this warld so wide
Has mevid w*ith* myght / on se and bi side.
NOE.   To dede ar thai dyght, / prowdist of pryde, —
Eu*er* ich a wyght / that eu*er* was spyde
     With syn ;
All ar thai slayn,
And put vnto payn.
VXOR.   ffrom thens agayn
     May thai neu*er* wyn ?   549

NOE.   Wyn ?   No, i-wis, / bot he that myght hase
Wold myn of thare mys / & admytte thaym to grace.
As he in bayll is blis, / I pray hym in this space,
In heven hye w*ith* his / to purvaye vs a place,
     That we,
With his sant*is* in sight
And his angels bright,
May com to his light :
     Amen, for charite.   558

Explicit processus Noe, sequitur Abraham.

HEGGE PLAYS.

————

Printed from MS. Cott. Vesp. D. viii. I have expanded curled *r* and *n* and crossed *h* and *ll*, because the scribe seems to have used them with a definite intention. In the footnotes, H. marks the readings of the edition of the old Shakespeare Society : " Ludus Coventriæ, . . . ed. J. O. Halliwell. London, 1841."

I have chosen to call the plays by the name of the earliest known owner of the MS., for I see no reason to connect them with Coventry, and " so-called Coventry Plays " is a clumsy expression.

————

[NOAH AND LAMECH.]

NOE.   God of his goodnesse and of grace grounde,
    By whoys gloryous power all*e* thyng is wrought,
In whom all*e* vertu plentevously [1] is ffounde,
    W*ith*owtyn whos [2] wyl may be ryth nought,
Thy seruaunt*es* saue, Lord, fro synful sownde
    In wyl, in werk, in dede *and* in thouht ;
Our*e* welth in woo lete nevyr be fownde ;
    Vs help, Lord, from synne *tha*t we be in brought,
        Lord God fful of myght !
    Noe, ser*es*, my name is knowe ;   [*Addressing the audience.*]
    My wyff *and* my chylder*e* here on rowe;
    To God we pray w*ith* hert ful lowe,
        To plese hym in his syght.   **13**

In me, Noe, *th*e secunde age
    Indede be-gynnyth as I ʒow say;

1 MS. plentevoufly.
2 MS. whof ; *probably for* whofe.

Afftyr Adam, with-outyn langage,
  The secunde fadyr am I, in fay.
But men of levyng be so owt-rage
  Bothe be nyght and eke be day,
That, lesse than synne the soner swage,
  God wyl be vengyd on vs sum way,
      In-dede.
    Ther may no man go therowte,
    But synne regnyth in every rowte ;
    In every place rownde a-bowte
      Cursydnes doth sprynge and sprede.   26

Vxor Noe.   Alle-myghty God, of his gret grace,
  Enspyre men with hertely wylle
For to sese of here trespace ;
  ffor synfulle levyng oure sowle xal spylle.
Synne offendyth God in his face
  And a-grevyth oure Lorde ffulle ylle ;
It causyth to man ryght grett manace
  And scrapyth hym out of lyvys bylle,
      That blyssyd book.
    What man in synne doth alle-wey scleppe,
    He xal gon to helle ful depp ;
    Than xal he nevyr after creppe [1]
      Out of that [2] brennyng brook.   39

I am ȝour wyff, ȝour childeryn these be ;
  On-to us tweyn it doth longe
Hem to teche in alle degre
  Synne to for-sakyn and werkys wronge.
Therfore, sere,[3] for loue of me,
  Enforme hem wele evyr [4] a-monge
Synne to for-sake and vanyte,
  And vertu to ffolwe, that thei ffonge
      Oure Lord God to plese.

----

[1] MS. crepp.   [3] MS. fere.
[2] H. the.   [4] MS. ovyr.

Noe. I warne ʒow, childeryn, on *and* all*e*,
Drede our*e* Lord God in hevy[n] hall*e*,
And in no forfete *tha*t we ne [1] ffall*e*
    Our Lord for to dysplese.   52

Chem.[2] A ! der*e* ffadyr, God for-bede
   *Tha*t we xulde do in ony wyse
Ony werke of synful dede
   Our*e* Lord God *tha*t xulde a-gryse.
My name is Chem, ʒo*ur* son of p*ri*se :
I xal werke after*e* ʒo*ur* rede ;
   And also, wyff, *th*e weyll*e* awyse
Wykkyd werkys *tha*t *tho*u non [3] brede,
      Nev*er* in no degr*e*.
     Vx*or* Seem. Forsothe,[4] ser*e*, be Goddys grace,
I xal me kepe from all*e* trespace
   *Tha*t xulde offende Goddys face,[5]
      Be help of *th*e Trynyte.   65

Cham. I am Cham, ʒo*ur* secunde son,[6]
   And purpose me, be Goddys myght,
Nevyr suche a dede for to don
   *Tha*t xuld [7] agreve God in syght.
Vx*or* Cham. I pray to God me grawnt *th*is bone,[8]
   That he me kepe in such*e* a plyght
Mornynge, hevenynge, mydday *and* none,
   I to affendyn hym day nor nyght.
     Lord God, I *th*e pray,
   Bothe wakynge *and* eke in slepe,
   Gracyous God, *tho*u me keppe,
     *Tha*t I nevyr in daunger crepe
      On dredfull*e* domys-day.   78

Iaphet. Iaphet, *th*i iij^{de} sone, is my name ;
   I pray to God, wher-so we be,

---

[1] MS. no.
[2] H. Shem.
[3] H. none.
[4] H. fforsothe.
[5] H. fface.
[6] H. sone.
[7] H. xulde.
[8] *Curl over* n *in* MS.

*Tha*t he vs borwe fro synfull*e* shame,
    And in vertuous [1] levynge evyr-mor*e* kepe me.
Vx[OR] IAPHET.   I am ʒ*our* wyff *and* pray *th*e same,
    *Tha*t God vs saue on sonde and se,
W*ith* no grevauns *tha*t we hy*m* grame ;
    He grawnt vs grace synne to fle.
        Lord God, now her*e* our*e* bone !
   NOE.   Gracyous God, *tha*t best may,
    W*ith* herty wyl to the we pray, —
    *Tho*u saue us sekyr bothe nyght *and* day,
        Synne *th*at we noon done.   91

[God speaks in heaven.]

DEUS.   Ow ! what menyht this mys-levyng man,
    Whiche myn hand made *and* byldyd in blysse?
Synne so sor*e* grevyht me, ʒo,[2] in certayn,
    I wol be vengyd of *th*is grett mysse.
Myn aungel der*e*, *th*ou xalt gan
    To Noe *tha*t my servaunt is ;
A shypp to make on hond to tan
    *Tho*u byd hym swyth [8] for hy*m and* his,
        ffrom drynchyng hem to saue ;
    ffor, as I am God off myght,
    I xal dystroye *th*is wer[l]d [4] down*e*-ryght ;
    Her*e* synne so sor*e* grevyht me in syght,
        *Th*ei xal no mercy haue.   104

*ffecisse ho*min*em nu*nc *penitet* [5] *me*,
    *Tha*t I made man sor*e* doth me rewe ;
Myn handwerk to sle sor*e* grevyth me,
    But *tha*t her*e* synne her*e* deth doth brewe.
Go sey to Noe as I bydde *th*e :
    Hy*m*-self, his wyf, his chylderyn [6] trewe,

---

    [1] MS. vertuo͡us.   [4] MS. *has* werd *as standard form.*
    [2] H. ʒa.   [5] H. pœnitet.
    [8] H. swythe.   [6] H. childeryn.

Tho viii [1] sowlys in shyp to be ;
 Thei xul not drede *th*e flodys fflowe,
  *Th*e fflod xal harme them nowht ;
 Of all*e* ffowlys *and* bestys thei take a peyr*e*
In shipp [2] to saue, bothe ffoule *and* ffayer*e*,
ffrom all*e* dowtys *and* gret dyspeyr*e*,
  This vengeauns or it be wrought.   117

   [The angel descends.]

ANGELUS *(ad Noe).* Noe ! Noe ! A shypp loke *tho*u make,
 And many a chaumbyr *tho*u xalt haue *the*rinne ;
Of euery kyndys best a cowpyl *tho*u take
 W*ith*-in *th*e shypp-bord,[3] her*e* lyvys to wynne ;
ffor God is sor*e* grevyd w*ith* man for his synne,
*Tha*t all*e th*is wyde werd xalbe dreynt w*ith* flood,
 Saff *tho*u *and th*i wyff xal be kept from *th*is gynne,
And also *th*i chylderyn w*ith* her*e* vertuys good.   125

NOE. How xuld I haue wytt a shypp for to make ?
 I am of ryght grett age, v. C. ȝere olde ;
It is not for me *th*is werk to vndyr-take ;
 ffor ffeyntnesse [4] of age my leggys gyn ffolde.
 ANGELUS. This dede ffor to do be bothe blythe *and*
  bolde;
God xal enforme *th*e *and* rewle *th*e ful ryght ;
 Of byrd *and* of beste take, as I *th*e tolde,
A peyr in-to *th*e shypp, *and* God xal *th*e qwyght.   133

NOE. I am ful redy, as God doth me bydde,
 A shypp for to make be myght of his grace.

   [Exit angelus.]

Alas ! *tha*t ffor synne it xal so be betydde
 *Tha*t vengeauns of flood xal werke *th*is manase.
 God is sor*e* grevyd w*ith* our*e* grett tresspas,
That w*ith* wylde watyr *th*e werd xal be dreynt.

---

  [1] H. viij.   [3] H. *omits* bord.
  [2] H. shypp.   [4] MS. ffeyynneſſe = ffeythnnesse.

A shypp*e* [1] for to make now lete us hens pas,
*Tha*t God a3ens us of synne haue no compleynt.   141

*Hic transit Noe cum familia sua pro naui ; quo exeunte, locum interludij
sub-intret statim Lameth conductus ab adolescente et di[cat]* [2] :

LAMETH.   Gret mornyng I make *and* gret cause I haue ;
    Alas ! now I se not, for age I am blynde ;
Blyndenes doth*e* make me of wytt forto rave ;
    Whantynge of eye-syght in peyn doth me bynde.
    Whyl I had syht, [3] myht nevyr man fynde
My pere of archerye in all*e* *th*is werd a-boute,
    ffor 3itt schet I nevyr at hert, [h]ar*e*, ner*e* hynde,
But yf *tha*t he deyd : of *th*is no man haue doute.   149

" Lameth, *th*e good archer*e* " my name was ovyr-all*e*,
    ffor *th*e best archer*e* my*n* name dede ev*er* sprede ;
Record of my boy her*e*, wytnes *th*is he xal,
    What merk *tha*t wer*e* set me, to deth it xuld blede.
    ADOLESCE*N*S.   It is trewe, mayst*er*, *tha*t 3e seyn indede ;
ffor *tha*t tyme 3e had 3our*e* bowe hent i*n* honde,
    If *tha*t 3o*ur* prycke had be half a myle in brede,
3e wolde *th*e pryk han hitte if 3e ny had stonde.   157

LAMETH.   I xuld nevyr a ffaylid, [4] what marke *tha*t ev*er* wer*e*
    sett,
    Whyl *tha*t I myght loke, *and* had my cler*e* syght ;
And 3itt, as me thynkyht, no man xuld shete bett
    Than I xuld do now if my*n* hand wer*e* sett aryght.
    Aspye som marke, boy, — my bowe xal [I] [5] bende wyght, —
And sett myn hand euyn to shete at som*e* best !
    And I dar ley a wago*ur* his deth for to dyght.
*Th*e marke xal I hitt, my lyff do I hest.   165

---

[1] MS. shypp.   [4] MS. affaylid, H. affayled.
[2] MS. di - - - ; H. dicens.   [5] *Supplied by* H.
[3] MS. syht y[t] myht ; H. syht, ther myht.

[The boy sees Cain.]

ADOLESCENS. Vndyr ȝon grett busche, mayst*er*, a best do I se ;
    Take me *thin* hand swyth *and* holde it ful stylle ;
Now is *thin* hand evyn as euyr it may be ;
    Drawe up *thin* takyll*e* ȝon best for to kylle.
    LAMETH. My bowe xal I drawe ryght w*ith* herty wylle ;
This brod arwe I shete *tha*t best ffor to sayll*e* ;
    Now, haue at *tha*t busch*e* ȝon best for to spylle !
A sharppe schote I shote, *ther*of I xal not fayll*e*.   173

CAYM. Out ! out ! *and* alas ! my*n* hert is on-sondyr ;
    W*ith* a brod arwe I am ded *and* sclayn.
I dye her*e* on grounde ; my*n* hert is all*e* to tundyr,
    W*ith* *th*is brod arwe it is clovyn on twayn.
    LAMETH. Herke, boy, cum telle me *the* trewth in certeyn ;
What man is he *tha*t *th*is cry doth *th*us make ?
    ADOLESCENS. Caym *tho*u hast kyllyd, I telle *the* ful pleyn*e* ;
W*ith* sharp shetyng his deth hath he take.   181

LAMETH. Haue I slayn Cayme ? Alas ! what haue I done ?
    *Tho*u stynkynge lurdeyn, what hast *tho*u wrought ?
*Tho*u art *th*e [cause] why I scle hym so sone ;
    *Th*er-for*e* xal I kyll*e* *th*e her*e*, *tho*u skapyst nowght.

*Hic Lameth cu*m *arcu suo* [1] *verberat adolescentem ad mortem, dicente adolescente :*

    ADOLESCENS. Out ! out ! I deye her*e*, my deth is now
        sought.
*Thi*s theffe w*ith* his bowe hath broke my brayn.
    Ther may non helpe be, my deth*e* is me brought ;
Ded her*e* I synke down, as man *tha*t is sclayn.   189

LAMETH. Alas ! what xal I do, wrecch*e*, wykkyd on woolde ?
    God wyl be vengyd ful sadly on me ;
ffor deth of Caym I xal haue vij folde

<hr>

[1] H. sua.

More peyn *th*an he had *th*at Abell*e* dede sle.
These to mennys deth full*e* sor*e* bought xal be ;
Vpon all*e* my blood God wyll*e* venge *th*is dede.
    Where-fore, sor*e* wepyng, hens wyl I fle,
And loke wher*e* I may best my hede sone heyde.   197

Hic recedat Lameth et *statim intrat Noe cum naui cantantes.*[1]

NOE.   With doolful hert, syenge sad *and* sor*e*,
    Grett morny*n*g I make for this dredful flood ;
Of man *and* of best is dreynte many a skore.
    All*e* *th*is werd [2] to spyll*e* *th*ese flodys be ful wood ;
    And all*e* is for synne of ma*n*nys wylde mood
*Tha*t God hath ordeyned *th*is dredfull*e* vengeau*n*ce.[3]
    In *th*is flood spylt is many a ma*n*nys blood ;
ffor synfull*e* levynge of man we haue gret grevau*n*s.   205

All*e* *th*is hundrýd ȝer*e* ryght her*e* haue I wrought
    This schypp for to make, as God dede byd me ;
Of all*e* maner best*es* a copyll*e* is in brought
    W*ith*-in my shypp-borde on lyve for to be.
    Ryght longe God hath soferyd, amendy*n*g to se,
All*e* *th*is hundyrd [4] ȝer*e* God hath shewyd grace.
    Alas ! fro gret syn man wyl not fle.
God doth *th*is vengeau*n*s for our*e* gret trespase.   213

VX*OR* NOE.   Alas ! for gret ruthe of *th*is gret vengeau*n*ce !
    Gret doyl it is to se *th*is watyr so wyde.
But ȝit thankyd be God of *th*is ordenau*n*ce,
    *Tha*t we be now savyd on lyve to a-byde.
    SEEM.   ffor grett synne of lechery all*e* *th*is doth betyde ;
Alas ! *tha*t evyr [5] such*e* synne xulde be wrought.
    *Th*is fflood is so gret on every a syde,[6]
*Tha*t all*e* *th*is wyde werd to car*e* is now brought.   221

[1] *See Notes.*	[4] H. hundryd.
[2] H.; MS. were.	[5] MS. ovyr.
[3] MS. vengeâuce.	[6] MS. asyde.

Vxo*R* Seem.   Be-cawse of chylderyn of God *tha*t weryn good
    Dede forfete ryght sor*e* what tyme *th*at *th*ei wer*e*
Synfully coupellyd ¹ to Caymys blood,
    Therfor*e* be we now cast in ryght grett care.
    Cham.   ffor synful levynge *th*is werde doth for-far*e*.
So grevous ² vengeau*n*s myght nevyr man se ;
    Ovyr all*e* *th*is werd wyde *ther* is no plot bar*e*.
W*ith* watyr *and* w*ith* flood God vengyd wyll*e* be.   229

Vxo*R* Cham.   Rustynes of synne is cawse of *th*ese wawys.
    Alas ! in *th*is fflood *th*is werd xal be lorn ;
ffor offens to God, brakyng his lawys,
    On rokkys ryght sharp is many a man torn.
    Iaphet.   So grevous fflodys wer*e* nevyr ȝett be-forn ;
Alas ! *tha*t lechery *th*is vengeau*n*s doth gynne.
    It wer*e* well*e* bettyr eu*er* to be vn-born
Than fforto forfetyn evyr-mor*e* in *tha*t synne.   237

Vxo*R* Iaphet.   Our*e* Lord God I thanke of his gret grace,
    *Tha*t he doth us saue from *th*is dredful payn*e*.
Hy*m* for to wurchipe in euery stede *and* place
    We beth gretly bownde w*ith* myght *and* w*ith* mayn.
    Noe.   xl*ti* days *and* nyght*es* hath lasted *th*is rayn,
And xl*ti* days *th*is grett flood begynnyth to slake.
    This crowe xal I sende out to seke sum playn ;
Good tydyng*es* to brynge *th*is massage I make.   245

*Hic emittat coruu*m et *paru*m *expectans iteru*m *dicat :*

This crowe on su*m* careyn is fall*e* for to ete ;
    *Th*er-fore a newe masanger*e* I wyll*e* fforth*e* now sende.
ffly fforth, *tho*u fayr dove, ovyr *th*ese water*ys* wete,
    *A*n*d* aspye afftere su*m* drye lond our*e* mornyng to amend.

Hic euolet columba ; ꝗua *redeunte* ³ *cum ramo viridj oliue,*⁴ [*dicat Noe :*]

Ioye now may we make of myrth *th*at *tha*t were frende ;
A grett olyve bush*e* *th*is dowe doth us brynge ;

---

¹ MS. compellyd ; *corr. by* Kittredge.   ³ MS. redeuite.
² MS. grevoûs.   ⁴ H. viride olivæ.

ffor ioye of *th*is tokyn ryght hertyly we tende.
Our*e* Lord God to worchep a songe lete vs sy*n*ge.   253

Hic decantent hos versus :

*Mare vidit, et fugit : Iordanis conu*ersus *est retrorsum.*
*Non nob*is, *Domine, non nob*is : sed *nomin*i *tuo da gl*oriam.

Et sic recedant cum naui.

BROME PLAY.

For this text I have used primarily the edition by Miss Lucy Toulmin Smith, in *Anglia*, VII, 316–337, and secondarily the edition (also by Miss Smith) in " A Commonplace Book of the Fifteenth Century . . . Printed from the Original MS. at Brome Hall, Suffolk, by Lady Caroline Kerrison. Edited with notes by Lucy Toulmin Smith. London and Norwich, 1886." In the footnotes, A. indicates the *Anglia* edition ; B., The Boke of Brome ; MS. indicates a reading found in the manuscript but relegated to the footnotes by Miss Smith. H. indicates the emendations of Holthausen, *Anglia*, XIII, 361.

As to the MS. Miss Smith says : " The crossed *ll* and *h* are constantly used, but for this date (1470 or 1480) it did not seem necessary to treat them otherwise than as *ll* and *h*."

[ABRAHAM AND ISAAC.]

ABRAHAM. Fad*er* of heuyn *omn*ipotent,
 W*ith* all my hart to the I call ;
Thow hast ʒoffe me both lond and rent,
And my lyvelod thow hast me sent ;
 I thanke the heyly eu*er*-mor*e* of all.   5

Fyrst off the erth *tho*u madyst Adam,
 And Eue also to be hys wyffe ;
All other creatur*es* [1] of them too cam ;
And now thow hast grant to me, Abrah*a*m,
 Her in thys lond to lede my lyffe.   10

In my age *tho*u hast g*r*antyd me thys,
 That thys ʒowng chyld w*ith* me shall won*e* ;
I love no-thyng so myche, i-wysse,
Excepe [2] *th*in owyn*e* selffe, der Fad*er* of blysse,
 As Ysaac her, my owyn*e* swete son*e*.   15

---

[1] B. creatures. *Such differences between the two prints I shall not record hereafter.*   [2] B. Except.

I haue dyu*er*se chyldryn moo,
    The wych I love not halffe so wyll ;
Thys fayer swet chyld he schereys me soo
In eu*er*y place wer that I goo,
    That noo dessece her may I fell.   20

And therfor,[1] Fadyr of heuyn, I the prey
    For hys helth and also for hys *grace* ;
Now, Lord, kepe hym both nygth and day,
That neu*er* dessese nor noo fray
    Cume to my chyld in noo place.   25

Now cu*m* on, Ysaac, my owyn*e* swet [2] chyld ;
    Goo we hom and take owr rest.
ISAAC.   Abrah*a*m, myn*e* owyn*e* fad*er* so myld,
    To folowe ȝow I am full prest,[3]
        Bothe erly *and* late.
      ABRAH*A*M.   Cume on, swete chyld, I love the best
        Of all the chyldryn that eu*er* I be-gat.   32

[God speaks above.]

DEUS.   Myn angell, fast hey the thy wey,
    And on-to medyll-erth anon *tho*u goo ;
Abrams hart now wyll I asay,
    Wether that he be stedfast or noo.   36

Sey I com*m*aw[n]dyd [4] hym for to take
    Ysaac, hys ȝowng sonne, *tha*t he love so wyll,
And w*ith* hys blood sacryfyce he make,
    Yffe ony off my freynchepe he [5] wyll ffell.   40

Schow hym the wey on-to the hylle
    Wer that hys sacryffyce schall be.

---

1 B. ther for.   2 B. swete.
3 MS. glad ; *cf. Englische Studien*, XIX, 150.
4 A. *inserts the* n, *but it is regularly omitted in this* MS.
5 A. B. yf *before* he.

I schall a-say now hys good wyll,
    Whether he lovyth [1] better hys chyld or me.
All men schall take exampyll be hym
    My commawmentes how they schall kepe.   46

[The angel begins to descend.]

ABRAHAM. Now, Fader of heuyn, that formyd all thyng,
    My preyeres I make to the a-ȝeyn,
For thys day my tender offryng
    Here mvst I ȝeve to the, certeyn.
A ! Lord God, all-myty Kyng,
    Wat maner best woll make the most fayn?
Yff I had ther-of very knoyng,
    Yt schuld be don with all my mayne
        Full sone anone.[2]
    To don thy plesyng on an hyll,
    Verely yt ys my wyll,
        Dere Fader, God in trinyte.   58

THE ANGELL. Abraham, Abraham, wyll thou rest !
    Owr Lord comandyth the for to take
Ysaac, thy ȝowng sone that thow lovyst best,
    And with hys blod sacryfyce that thow make.   62

In-to the lond of V[i]syon [3] thow goo,
    And offer thy chyld on-to thy Lord ;
I schall the lede and schow all-soo.
    Vnto Goddes hest, Abraham, a-cord,   66

And folow me vp-on thys grene.
    ABRAHAM. Wolle-com to me be my Lordes **sond,**
    And hys hest I wyll not with-stond ;
    ȝyt Ysaac, my ȝowng sonne in lond,
A full dere chyld to me haue byn.   71

[1] A. B. lovyd.
[2] *For* anone, H. *suggests* by me, *to rhyme with* 58.
[3] *Corr. by* H.

I had lever, yf God had be plesyd,
    For to a for-bore all the good that I haue,
Than Ysaac my sone schuld a be desessyd,
    So God in heuyn my sowll mot saue !   75

I lovyd neuer thyng soo mych in erde,[1]
    And now I mvst the chyld goo kyll.
A ! Lord God, my conseons ys stronly steryd,
And ȝyt, my dere Lord, I am sore [2] a-ferd
    To groche ony thyng a-ȝens ȝowr [3] wyll.   80

I love my chyld as my lyffe,
    But ȝyt I love my God myche more,
For thow my hart woold make ony stryffe,
ȝyt wyll I not spare for chyld nor wyffe,
    But don after my Lordes lore.   85

Thow I love my sonne neuer so wyll,
    ȝyt smythe of hys hed sone I schall.
A ! Fader of heuyn, to the I knell,
An hard dethe my son schall fell
    For to honor the, Lord, with-all.   90

THE ANGELL.   Abraham ! Abraham ! thys ys wyll seyd,
    And all thys comamentes loke that thou kepe ; [4]
But in thy hart be no-thyng dysmayd.[5]
ABRAHAM.   Nay, nay, for-soth, I hold me wyll plesyd [6]
    To plesse [7] my God to the best that I haue.[8]   95

For thow my hart be heuely sett
    To see the blood of my owyn dere sone,
ȝyt for all thys I wyll not lett,   [Exit angel.]
But Ysaac, my son, I wyll goo fett,
    And cum asse fast as euer we can.   100

---

[1] MS. erthe.
[2] A. sere.
[3] B. ȝowre.
[4] Qy.: loke thou obay.
[5] H. for MS. dysmasyd.
[6] Qy.: a-payd.
[7] MS. pelsse.
[8] Qy.: may.

Now, Ysaac, my owyne son dere,
　　Wer art thow, chyld?　Speke to me.
YSAAC.　My fayer [1] swet fader, I am here,
　　And make my preyrys to the Trenyte.　　　　　104

ABRAHAM.　Rysse vp, my chyld, and fast cum heder,
　　My gentyll barn that art so wysse,
For we to, chyld, must goo to-geder
　　And on-to my Lord make sacryffyce.　　　　　108

YSAAC.　I am full redy, my fader, loo !
　　3evyn at 3owr handes I stand rygth here,
And wat-so-euer 3e byd me doo,
　　Yt schall be don with glad cher,
　　　　Full wyll and fyne. [2]
　　ABRAHAM.　A ! Ysaac, my owyn son soo dere,
　　　　Godes blyssyng I 3yffe the, and myn.　　　　　115

Hold thys fagot vp-on thi bake,
　　And her my-selffe fyer schall bryng.
YSAAC.　Fader, all thys her wyll I packe ;
　　I am full fayn to do 3owr bedyng.
　　ABRAHAM.　A ! Lord of heuyn, my handes I wryng,
　　　　Thys chyldes wordes all to-wond my harte.　　　　　121

Now, Ysaac son,[3] goo we owr wey
　　On-to 3on mownte, with all owr mayn.
YSAAC.　Go we,[4] my dere fader, as fast as I may ;
　　To folow 3ow I am full fayn
　　　　All-thow I be slendyr.
　　ABRAHAM.　A ! Lord, my hart brekyth on tweyn,[5]
　　　　Thys chyldes wordes, they be so tender.　　　　　128

　　　　　　[They arrive at the Mount.]

A ! Ysaac, son, a-non ley yt down,
　　No lenger vp-on thi backe yt hold,[6]

[1] B. fader.　　　　[4] B. Gowe.
[2] A. syne.　　　　[5] MS. tewyn ; corr. by A.
[3] B. on.　　　　[6] MS. bere ; corr. by Kittredge (cf. v. 116).

For I mvst make redy bon
    To honowr my Lord God as I schuld.[1]   132

YSAAC.   Loo, my der*e* fad*er*, wer yt ys !
    To cher ʒow all-wey I draw me ner ;
But, fad*er*, I m*er*vell sor*e* of thys,
    Wy *tha*t ʒe make thys heuy cher*e* :   136

And also, fad*er*, eu*er*-mor*e* dred I :
    Wer ys ʒowr qweke best *tha*t ʒe schuld kyll?
Both fyer and wood we haue redy,
    But queke best haue we non on *thi*s hyll.   140

A qwyke best, I wot wyll, must be ded
    Ʒowr sacryfyce for to make.[2]
ABRAH*A*M.   Dred the nowyth, my chyld, I the red,
Owr Lord wyll send me on-to thys sted
    Su*m*m man*er* a best for to take,
        Throw hys swet sond.
     YSAAC. Ʒa, fad*er*, but my hart begynnyth to quake
    To se *tha*t scharpe sword in ʒowr hond.   148

Wy ber*e* ʒe ʒowr sword drawyn soo?
    Off ʒowr*e* co*n*wnau*n*s I haue mych wond*er*.
ABRAH*A*M.   A ! Fad*er* of heuyn, so [3] I am woo !
    Thys chyld her brekys my harte on-sonder.[4]   152

YSAAC.   Tell me, my der*e* fad*er*, o*r* that ʒe ses,
    Ber ʒe ʒowr sword draw[yn] [5] for me?
ABRAH*A*M.   A ! Ysaac, swet son, pes ! pes !
    For i-wys thow breke my harte on thre.   156

YSAAC.   Now trewly, su*m*-wat,[6] fad*er*, ʒe thynke,
    That ʒe morne thus mor*e* and mor*e*.

---

[1] A. *suggests* that I fere *for* as I schuld. H. *prefers* as dewli were.
[2] *Lines* 141, 142 *reversed in* MS.; *corr. by* A.
[3] MS. os; *corr. by* A.
[4] A. B. on too; H.'s *correction on basis of Chester Play.*
[5] *Corr. by* H.   [6] B. su*m*-what.

ABRAHAM. A ! Lord of heuyn, thy grace let synke,
    For my hart was [1] neue*r* halffe so sor*e*.   160

YSAAC. I p*r*eye ȝow, fad*er*, *tha*t ȝe wyll let me *tha*t wyt,
    Wyther schall I haue ony harme or noo.
ABRAHAM. I-wys, swet son, I may not tell the ȝyt,
    My hart ys now soo full of woo.   164

YSAAC. Der*e* fad*er*, I prey ȝow, hyd yt [2] not fro me,
But su*m* of ȝowr thɑwt *tha*t ȝe tell me.
ABRAHAM. A ! Ysaac, Ysaac, I must kyll the !
    YSAAC. Kyll me, fad*er*? alasse ! wat haue I don*e*?   168

Yff I haue trespassyd a-ȝens ȝow owt,
    W*ith* a ȝard ȝe may make me full myld ;
And w*ith* ȝowr scharp sword kyll me nogth,
    For i-wys, fad*er*, I am but a chyld.   172

ABRAHAM. I am full sory, son, thy blood for to spyll,
    But truly, my chyld, I may not chese.
YSAAC. Now I wold to God my mod*er* wer*e* her on *th*is [3] hyll!
    Sche woold knele for me on both hyr kneys
        To save my lyffe.
And sythyn that my mod*er* ys not her*e*,
I prey ȝow, fad*er*, schonge ȝow*er* cher*e*,
    And kyll me not w*ith* ȝowyr knyffe.   180

ABRAHAM. For-sothe, son, but ȝyf I the kyll,
    I schuld g*r*eve God rygth sor*e*, I drede ;
Yt ys hys co*m*mawment and also hys wyll
    That I schuld do thys same dede.   184

He co*m*mawdyd me, son, for serteyn,
    To make my sacryfyce w*ith* thy blood.
YSAAC. And ys yt Godd*es* wyll *tha*t I schuld be slayn?
    ABRAHAM. Ȝa, [4] truly, Ysaac, my son soo good,
    And ther-for my hand*es* I wryng.   189

[1] B. wos.   [3] A. ys; B. yis = *th*is.
[2] A. B. hydygth.   [4] B. Ȝa.

YSAAC. Now, fad*er*, aȝens my Lord*es* wyll [1]
I wyll neu*er* groche, lowd nor styll ;
    He mygth a sent me a bett*er* desteny
Yf yt had a be hys plecer.[2]   193

ABRAH*A*M. For-sothe, son, but yf Y [3] ded *th*is dede,
    Grevosly dysplessyd owr Lord wyll be.
YSAAC. Nay, nay, fad*er*, God for-bede
    That eu*er* ȝe schuld gr*e*ve hym for me.   197

Ȝe haue other chyldryn, on or too,
    The wyche ȝe schuld love wyll be kynd.
I prey ȝow, fad*er*, make ȝe no woo,
For, be I onys ded and fro ȝow goo,
    I schall be sone owt of ȝowr mynd.   202

Ther-for doo owr Lord*es* byddyng,
    And wan I am ded, than p*r*ey for me ;
But, good fad*er*, tell ȝe my mod*er* no-thyng,
Say [4] *tha*t I am in a-nother cu*n*tre dwellyng.[5]
    ABRAH*A*M. A ! Ysaac, Ysaac, blessyd mot thow be !   207

My hart be-gynnyth [6] stronly to rysse,
    To see the blood off thy blyssyd body.
YSAAC. Fadyr, syn yt may be noo other wysse,
    Let yt passe ou*er* as wyll as I.   211

But, fad*er*, or I goo on-to my deth,
    I prey ȝow blysse me w*ith* ȝowr hand.
ABRAH*A*M. Now, Ysaac, w*ith* all my breth
    My blyssyng I ȝeve *th*e vpon thys lond
        And God*es* also ther-to, i-wys.
    Ysaac, Ysaac, son*e*, vp thow stond,
        Thy fayer swete mowthe *th*at I may kys.   218

---

[1] *Qy.:* decre.   [4] B. Sey.
[2] *Qy.:* wyll.   [5] MS. dewllyng; *corr. by* A.
[3] B. I.   [6] MS. begynnyd; A. *suggests* begynnys.

YSAAC.   Now for-wyll, my owyn*e* fad*er* so fyn,
    And grete wyll my mod*er* in erde.[1]
But I prey 3ow, fad*er*, to hyd my eyne,
    That I se not *th*e stroke of 3owr scharpe swerd,[2]
        That my fleysse schall defyle.
ABRAH*A*M.   Son*e*, thy word*es* make me to wepe [3] full sor*e* ;
Now, my der*e* son Ysaac, speke no mor*e*.
YSAAC.   A ! my owyn*e* der*e* fad*er*, wer*e*-fore ?
    We schall speke to-gedyr her but a wylle.   227

And sythyn that I must nedysse be ded,
    3yt, my der*e* fad*er*, to 3ow I prey,
Smyth*e* but fewe [4] strok*es* at my hed,
    And make an end as sone as 3e may,
        And tery not to longe.
    ABRAH*A*M.   Thy meke word*es*, chyld, make me afray; [5]
        So, " welawey !" may be my songe,   234

Excepe alo*n*ly Godes wyll.
    A ! Ysaac, my owyn swete chyld,
3yt kysse me a-3en vp-on thys hyll !
    In all thys war[l]d [6] ys no*n* soo myld.   238

YSAAC.   Now truly, fad*er*, all thys teryyng
    Yt doth my hart but harme ;
I prey 3ow, fader, make an enddyng.
    ABRAH*A*M.   Cume vp, swet son, on-to my arme.   242

I must bynd thy handes [7] too,
    All-thow thow be neu*er* soo myld.
YSAAC.   A ! m*er*cy, fad*er* ! wy schuld 3e do soo ?
    ABRAH*A*M.   That thow schuldyst not let,[8] my chyld.   246

[1] A. B. erthe.
[2] A. B. sword.
[3] B. weep.
[4] A. B. feve.
[5] A. B. afrayed.
[6] ward *is the regular form of* world *in this* MS.
[7] B. hands.
[8] A. B. *insert* [me].

YSAAC.   Nay, i-wysse, fad*er*, I wyll not let ȝow ;
    Do on for me ȝowr wyll,
And on the p*ur*pos that ȝe haue set ȝow
    For God*es* love kepe yt forthe styll.   250

I am full sory thys day to dey,
    But ȝyt I kepe not my God to greve ;
Do on ȝowr lyst for me hardly,
    My fayer swete fad*er*, I ȝeffe ȝow leve.   254

But, fad*er*, I prey ȝow eu*er*-mor*e*,
    Tell ȝe my mod*er* no dell ;
Yffe sche wost yt,[1] sche wold wepe full sor*e*,
    For i-wysse, fad*er*, sche lovyt me full wylle,
        God*es* blyssyng mot sche haue ![2]   259

Now for-wyll, my mod*er* so swete,
    We too be leke no mor to mete.
ABRAH*A*M.   A ! Ysaac, Ysaac ! son, *tho*u makyst me to gret,
    And w*ith* thy word*es* thow dystempurst me.   263

YSAAC.   I-wysse, swete fad*er*, I am sory to g*r*eve ȝow,
    I cry ȝow m*er*cy of that I haue donne,
And of all trespasse *tha*t eu*er* I ded meve ȝow ;
    Now, der*e* fad*er*, for-ȝyffe me *tha*t I haue donne.
        God of heuyn be w*ith* me !   268

ABRAH*A*M.   A ! der*e* chyld, lefe of thy monys ;
In all thy lyffe thow grevyd me neu*er* onys ;
Now blyssyd be thow, body and bonys,
    That eu*er* thow wer*e* bred and born !
Thow hast be to me chyld full good.
    But i-wysse, chyld, thow I morne neu*er* so fast,
    ȝyt must I ned*es* her*e* at the last
In thys place sched all thy blood.   276

---

[1] A. B. wostyt.
[2] H. *suggests* haue mot sche, *to rhyme with* 263.

Ther-for, my der*e* son, her*e* schall *tho*u lye.
 On-to my warke I must me stede,
I-wysse I had as leve my-selffe to dey —
  Yff God wyll be[1] plecyd wyth my dede —
  And myn owyn body for to offer.
 YSAAC. A ! mer*c*y, fad*er*, morne ȝe no mor*e*,
 ȝowr wepyng make[2] my hart sor*e*,
  As my owyn deth that I schall suffer.   284

ȝowr kerche, fad*er*, a-bowt my eyn ȝe wynd !
 ABRAH*A*M. So I schall, my swettest chyld in erde.[3]
YSAAC. Now ȝyt, good fad*er*, haue thys in mynd,
 And smyth me not oftyn w*it*h ȝowr scharp swerd,[4]
  But hastely that yt be sped.

   *Her*e *A braham leyd a cloth on Ysaac*es *face, thus seyyng :*

ABRAH*A*M. Now for*e*-wyll, my chyld, so full of g*ra*ce.
YSAAC. A ! fad*er*, fad*er*, torne downgward my face,
  For of ȝowr scharpe sword I am eu*er* a-dred.   292

ABRAH*A*M. To don thys dede I am full sory,
 But, Lord, thyn hest I wyll not w*it*h-stond.
YSAAC. A ! Fad*er* of heuyn, to the I crye,
  Lord, reseyve me in-to[5] thy hand.   296

ABRAH*A*M. Loo ! now ys the tyme cu*m* certeyn
 That my sword in hys necke schall bite.[6]
A ! Lord, my hart reysyth ther-ageyn,[7]
 I may not fynd yt[8] in my harte to smygth, —
  My hart wyll not now ther-too.
 ȝyt fayn I woold warke my Lord*es* wyll ;
 But thys ȝowng innosent lygth so styll,
 I may not fynd yt[8] in my hart hym to kyll.
  O ! Fad*er* of heuyn ! what schall I doo ?   305

---

  [1] B. *omits* be.   [5] A. *omits* to.
  [2] H. maketh.   [6] MS. synke ; *corr. by* H.
  [3] A. B. erthe.   [7] B. the ageyn.
  [4] A. B. sword.   [8] A. B. fyndygth.

YSAAC.   A ! mercy, fader, wy tery ʒe so,
　　And let me ley thus longe on this hethe?
Now I wold to God the stroke were doo !
Fader, I prey ʒow hartely, schorte me of my woo,
　　And let me not loke thus after my degth.　　　　　　310

ABRAHAM.   Now, hart, wy wolddyst not thow breke on thre ?
　　ʒyt schall th[o]u not make me to my God on-myld.
I wyll no lenger let for the,
For that my God a-grevyd wold be ;
　　Now hoold tha stroke, my owyn dere chyld.　　　　315

Her Abraham draw [1] hys stroke and the [2] angell toke the sword in hys hond
soddenly.

THE ANGELL.   I am an angell, thow mayist se blythe,
　　That fro heuyn to the ys senth.
Owr Lord thanke the an C sythe
　　For the kepyng of hys commawment.　　　　　　319

He knowyt thi wyll and also thy harte,
　　That thow dredyst hym above all thyng ;
And sum of thy hevynes for to departe
　　A fayr ram ʒynder I gan brynge ;　　　　　　　323

He standyth teyed, loo ! a-mong the breres.
　　Now, Abraham, a-mend thy mood,
For Ysaac, thy ʒowng son that her ys,
　　Thys day schall not sched hys blood ;　　　　　327

Goo, make thy sacryfece with ʒon [3] rame.
Now for-wyll, blyssyd Abraham,
　　For on-to heuyn I goo now hom ;
　　　The way ys full gayn.
　　　　Take vp thy son soo free.　　　[*Exit.*]　　332

ABRAHAM.   A ! Lord, I thanke the of thy gret grace,
　　Now am I yeyed [4] on dyuers wysse ;

---

[1] B. *drew.*　　　[2] B. *the.*　　　[3] A. ʒou.　　　[4] *Qy.: for* ethed = eased.

A-rysse vp, Ysaac, my der*e* su*n*ne, a-rysse ;
    A-rysse vp, swete chyld, and cu*m* to me.   336

YSAAC. A ! me*r*cy, fad*er*, wy smygth ȝe nowt ? [1]
    A ! smygth on, fad*er*, onys w*ith* ȝowr knyffe.
ABRAH*A*M.   Pesse, my swet son,[2] and take no thowt,[3]
    For owr Lord of heuyn hath grant *th*i lyffe
      Be hys angell now,   341

That *tho*u schalt not dey *th*is day,[4] su*n*ne, truly.
YSAAC. A ! fad*er*, full glad than wer I,
    I-wys, fad*er*, I sey, i-wys,
      Yf thys tale wer trew.
    ABRAH*A*M.   An hundyrd tymys, my son fayer of hew,
    For joy *th*i mowth [5] now wyll I kys.   347

YSAAC. A ! my der*e* fad*er*, Abraha*m*,
    Wyll not God be wroth *th*at we do thus ?
ABRAH*A*M.   Noo, noo ! har[de]ly, my swyt son,
    For ȝyn same rame he hath vs sent [6]
    Hether down to vs.[7]   352

ȝyn best schall dey her*e* in *th*i sted,
    In the wor*th*schup [8] of owr Lord a-lon ;
Goo, fet hym hethyr, my chyld, in-ded.
YSAAC.   Fad*er*, I wyll goo hent hym be the hed,
    And bryng ȝon best w*ith* me a-non.   357

        [*Isaac catches the ram.*]

A ! scheppe, scheppe, blyssyd [9] mot *tho*u be,
    That eu*er* thow wer*e* sent down hed*er* !
Thow schall thys day dey for me,
In the worchup of the holy Trynyte.

[1] MS. not ȝyt ; *corr. by* H.
[2] A. B. sir.   [4] B. dey.
[3] H. *proposes* dowt.   [5] B. mowt.
[6] H. *proposes :* For he hath sent us ȝyn same rame.
[7] *Qy.* : Noo, noo, swyt son, for ȝyn same rame
        He hath sent hether down to vs.
[8] MS. worpschup ; *corr. by* A.   [9] B. blessed.

    Now cu*m* fast and goo we to-ged*er*
      To my Fad*er* of heuyn.[1]
Thow *tho*u be neu*er* so jentyll and goo*d*,
3yt had I leu*er* thow schedyst *th*i blood,
    I-wysse, scheppe, than I.   366

Loo ! fad*er*, I haue browt her*e* full smerte
    Thys jentyll scheppe,[2] and hym to 3ow I 3yffe ;
But, Lord God, I thanke *th*e [3] *with* all my hart,
    For I am glad that I schall leve
    And kys onys my der*e* moder.
    ABRAH*A*M.   Now be rygth myry, my swete chyld,
    For thys qwyke best *tha*t ys so myld
    Her*e* I schall pr*e*sent be-for*e* all other.   374

YSAAC. And I wyll fast be-gynne to blowe ;
    Thys fyer schall brene a full good spyd.
But, fad*er*, wyll I stowppe down*e* lowe,
3e wyll not kyll me *with* 3owr sword, I trowe?
    ABRAH*A*M.   Noo, har[de]ly, swet son, haue no dred,
    My mornyng ys past.
    YSAAC.   3a ! but I woold *tha*t sword wer in a gled,[4]
    For, i-wys, fad*er*, yt make me full yll a-gast.   382

    *Her*e *Abraham mad hys offryng, knelyng and seyyng thus :*

ABRAH*A*M. Now, Lord God of heuen in Trynyte,
    All-myty God omnipotent,
My offeryng I make in the worchope of the,
    And *with* thys qweke best I the pr*e*sent.
    Lord, reseyve thow myn intent,
    As [thow] art God and grownd of owr gr*a*ce.   388

---

[1] *Qy.:* To my fad*er* in hy.
[2] *As two lines in* A. B., *the first ending here. From here my numbering is one line behind Miss Smith's.*
[3] B. ye.
[4] A. B. glad = gled.

[God speaks from above.]

DEUS.   Abrah*a*m, Abrah*a*m, wyll mot thow sped,
    And Ysaac, *th*i ȝowng son the by !
Trvly, Abrah*a*m, for thys dede
I schall mvltyplye ȝowr*es* bother*es* sede
    As thyke as sterr*es* be in the skye,
        Bothe more and lesse ;
    And as thyke as gravell in the see,
    So thyke mvltyplyed ȝowr sede schall be ;
        Thys grant I ȝow for ȝowr goodnesse.   397

Off ȝow schall cume frowte gret [won],
    And eu*er* be in blysse w*ith*-owt ȝynd.
For ȝe drede me as God a-lon
And kepe my co*m*mawment*es* eu*er*yschon,
    My blyssyng I ȝeffe, wer-so-eu*er* ȝe wend.[1]   402

ABRAH*A*M.   Loo ! Ysaac, my son, how thynke ȝe
    Be thys warke that we haue wrogth ?
Full glad and blythe we may be,
    Aȝens *th*e wyll of God *tha*t we grucched nott,
        Vp-on thys fayer hetth.
    YSAAC.   A ! fad*er*, I thanke owr Lord eu*er*y dell,
    That my wyt servyd me so wyll
        For to drede God mor*e* than my detth.   410

ABRAH*A*M.   Why ! der*e*-wordy son, wer thow a-dred ?
    Hardely, chyld, tell me thy lore.
YSAAC.   Ȝa ! be my feyth, fad*er*, now haue [2] I red,
    I wos neu*er* soo afrayd be-for*e*
        As I haue byn at ȝyn hyll.
    But, be my feyth, fad*er*, I swer*e*
    I wyll neu*er*-mor*e* cume ther*e*
        But yt be a-ȝens my wyll.   418

---

[1] A. B. goo; *corr. by* H.   [2] A. B. hath.

ABRAHAM.   3a ! cum on with me, my owyn swet sonn,
And hom-ward fast now let vs goon.

    YSAAC.   Be my feyth, fader, ther-to I grant,
I had neuer so good wyll to gon hom,
       And to speke with my dere moder.

    ABRAHAM.   A ! Lord of heuyn, I thanke the,
For now may I led hom with me
Ysaac, my 3ownge sonn so fre, —
      The gentyllest chyld a-bove all other,[1]
        Thys may I wyll a-voee.   428

Now goo we forthe, my blyssyd sonn.
YSAAC.   I grant, fader, and let vs gon,
    For be my trowthe wer I at home,
    I wold neuer gon owt vnder that forme.
      I pray God 3effe vs grace euer-mo,
      And all thow that we be holdyng to.   434

[Exeunt. Enter Doctor.]

DOCTOR.   Lo ! sovereyns and sorys, now haue we schowyd
    Thys solom story [2] to grete and smale ;
It ys good lernyng to lernd and lewyd
    And the wysest of vs all,
      Wyth-owtyn ony berryng.
For thys story schoyt 3owe [her]
How we schuld kepe to owr po[we]re
      Goddes commawments with-owt grochyng.   442

Trowe 3e, sores, and God sent an angell
    And commawndyd 3ow 3owr chyld to slayn,[3]
Be 3owr trowthe ys ther ony of 3ow
    That eyther wold groche or stryve ther-ageyn ?
How thyngke 3e now, sorys, ther-by ?

       [1] MS. erthe; *corr. by* A.
       [2] A. B. *have* hath schowyd *after* story ; *corr. by* H.
       [3] A. B. to smygth of 3owr chyldes hed ; *corr by* H.

I trow ther be iij or iiij or moo.
And thys women that wepe so sorowfully
   Whan that hyr chyldryn dey them froo,
      As nater woll[1] and kynd, —
   Yt ys but folly, I may well awooe,
   To groche a-ȝens God or to greve ȝow,
   For ȝe schall neuer se hym myschevyd, wyll I know,
      Be lond nor watyr, haue thys in mynd ;   455

And groche not a-ȝens owr Lord God
   In welth or woo, wether that he ȝow send,
Thow ȝe be neuer so hard be-stad ;
   For when he wyll, he may yt a-mend,
Hys comawmentes trevly[2] yf ȝe kepe with goo[d][3] hart,
   As thys story hath now schowyd ȝow be-for[n]e,[4]
And feytheffully serue hym qwyll ȝe be qvart,
   That ȝe may plece God bothe euyn and morne.
   Now Jesu, that weryt the crown of thorne,
      Bryng vs all to heuyn blysse !   465
        Finis.

[1] woll *twice in* MS.   [3] *So* A. B.
[2] B. treuly.   [4] *Corr. by* H.

TOWNELEY PLAYS.

For information as to the text, see above, p. 13. The fragmentary condition of the first piece, Isaac, is due to the loss of two leaves of the MS. at this place.

I.

[ISAAC.]

. . . .

[ISAAC.] Com nere, son, and kys me,
That I may feyle the smell of the.
The smell of my son is lyke
To a feld with flouris, or hony bike.
Where art thou, Esaw, my son?
IACOB.   Here, fader, and askis youre benyson.
ISAAC.   The blyssyng my fader gaf to me,
God of heuen & I gif the :
God gif the plente grete
Of wyne, of oyll, and of whete ;   10
And graunt thi childre all
To worship the, both grete and small ;
Who-so the blyssys, blyssed be he ;
Who-so the waris, wared be he.
Now has thou my grete blyssyng,
Loue the shall all thyne ofspryng ;
Go now wheder thou has to go.
IACOB.   Graunt mercy, sir, I will do so.

Recedet Iacob. [Esau advances.]

ESAW.   Haue ete, fader, of myn huntyng,
And gif me sythen your blyssyng.   20

ISAAC. Who is that?
ESAW.   I, youre son,
Esaw, bryng*is* you venyson.
ISAAC. Who was that was right now here
And broght me bruet of a dere?
I ete well, and blyssyd hym ;
And he is blyssyd, ich a lym.
ESAW. Alas! I may grete and sob.
ISAAC. Thou art begylyd thrugh Iacob
That is thyne awne german brother.
ESAW. Haue ye kepyd me none other   30
Blyssyng then ye set hym one?
ISAAC. Sich another haue I none ;
Bot God gif the to thyn handband
The dew of heuen & frute of land ;
Other then this can I not say.
ESAW. Now, alas and walo-way!
May I with that tratoure mete,
My faders dayes shall com *with* grete,
And my moders also ;
May I hym mete, I shall hym slo.   40

[Esau retires. Rebecca advances.]

REBECCA. Isaac, it were my deth
If Iacob weddeth in kynd of Heth ;
I will send hym to Aran,
There my brothere dwellys, Laban ;
And there may he s*er*ue in peasse
Till his brothers [1] wrath will seasse.
Why shuld I apon a day
Loyse both my sonnes? bett*er* nay.
ISAAC. Thou says soth, wife ; call hym hed*er*,
And let vs tell hym where & whed*er*   50
That he may fle Esaw,
That vs both het*is* bale to brew.

---

[1] E. E. T. S. brother's.

REBECCA.   Iacob, son! thi fad*er* & I
Wold speke w*ith* the ; com, stand vs by !

[*Jacob advances.*]

Out of contry must thou fle,
That Esaw slo not the.
IACOB.   Whederward shuld I go, dame?
REBECCA.   To Mesopotameam ;
To my brothere, and thyn eme,
That dwellys besyde Iordan streme ;   60
And ther may thou with hym won,
To Esaw, myne other son,
fforget, and all his wrath be dede.
IACOB.   I will go, fad*er*, at youre rede.
ISAAC.   Yei, son, do as thi mod*er* says ;
Com kys vs both, & weynd thi ways.

*Et osculat*ur.

IACOB.   Haue good day, s*ir* and dame !
ISAAC.   God sheld the, son, from syn and shame !
REBECCA.   And gif the grace good man to be,
And send me glad tything*is* to [1] the.   70

Explicit Isaac.

II.

[JACOB.] [2]

IACOB.   Help me, Lord, Adonay,
And hald me in the right way
To Mesopotameam !
ffor I cam neu*er* or now where [3] I am ;
I cam neu*er* here in this contre.
Lord of heuen, thou help me !
ffor I haue maide me, in this strete,
Sore bonys & warkand feete.

[1] *Qy.:* fro.
[2] E. E. T. S. Sequit*ur* *Iacob.*
[3] *Qy.: change* now where *to* where now *for metre.*

The son is downe, what is best?
Her purpose I all nyght to rest ;   10
Vnder my hede this ston shal ly ;
A nyght*is* rest take will I.

        [He sleeps. God appears and speaks.]

DEUS. Iacob, Iacob, thi God I am,
Of thi forfad*er* Abraham,
And of thi fad*er* Isaac.
I shall the blys for thare sake.
This land that thou slepys in
I shall the gif, and thi kyn ;
I shall thi seede multyply,
As thyk as powd*er* on erth may ly ;   20
The kynd of the shall sprede wide,
ffrom eest to west on eu*er*y syde,
ffrom the south vnto the north, —
All that I say, I shall forth, —
And all the folk*is* of thyne ofspryng,
Shal be blyssyd of thy blyssyng.
Iacob, haue thou no kyns drede !
I shall the clethe, I shall the fede ;
Whartfull shall I make thi gate ;
I shal the help erly and late ;   30
And all in qwart shall I bryng the
Home agane to thi countre.
I shall not fayll, be thou bold,
Bot I shall do as I haue told.

        Hic vigilet.

IACOB. A ! Lord, what may this mene ?
What haue I herd in slepe, and sene ?
That God leynyd hym to a stegh
And spake to me, it is no leghe !
And now is here none othere gate
Bot God*is* howse and heuens yate.   40

Lord, how dredfull is this stede !
Ther I layde downe my hede,
In God*is* lovyng I rayse this stone,
And oyll will I putt theron.
Lord of heuen, that all wote,
Here to the I make a hote :
If thou gif me mete and foode,
And close to body, as I behoued,
And bryng me home to kyth and kyn
By the way that I walk in,   50
Without skathe and in quarte,
I p*ro*myse to the *with* stedfast hart,
As thou art Lord and God myne
And I Iacob, thi trew hyne,
This stone I rayse in sygne to-day
Shall I hold holy kyrk for ay ;
And of all that newes me
Rightwys tend shall I gif the.

[*An interval of about twenty years.*]

*Hic egrediat*ur *Iacob de Aran in* te*rram natiuita*tis *sue.*

[IACOB.]   A ! my Fad*er*, God of heuen,
That saide to me thrugh thi steven,   60
When I in Aran was dwelland,
That I shuld turne agane to land
Ther I was both fed and born*e*,
Warnyd thou me, Lord, beforn*e*,
As I went toward Aran
With my staff, and passyd Iordan ;
And now I com agane to kyth
With two ostes of men me with.
Thou hete me, Lord,[1] to do well w*ith* me,
To multyplye my seede as sand of see ;   70
Thou saue me, Lord, thrugh vertew,
ffrom veniance of Esaw,

---

[1] *Qy. · omit* Lord.

That he slo not, for old greme,
These moders *with* thare barne-teme.
RACHELL.   Oure anguysh, sir, is many-fold,
Syn that oure messyngere vs told
That Esaw wold you slo,
With foure hundreth men and mo.
IACOB.   ffor soth, Rachell, I haue hym sent
Of many beest*is* sere p*r*esent.   80
May tyde he will oure gift*is* take,
And right so shall his wrath slake.
Where ar oure thyng*is*, ar thay past Iordan?
LYA.   Go and look, sir, as ye can.

Hic scrutetur superlectile, et *luctetur angelus cum eo.*

DEUS.   The day spryng*is*; now lett me go.
IACOB.   Nay, nay, I will not so
Bot thou blys me or thou gang;
If I may, I shall hold the lang.
DEUS.   In tokynyng that thou spek*is with* me
I shall toche now thi thee,   90
That halt shall thou eu*er*more,
Bot thou shall fele no sore.
What is thy name, thou me tell?
IACOB.   Iacob.
DEUS.   Nay, bot Israell.
Syn thou to me sich strengthe may kythe,
To men of erth thou must be stythe.
IACOB.   What is thy name?
DEUS.   Whi ask*is* thou it?
'Wond*er*full,' if thou wil wyt.
IACOB.   A, blys me, Lord!
DEUS.   I shall the blys,
And be to the full p*r*opyce,   100
And gyf the my blyssyng for ay;
As lord and he that all may,
I shall[1] grayth thi gate,

[1] *Qy.: insert* goodly.

And full well ordeyn thi state.
When thou has drede, thynk on me,
And thou shal full well saynyd be.
And look thou trow well my sayes ;
And farewell now, the day dayes.

IACOB. Now haue I a new name, Israell ;
This place shall [hight] [1] Fanuell,   110
ffor I haue seyn in this place
God of heuen face to face.

RACHELL. Iacob, lo ! we haue tythand
That Esaw is here at hand.

Hic diuidit turmas in tres partes.

IACOB. Rachell, stand thou in the last eschele,
ffor I wold thou were sauyd wele ;
Call Ioseph and Beniamin,
And let theym not fro the twyn.
If it be so that Esaw
Vs before all to-hew,   120
Ye that ar here the last
Ye may be sauyd if ye fle fast.

Et *vadat Iacob osculand* [o] *Esaw ; venit Iacob, flectit genua exorando Deum; et
leuando, occurrit illi Esaw in amplexibus.*

IACOB. I pray the, Lord, as thou me het,
Thou [2] saue me and my gete.

ESAW. Welcom, brother, to kyn and kyth,
Thi wife and childre that comes the with.
How has thou faren in far land?
Tell me now som good tythand.

IACOB. Well, my brother Esaw,
If that thi men no bale me brew.   130

Dicit seruis suis.

ESAW. Wemo ! felows, hold youre hend,
Ye se that I and he ar frend,

---

[1] *Supplied by* E. E. T. S.   [2] MS. that.

And frenship here will we fulfill,
Syn that it is God*is* will.

IACOB.   God yeld you, brothere, that it so is
That thou thi hyne so wold kys.

ESAW.   Nay, Iacob, my dere brothere,
I shall the tell all anothere :
Thou art my lord thrugh destyny.
Go we toged*er*, both thou and I,   140
To my fad*er* and his wife,
That lofys the, brother, as thare lyfe.

Explicit Iacob.

CHESTER WHITSUN PLAYS.

Reprinted from " The Chester Plays. Reëdited from the MSS. by the late Dr. Hermann Deimling, Part I, E. E. T. S., 1892." I have printed only MS. Harl. 2124, because, although written in 1607, it represents, I believe, a more primitive form of this play than the other MSS. The Duke of Devonshire's MS. (written by Edward Gregorie, 1591) was not collated by Deimling; consequently I do not know which version of our play it presents, but Pollard's partial collation seems to indicate that it would agree with the others. Only occasionally have I recorded the readings of the other MSS. For convenience I have used Deimling's symbols; thus, H.= Harl. 2124 (partly written by James Miller, 1607), B.= Bodley 175 (written by Wm. Bedford, 1604), W. = Brit. Mus., Addit. 10,305 (written by George Bellin, 1592), h.= Harl. 2013 (written by George Bellin, 1600). D. indicates Deimling's text, which agrees with H., unless otherwise specified. I have made no changes without notification, except in punctuation, capitals, and mode of indicating stanza-structure.

Pagina Quinta de Mose et Rege Balaak et Balaam Propheta.   The Cappers.

DEUS.   Moyses, my servaunte life *and* dere,
And all the people that be here,
You wott in Egipte when you were,
　　Out of thralldome I you broughte.
I wyll, you honour no God saue me,
Ne mawmentrye none make yee,
My name in vayne nym[1] not yee,
　　For that me lykes naughte.

I will, you hold yo*ur* holy daye,
And worshipp also, by all waye,
Father and mother all that you maye,
　　And slaye no man no-where.

8

　　　　　　　　[1] H. myn ; B. W. h. nam.

Fornication you shall flee ;
No mens goods steale yee ;
Ne in no place abyde ne bee
    Falce wytnes for to beare.   16

Your neigheboures [1] wyves covettes noughte,
Servant ne good that he hath boughte,
Oxe ne asse, in deede ne thoughte,
    Nor any-thinge that is his,
Ne wrongefullie to haue his thinge
Agayne his will and his lykinge.
In all these doe my byddinge,
    That you doe not amisse.   24

Tunc princeps Sinagogæ statuet eum [2] in loco et quasi pro populo loquatur ad
Dominum et Moysen.

PRINCEPS SINAGOGÆ.   Ah ! good Lord, much of mighte,
Thou comes with so great lighte !
We bene so afraide of this sighte,
    No man dare speake ne see ; [3]
God is so grym with us to deale,
But Moyses, master, with us thou mele, —
Els we dyen many and feele,
    So afrayde bene all wee.   32

Tunc Moyses stans super montem loquatur ad populum.

MOYSES.   Gods folke, drede you noughte ;
To prove you with, God hath this wrought,
To make you afrayd in deede and thoughte,
    Aye for to avoyde synne.
By this sight you may now see
That he is pereles of postye ;
Therfore his teachinge look done yee,
    Thereof that you not blyn.   40

---

[1] D. neightboures.
[2] H. eu; D. *prints* eum, *but suggests* eo ; Zupitza *suggested* se.
[3] MS. looke; *corr. by* D.

P*RI*NCEPS SINAGOG*Æ*.   Ah! highe Lord, God almighte,
That Moyses shynes wondrous bright!
I may no way for great lighte
        Now looke upon hym.
And horned he semes in our sighte!   Exodus, 34. 29.
Sith he came to the hyll, dight
Our lawe he hase, I hope, aright,
        For was he never so grym.   48

*Mo*YSES.   You, Gods folke of Israell,
Hearkens to me that loven heale ;
God bade you sholde doe, everye deale,
        As that I shall saye.
Six dayes boldelye worches all,
The seaventh Sabaoth you shall call ;
That daye for ought that may befall
        Hallowed shalbe aye.   56

That doth not this deede deade shall be.
In houses fire shall no man see.
First fruytes to God offer yee,
        For so hym-selfe bade.
Gould *and* silver offers also,
Purple, bisse, and other moe,
To hym that shall save you from woe
        And helpe you in yo*u*r neede.   64

*Ex*POSITOR.   Lordinges, this comaundment
Was of the Old Testamente,
And yet is used w*i*th good entent
        W*i*th all that good bene.
This storye all if we shold fong,
To playe this moneth it were to longe ;
Wherfore most frutefull there amonge
        We taken, as shall be sene.   72

Also we read in this storie,
God in the Mownt of Synai

Toke Moises these comaundment*is* verelye,
 Wrytten w*i*th his owne hande
In tables of ston, as reade I ;
But when men honoured mawmentry,
He brake them in anger hastelye,
 For that he wold not wonde.   80

But afterward sone, leeve ye me,
Other tables of stone made he,
In w*hi*ch God bade wrytten shold be
 His wordes that were before,
The which tables shryned were
After as God can Moyses leare ;
And that shryne to them was deare
 Thereafter evermore.   88

Tunc Moyses descendet de monte, et ex altera parte montis dicet rex Balaac equitando.

BALAACK REX.   I, Balaack, king of Moab land,
All Israell and I had in [1] hand,
I am so wroth, I wold not wond
 To slaye them, ech wighte ;
For their God helpes them stiflye
Of other landes to haue mastrye,
That it is bootles, witterlie,
 Against them for to fighte.   96

What nation soever dose them noye,
Moyses prayes anone in hye,
Therefore haue they sone the victorie
 And other men [2] haue the worse,
Therfore how will I wroken be,
I am bethought, as mot I the !
Balaam I will shall come to me
 That people for to curse,   104

[1] D. I had it in my; B. W. h. and I hand in.
[2] D. *has* they *after* men.

For sworde ne knife may not avayle   *[Fluryshe.]*[1]
These ilke shroes for to assaile ;
That fowndes to fight he shall faile,
    For sicker is hym no boote.
All nations they doe any,   *[Cast up.]*[1]
And my-selfe they can destroie,
As ox that gnawes biselie
    The grasse right to the roote.   112

Who-so Balaam blesses, i-wis,[2]
Blessed sickerlie that man is ;
Who-so he curses, fareth amisse :
    Such loos over all hase he.   Numbers, 22. 6.
Therfore goe fetch hym, bachler,
That he may curse the people here ;
For, sicker, on them in no manner
    Mon we not wroken be.   120

MILES.   Syr, on yo*ur* errand I will gone ;
Yt shall be well done, and that anone,
For he shall wreak you on yo*ur* fone,
    The people of Israell.
BALAACK.   Yea, looke thou het hym gold **gret wone,**
And riches for to lyve upon,
To destroy them if he can,
    The freakes that be so fell.   128

                Tunc ibit ad Balaam.

MILES.   Balaam, my lorde greetes well thee
And prayes the right sone at hym to be,
To curse the people of Iudy,
    That do hym great anoye.
BALAAM.   Forsooth, I tell the, bacheler,
That I may haue no power
But if Gods will were ;
    That shall I witt in hye.   136

      [1] *Not in* H.; *supplied from the other* MSS.
      [2] D. I wis.

[1] [*Tunc ibit Balaam ad consulendum Domi*num *in oratione, et sedens*[2] *dicat Deus.*
Balaam prayeth to God one his knees.]

DEUS (*in supremo loco*). Balaam, I comaund the,
King Balaak his bydding that thou flee ;
That people that is blessed of me
    Curse thou not by no waye.
BALAAM. Lord, I must doe thy byddinge,
Thoughe it be to me unlykeing ;
For, truly, much wynninge
    I might haue had to-daye.   **144**

DEUS. Thoughe the folke be my foe,
Thou shalt haue leaue thydder to goe,
But looke that thou doe right soe
    As I haue thee taughte.
BALAAM. Lord, it shall be done in height,
This asse shall beare me aright.
Goe we together anone, s*i*r knight,
    For now leave I haue coughte.   **152**

Tunc equitabunt versus regem, et eundo dicat Balaam :

Now, by the law I leve upon,
Sith I haue leaue for to gone,
They shalbe cursed every one,
    And I ought wyn maye.
If Balaak hold that he has heighte
Gods hest I set at light ;
Warryed they shalbe this night
    Or that I wend awaye.   160

*Tunc angelus obuiabit Balaam cu*m *gladio extracto in manu, et stabit ,*sin*a.*

Goe forth, Burnell, goe forth, goe !
What the dyvell ! my asse will not goe ;
Served she me never soe.

      1 *Not in* H.; *supplied from the other* MSS.
      2 B. scedens; W. sedentes; h. *omits.*

What sorrow so her dose nye?
Rise up, Burnell! make thee bowne,
And helpe to beare me out the towne;
Or, as brok I my crowne,
 Thou shalt full sore abye!   **168**

Tunc percutiet asinam, et loquetur aliquis in asina.

ASINA. Maister, thou dost evell, witterly,
So good an ass as me to nye,
Now hast thou beaten me thry
 That beare thee thus aboute.
BALAAM. Burnell, whye begiles thou me,
When I haue most nede to the?
ASINA. That sight that I before me see
 Makes me downe to lowte.   **176**

Am I not, m*aste*r, thyne owne ass,
That ever before ready was
To beare the whether thou woldest pas?
 To smyte me now yt is shame.
Thou wottest well, m*aste*r, pardy,
Thou haddest never ass like to me,
Ne never yet thus served I thee;
 Now I am not to blame.   **184**

Tunc Balaam videns angelum evaginatum gladium habentem, adorans dicat:

BALAAM. Ah! Lord, to thee I make avowe,[1]
I had no sight of thee erre now;
Lyttle wist I it was thou
 That feared my asse soe.
ANGELUS. Why hast thou beaten thy asse thry?
Now I am comen thee to nye,
That changes thy purpose falcelye,
 And woldest be my foe.   **192**

---

[1] D. a vowe.

And the ass had not downe gone,
I wold haue slayne the here anone.
BALAAM.   Lord, haue pittye me upon,
　　For sinned I haue sore !
Is it thy will that I forth goe?
ANGELUS.   Yea ; but looke thou doe this folk no woe
Otherwise then God bade thee tho
　　And saide to thee before.　　　　　　　　200

　　　　Tunc Balaam et miles ibunt, Balaack venit in obuiam.

BALAACK.   Ah ! welcome, Balaam, my frend !
For all myne anguish thou shalt end,
If that thy will be to wend,
　　And wreake me of my foe.
BALAAM.   Nought may I speake, so haue I win,
But as God puttes me in,
To forby all and my kin ;
　　Therfore, sure, me is woe.　　　　　　　208

BALAACK.   Come forth, Balaam, come with me !
For on this hill, so mot I thee,
The folke of Israell thou shalt see ;
　　And curse them, I thee praye.
Thou shalt haue riches, golde and fee,
And I shall aduance thy dignytye,
To curse men, — cursed they may be
　　That thou shalt see to-day.　　　　　　216

　　Tunc adducens secum Balaam in montem et ad australem partem respiciens
　　　　　　　　dicat ut sequitur.[1]

BALAAM.   How may I curse them in this place,
The people that God blessed hase?
In them is both might and grace,
　　And that is alwayes seene.

　[1] *This stage direction seems to indicate that a speech of Balaac's has
dropped out, — perhaps the stanza contained in the other version:*
　　　　　　　Lo ! Balaam, thou seest here
　　　　　　　God*is* people all in feare,

Wytnes I may none beare
Against God that thus [1] can were
His people that no man may deare
    Ne troble wïth no teene.   224

I saye these folkes shall haue their will,
That no nation shall them gryll ;
The goodnes that they shall fulfill
    Nombred may not be ;
Their God shall them kepe and save.
No other repreve shall they non [2] have ;
But such death as they shall haue
    I praye God send me.   232

BALAACK.   What the devill [3] eyles the, poplart ?
Thy speach is not worth a fart,
Doted I wot well thou art,
    For woodlie thou has wrougt.
I bade thee curse them, every one,
And thou blest them, blood and bone ;
To this north syde thou shalt anon,
    For here thy deed is nought.   240

Tunc adducet eum ad borealem partem.

BALAAM.   Herken, Balaack, what I say ;
God may not gibb by no waye,
That he saith, is veray,
    For he may not lye.

        Cittie, castell, *and* riuer ;
           Looke now how likes thie.
        Curse them now at my prayer,
        As thou wilte be to me full dere
        And in my realme most of power
        And greatest under me.

Tunc Balaam versus austrum : dicat Balaham :

[1] D. this.   [2] *So* B. W. h.; H. *has* may I not.   [3] D. devilles.

To bless his folk he me sent ;
Therfore I saie, as I am kent
That in this land, verament,
    Is used no mawmentry :   Numbers, 23. 19. **248**

To Iacobs blood and Israell
God shall send ioy and heale ;
And as a lyon in his weale
    Christ shalbe haunsed hye,
And rise also in noble araye
As a prynce to wyn great paye,
Overcome his enemyes, as I say,   Numbers, 24. 9.
    And them bowndly bye.   **256**

BALAACK. What the devill is this? Thou cursest them naught,
Nor blessest them nether, as me thought.
BALAAM. Syr kinge, this I thee beheight
    Or that I come here.
BALAACK. Yet shalt thou to an-other place,
Ther Gods power for to embrace.
The dyvell geve the hard grace
    But thou doe my prayer !   **264**

Ad occidentalem partem.

BALAAM. Ah ! Lord, that here is fayre wonning,
Halls, chambers of great lyking,
Valleyes, woodes, grass springing,
    Fayre yerdes [1] and eke river !   Numbers, 24. 5, 6.
I wot well God made all this
His folk to lyue in ioye and blisse.
That warryeth them, warried is ;
    That blesseth [2] them, to God is deare.   **272**

BALAACK. Popelard ! thou preachest as a pie ;
The deuill of hell thee destroy !
I bade thee curse myne enemye ;
    Therfore thou came me to.

      [1] D. yordes.   [2] D. blessest.

Now hast thou blessed them here thry,
For thou meanes me to nye.
BALAAM.   So tould I the before twye,
     I might none other doe.   280

BALAACK.   Out ! alas ! what dyvell ayles thee?
I haue het thee gold and fee
To speake but wordes two or three,
     And thou makes much distance.
Yet once I will assay thee,
If any boote of bale will be ;
And if thou falcely now faile me,
     Mahound geue thee mischance !   288

Tunc Balaam ad cælum respiciens prophetando:

BALAAM.   *Orietur Stella ex Iacob, et exurget Homo de Is-*
    *raell, et confringet omnes duces alienigenaru*m,[1] *et erit*
    omnis terra possessio[2] *eius.*
Now one thinge I will tell you all,   Numbers, 24. 18.
Hereafter what shall befall :
A starre of Iacob springe shall,
     A man of Israell ;
He shall overcome and haue in band
All kinges, dukes of strang land,
And all the world haue in his hand,
     As lord to dight and deale.   296

[The other prophets enter, attended by the Expositor.][3]

ESAYAS.   I saye a mayden meeke and mylde
Shall conceave and beare a childe,
Cleane, w*i*thout workes wilde,
     To wyn mankinde to wayle ;

[1] D. alieginarum.

[2] D. professio, *but suggests* possessio.

[3] *It is, however, possible — even likely — that all were present on the stage from the beginning.*

Butter and hony shall be his meate,   Isaiah, 7. 14 ff.
That he may all evill forgeat,
Our soules out of hell to get,
    And called Emanuell.   304

EXPOSITOR.   Lordinges, these wordes are so veray
That exposition, in good faye,
None needes, but you know may
    This word Emanuell.
Emanuell is as much to saye
As " God with us night and day " ;
Therfore that name for ever and aye
    To his sonne cordes wondrous [1] well.   312

EZECHIELL.   [2] *Vidi porta*m *in domo* Domi*ni clausa*m *et
    dixit angelus ad me, " Porta hæc non aperietur sed
    clausa erit "* et ct.   *Ezechiel capitulo 2.*

I, Ezechiell, sothlie see   Ezekiel, 44. 2.
A gate in Gods house on hye ;
Closed it was, no man came nye ;
    Then told an angell me :
" This gate shall no man open, i-wis,[3]
For God will come and goe by this,
For him-self it reserved is,
    None shall come there but hee."   320

EXPOSITOR.   By this gate, lords, verament,
I understand in my intent
That way the Holy Ghost in went
    When God tooke flesh and bloode
In that sweet mayden Mary.
She was that gate, witterly,
For in her he light graciouslie
    Mankind to doe good.   328

[1] *Qy.: omit* wondrous.
[2] *In* D. *this precedes* EZECHIELL.
[3] D. I wis.

IHEREMIA.   *Deducant*[1] *oculi mei lacrimas per diem et noctem, et non taceant; contritione magna contrita est virgo filia populi mei et plaga* et *ct.*

My eyes must run and sorrow aye   Ierem. 14. 17.
W*i*thout ceasing, night and daye,
For my daughter, soth to saye,
    Shall suffer great anye ;
And my folke shall doe, in faye,
Thinges that they ne know may
To that mayden, by many waye,
    And her sonne, sickerlie.   336

EXPOSITOR.   Lordinges, this prophesie, i-wis,[2]
Touches the Passion nothing amisse,
For the prophet see well this
    What shall come, as I reade :
That a childe borne of a maye
Shall suffer death, sooth to saye ;
And they that mayden shall afray,
    Haue vengeance for that deede.   344

IONAS.   *Clamaui de tribulacione mea ad Dominum et exaudiuit ; de ventre inferi clamavi et exaudisti vocem meam et proiecisti me.*

I, Ionas, in full great any   Ion. 2. 2.
To God I prayed inwardlie,
And he me hard through his mercy
    And on me did his grace.
In myddes the sea cast was I
For I wrought inobedyentlie,
But in a whalles bellye
    Three dayes saved I was.   352

EXPOSITOR.   Lordinges, what this may signifie
Christ expoundes apertelie,
As we reade in the Evangely
    That Christ him-self can saie :

    [1] D. Deducunt.   [2] D. I wis.

Right as Ionas was dayes three
In wombe of whall, so shall he be
In earth lyinge, as was he,
    And rise the third daye. 360

DAUID. *De summo cælo egressio eius, et occursus eius ad*
    *su*m[m]*um eius. Psal.*

I, Davyd, saie that God almighte   Psalm, 18. 7.
From *the* highest heaven to earth will light,
And thidder againe w*i*th full might,
    Both God and man in feare ;
And after come to deeme the righte.
May no man shape them[1] of his sight
Ne deeme[2] that to mankind is dighte,
    But all then must apeare. 368

EXPOSITOR. Lordes, this speach is so veray
That to expound it to yo*u*r pay
It needes nothing in good faye,
    This speach is so expresse.
Each man by it knowe may
That of the Ascension, soth to saie,
David prophesied in his daye,
    As yt rehearsed was. 376

IOELL. *Effundam de spiritu meo super omnem carnem, et*
    prophetabunt filij vestri.

I, Ioell, saie this sickerlye :   Ioel, 2. 28.
That my Ghost send will I
Upon mankinde merciably
    From heaven, sitting in see ;
Then shold [y]our childre prophesie,
Ould men meet swevens,[3] wytterly,
Yong se sightes that therby
    Many wise shall be. 384

EXPOSITOR. Lordinges, this prophet speakes here
In Gods person, as it were,

---

[1] Kittredge *suggests* scape then. [2] *Qy.:* doome. [3] H. sweens; *corr. by* D.

And prophesies that he will apeare
    Ghostlie to mankinde.
This signes non other, in good faye,
But of his deede on Whitson-day,
Sending his Ghost, that we ever may
    On hym haue sadlie mynd.   392

MICHEAS.   [1] *Tu, Bethlem, terra Iuda, nequaqua*m *minima*
    es in principibus Iuda ; ex te enim exiet Dux qui reget
    *populu*m *meum Israell.*

I, Micheal, through my mynde   Mich. 5. 2 ; Matth. 2. 6.
Will saye that man shall sothlie finde
That a childe of kinges kinde
    In Bethlem shall be borne,
That shall be duke to dight *and* deale,
And rule the folke of Israell,
Also wyn againe mankindes heale,
    That through Adam was lorne.   400

EXPOSITOR.   Lordinges, two thinges apertlie
You may see in this prophesie :
The place certifies thee sothlie
    Where Christ borne will be ;
And after his ending, sickerlie,
Of his deedes of great mercy,
That he shold sit soveraynly
    In heauen, thereas is he.   408

Moe prophet*is*, lordinges, we might play,
But yt wold tary much the daye ;
Therfore six, sothe to say,
    Are played in this place.
Twoo speakes of his Incarnation,
Another of Christe[s] Passion,
The fourth of the Resurrection.
   .   .   .   . [2]   416

[1] H. *seems to have* In ; *corr. by* D.
[2] D. *points out that a line is missing in* MS.

The fifte speakes expreslie
How he from *the* highest heavenlye
Light into earth us to forby,
    And after thydder steigh
With oure kinde to heaven-blisse.
More loue might he not shew, i-wis,[1]
But right there-as hym-selfe is
    He haunshed our kinde on high.   424

The sixt shewes, you may see,
His Goste to man send will he,
More stidfast that they shalbe
    To loue God evermore.
Thus that beleve [2] that leven we
Of Gods deedes that had pittye
One man, when that he made them free,
    Is prophesied here before.   432

BALAACK.   Goe we forth ! it is no boote
Longer with this man to moote ;
For God of Iewes is crop and roote,
    And lord of heaven and hell.
Now see I well no man on lyue
Gaynes w*i*th him for to stryve ;
Therefore here, as mot I thryue,
    I will no longer dwell.   440

EXPOSITOR.   Lordinges, much more matter
Is in this story then you see here ;
But the substance, w*i*thout were,
    Is played you beforne.
And by these prophesies, leav you me,
Three kinges, as you shall played see,
Presented at his Nativitye
    Christ, when he was borne.   448

Finis paginæ quintæ.

[1] D. I wis.   [2] D. beleven.

HEGGE PLAYS.

Printed from MS. Cott. Vesp. D. viii ; see p. 31, above. H. denotes the readings of Halliwell's edition. P. denotes the readings of Pollard, who printed the first 139 lines in " English Miracle Plays, Moralities and Interludes, ed. A. W. Pollard, Oxford, 1890 (2d ed. 1895)." K. denotes the readings of Kölbing, *Englische Studien*, XXI, 166. The few unnoted variants are confined, I think, to cases in which my copyist did not regard the curl or stroke as sufficient to indicate final -*e*.

[The Salutation and Conception.]

Contemplacio. ffowre thowsand sex vndryd four*e* ʒer*e*,[1] I telle,
    Man ffor his offens *and* ffowle foly
Hath leyn [2] yer*es* in *th*e peynes of helle,
    And wer*e* wurthy to ly *th*er*in* endlesly ;
    But thanne xulde perysche ʒo*ur* grete mercye.[3]
Good Lord, haue on man pyte,
    Haue mende of *th*e prayo*ur* seyd by Ysaie :
Lete mercy meke *th*in hyest mageste.   8

Wolde God *th*ou woldyst breke *th*in hefne myghtye,
    And com down her*e* in-to erth
And levyn ʒer*es* thre *and* threttye,
    Thyn famyt ffolke w*ith th*i fode [4] to fede.
    To staunche *th*eir [5] thryste lete *th*i syde blede ;
ffor erste [6] wole not be mad redempc*i*on.
    Cu*m* vesyte [7] vs in *th*is tyme of nede ;
Of *th*i careful creatur*es*, Lord, haue compassyon.[8]   16

---

[1] K. *omits* ʒere.
[2] MS. loyn.
[3] H. mercy.
[4] H. ffode.
[5] MS. *th*i.
[6] H. P. erst.
[7] H. vysite; P. vesite.
[8] *A curl over* on.

A ! woo to vs wrecchis [1] that wrecchis be,
 ffor God hath addyd ssorwe [2] to sorwe.
I prey *the*, Lord, *th*i sowlys [3] com se,
 How *th*ei ly *and* sobbe bothe eue *and* morwe.[4]
*With th*i blyssyd blood from balys [5] hem borwe,
Thy careful creaturys cryenge in captyvyte ;
 A ! tary not, gracyous Lord, tyl it be to-morwe !
The devyl hath dysceyved hem be his iniquite.   24

" A ! " q*uo*d Ieremye, " who xal gyff wellys to my*n* eynes
 *Tha*t I may wepe bothe day *and* nyght
To se our*e* bretheryn in so longe peynes ? "
 Her*e* myschevys a-mende may *th*i mech*e* myght.
 As grett as *th*e se, Lord, was Adamys contryssyon ryght.
ffrom our*e* hed is falle [6] *th*e crowne ;
 Man is comeryd in synne ; I crye to *th*i syght,
Gracyous Lord ! gracyous Lord ! gracyous Lord, come downe ! 32

VIRTUTES.   Lord, plesyth [7] it *th*in*e* hy3 domynac*i*on
 On man, *tha*t *tho*u made, to haue pyte !
Patryarchys *and* prophetys han mad supplycac*i*on ;
 Our*e* offyse is to presente her*e* prayer*es* to the.
 Aungelys, archaungelys, we thre
*Tha*t ben in *th*e fyrst ierarchie,
 ffor man to *th*in hy mageste
" Mercy ! mercy ! mercy ! " we crye.   40

The aungel, Lord, *tho*u made so gloryous,
 Whos synne hath mad hy*m* a devyl in helle,
He mevyd man to be so contraryous.
 Man repentyd ; *and* he in his obstynacye doth dwelle.
 Hese grett males, good Lord, repelle,
And take man on-to *th*i grace ;
 Lete *th*i mercy make hy*m* w*ith* au*n*gelys dwelle,
Of Locyfer*e* to restor*e* *th*e place.   48

---

[1] K. *strikes out* wrecchis.   [2] H. ssorowe.   [3] P. sowles.
 [4] H. P. morewe; both eue & morwe *is written in another hand over the cancelled words:* ffor syknes & sorwe.   [5] MS. babys; *corr. by* H.
 [6] H. P. ffalle.   [7] K. plese.

PATER.   *Propter miseriam inopum*
          Et gemitum pauperum
          *Nu*nc *exurgam.*[1]

ffor *th*e wretchydnes of *th*e nedy
    And *th*e porys lamentac*i*on
Now xal I ryse *tha*t am almyghty.
    Tyme is come of reconsyliac*i*on ;
    My p*r*ophetys w*ith* prayers haue made supplicac*i*on,
My contryte creaturys crye all*e* for comforte,
    All my*n* aungellys in hefne, w*ith*-owte cessac*i*on,
They crye *tha*t grace to man myght exorte.   59

VERITAS.   Lord, I am *th*i dowter*e*, Trewth,
    *Th*ou wylt[2] se I be not lor*e* ;
Thyn vnkynde creatur*es* to save wer*e* rewthe ;
    The offens of man hath grevyd *th*e sor*e*.
    Whan Adam had synnyd, *tho*u seydest yor*e*
*Tha*t he xulde deye *and* go to helle ;
    And now to blysse hym to restor*e* —
Twey contraryes mow not to-gedyr dwelle.   67

Thi[3] Trewthe, Lord, xal leste w*ith*-owtyn ende ;
    I may in no wyse ffro *th*e go.
*Tha*t wretche[4] *tha*t was to *th*e so vnkende,
    He may not haue to moche[5] wo.
    He dyspysyd *th*e *and* plesyd *th*i ffo.
*Th*ou art his creato*ur and* he is *th*i creature ;
    *Th*ou hast lovyd Trewthe, it is seyd, evyr-mo ;
Ther-for*e* in peynes lete hym evyr-mor*e* endur*e*.   75

MISERICORDIA.   O ffadyr of Mercy, *and* God of Comforte,
    *Tha*t counsell*e*[6] us in eche trybulac*i*on,
Lete ʒo*ur* dowter*e*, Mercy, to ʒow resorte ;
    And on man, *tha*t is myschevyd, haue compassyon.

----

[1] MS. exergam; *corr. by* H.   [4] H. P. wrecche.
[2] H. P. wilt.   [5] H. P. meche.
[3] H. P. Thy.   [6] K. *emends to* counsellest.

Hym grevyth fful gretly his transgressyon ;
Alle hefne *and* erthe crye ffor Mercy ;
Me semyth *ther* xuld be non excepc*i*on,
Ther prayers ben offeryd so specyally. 83

Trewthe [1] sseyth she hath evyr be, than.
I graunt it wel ; she hath be so.
*And tho*u seyst endlesly *tha*t Mercy *tho*u hast kept ffor man ;
Than, mercyabyl Lorde, kepe us bothe to !
Thu seyst, *Veritas mea* et *M*isericord*ia mea cu*m *ip*so ;
Suffyr not *th*i sowlys than in sorwe to slepe ;
*Tha*t helle hownde *tha*t hatyth *th*e — byddyth [2] hy*m* ho !
*Th*i love, man, no lenger*e* lete hy*m* kepe. 91

IUSTICIA. Mercy, me merveylyth [3] what ȝow movyth !
ȝe know wel I am ȝo*ur* syster*e*, Ryght-wysnes.
God is ryghtful [4] *and* ryghtffulnes lovyth ;
Man offendyd hym *tha*t is endles ;
Therfor*e* his endles punchement may nevyr sees.
Also he forsoke his Maker*e tha*t made hym of clay,
And *th*e devyl to his mayst*er* he ches.
Xulde he be savyd ? Nay, nay, nay ! 99

As wyse as is God he wolde a be ;
This was *th*e abhomynabyl p*re*su*m*pc*i*on.
It is seyd — ȝe know wel *th*is of me —
*Tha*t *th*e Ryghtwysnes of God hath no diffynic*i*on ;
Therffor*e* lette [5] *th*is be our*e* conclusyon*e* :
He *tha*t sor*e* synnyd, ly stylle in [6] sorwe.
He may nevyr make a seyth be [7] reson*e* ;
Whoo myght thanne thens hym borwe ? 107

M*ISERICORD*IA. Systyr Ryghtwysnes, ȝe ar*e* to vengeable.
Endles synne God endles may restor*e* ;
Above alle hes*e* werkys God is mercyabyl.

---

[1] MS. Threwthe.
[2] K. *emends to* bydde.
[3] H. mervelyth.
[4] H. P. ryghtfful.
[5] H. P. late.
[6] *A stroke over* n.
[7] H. *proposes* subtyl *for* seyth be.

*Th*ow he for-sook God be synne, be feyth he for-sook
    hy*m* nev*er th*e mor*e* ;
And *th*ow he *p*resumyd nevyr so sor*e*,
ȝe must consyder *th*e frelnes of mankende.
    Lerne,[1] *and* ȝe lyst, — *th*is is Goddys lor*e*, —
*Th*e Mercy of God is w*ith*-owtyn ende.   115

PAX.[2]   To spar*e* ȝo*ur* speches, syster*e*s, it syt ;
    It is not onest, in Vertuys to ben dyscenc*i*on.
The Pes of God ovyr-comyth all*e* wytt.
    *Th*ow [8] Trewth *and* Ryght sey grett reson*e*,
    ȝett Mercy seyth best to my pleson ;
ffor yf mannys sowle xulde abyde in helle,
    Be-twen God *and* man evyr xulde be dyvysyon,
And than myght not I, Pes, dwelle.   123

Ther*e*-for*e* me semyth best, ȝe thus acorde,
    Than hefne *and* erthe ȝe xul qweme :
Putt bothe ȝo*ur* sentens in our*e* Lorde,
    And in his hyȝ wysdam-lete hym deme, —
    This is most syttynge,[4] me xulde seme, —
And lete se how we ffowr*e* may all*e* abyde.
    *Th*at mannys sowle it [5] xulde p*er*ysche it wor*e* sweme,
Or *th*at ony of vs ffro other*e* xulde dyvyde.   131

VERITAS.   In trowthe, her*e*-to I consente ; [6]
    I wole prey our*e* Lorde it may so be.
IUSTICIA.   I, Rygtwysnes,[7] am wele contente,
    ffor in hym is very equyte.
    M*I*SE*R*ICO*RD*IA.   And I, Mercy, ffro *th*is counsel wole
      not fle,
Tyl Wysdam hath seyd I xal ses.
    PAX.   Her*e* is God now ; her*e* is Vnyte ;
Hefne *and* erth is plesyd w*ith* Pes.   139
                  [*They appear before the Son.*]

[1] H. P. Lerne ; MS. Lorne.   [4] H. fyttynge.
[2] *A stroke over* AX.   [5] K. *strikes out* it.
[8] H. Thou.
[6] *Qy.:* I, Trowthe, herevnto I (*or* do) consente.
[7] H. P. Ryghtwysnes.

FFILIUS. I thynke *th*e thoughtys of Pes, *and* nowth of
    Wykkydnes !
    This I deme to ses ȝo*ur* contraversy : —
If Adam had not deyd, peryschyd had Ryghtwysnes,
    And also Trewth*e* had be lost *ther*-by, —
    Trewth and Ryght wolde chastyse ffoly ;
ȝiff a-nother deth come not, Mercy xulde perysch*e* ;
    *Th*an Pes wer*e* exyled ffynaly : [1]
So tweyn dethis must be, ȝow fowr*e* to cherysch*e*.   147

But he *tha*t xal deye, ȝe must knawe
    *Tha*t in hym may ben non iniquyte,
*Tha*t helle may holde hym be no lawe,
    But *tha*t he may pas at hese lyberte.
    Qwer*e* swyche on is, provyde [2] and se,
And hese deth for mannys deth xal be redempc*i*on ;
    All*e* hefne *and* erth seke now ȝe.
Plesyth it ȝow *th*is con*n*clusyon ?   155

               [*They seek ; and, returning, say :*]

VERITAS. I, Trowthe, haue sowte *th*e erthe w*ith*-owt *and*
    w*ith*-inne,
    And in sothe *ther* kan non be fownde
*Tha*t is of o day byrth w*ith*-owte synne,
    Nor to *tha*t deth wole be bownde.
    M*ISERICORD*IA. I, Mercy, haue ronne *th*e hevynly re-
    gyon rownde,
And ther is non of *tha*t charyte
    *Tha*t ffor man wole suffre a deddly wounde ;
I can nott wete how *th*is xal be.   163

IUSTICIA. Sur*e* [3] I can fynde non sufficyent,
    ffor servauntys vnprofytable we be ech*e* on ;
Hese [4] love nedyth to be ful ardent
    That for man to helle wolde gon.

---

    [1] H. ffynyaly.   [3] *In* MS. *this looks like* Our*e*.
    [2] MS. H. his p*r*evyde.   [4] MS. He ; H. Hes.

PAX.   That God may do, is non but on ;
*Ther*fore — *th*is is be hys avyse —
   He *tha*t ʒaff *th*is cou*n*selle, lete hy*m* ʒeve *th*e comforte
      alon,
ffor *th*e conclusyon in hym of all*e* *th*ese lyse.   171

FFILIUS.   It peyneth me *tha*t man I made ; [1]
   *Tha*t is to seyn, peyne I must suffre sor*e*. [2]
A counsel of *th*e Trinite must be had,
   Whiche of vs xal man restor*e*.
      PATER.   In ʒo*ur* wysdam, son, man was mad thor*e*,
And in wysdam was his temptac*i*on ;
   *Ther*for, sone, sapyens ʒe must ordeyn her*e*-fore,
And se how of man may be salvac*i*on. [3]   179

FILIUS.   ffadyr, he *tha*t xal do *th*is must be both God *and*
      man.
   Lete me se how I may wer*e* *tha*t wede ;
And syth*e* in my wysdam he be-gan,
   I am redy to do *th*is dede.
      SP*IRIT*US S*A*N*CT*US.   I, the Holy Gost, of ʒow tweyn
         do pr*o*cede ;
This charge I wole take on me ;
   I, Love, to ʒo*ur* lover xal ʒow lede :
*Th*is is *th*e assent of our*e* Vnyte.   187

M*ISERICORD*IA.   Now is *th*e loveday mad of us fowr*e*
      fynialy ;
   Now may we leve in pes, as we wer*e* wonte ;
Misericordia et *Veritas obviauerunt sibi*,
   Iusticia et *Pax osculate* [4] *sunt*.   191

           Et *hic osculabunt pariter omnes.*

PATER.   ffrom vs, God, au*n*gel Gabryel, *tho*u xalt be sende
      Into *th*e countre of Galyle, —
The name of *th*e cyte Naʒareth is kende, —

---

[1] H. mad.   [3] H. salvation.
[2] MS. for*e* ; *corr. by* H.   [4] H. osculatæ.

To a mayd,; weddyd to a man is she,
Of whom *the* name is Ioseph, se,
Of *the* hous of Davyd bore.
The name of *the* mayd ffre
Is Mary, *that* xal al restore.   199

FFILIUS.   Say *that* she is *with*-owte wo *and* ful of grace,
And *that* I, *the* Son of *the* Godhed, of her*e* xal be bor*e*.
Hyȝe *the*, *tho*u wer*e* ther*e* a-pace,
Ellys we xal be ther*e* the be-ffor*e*,[1]
I haue so grett hast to be man thor*e*
In *that* mekest *and* purest virgyne.
Sey her*e*, she xal restor*e*
Of ȝow aungellys *the* grett ruyne.   207

SPIRITUS SANCTUS.   And if she aske *the* how it myth be,
Telle her*e*, I, *the* Holy Gost, xal werke al this ;
Sche xal be savyd thorwe our*e* Vnyte.
In tokyn, her*e* bareyn cosyn Elyȝabeth is
Qwyk *with* childe in her*e* grett age, i-wys.
Sey her*e*, to vs is no-thynge impossyble.
Her*e* body xal be so ful-fylt *with* blys
*Tha*t she xal sone thynke *th*is sownde credyble.   215

GABRIEL.   In thyn hey inbassett,[2] Lord, I xal go,
It xal be do *with* a thought ;
Be-holde now, Lord, I go her*e* to,
I take my fflyth [3] *and* byde nowth.   219

                              [*Gabriel descends to Mary.*]

Ave, Maria, gratia plena, Dominus tecum!
Heyl, fful of grace, God is *with* the !
Amonge all*e* women blyssyd art thu !
Her*e* *th*is name Eva is turnyd Ave ;
*Tha*t is to say, *with*-owte sorwe ar ȝe now.   224

Thow sorwe in ȝow hath no place,
ȝett of ioy, lady, ȝe nede more ;

───────────────

[1] H. before.   [2] H. inbasset.   [3] H. flyth.

Therfore I adde and sey " ful of grace,"
    ffor so ful of grace was nevyr non bore.
3ett who hath grace, he nedyth kepyng sore ;
Therfore I sey " God is with the,"
    Whiche xal kepe 3ow endlesly thore.
So amonge alle women blyssyd are 3e.   232

MARIA.   A ! mercy, God ! this is a mervelyous herynge ;
    In the aungelys wordys I am trobelyd her ;
I thynk, ' how may be this gretynge ? '
    Aungelys dayly to me doth aper,
    But not in the lyknes of man ; that is my fer ;
And also thus hy3ly to comendyd be,
    And am most vn-wurthy.[1]   I can not answere ;
Grett shamfastnes and grett dred is in me.   240

GABRYEL.   Mary, in this take 3e no drede,
    ffor at God grace ffownde haue 3e,
3e xal conceyve in 3our wombe, indede,
    A childe, the sone of the Trynyte.
    His name of 3ow Iesu clepyd xal be ;
He xal be grett, the son of the Hyest, clepyd of kende ;
    And of his ffadyr Davyd the Lord xal 3eve hym the se,
Reynyng in the hous of Iacob, of whiche regne xal be non [2]
        ende.   248

MARIA.   Aungel, I sey to 3ow :
    In what manere of wyse xal this be ?
ffor knowyng of man I haue non now ;
    I haue evyr-more kept, and xal, my virginyte.
    I dowte not the wordys 3e hau[e] [3] seyd to me,
But I aske how [4] it xal be do.
    GABRYEL.   The Holy Gost xal come fro above to the,
And the vertu of hym Hyest xal schadu the so ;   256

            [1] H. unwirthy.   [3] H. han.
            [2] MS. *illegible*.   [4] H. *says* how *is omitted in* MS.

Therfore *tha*t Holy Gost of *th*e xal be bor*e*,
    He xal be clepyd *th*e Son of God sage.
And se, Ely3abeth, 3o*ur* cosyn thor*e*,
    She hath conseyvid a son in hyr*e* age ;
      This is the sexte monyth of her*e* passage, —
Of her*e* *tha*t clepyd was bareyn ;
    No-thynge is i*m*possyble to Goddys vsage.
They thynkyth longe to her*e* what 3e wyl seyn.   264

    *Her*e th*e aungel makyth a lytyl restynge,* and *Mary be-holdyth hy*m, and
      th*e aungel seythe :*

Mary, com of *and* haste the,
    And take hede in thyn entent
How [1] *th*e Holy Gost, — blyssyd he be ! —
    A-bydyth *th*in answer*e and th*in assent.
Thorwe wyse werke of dyvinyte
    The Secunde P*er*sone, verament,
Is mad man by fratirnyte [2]
    W*ith*-inne *th*i-self, in place present.   272

fferther-mor*e*, take hede *th*is space
    How [1] all*e the* blyssyd spyrytys of vertu
That ar*e* in hefne by-ffor*e* Goddys face,
    And all*e th*e gode levers *and* trew
That are her*e* in *th*is erthely place,
    Thyn owyn kynrede — *th*e sothe ho knew, —
And *th*e chosyn sowlys *th*is tyme of grace
    *Tha*t ar*e* in helle *and* byde *ther* rescu,   280

As Adam, Abrah*a*m *and* Davyd, in-fer*e*,
    And many other*e* of good reputac*i*on,
*Tha*t *th*in answer*e* desyr*e* to her*e*
    And *th*in assent to *th*e Incarnac*i*on,
In which*e* *th*ou standyst as p*r*eserver,[3]
    Of all*e* man-kende savac*i*on.

    [1] MS. H. Whow.   [2] H. fraternyte.   [3] MS. p*er*sever*e*.

Gyff me my*n* answer*e* now, lady der*e*,
  To all*e* these creatur*es* comfortac*i*on.   288

MARIA.   W*ith* all*e* mekenes I clyne to *th*is a-corde,
  Bowynge down my face w*ith* all*e* benyngnyte.
Se her*e* *th*e hand-mayden of our*e* Lorde ;
  Aftyr *th*i worde be it don to me !
    GABRYEL.   Gramercy, my lady ffre !
Gramercy of ʒo*ur* answer*e* on hyght !
  Gramercy of ʒo*ur* grett humylyte !
Gramercy, ʒe lanterne off[1] lyght !   296

        Here the *Holy Gost discendit* w*ith* *iij bemys to O*ur *Lady,* the *Sone of*
        the *Godhed next*[2] w*ith* *iij bemys to* the *Holy Gost,* the *Fadyr Godly*
        w*ith* *iij bemys to* the *Sone ; and so entre all*e *thre to her*e *bosom ;* and
        Mary seyth :

MARIA.   A ! now I ffele in my body be
  Parfyte God *and* parfyte man,
Havyng al[3] schapp*e* of chyldly carnalyte.
  Evyn al at onys, *th*us God be-gan ;   300

Nott takynge ffyrst o membyr *and* sythe a-nother,
  But parfyte childhod ʒe haue anon.
Of ʒo*ur* hand-mayden now ʒe haue mad ʒo*ur* modyr,
  W*ith*-owte peyne, in fflesche *and* bon.
  Thus conceyved nevyr woman non
*Tha*t evyr was beynge in *th*is lyff ;
  O my*n* hyest ffadyr, in ʒo*ur* tron*e*,
It is worthy, ʒo*ur* Son — now my son — haue a p*r*erogatyff !   308

I can not telle what ioy, what blysse,
  Now I fele in my body.
Aungel Gabryel, I thank ʒow for thys ;
  Most mekely recomende me to my Fader*es* mercy !
  To haue be *th*e modyr of God fful lytyl wend I.
Now my*n* cosyn Elyʒabeth ffayn wold I se,
  Now sche hath conseyvid as ʒe dede specyfy.
Now blyssyd be *th*e hyʒ Trynyte !   316

        [1] H. of.   [2] MS. nest ; H. vest.   [3] H. alle.

GABRYEL.   ffare-weyl, turtyl, Goddys dowter*e* der*e* !
    ffar*e*-wel, Goddys modyr, I *th*e honowr*e* !
ffar*e*-wel, Goddys sustyr and his pleynge fer*e* !
    ffar*e*-wel Goddys chawmer*e* and his bowr*e* !   320

MARIA.   ffar*e*-wel, Gabryel, specyalye !
    ffar*e*-wel, Goddys masanger*e* expresse !
I thank ȝow for ȝo*ur* traveyl hye ;
    Gramercy of ȝo*ur* grett goodnes,   324

And namely of ȝo*ur* comfortabyl massage !
    ffor I vndyrstande, by inspyrac*i*on,
*Tha*t ȝe knowe by synguler*e* pr*e*vylage
    Most of my sonys Incarnac*i*on.
I p*ra*y ȝow take it in-to vsage,
    Be a-custom ocupac*i*on,
To vesyte me ofte be mene passage ;
    ȝo*ur* pr*e*sence is my comfortac*i*on.   332

GABRIEL.   At ȝo*ur* wyl, lady, so xal it be.
    ȝe gentyllest of blood *and* hyest of kynrede
*Tha*t reynyth in erth in ony degre,
    Be pryncypal incheson of *th*e Godhede,   336

I comende me on-to ȝow, *tho*u trone of *th*e Trinyte,
    O mekest mayde, now *th*e modyr of Ie*s*u ;
Qwen of hefne, lady of erth, *and* empres of helle be ȝe ;
    Soco*ur* to all*e* synful *tha*t wole to ȝow sew ;
Tho*ur* [1] ȝo*ur* body beryth *th*e babe [2] our*e* blysse xal renew :
To ȝow, modyr of mercy, most mekely I recomende,[3]
    And, as I began, I ende, with an " Ave ! " new,
Enionyd [4] hefne *and* erth ; w*ith tha*t I ascende.   344

*Aue, Maria, gr*at*ia plena !* ⎫
*Domin*u*s tecu*m, *uirgo serena !* [5] ⎬ *Angeli cantando ista*m *sequenciam.*
    ⎭

---

[1] H. Thoro.
    [2] *Qy.* Thour the babe your body beryth ; *but* Kittredge *assumes ellipsis of*
that *after* body, *which seems better.*
    [3] *Qy.* me comende.   [4] H. Enjoynd.   [5] MS. fefena.

TOWNELEY PLAYS.

For information as to the text, see above, p. 13. The notes marked K. are from Kölbing's papers in *Englische Studien*, XVI, 278 ff. and XXI, 162 ff.

This play is preceded in the MS. by another on the same subject, which was perhaps played in alternation with this. At the end of the first the MS. has "*Explicit Vna pagina pastor*um," followed by "*Incipit Alia eor*undem."

[THE SECOND SHEPHERDS' PLAY.]

[Enter First Shepherd alone.]

1.[1] PASTOR.   Lord, what ! these weders ar cold ! / and I am
    yll happyd ;
I am nere-hande dold, / so long haue I nappyd ;
My legys thay fold, / my fyngers ar chappyd ;
It is not as I wold, / for I am al lappyd
    In sorow,
In stormes and tempest,
Now in the eest, now in the west.
Wo is hym has neu*er* rest
    Myd-day nor morow !

9

Bot we sely shepardes [2] / that walkys on the moore,
In fayth, we are nere-hand*ys* / [3] outt of the doore ;
No wonder, as it standys, / if we be poore,
ffor the tylthe of oure land*ys* / lyys falow as the floore,
    As ye ken.

---

[1] MS. *Primus; similarly below.*
[2] *Qy.* husbandys ; *cf.* 22.
[3] K. *inserts* ay.

We ar so hamyd,
ffor-taxed and ramyd,
We ar mayde hand-tamyd
    With thyse gentlery men.   18

Thus thay refe vs oure reste, / Oure Lady theym wary !
These men that ar lord-fest / thay cause the ploghe tary.
That men say is for the best, / we fynde it contrary ;
Thus ar husband*ys* opprest / in po[i]nte [1] to myscary
    On lyfe.
Thus hold thay vs hunder,
Thus thay bryng vs in blond*er* ;
It were greatte wonder
    And eu*er* shuld we thryfe.   27

[2] ffor may he gett a paynt slefe / or a broche now on dayes,
Wo is hym that hym grefe / or onys agane says !
Dar noman hym reprefe, / what mastry he mays ;
And yit may noman lefe / oone word that he says,
    No letter.
He can make purveance,
W*ith* boste and bragance,
And all is thrugh mantenance
    Of men that are gretter.   36

Ther shall com a swane / as prowde as a po,
He must [3] borow my wane, / my ploghe also ;
Then I am full fane / to graunt or he go.
Thus lyf we in payne, / ang*er*, and wo,
    By nyght and day.
He must haue if he langyd,
If I shuld forgang it ;
I were better be hangyd
    Then oones say hym nay.   45

---

[1] E. E. T. S.
[2] K. *wishes to reverse the order of this stanza and the next.*
[3] K. *wishes to read* will.

It dos me good, as I walk / thus by myn oone,
Of this warld for to talk / in maner of mone.
To my shepe wyll I stalk / and herkyn anone ;
Ther abyde on a balk / or sytt on a stone
    ffull soyne.
ffor I trowe, perde,
Trew men if thay be,
We gett more compane
    Or it be noyne.   54

[Enter Second Shepherd soliloquizing.]

II. PASTOR.   Benste and Dominus ! / what may this bemeyne ?
Why fares this warld thus ? / Oft haue we not sene !
Lord, thyse weders [1] are spytus / and the weders full kene ;
And the frostys so hydus / thay water myn eeyne,
    No ly.
Now in dry, now in wete,
Now in snaw, now in slete ;
When my shone freys to my fete,
    It is not all esy.   63

Bot as far as I ken, / or yit as I go,
We sely wedmen / dre mekyll wo ;
We haue sorow then and then, / it fallys oft so.
Sely Capyle, oure hen, / both to and fro
    She kakyls ;
Bot begyn she to crok,
To groyne or [to clo]k,[2]
Wo is hym is of [3] oure cok,
    ffor he is in the shekyls.   72

These men that ar wed / haue not all thare wyll ;
When they ar full hard sted, / thay sygh full styll ;
God wayte thay ar led / full hard and full yll ;
In bower nor in bed / thay say noght ther-tyll.

---

[1] *Qy.* winters *for this* weders, *or* windes *for the other; cf.* l. 128.
[2] E. E. T. S.   [3] *Qy. omit* is of.

This tyde,
My parte haue I fun,
I know my lesson.
Wo is hym that is bun,
    ffor he must abyde.   81

Bot now late in oure lyfys — / a meruell to me,
That I thynk my hart ryfys / sich wonders to see;
What that destany dryfys, / it shuld so be ! —
Som men wyll have two wyfys, / and som men thre,
    In store ;
Som ar wo that has any ;
Bot so far can I,
Wo is hym that has many,
    ffor he felys sore.   90

Bot, yong men, of wowyng,[1] / for God that you boght,
Be well war of wedyng / and thynk in youre thoght :
" Had I wyst " is a thyng / it seruys of noght.
Mekyll styll mowrnyng / has wedyng home broght,
    And grefys,
With many a sharp showre ;
ffor thou may cach in an owre
That shall [savour][2] fulle sowre
    As long as thou lyffys.   99

ffor, as euer red I pystyll, / I haue oone to my fere,
As sharp as a thystyll, / as rugh as a brere ;
She is browyd lyke a brystyll, / with a sowre-loten chere ;
Had she oones wett hyr whystyll, / she couth syng full clere
    Hyr pater noster.
She is as greatt as a whall ;
She has a galon of gall ;
By hym that dyed for vs all,
    I wald I had ryn to I had lost hir.   108

---

[1] *But* Kittredge *suggests that it is equivalent to* yong men a-wowyng.
[2] *The word in brackets is illegible in the* MS; *supplied by* E. E. T. S.

I. Pastor.   God looke ouer the raw ! / ffull defly ye stand.
II. Pastor.   Yee, the dewill in thi maw, / so tariand !
Sagh thou awro of Daw? /
I. Pastor.   Yee, on a ley-land
Hard I hym blaw ; / he commys here at hand,
    Not far ;
Stand styll.
II. Pastor.   Qwhy?
I. Pastor.   ffor he commys, hope I.
II. Pastor.   He wyll make vs both a ly
    Bot if we be war.   117

[Enter Third Shepherd soliloquizing.]

III. Pastor.   Crystys crosse me spede / and Sant Nycholas !
Ther-of had I nede, / it is wars then it was.
Whoso couthe take hede / and lett the warld pas,
It is euer in drede / and brekyll as glas,
    And slythys.
This warld fowre neuer so,
With meruels mo and mo,
Now in weyll, now in wo,
    And all thyng wrythys.   126

Was neuer syn Noe floode / sich floodys seyn,
Wyndys and ranys so rude / and stormes so keyn ;
Som stamerd, som stod, / in dowte, as I weyn ;
Now God turne all to good ! / I say as I mene,
    ffor ponder :
These floodys so thay drowne,
Both in feyldys and in towne,
And berys all downe,
    And that is a wonder.   135

We that walk on the nyghtys / oure catell to kepe,
We se sodan syghtys / when othere men slepe.[1]
Yit me thynk my hart lyghtys ; / I se shrewys pepe.

     [1] *Originally* slepys; *altered in red ink.*

Ye ar two all ¹ wygh*tys* ; / I wyll gyf my shepe
   A turne.
Bot full yll haue I ment ;
As I walk on this bent,
I may lyghtly repent,
   My toes if I spurne.   144

A, s*ir*, God you saue, / and mast*er* myne !
A drynk fayn wold I haue / and somwhat to dyne.
I. PAST*OR*. Crys*tys* curs, my knaue, / thou art a ledyr
     hyne !
II. PAST*OR*.   What ! the boy lyst rave ? / Abyde vnto syne ;
   We haue mayde it.
Yll thryft on thy pate !
Though the shrew cam late,
Yit is he in state
   To dyne, if he had it.   153

III. PAST*OR*.   Sich s*er*uand*ys* as I, / that swettys and swynkys,
Etys oure brede full dry, / and that me forthynkys ;
We ar oft weytt and wery / when mast*er*-men wynkys ;
Yit co*m*mys full lately / both dyners and drynkys.
    Bot nately
Both oure dame and oure syre,
When we haue ryn in the myre,
Thay can nyp at oure hyre,
   And pay vs full lately.   162

Bot here my trouth, master, / for the fayr that ye make,
I shall do theraf*ter*, — / wyrk as I take ;
I shall do a lytyll, s*ir*, / and emang eu*er* lake ;
ffor yit lay my soper / neu*er* on my stomake
    In feyldys.
Wherto shuld I threpe ?
W*ith* my staf can I lepe,
And men say " Lyght chepe
   Letherly for-yeldys."   171

         ¹ Kittredge *suggests* tall.

I. PASTOR.   Thou were an yll lad / to ryde on wowyng
W*ith* a man that had / bot lytyll of spendyng.
II. PASTOR.   Peasse, boy, I bad ; / no more iangling,
Or I shall make the full rad, / by the heuens [1] kyng !
    W*ith* thy gawdys.
Wher ar oure shepe, boy ?   We skorne.
III. PASTOR.   Sir, this same day at morne
I thaym left in the corne,
    When thay rang lawdys ;   180

Thay haue pasture good, / thay can not go wrong.
I. PASTOR.   That is right. By the roode ! / thyse nyght*ys* ar long !
Yit I wold, or we yode, / oone gaf vs a song.
II. PASTOR.   So I thoght as I stode, / to myrth vs emong.
    III. PASTOR.   I grauntt.
I. PASTOR.   Lett me syng the tenory.
II. PASTOR.   And I the tryble so hye.
III. PASTOR.   Then the meyne fallys to me ;
    Lett se how ye chauntt.[2]   189

       *Tunc intrat Mak, in clamide se sup*er *toga*m *vestitus.*

MAK.   Now, Lord, for thy naymes sevyn,[3] / that made both
       moyn & starnes
Well mo then I can neuen, / thi will, Lorde, of me tharnys ;
I am all vneuen ; / that moves oft my harnes.
Now wold God I were in heuen, / for there [4] wepe no barnes
    So styll.
I. PASTOR.   Who is that, pypys so poore ?
MAK.   Wold God ye wyst how I foore !
Lo, a man that walk*ys* on the moore,
    And has not all his wyll !   198

II. PASTOR.   Mak, where has thou gon [5] ? / tell vs tythyng.
III. PASTOR.   Is he co*m*men? Then ylkon / take hede to his
    thyng.

     [1] E. E. T. S. heuen's.
     [2] *The song was probably sung, but it is not given in the* MS.
     [3] MS. vij.   [4] MS. the.   [5] MS. gom.

Et *accip*it *clamide*m *ab ip*so.

MAK. What ! ich be a yoman, / I tell you, of the king ;
The self and the same, / sond from a greatt lordyng,
  And sich.
ffy on you ! goyth hence
Out of my presence !
I must haue reuerence ;
  Why, who be ich?   207

I. PASTOR. Why make ye it so qwaynt? Mak, ye do
   wrang.
II. PASTOR. Bot, Mak, lyst ye saynt? / I trow that ye lang.
III. PASTOR. I trow the shrew can paynt, / the dewyll myght
   hy*m* hang !
MAK. Ich shall make complaynt / and make you all to
   thwang
  At a worde,
And tell euyn how ye doth.
I. PASTOR. Bot, Mak, is that sothe?
Now take outt that sothren tothe,
  And sett in a torde !   216

II. PASTOR. Mak, the dewill in youre ee ! / a stroke wold I
   leyne you.
III. PASTOR. Mak, know ye not me? / by God, I couthe
   teyn you.
MAK. God looke you all thre ! / me thoght I had sene you, —
Ye ar a fare compane. /
I. PASTOR.   Can ye now mene you?
  II. PASTOR. Shrew, iape !
Thus late as thou goys,
What wyll men suppos?
And thou has an yll noys
  Of stelyng of shepe.   225

1 MS. teyle ; *but the letters* le *have been written over the original by a later hand.*

MAK.   And I am trew as steyll, / all men waytt !
Bot a sekenes I feyll / that hald*ys* me full haytt,
My belly farys not weyll, / it is out of astate.
III. PAST*OR*.   Seldom lyys the dewyll / dede by the gate.
     MAK.   Therfor
ffull sore am I and yll
If I stande stone styll ;
I ete not an nedyll
     Thys moneth and more.   234

I. PAST*OR*.   How farys thi wyff ? by my hoode, / how farys
          sho ?
MAK.   Lyys walteryng, by the roode, / by the fyere, lo !
And a howse full of brude / she drynkys well to ;
Yll spede othere good / that she wyll do
     Bot so !
Etys as fast as she can,
And ilk yere that co*m*mys to man
She bryng*ys* furth a lakan,
     And som yeres two.   243

Bot were I not more gracyus / and rychere be far,[1]
I were eten outt of howse / and of harbar ;
Yit is she a fowll dowse / if ye com nar ;
Ther is none that trowse / nor knowys a war
     Then ken I.
Now wyll ye se what I profer ? —
To gyf all in my cofer
To-morne at next to offer
     Hyr hed-mas pe*n*ny.   252

II. PAST*OR*.   I wote so forwakyd / is none in this shyre :
I wold slepe, if I takyd / les to my hyere.
III. PAST*OR*.   I am cold and nakyd / and wold haue a fyere.
I. PAST*OR*.   I am wery for-rakyd, / and run in the myre.
     Wake thou !

                    [1] E. E. T. S. befar.

II. PASTO*R*.   Nay, I wyll lyg downe by,
ffor I must slepe truly.
III. PASTO*R*.   As good a mans [1] son was I
       As any of you.   261

Bot, Mak, com hed*er* ! betwene / shall thou lyg downe.
MAK.   Then myght I lett you, bedene, / of that ye wold
          rowne,[2]
       No drede.
ffro my top to my too,
*Man*us *tuas co*m*mendo*,
Poncio Pilato,
          Cryst crosse me spede !   268

          *Tu*nc *surg*it, *pastorib*us *dormie*nfibus, et *dic*it :

Now were tyme for a man / that lakkys what he wold [3]
To stalk pr*e*uely than / vnto a fold
And neemly to wyrk than / and be not to bold,
ffor he might aby the bargan, / if it were told,
       At the endyng.
Now were tyme for to reyll ;
Bot he ned*ys* good counsell
That fayn wold fare weyll,
       And has bot lytyll spendyng.   277

Bot abowte you a serkyll / as rownde as a moyn,[4]
To I haue done that I wyll, / tyll that it be noyn,
That ye lyg stone styll / to that I haue doyne,
And I shall say thertyll / of good word*ys* a foyne
       On hight :

1 E. E. T. S. man's.
2 E. E. T. S. *notes that two lines are missing and refers to a similar*
stanza (No. 15) *in the first Shepherds' Play. In both cases lines have been*
lost, I think.
3 *From this point on, Pollard's numbering is* 11 *ahead of* E. E. T. S.,
possibly because he miscounted the stanzas by one and did not notice that
the immediately preceding stanza contains only 7 lines.
4 K. *corrects the spelling of these four rhyme-words by omitting* y.

Ou*er* youre heyd*ys* my hand I lyft,
Outt go youre een, fordo your syght ; —
Bot yit I must make bett*er* shyft
    And it be right.   286

Lord, what ! thay slepe hard ! / that may ye all here.
Was I neu*er* a shepard, / bot now wyll I lere ;
If the flok be skard, / yit shall I nyp nere.
How ! drawes hederward ! / Now mend*ys* oure chere
    ffrom [1] sorow.
A fatt shepe I dar say !
A good flese dar I lay !
Eft-whyte when I may,
    Bot this will I borow.   *[Mak goes home.]* 295

How, Gyll, art thou in ? / gett vs som lyght.
VXOR EIUS.   Who makys sich dyn / this tyme of the nyght?
I am sett for to spyn ; / I hope not I myght
Ryse a penny to wyn. / I shrew them on hight
    So farys !
A huswyff that has bene
To be rasyd thus betwene !
Here may no note be sene
    ffor sich small charys.   304

MAK.   Good wyff, open the hek ! / seys thou not what I
      bryng ?
VXOR. I may thole the dray the snek. / A, com in, my
      swetyng !
MAK.   Yee, thou thar not rek / of my long standyng.
VXOR. By the nakyd nek / art thou lyke for to hyng.
    MAK. Dò way ;
I am worthy my mete,
ffor in a strate can I gett
More then thay that swynke and swette
    All the long day.   313

                  [1] MS. ffron.

[He shows her the sheep.]

Thus it fell to my lott, / Gyll, I had sich grace.

VXOR.   It were a fowll blott / to be hanged for the case.

MAK.   I haue skapyd, Ielott, / oft as hard a glase.

VXOR.   Bot so long goys the pott / to the wat*er*, men says,
    At last

Comys it home broken.

MAK.   Well knowe I the token,

Bot let it neu*er* be spoken ;
    Bot com and help fast.   322

I wold he were slayn, / I lyst well ete ;

This twelmo[n]the [1] was I not so fayn / of oone shepe mete.

VXOR.   Com thay or he be slayn / and here the shepe blete —

MAK.   Then myght I be tane ; / that were a cold swette !
    Go spar

The gaytt doore.

VXOR.   Yis, Mak,

ffor and thay com at thy bak —

MAK.   Then myght I by, for all the pak,
    The dewill of the war.   331

VXOR.   A good bowrde haue I spied, / syn thou can none ;

Here shall we hym hyde / to thay be gone, —

In my credyll abyde, — / lett me alone,

And I shall lyg besyde / in chylbed, and grone.

    MAK.   Thou red ;

And I shall say thou was lyght

Of a knaue childe this nyght.

VXOR.   Now well is me day bright,
    That eu*er* was I bred !   340

This is a good gyse / and a far cast ;

Yit a woman avyse / helpys at the last !

I wote neu*er* who spyse : / agane go thou fast.

MAK.   Bot I com or thay ryse, / els blawes a cold blast !
    I wyll go slepe.

              1 *Corr. by* K.

[Mak returns to the shepherds, and resumes his place.]

Yit slepys all this meneye,
And I shall go stalk *pr*euely,
As it had neu*er* bene I
    That caryed thare shepe.   *[Sleeps.]* 349

I. PASTO*R*.   *Resurrex a mortru*is ! / Haue hald my hand.
*Iudas carnas d*omin*us* ! / I may not well stand :
My foytt slepys, by Ih*esus*,[1] / and I water fastand.
I thoght that we layd vs / full nere Yngland.
    II. PASTO*R*.   A ye !
Lord, what ! I haue slept weyll ;
As fresh as an eyll,
As lyght I me feyll
    As leyfe on a tre.   358

III. PASTO*R*.   Benste be here-in ! / so my [body][2]
    qwakys,
My hart is outt of skyn, / what-so it makys.
Who makys all this dyn ? / So my browes blakys.
To the dowore wyll I wyn. / Harke felows, wakys !
    We were fowre :
Se ye awre of Mak now?
I. PASTO*R*.   We were vp or thou.
II. PASTO*R*.   Man, I gyf God a-vowe,
    Yit yede he nawre.   367

III. PASTO*R*.   Me thoght he was lapt / in a wolfe skyn.
I. PASTO*R*.   So are many hapt / now, namely within.
III. PASTO*R*.[3]   When we had long napt, / me thoght w*ith*
    a gyn
A fatt shepe he trapt / bot he mayde no dyn.
    II. PASTO*R*.[4]   Be styll ;
Thi dreme mak*ys* the woode ;
It is bot fantom, by the roode.
I. *P*ASTO*R*.   Now God turne all to good,
    If it be his wyll !   376

---

[1] MS. ihc.   [2] Kittredge; E. E. T. S. [hart?].
[3] E. E. T. S. II. PASTOR.   [4] E. E. T. S. III. PASTOR.

II. PAST*OR*.   Ryse, Mak ; for shame ! / thou lyg*ys* right
  lang.

MAK.   Now Cryst*ys* holy name / be vs emang !
What is this, for Sant Iame ? / I may not well gang !
I trow I be the same. / A ! my nek has lygen wrang
  Enoghe,
Mekill thank ! syn yist*er* euen.
Now, by Sant Strevyn,
I was flayd w*ith* a swevyn,
  My hart out of-sloghe :   385

I thoght Gyll began to crok / and trauell full sad,
Welner at the fyrst cok, / of a yong lad
ffor to mend oure flok. / Then be I neuer glad ;
I haue tow on my rok / more then eu*er* I had.
  A, my heede !
A house full of yong tharnes,[1]
The dewill knok outt thare harnes !
Wo is hym has many barnes,
  And therto lytyll brede !   394

I must go home, by youre lefe, / to Gyll, as I thoght.
I pray you looke my slefe / that I steyll noght ;
I am loth you to grefe / or from you take oght. [*Exit.*]
III. PAST*OR*.   Go furth, yll myght thou chefe ! / Now wold
   I we soght,
  This morne,
That we had all oure store.
I. PAST*OR*.   Bot I will go before ;
Let vs mete.
II. PAST*OR*.   Whore ?
  III. PAST*OR*.   At the crokyd thorne.   403

MAK.   Vndo this doore ! who is here ? / how long shall I
  stand ?
VXOR EIUS.   Who makys sich a bere ? / now walk in the
  wenyand !
      [1] E. E. T. S. tharmes.

MAK.   A, Gyll, what chere? / it is I, Mak, youre husbande.
VXOR.   Then may we se [1] here / the dewill in a bande,
    Syr Gyle ;
Lo, he commys with a lote
As he were holden in the throte.
I may not syt at my note
    A hand-lang while.   412

MAK.   Wyll ye here what fare she makys / to gett hir a
    glose?
And dos noght bot lakys / and clowse hir toose.
VXOR.   Why, who wanders, who wakys, / who commys, who
    gose?
Who brewys, who bakys? / what makys me thus hose?
    And than,
It is rewthe to beholde,
Now in hote, now in colde.
ffull wofull is the householde
    That wantys a woman.   421

Bot what ende has thou mayde / with the hyrdys, Mak?
MAK.   The last worde that thay sayde / when I turnyd my
    bak,
Thay wold looke that thay hade / thare shepe all the pak.
I hope thay wyll nott be well payde / when thay thare shepe
    lak,
    Perde.
Bot how-so the gam gose,
To me thay wyll suppose,
And make a fowll noyse,
    And cry outt apon me.   430

Bot thou must do as thou hyght. /
VXOR.   I accorde me thertyll,
I shall swedyll hym right / in my credyll.
If it were a gretter slyght, / yit couthe I help tyll.
I wyll lyg downe stright ; / com hap me.

             [1] E. E. T. S. be; *emend. by* Kittredge.

Mak.   I wyll.
    Vxor.   Behynde !
Com Coll and his maroo,
Thay will nyp vs full naroo.
Mak.   Bot I may cry out haroo,
    The shepe if thay fynde.   439

Vxor.   Harken ay when thay call ; / thay will com onone.
Com and make redy all / and syng by thyn oone ;
Syng lullay thou shall, / for I must grone
And cry outt by the wall / on Mary and Iohn,
    ffor sore.
Syng lullay on fast
When thou heris at the last ;
And bot I play a fals cast,
    Trust me no more.   448

III. Pastor.   A, Coll, good morne ! / Why slepys thou nott ?
I. Pastor.   Alas, that euer was I borne ! / we haue a fowll
    blott.
A fat wedir haue we lorne. /
III. Pastor.   Mary, Godys forbott !
II. Pastor.   Who shuld do vs that skorne ? / that were a
    fowll spott.
    I. Pastor.   Som shrewe.
I haue soght with my dogys
All Horbery Shrogys,
And of fefteyn ¹ hogys
    ffond I bot oone ewe.   457

III. Pastor.   Now trow me, if ye will ; / by Sant Thomas
        of Kent,
Ayther Mak or Gyll / was at that assent.
I. Pastor.   Peasse, man, be still ! / I sagh when he went ;
Thou sklanders hym yll ; / thou aght to repent
    Goode spede.

                    ¹ MS. xv.

II. Pastor.   Now as euer myght I the,
If I shuld euyn here de,
I wold say it were he
    That dyd that same dede.   466

III. Pastor.   Go we theder, I rede, / and ryn on oure feete.
Shall I neuer ete brede / the sothe to I wytt.
I. Pastor.   Nor drynk in my heede / with hym tyll I mete.
II. Pastor.   I wyll rest in no stede / tyll that I hym grete,
    My brothere.
Oone I will hight :
Tyll I se hym in sight
Shall I neuer slepe one nyght
    Ther I do anothere.   475

III. Pastor.   Will ye here how thay hak ? / Oure syre lyst
    croyne.
I. Pastor.   Hard I neuer none crak / so clere out of toyne ;
Call on hym.
II. Pastor.   Mak ! / vndo youre doore soyne.
Mak.   Who is that spak / as it were noyne
    On loft ?
Who is that ? I say.
III. Pastor.   Goode felowse, were it day.
Mak.   As far as ye may,
    Good, spekys soft,   484

Ouer a seke womans [1] heede / that is at mayll-easse ;
I had leuer be dede / or she had any dyseasse.
Vxor.   Go to an othere stede, / I may not well qweasse.
Ich fote that ye trede / goys thorow my nese
    So hee !
I. Pastor.   Tell vs, Mak, if ye may,
How fare ye, I say ?
Mak.   Bot ar ye in this towne to-day ?
    Now how fare ye ?   493

Ye haue ryn in the myre / and ar weytt yit ;
I shall make you a fyre / if ye will syt.

        [1] E. E. T. S. woman's.

A nores wold I hyre, / thynk ye on yit ;
Well qwytt is my hyre, — / my dreme this is itt, —
    A seson.
I haue barnes, if ye knew,
Well mo then enewe,
Bot we must drynk as we brew,
    And that is bot reson.   502

I wold ye dynyd or ye yode ; / me thynk that ye swette.
II. PASTOR.   Nay, nawther mendys oure mode / drynke nor
        mette.
MAK.   Why, sir, alys you oght bot goode ? /
III. PASTOR.   Yee, oure shepe *that*
        we gett
Ar stollyn as thay yode ; / oure los is grette.
    MAK.   Syrs, drynk*ys* !
Had I bene thore,
Som shuld haue boght it full sore.
I. PASTOR.   Mary, som men trowes that ye [1] wore,
    And that vs forthynk*ys*.   511

II. PASTOR.   Mak, som men trowys / that it shuld be ye.
III. PASTOR.   Ayther ye or youre spouse, / so say we.
MAK.   Now if ye haue suspowse / to Gill or to me,
Com and rype oure howse / and then may ye se
    Who had hir.
If I any shepe fott,
Aythor cow or stott, —
And Gyll, my wyfe, rose nott
    Here syn she lade hir, —   520

As I am true and lele, / to God here I pray
That this be the fyrst mele / that I shall ete this day.
I. PASTOR.   Mak, as haue I ceyll, / avyse the, I say ;
He lernyd tymely to steyll / that couth not say nay.

                    [1] K. *inserts* it.

VXOR.   I swelt!
Outt, thefys, fro my wonys!
Ye com to rob vs, for the nonys.
MAK.   Here ye not how she gronys?
  Youre hartys shuld melt.   529

VXOR.   Outt, thefys, fro my barne! / negh hym not thor.
MAK.   Wyst ye how she had farne, / youre hartys wold be
   sore.
Ye do wrang, I you warne, / that thus *com*mys before
To a woman that has farne / — bot I say no more!
  VXOR.   A, my medyll!
I pray to God so mylde,
If eu*er* I you begyld,
That I ete this chylde
  That lyg*ys* in this credyll.   538

MAK.   Peasse, woman, for God*ys* payn, / and cry not so:
Thou spyllys thy brane / and mak*ys* me full wo.
II. PASTO*R*.   I trow oure shepe be slayn. / What finde ye
   two?
III. P*ASTOR*.   All wyrk we in vayn; / as well may we go.
  Bot hatters,
I can fynde no flesh,
Hard nor nesh,
Salt nor fresh,
  Bot two tome platers.   547

Whik catell bot this, / tame nor wylde,
None, as haue I blys, / as lowde as he smylde.
VXOR.   No, so God me blys / and gyf me ioy of my chylde!
I. PASTOR.   We haue m*er*kyd amys; / I hold vs begyld.
  II. PASTOR.   Syr, don.
Syr, Oure Lady hym saue!
Is youre chyld a knaue?
MAK.   Any lord mygҺt hym haue,
  This chyld to his son;   556

When he wakyns he kyppys / that ioy is to se.
III. PASTOR. In good tyme to hys hyppys / and in cele !
Bot who was his gossyppys / so sone rede ?
MAK. So fare fall thare lyppys ! /
I. PASTOR.   Hark now, a le !
   MAK. So God thaym thank,
Parkyn, and Gybon Waller, I say,
And gentill Iohn Horne, in good fay,
He made all the garray,
   With the greatt shank.   565

II. PASTOR. Mak, freyndys will we be, / ffor we ar all oone.
MAK. We ! now I hald for me, / for mendys gett I none.
ffare-well all thre ! / all glad were ye gone.   [*The shepherds go out.*]
III. PASTOR. ffare wordys may ther be, / bot luf is ther none
   *Th*is yere.
I. PASTOR. Gaf ye the chyld any-thyng?
II. PASTOR. I trow, not oone farthyng.
III. PASTOR. ffast agane will I flyng,
   Abyde ye me there.   [*Goes back to the house.*] 574

Mak, take it to no grefe, / if I com to thi barne.
MAK. Nay, thou dos me greatt reprefe / and fowll has thou
      farne.
III. PASTOR. The child will it not grefe, / that lytyll day-starne.
Mak, *with* youre leyfe, / let me gyf youre barne
   Bot sex[1] pence.
MAK. Nay, do way ; he slepys.
III. PASTOR. Me thynk he pepys.
MAK. When he wakyns he wepys ;
   I pray you go hence.   [*The other shepherds come back.*] 583

III. PASTOR. Gyf me lefe hym to kys, / and lyft vp the
      clowtt.   [*Seeing the sheep.*]
What the dewill is this ? / he has a long snowte.

[1] MS. vj.

I. Pastor.   He is merkyd amys ; / we wate ill abowte.

II. Pastor.   Ill spon weft, iwys,/ ay commys foull owte.
>   Ay, so !

He is lyke to oure shepe !

II. Pastor.   How, Gyb ! may I pepe?

I. Pastor.   I trow, kynde will crepe
>   Where it may not go.   592

II. Pastor.   This was a qwantt gawde / and a far cast.

It was a hee frawde. /

III. Pastor.   Yee, syrs, wast.

Lett bren this bawde, / and bynd hir fast.

A ! fals skawde, / hang at the last !
>   So shall thou.

Wyll ye se how thay swedyll

His foure feytt in the medyll?

Sagh I neuer in a credyll
>   A hornyd lad or now.   601

Mak.   Peasse byd I ! what, / lett be youre fare !

I am he that hym gatt, / and yond woman hym bare.

I. Pastor.   What dewill shall he hatt? / Mak ?   Lo
>   God, Makys ayre !

II. Pastor.   Lett be all that. / Now God gyf hym care,
>   I sagh.

Vxor.   A pratty childe is he

As syttys on a womans kne ;

A dyllydowne, perde,
>   To gar a man laghe.   610

III. Pastor.   I know hym by the eere-marke ; / that is a
>   good tokyn.

Mak.   I tell you, syrs, hark ! / hys noyse was brokyn ;

Sythen told me a clerk / that he was forspokyn.

I. Pastor.   This is a fals wark ; / I wold fayn be wrokyn ;
>   Gett wepyn !

Vxor.   He was takyn with an elfe,

I saw it myself ;

When the clok stroke twelf
  Was he forshapyn.   619

II. PASTOR.   Ye two ar well feft / sam in a stede.
I. PASTOR.[1] Syn thay manteyn thare theft, / let do thaym
      to dede.
MAK.   If I trespas eft, / gyrd of my heede !
With you will I be left. /
III. PASTOR.[2]   Syrs, do my reede :
  ffor this trespas
We will nawther ban ne flyte,
ffyght nor chyte,
Bot haue done as tyte,
  And cast hym in canvas.   628

                    [*They toss Mak in a sheet.*]
[I. PASTOR.] Lord, what ! I am sore, / in poynt for to bryst.
In fayth, I may no more ; / therfor wyll I ryst.
II. PASTOR.   As a shepe of sevyn[3] skore / he weyd in my
      fyst.
ffor to slepe ay-whore / me thynk that I lyst.
    III. PASTOR.   Now I pray you,
Lyg downe in this grene.
I. PASTOR.   On these thefys yit I mene.
III. PASTOR.   Wherto shuld ye tene ?
  Do[4] as I say you?   637

            Angelus cantat " Gloria in exelsis" ; postea dicat :
ANGELUS.   Ryse, hyrd-men heynd ! / for now is he borne
That shall take fro the feynd / that Adam had lorne :
That warloo to sheynd / this nyght is he borne ;
God is made youre freynd / now at this morne.
    He behestys,
At bedlem go se,

                    [1] E. E. T. S. III. PASTOR ; *see Notes.*
                    [2] E. E. T. S. I. PASTOR.
                    [3] MS. vij.
                    [4] E. E. T. S. So.

Ther lyg*ys* that fre
In a cryb full poorely
 Betwyx two bestys.   646

I. PASTOR. This was a qwant stevyn / that eu*er* yit I hard.[1]
It is a m*er*uell to neuyn, / thus to be skard.
II. PASTOR. Of God*ys* son of heuyn / he spak vpward.
All the wod on a leuyn / me thoght that he gard
 Appere.
III. PASTOR. He spake of a barne
In Bedlem, I you warne.
I. PASTOR. That betokyns yond starne ;
 Let vs seke hym there.   655

II. PASTOR. Say, what was his song? / hard ye not how he
  crakyd it,
Thre brefes to a long? /
III. PASTOR.   Yee, mary, he hakt it ;
Was no crochett wrong, / nor no-thyng that lakt it.
I. PASTOR. ffor to syng vs emong, / right as he knakt it,
 I can.
II. PASTOR. Let se how ye croyne ;
Can ye bark at the mone?
III. PASTOR. Hold youre tonges, haue done !
 I. PASTOR. Hark aft*er*, than !   664

II. PASTOR. To Bedlem he bad / that we shuld gang ;
I am full fard / that we tary to lang.
III. PASTOR. Be mery and not sad, / of myrth is oure sang,
Euer-lastyng glad / to mede may we fang,
 W*ith*outt noyse.
I. PASTOR. Hy we thed*er* for-thy, —
If we be wete and wery, —
To that chyld and that lady !
 We haue it not to lose.   673

----

[1] That euer yit I hard *was originally* he spake vpward, *from* l. 649, *but this has been crossed out with red ink.* K. *changes* a qwant stevyn *to* the qwantest stevyn ; *but why not change* that euer *to* as euer, *if emendation must be made?*

II. PASTOR. We fynde by the prophecy — / let be youre
    dyn —
Of Dauid and Isay / and mo then I myn,
Thay prophecyed by clergy / that in a vyrgyn
Shuld he lyght and ly, / to slokyn oure syn
        And slake it,
Oure [1] kynde from wo ;
ffor Isay sayd so :
Ecce [2] *virgo*
    Concipiet a chylde that is nakyd.   682

III. PASTOR. ffull glad may we be / and abyde that day
That lufly to se, / that all myghtys may.
Lord, well were me / for ones and for ay,
Myght I knele on my kne / som word for to say
        To that chylde.
Bot the angell sayd,
In a cryb wos he layde,
He was poorly arayd,
    Both mener [3] and mylde.   691

I. PASTOR. Patryarkes that has bene / and prophetys be-
    forne,
Thay desyryd to haue sene / this chylde that is borne.
Thay ar gone full clene ; / that haue thay lorne.
We shall se hym, I weyn, / or it be morne,
        To tokyn.
When I se hym and fele,
Then wote I full weyll
It is true as steyll
    That prophetys haue spokyn :   700

To so poore as we ar / that he wold appere,
ffyrst fynd, and declare / by his messyngere.
II. PASTOR. Go we now, let vs fare ; / the place is vs nere.

[1] K. *inserts* To kepe, *or* To fre, *before* Oure.
[2] E. E. T. S. Citè ; *corr. by* K.
[3] K. *suggests* meke.

III. PASTOR.   I am redy and yare ; / go we in-fere
     To that bright.
Lord, if thi wyll it[1] be,
We ar lewde all thre :
Thou grauntt vs somkyns gle
     To comforth thi wight.   709

[They enter the stable.]

I. PASTOR.   Hayll, comly and clene ! / hayll, yong child !
Hayll, Maker,[2] as I meyne ! / of a madyn so mylde !
Thou has waryd, I weyne, / the warlo so wylde ;
The fals gyler of teyn, / now goys he begylde.
     Lo, he merys ;
Lo, he laghys, my swetyng !
A wel fare [3] metyng !
I haue holden my hetyng.
     Haue a bob of cherys !   718

II. PASTOR.   Hayll, sufferan Sauyoure, / ffor thou has vs
               soght !
Hayll, frely foyde and floure, / that all thyng has wroght !
Hayll, full of fauoure, / that made all of noght !
Hayll ! I kneyll and I cowre. / A byrd haue I broght
     To my barne.
Hayll, lytyll tyne mop !
Of oure crede thou art crop :
I wold drynk on thy cop,
     Lytyll day-starne !   727

III. PASTOR.   Hayll, derlyng dere, / full of godhede !
I pray the be nere / when that I haue nede.
Hayll ! swete is thy chere ! / My hart wold blede
To se the sytt here / in so poore wede,
     With no pennys.

[1] E. E. T. S. wylles.
[2] K. *inserts* born.
[3] E. E. T. S. welfare.

Hayll ! put furth thy dall !
I bryng the bot a ball :
Haue and play the with-all,
        And go to the tenys.   736

MARIA.   The Fader of heuen, / God omnypotent,
That sett all on seuen, / his Son has he sent.
My name couth he neuen / and lyght.or he went.
I conceyuyd hym full euen, / thrugh myght as he ment ;
        And now he is borne.
He kepe you fro wo !
I shall pray hym so.
Tell, furth as ye go,
        And myn on this morne.   745

I. PASTOR.   ffarewell, lady, / so fare to beholde,
With thy childe on thi kne ! /
II. PASTOR.   Bot he lygys full cold.
Lord, well is me ! / now we go, thou behold.
III. PASTOR.   ffor sothe, all redy !·/ it semys to be told
        Full oft.
I. PASTOR.   What grace we haue fun !
II. PASTOR.   Com furth, now ar we won.
III. PASTOR.   To syng ar we bun :
        Let take on loft !   754
                        Explicit pagina Pastorum.

COVENTRY. CORPUS CHRISTI PLAYS.

Reprinted from "A Dissertation on the Pageants or Dramatic Mysteries
Anciently performed at Coventry . . . by Thomas Sharp. Coventry, 1825." In
the notes S. indicates such of Sharp's readings as I have changed. The date of
the MS. is given at the end of the play.

It will aid the reader if he bears in mind that in this play *w* and *v* are often
interchanged, and that such words as *holy*, *home* are sometimes spelt *wholle*, *whom*.
In general, the sound will be a better guide to the meaning than the spelling. *The*
is a frequent spelling for *they*, and occurs occasionally for *them;* in such cases I
have added a letter in brackets to aid the reader.

[THE PAGEANT OF THE SHEARMEN AND TAYLORS.]

ISAYE. The Sofferent thatt seithe ev*er*e seycrette,
　　　　He saue you all and make you p*er*fett *and* stronge,[1]
And geve us [2] *grace* w*ith* his marce forto mete !
　　　　For now in grett mesere mankynd ys bownd ;
　　　　The sarpent hathe gevin vs soo mortall a wonde
That no creature ys abull vs forto reyles
Tyll thye right vncion of Jvda dothe seyse.　　　　　　　　7

Then schall moche myrthe and joie in-cresse ;
　　　　And the right rote in Isaraell sprynge,
Thatt schall bryng forthe the greyne off whollenes ;
　　　　And owt of danger he schall vs bryng
　　　　In-to thatt reygeon where he ys kyng
Wyche abowe all othur far dothe a-bownde,
And thatt cruell Sathan he schall confownde.　　　　　　14

Where-fore I cu*m* here apon this grownde
　　　　To comforde eyu*er*e [3] creature off birthe ;

----

[1] *Qy.* sounde.　　　　　[2] S. geven*us*.　　　　　[3] S. eyерue.

For I, Isaye the *pr*ofet, hathe fownde
   Many swete matt*er*s whereof we ma make myrth
      On this same wyse ;
For, thogh that Adam be demid to deythe
W*ith* all his childur, asse Abell *and* Seythe,
Yett *Ecce virgo consepeet*, —
      Loo, where a reymede schall ryse !   **23**

Be-holde, a mayde schall conseyve a childe
   And gett vs more *gr*ace then eyu*er* men had,
And hir meydin-[h]od nothing defylid.
Sche ys deputyd to beare the Sun, Almyghte God.
   Loo ! sufferntis,[1] now ma you be glad,
For of this meydin all we ma be fayne ;
   For Adam, *tha*t now lyis in sorrois full sade,
Hir gloreose birth schall reydeme hym ageyn
      From bondage and thrall.
   Now be myrre eyu*er*e mon,[1]
For this dede bryffly in Isaraell schalbe done,
And before the Fathur in trone,
      Thatt schall glade vs all.   **36**

More of this matt*er* fayne wolde I meve,
   But lengur tyme I haue not here for to dwell.
That Lorde *tha*t ys m*ar*cefull his m*ar*ce soo in vs ma p*re*ve
   For to sawe owre sollis from the darknes of hell ;
        And to his blys
          He vs bryng
       Asse he ys
          Bothe lord *and* kyng,
          And shall be eyu*er*lastyng,
          *In secula seculo*rum, *amen !* [2]   **46**

---

[1] *A curl over* n.
[2] *These six lines* (41–46) *as two in* S., *the first ending with* king.

[Exit Isaiah ; enter Gabriel to Mary.]

GABERELL.   Hayle, Mare, full of grace !
    Owre Lord God ys wit*h* the ; [1]
Aboue all wemen [2] *tha*t eyu*er* wasse,
    Lade, blesside mote thow be !   50

MARE.   All-myght Fathur and King of blys,
    From all dysses *tho*u saue me now !
For inwardely my spretis trubbuld ys,
    Thatt I am amacid *and* kno nott how.   54

GABERELL.   Dred the nothyng, meydin, of this ;
    From heyvin a-bowe hyddur am I sent
Of ambassage from that Kyng of blys
    Unto the, lade *and* ver*g*in reyu*er*ent !
    Salutyng the here asse most exselent,
Whose ve*r*tu aboue all othur dothe abownde.
Wherefore in the *gr*ace schalbe fownde ;
For thow schalt conseyve apon *thi*s grownd
    The Second Pe*r*sone of God in trone ;
    He wylbe borne of the alone ;
        Wit*h*-owt sin *tho*u schalt hy*m* see.[3]
    Thy *gr*ace *and* thi goodnes wyl neyu*er* be gone,
    But eyu*er* to lyve in ve*r*genete.   67

MARE.   I marvell soore how thatt mabe.
    Man*us* cu*m*pany knev I neyu*er* yett,
Nor neyu*er* to do, kast I me,
    Whyle thatt owre Lord sendith me my wytt.   71

GABERELL.   The Wholle Gost in the schall lyght,
    And schado thy soll soo wit*h* ve*r*tu
From the Fathur thatt ys on hyght.
    These wordis, turtill, the[y] be full tru.   75

---

[1] *Lines* 47, 48 *as one in* S.
[2] *Curl over* n.
[3] *Lines* 64, 65 *as one in* S.

This chylde that of the schalbe borne
  Ys the Second Per*s*one in Trenete ;
He schall saue that wase forlorne
  And the fyndis powar dystroie schall he.   79

These wordis, lade, full tru the[y] bene,
  And furthur, lade, here in thy noone lenage
Be-holde Eylesabeth, thy cosyn clene,
  The wyche wasse barren *and* past all age,   83

And now w*ith* chyld sche hath bene
Syx monethis and more, asse schalbe sene;
  Where-for, discomforde *th*e not, Mare !
  For to God onpossibull nothyng mabe.   87

MARE.   Now, and yt be thatt Lordis wyll
  Of my bodde to be borne *and* forto be,
Hys hy pleysuris forto full-fyll
  Asse his one hande-mayde I submyt me.   91

GABERELL.   Now blessid be *th*e tyme sett
  That *th*ou wast borne in thy degre !
For now ys the knott surely knytt,
  And God conseyvide in Trenete.   95

Now fare-well, lade off myghtis most !
  Vnto the God-hed I the be-teyche.
MARE.   Thatt Lord the gyde in eyu*er*e cost,
  And looly he leyde me *and* be my leyche !   99

*Here the angell dep*artyth*, and J*oseff *cu*myth in *and seyth :*

JOSOFF.   Mare, my wyff so dere,
How doo ye, dame, and whatt chere
  Ys w*ith* you this tyde ?
MARE.   Truly, husebonde, I am here
  Owre Lordis wyll forto abyde.   104

JOSOFF.   What ! I troo thatt we be all schent !
Sey, womon ;[1] who hath byn here sith I went,
　　To rage wyth thee?
MARE.   Syr, here was nothur man[1] nor mans eyvin,
But only the sond of owre Lorde God in heyvin.
JOSOFF.   Sey not soo, womon ; for schame, ley be !   110

Ye be w*ith* chyld soo wondurs grett,
Ye nede no more *the*rof to tret
　　Agense all right.
For sothe, this chylde, dame, ys not myne.
Alas, that eyu*er* w*ith* my nynee
　　I suld see *thi*s syght !   116

Tell me, womon ;[1] whose ys this chyld?
MARE.   Non but youris, husebond soo myld,
　　And thatt schalbe seyne, [ywis].
JOSOFF.   But myne? allas ! alas ! why sey ye soo?
Wele-awey ! womon, now may I goo,
　　Be-gyld as many a-nothur ys.   122

MARE.   Na, truly, sir, ye be not be-gylde,
Nor yet w*ith* spott of syn I am not defylde ;
　　Trust yt well, huse-bonde.
JOSOFF.   Huse-bond, in feythe ! *and tha*t acold !
A ! weylle-awey, Josoff, as thow ar olde !
　　Lyke a fole now ma I stand
　　　　And truse.[2]
　　But, in feyth, Mare, *tho*u art in syn ;
　　Soo moche ase I haue cheyrischyd *the*e, dame, *and* all *th*i
　　　　kyn,
　　　　Be-hynd my bake to s*er*ve me thus !   132

All olde men, insampull take be me, —
How I am be-gylid here may you see ! —
　　To wed soo yong a chyld.

　　　　　[1] *Curl over* n.　　　　　[2] *Lines* 128, 129 *as one in* S.

Now fare-well, Mare, I leyve the here alone, —
[Wo] worthe the, dam, and thy warkis ycheone ! —
    For I woll noo-more be be-gylid [1]
    For frynd nor fooe.[2]
Now of this ded I am soo dull,
And off my lyff I am soo full,
    No farthur ma I goo.[3]   142

[Lies down to sleep ; to him enters an angel.]

I. ANGELL.[4]   Aryse up, Josoff, *and* goo whom ageyne
    Vnto Mare, thy wyff, that ys so fre.
To comford hir loke *tha*t thow be fayne,
    For, Josoff, a cleyne meydin ys schee :
Sche hath conseyvid w*ith*-owt any trayne
    The Seycond P*er*son in Trenete ;
Jh*e*su schalbe hys name, sarten,
    And all thys world sawe schall he ;
        Be not agast.[5]
JOSOFF.   Now, Lorde, I thanke the w*ith* hart full sad,
For of these tythyngis I am soo glad
    That all my care awey ys cast ;
    Wherefore to Mare I woll in hast.   155

[Returns to Mary.]

A ! Mare, Mare, I knele full loo ;
    Forgeve me, swete wyff, here in *thi*s lond !
Marce, Mare ! for now I kno
    Of youre good gou*er*nance and how yt doth stond.   159

    Thogh [6] thatt I dyd the mys-name,
Marce, Mare ! Whyle I leve,
Wyll I neyu*er*, swet wyff, the greve
    In ernyst nor in game.[5]
MARE.   Now, that Lord in heyvin, sir, he you forgyve !

---

1 S. be gylid be.   2 138, 139 *as one in* S.
3 *Lines* 141, 142 *as one in* S.
4 S. ANGELL J ; *so below for both angels and shepherds.*
5 *These two lines as one in* S.   6 S. Thoght.

And I do for-geve yow in hys name
    For euermore.[1]

JOSOFF.   Now truly, swete wyff, to you I sey the same.   167

But now to Bedlem must I wynde
    And scho my-self, soo full of care ;
And I to leyve you, this grett, behynd, —
    God wott, the whyle, dame, how you schuld fare.   171

MARE.   Na, hardely, husebond, dred ye nothyng ;
    For I woll walke with you on the wey.
I trust in God, all-mighte kyng,
    To spede right well in owre jurney.   175

JOSOFF.   Now I thanke you, Mare, of your goodnes
    That ye my wordis woll nott blame ;
And syth that to Bedlem we schall vs dresse,
    Goo we to-gedur in Goddis wholle name.   179

[They set out, and travel a while.]

Now to Bedlem have we leygis three ;
    The day ys ny spent, yt drawyth toward nyght ;
Fayne at your es, dame, I wold that ye schulde be,
    For you grone [2] all werely, yt semyth in my syght.   183

MARE.   God haue marcy, Josoffe, my spowse soo dere ;
    All profettis herto dothe beyre wyttnes,
The were tyme now draith nere
    That my chyld wolbe borne, wyche ys Kyng of blis.   187

Vnto sum place, Josoff, hyndly me leyde,
    Thatt I moght rest me with grace in this tyde.
The lyght of the Fathur ouer hus both spreyde,
    And the grace of my sun with vs here a-byde !   191

JOSOFF.   Loo ! blessid Mare, here schall ye lend,
    Cheff chosyn of owre Lorde and cleynist in degre ;
And I for help to towne woll I wende.
    Ys nott this the best, dame ? whatt sey ye ?   195

---

[1] *Lines* 165, 166 *as one in* S.   [2] S. groue ; *possibly for* growe?

MARE.   God haue marce, Josoff, my huse-bond soo meke !
    And hartely I p*ra* you, goo now fro me.
JOSOFF.   That schalbe done in hast, Mare so swete !
    The comford of the Wholle Gost leyve I w*ith* the.   199

Now to Bedlem streyght woll I wynd
    To gett som helpe for Mare soo free.
Su*m* helpe of wem*m*en God may me send,
    That Mare, full off *gra*ce, pleysid ma be.   203

      [In another part of the place a shepherd begins to speak.]

I. PASTOR.   Now God, that art in Trenete,
Thow sawe my fellois and me !
For I kno nott wheyre my scheepe nor the[y] be,
    Thys nyght yt ys soo colde.
Now ys yt nygh the myddis of the nyght ;
These wedurs ar darke and dym of lyght,
Thatt of them can hy haue noo syght,
    Standyng here on this wold.   211

But now to make there hartis lyght,
Now wyll I full right
    Stand apon this looe,[1]
And to them cry w*ith* all my myght, —
    Full well my voise the[y] kno :
    W*hat* hoo ! fellois ! hoo ! hooe ! hoo !   217

      [Two other shepherds appear (in the street).]

II. PASTOR.   Hark, Sym, harke ! I here owre brothur on the
      looe ;
This ys hys woise, right well I knoo ;
There-fore toward hym lett vs goo,
    And follo his woise a-right.
See, Sym, se, where he doth stond !
I am ryght glad we haue hym fond !
Brothur, where hast thow byn soo long,
    And hit ys soo cold this nyght ?[2]   225

---

[1] *Lines* 213, 214 *as one in* S.   [2] S. And this nyght hit ys soo cold.

I. PASTOR.   E ! fryndis, *the*r cam a pyrie of wynd w*ith* a
    myst suddenly,[1]
Thatt forth off my weyis went I
And grett heyvenes then [2] made I
    And wase full sore afryght.[3]
Then forto goo wyst I nott whyddur,
But trawellid on this loo hyddur *and* thyddur ;
I wasse so were of this cold weddur
    Thatt nere past wasse my might.   233

III. PASTOR.   Brethur, now we be past *tha*t fryght,
And hit ys far w*ith*-in the nyght,
Full sone woll spryng the day-lyght,
    Hit drawith full nere the tyde.
Here awhyle lett vs rest,
And repast owreself of the best ;
Tyll thatt the sun ryse in the est
    Let vs all here abyde.   241

   *There the schep*p*ardis drawys furth there meyte* and *doth eyte* and *drynk ;*
   and asse the[y] *drynk, the*[y] *fynd the star,* and *sey thus :*

III. PASTOR.   Brethur, loke vp and behold !
    Whatt thyng ys yondur thatt schynith soo bryght?
Asse long ase eyu*er* I haue wachid my fold,
    Yett sawe I neyu*er* soche a syght
        In fyld.[4]
A ha ! now ys cu*m* the tyme *tha*t old fathurs hath told,
Thatt in the wynturs nyght soo cold
A chyld of meydyn [5] borne be he wold
        In whom all p*ro*feciys schalbe fullfyld.   250

I. PASTOR.   Truth yt ys w*ith*-owt naye,
Soo seyd the p*ro*fett Isaye,
    Thatt a [6] chylde schuld be borne of a made soo bryght

---

[1] *Curl over* n.   [4] *Lines* 245, 246 *as one in* S.
[2] S. in.   [5] *Curl over* n.
[3] S. afrayde.   [6] S. *has* I.

In wentur ny the schortist dey
    Or elis in the myddis of the nyght.   255

II. PASTOR.   Loovid be God, most off myght,
That owre *gra*ce ys to see thatt syght ;
Pray we to hym, ase hit ys right,
    Yff thatt his wyll yt be,
That we ma haue knoleyge of this syngnefocacion
And why hit aperith on this fassion ;
And eyu*er* to hym lett vs geve lawdacion,
    In yerthe whyle thatt we be.   263

There the angelis syng " Glorea in exselsis Deo."

III. PASTOR.   Harke ! the[y] syng abowe in the clowdis
        clere !
Hard I neyuer of soo myrre a quere.
Now, gentyll brethur, draw we nere
    To here there armonye.
I. PASTOR.   Brothur, myrth and solas ys cu*m* hus among ;
For be the swettnes of *the*r songe,
Goddis Sun ys cu*m*, whom we haue lokid for long,
    Asse syngnefyith thys star *tha*t we do see.
II. PASTOR.   "*Glore, glorea in exselsis*," *tha*t wase *the*r
        songe ;
    How sey ye, fellois, seyd the[y] not thus ?
I. PASTOR.   Thatt ys welseyd ; now goo we hence
To worschipe thatt chyld of hy manyffecence,
And that we ma syng in his p*r*esence
    "*Et in tarra pax omynibus.*"   277

There the scheppardis syngis "Ase I owt Rodde," [1] and *Josoff seyth:*

JOSOFF.   Now, Lorde, this noise *tha*t I do here,
    With this grett solemnete,
Gretly amendid hath my chere ;
    I trust hy nevis schortly wolbe.   281

[1] *For the song, see* p. 151.

There the angellis syng " Gloria in exsellsis" ageyne.

MARE.   A ! Josoff, husebond, cu*m* heddur anon ;
    My chylde ys borne *that* ys Kyng of blys.
JOSOFFE.   Now welcu*m* to me, the Makar of mon,
W*ith* all the omage thatt I con ;
    Thy swete mothe here woll I kys.   286

MARE.   A ! Josoff, husebond, my chyld waxith cold,
    And we haue noo fyre to warme hym w*ith*.
JOSOFF.   Now, in my narmys I schall hym fold,
    Kyng of all kyngis be fyld *and* be fryth ;
He myght haue had bettur, *and* hymselfe wold,
    Then the breythyng of these bestis to warme hy*m* w*ith*. 292

MARE.   Now, Josoff, my husbond, fet heddur my chyld,
    The Maker off man and hy Kyng of blys.
JOSOFF.   That schalbe done anon, Mare soo myld,
    For the brethyng of these bestis hath warmyd [hym]
        well, i-wys.   296

[Angels appear to the shepherds.]

I. ANGELL.   Hyrd-men [1] hynd,
Drede ye nothyng [2]
    Off thys star thatt ye do se ;
For thys same morne
Godis Sun ys borne [3]
    In Bedlem of a meydin fre.   302

II. ANGELL.   Hy you thyddur in hast ;
    Yt ys hys wyll ye schall hym see
Lyinge in a cribbe of pore reypaste,
    Yett of Davithis lyne cu*m*on [1] ys hee.   306

[The shepherds approach and worship the Babe.]

I. PASTOR.   Hayle, mayde-mothur *and* wyff soo myld !
    Asse the angell seyd, soo haue we fonde.

[1] *Curl over* n.
[2] *Lines* 297, 298 *as one in* S.
[3] *Lines* 300, 301 *as one in* S.

I haue nothyng to present w*ith th*i chylde
    But my pype ; hold, hold, take yt in thy hond ;
    Where-in moche pleysure *that* I haue fond ;
And now, to oonowre thy gloreose byrthe,
Thow schallt yt haue to make the myrthe.   313

II. PASTOR.   Now, hayle be thow, chyld, *and* thy dame !
    For in a pore [1] loggyn here art thow leyde,
Soe the angell seyde *and* tolde vs thy name ;
    Holde, take thow here my hat on thy hedde !
    And now off won thyng thow art well sped,
For weddur thow hast noo nede to complayne,
For wynde, ne sun, hayle, snoo and rayne.   320

III. PASTOR.   Hayle be thow, Lorde ou*er* watur *and* landis !
    For thy cu*m*yng all we ma make myrthe.
Haue here my myttens to pytt on *th*i hondis,
    Othur treysure haue I non to present the w*ith.*   324

MARE.   Now, herdmen hynd,
    For youre comyng
        To my chylde schall I p*ra*e,
    Asse he ys heyvin kyng,
        To grant you his blessyng,
And to hys blys *tha*t ye may wynd
        At your last day.   331

*There the schep*p*ardis syngith* [2] *ageyne and goth forthe of* the *place ; and
the ij.* pro*fettis cu*m*yth in and seyth thus :*

I. PROFETA.   Novellis, novellis
Of wonderfull m*er*vellys,[3]
    Were hy *and* defuce vnto the heryng !
Asse scripture tellis,
These strange novellis
    To you I bryng.[4]   337

[1] S. apore.
[2] *For this song, see* p. 152.
[3] *Lines* 332, 333 *as one in* S.
[4] *Lines* 335, 337 *as one in* S.

II. P*R*OFETA.   Now hartely, sir, I desyre to knoo,
Yff hytt wolde pleyse you forto schoo,
 Of what maner a thyng.
  I. P*R*OFETA.   Were mystecall vnto youre heryng, —
  Of the natevete off a kyng.   342

II. P*R*OFETA.   Of a kyng? Whence schuld he cu*m*?
  I. P*R*OFETA.   From thatt reygend ryall *and* mighty
    mancion,
The sede seylesteall and heyvinly vysedome,
 The Second Person *and* Godis one Sun,
For owre sake now ys man be-cum.[1]   347

This godly spere
Desendid here [2]
Into a v*er*gin clere.
 Sche, on-defyld [3]
. . . . . .[4]
Be whose warke obskevre
Owre frayle nature
 Ys now begilde [5]
  II. P*R*OFETA.   Why, hathe sche a chylde? 355

I. P*R*OFETA.   E ! trust hyt well ;
 And neu*er* the las [6]
 Yet ys sche a mayde evin asse sche wasse,
And hir sun the kyng of Isaraell.   359

II. P*R*OFETA.   A wondur-full marvell
 How thatt ma be, [7]
And far dothe exsell
 All owre capasete : [7]
 How that the Trenete,
  Of soo hy regallete, [7]
 Schuld jonyd be [8]
  Vnto owre mortallete ! [7]   367

---

[1] *Curl over* m.
[2] *Lines* 348, 349 *as one in* S.
[3] *Lines* 350, 351 *as one in* S.
[4] *Line missing.*
[5] *Lines* 353, 354 *as one in* S.
[6] *Lines* 356, 357 *as one in* S.
[7] *This and the preceding line as one in* S.
[8] S. be jonyd.

I. PROFETA.   Of his one grett marce,
  As ye shall se *th*e exposyssion,[1]
Throgh whose vmanyte
All Adam*us* p*r*ogene[1]
  Reydemyd schalbe owt of p*er*dyssion.   372

Syth man[2] did offend,
Who schuld amend[1]
  But the seyd mon[2] and no nothur?
For the wyche cawse he
Incarnate wold be[1]
  And lyve in mesere asse man*us* one brothur.   378

II. PROFETA.   Syr vnto the deyite,
I beleve p*ar*fettle,[1]
  Onpossibul to be there ys nothyng;
How be yt this warke
Vnto me ys darke[1]
  In the opp*er*acion or wyrkyng.
I. PROFETA.   Whatt more reypriff
Ys vnto belyff
  Then[2] to be dowtyng?[3]   387

II. PROFETA.   Yet dowtis oftym*us* hathe derevacion.
I. PROFETA.   Thatt ys be *th*e meynes of comenecacion[2]
Of trawthis to haue a dev p*r*obacion
  Be *th*e same dowts reysoning.
    II. PROFETA.   Then to you thys won thyng:
Of whatt nobull *and* hy lenage ys schee
Thatt myght *thi*s ve*r*abull[4] p*r*encis modur be?   394

I. PROFETA.   Ondowtid sche ys cu*m* of hy parrage,
Of the howse of Davith *and* Salamon the sage;
And won off the same lyne joynid to hir be mareage;

---

[1] *This and the preceding line as one in* S.
[2] *Curl over* n.   [4] *Qy.* renable, *see Notes.*
[3] *Lines* 385-387 *as one in* S.

Of whose trybe
We do subscrybe [1]
This chy[l]dis lenage.[2]　　　　　　　　　　400

II. PROFETA.　And why in thatt wysse?
I. PROFETA.　For yt wasse the gysse
　　To conte the parant on the manys lyne,
　　And nott on the feymy[ny]ne,
　　　　Amonst vs here in Isaraell.
II. PROFETA.　Yett can I　nott aspy　be noo wysse
How thys chylde borne schuldbe wit*h*-ow[t] naturis prejudyse.
I. PROFETA.　Nay, no prejvdyse vnto nature, I dare well sey;
For the kyng of nature may
　　　　Hawe all at his one wyll.[3]
　　Dyd not *th*e powar of God
　　Make Aronis rod
Beyre frute in on day?[4]　　　　　　　　　　413

II. PROFETA.　Truth yt ys in-ded.
I. PROFETA.　Then loke you and rede.
II. PROFETA.　A ! I per*s*eyve the sede
　　Where apon thatt you spake. [5]
Yt wasse for owre nede
　　*Tha*t he frayle nature did take,[5]
And his blod he schuld schede
　　Amens forto make [5]
　　　　For owre transegression ;
　　Ase yt ys seyd in profece
　　*Tha*t of the lyne of Jude [5]
　　Schuld spryng a right Messe,
　　Be whom all wee
　　　　Schall [6] haue reydemcion,[5]　　　　427

I. PROFETA.　S*i*r, now ys the tyme cu*m*,
*An*d the date there-of run,[7]
　　Off his Natevete.

---

[1] S. subscryve.
[2] *Lines* 398–400 *as one in* S.
[3] *Lines* 409, 410 *as one in* S.
[4] *Lines* 411–413 *as one in* S.
[5] *This and the preceding line as one in* S.
[6] S. schalld.　　[7] *Curl over* n.

II. PROFETA. Yett I beseke you hartele
  *Tha*t ye wold schoo me how [1]
Thatt this strange nowelte
  Were broght vnto you.[1]   434

I. PROFETA. This othur nyght soo cold
Hereby apon a wolde
Schepp*ar*dis wachyng there fold,
  In the nyght soo far
  To them aperid a star,
  And eyu*er* yt drev them nar ;
Wyche star the[y] did behold
Bryght*er*, *th*e[y] sey, M folde
  Then the sun so clere
  In his mydday spere,
And the[y] these tythyngis tolde.   445

II. PROFETA. What, seycretly?
I. PROFETA. Na, na, hardely ;
  The[y] made there-of no conseil ;
For the[y] song ase lowde
Ase eyu*er* the[y] cowde,
  Presyng the kyng of Isaraell.   451

II. PROFETA. Yett do I marvell
In what pyle or castell
  These herdmen [2] dyd hym see.

I. PROFETA. Nothur in hallis nor yett in bowris
  Borne wold he not be,
Nothur in castellis nor yet in towris
  *Tha*t semly were to se ;   458

But att hys Fathurs wyll,
The *pr*ofeci to full-fyll,
  Be-twyxt an ox and and an as
  Ihe*s*u, *thi*s kyng, borne he was.
Heyvin he bryng us tyll !   463

---

[1] *This and the preceding line as one in* S. [2] *Curl over* n.

II. PROFETA.   Sir, a ! but when these sheppardis had seyne
    hym there,
In-to whatt place did the[y] repeyre?
I. PROFETA.   Forthe the[y] went and glad the[y] were,
    Going the[y] did syng ;
With myrthe and solas the[y] made good chere
    For joie of that new tything ;   469

And aftur, asse I hard the[m] tell,
He reywardid them full well :
He graunt them hevyn ther-in to dwell ;
    In ar the[y] gon with joie and myrthe,
And there songe hit ys " Neowell."   474

There the profettis gothe furthe and *Erod* cumyth in, and the *messenger*.

NONCEOSE.[1]   Faytes pais, dñyis,[2] baronys de grande rey-
    nowme !
Payis, seneoris, schevaleris de nooble posance![3]
Pays, gentis homos,[4] companeonys petis egrance ![5]
Je vos command dugard treytus [6] sylance.
Payis, tanque vottur nooble Roie syre ese presance ![7]
Que nollis[8] persone ese non fawis perwynt[9] dedfferance,
Nese [10] harde de frappas ;[11] mayis gardus to to[12] paceance, —

---

[1] In reading this proclamation I have had the aid of both Professor Kittredge and Professor Sheldon.   As this aid, however, was given a year or two
ago in the form of a pretty lively oral discussion of the most perplexing of
the difficulties, and as I unfortunately neglected to take any notes at the
time, I find myself unable, except in one or two cases, to remember to which
of the two each suggestion belongs.   Of course they are not responsible for
any mistakes that may appear here.   I have printed the text with no change
except in punctuation.   The footnotes deal with all difficulties that seem
beyond the scope of even a beginner in French.

[2] Sheldon *suggests that this is the* pl. *of* O.F. dame, damne, *influenced by
the spelling of some form of* Lat. dominus.

[3] puissance.   [8] nulle.   [11] frapper.

[4] *The second* o *is probably only a careless form of* e.

[5] et grands.   [9] Kittredge : ici non fasse point.

[6] de garder trestous.   [10] Ne se.   [12] gardez tote.

[7] roi seit ici present.

Mayis gardus [1] voter seneor to cor[2] reyue*r*ance ;
Car elat vottur Roie to to puysance.[3]
Anoñ de leo,[4] pase tos ! je vose cum*m*ande,
E lay Roie erott la grandeaboly vos vmport.[5]   485

ERODE. *Qui statis* [6] *in Jude et Rex Iseraell,*
　　And the myghttyst conquerowre *th*at eyue*r* walkid on
　　　　ground ;
For I am evyn he thatt made bothe hevin *and* hell,
　　And of my myghte powar holdith vp *thi*s world rownd.
Magog *and* Madroke, bothe *th*e[m] did I confownde,
And w*ith* this bryght bronde there bonis I brak on-sund*e*r,
Thatt all the wyde worlde on those rappis did wond*e*r.   492

I am the cawse of this grett lyght and thund*e*r ;
　　Ytt ys throgh my fure *th*at the[y] soche noyse dothe
　　　　make.
My feyrefull contenance *th*e clowdis so doth incu*m*bur
　　*Th*at oftym*u*s for drede *th*er-of the verre yerth doth
　　　　quake.
Loke, when I w*ith* males this bryght brond doth schake,
All the whole world from the north to *th*e sowthe
I ma them dystroie w*ith* won worde of my mowthe !   499

To reycownt vnto you myn innevmerabull substance, —
　　Thatt were to moche for any tong to tell ;
For all the whole Orent ys vnd*e*r myn obbeydeance,
　　And prynce am I of purgatorre *and* cheff capten of hell ;
And those tyraneos trayturs be force ma I compell[7]
Myne enmyis[8] to vanquese *and* evyn to dust them dryve,
And w*ith* a twynke of myn iee not won to be lafte alyve.   506

---

[1] *A preposition before the indirect object seems unnecessary.*
[2] tote.　　　　　　　[3] Sheldon : Car il est votre roi tout puissant.
[4] A (= au) nom de lui (Sheldon *suggests* loi *instead of* lui).
[5] Sheldon *suggests that the line properly ends with* grand (*modifying* Erott
and rhyming with 484), — diable vos emporte! *being merely an unattached
pleasantry addressed to the audience.*
[6] Qui statis *is in red in* S.
[7] *Curl over* m.　　　　　　[8] *Curl over* n.

Behold my contenance and my colur,
    Bryghtur then the sun in the meddis of *th*e dey.
Where can you haue a more grettur succur
    Then to behold my *per*son that ys soo gaye?
    My fawcun *and* my fassion, w*ith* my gorgis araye,—
He thatt had the g*r*ace all-wey *the*r-on to thynke,
Lyve he [1] myght all-wey w*ith*-owt othur meyte or drynke.   513

And thys my tryomfande fame most hylist dothe a-bownde
    Throgh-owt this world in all reygeons abrod,
Reysemelyng the fau*er* of thatt most myght Mahownd ;
    From Jubytor be desent *and* cosyn to the grett God,
    And namyd the most reydowndid king Eyrodde,
Wyche thatt all pryncis hath und*er* subjeccion
And all there whole powar vndur my p*r*oteccion.   520

And therefore, my hareode, here, callid Calcas,
    Warne thow eyu*er*[e] porte thatt noo schyppis a-ryve,
Nor also aleond strang*er* throg my realme pas,
    But the[y] for there truáge do pay markis fyve.
        Now spede the forth hastele,
        For the[y] thatt wyll the contrare
        Apon a galowse hangid schalbe,
And, be Mahownde, of me the[y] gett noo g*r*ace !   528

NONCIOS.   Now, lord and mastur, in all the hast
    Thy worethe wyll ytt schall be wroght,
And thy ryall cuntreyis schalbe past
    In asse schort tyme ase can be thoght.   532

ERODE.   Now schall owre regeons throgh-owt be soght
    In eyu*er*[e] place bothe est *and* west ;
Yff any katyffis to me be broght,
    Yt schalbe nothyng for there best.
    And the whyle thatt I do resst,
Trompettis, viallis and othur armone
Schall bles the wakyng of my mai*e*ste.   539

                [1] S. the.

Here Erod goth awey and *the iij Kyngis speykyth in* the *strete.*

I. REX.   Now blessid be God of his swet sonde,
   For yondur a feyre bryght star I do see !
Now ys he comon[1] vs a-monge,
   Asse the *p*rofet[2] seyd thatt yt schuld be.   543

A seyd[3] there schuld a babe be borne,
   Comyng of the rote of Jesse,
To sawe mankynd that wasse for-lorne ;
   And truly come*n* now ys he.   547

Reyu*e*rence and worschip to hym woll I do
   Asse God and man, thatt all made of noght.
All the *p*rofettis acordid and seyd evyn soo,
   That w*it*h hys *p*resseos blod mankynd schuld be boght.   551

He grant me g*ra*ce,
   Be yond*e*r star *tha*t I see,[4]
And in-to thatt place
   Bryng me [5]
   Thatt I ma hym worschipe w*it*h umellete
And se hys gloreose face.   557

II. REX.   Owt off my wey I deme thatt I am,
   For toocuns of thys cuntrey can I non see ;
Now, God, thatt on yorth madist man,
   Send me su*m* knoleyge where thatt I be !   561

Yondur, me thynke, a feyre, bryght star I see,
   The wyche be-tocunyth the byrth of a chyld
Thatt hedur ys cu*m* to make man fre ;
   He borne of a mayde,[6] and sche nothyng defyld.   565

To worschip thatt chyld ys myn in-tent ;
   Forth now wyll I take my wey.
I trust su*m* cu*m*pany God hathe me sent,
   For yond*e*r I se a kyng labur on the wey ;   569

----

[1] *Curl over* m.   [4] *Lines* 552, 553 *as one in* S.
[2] S. p*r*ofettis.   [5] *Lines* 554, 555 *as one in* S.
[3] S. Aseyd.   [6] S. amayde.

To-warde hym now woll I ryde.
    Harke ! cu*m*ly kyng, I you pray,
In-tò whatt cost wyll ye thys tyde,
    Or weddur lyis youre jurney?   573

I. REX.   To seke a chylde ys myne in-tent
Of whom the p*r*ofetis hathe ment ;
The tyme ys cu*m*, now ys he sent,
    Be yondur star here ma [you]¹ see.
II. REX.   Sir, I prey you, w*ith* your lysence,
To ryde w*ith* you vnto his presence ;
To hym wyll I offur frank-in-sence,
    For the hed of all Whole Churche schall he be.   581

III. REX.   I ryde wanderyng in veyis wyde,
    Ou*er* montens and dalis ; I wot not where I am.
Now, Kyng off all kyngis, send me soche gyde
    Thatt I myght haue knoleyge of thys cuntreys name.   585

A ! yondur I se a syght, be semyng all afar,
    The wyche be-tocuns sum nevis, ase I troo ;
Asse me thynke, a chyld peryng in a stare.
    I trust he be cu*m* *tha*t schall defend vs from woo.   589

To kyngis yondur I see,
    And to them woll I ryde
Forto haue there cu*m*pane ;
    I trust *th*e[y] wyll me abyde.²
Hayle, cu*m*ly kyngis augent !⁸
Good surs, I pray you, whedd*er* ar ye ment?   595

I. REX.   To seke a chylde ys owre in-tent,
    Wyche be-tocuns yond*er* star, asse ye ma see.
II. REX.   To hym I purpose thys present.
    III. REX.   Surs, I pray you, and thatt ryght vmblee,
    W*ith* you thatt I ma ryde in cu*m*pane.
    [? ALL.]   To all-myghte God now prey we
    Thatt hys pressiose p*er*sone we ma se.   602

¹ *Supplied by* S.   ² *Lines* 590–593 *as two in* S.   ⁸ *Qy.* and gent.

Here Erode cumyth *in ageyne* and *the messengere seyth:*

NUNCIOS. Hayle, lorde most off myght !
Thy commandement ys right ;
In-to thy land ys comyn *this* nyght
   iij kyngis and w*ith* them a grett cumpany.
EROD. Whatt make those kyngis in this cuntrey?
NONCIOS. To seke a kyng and a chyld, the[y] sey.
   ERODE. Of whatt age schuld he bee?
   NONCIOS. Skant twellve deyis old fulle.   610

EROD. And wasse he soo late borne ?
NONCIOS. E, syr, soo the[y] schode me thys same dey in
     the morne.
EROD. Now, in payne of deyth, bryng them me beforne ;
   And there-fore, harrode, now hy the in hast,
In all spede thatt thou were dyght
   Or thatt those kyngis the cuntrey be past ;
Loke thow bryng them all iij before my syght ;   617

And in Jerusalem [1] inquere more of that chyld.
But I warne the that thy wordis be mylde,
For there must [2] thow hede and crafte wey[lde]
How to for-do his powere ; and those iij kyngis shalbe begild. 621

NONCIOS. Lorde, I am redde att youre byddyng
To sarve the ase my lord and kyng ;
For joye there-of, loo, how I spryng
W*ith* lyght hart *and* fresche gamboldyng
   Alofte here on this molde !
ERODE. Then sped the forthe hastely,
And loke *tha*t thow beyre the eyvinly ;
And also I pray the hartely
Thatt thow doo comand me
   Bothe to yong and olde. [8]   631

[1] S. Jerusalen.   [2] S. mast.
[8] *Lines 629–631 as two in* S., *the first ending with* doo.

[The messenger goes to the kings.]

NUNCIOS.　Hayle, syr kyngis, in youre degre ;
　　Erood, kyng of these cuntreyis wyde,
Desyrith to speyke w*i*th you all thre,
　　And for youre comyng he dothe abyde.　　　635

I. REX.　Syr, att his wyll we be ryght bayne.
　　Hy us, brethur, vnto thatt lordis place ;
To speyke w*i*th hym we wold be fayne ;
　　Thatt chyld thatt we seke, he grant us of his g*r*ace !　　639

[They go to Herod.]

NUNCIOS.　Hayle, lorde w*i*th-owt pere !
　　These iij kyngis here have we broght.
ERODE.　Now welcu*m*, syr kyngis, all in-fere ;
　　But of my bryght ble, surs, bassche ye noght !　　643

Sir kyngis, ase I vndurstand,
A star hathe gydid you into my land,
Where-in grett harting[1] ye haue fonde
　　Be reysun of hir beym*us* bryght.
Wherefore I pray you hartely
The vere truthe thatt ye wold s*er*tefy,
How long yt ys surely
　　Syn of that star you had furst syght.　　　651

I. REX.　S*i*r kynge, the vere truthe to sey
　　And forto schoo you ase hit ys best,
This same ys evin the xij[th] dey
　　Syth yt aperid to vs to be west.　　　655

ERODE.　Brethur, then ys there no more to sey,
But w*i*th hart and wyll kepe ye your jurney
And cu*m* whom by me this same wey,
　　Of your nevis thatt I myght knoo.

　　　　　　　[1] S. harie.

You schall tryomfe in this cuntre
And with grett conquorde bankett with me,
And thatt chyld myself then woll I see
    And honor hym also.   663

II. REX.   Sir, youre commandement we woll fullfyll
And humbly abaye owreself there-tyll.[1]
He thatt weldith all thyng at wyll
    The redde way hus teyche,[2]
Sir kyng, thatt we ma passe your land in pes !
ERODE.   Yes, and walke softely eyvin at your one es ;   669

Youre pase-porte for a C deyis
    Here schall you haue of clere cummand,
Owre reme to labur any weyis
    Here schall you haue be spesschall grante.   673

III. REX.   Now fare-well, kyng of hy degre,
    Humbly of you owre leyve we take.
ERODE.   Then adev, sir kyngis all thre ;
And whyle I lyve, be bold of me !
There ys nothyng in this cuntre
    But for youre one ye schall yt take.   679

              [Exeunt the three kings.]

Now these iij kyngis ar gon on ther wey ;
    On-wysely and on-wyttely haue the[y] all wroghte.
When the[y] cum ageyne, the[y] schall dy that same dey,
    And thus these vyle wreychis to deyth the[y] schalbe broght,—
        Soche ys my lykyng.
    He that agenst my lawis wyll hold,
    Be he kyng or keysar neyuer soo bold,
    I schall them cast in-to caris cold
        And to deyth I schall them bryng.   688

     There Erode goth his weyis and the iij kyngis cum in ageyne.

I. REX.   O blessid God, moche ys thy myght !
Where ys this star thatt gawe vs lyght ?   690

     [1] *Qy.* there-to.   [2] *Qy.* show.

II. REX. Now knele we downe here in this presence,
Be-sekyng that Lord of hy mangnefecens [1]
That we ma see his hy exsellence
    Yff thatt his swet wyll be. [2]   694

III. REX. Yondur, brothur, I see the star,
Where-by I kno he ys nott far ;
Therefore, lordis, goo we nar
    Into *this* pore place.   698

     There the iij kyngis gois in to the jesen, to Mare and hir child.

I. REX. Hayle, Lorde thatt all this worlde hath wroght !
    Hale, God and man to-gedur in-fere !
For thow hast made all thyng of noght,
    Albe-yt thatt thow lyist porely here ;
A cupe-full [3] golde here I haue the broght
    In toconyng thow art w*ith*-owt pere.   704

II. REX. Hayle be thow, Lorde of hy mangnyffecens ! [4]
    In toconyng of p*re*ste[h]od *and* dyngnete of offece
To the I offur a cupe full off in-sence,
    For yt be-hovith the to haue soche sacrefyce.   708

III. REX. Hayle be thow, Lorde longe lokid fore !
    I haue broght the myre for mortalete,
In to-cunyng thow schalt mankynd restore
    To lyff be thy deyth apon [5] a tre.   712

MARE. God haue ma*r*ce, kyngis, of yowre goodnes ;
    Be the gydyng of the godhed hid*d*er are ye sent ;
The p*ro*vyssion off my swete sun your weyis whom [6] reydres,
    And gostely reywarde you for youre present !   716

      [As the kings go away, they say :]

I. REX. Syr kyngis, aftur owre p*ro*mes
    Whome be Erode I mvst nedis goo.

---

1 S. maugnefecens.   4 S. maugnyffecens.
2 S. wylbe.   5 *Curl over* n.
3 S. *inserts* [of].   6 *Curl over* m.

II. REX.   Now truly, brethur,[1] we can noo las,
 But I am soo for-wachid [2] I wott not wat to do. 720
III. REX.   Ryght soo am I ; where-fore I you pray,
 Lett all vs rest vs awhyle upon *thi*s grownd.
I. REX.   Brethur, you*er* seying ys right well vnto my pay.
 The *gra*ce of thatt swet chylde saue vs all sownde ! 724

   [*While they sleep, the angel appears.*]

ANGELL*US*.   Kyng of Tawrus, S*ir* Jesp*ar*,
Kyng of Arraby, S*ir* Balthasar,
Melchor, Kyng of Aginare,
 To you now am I sent.
For drede of Eyrode, goo you west whom ;
In-to those p*ar*ties when ye cu*m* downe,
Ye schalbe byrrid w*ith* gret reynowne ;
 The Wholle Gost thus knoleyge hath sent. [*Exit.*] 732

I. REX.   Awake, s*ir* kyngis, I you praye,
 For the voise of an angell I hard in my dreyme.
II. REX.   Thatt ys full tru thatt ye do sey,
 For he reyherssid owre names playne. 736

III. REX.   He bad thatt we schuld goo downe be west
 For drede of Eyrodis fawls be-traye.
I. REX.   Soo forto do yt ys the best ;
 The child that we haue soght, gyde vs the wey ! 740

Now fare-well, the feyrist, of schapp so swete !
 And thankid be Jh*e*su of his sonde,
That we iij to-ged*er* soo suddenly schuld mete,
 Thatt dwell soo wyde *and* in straunge lond, 744

And here make owre presentacion
 Vnto this kyngis son clensid soo cleyne
And to his mod*er* for ovre saluacion ;
 Of moche myrth now ma we meyne,
Thatt we soo well hath done this obblacion. 749

   [1] S. berthur.   [2] S. far wachid.

II. REX.   Now farewell, S*i*r Jaspar, brothur, to yoeu,
    Kyng of Tawrus the most worthe ;
S*i*r Balthasar, also to you I bow ;
    And I thanke you bothe of youre good cu*m*pany
        Thatt we togeddur haue had.
    He thatt made vs to mete on hyll,
    I thanke hym now and eyu*er* I wyll ;
    For now may we goo w*ith*-owt yll,
        And off owre offerynge be full glad.[1]   758

III. REX.   Now syth thatt we mvst nedly goo
    For drede of Erode thatt ys soo wrothe,
Now fare-well brothur, *and* brothur also,
    I take my leve here at you bothe
        This dey on fete.[2]
    Now he thatt made vs to mete on playne
    And offur[3] to Mare in hir jeseyne,
    He geve vs g*ra*ce in heyvin a-gayne
        All to-geyd*er* to mete !   767

        [*They go out, and Herod and his train occupy the pageant.*]

NU*N*CIOS.   Hayle, kyng, most worthist in wede !
    Hayle, manteinar of curt*e*se[4] throgh all *thi*s world wyde !
Hayle, the most myghtyst that eyu*er* bestrod a stede !
    Ha[y]ll,[5] most monfullist mon in armor man to abyde !
        Hayle, in thyne hoonowre !
    Thesse iij kyngis *tha*t forthe were sent
    And schuld haue cu*m* ageyne before *th*e here p*re*sent,
    Anothur wey, lorde, whom the[y] went,
        Contrare to thyn honowre.   776

ERODE.   A-nothur wey? owt ! owt ! owtt !
    Hath those fawls traytvrs done me *thi*s ded ?
I stampe ! I stare ! I loke all abowtt !

---

[1] S. fayne.   [2] S. fote.   [3] S. offurde.
[4] *The contraction here is really that for* er, *but it has already occurred about a dozen times in words like* toged*er*.   [5] *Corr. by* S.

Myght I them take, I schuld them bren at a glede!
I rent! I rawe! *and* now run I wode!
A! thatt these velen trayturs hath mard *thi*s my mode!
  The[y] schalbe hangid yf I ma cu*m* them to! 783

Here Erode ragis in the *pagond* and *in the strete also.*

E! and thatt kerne of Bedlem, he schalbe ded
  And thus schall I for-do his p*ro*fece. 785

How sey you, s*i*r knyghtis? ys not this the best red,
Thatt all yong chyldur for this schuld be dede,
  Wyth sworde to be slayne?
  Then schall I, Erod, lyve in lede,
  And all folke me dowt and drede,
  And offur to me bothe gold, rychesse *and* mede;
  Thereto wyll the[y] be full fayne. 792

I. MYLES. My lorde kyng, Erode be name,
  Thy wordis agenst my wyll schalbe;
To see soo ma*n*y yong chyld*er* dy ys schame,
  Therefore consell *the*r-to gettis *tho*u non of me. 796

II. MYLES. Well seyd, fello, my trawth I plyght.
  S*i*r kyng, p*er*seyve right well you may,
Soo grett a mord*er* to see of yong frute
  Wyll make a rysyng in *th*i noone cuntrey. 800

ERODE. A rysyng? Owt! owt! owt! 801

There Erode ragis ageyne and then seyth thus:

Owt! velen wrychis, har apon you I cry!
  My wyll vtturly loke *tha*t yt be wroght,
Or apon a gallowse bothe you schall dy,
  Be Mahownde most myghtyste, *tha*t me dere hath boght. 805

I. MYLES. Now, cruell Erode, syth we schall do this dede!
  Your wyll nedefully in this realme mvste be wroght;
All the chyld*er* of *tha*t age dy the[y] mvst nede;
  Now w*ith* all my myght the[y] schall be vpsoght. 809

II. MYLES.   And I woll sweyre here apon your bryght swerde,[1]
   All the chylder thatt I fynd, sclayne the[y] schalbe ;
Thatt make many a moder to wepe and be full sore aferde [2]
   In owre armor bryght when the[y] hus see.   813

ERODE.   Now you have sworne, forthe that ye goo,
   And my wyll thatt ye wyrke bothe be dey and nyght,
And then wyll. I for fayne trypp lyke a doo.
   But whan the[y] be ded I warne you bryng [t]ham be-fore
         my syght.   817

   *[Herod and his train go away, and Joseph and Mary are, while asleep,
   addressed by an angel.]*

ANGELLUS.   Mare and Josoff, to you I sey,
   Swete word from the Fathur I bryng you full ryght :
Owt of Bedlem in-to Eygype forth goo ye the wey
   And with you take the King, full of myght,
         For drede of Eroddis rede !
JOSOFF.   A-ryse up, Mare, hastely and-sone ;
   Owre Lordis wyll nedys mvst be done,
         Lyke ase the angell vs bad.   825

MARE.   Mekely, Josoff, my none spowse,
   Towarde that cuntrey let vs reypeyre ;
Att Eygyp [8] to sum cun [8] off howse,
   God grant hus grace saff to cum there !   829

   Here the wemen cum in wythe there chyldur, syngyng them ; [4] *and Mare
   and Josoff goth awey cleyne.*

I. WOMON.   I lolle my chylde wondursly swete,
And in my narmus I do hyt kepe,
   Be-cawse thatt yt schuld not crye.
II. WOMAN.   Thatt babe thatt ys borne in Bedlem, so meke,
   He saue my chyld and me from velany !   834

III. WOMAN.   Be styll, be styll, my lyttull chylde !
   That Lorde of lordis saue bothe the and me !

---

[1] S. sworde.   [8-8] S. sum tocun ; *emend. by* **Kittredge.**
[2] *Two lines in* S.   [4] *For the song, see p.* 151.

For Erode hath sworne w*ith* wordis wyld
    Thatt all yong chyldur sclayne *th*e[y] schalbe.   838

I. MYLES.   Sey, ye wyddurde wyvis, whydd*er* ar ye a-wey?
    What beyre you in youre arm*us* nedis mvst we se.
Yff the[y] be man-chyldur,[1] dy the[y] mvst *thi*s dey,
    For at Eroddis wyll all thyng mvst be.   842

II. MYLES.   And I in handis wonys them [2] hent,
    Them forto sley noght woll I spare ;
We mvst full-fyll Erodis com*m*andement,
    Elis be we asse trayturs *and* cast all in care.   846

I. WOMAN.   S*i*r knyghtis, of youre curtessee,
Thys dey schame not youre chevaldre,
But on my chyld haue pytte
        For my sake in this styde ;
For a sympull sclaghtur yt were to sloo
Or to wyrke soche a chylde woo,
*Tha*t can nod*er* speyke nor goo,
        Nor neu*er* harme did.   854

II. WOMAN.   He thatt sleyis my chyld in syght,
Yff thatt my strokis on hym ma lyght,
Be he skwyar or knyght,
        I hold hym but lost.
Se, thow fawls losyngere,
A stroke schalt thow beyre me her*e*
        And spare for no cost.   861

III. WOMAN.   Sytt he neyu*er* soo hy in saddull,
But I schall make his braynis addull,
A nd here w*ith* my pott-ladull
        W*it*h hym woll I fyght.
I schall ley on hym a[s] thogh [3] I wode were,
W*it*h thys same womanly geyre ;
There schall noo man steyre,
        Wheddur thatt he be kyng or knyght.   869

---

[1] *Curl over* n.   [2] *Curl over* m.   [3] S. athog.

I. MYLES.   Who hard eyu*er* soche a cry
　　Of wemen thatt there chyldur haue lost,
And grettly reybukyng chewaldry
　　Throgh-owt this reme in eyu*ere* [1] cost,
　　Wyche many a mans lyff ys lyke to cost?
For thys grett wreyche *tha*t here ys done
I feyre moche wengance *the*r-off woll cu*m*.   876

II. MYLES.   E ! brothur, soche talis may we not tell ;
　　Where-fore to the kyng lett vs goo,
For he ys lyke to beyre the p*er*ell,
　　Wyche wasse the cawser that we did soo.
　　Yett must the[y] all be broght hym to
W*ith* waynis and waggyns fully fryght ;
I tro there wolbe a carefull syght.   883

　　　　　　[They go to Herod.]

I. MYLES.   Loo ! Eyrode, kyng, here mast thow see
　　How many M' thatt we haue slayne.
II. MYLES.   And nedis thy wyll full-fyllid must be ;
　　There ma no mon sey there-ageyne.   887

　　　　　　[Enter Nuntius.]

NU*N*CIOS.   Eyrode, kyng, I schall the tell,
　　All thy dedis ys cu*m* to noght ;
This chyld ys gone in-to Eygipte to dwell.
　　Loo ! s*i*r, in thy none land what wondurs byn wroght !   891

EROD.   Into Eygipte? alas, for woo !
　　Lengur in lande here I canot abyde ;
Saddull my palfrey, for in hast wyll I goo,
　　Aftur yondur trayturs now wyll I ryde,
　　　　Them for to sloo.
　　Now all men hy fast
　　In-to Eygipte in hast !
　　All thatt cuntrey woll I tast,
　　　　Tyll I ma cu*m* them to.   900

　　　　　　[1] S. eyu*er*.

Fynes lude de taylars and scharmen.

Tys[1] matter / nevly correcte be Robart Croo / the xiiijth dey of marche / fenysschid in the yere of owre lorde god / MCCCCC & xxxiiij^{te} / then beyng mayre mastur Palmar / also mastris of the seyd fellyschipp Hev Corbett / Randull Pynkard and / John Baggeley.

Theise Songes / belonge to / the Taylors *and* Shearemens Pagant. / The first and the laste the Shepheards singe / and the second or middlemost the Women singe.

THOMAS MAWDYCKE / die decimo tertio Maij anno d*o*m*i*ni millessimo quingentesimo nonagesimo primo. / Praetor fuit ciuitatis Couentriæ D. Mathaeus[2] Richardson, tunc Consules / Johanes Whitehead *et* Thomas Crauener.

SONG I.

As I out rode this enderes night,
Of thre ioli sheppardes I saw a sight,
And all a-bowte there fold a star shone bright ;
    They sange terli terlow ;
    So mereli the sheppards ther pipes can **blow.**   5

SONG II.

Lully, lulla, tho*w* *littell tine child,*
By by, lully, lullay, tho*w* *littell tyne child,*
    By by, lully, lullay !

---

[1] S. T[h]ys.   [2] S. Mathaens.

O sisters too,
How may we do [1]
   For to preserve *th*is day
This pore yongling
For whom we do singe [1]
   By by, lully, lullay?   6

Herod, the king,
In his raging,[1]
   Chargid he hath this day
His men of might
In his owne sight [1]
   All yonge children to slay,—   12

That wo is me,
Pore child, for thee,[1]
   And ever morne and may [2]
For thi parting
Nether say nor singe,[1]
   By by, lully, lullay.   18

Song III.

Doune from heave*n*, from heave*n* so hie,
Of angeles *th*er came a great companie,[3]
W*ith* mirthe and ioy and great solemnitye,
   The[y] sange terly terlow,
So mereli the sheppards *th*er pipes ca*n* blow.   5

[1] *This and the preceding as one line in* S.
[2] S. say; *corr. by* Kittredge.
[3] *Curl over* m.

YORK CORPUS CHRISTI PLAYS.

Reprinted from "York Plays . . . ed. [Miss] Lucy Toulmin Smith, Clarendon Press, 1885." In the footnotes, Y. indicates this edition, which, unless the contrary is stated, represents the MS.; Ha. indicates J. Hall's review, *Englische Studien*, IX, 484 ff.; He. indicates "Studien zu den York Plays, von O. Herttrich. Breslau, 1886"; Ho. indicates F. Holthausen's emendations, *Archiv für das Studium der neueren Sprachen*, LXXXV, 411 ff., LXXXVI, 280 ff., and " Philologische Studien; Festgabe für Eduard Sievers, Halle, 1896," 30 ff.; K. indicates E. Kölbing's emendations, *Englische Studien*, XX, 179 ff.; T. indicates the corresponding play in the Towneley cycle, but its readings are only occasionally recorded.

[THE RESURRECTION.]

[Enter Pilatus, Cayphas, and Anna with attendants.]

PIL.   Lordingis, listenys nowe vnto me,
I comaunde ʒou, in ilke degre ;
Als domesman chiffe in *th*is contre,
　　　For counsaill kende,
Atte my bidding ʒou awe to be
　　　And baynly bende.   6

And, sir Cayphas, chiffe of clergye,
Of youre counsaill late here in hye,
By oure [1] assente sen we dyd dye
　　　Ihesus *th*is day,
*Th*at we [2] mayntayne — and stand *th*erby —
　　　*Th*at werke all-way.   12

CAYPH.   ʒis, sir, *th*at dede schall we mayntayne ;
By lawe it was done all be-dene,

---

[1] He. K. ʒoure.   [2] K. Yff ʒe.

ȝe wotte youre-selue, with-outen wene,
    Als wele as we.
His sawes are nowe vppon hym sene,
    And ay schall be.   18

ANNA. *Th*e pepull, sir,[1] in *th*is same steede
Be-fore ȝou saide with a hole hede
*Th*at he was worthy to be dede,
    And *th*erto sware.
Sen all was rewlid by right[w]is[2] rede,
    Nevyn it nomore.   24

PIL. To neuyn me thinketh it nedfull thyng;
Sen he was hadde to beriyng,
Herde we nowthir of olde ne ȝing
    Tidynges[3] be-twene.
CAYPH. Centurio, sir, will tidingis bringe[4]
    Of all be-dene.   30

We lefte hym *th*ere for man moste wise,
If any rebelles[5] wolde ought rise
Oure rightwise dome for to dispise
    Or it offende,
To sese *th*ame till *th*e nexte assise
    And *th*an make ende.   36

[Enter Centurio.]

CENT. [*To himself.*] A! blissid Lorde Adonay,
What may *th*es meruayles signifie
*Th*at her was schewed so oppinly
    Vn-to oure sight
*Th*is day whanne *that* *th*e man gune dye
    *Th*at Ihesus highte?   42

---

[1] Y. sirs.
[2] *Corr. by* Ha.
[3] Y. Thithynges; Ho. Tithynges.
[4] Y. bringe thidingis; Ho. bringe tiding.
[5] T. *has* rybaldes.

Itt is a misty thyng to mene ;
So selcouth a sight was neuere sene,
*Th*at [1] oure princes and prestis be-dene
　　Of *th*is affray
I woll go weten, with-outen wene,
　　What *th*ei can saye.　　　　　　　　　48

[He salutes Pilate and the priests.]

God saue ȝou, sirs, on ilke a side !
Worschippe and welthe in worldis wide
With mekill mirthe myght ȝe abide
　　Both [2] day and nyght !
PIL.　Centurio, welcome this tide,
　　Oure comely knyght !　　　　　　　54

ȝe haue bene miste vs here [3] among.
CENT.　God giffe you grace grathely to gang !
PIL.　Centurio, [o]ure frende full lang,
　　What is your will ?
CENT.　I drede me *th*at ȝe haue done wrang
　　And wondir ill.　　　　　　　　60

CAYPH.　Wondir ill ? I pray *th*e, why ?
Declare it to *th*is company.
CENT.　So schall I, sirs, telle ȝou trewly,
　　With-owten trayne :
*Th*e rightwise mane *th*anne mene I by
　　*Th*at ȝe haue slayne.　　　　　　66

PIL.　Centurio, sesse of such sawe.
*Th*ou arte a lered man in *th*e lawe,
And if we schulde any witnes drawe
　　Vs to excuse,
To mayntayne vs euermore *th*e [4] awe
　　And noȝt reffuse.　　　　　　　72

---

[1] K. *inserts* to.
[2] Y. Boght; *corr. by* K.　*The whole line is in a later hand than the rest of the* MS.
[3] K. *reads* here vs.　　　　　　[4] Ho. *reads* ye.

Cent.   To mayntayne trouthe is wele wor*th*i ;
I saide ȝou, whenne I sawe hym dy,
*Th*at he was Goddis sone Almyghty
              *Th*at hanged[1] *th*ore ;
Ȝitt saie I soo, and stande *th*erby
              For-euermore.   78

Cayph.   Ȝa, sir, such reasouns may ȝe rewe.
Ȝe schulde noght neueyn such note enewe[2]
But ȝe couthe any tokenyngis trewe
              Vnto vs tell.
Cent.   Such woundirfull cas neuere ȝit ȝe knewe
              As now befell.   84

Anna.   We pray *th*e, tell vs of what thyng.
Cent.   All elementis, both olde and ȝing,
In ther maneres *th*ai made mornyng
              In ilke a stede ;
And knewe, be countenaunce, *th*at *th*er kyng
              Was done to dede.   90

*Th*e sonne for woo he waxed all wanne ;
*Th*e mone and sterres of schynyng blanne ;
*Th*e erthe tremeled and also manne[3]
              Be-gan to speke ;
*Th*e stones *th*at neuer was stered or *th*anne
              Gune[4] a-sondir breke ;   96

And dede-men rose, both grete and small.
Pil.   Centurio, be-ware with-all !
Ȝe wote oure clerkis *th*e clipsis *th*ei call
              Such sodayne sight.
Both sonne and mone *th*at sesonne[5] schall
              Lak of *th*er light.   102

---

[1] Y. hangeth; *corr. by* K.   [4] *Qy. omit* Gune.
[2] T. *has* notes newe.   [5] Ho. sesoune.
[3] T. And erthe it tremlyd as a man ; *qy.* And erthe it tremeled as the man.

CAYPH.   ȝa, and if dede men rose bodily,
*Th*at myght be done thurgh so[r]cery ;[1]
*Th*erfore we sette no thyng *th*erby,
          To be abaiste.
CENT.   All *th*at I tell, for trewthe schall I
          Euermore traste.   108

For[2] this ilke werk *th*at ȝe did wirke
Nought allone *th*e sonne was mirke,
But howe youre vaile raffe in youre kirke
          That witte I wolde.
PIL.   Swilke tales full sone will make vs irke
          And *th*ei be talde.   114

ANNA.   Centurio, such speche withdrawe ;
Of all *th*es wordes we haue none awe.
CENT.   Nowe, sen ȝe sette noght be my sawe,
          Sirs, haue gode day !
God[3] graunte you grace *th*at ȝe may knawe
          *Th*e soth alway.   120

ANNA.   With-drawe *th*e faste, sen *th*ou *th*e dredis,
For we schall wele mayntayne oure dedis.   [*Exit Centurio.*]
PIL.   Such wondir reasouns as he redis
          Was neuere beforne.
CAIPH.   To neven *th*is noote no more vs nedis,
          Now*th*ere even ne morne.   126

*Th*erfore loke nomanne make ille[4] chere.
All *th*is doyng may do no dere ;
But to be-ware ȝitt of more were
          *Th*at folke may fele,
We pray you, sirs, of *th*es sawes sere
          Avise ȝou wele.   132

---

1 *Corr. by* K.; *but* socery *occurs often.*
2 Y. I**ᴎ** ; T. Not for.
3 *Supplied by* K.
4 Y. ilke; *corr. by* Ho.

And to *th*is tale takes hede in hye,
For Iesu saide even opynly
A thyng *th*at greues all *th*is Jury,
    And riȝte so may, —
*Th*at he schulde rise vppe bodily
    With-in [1] *th*e thirde day.   138

And be it so, als motte I spede,
His lattar deede is more to drede
*Th*an is the firste, if we take hede
    Or tente *th*erto.
To neuyn *th*is noote me thynke maste nede
    And beste to do.   144

ANNA. Ȝa, sir, all if [2] *th*at he saide soo,
He has no myght to rise and goo.
But if his menne stele hym vs froo
    And bere away,
*Th*at were tille us and o*th*er moo
    A foule [a]ffraye ; [3]   150

For *th*anne wolde *th*ei saie, euere-ilkone,
*Th*at he roose by hym-selffe allone ;
*Th*erfore latte hym be kepte anone
    With knyghtes hende,
Vnto thre daies be comen and gone
    And broght till ende.   156

PIL. In certayne, sirs, right wele ȝe saie ;
For *th*is ilke poynte nowe [to] [4] purvaye,
I schall ordayne, if that [5] I may,
    He schall not ryse,
Nor none schalle wynne hym *th*ens away
    On no-kyns wise.   162

---

[1] Kittredge *suggests* Qn.   [3] K. T. enffraye.   [4] Y.
[2] Y. if all.   [5] K.; Y. if; Ho. it if.

[*He speaks to the soldiers.*]

Sir knyghtis, *th*at are in dedis dowty,
Chosen for chiffe of cheualrye,
As we ay in youre force affie
    Bo*th*e day and nyght,
[1] Wendis and kepis Jesu body
    With all youre myghte ;   **168**

And for thyng *th*at euere be maye
Kepis hym wele to *th*e thirde day,
And latis noman take [2] hym away
    Oute of *th*at stede ;
For, and *th*ei do, suthly I saie,
    3e schall be dede.   **174**

I. MILES.   Lordingis, we saie 3ou for certayne,
We schall kepe hym with myght [3] and mayne;
*Th*er schall no traitoures with no trayne
    Stele hym vs froo.
Sir knyghtis, takis gere *th*at moste may gayne,
    And lates vs goo.   **180**

II. MIL.   3is, certis, we are all redy bowne ;
We schall hym kepe till oure rennowne.

[*The soldiers go to the Sepulchre.*]

On ilke a side latte vs sitte doune
    Now all in-fere,
And fownde [4] we schall to [5] crake his croune,
    Whoso comes here.   **186**

[*The soldiers sit down and fall asleep.*]

Tunc "*Iesu resurgente.*" [6]

---

[1] K. *prefixes* Ye.   [3] Y. myghtis; *corr. by* K.
[2] Y. takis; *corr. by* Ho.   [4] K.; Y. sone.   [5] *Om.* Y.
[6] Miss Smith *says:* " *The marginal note in later hand here,* ' tunc angelus cantat Resurgens.' *See lines* 383–386." *This is supported by* T., *which has:* " Tunc cantabunt angeli ' Jesus resurgens.' "

[Enter the three Marys going to the Tomb.]

I. MAR.   Allas ! to dede I wolde be dight,
So woo in worlde [1] was neuere wight ;
Mi sorowe is all for *th*at sight
    *Th*at I gune see,
Howe Criste, my maistir, moste of myght,
    Is dede fro me.   192

Allas, *th*at I schulde se his pyne,
Or yit *th*at I his [2] liffe schulde tyne !
Of ilke a myscheue he is [3] medicyne
    And bote of all,
Helpe and halde to ilke a hyne
    On hym wolde call. [4]   198

II. MAR.   Allas ! who schall my balis bete,
Whanne I thynke on his woundes wete ?
Jesu, *th*at was of loue so swete
    And neuere did ill,
Es dede and grauen vnder *th*e grete
    With-outen skill.   204

III. MAR.   With-owten skill *th*e Jewes ilkone
*Th*at louely lorde has newly slone, [5]
And trespasse did he neuere none
    In no-kyn steede.
To whome nowe schall I make my mone,
    Sen he is dede ?   210

I. MAR.   Sen he is dede, my sisteres dere,
Wende we will on mylde manere,
With oure a-noynementis faire *and* clere
    *Th*at we haue broght,
To noynte his wondis, on sides sere
    *Th*at Jewes hym wroght.   216

---

[1] Y. werke ; T. warld ; *pointed out by* He.
[2] Ho. my.   [3] Ho. T. was.
[4] MS. *th*at on hym on wolde call ; *corr. by* Y.
[5] K. T. ; Y. slayne.

II. MAR.[1] Goo we same, my sisteres free.
Full sare [2] vs longis his corse to see,
But I wotte noght howe beste may be ;
     Helpe haue we none,
And who schall nowe here of vs thre
     Remove *th*e stone ?   **222**

III. MAR. *Th*at do we noght but we wer moo,
For it is huge and heuy also.
I. MAR. Sisteris ! a ʒonge child, as we goo
     Makand mornyng,
I see it sitte wher we wende to,
     In white clothyng.   **228**

II. MAR. Sisters, sertis, it is noght to hide,
*Th*e heuy stone is putte beside !
III. MAR. Sertis, for thyng *th*at may be-tyde
     Nere will we wende,
To layte *th*at luffely and with hym bide
     *Th*at was oure ffrende.   **234**

[They approach nearer the Sepulchre.]

ANGEL. ʒe mournand women in youre *th*ought,
Here in *th*is place whome haue ʒe sought ?
I. MAR. Jesu, *th*at unto [3] dede was [4] brought,
     Oure Lord so free.
ANG. Women, certayne here is he noght ;
     Come nere and see.   **240**

He is noght here, *th*e soth to saie ;
*Th*e place is voide *th*at he in laye.
*Th*e sudary here se ʒe may,
     Was on hym laide.
He is resen and wente his [5] way,
     As he ʒou saide.   **246**

---

[1] Y.; MS. *Prima* Maria ; *see Notes.*   [4] T.; Y. is.
[2] Y. faire ; T. sore ; *pointed out by* He.   [5] MS. *repeats* his.
[3] K. T.: Y. to.

Euen .as he saide, so done has hee ;
He is resen thurgh grete poostee.
He schall be foune in Galile,
    In flesshe and fell.
To his discipilis nowe wende ȝe,
    And *th*us *th*ame tell.   252

I. MAR.   Mi sisteres dere, sen it is soo,
*Th*at he is resen dede *th*us froo,
As *th*e aungell tolde me and yow too, —
    Oure lorde so free, —
Hens [1] will I neuer goo
    Or I hym see.   258

II. MAR.   Marie, vs thare no lenger lende ; [2]
To Galile nowe late vs wende.
I. MAR.   Nought tille I see *th*at faithfull frende,
    Mi lorde *and* leche.
*Th*erfore all *th*is, my sisteres hende,
    *Th*at ȝe forth preche.[3]   264

III. MAR.   As we haue herde, so schall we saie.
Marie oure sistir, haue goode daye !
I. MAR.   Nowe verray God, as he wele maye,
    Man most of myght,[4]   267 *a*
He wisse you, sisteres, wele in youre waye
    And rewle ȝou right !   269

[Exeunt second and third Marys.]

Allas ! what schall nowe wor*th*e on me ?
My kaytiffe herte will breke in three
Whenne I thynke on *th*at body free,
    How it was spilte,
Both feete and handes nayled tille a tre,
    Withouten gilte !   275

[1] He. *wishes to insert* furthe.
[2] MS. layne ; *corr. by* Y.
[3] Ho. T. Loke *th*at ȝe preche.
[4] *Line missing in* MS. ; *supplied by* Y. *from* T.

With-outen gilte *th*e trewe was tane,
For trespas did he neuere nane. [1]
*Th*e woundes he suffred, — many ane, — [2]
  Was for my misse ;
It was my dede [3] he was for slayne [4]
  And no-thyng his.   281

How might I, but I loued *th*at swete,
*Th*at for my loue tholed woundes wete
And sithen be grauen vndir *th*e grete,
  Such kyndnes kithe ?
*Th*er is no-thing to *th*at we mete
  May make me blithe.   287

       [*The soldiers awaken.*]

I. Mil. What ! oute ! allas ! what schall I saie ?
Where is *th*e corse *th*at here in laye ?
II. Mil. What ayles *th*e, man ? Is he awaye
     *Th*at we schulde tente ?
I. Mil. Rise vppe and see.
II. Mil.   Harrowe ! for ay
    I telle vs schente.   293

III. Mil.[5] What deuill is *th*is ? what aylis ȝou twa [6]
Such noyse and crye *th*us for to ma ? [7]
I. Mil. For he is gone. [8]
III. Mil.   [9] Allas ! wha ?
   II. Mil. He *th*at here laye.[9]
IV. Mil. Whe ! harrowe ! deuill ! [10] how swa   298
    Gat he away ? [10]   298 *a*

---

[1] Y. none.
[2] Y. one.
[3] He. T. gylt.
[4] K ; Y. for-slayne.
[9-9] T. ; Y. Allas whare is he *th*at here laye ?
[10-10] T. ; Y. whare is he away ?

[5] *On this stanza, see Notes.*
[6] Y. twoo.
[7] Y. to make too ; T. to may.
[8] T. ; Y. Why is he gone ?

III. MIL.[1]   What ! is he *th*us-gatis fro vs wente,
*Th*at fals traitour *th*at here was lente,
And we trewly here for to tente
   Had vndir-tane ?
Sekirlie,[2] I telle vs schente
   Holy, ilkane.   304

I. MIL.[3]   Allas ! what schall we do *th*is day
*Th*at *th*us *th*is warlowe is wente his waye?
And sauely, sirs, I dare wele saie,
   He rose allone.
II. MIL.   Witte sir Pilate of *th*is affraye,
   We mon be slone.   310

III. MIL.   Why,[4] canne none of vs no bettir rede ?
IV. MIL.   *Th*er is not ellis but we be dede.
II. MIL.   Whanne *th*at he stered oute of *th*is steede,
   None couthe it kenne.
I. MIL.   Allas ! harde happe was on my hede
   Amonge all menne.   316

Fro sir Pilate witte of *th*is dede,
*Th*at we were slepande whanne he ȝede,
He will[5] forfette, with-outen drede,
   All that we haue.
II. MIL.   Vs muste[6] make lies, for *th*at is nede,
   Oure-selue to saue.   322

III. MIL.   ȝa, that rede I[7] wele, also[8] motte I goo.
IV. MIL.   And I assente *th*erto alsoo.
II. MIL.   An hundereth, schall I saie, and moo,
   Armed[9] ilkone,
Come and toke his corse vs froo
   And[10] vs nere slone.[11]   328

---

[1] MS.; *changed by* Y. *to* II. MIL., *but see Notes.*
[2] K. *inserts* sirs.
[3] T.; Y. III. MIL.
[4] K. *omits* Why.
[5] T. We mon ; *preferred by* He.
[6] Ho. bus.
[7] Y. I rede I ; T. He. red I.
[8] T. so ; Ho. als.
[9] T. K. Welle armed.
[10] He. Had.
[11] T.; Y. slayne.

I. MIL. Nay, certis, I halde *th*ere none so goode
As saie *th*e soth even as it stoode,
Howe *th*at he rose with mayne and mode
    And wente his way.
To sir Pilate, if he be wode,
    *Th*is dar I saie.   334

II. MIL. Why, dare *th*ou to sir Pilate goo
With thes tydingis and saie hym soo?
I. MIL. So rede I, for,[1] if he vs sloo,
    We dye but onys.
III. MIL. Nowe, he *th*at wrought vs all *th*is woo,
    Woo worthe his bonys !   340

IV. MIL. Go we *th*anne, sir knyghtis hende,
Sen *th*at [2] we schall to sir Pilate wende.
I trowe *th*at we shall parte no frende [8]
    Or *th*at we passe.
I.[4] MIL. And I schall hym [5] saie ilke word tille ende
    Even as it was.   346

              [They go to Pilate.]

Sir Pilate, prince withouten pere,
Sir Cayphas and Anna, in-fere,
And all ȝe lordyngis *th*at are here,
    To neven by name,
God saue ȝou all, on sidis sere,
    Fro synne and schame !   352

PIL. Ȝe are welcome, oure knyghtis kene !
Of mekill mirthe nowe may ȝe mene ;
Therfore some tales telle vs be-twene,
    Howe ȝe haue wroght.
I. MIL. Oure wakyng, lorde, with-outen wene,
    Is worthed [6] to noȝt.   358

1 *Inserted by* K. ; Ho. *inserts* do *after* he.
2 *Om.* T.   5 *Om.* T. K.
8 Y. frendes ; *corr. by* K. *from* T.   6 He. T. worthe.
4 *Speaker added by late hand.*

CAYPH.   To noght? allas ! Sesse of such sawe !
II. MIL.   *The* prophete Jesu, *th*at ȝe wele knawe,
Is resen and gone, for all oure awe,
    With mayne and myght.
PIL.   *Th*erfore *the* deuill hym-selffe *th*e drawe,
    Fals recrayed knyght !   364

Combered cowardis I you call!
Haue ȝe latten hym goo fro you all?
III. MIL.   Sir, *th*er was none *th*at did but small
    When *th*at he ȝede.
IV. MIL.   We wer so ferde, downe ganne we falle
    And dared for drede.   370

ANNA.   Hadde ȝe no streng[t]he hym to gayne-stande?
Traitoures ! ȝe myght haue boune in bande
Bothe hym and *th*ame *th*at ȝe *th*er fande,
    And sessid *th*ame sone.
I. MIL.   *Th*at dede all erthely men leuand
    Myght noȝt haue done.   376

II. MIL.   We wer so radde euer-ilkone,
Whanne *th*at he putte beside *th*e stone,
We wer so stonyd we durst stirre none,
    And so abasshed.
PIL.   What! rose he by hym-selfe allone?
    I. MIL.   ȝa, sir, *th*at [1] be ȝe traste.   382

IV. MIL.   We herde never sen we were borne,
Nor all oure faderes vs be-forne,
Suche melodie, mydday ne morne,
    As was made *th*ere.
CAYPH.   Allas ! *th*anne is oure lawes lorne
    For-euere-mare.   388

II. MIL.   What tyme he rose good tente I toke ;
*Th*e erthe *th*at tyme tremylled and quoke.

        [1] K. *omits th*at.

All kyndely force *th*an me for-soke,
  Tille he was gone.
III. MIL. I was a-ferde, I durste not loke,
  Ne myght had none ;   394

I myght not stande, so was I starke.
PIL. Sir Cayphas, ȝe are a connyng clerke, —
If we amisse haue tane oure merke, —
  I trowe same [1] faile ;
*Th*erfore what schalle wor*th*e nowe [2] of *th*is werke,
  Sais your counsaille.   400

CAYPH. To saie *th*e beste, forsothe, I schall,
That schall be prophete [3] to vs all :
ȝone knyghtis behoues *th*ere wordis agayne [4] call,
  Howe he is miste :
We nolde for thyng *th*at myght be-fall
  *Th*at no man wiste.   406

ANNA. Now, sir Pilate, sen *th*at it is soo,
*Th*at he is resynne [in-]dede us froo,
Comaundis ȝoure knyghtis to saie wher *th*ei goo
  *Th*at he was tane
With xx^ti m^l. men, and mo,
  And *th*ame [5] nere slayne.   412

And therto of our tresorie
Giffe to *th*ame a rewarde for-thy.
PIL. Nowe of *th*is purpose wele plesed am I,
  And forther *th*us : [6]

    [*To the soldiers.*]

Sir knyghtis, *th*at are in dedis dowty,
  Takes tente to vs,   418

---

[1] Ho. sanz.   [3] *Of course a bad spelling of* profit.
[2] *Om.* K.   [4] K. gayne.   [5] He. *th*ai.
[6] He. T. It shalbe thus, *which is probably right.*

And herkenes what *th*at ӡe shall saie
To ilke a man,[1] both nyӡt and daye :
That [2] ten m[l]. men in good araye
      Come ӡou vntill,
With forse of armys bare hym awaye
      Agaynst your will.   424

Thus schall ӡe saie in ilke a lande,
And *th*erto, on *th*at same comenaunde,
A thousande pounde haue in youre hande
      To your rewarde ;
And frenschippe, sirs, ӡe vndirstande,
      Schall not be spared.   430

CAIPH.[3]   Ilkone youre state we schall amende ;
And loke ӡe saie as we ӡou kende.
I. MIL.   In what contre so ӡe vs sende,
      Be nyght or daye,
Wherso we come, wherso we wende,
      So schal we saie.   436

PIL.   Ӡa, and where-so ӡe tarie in ilke contre,
Of oure doyng in no degre
Dois *th*at nomanne *th*e wiser be,
      Ne freyne be-forne ;
Ne of *th*e sight *th*at ӡe gonne se,
      Nevynnes it [4] now*th*ere even ne morne ;   442

For we schall mayntayne ӡou alwaye,
And to *th*e pepull schall we saie
It is gretely agaynste oure lay
      To trowe such thing.
So schall *th*ei deme, both nyght and day,
      All is lesyng.   448

[1] Y. aman.   [3] *Late hand.*
[2] *Om.* K.   [4] Ho. *omits* Nevynnes it.

Thus schall *the* sothe be bought and solde,
And treasoune schall for trewthe be tolde ;
*Th*erfore ay in youre hartis ȝe holde
    *Th*is counsaile clene.
And fares nowe wele, both younge and olde,
    Haly be-dene !   454

CHESTER WHITSUN PLAYS.

Printed from MS. Hengwrt 229, the property of W. R. M. Wynne, Esq. The date of the MS. is, according to Dr. Furnivall, 1475 or a little later; Mr. Warner, of the British Museum, assigns it to the end of the fifteenth century. It is, therefore, at least a century older than the oldest of the five complete MSS. of this collection. Another claim to interest is indicated in a note by Dr. Furnivall : "Mr. Wynne's MS. must have been owned by some player or manager, who doubled it up and carried it about in his pocket, used it with hot hands, and faded its ink. I suppose it's the only copy of the kind."

Mr. Wynne, whose kindness I cannot adequately acknowledge, wishes the print to represent the MS. as exactly as possible. I have accordingly given the text without change, except that I have not attempted to reproduce the forms of the letters — long *f*, for example — and that I have supplied the punctuation, there being none in the MS. Final *ll* is usually crossed, and final *m* and *n* flourished, but it seemed unnecessary to indicate these; only exceptional peculiarities are pointed out. The capitals, it will be observed, are those of the MS. Such corrections and additions as seemed absolutely necessary for the ordinary reader have been supplied in the footnotes, where will also be found a sufficient number of readings from the other MSS. to indicate in a general way the relations of this MS. to the two classes established by Deimling. A full collation seemed unnecessary, in view of the nature of this book and of the likelihood that we shall ere long have the second part of Deimling's edition. Suffice it to say here that this MS. is more closely related to H. than to B. W. h.

In the footnotes, Wr. indicates Wright's edition (2 vols., Shakespeare Society, 1843); W. indicates Dr. Furnivall's reading of MS. Addit. 10,305, — the basis of Wright's text; H. indicates MS. Harl. 2124; cf. p. 66, above. The occasional remarks on the different ways in which the same word has been read are intended to help the reader to a conception of the actual appearance of the MS.

[ANTICHRIST.]

[1]Incipit pagina XX . . .[2] De salla . . . [3]Ante*christi*.

Primo equitando incipiat Ant . . . :[4]

p. 1. De celso trono poli, pollens clarior sole —
Age vobis [5] monstrare — descendi vos iudicare.

[1] *All Latin is written in big letters.*
[2] *In* Wr. *it is* XXIV, *but the* MS. *he follows calls it* XXIII.
[3] *Qy.* fallacia.   [4] Antechristus.
[5] Wr. Age vos ; *both words almost illegible in* MS.

Reges et principes sunt subditi sub me viuentes ;
Sites [1] sapientes vos, sem*per* in me credentes,
Et faciam flentes gaudere at*que* dolentes ;
Sic omnes gentes gaudebunt in me sperantes.
Descendi presens Rex pius et perlustrator ;
Prinnceps eternus Vocor, cristus, vester Saluator.   8

All ledys in londe, now bese light,
That wyllyn be Rulyde throghe out the Right :
Youre [2] Savyor nowe in youre sight
      Here may ye sauely see ;
Messyas, criste [2] and most of might,
That in the [2] lawe wos youe behyght,
All monkynde Ioy to dyght
      Is comyn, for I am hee.   16

Off me was spokyn in prophecye
Off Moyses, davyd and ysaye ;
I am [3] he they call messye,
      fforbyer of Israell.
That [4] levyn on me stydfastly,
I shall them saue frome all Any,
And siche [5] joye Right as haue I
      with hem [6] I thinke to dele.   24

*De me enim d*icitu*r Ezechiel tricesimo sexto :*
"*Tollam vos de gentib*us*, et congregabo vos de
vniuersis terris, et redua*m [7] *vos in terra*m *v*estra*m.*"

But one hath lyggydd [8] hym here in londe, —
Ihe*s*u he hight, I vnderstond, —
To fforther falsed [9] he confounde [10]

1 Wr. Sitis ; *almost illegible in* MS.
2 *The beginning of these lines almost illegible.*
3 I am *is almost illegible.*   4 Wr. Those that.   5 Wr. *omits* siche.
6 *This is the only example of* hem (= them) *in this* MS.
7 *The correct reading,* reducam, *is written below this word in* MS.
8 *Corrected in* MS. *from* laykyd.   9 Wr. falsehoode.
10 *Read* can (= gan) fonde; Wr. *has* can founde.

And ferde withe ffantasye.
His wykydneȝ he wolde not wonde [1]
Till he wos takyn and putt in bonde [1]
And Slayne throghe ver*tue* of my sonde.[1]
        This ys sothe sycurlye.   32

My peple of Iues he cothe twynne,
p. 2.   That theyr land come they neu*er* in ;
Then on theym nowe most I myn
        And Restoure theym agayn.
To bylde this temple wyll I not blyn,
And as god hon*ur*yd be therin ;
And endless wele I shall them wyn,
        All that to me bene bayne.   40

        *De me e*tia*m* [2] *d*icitu*r in psalmo:* "*Adorabo ad
templu*m *Sanctu*m *tuu*m *in timore tuo.*"

One thing me gladys, be ye bolde,
As Danyell, the prophett, ffore me tolde,
All women in worlde me loue shulde
        when I were comyn Rowland.[8]
This prophesye I shall well holde,[4]
which ys most lykyng to yonge & olde.
I thinke to ffaast mo*n*ye folde [5]
        And theyr ffayrnesse to ffounde.   48

Also he told them,[4] leue ye me,
That I of giftis shulde be free, —
whiche prophesye don shalbe
        When I my Realme [4] haue wonnen, — [6]
And that I [4] shulde [4] graunte [4] men poste,[7]
Ryvyd Riches, lond and ffee ; —

---

[1] *The* o *in these words looks like* e.   [2] *Perhaps* enim *as in* **Wr.**
[8] **Wr.** *has l.* 48 *as both* 44 *and* 48 ; **H.** *gives the correct reading:* When I
were come in land.   [5] **Wr.** I thinke faste manye to holde.
[4] *Almost illegible.*
[6] **H.** *has* nommen ; *the word is so uncertain in* MS. *that it was at first
read* memory.   [7] **Wr.** mercy ; **H.** *agrees with* MS.

That shall [1] be done,[1] that ye shall see,
    Whan I am hether comen.[2]   56

    Danielis [1] *tercio decimo* : " *dabit eis potestatem mult . .*[1] *et terram diuidet gratuita*m."

Whatt saye ye, kingis that here ben lente?
Ar not my wordys at youre Assente?
That I [1] am [1] criste omnypotente, —
    Leve ye not thus Ichon [1] ?
PRIMUS REX.   We leuen, lorde, w*ith*out lett,
That crist he ys not comyn yet.
Yff thowe be he, thowe shalbe sett
    In temple as god Alon.   64

SECUNDUS REX.   Iff thowe be crist, callyd messye,
That from oure bale shall vs bye,
Doe [1] byfore us some maistrye,
    A signe [1] that we may see.
p. 3.   TERCIUS REX.   Then will I leue that hitt ys so
yf thowe do wonders or thow goo ;
So that thow saue vs of oure woo,
    Then honoryd shall thowe be.   72

QUARTUS REX.   ffowle haue we levyd mony a yer*e*
And of oure wenyng bene in were ;
And thowe be crist now comyn here,
    Then may thowe stynt all striffe.
ANTE*CHRISTU*S.   That I am Crist, and Crist wilbe,
By v*er*rey signes sone shall ye see,
ffor dede [3] men thrughe my poste
    Shall Ryse from dethe to lyue.   80

Now wyll I turne all thrughe my myght
Trees downe, the Rote vp Right, —
That ys marvell to youre sighte, —

---

[1] *Almost illegible.*   [2] *The line is almost illegible.*
[3] *This was at first read as* alle; Wr. *has* dead.

And ffrute groing vpon :
So shall they growe and Multiplie [1]
Throghe my might and my maistrey, —
I putt you out of hereysye
    to here [2] me Apon.   88

and bodyes that ben dede and slayne,
Yff I may Rayse theym vp Agayne,
Thow honorys me with myght & mayn ;
    Then shall no mon yow gryue.
fforsothe then after will I dee
And Ryse Agayn thrughe my poostye.
Yff I may do thus mareulosly,
    I Redd yow on me leue.   96

Men buryed in graue, as ye may see,
What Maistrye ys nowe, hope ye,
To Rayse theym vp thrughe my postye
    And all thrughe my none Accorde?
Whyther I in my godhede be,
By euery signe ye shall se.
Ryse vp, ye dede men, & honures me
    And knoys me for youre lorde.   104

Tunc Resurgendo dicat primus Mortuus.

A! lord, to the I aske mercye ;
I wos dede, but nowe lyue I !
Nowe wot I well and wytterly
    That Crist ys hyther comyn.
p. 4. SECUNDUS MORTUUS. Hym honore we and all Men,
Devotly kneling on oure knen.
Wurshipte be thowe then, Amen !
    Crist, that oure name has nomen. [3]   112

---

[1] *A stroke through the second* l.
[2] *Corrected in margin to* leeve.
[3] Wr. Christe our name is comen.

ANTECRISTUS.   That I shall fulfill holly wrytt,
Ye shall wott and knowe well hyt ;
ffor I am wall of welle and wytt [1]
    And lord of euery londe ;
And as the prophet Sophanye
Spekis of me full wytturlye,
I shall Reherse here Redylye
    That Clerkys shall vnderstond :   120

Sophonie tercio : expectame [2] *in die Resurreccionis
mee in futurum, quia iudicium* [3] *ut congregem gentes
et colligam Regna.*

Nowe will I dye that ye shall see,
And Ryse agayne thrughe my poostye.
I wyll in graue that ye put me
    And wurship me Alon ;
ffor in this temple a tombe ys made,
There in my bodye shalbe leyde.
Then wyll I Ryse as I haue sayde, —
    Take tente to me ychon, —   128

And after my Resurreccion,
Then wyll I sytt with gret Renovne,
And my gost sende to yow downe [4]
    In forme of fyer full sone.
I dye ! I dye ! nowe am I dede !   133

PRIMUS REX.   Nowe sithe this worthy lorde ys dede
And his [4] grace ys withe us lede,
To [4] take hys body it ys my Rede [5]
    And burye it in a graue.
SECUNDUS REX.   fforsothe and so to us he saide,
In a toumbe he wolde be laide.

---

[1] Wr. wall [of] wayle and witte ; *read* welle of wele and wytt.
[2] *Read* expecta me.   [4] *Almost illegible.*
[3] Wr. *also omits* meum.   [5] *This was at first read as* bedde.

Nowe goo we forthe all at a brayde !
ffrome dyssese he may us saue.   141

Tunc transeunt ad Antechristum.

TERCIUS REX.   Take we the bodye of this swete
And ley it low vndre the greet !
Nowe, lorde, comforde us, we the biseke,
    And send vs of thy grace.

p. 5. QUARTUS REX.   And if he Rise sone[1] thrughe his
                myght
ffrome dethe to lyve, as he hyght,
Hym wyll I honour day and nyght
    As god in euery place.   149

Tunc recedent de tumulo usque ad terram, et dicat

PRIMUS REX.   Nowe wot I well that he ys dede,
ffor nowe in greve we haue hym layde.
Yff he[2] Ryse as he hasse sayd,
    He ys[2] of fulgret[3] myghte.
SECUNDUS REX.   I can not leffe hym apon
But yf he Ryse hym selffe alon,
As he hass sayde to monyon,
    And shoo hym here in syght.   157

TERCIUS REX.   Tyll that oure sauyore be Ryson
                agayne,
In fayth, my hart may not be fayne
.   .   .   .[4]

    But I hym see withe yee.
QUARTUS REX.   I most morne withe All my mayne
Till Crist be Rison vp Agayn.
Off that myracle make us fayne,
    Ryse vp,[2] lorde, that we may see.   164

---

[1] *A curve over* n.   [2] *Almost illegible.*   [3] *Read* ful gret.
[4] *The MS.* (W.) *printed by* Wr. *also omits this line ;* Wr. *supplied it from*
H., *as follows :* My body eke will not be bayne.

Tunc Antechristus leuat caput suum surgens a mortuis.

ANTECHRISTUS. I Rise nowe ! Reuerence dose to me !
God glorify, fyrst, last, in [1] degre.
Iff I be crist, nowe levys ye,[2]
 And warchis after the wyse ! [3]
PRIMUS REX. A ! lord, welcome most thowe be !
That thow art god, nowe leue we.
Therefore go sit vp in thy see,
 And kepe oure sacryfyse.   172

Tunc transient ad Antechristum.

SECUNDUS REX. Forsoth in seyte thowe shaltbe sett,
And honoryd bothe with lambe & gete,[4]
As moseyes lawe that lastyth yet,
 As he as [5] sayde beffore.[6]
TERCIUS REX. O gracius lorde, go sytt downe then,
And we shall, kneling on oure knen,
wurship the as thyn owne men
 And worche after thy lore.   180

Tunc assendit Antechristus ad . . . .[7]

p. 6. ET TERCIUS [8] REX. Hethur we be comyn with
   good entent
To make oure sacryfice, lord excellent,
Withe this lambe that I haue here hente,
 Knelyng the before.
Thowe graunte vs grace to do & saye

---

[1] Wr. glorified, created of ; H. glorified, greatest of. *The latter is probably correct and the original of the reading of our* MS. Dr. Furnivall, *however, thinks* MS. *really has* glorify kreatyd in.

[2] Wr. H. ye me.   [3] Wr. my will.

[4] Wr. honoured with lande (*for* laude) greate.

[5] Wr. hath ; *read* has.

[6] *This line in another hand, which* Dr. Furnivall *thinks later.*

[7] Wr. cathedram. *In* MS. *this stage direction follows* Et Tercius Rex, *on the same line.*

[8] H. *has* Primus ; Wr. *has no speaker's name.*

That it be plesing to the aye,
To thy blysse that come we may
     And never fro it be loore.   188

ANTE*CHRISTU*S.   I lord, I god, I hyght Iustyce,
I crist, that made the dede to Rise,
Here I Receyue youre sacryfyce,
     And blesse you ffleshe and fell

*Tunc transiunt de Ante*christ*o.*

Ye kyngis, also to you I tell,
I wyll nowe send my holly goost
To knowe me lord, of myghtist[1] most,
     off heven, yerthe and hell.   196

*Tunc emittit spiritu*m *dicens :*

    "*Dabo vobis cor novu*m *et spritu*m *novu*m *In medio Vestri.*"

QUARTUS REX.   A, god ! a, lorde, mycle of myght !
This holye gost is in me pight ;
Me thinks my hart ys verry light
     Sithe it come into me.
PRIM*US* REX.   Lord, we the honor day and nyght,
ffor thowe shewys vs in sight,
Right as moyses vs behyght.
     Honoryd most thowe bee !   204

ANTE*CHRISTU*S.   Yet worthie werkis to youre will
Off prophcie I will[2] fullfill :
As Danyell prophycied you till
     That londys[3] I shulde devyse,
That phrophecye it shalbe done,
That ye shall se Right sone.
Wurshipis me all that ye mone,
     And do after the wise.   212

---

[1] *Read* myghtis, *as in* Wr.   [2] Wr. shall.   [3] Wr. baundes.

Ye kyngis, I shall avaunte [1] you All,
And, for youre Regnis be but Small,
Citie3, castells shall you befall,
    with Towne3 and Towre3 gay,

p. 7.   And make you lordis of lordishipis ffere,[2] —
And well it ffalles for my power ; —
And loke ye do as I you lerr,[3]
    And harkens what I say.[4]   220

I am verey god of myght ;
All thinge I made thrugh my myght,
Son and mone, day and nyght ;
    To blisse I may you bring.
Therfor, kyngis noble [5] and gay,
Yoken [6] youre peple [5] that [7] I saye,
That I am crist, god verey,
    And tell theym such tything.[8]   228

My peple [5] of Iwes were put me frome ;
Therfor gret Ruthe I haue theym on.
Whythur they wyll leue me vpon
    I wyll fulsone Assaye ;
ffor All that wyll leue me vpon
Wordely welthe shall theym fall on,
And to my blysse shall they come
    To dwell withe me for Aye.[10]   236

And the giftes that I behighte
Ye shall haue, as ys good Right,
Hens or I goo oute of youre sight ;
    Ichon shall knowe [11] his doole :
To the I gyffe lambardye ;
And to the, denmarke and hungrye ;

---

[1] Wr. advanse ; *read* avaunce ; MS. *clearly has* t *not* c.
[2] H. fayre.   [7] H. what.
[3] H. bad.   [8] 225-228 *are not in* Wr. (W.)
[4] 217-220 *are not in* Wr. (W.) [10] *This stanza is not in* Wr. (W.)
[5] *A stroke through* l.   [11] H. haue ; Wr. knowe.
[6] H. Token.

And take patmouse [1] & Italye,
And Rome hit shall be hyse.[2]   244

SECUNDUS REX.   Gra*u*nt marsye, lorde, youre gifte
        to day!
Honor the we wyll Alway,
ffor we were nevyr so Rych, in ffay,
        Ne non of all oure kynde.
[8] ANTE*CHRISTU*S.   Therefor be true and stydfast Aye
And levys trulye on my laye,
ffor I wyll harken on you to day
        Stydfast yf I you ffynd.   252

*Tu*nc *sedeat A*nte*christus; et veniant Enoke et Elysas, Quoru*m *dicat
enoke :*

Almyghtye god in maiestye,
That made the hevon and yerthe to be,
ffyre, water, ston and tree
        And mon Als, throghe thy myght,
The poyntys of thy prevytye
Any erthely mon to see
p. 8.   Is impossible, as thynk*is* me,
        To ony worldely wighte.   260

Gracius lorde, that arte so gud,
That who [4] so long in fleshe and blude
Hasse grauntyd lyue and hevonly ffode,
        Lett never oure thought*is* be fylyde;
But gyue vs, lorde, might & mayn,
Orr we of this shrewe be slayne,
To convert thy peple [5] Agayne,
        That he hasse thus begylyd.   268

---

[1] Wr. take thou Ponthous.

[2] H. Wr. thyne; *I cannot suggest the emendation required by the rhyme.*

[8] *In the left margin opposite* 249, 250, 251 *are three words, which* Dr. Furnivall *suggests may be the names of actors. From the analogy of the other
Chester Plays (cf. the Balaam pageant, p. 70, above, and that of the Three
Kings) I should rather infer that they are stage directions. These words
in transcript look like* hoore ande offod.

[4] *Qy.* us.   [5] *A stroke through* l.

Sythe the worldis begynnyng
I haue lyvyd in grett lyking,
Thrugh helpe of highe hevon kyng,
    In paradyce, with out Anye,
Tyll we hard tokening
Off this theeffys commyng,
That nowe in erthe ys Reynyng
    And goddis folke [1] distryes.[2]   276

To paradyce takyn I wos that tyde
This theffys comyng to Abyd,
And helye, my brother, here me bysyde,
    wos after sende to me.
wythe this Champion we most Chyde,
That nowe in worlde walkys wyde,
To disspreve his pompe and [3] pryde
    And payre all his poostye.   284

HELYAS.[4]   O lorde, that Maddist Althinge,
And long hasse lent vs lyving,
Lett nevure [5] the Devyle power [3] spryng
    This man hass hym with in.
God gyve you grace, bothe olde & yonge,
To knowe discayte in hys doynge,
That ye may come to that lykynge
    Off blisse that nevere shall blyn.   292

I warne you, all men, wytterly,
This hys Ennoke, I am helye,
Ben comyn thys herrours [6] to distrye
    That he to you nowe shewe3.
He callis hym selffe crist & messye ;
He lye3, forsothe, Appertelye :

---

[1] A stroke through l.
[2] Wr. And doth Godes folkes destroye; of course the final s is to be
stricken out ; whether doth is to be inserted may admit of doubt, considering
the numerous instances of 3. s. pr. Ind. without either s or th.
[3] Almost illegible.   [5] This was at first read as us dure.
[4] A curve over as.   [6] Wr. his errores.

He ys the Devull you to Anye ;
 And for non other hym knoys !   300

p. 9. TERTIUS REX. A ! men,[1] what speke ye of helye
And[1] ennoke ? they ben[2] in companye.
Off oure blude they ben wetterlye,
 And we be of theyre kynde.
QUARTUS REX. We Redon in bokys of oure lawe
That they to hevon were I drawe ;
And yet ben ther, ys the comyn sawe,
 Wrytyn as men may ffynde.   308

ENNOKE. We be the men, forsoth I wysse,
Be comyn to tell ye don Amysse
And bring youre sowlys to hevon blisse,
 Yff it were ony bote.
HELYAS. This devuls lym that comyn ys,
That saye3 hevon and yerthe ys hys,
Nowe been we Redye, leve ye this,
 Agaynst hym for to Mote.   316

PRIMUS REX. Yff that we Redye[3] wytt monn,
By preues of Disputacion,
That ye haue skyll and Reason,
 With you we will Abyde.
SECUNDUS REX. And if youre skyllys may do hym
  downe,
To dye withe you we wilbe bowne,
In hope of Sawle[4] saluacioun,
 What so euer betyd.   324

ENNOKE. To do hym downe we shall Assay,
Thrugh myght of Ihesu borne of A maye,
By Right and Reason, as ye shall say, —
 And that ye shall well here ;
And for that cause hyther were we sent

---

[1] *Almost illegible.*   [3] Wr. heare.
[2] Wr. bene bouth.   [4] Wr. *omits* sawle.

By Ihesu crist omnipotente,
And that ye shall not all be shente :
  He thought[1] you all full dere.   332

Bese glade, therefor, and makis gud chere,
And do, I Redd,[2] as I you lere ;
ffor we ben comyn in gud manere
  To saue you euerychon.
And drede you noght for that falsse fynde,
ffor ye shall se hym cast Behynde
Or we departe and from hym wynde,
  And shame shall hym light on.   340

*Et sic transibunt Ennoke et Helyas Ad Ante*christum, *quoru*m *dicat
Ennoke :*

p. 10. [3] Say, thowe verey devuls lyme,
  That sittis so grisly and [4] grym,
  ffrom hym thowe come & shall to hym,
    ffor mony A sowle thowe decevys.[5]
  Thowe hasse deceyuyd men mony a day,
  And made the peple [6] to thy pay,
  And wychyd theym into A wrang wey
    Wykkydly with thy wylys.   348

ANTECHRISTUS. A! fals fayteors, from me ye fflee !
Am I not most in maiestye ?
What men dar meyn theym thus to me
  Or make such distaunce ? [7]
HELIAS. ffye on the, fayture, fye on the,
The devuls owne nurre !
Thrughe hym thowe preches & hast postye
  A whyle thrughe sufferaunce.   356

ANTECHRISTUS. You ypocritis, that so cryn,
losells, lurdans, lowdelye you lyne !

---

[1] Wr. bought.   [2] Wr. And I doe read.
 [3] *In left margin a later hand has written some words which* in *Dr.*
Furnivall's *transcript look like:* hore ha sde son s m.   [4] Wr. and so.
 [5] *Read* begylys.   [6] *A stroke through* l.   [7] *A stroke over* un.

To spyll my lawe you Asspyne.[1]
 That speeche ys gud to spare !
You that my true fayth desyne [2]
And nedeles my folke devyen,[3]
ffrom hens hastely but ye hyne,
 To you comys sorowe & care.   364

ENNOKE. Thy sorowe and care cu*m* on thy hede,
ffor falsly thrughe thy wykkyd Redde
 The peple [4] ys put to pyne.[5]
I wolde the [6] body were from the [6] hede,
XX mylys from hit layde
 Tyll I hit broght Agayn.   370

ANTE*CHRISTU*S. Oute on the, wysarde,[7] w*ith* thy
  wylis !
ffor falsly my peple thowe begylus ;
 I shall the hastely honge !
p. 11. And that lurdayn *that* stondys the bye,
He puttys my folke to gret Anye
 Withe his false flate*r*and tong.   376

But I shall teche you curtesye,
youre sauyor to knowe anon in hye,
ffals Theffe3 w*ith* youre herysye,
 And if ye darr Abyde !   380

HELYAS. Yes, forsothe, for All thy pryde,
 Thrughe grace of God Almyght
Here we purpose for to Abyde,
And all the werld, that ys so wyde,
Shall wondre on the on eu*er*y syde,
 Sone in all mennys sight.[8]   386

---

[1] Wr. spine.
[2] MS. *clearly has* ſ, *but read* defyne (= defy) *with* Wr. H.
[3] *This was at first read as* denyen ; Wr. *has* devyne.
[4] *A stroke through* l. [5] Wr. paine. [6] Wr. thy. [7] Wr. rasarde.
[8] *The stanza lacks the first two lines in* Wr. *also.*

ANTE*CHRISTU*S.   Out on you, theffys bothe ij !
Iche man may se ye be soe
    All by youre Araye ;
Muffelyd in mantyls, non such I knowe ;
I shall make you lowte full loo
Or I departe you all froo,
      To knowe me lorde for Aye.   393

ENNOKE.   We ben no theffys, I the tell,
Thowe fals fend comyn from hell !
Wythe the we purpous more to mell,
    My felow and I in fere,
To knowe thy power and thy myght,
As we these kyngis have behight ;
And thereto we ben Redy dighte,
      That all men nowe may here.   401

ANTE*CHRISTU*S.   My myght ys most, I tell to the ;
I dyed, I Rose, thrughe my poostye,
That all these kyng*is* sawe w*ith* theyr ee,
    And eu*er*y mon and wiffe ;
And myracles[1] and m*ar*vels I did Also.
I consell you, ther*e*for, bothe ij,
To wurship me and no moo,
      And lett vs nowe no more stryue.   409

HELYAS.   They were no myracles but m*ar*vells[2] thing*is*
That thowe shewyd to these kyngis

  .   .   .   .   [3]

    Thrughe the fendys crafte.
p. 12.   And as the floure nowe springys,
ffallith, fadithe [4] and hyngys,
    So do thy Ioy nowe [5] Ragnes
      That shalbe from the Rafte.   416

---

[1] *A stroke through* l.   [4] Wr. faith.
[2] Wr. marvayles.   [5] Wr. So thy joye it; H. So thy joye now it.
[3] *This line, missing also in* Wr., *is supplied by* H.: into falsehood
thou them bringes.

ANTE*CHRISTU*S.   Oute on the, theffe, that sett*is* so
    styll !
Why wylte *tho*u not one wurde speke theym tyll,
.   .   .   .[1]
    That comyn me to Reprove ?[2]
DOCTOR.   O Lorde, maistre ! what shall I say then ?
ANTE*CHRISTU*S.   I beshrewe bothe thy kenne,[3]
Arte thowe nowe for to kenn?
    In faythe, I shall the greve !   423

Off my godhed I made the wysse
And sett the eu*er* at Micle[4] price ;
Nowe I wolde fele thy gud advyce,
    And here what thowe wolde saye.
These lowlers they wolde full fayne me greue,
And nothing on me will they leue,
But eu*er* ben Radye me to Repreue
    And all the peple[4] of my lawe.[5]   431

DOCTOR.   O Lord, that art so mycle of myghte,
Me thynke thowe shullest not Chyde nor fyghte,
But curs theym, lorde, thrugh thy myght,
    Then[6] shall they far*e* full yll ;
for those that thowe Blesses they shall well spede,
And those that thowe cursys they be best dede :
This ys my co*n*cell and my Rede
    Yendre herytyk*is* to spyll.   439

ANTECRYSTUS.   The same I purposyd, lerne[7]
    thowe me ;
All thing I knowe thrugh my postye ;
But yet I thoghte thy witt to see,
    What wos thyn entent.

---

[1] *This line, missing in* Wr. *also, is supplied by* H. : but lett them
speak all thei will.   [2] *Read* repreve.
[3] *Later hand has written in margin* knees ; H. *has* knenne.
[4] A *stroke through* l.   [5] *Read* laye.
[6] *Almost illegible.*   [7] *Read* leeve, *with* Wr.

Hit shalbe downe[1] ful sicurlye, —
The sentence gyvon full openly,
with my mouthe trulye,
    Apon theym shalbe hente.   447

My curse I gyue you to mend your Melys,
ffrom youre hede vnto youre helys!
    walke ye furthe youre[2] way!
ENOKE. Ye! thowe shalt nevur com *in Celis*,
ffor falsly with thy wylus[3]
    The peple[4] ys put in pyne.[5]   453

p. 13. ANTECRISTUS. Out on you, Thevys! why far ye
    thus?
Whither hade ye leuer haue payne or blisse?
I may you saue from all Amys;
    I made the day and yke the nyght,
And All thing that ys on yerthe groyng, —
fflowre3 freshe that fayr can spryng, —
Also I made all other thing,[6]
    They sterrus that be so bryght.   461

HELYAS. Thowe list! vengeaunce on the befall!
Oute on the, wreche! wrothe the I shall.
Thowe callis the kyng & lord of all;
    A ffynde ys the withein!   465

ANTECHRISTUS. Thowe liest falsly, I the tell!
Thowe wilbe dampnyd into hell.
I made the, mon, of fleshe & fell,
    And all That ys lyvyng;
ffor other god[7] haue you non;
Therefor wurship me Alon,
The wyche hasse made the water and ston,
    And all at my lykyng.   473

---

[1] Wr. done.   [4] *A stroke through* l.
[2] *Instead of* youre, Wr. *has* in twentie devilles.
[3] *After this* H. *has:* all this people thou begyles and puttes them all to
paine.   [5] Wr. paine.   [6] *This line is not in* Wr.   [7] Wr. Godes; H. godds.

ENNOKE.   fforsothe thowe lyes fulfalsly ! [1]
Thowe art A ffende commyn to Any
Goddis peple that stondis us bye ;
   In hell I wolde thou were.
HELYAS.   ffye on the, felon ! fye on the ! fye !
ffor All thy wychecrafte & socerye,[2]
To mote [3] with the I am Redye,
   That All the peple may here.   481

ANTECHRISTUS.   Out on you, harlottys ! whens come
     ye ?
Where [4] haue you other god then [5] me ?
ENNOKE.   Yes ; crist, god in trenyte,
   Thow ffalse ffayture Attaynte !
That send his [6] son from hevon see,
That for mon kynd dyed on Rode tree,
That shall fullsone make the to flee,
   Thowe ffeaytir false and ffaynte !   489

p. 14.   ANTECHRISTUS.   Rybaldis Riuelid [7] out of Raye,
What ys the trenyte to saye ?
HELYAS.   Thre persons, as thowe leue may,
   In on godhede in ffere :
ffather and son, that ys no nay,
And the holly goost, stryrring Aye :
That ys one god verey ;
   Ben all thre namyd here.   497

ANTECHRISTUS.   Out on you, thevys ! what say ye ?
Wyll ye haue bothe one [8] god And iije ?
   Howe darr ye so say ?
Maddmen, therefor levys [9] on me

---

[1] Wr. *omits* ful.   [2] Wr. sorcerye; *but cf.* p. 157, l. 104.
[3] *This looks a little more like* mote *than* mete; Wr. *has* mote.
[4] Wr. *also has this form of* whether.
[5] Wr. any other godes but.
[6] MS. *has a second* his, *under-dotted for omission by a later hand.*
[7] Wr. ruled.
[8] *A stroke over* e.   [9] Wr. Madmen, maddmen, leeve.

That am one god, — so is not he !
Then may ye lyue in Ioye & lee,
    All th*is* londe I darr lay.   504

ENNOKE.   Nay, tyrand ; vnde*r*stond *tho*u this :
But[1] beginnyng h*is* godhed ys
And also boute[1] ending, ywys ;
    Thus fully levon we.
And thowe, that genderyd[2] wos Amys,
Hasse[3] beginnyng & nowe that[4] blisse,
And[5] ende shall haue — no drede there ys —
    ffull[6] ffoule, as men shall se.   512

ANTE*CHRISTU*S.   Whrecchys, golys,[7] ye ben blent !
Goddis son I am, from hym sente.
Howe darr you maynten youre entente,
    Sithe he and I ben won ?[8]
Haue I not, sithe I cam hym froo,
Made the dede to speke[9] and goo ?
And tho[10] men I sende[11] my goste Also
    That levyd[12] me Apon.   520

HELYAS.   fye on the, felone ! fye on the ! fye !
ffor thrughe his myght & h*is*[13] maistrye,[14]
By sufferaunce[15] of god Allmyghtye,
    The people[16] ys blent thrughe the.
Yff tho[17] men be Raysyd, witt*er*lye,
W*ith*outen the devuls ffantasye,
Here shall be prevyd App*er*tely,
    That all men shall see.   528

[1] Wr. Without.
[2] Wr. ingendred.
[3] Wr. haste.
[4] Wr. this.
[5] Wr. An.
[6] Wr. Fully.
[7] Wr. glowes.
[8] Wr. one.
[9] Wr. rise.
[10] Wr. to.
[11] Wr. sente.
[12] Wr. leeve.
[13] Wr. *omits* his.
[14] *This was at first read* marsaye.
[15] *A stroke over* aun.
[16] *A stroke through* l.
[17] Wr. thoes ; W. thees.

p. 15. ANTE*CHRISTU*S.   A !¹ ffolys, I Redd you leue me
Apone,
That myracles haue shewyd ² manyon
To the peple eu*er*ychone,
To put theme out of Doute.
Therefor, I Rede you, hastely
Convert*is* to me most myghty ;
I shall you saue from Anye,
And¹ that I am Aboute.   536

ENNOKE.   Nowe, of thy Myracles I wold see.
HELIAS.   Therfor comyn hether be we,
To se ⁸ what ys thy grete postye,
And some therof to lere.
ANTE*CHRISTU*S.   Sone may ye se if you will byde ;
ffor I wyll nother fyght nor chyde.
Offt⁴ all the worlde that ys so wyde
Therin ys not my pere.   544

ENNOKE.   Bryng ffurthe those men here in our syght
That *tho*u hase Raysyd Agayn ⁵ the Ryght ;
Yf thowe be of so ⁶ mycle might
To make theym ete and drynke,
ffor verey god we wyll the knowe, —
such A sygne yf thow wyll shewe, — ⁷
And do the Reu*er*ence on A Rowe,
All at thy lykyng.   552

ANTE*CHRISTU*S.   Wrecches dampnyd all be ye,
But noght for that yt fallyth me,
As *gra*cius god, Abyding be
Yf ye wyll mende youre liffe.
Ye dede men, Ryse thrughe my postye,
And ⁸ ete and drynke that men may see,

---

¹ *Almost illegible.*   ⁵ Wr. againste.
² Wr. showed to.   ⁶ Wr. *omits* so.
³ Wr. Doe *for* To se.   ⁷ *This was at first read* showe.
⁴ *Perhaps for* Offᵉ ; Wr. Of.   ⁸ Wr. Come.

And proue me worthest in deyte ;[1]
 So shalle we stynt All stryffe.   560

PRIMUS MORTUUS. Lorde, thy bydding I will do Aye,
And for to ete I will Assaye.
SECUNDUS MORTUU*S*.[2] And I also, all that I maye,
 Wyll do thy byddyng here.
p. 16. HELIAS. Hand here brede, bothe two ;
But I most blesse hyt or I goo,
That the fende, mankynd*is* ffoo,
 One hit haue no powere.   568

Thys brede I blesse now w*ith* my honde
In Ih*e*sus name, I vnderstonde,
The wych ys lorde of see and londe
 And kyng in hevon so hye :
*In no*min*e patris*, that all hathe wroghte,
Et filii virginis, that dere vs boughte,
*Et spyrytus san*c*ti*, ys all my thoghte, —
 One god and parsons thre.   576

PRIMUS [3] MORTUU*S*.[2] Alas ! put that [4] oute of my
    syghte ;
To loke on yt I am not light, —
That Pryntte that ys vpon yt [5] pight
 Hit puttythe me to grett ffere.
SECUNDUS MORTUU*S*.[2] To loke on hit I am not light,
That brede to Me yt ys so bryght,
And ys my ffoe bothe day and nyght
 And puttys me to grete dere.[6]   584

ENNOKE. Nowe, ye men that haue donne mis,[7]
Ye seey [8] well what h*is* powere ys.

---

1 Wr. worthye of dietie.
2 MS. mortuu*us*.   5 vpon yt *is almost illegible.*
3 MS. Pr*i*mus*us*.   7 Wr. amisse.
4 Wr. that bread.   8 Wr. see.
6 *Written over another word ;* Wr. *has* dreade ; dere *is right.*

Convert*is* to hym, I Rede I wysse,
 That you on Rode haue [1] boughte.
TERCIUS REX. A ! [2] now we knowyn apertly
We haue ben broghte in herysye ;
w*ith* you to dethe we will for thy,
 And neu*er* eft turne ourre thought.   592

QUART*US* REX. Nowe, Ennoke and helye, it ys no
  nay,
Haue [3] tayntyd the Tyrant, th*is* same day.
Blest be Ih*e*su borne of A may,
 On hym I leue A pon ! [4]
PRIM*US* REX. Thowe fayture, that ferde [5] w*ith* fan-
  tesye,
W*ith* socerye, wycchrafte [6] & nygrymancye,
Thowe hasse vs led [7] in heresye, —
 ffye on thy werkys ychon !   600

p. 17. SECU*N*DUS REX. Ih*e*su, for thy mycle grace,
fforgeve vs all oure tresspas,
And bryng us to the hye hevynly place
 As thowe art god And mon !
Nowe am I wyse made thrughe thy myght ;
Blessyd be thowe,[8] Ih*e*su, day and nyght !
This [9] grysely grome grayth*is* hym*e* to fyght
 To sle [9] us here Anon.   608

TERCI*US* REX. Off oure lyvys lett us not Reche,
Thoghe we be slayne of such A wreche
ffor Ih*e*su sake, that may vs leche,[9]
 Oure sowlys to bryng to blysse !
QUARTUS REX. That wos well sayde & so I sente ; [10]

---

[1] Wr. hath, *and so* Dr. Furnivall *reads here.*
[2] Wr. And, *which* Dr. Furnivall *is inclined to see here.*
[3] Wr. You have.
[4] Wr. *has the same line.*
[5] Wr. Thou feature, fere.
[6] *Error of scribe.*
[7] le *above the line.*
[8] Wr. *omits* thowe.
[9] *Almost illegible.*
[10] Wr. assente.

To dye, for sothe, ys myn intent
ffor Christes[1] loue[1] om*ni*potende,[1]
   In cause that ys Ryghtwyse.   616

ANTECRISTUS. A ![2] falsse faytures, turne you nowe?
Ye shalbe slayne, I make A vowe ;
And those Traytours that turnyd you,
   I shall make theym vnfayn,
That all other by verey sight
Shall knowe that I am most of myght,
ffor w*ith* this sworde nowe wyll I fyght ;
   ffor all ye shalbe Slayne.   624

*Tunc A*nte*christu*s *occidet Enoke et Eliam et omnes*[3] *conversos cu*m
gladio, et Redebit ad chathedram; cui[4] *dicat Michaell cu*m *gladio in
manu sua dextra :*[5]

MICHAELL.   Antecrist, nowe ys comyn thy day ;
Reigne no longer thowe ne maye !
He that hath laad the Alwey,
   Nowe hym thowe most go to.
No mo men shalbe shente[6] by the ;
My lorde wyll, dede *tha*t *tho*u be ;
He that hath gyvon the th*is*[7] poste
   Thy soule shall vnder foo.   632

In syn Ingendirt furst *tho*u wos,
In syn Als[8] lade thy lyfe thowe hasse,
p. 18. In Syn nowe An ende thowe mas,
   That marryd hasse monyon.
Thowe hasse eu*er* s*er*uyd sathanas
And had hys power in eu*er*y place ;
Ther*e*fo[9] thowe gayttys nowe no grace, —
   w*ith* hym thowe most gon.[10]   640

---

[1] *Almost illegible.*
[2] *This was at first read as* Ve, *which may be a bad spelling of the ex-
clamation* we; Wr. *has* A !
[3] Wr. *omnes reges.*
[4] Wr. *cum.*
[5] Wr. *in dextera sua.*
[6] Wr. slayne.
[7] Wr. his.
[8] Wr. *omits* Als.
[9] *Error of scribe.*
[10] *In* Wr. *lines 637–640 follow* 648.

iij yere and An halffe on, wytt*er*lye,
Thowe hasse hadde leue to distrye
Godd*is* people [1] wykkydlye
    Thrughe thy fowle Reede ;
Nowe thowe shalt knowe and wytt in hye
That more ys goddys Maystrye [2]
Then eke the devuls & thyn therebye,
    ffor [3] nowe shalt thowe be dede.   648

*Tu*nc *Mychaell occidet* [4] *A*nte christu*m*, *et in Occidendo dicat* [5] *A*nte-
christu*s* Help ! Help ! [6]

Help ! sathanas and lucyfer,
Belsabub, bolde bacheler, [7]
Ragnayll,[8] thowe art my dere !
    Nowe fare I wondre evull !
Alas ! Alas ! were is my powere ?
Alas, my wytt ys in A were !
Nowe bodye and sowle, bothe in fere,
    And all gose to the Devyll !   656

*Tu*nc *morietur A*nte christu*s*, *et veniant* [9] *duo Demones, quoru*m *dicat*
primus demon : [10]

Anon ! maister, Anon ! anon !
ffrom hell grounde I herde the groune ;
I thoghte I wolde not com*e* myself Alon
    ffor wurship of thyn Astate.
W*ith* vs to hell thowe shalt gon.
ffor this deth we make gret mon,
To wyn moo sowlys into oure won ; [11]
    But nowe hit ys to late.   664

Secu*n*dus demon. W*ith* me thowe shall ; fro me
    thowe come ;
Off me shall come thy last Dome,

---

[1] *A stroke through* l.
[2] Wr. magistie ; W. magistrie.
[3] Wr. *omits* ffor.
[4] Wr. occidit.
[5] Wr. clamat ; W. clamavit.
[6] Wr. helpe *twice more.*
[7] Wr. balacher.
[8] Wr. Ragnell, Ragnell.
[9] Wr. *venient.*
[10] Wr. *et dicunt ut sequitur.*
[11] Wr. pon.

ffor thowe hasse well des*er*uyd !
And thrughe my might & my poste
Thowe hasse lyuyd in dignyte
And mony a Sawle deceyuyd.   670

p. 19. PRIM*US* DEMON.   This body was getton by myn
            Assente
In clene horedom verament ;
Off mother wombe or that he wente,
      I wos hym w*ith* in,
And taghte hym*e* Ay w*ith* [1] myn entente
Syne, by wyche he shalbe shente ;
ffor he dyd my coma*u*ndemente
      His sowle shall neu*er* blyn.   678

SECU*N*D*US* DEMON.   Nowe, felow, in faythe, gret
            mon we may make
ffor this lorde of a state [2] that stond*is* in [3] styde ;
Mony A fatt morsell we haue had for h*is* sake
      Off Sowlys that shulde haue be sauyd ; — in hell
            be *th*ie [4] hyd.[5]   682

            *A nimam ei*us *tu*nc *capiat.*[6]

PRIM*US* DEMON.   His sowle w*ith* sorowe in honde
            haue I hente ;
He [7] pena*u*nce and payne sone shall he fele ;
To Lucyffer, that lord, yt shalbe presente,
      That bren shall as a bronde ; — h*is* sorow shall
            not kele.[8]   686

SECU*N*D*US* DEMON.   This proctor of prophecye hasse
            procuryd monyon
On h*is* lawe for to leue, and lost [9] for h*is* sake.

[1] Wr. eever *for* Ay w*ith*.   [7] Wr. (H.) Yea.
[2] Wr. of estate.   [8] Wr. (H.) feele.
[3] Wr. in this.   [9] Wr. (H.) lose.
[4] *Read* thei.
[5] Wr. shoulde bene hange in hel by the head.
[6] Wr. *from* H.: *Tunc aufertur corpus Antechristi a demonibus.* **W.**
lacks lines 683–694 ; Wr. *prints them from* H.

Theyre sowlys ben in sorowe, And h*is* shalbe sone.
　　Such maisters[1] thrughe my myght mo*n*ion I[2]
　　make.   690

PRIM*US* DEMON.   W*ith* lucyfer, that lorde, long shall
　　he lenge ;
In a sete Ay w*ith* sorowe w*ith* hym shall he sytt.
SEC*UN*DUS DEMON.   Ye, by the halse[3] in hell shall
　　he henge,
In a du*n*gen full depe, ryght in hell pytt.   694

PRIM*US* DEMON.   To hell wyll I hye w*ith* out ony
　　fayle,[4]
W*ith* th*is* present of pryce thedure[5] to bryng.
S*E*C*UN*DUS DEMON.   Thowe take hym by the tope &
　　I by the tayle ;
An soryfull song, in faythe, shall he senge.   698

[6] PRIM*US* DEMON.   A ! felowe, A doule[7] loke that
　　thowe[8] dele
　　To all this fayr compayny, hence or[9] *tho*u
　　wynde ![10]
SEC*UN*DUS DEMON.   Ye, sorowe and care eu*er* shall
　　they sele ;[11]
　　In hell shall they dwell at theyr last ende !   702

*Tu*nc *ibunt demones Ad infer#u*m *ad A#imam[12] A#te*christi; *et su*r*ge*nt
*ennoke et helyas, quoru*m *Dicat Ennoke :*

p. 20. ENNOKE.   A ! lorde, that all[13] shall lede
　　And bothe deme[14] the quycke and dede,

1 Wr. (H.) maystryes.   8 Wr. (H.) thou now.
2 Wr. (H.) do I.   9 Wr. (H.) er.
8 Wr. (H.) heeles.   10 Wr. (H.) wend.
4 Wr. (W.) fay[l]e.   11 MS. *clearly* sele ; *but read* fele.
5 Wr. (W.) theither.   12 *Read* cum anima.
　6 *These four lines with the stage direction after* 702 *are not in* W.
H. *apparently lacks only the stage direction.*   18 H. alle the world.
　7 Wr. (H.) dole.   14 H. deme both.

That Reue*r*ence the, thowe on theym Rede
    And theym thrughe Right Releuyd![1]
I wos dede and Right here slayne,
But thrughe thy myghte, lord,[2] & thy mayne
Thowe hasse me Raysyd vp Agayne.
    The wyll I loue and leue !   710

HELYAS.   Ye, lorrde, blessyd most *tho*u be!
My fleshe nowe gloryfyed I see.
Witt*is* ne[3] sleightte[4] ageeynste[4] the
    Conspyryd[4] may be no way.
Alle that levon in the stydfastly
Thow helpis, lorde, ffrom all Any,
ffor dede I wos and nowe lyue I.
    Honuryd[4] be thowe Aye ![5]   718

MYCHAELL.   Ennoke and helye, com ye Anon ;
My lorde wyll that ye[4] with[4] me gon
To hevens[4] blysse, botthe[4] blude & bon,
    Eu*er* mo there to be.[6]
Ye[4] have[4] ben[4] long, — for ye ben wyse, —
Dwellyng[4] in erthlye paradyce ;
But[4] to heven,[4] there hym selffe ys,
    Nowe[4] shall ye goe withe me.   726

*Tu*nc *ibit Angelus adducens ennok et Helyam ad celu*m *cantans :* "*Gau-*
d•*te iusti in d*omi*no,*" &c.[7]
                                    Explicit.

[1] So Wr.; *but read* releeve with H.   [4] *Almost illegible.*
[2] Wr. *omits* lord.   [5] Wr. ever.
[3] Wr. Witte ner; with no *is possible.*
[6] *The whole line is almost illegible.*
[7] Wr. *Tunc abducens eos* (W. omne*s*) *ad celu*m *cantabit* (W. **cantebit**)
angelus (W. *angellus*) : "*Gaudete iusti in D*omi*no.*"

YORK CORPUS CHRISTI PLAYS.

For information as to the source of the text and the meaning of the symbols, see
p. 153.

[THE JUDGMENT DAY.] [1]

The Merceres.

Deus incipit.

[DEUS.] Firste when I *th*is worlde hadde wroght, —
    Woode and wynde and wateris wan,
And all-kynne thyng *th*at nowe is oght, —
    Fulle wele me *th*oght *th*at I did *th*anne ;
Whenne *th*ei were made, goode me *th*ame [2] *th*oght.
    Sethen to my liknes made I man ;
And man to greue [3] me gaffe he noght :
    *Th*erfore me rewis *th*at I began. [4]   **8**

Whanne I had made man at my will,
    I gaffe hym wittis hym-selue to wisse,
And Paradise I putte hym till,
    And bad hym halde it all as his.
But of *th*e tree of goode and ill
    I saide, "What tyme *th*ou etis of *th*is,
Manne, *th*ou spedes *th*i-selue to spill, —
    *Th*ou arte broght oute of all [5] blisse."   **16**

---

[1] *Supplied by* Y.
[2] Ho. *th*ai.
[3] K. *wishes to read* plese.
[5] K. *inserts* thi.
[4] **Y.** *has* I *th*e worlde began; K. *omits either* the worlde *or* *Th*erfore.

Belyue brak manne my bidding ;
    He wende haue bene a god *th*erby,
He wende haue wittyne of all-kynne thyng,
    In worlde to haue bene als wise as I :
He ete the appill I badde schulde hyng ;
    *Th*us was he begilid thurgh glotony.
Sithen both hym and his ospring
    To pyne I putte *th*ame all for-thy,   **24**

To lange and late me *th*oghte it goode [1]
    To catche *th*ois caitiffis oute of care.
I sente my sone, with full blithe moode,
    Till er*th*e to salue *th*ame of *th*are sare ;
For rew*th*e of *th*ame he reste on roode
    And boughte *th*ame with his body bare ;
For *th*ame he shedde his harte bloode : [2]
    What kyndinesse myght I do *th*ame mare ?   **32**

Sethen aftirwarde he heryed hell,
    And toke oute *th*ois wrechis *th*at ware *th*are-inne ;
*Th*er faughte *th*at free with feendis feele
    For *th*ame *th*at ware sounkyn for synne.
Sethen in erthe *th*an gonne he dwelle,
    Ensaumpill he gaue *th*ame heuene to wynne,
In tempill hym-selffe to teche and tell,
    To by *th*ame blisse *th*at neuere may blynne.   **40**

Sethen haue *th*ei founde me full of mercye,
    Full of grace and for-giffenesse ;
And *th*ei als wrecchis, wittirly,
    Has ledde *th*er liffe in lithirnesse ;
Ofte haue *th*ei greued me greuously :
    *Th*us have *th*ei quitte me my kyndinesse ;
*Th*er-fore no lenger, sekirlye,
    Thole will I *th*are wikkidnesse.   **48**

---

[1] K. *reads* yoode.   [2] Ho. ; Y. harte and bloode.

Men seis *th*e worlde but vanite,
    Ʒitt will no-manne be ware *th*er-by ;
Ilke a day *th*er mirroure may *th*ei se,
    Ʒitt thynke *th*ei noʒt *th*at *th*ei schall dye.
All *th*at euere I saide schulde be
    Is nowe fulfillid thurgh prophicie ;
Ther-fore nowe is it tyme to me
    To make endyng of mannes folie.   56

I haue tholed mankynde many a ʒere
    In luste and likyng for to lende,
And vnethis fynde I ferre or nere
    A man *th*at will his misse amende ;
In erthe I see butte synnes seere :
    Therfore myne aungellis will I sende
To blawe *th*er bemys, *th*at all may here.
    The tyme is comen I will make ende.   64

Aungellis, blawes youre bemys belyue,
    Ilke a creatoure for to call !
Leerid and lewde, both man and wiffe,
    Ressayue *th*er dome *th*is day thei schall,—
Ilke a leede *th*at euere hadde liffe ;
    Bese none for-getyn, grete ne small.
Ther schall *th*ei see *th*e woundes fyve
    *Th*at my sone suffered for *th*em all.   72

And sounderes *th*ame be-fore my sight !
    All same in blisse schall *th*ei not be.
My blissid childre, as I haue hight,
    On my right hande I schall *th*ame see ;
Sethen schall ilke a weried wight
    On my lifte side for ferdnesse flee.
*Th*is day *th*er domys *th*us haue I dight,
    To ilke a² man as he hath serued me.   80

¹ K. *rejects* a.

I.[1] ANG.   Loued be *th*ou, Lorde, of myghtis moste,
　　*Th*at aungell made to messengere !
Thy will schall be fulfillid in haste,
　　*Th*at heuene and erthe and helle schall here.

[He makes the proclamation.]

Goode and ill, euer ilke a gaste,[2]
　　Rise, fecche [3] youre flessh, *th*at was youre feere !
For all *th*is worlde is broght to waste.
　　Drawes to youre dome ! it neghes nere.   88

II. ANG.   Ilke a creature, both olde and yhing,
　　Be-lyue I bidde ʒou *th*at ʒe ryse ;
Body and sawle with ʒou ʒe bring,
　　And comes be-fore *th*e high justise !
For I am sente fro heuene kyng
　　To calle ʒou to *th*is grette assise ;
*Th*erfore rise vppe, and geue rekenyng
　　How ʒe hym serued vppon sere wise.   96

[The dead rise and speak.]

I. ANIMA BONA.   Loued be *th*ou, Lorde, *th*at is so schene,
　　*Th*at on *th*is manere made vs to rise,
Body and sawle to-gedir, clene,
　　To come before *th*e high justise.
Of oure ill dedis, Lorde, *th*ou not mene,
　　That we haue wroght vppon sere wise ;
But graunte vs for thy grace bedene
　　*Th*at we may wonne in paradise.   104

II. AN. BONA.   A ! loued be *th*ou, Lorde of all,
　　*Th*at heuene and erthe and all has wroght,
*Th*at with *th*yne aungellis wolde vs call
　　Oute of oure graues, hidir to be broght.

1 *I have not followed* Y. *always in the abbreviations of the names.*
2 Y. euery ilke agaste ; He. euery ilke a gaste.
3 Y. Rise and fecche ; K. *rejects the first* youre.

Ofte haue we greued *th*e grette and small, —
    Ther-aftir, Lorde, *th*ou deme vs noght !
Ne suffir vs neuere to fendis to be thrall,
    *Th*at ofte in er*th*e with synne vs soght !   112

1. ANIMA MALA.   Allas, allas ! that we were borne !—
    So may we synfull kaytiffis say.
I here wele be *th*is hydous horne
    Itt drawes full nere to domesday.
Allas ! we wrecchis *th*at ar for-lorne,
    *Th*at never ȝitt serued God to paye,
But ofte we haue his flessh for-sworne ;
    (Allas, allas, and welaway !)   120

What schall we wrecchis do for drede,
    Or whedir for ferdnes may we flee,
When we may bringe forthe no goode dede
    Before hym *th*at oure juge schall be ?
To aske mercy vs is no nede,
    For wele I wotte dampned be we.
Allas, that we swilke liffe schulde lede
    *Th*at dighte vs has *th*is destonye !   128

Oure wikkid werkis *th*ei will vs wreye,
    *Th*at we wende never schuld haue bene weten ;
*Th*at we did ofte full pryuely,
    Appertely may we se *th*em wreten.
Allas, wrecchis, dere mon we by !
    Full smerte with helle-fyre be we smetyn.
Nowe mon neuere saule ne body dye,
    But with wikkid peynes euermore be betyne.   136

Allas ! for drede sore may we quake ;
    Oure dedis beis oure dampnacioune.
For oure mys menyng [1] mon we make ;
    Helpe may none excusacioune.

---

[1] Y. mys-meuyng ; Ho. mys-menyng ; *but* mys *is a noun, and* mon *a verb.*

We mon be sette for our synnes sake
    For-euere fro oure saluacioune,
In helle to dwelle with feendes blake,
    Wher neuer schall be redempcioune.   144

II. AN. MALA.   Als carefull caitiffis may we ryse,
    Sore may we ringe oure handis and wepe ;
For cursidnesse and for covetise
    Dampned be we to helle full depe.
Rought we neuere of Goddis seruise,
    His comaundementis wolde we noȝt kepe ;
But ofte *th*an made we sacrafise
    To Satanas when othir slepe.[1]   152

Allas ! now wakens all oure were ;
    Oure wikkid werkis may we not hide,
But on oure bakkis vs muste [2] *th*em bere,
    Thei wille vs wreye on ilke a side.
I see foule feendis *th*at wille vs feere,
    And all for pompe of wikkid pride.
Wepe we may with many a teere ;
    Allas, *th*at we *th*is day schulde bide !   160

Before vs playnly bese fourth brought
    *Th*e dedis *th*at vs schall dame be-dene.
That eres has herde or harte has *th*oght
    Sen any tyme *th*at we may mene,
*Th*at fote has gone or hande has wroght,
    That mouthe has spoken or ey has sene, — [3]
*Th*is day full dere thanne bese it boght.
    Allas, vnborne and we hadde bene ![4]   168

III. ANG.   Standis noght to-gedir ! parte you in two !
    All sam schall ȝe noght be in blisse.

[1] T. othere can slepe; Ho. othir did (*or* can) slepe.
[2] Ho. bus; *but* T. *also has* must.
[3] T. *interchanges* 164 *and* 166.
[4] He. *prefers* T.: Allas vnborne then had I bene! Ho. *rejects this.*

Oure Lorde[1] of heuene woll it be soo,
    For many of yowe has wroght amys.
Ye[2] goode, on his right-hande ʒe goe,
    *Th*e way till heuene he will you wisse ;
ʒe weryed wightis, ʒe flee hym froo
    On his lefte-hande, as none of his.   176

DEUS.[3] *Th*is woffull worlde is brought till ende ;
    My Fadir of heuene he woll it be.
*Th*erfore till er*th*e nowe will I wende,
    Mi-selue to sitte in mageste.
To deme my domes I woll descende ;
    *Th*is body will I bere with me ;
How it was dight, mannes mys to mende,
    All mankynde *th*ere schall it see.   184

       [Jesus descends to earth in a cloud, and, before assuming the Judgment Seat, speaks :]

DEUS. Mi postelis and my darlyngis dere,
    *Th*e dredful dome *th*is day is dight.
Both heuen and erthe and hell schall here
    How I schall hold *th*at I haue hight,
That ʒe schall sitte on seetis sere
    Be-side my-selffe, to se *th*at sight,
And for to deme folke ferre and nere
    Aftir *th*er werkyng wronge or right.   192

I saide also whan I you sente
    To suffre sorowe for my sake,
All *th*o *th*at wolde *th*ame right repente
    Schulde with you wende and wynly wake ;
And to youre tales who toke no tente
    Shulde fare to fyre with fendis blake.

---

[1] Y. My fadir ; *the text is from* T. (*by* He.)
[2] Y. *Th*e.
[3] **Miss Smith** *points out that this is not God the Father, who appeared at the beginning of the pageant, but God the Son.*

Of mercy nowe may no3t be mente ;
  Butt, aftir wirkyng, welth or wrake.   200

[1] My hetyng haly schall I fullfille ;
  Therfore comes furth and sittis me by
To here *th*e dome of goode and ill.
I. APOSTOLUS.   [2] I loue *th*e, Lord God all-myghty ;
  Late and herely, lowde and still,
To do thy bidding bayne am I ;
  I obblissh me to do *th*i will
With all my myght, als is worthy.   208

II. APOST.   [3] A ! myghtfull God, here is it sene
  *Th*ou will fulfille *th*i forward right,
And all *th*i sawes *th*ou will maynteyne.
  I loue *th*e, Lorde, with all my myght,
*Th*at for [4] vs *th*at has erthely bene
  Swilke dingnitees ·has dressed and dight.
DEUS.   Comes fourthe !   I schall sitte 3ou betwene,
  And all fulfille *th*at I haue hight.   216

Hic ad sedem iudicii cum cantu angelorum.

[*Meanwhile the devils prepare to attend the Judgment.*]

I. DIABOLUS.   Felas, arraye [5] vs for to fight,
  And go we faste oure fee to fange ;
*Th*e dredefull dome *th*is day is dight,
  I drede me *th*at we dwelle full longe.
II. DIAB.   We schall be sene euere in *th*er sight,
  And warly waite, — ellis wirke we wrange ; —
For if *th*e domisman do vs right,
  Full grete partie with vs schall gang.   224

---

[1] *Marginal note in later hand:* What they shall haue for y[r] folly.
[2] *In margin :* Hic caret O soverand Savyo[r] de novo facto.
[3] *In margin :* de novo facto.
[4] Y. *Th*er-fore ; Ha. Thou for vs that has not ; Ho. (*and* K.) *as above,
but both seem to take* the (212) *as def. article instead of pronoun.*
[5] K. *inserts* we.

iii. Diab.   He schall do right to foo and frende,
    For nowe schall all *th*e soth be sought.
All weried wightis with vs schall wende,
    To payne endles *th*ei schall be broght.[1]   228

Deus.   Ilke a creature, takes entent
    What bodworde I to you[2] bringe :
*Th*is wofull worlde away is wente,
    And I am come as crouned kynge.
Mi Fadir of heuene he has me sente
    To deme youre dedis and make ending.
Comen is *th*e day of jugement ;
    Of sorowe may ilke a synfull synge.   236

The day is comen of kaydyfnes,[3]
    All *th*am to care *th*at are vnclene,
*Th*e day of bale and bittirnes, —
    Full longe abedyn has it bene ! —
*Th*e day of drede to more and lesse,
    Of care,[4] of trymbelyng and of tene,
*Th*at ilke a wight *th*at weried is
    May say, Allas, this day is sene !   244

Here may ʒe se my woundes wide,
    *Th*e whilke I tholed for youre mysdede,
Thurgh harte and heed, foote, hande and hide,
    Nought for my gilte butt for youre nede.
Beholdis both body, bak, and side, —
    How dere I bought youre brotherhede !
*Th*es bittir peynes I wolde abide ;
    To bye you blisse, *th*us wolde I bleede.   252

[1] "*In margin :* Hic caret de novo facto, Alas that I was borne, dixit prima anima mala et ijda anima mala, de novo facto. *And indeed four lines are wanting to the stanza, as shown by the rimes, though there is no blank.*" — Y.

[2] K. *inserts* shall *from* T.

[3] Ho. *corrects the spelling to* kaytyfnes.

[4] Y.: " *The copyist first wrote* ire (*a reminiscence of* dies iræ)."

Mi body was scourged with-outen skill ;
    As theffe full thraly was [I] [1] thrette ;
On crosse *th*ei hanged me on a hill,
    Blody and bloo, as I was bette,
With croune of thorne throsten full ill ;
    This spere vnto my side was sette ;
Myne harte bloode spared *th*ei noght [2] to spill :
    Manne, for thy loue wolde I not lette.   260

The Jewes spitte on me spitously,
    *Th*ei spared me nomore *th*an a theffe.
When *th*ei me strake, I stode [3] stilly ;
    Agaynste *th*am did I no-thyng greve.
Behalde, mankynde, *th*is ilke is I,
    *Th*at for *th*e suffered swilke mischeue :
*Th*us was I dight for thy folye ;
    Man, loke, thy liffe was me [4] full leffe.   268

*Th*us was I dight *th*i sorowe to slake ;
    Manne, *th*us behoued *th*e borowed to [5] be.
In all my woo toke I no wrake ;
    Mi will itt was for *th*e loue of *th*e.
Man, sore aught *th*e for to quake, [6]
    *Th*is dredfull day *th*is sight to see.
All *th*is I suffered for *th*i sake ;
    Say, man, what suffered *th*ou for me ?   276

Mi blissid childre on my right hande,
    Youre dome *th*is day ȝe thar not drede,
For all youre comforte is command,
    Youre liffe in likyng schall ȝe lede.

---

[1] *Supplied by* Y. *from* T.
[2] Ho. *from* T. ; Y. *has* spared noght thei for to.
[3] Y. stode full stilly ; *omission suggested in footnote.*
[4] Y. was to me ; *omission suggested in footnote.*
[5] K. *from* T. ; Y. to borowed.
[6] T. *has* Man, for sorow aght the to qwake.

Commes to *th*e kyngdome ay lastand
    *Th*at ȝou is dight for youre goode dede.
Full blithe may ȝe be where ȝe stande,
    For mekill in heuene schall be youre mede.   284

Whenne I was hungery, ȝe me fedde ;
    To slake my thirste youre harte was free ;
Whanne I was clothles, ȝe me cledde,
    ȝe wolde no sorowe vppon me see ;
In harde prisoun [1] whan I was stedde,
    Of my paynes [2] ȝe hadde pitee ;
Full seke whan I was brought in bedde,
    Kyndely ȝe come to coumforte me.   292

Whanne I was wikke [3] and werieste,
    ȝe herbered me full hartefully ;
Full gladde *th*anne were ȝe of youre geste,
    And pleyned my pouerte piteuously ;
Be-lyue ȝe brought me of *th*e beste,
    And made my bedde full esyly.
*Th*erfore in heuene schall be youre reste,
    In joie and blisse to be me by.   300

I. ANIMA BONA.   Whanne hadde we, Lorde, *th*at all has
        wroght,
    Meete and drinke *th*e with to feede,
Sen we in er*th*e hadde neuere noght
    But thurgh *th*e grace of thy godhede ?
II. AN. BONA.   Whanne waste *th*at we *th*e clothes brought ?
    Or visite *th*e in any nede ?
Or in *th*i sikenes we *th*e sought ?
    Lorde, when did we [to] *th*e *th*is dede ?   308

DEUS.   Mi blissid childir, I schall ȝou saye
    What tyme *th*is dede was to me done :

---

[1] He. *from* T. ; Y. presse.

[2] Y. paynes *corrected in* MS. *from* penaunce. T. *has* penaunce, *which* K. *prefers.*

[3] Ho. *wishes to substitute* wille *from* T., *which he says equals* wilde.

When any *th*at nede hadde, nyght or day,
    Askid ȝou helpe and hadde it sone ;
Youre fre hartis saide *th*em neuere nay
    Erely ne late, mydday ne none ;
But als ofte sithis as *th*ei wolde praye,
    *Th*ame thurte but bide, and haue *th*er bone.   316

Ȝe cursid caytiffis of Kaymes kynne,
    *Th*at neuere me comforte in my care,
I and ȝe for-euer will twynne,
    In dole to dwelle for-euermare.
Youre bittir bales schall neuer blynne
    *Th*at ȝe schall haue whan ȝe come *th*are.
*Th*us haue ȝe serued for youre synne,
    For derffe dedis ȝe haue done are.   324

Whanne I had mistir of mete and drynke,
    Caytiffis, ȝe cacched me fro youre ȝate ;
Whanne ȝe were sette as sirs on benke,
    I stode *th*er-oute werie and wètte ;
Was none of yowe wolde on me thynke,
    Pyte to haue of my poure state :
*Th*er-fore till hell I schall you synke, —
    Weele are ȝe worthy to go *th*at gate.   332

Whanne I was seke and soriest,
    Ȝe visitte me noght, — for I was poure ;
In prisoune faste when I was feste,
    Was none of you loked howe I fore ;
Whenne I wiste neuere where to [1] reste,
    With dyntes ȝe draffe me fro your dore ;
Butte euer to pride *th*anne were ȝe preste ;
    Mi flessh, my bloode, ofte ȝe for-swore.   340

Clothles whanne I was ofte, and colde,
    At nede of you [2] ȝede I full naked, —

---

[1] T.; Y. where for to.
[2] K. *thinks this unintelligible and suggests, on basis of* T., **For you nere-**
hand, *etc.*

House ne herborow, helpe ne holde,
    Hadde I none of you, *th*of I quaked.
Mi mischeffe sawe ye many-folde ;
    Was none of you my sorowe slaked,
Butt euere for-soke me, yonge and alde.
    *Th*erfore schall ȝe nowe be for-saked.   348

I. ANIMA MALA.   Whan had *th*ou, Lorde, *th*at all thyng has,
    Hungir or thirste, sen *th*ou God is ?
Whan was that[1] *th*ou in prisonne was ?
    Whan was *th*ou naked or herberles ?
II. AN. MALA.   Whan was it we sawe *th*e seke, allas ?
    Whan kid we *th*e *th*is vnkyndinesse ?
Werie or wette to late *th*e passe, —
    When did we *th*e *th*is wikkidnesse ?   356

DEUS.   Caitiffis,[2] als ofte als it be-tidde
    *Th*at nedfull aught askid in my name,
ȝe herde *th*em noght, youre eris ȝe hidde,
    Youre helpe to *th*ame was noȝt at hame, —
To me was *th*at vnkyndines kyd !
    *Th*ere-fore ye bere[3] this bittir blame.
To the lest of myne when ȝe oght did[4]
    To me ȝe did *th*e selue and same.[5]   364

Mi chosen childir, comes vnto me !
    With me to wonne nowe schall ȝe wende ;
*Th*ere joie and blisse schall euer be
    Youre liffe in lyking schall ȝe lende.
ȝe cursed kaitiffis, fro me ȝe flee,
    In helle to dwelle with-outen ende ;
*Th*er ȝe schall neuere butt sorowe see
    [6]And sitte be Satanas *th*e fende.   372

[1] *Inserted by* Ho. *from* T.
[2] Y. Caistiffis.
[3] T.; Y. *omits* ye; Ho. ye beres.
[4] He. *from* T.; Y. To leste or moste whan ȝe it did.
[5] T.; Y. and *th*e same.
[6] *In margin:* nota, miseremini mei, etc.

Nowe is fulfillid all my for-*th*oght,
    For endid is all erthely thyng.
All worldly wightis *th*at I haue wroght
    Aftir *th*er werkis haue nowe wonnyng :
Thei *th*at wolde synne and sessid noght,
    Of sorowes sere now schall *th*ei syng ;
And *th*ei *th*at mendid *th*ame whils *th*ei moght,
    Schall belde and bide in my blissing.   380

Et sic facit finem cum melodia angelorum transiens a loco ad locum.

PART II.

DIGBY PLAYS.

Reprinted from " The Digby Mysteries, ed. by F. J. Furnivall, New Shakspere Society, 1882." In the footnotes, F. indicates this edition, which represents the MS. unless the contrary is stated; S. indicates " Die Digby-Spiele. Diss. v. K. Schmidt, Berlin, 1884." The MS. is assigned to the last decade of the fifteenth century. I have disregarded scribal flourishes and tags.

[THE CONVERSION OF ST. PAUL.][1]

[*First Station.*]

[*Enter* POETA *as* PROLOGUE.]

POETA.[2] *Rex glorie*, Kyng omnipotent,
　　Redemer of *th*e world by thy[3] pouer diuine,
And Maria, *tha*t pure vyrgy[*n*],[1] quene most excelle*n*t,
　　Wyche bare *tha*t blyssyd babe, I*e*su, *tha*t for vs sufferd
　　　　pyne,[4]
Vnto whoys goodnes I do inclyne,
Besechyng *tha*t Lord, of hys pytous influens,
To p*r*eserue & gou*er*ne thys wyrshypfull audyens.　　　　7

Honorable frend*es*, besechyng yow of lycens
　　To p*r*ocede[5] owr p*r*ocesse, we may, vnder yo*ur* cor-
　　　　recc*i*on,
[Show] the conu*er*syon of Seynt Paule, as *th*e Byble gyf
　　　　experyens.
　　Whoo lyst to rede *th*e booke *A*c*tu*m *Appostolorum*,
　　Ther shall he haue *th*e very notycyon ;

---

[1] *Supplied by* F.　　　　[4] F. payne.
[2] *Beside this a later hand wrote* Myles Blomefylde.
[3] F. the.　　　　[5] *Misunderstood by* S., p. 24.

But, as we can, we shall vs redres,
Brefly wi*th* yowr fauo*u*r begynyng owr pr*o*ces.   [*Exit.*]   14

*Dau*nce.[1]

Here entryth Saule, goodly besene in the *best wyse lyke an aunterous knyth, thus sayyng :*

SAULUS.   Most dowtyd man I am lyuy*ng* vpon the ground,
     Goodly besene wi*th* many a riche garnement ;[2]
My pere on lyue I trow ys nott found ;
     Thorow *th*e world, fro *th*e oryent to *th*e occydent,
     My fame ys best knowyn vndyr *th*e fyrmament ;
I am most drad of pepull vnyue*r*sall,
They dare not dysp[l]ease me[3] most noble.   21

Saule ys my name, — I wyll *tha*t ye notyfy, —
     Whych conspyreth the dyscyplys wi*th* thret*e* & menac*e* ;[4]
Be-fore *th*e prync*es* of prest*es* most noble & hye[5]
     I bring them to punyshement for ther trespace.
     We wyll them nott suffer to rest in no place,
For they go a-bou3te to pr*e*che & gyff exemplis,
To destroye our lawes, sinagoges and templis.   28

By the god Bellyall, I schall make pr*o*gresse
     Vnto the princes, both Caypha and Anna,
Wher I schall aske of them, in suernes,
     To pe*r*sue thorow all Dammask & Liba,
     And thus we schall soone aft*er* than[6]
Bryng them *tha*t so do lyff in-to Ierusalem,
Both man and child that I fynd of them.   35

*Her cu*mmyth *Sale to Caypha &* Anna, *p*rest*es of* the *tempyll.*

Nobyll pr*e*lat*es* and prync*es* of regalyte,
     Desyryng and askyng of yo*u*r benyngne wurthynes

---

[1] *In a later hand.*
[2] F. garlement.
[3] F. my.
[4] F. thret*es* *and* menac*es*.
[5] F. hye *and* noble.
[6] *This unrhymed line may, as* **Kittredge** *suggests, have taken the place of the original.*

Yo*u*r letters & epystolys of most sou*er*ente
    To subdue rebellyous [1] that wyll, of frawardnes,
    A-gaynst o*u*r lawes rebell or transgresse,
Nor wyll not inclyne but mak obiecc[*i*]on, — [2]
To pursue all such I wyll do p*r*otecc*i*on.   42

CAYPHA.   To yo*u*r desyer we gyf p*er*fyth sentens,
    Accordyng to yo*u*r petyc*i*ons that ye make postulac*i*on,
By-cause we know yo*u*r trewe delygens
    To p*er*sue all tho *tha*t do reprobac*i*on
    A-gayns ow*u*r lawes by ony redarguac*i*on ;
Wherefor shortly we gyf in co*m*mandment
To put down them *tha*t be dy[s]obedyent.[2]   49

ANNA.   And by thes letturs, *tha*t be most reuerre*n*t,
    Take them in hand, full agre *ther*-to.
Co*n*streyn all rebellys by ow*u*r hole assent ;
    We gyf yow full power so to doo ;
    Spare not, hardly, for frend nor foo ;
All thos ye fynd of *tha*t lyfe in thys realme,
Bounde loke ye bryng them in-to Ierusalem.   56

              Her Saule resayuyth ther letters.

SAULUS.   Thys p*re*cept here I take in hande
    To fullfyll aft*er* yow*u*r wyll*es* both,
Wher I shall spare w*ith*-in *th*is londe
    Nother man nor woman, — to *th*is I make an oth, —
    But to subdue I wyll not be loth.
Now folow me, knytys & s*er*uant*es* trewe,
In-to Damaske as fast as ye can sewe.   63

I. MILES.[3]   Vnto yo*u*r co*m*mau*n*dme*n*t I do obeysaunce ;
    I wyll not gaynsay nor make delac*i*on,
But w*ith* good mynd & harty plesaunce

---

      [1] F. rebellyons.   [2] *Corr. by* F.
      [3] F. P*r*im*us* miles ; *similarly below.*

I shall yow succede & make perambulacion
Thorow-oute Damaske with all delectacion,
And all that [1] rebell & make resystens,
ffor to oppres I wyll do my delygens.   70

II. MILES.   And in me shalbe no neclygens,
　　But to thys precept my-self I shall applye,
To do your behest with all conuenyens,
　　With-owt eny frowardnes or eny obstynacy, —
　　Non shall appere in me, but, verely,
With all my mynd I yow insure,
To resyst tho rebelles I wyll do my cure.   77

SAULUS.   Truly to me yt ys grett consolacion
　　To here thys report that ye do avauns.
ffor your sapyencyall wyttes I gyf commendacion;
　　Euer at my nede I haue founde yow constant.
　　But, knytes & seruauntes,[2] that be so plesaunt,
I pray yow anon my palfray ye bryng,
To spede my iurney with-owt lettyng.   84

　　　Here goyth Sale forth a lytyll a-syde for to make hym redy to ryde, the
　　　　seruuant thus seyng:

SERUUS.   How, hosteler, how!   A peck of otys & a botell
　　　　of haye !
　　Com of a-pase, or I wyll to a-nother inne !
What, hosteler ! why commyst not thy way?
　　Hye the faster, I beshrew thi skynne !
STABULARYUS.   I am non hosteler, nor non hostelers kynne,
But a ientylmanys seruuant, i[f] thou dost know !
Such crabyysh wordes do aske a blow.   91

SERUUS.   I cry yow mercy, sir !   I wyst well sum-what ye
　　　　were,
　　Owther a gentylman—or a knaue, me thynkyth by your
　　　　physnomy !

---

[1] F. thoo, *emend. by* Kittredge.
[2] F. *seruuantes; hereafter I shall follow* F.

Yf on loke yow in *th*e face *tha*t neu*er* se yow ere,
 Wold thynk ye were at *th*e next dore by.
 In good fayth, I wenyd yow had bene an hosteler, verely :
I sye suche a-nother ientylman w*it*h yow a barowfull bare
Of horsdowng & dogg*es* tord*es* & sych other gere.   98

And how yt happenyd, a m*er*velous chance be-tyde :
 Yo*ur* felow was not suer of foote, & yet he went very
  brode,[1]
But in a cow-tord both dyd ye slyde,
 And, as I wene, yo*ur* nose *ther*-in rode, —
 Yo*ur* face was be-payntyd w*it*h sowters code.
I sey neu*er* sych a sy3t, I make God a-vow ;
Ye were so be-grymlyd & yt had bene a sowe.   105

STAB. In fayth, *tho*u neu*er* syest me tyll *th*is day !
 I haue dwellyd w*it*h my master thys vij 3ere & more ;
ffull well I haue pleasyd hym, he wyll not say nay,
 And mykyll he makyth of me therfore.
 SERU*US*. By my trowth, *th*an be ye changyd to a new
  lore?
A s*er*uand ye are, & *tha*t a good,
Ther ys no better lokyth owt of a hood.   112

STAB. ffor soth, & a hood I vse for to were,
 ffull well yt ys lynyd w*it*h sylk & chamlett ;
Yt kepyth me fro the cold, *tha*t *th*e wynd doth me not dere,
 Nowther frost nor snow *tha*t I therby do sett.
 SERU*US*. Yea, yt ys a dobyll hood & *tha*t a fett !
He was a good man *tha*t made yt, I warant yow ;
He was noth*er* horse ne mare,[2] nor yet yokyd sow ! 119

*Here co*mm*yth the fyrst knyth to the stabyl-grom, sayng :*

1. MILES. Now, stabyll-grom, shortly bryng forth away
 The best horse, for ow*ur* lorde wyll ryde !

---

[1] *Substituted in* MS. *for* wyde.
[2] MS. nare; *corr. by* F.

STAB.   I am full redy ; here ys a palfray,
  There can no man a better bestryde ;
He wyll conducte owur lorde & gyde
Thorow the world ; he ys sure & abyll ;
To bere a gentyllman he [is] [1] esy & prophetabyll. 126

   Her the knyth cummyth to Saule with a horse.

I. MILES.   Behold, sir Saule, your palfray ys com,
  Full goodly besene, as yt ys yowr desyer,
To take yowur vyage thorow euery regyon.
  Be nott in dowt, he wyll spede your mater ;
  And we, as your seruauntes, with glad chere
Shall gyf attendance, — we wyll nott gaynsay,
But folow you where ye go be nyȝt or day. 133

SAULUS.   Vnto Damask I make my progressyon,
  To pursue all rebellyous, beyng froward & obstynate,
Agayns our lawes be ony transgressyon.
  With all my delygens my-self I wyll preparate [2]
  Concernyng my purpose to oppres & separate ;
Non shall reioyce that doth offend,
But vtterly to reproue with mynde & intende. 140

   Her Sale rydyth forth with hys seruantes a-bowt the place, [&][1] *owt of*
   the *pl[ace].*[1]

CAYPHA.   Now Saule hath takyn hys wurthy wyage
  To pursue rebellyous, of what degre thei be ;
He wyll non suffer to raygne nor haue passage
  With-in all thys regyon, we be in sertayn[te].
  Wherefor I commende hys goodly dygnyte,
That he thus aluay takyth in hande
By hys power to gouerne thus all thys lande. 147

ANNA.   We may lyue in rest by hys consolacion ;
  He defendyth vs ; where-for we be bownde
To loue hym intyrely with our harttes affeccion,
  And honour hym as champyon in euery stownde.

   [1] *Supplied by* F.   [2] F. p*repare.*

Ther ys non suche lyuyng vpon *the* grownde
That may be lyke [1] hym nor be hys pere,
Be est nor west, ferre nor nere.   154

POETA (*si placet*).

CO*N*CLUSYON.

Daunce.[2]

[POETA.] ffynally, of *th*is stac[*i*]on thus we mak a conclusyon,
     Besechyng thys audyens to folow & succede,
W*ith* all yo*ur* delygens, *th*is gen*e*rall p*r*ocessyon.
     To vnderstande *th*is matter, wo lyst to rede
     The Holy Bybyll for *the* better spede,
Ther shall he haue *the* p*er*fyth intellygens.
And *th*us we comyt yow to Crystys magnyfycens.   161

     ffinis istius stacionis et altera sequitur,

[*Second Station.*][3]

[PROLOGUE.]

POETA.   Honorable frend*es*, we beseche yow of audyens
     To here o*ur* intenc*i*on & also o*ur* prosses.
Vpon o*ur* matter, be yo*ur* fauorable lycens,
     A-nother p*ar*t of *th*e story we wyll redres :
     Here shalbe brefly shewyd w*ith* all o*ur* besynes,
At thys pagent, Saynt Poullys co*n*uercyon.
Take ye good hede & ther-to gyf affecc*i*on.   [*Exit.*]   168

     *Here co*mmyth Saule rydyng in, with hys seruantes.*

SAUL*US*.   My purpose to Damask fully I intende ;
     To pursewe the dyscypulys my lyfe I apply.
ffor to breke down the chyrchys thus I co*n*descende,
     Non I wyll suffer that [they][3] shall edyfey ;

     ----

[1] *A late hand has added* to *above the line.*
[2] *In later hand.*
[3] *Supplied by* F.

Perchaunce owur lawes than my3te [peyre] [1] ther-by,
And the pepull also turne & co*n*uerte,
Whych shuld be gret heuynes vnto my*n* hart.   175

Nay, *tha*t shall nott be butt layd a-part !
   *Th*e prynces haue gouyn me full potestac*i*on.
All that I fynd, *th*ei shall nott start,
   But bounde, to Ierusalem, w*ith* furyous vyolac*i*on,
   Be-for Cesar, Caypha & Annas [haue] p*r*esentac*i*on.
Thus shalbe subduyd tho wretchys of *tha*t lyfe,
That non shall in-ioy, nother man, chy[l]de nor wyfe.   182

   *Here co*mmyth a feruent [flame] wi*th* gret tempest, and Saule faulyth
   down of hys horse ; tha*t* done, Godhed spekyth in heuyn.

DE*US*.   Saule ! Saule ! why dost *tho*u me pursue ?
   Yt ys hard to pryke a-gayns *th*e spore !
I am *th*i Savyo*ur*, *tha*t ys so trwe,
   Whych made heuyn & erth & eche creature.
   Offende nott my goodnes ; I wyll *th*e recure !
SAULUS.   O Lorde, I am a-ferd, I trymble for fere.
What woldyst I ded ? Tell me here !   189

DEUS.   A-ryse & goo *tho*u wyth glad chere
   In-to the cyte a lytyll be-syde,
And I shall *th*e socor in eu*er*y dere,
   That no maner of yll xal be-tyde ; [2]
   And I wyll ther for the p*r*ouyde
By my grete goodnes what *tho*u shalt doo.
Hy *th*e as fast theth*er* as *tho*u mast goo.   196

SAUL*US*.   O mercyfull God, what aylyth me ?
   I am lame, my legg*es* be take me fro ;
My sygth lykwyse, — I may nott see ;
   I can nott tell whether to goo.
   My men hath forsake me also.
Wheth*er* shall I wynde, or whether shall I pas ?
Lord, I beseche the, helpe me, of thy grace.   203

   [1] *Supplied by* Kittredge.   [2] F. xalbe-tyde.

I. MILES.[1]   Syr, we be here to help the in *th*i nede
    W*ith* all o*u*r affyance ; we wyll not seise.[2]
SAUL*US*.   Than, in Damask, I pray yow, me lede,
    I' [3] God*es* name, accordyng to my p*ro*myse.
    II. MILES.   To put forth yow*u*r hand loke ye dresse !
Cu*m* on yo*u*r way ; we shall yow bryng
In-to *th*e cyte wit*h*-owt taryng.   210

    *Here the knyght*es *lede forth Sale in-to a place, &* Cryst apperyth to*
    Annanie, sayng :

DEUS.   Ananie ! Ananie ! where art *th*ou, Ananie ?
ANAN.[4]   Here, Lord, I am here, trwly !   212

DEUS.   Go thy way & make *th*i curse,
    As I shall assyng *th*e by myn aduysse,
Into *th*e strete *qui dicitur rectus,*
    And in a certayn house, of warantyse,
    Ther shall ye fynd Saule in humble vyse,
As a meke lamb, *tha*t a wolf before was namyd.
Do my behest ; be nothyng a-shamyd !   219

He wantyth hys syth, by my punyshment co*n*strayned.
    P*r*ayeng vnto me, I assure, *th*ou shalt hym fynd.
W*ith* my stroke of pyte sore ys he paynyde,
    Wantyng hys sygth, for he ys truly blynyde,
    ANAN.   Lord, I am aferd, for aluay i*n* my mynd
I here so myche of hys furyo*us* cruelte,
*Tha*t, for spekyng of *th*i name, to deth he wyll put me.   226

DEUS.   Nay, Ananie ; nay, I assure *th*e !
    He wulbe glad of thy cu*m*myng.
ANAN.   A ! Lord, but I know of a certayn[te]
    That thy seynt*es* in Ierusalem to deth he doth bryng.
    Many yllys of hym I haue be kennyng,

    [1] F. j*us* miles ; *so below.*
    [2] MS. *apparently* serse ; *corr. by* F.
    [3] *But the stroke for* n *may have been omitted.*
    [4] F. Ananias, *here and below.*

ffor he hath the pour of the p*rinces* alle
To saue or spylle, — do which he schall.   233

DEUS.   Be nothyng a-drad, he ys a chosen wessell,
     To me assyngned by my godly elecc*i*on.
He shall bere my name be-fore the kyng*es* & chyld*er* of Israell,
     By many sharpe shour*es* sufferyng correcc*i*on,
     A gret doctor, of benyngne conplecc*i*on,
The trwe precher of the hye deuynete,
A very pynacle of *th*e fayth, I ensure the.   240

ANAN.   Lorde, thy co*m*mandme*n*t I shall fullfyll ;
     Vn-to Saule I wyll take my waye.
DEUS.   Be nothyng i*n* dowte for good nor yll !
     Fare-well, Ananie ; tell Saule what I do say.

          *Et exiat De*us.

ANAN.   Blyssyd Lord, defende me, as *tho*u best may !
Gretly I fere hys cruell tyra*n*ny ;
But to do *th*i precept my-self I shall applye.   247

        Here Ananias goth toward Saule.

I. MILES.   I maruayle gretly what yt doth mene,
     To se ow*u*r master in thys hard stounde.
The wond*er* grett lythtys *tha*t were so shene
     Smett hym doune of hys hors to *th*e grownde ;
     And me thowt that I hard a sounde
Of won spekyng w*ith* voyce delectable,
Whych was to [vs] wonderfull myrable.   254

II. MILES.   Sertenly thys ly3t was ferefull to see,
     The sperkys of fyer were very ferue*n*t ;
Yt inflamyd so greuosely about *th*e cou*n*tre
     That, by my trowth, I went we shuld a ben bre*n*t.
     But now, serys, lett vs relente
Agayne to Caypha & Anna, to tell *th*is chau*n*ce
How yt be-fell to vs thys greuau*n*s.   261

Her Saule ys in contemplacion.[1]

SAUL*US*. Lord, of *th*i cou*n*fort moch I desyre,
    *Tho*u my3ty P*r*ince of Israell, Kyng of pyte,
Whyche me hast punyshyd as *th*i presoner
    That nother ete nor dranke thys dayes thre ;
    But, gracyos Lorde, of *th*i vysytacyon I thanke the ;
Thy s*er*uant shall I be as long as I haue breth,
Thowgh I therfor shuld suffer dethe.   268

*Here co*m*myth Anania to Saule, sayeng :*

ANAN. Pease be in thys place & goodly mansyon !
    Who ys w*ith*-in ? Speke, in Crystys holy name !
SA[U]L*US*.[2] I am here, Saule. Cu*m* in, on Godd*es* benyson !
    What ys yo*ur* wyll ? Tell, w*ith*-owten blame.
    ANAN. ffrom Almyghty God, s*er*tanly, to the sent I am,
And Ananie men call me wher-as I dwell.
SAUL*US*. What wold ye haue ? I pray yow me tell.   275

ANAN. Gyfe me yo*ur* hand for yo*ur* awayle !
    For, as I was co*m*mau*n*dyd, by hys *gra*cyos sentens
I byd[3] the be stedfast, for *tho*u shalt be hayle.
    ffor thys same cause he sent me to *th*i presens ;
    Also he bad the remember hys hye excellens,
Be *th*e same tokyn *tha*t he dyd *th*e mete
Toward *th*e cyte, when he apperyd in *th*e strete.   282

Ther mayst *tho*u know hys power celestyall,
    How he dysposyth euery-thyng as hym lyst ;
No-thyng may w*ith*stand hys my3te essencyall.
    To stond vp-ryght, or els doun to thryste,
    Thys ys hys pow*ur*, yt may not be myste,
ffor who *tha*t yt wantyth, lackyth a frende.
Thys ys *th*e massage *tha*t he doth *th*e sende.   289

SAULUS. Hys marcy to me ys ryght welcom ;
    I am ryght glad *tha*t yt ys thus.

---

[1] MS. comtemplac*i*on ; *corr. by* F.   [2] *Corr. by* F.   [3] F. & bad.

Hic aparebit Spiritus Sanctus super eum [in the form of a dove].

ANAN.   Be of good chere & perfyte iubylacion,
    Discendet super te Spirytus Sanctus,
    Whych hath with hys¹ grace illumynyd vs.
Put fo[r]th² thi hond & goo wyth me ;
A-gayne to thy syght here I restore the.   296

SAULUS.   Blyssyd Lord, thankys to yow euer be !
    The swame ys fallyn from my eyes twayne ;
Where I was blynyd & cowd nott see,
    Lord, thou hast sent me my syght agayne.
    ffrom sobbyng & wepyng I can not refrayne
My pensyue hart, full of contryccion ;
ffor my offences my body shal haue punycyon ;   303

And, where I haue vsed so gret persecucyon
    Of thi descyplys thorow all Ierusalem,
I wyll [aid]² & defende ther predycacyon
    That th[e]y² dyd tech on all this reme :
    Wherefor, Ananie, at the watery streme
Baptyse me, hartely I the praye,
A-mong your numbyr that I electe & chosen be may.   310

ANAN.   On-to this well of mych vertu
    We wyll vs hye with all our delygens.
SAULUS.   Go yow be-fore, & after I shall sewe,
    Laudyng & praysyng our Lordes benevolens.
    I shall neuer offend hys myȝty magnyfycens,
But aluay obserue hys preceptys & kepe.
ffor my gret vnkyndnes my hart doth wepe.   317

ANAN.   Knele ye down vpon thys grownde,
    Receyuyng thys crystenyng with good intent,
Whyche shall make yow hole of your dedly wound,
    That was infecte with venom nocent.

¹ MS. hys hys ; *corr. by* F.
² *Corr. by* F.

Yt purgyth synne ; and fend*es* poure [1] so fraudelent
It putyth a-syde, — where thys doth at-tayne,
In euery stede, he may not obtayne.   324

I crysten yow w*ith* mynd full p*er*fyght,
    Reseyuyng yow in-to ow*u*r relygyon,
Euer to be stedfast & neuer to flyt,
    But euer constant w*ith*-owt varyacyon.
    Now ys fullfyllyd all o*u*r obseruacyon ;
Concludyng, *tho*u mayst yt ken,
*In no*m*ine Patris et Filii et S*p*iritus S*anc*ti, Amen !*   331

SAULUS.   I am ryght glad as foule on flyte
    That I haue receyuyd *th*is blyssyd sacrem*en*t.
ANAN.   Com on yo*u*r way, Saule ; for nothyng lett !
    Take yow sum cou*m*forth for yo*u*r bodyes noryschm*en*t.
    Ye shall abyde w*ith th*e dyscyplys, verament,
Thys many dayes in Damask cyte,
Vn-tyll *th*e tyme more p*er*fyt ye may be.   338

SAULUS.   As ye co*m*mande, holy father Ananie ;
    I full[y] assent at yow[r] [2] request,
To be gydyd & rulyd as ye wyll haue me,
    Evyn at yo*u*r pleasur, as ye thynk best.
    I shall not offend for most nor lest.
Go forth yow*u*r way ; I wyll succede
In-to what place ye wyll me lede.   345

CO*N*CLUSYO[N].
Daunce.[8]

POETA.   Thus Saule ys co*n*uertyd, as ye se expres,
    The very trw s*er*uant of our Lord I*es*u ;
Non may be lyke to hys p*er*fy3t holynes,
    So nobyll a doctor, co*n*stant & trwe ;
    Aftyr hys co*n*ue*r*syon neu*er* mutable, but styll insue

---

[1] F. pour*es*.   [2] *Corr. by* F.
[8] F. *has no note as to the hand.*

The lawys of God to teche euer more & more,
As Holy Scryptur tellyth,[1] who-so lyst to loke *ther*-fore.   352

Thus we comyte yow all to *th*e Trynyte,
   Conkludyng thys stac*i*on as we can or may,
Vnder *th*e correccyon of them *tha*t letteryd be ;
   How-be-yt vnable, as I dare speke or say,
   The co*m*pyler here-of shuld translat veray
So holy a story, but w*ith* fauorable correccyon
Of my fauorable [2] masters of *the*r benygne supplexion.   359

     *ffinis isti*us secun*de staci*on*is* et *sequitur tarcia.*

[*Third Station.*][3]

[PROLOGUE.]

POETA.   The myght of the Fadir*es* potenciall deite
   P*r*es*er*ue thys honorable & wurshypfull co*n*gregac*i*on
That here be p*r*esent of hye & low degre,
   To vnderstond thys pagent at thys lytyll stac*i*on,
   Whych we shall p*r*ocede w*ith* all o*u*r delectac[i]on,[4]
Yf yt wyll plese yow to gyf audyens fauorable.
Hark wysely ther-to ; yt ys good & p*r*ofetable.   [*Exit.*]   366

   [Caypha and Anna, to whom enter the knights.]

I. MILES.   Nobyll p*r*elat*es*, take hede to ow*u*r sentens !
   A wundyrfull chau*n*ce fyll & dyd be-tyde
Vn-to owr master, Saull, when he depa*r*tyd hens,
   In-to Damaske p*ur*posyd to ryde :
   A m*er*uelous ly3t fro theleme*n*t dyd glyde,
Whyche smet doun [5] hym to grunde, both horse & man,
W*ith* the ferfulest wether *tha*t eu*er* I in cam.   373

---

    [1] F. tellyd.   [4] *Corr. by* F.
    [2] *Qy.* honorable.   [5] MS. doum; *corr. by* F.
    [3] *Supplied by* F.

II. MILES.   It rauysshid hym and hys spirit*es* did be-nome ;
    A swete, dulcet voyce spake hym vnto
And askyd wherfor he made suche p*er*secucyon
    A-geynst hys dyscyplys & why he dyd soo.
    He bad hym in-to Damaske to Ananie goo,
And ther he shuld reseyue baptym, truly.[1]
And now clene a-geyns ow*u*r lawys he ys trwly.   380

CAYPHA.   I am sure thys tale ys not trw !
    What ! Saule conuertyd from o*u*r law?
He went to Damask for to p*u*rsue
    All the dyscyplys that dyd w*ith*-draw
    Fro ow*u*r fayth, — thys was hys sawe.
How say ye, Anna, to thys mater? *Thi*s ys a m*er*velos
       chans ;
I can not beleve *tha*t thys ys of assurans.   387

ANNA.   No, Caypha ; my mynde trwly do [I][2] tell :
    That he wyll not turne in no maner wyse,
But rather to deth put & expell
    All myscreaunt*es* & wretchys *tha*t doth aryse
    Agaynst o*u*r lawes by ony enterpryse.
Say the trwth w*ith*-[owt][2] ony cause frawdelent,
Or els for yo*u*r talys ye be lyke to be shent !   394

I. MILES.[3]   Ellys ow*u*r bodyes may [ye] put to payn !
All *tha*t we declare I sye yt w*ith* my nye ;
Nothyng offendyng, but trwly do iustyfye.   397

CAYPHAS.   By the gret God, I do maruayle gretly !
    And thys be trw *tha*t ye do reherse,
He shall repent hys rebellyous treytory,
    That all shalbe ware of hys falsnes.
    We wyll not suffer hym to obtayne dowtles,
ffor meny p*er*ellys *tha*t myght be-tyde
By hys subtyll meanys on eu*er*y syde.   404

---

[1] *Qy.* duly.   [2] *Supplied by* F.
[3] *Apparently four lines are missing here.*

ANNA.   The law ys commyttyd to owur aduysment ;
    Wherfor we wyll not se yt decay, —
But rather vphold yt, help & augment, —
    That ony reprofe to vs fall may
    Of Cesar, themprour, by ny3t or day.
We shall to such matters harke & attende,
Accordyng to the lawes our wyttes to spende.   411

        ¹ *Here to enter a dyvel* ² *with thunder & fyre, & to avaunte* ³ *hym-sylfe,*
      saying as folowyth ; &, hys spech spokyn, to syt downe in a chayre.

BELYALL.   Ho ! ho ! beholde me, the my3te prince of the
    partes in-fernall !
    Next vnto Lucyfer I am in magestye ;
By name I am nominate the god Belyall ;
    Non of more my3te nor of more excellencye !
    My powre ys princypall & now of most soferaynte.
In the temples & synogoges who deneyth me to honore,
My busshopes thorow my motyon thei wyl hym sone devoure.   418

I have movyd my prelates, Cayphas & Anna,
    To persew & put downe by powre ryall,
Thorow the sytyes of Damask & Liba,
    All soch as do worship the hye God supernall.
    Ther deth ys conspyryd with-owt any fauoure at all ;
My busshopys hathe chosyne won most rygorus
Them to persew, howse name ys Saulus.   425

Ho ! thus as a god, most hye in magestye,
    I rayne & I rule ouer creatures humayne.
With souerayne sewte sow3te to ys my deyte ;
    Mans mynd ys applicant as I lyst to ordeyne.
    My law styll encreasyth ; wherof I am fayne;
Yet of late I haue hard of no newys truly,
Wherfor I long tyll I speke with my messenger Mercurye.   432

    ¹ *From here through the stage direction following* l. 502 *is by a later*
hand, written on three separate inserted leaves.
    ² *In margin:* Diabolus.   ⁸ F. avaunce.

Here shall entere a-nother devyll, callyd Mercury, with a fyeryng, com-
myng in hast, cryeng & roryng, & shal say as folowyth :

MARCURY.   Ho ! ow3t ! ow3t ! alas thys sodayne chance !
　　Well may we bewayle *th*is cursyd adue*n*ture !
BELYAL.   Marcurye, what aylys*e tho*u ? Tell me thy grevau*n*ce !
　　Ys *ther* any *tha*t hath wrow3te vs dyspleasure ?
　　MERC.   Dyspleasure i-nowgh, *ther*of ye may be sure !
Our law at lengthe yt wylbe clene downe layd,
For yt decayth sore, & more wyl, I am a-frayd.   439

BEL.   Ho ! how can *tha*t be ? Yt ys not possyble !
　　Co[*n*]syder,[1] *tho*u foole, *th*e long co*n*tynuance.
Decaye, q*u*od a ? Yt ys not credyble !
　　Of fals tydyng*es tho*u makyst here vtterance.
　　Behold how the peple hath no pleasau*n*ce
But in syn & to folow our desyere,
Pryde & voluptuosyte *ther* hart*es* doth so fyre.   446

Thow3e on do swau*er* away from our lore,
　　Yet ys our powre of suche nobylyte
To have hym a-gayne & twoo therfore
　　*Tha*t shal p*r*eferre *th*e p*r*ayse of owre maiestye.
　　What ys *th*e tydyng*es* ? Tell owt ! Lett vs see !
Why arte *tho*u amasyd so ? Declare afore vs
What fury ys fallyn *tha*t troblyth *th*e thus !   453

MERCURY.   Ho ! ow3t ! ow3te ! He *tha*t I most trustyd to
　　And he *tha*t I thow3te wold haue ben to vs most specyall
Ys now of late turnyd & our cruell foo ;
　　Our specyall frynd, our chosen Saull,
　　Ys be-co*m*me s*er*uante to *th*e hye God et*er*nall.
As he dyd ryde on our enemyes p*er*secutyon,
He was sodenly strykyn by the hye p*r*ovysyon,   460

And now ys baptysyd, & p*r*omys he hath made
　　Neu*er* to vary ; & soch grace he hath opteynyd
*Tha*t ondowtyd hys fayth from hy*m* can not fade.

1 *Corr. by* F.

Wherfor to complayne I am constraynyd,
For moch by hym shuld we haue prevaylyd.
BELYAL.   Ho ! ow3t ! ow3t ! What ! haue we loste
Our darlyng most dere whom we lovyd moste ?   467

But ys yt of trowth *that* *thou* doyst here specyfye ?
      MERCURY.   Yt ys so, ondow3tyd.   Why shuld I fayne ?
For thow3te I can do non o*ther* but crye !
            *Here the*i shal rore &° crye, &° then Belyal shal saye :

      BELYAL.   Ow3te ! *Thi*s grevyth vs worse *tha*n hell-
            payne !
      The conuersyon of [a] synner, certayne,
Ys more payne to vs & persecutyon
Than all *th*e furyes of *th*e infernall dongyon.   474

MERCURY.   Yt doyth not avayl vs thus to lament,
      But lett vs provyd for remedy shortlye.
Wherfor let vs both by on assent
      Go to *th*e busshopys & moue *th*em pryvelye
      *Tha*t by some sotyl meane *th*ei may cause hy*m* to dye.
Than shal he in our law make no dysturbau*n*ce,
Nor here-after cause vs to haue more greuau*n*ce.   481

BELYAL.   Wel sayd, Mercurye ! Thy cowncel ys profytable.
      Ho, Saul ! *tho*u shalt repent thy vnstablenes !
Thou hadyst ben bett*er* to haue byn confyrmable
      To our law ; for thy[1] deth, dowtles,
      Yt ys conspyryd to reward thy falsnes.
Thowgh on hath dyssayvyd vs, yet now-a-days
Twenti[2] doyth gladly folow oure layes :   488

Some by pryde, some thorowgh envye,
      Ther rayneth thorow my myght so moch dysobedyau*n*ce ;
Ther was neu*er* a-mong crystyans lesse charyte
      Than ys at *thi*s howre ; & as for co*n*cupysence,
      [He] rayneth as a lord thorow my violence ;

            ¹ F. thys.   ² F. xxti

Glotony & wrath eue*r*y man doth devyse ;
And most now ys praysyd my cosyn Covytyce. 495

Cu*m*, Me*r*cury, let vs go & do as we haue sayd ;
To delate yt any lenger yt ys not best.
ME*R*CURY. To bryng yt a-bow3t I wold be wel apayd ;
Tell yt be done let vs not rest.

. . . . [1]

BELYAL. Go we than shortly ! Let vs depa*r*te
Hys deth to devyse, syth he wyl not revart. 502

Here th*ei shal vanyshe away with a fyrye flame &* a* te*m*pest.*[2]
[3] *Her apperyth Saule in a* [4] *disciplis wede, sayng :*

SAULUS. [5] That Lord that ys shaper of see & of sond
And hath wrowth w*ith* hys woord all thyng at hys wyll,
Saue thys semely [6] *tha*t here syttyth or stonde,
ffor his meke marcy, *tha*t we do not spyll !
Grant me, good Lord, thy pleasur to fulfyll,
And send me suche speche that I *th*e trwth say,
My entenc*i*ons proph[i]table [7] to meve yf I may. 509

Welbelouyd frend*es*, ther be vij mortall synnes,
Whych be p*r*ovyd pryncypall & p*r*inc*es* of poysonnes :
Pride, *tha*t of bytternes all bale begynnes, —
W*ith*-holdyng all fayth, yt fedyth & foysonnes,
As Holy Scryptur beryth playn wyttnesse :
Inicium omni*um peccatoru*m su*p*erb*ya* [8] *est*,
That often dystroyeth both most & lest.[9] 516

---

[1] *Indicated by* F.
[2] *Here ends the insertion by the late hand.*
[3] *From here through* l. 516 *was originally written immediately after*
l. 411, *but was crossed out there and repeated here by the late hand. Both*
stanzas are rejected by S. *In the footnotes* L. *indicates the reading of the*
later copy.

[4] L. hys.	[7] *Corr. by* F.
[5] *Om. by* L.	[8] L. subia.
[6] L. asembly.	[9] L. man & best.

Off all vyces & foly pride ys the roote.
    Humylyte may not rayn ner yet indure ;
Pyte, alak, that ys flower & boot,
    Ys exylyd wher pride hath socour.
      Omnis qui se exaltat humiliabitur :
Good Lord, gyf vs grace to vnderstond & perseuer,
Thys wurd as *thou* bydyst to fulfyll euer, —   523

Who-so in pride beryth hym to hye,
    W*ith* mys[c]heff [1] shalbe mekyd, as I mak mensyon ;
And I therfor assent & fully certyfy
    In text, as I tell, the trw entencyon
    Of perfy3t goodnes & very-locucyon :
Noli, tibi dico, in altum sapere, sed time, —
Thys ys my consell, — bere the not to hye,   530

But drede alway synne & folye,
    Wrath, enuy, couytys, and slugyshnes ;
Exeunt owt of thy sy3t glotony & lechery,
    Vanytye & vayneglory and fals idylnes.
    Thes be the branchys of all wyckydnes ;
Who *that* in hym thes vyces do roote,
He lackyth all grace & bale ys *the* boote.   537

" Lern at my-self, for I am meke in hart,"
    Owr Lorde to hys ser*uantes* thus he sayth,
"ffor meknes I sufferyd a spere at my hart ;
    Meknes all vyc*es* anullyth & delayeth,
    Rest to soulys [ye] shall fynd yt,[2] in fayth :
Discite a me, quia mitis sum, et *corde humilis ;*
Et invenietis requiem animabus vestris."   544

So owur Sauyour shewyth vs example [3] of meknes,
    Thorow grace of hys godnes mekly ys [4] groundys ;
Trwly yt wyll vs saue fro *the* synnes sekenes,

---

        [1] *Corr. by* F.   [3] F. exampls.
        [2] F. yt shall fynd.   [4] *Qy.* yt.

ffor [1] pryde & hys progeny mekenes confoundys :
Quanto maior es, tanto humilia te in omnibus, —
The gretter *thou* art, the lower loke thu be,
Bere the neu*er th*e hyer for *th*i degre. 551

ffro sensualyte of fleshe thy-self loke *tho*u lede,
   Vnlefully therin vse not thy lyfe ;
Whoso therin delyteth, to deth he must nede ;
   It consumyth natur, the body sleyth w*ith*-owt knyf ;
   Also yt styntyth nott but manslawt*er* & stryf :
Omnis fornicator aut immundus non habet hereditatem
     Christ*i*, —
No*n* shall in heuyn posses that be so vnthryfty. 558

ffle fornycac[i]on, nor be no letchour,
   But spare yo*u*r speche & speke nott theron :
Ex habundancia cordis os loquitur ;
   Who movyth yt oft, chastyte louyth non,
   Of *th*e hart*es* habundans *th*e tunge makyth locuc*i*on,
What manys mynde ys laboryd, therof yt spekyth ; —
That ys of suernes, as Holy Scryptur tretyth. 565

Wherfor I reherse thys w*ith* myn owyn mowthe :
   *Caste viuentes templu*m *Dei sunt.*
Kepe clene yo*u*r body from synne vncuth,
   Stabyll yo*u*r syght*es* & look ye not stunt,
   ffor of a s*er*taynte I know, at a brunt,
Oculus est nuncius peccati, —
That the iey ys eu*er th*e messenger of foly 572

Enter Seruus sacerdotum.

S*ERUUS.*   Whate ! Ys not thys Saule *tha*t toke hys vyage
   In-to Ier*u*sa*l*em,[2] the dyscyplys to oppresse ?
Bounde he wold bryng them yf ony dyd rage
   Vpon Cryst, — *th*is was hys processe
   To *th*e p*r*inc*es* of p*r*estys, he sayde dowtles, —

---

[1] MS. ffror ; *corr. by* F.
[2] F. *points out that this is a mistake for* Damascus, *but see Notes.*

Thorow all Damask & also Ier*usa*lem
Subdwe all templys *tha*t he founde of them.   579

SA[U]LUS.[1]   Yes, s*er*taynly, Saule ys my p*ro*per name,
    That had in powr the full dominion —
To hyde yt fro you yt were gret shame
    And mortall synne, as in my opynyon, —
    Vnder Cesar & p*ri*st*es* of the relygeon
And templys of Iues, *tha*t be very hedyous,
A-gayns almyghty Cryst, *tha*t kyng so p*re*cyous.   586

S*ERUUS*.   To Anna & Caypha ye must make yo*ur* recurse ;
    Com[2] on yo*ur* way, & make no delac*i*on !
SAUL*US*.   I wyll yow succede, for better or wors,
    To the prync*es* of p*ri*st*es* w*ith* all delectac*i*on.

                    [*They go to **Anna** and Caypha.*]

    S*ERUUS*.   Holy p*ri*st*es* of hye potestac*i*on,
Here ys Saule !   Lok on hym wysely ;
He ys a-nother man than he was, verely.   593

SAULUS.   I am *th*e s*er*uant of Ihesu Almyghty,
    Creator & maker of see & sonnd,
Whiche ys kyng conctypotent of heuyn glory,
    Chef co*m*fort & solas both to fre & bonde,
    A-gayns whos power nothyng may stonde ;
E*m*p*er*owr he ys both of heuyn & hell,
Whoys goodnes & grace al thyng doth excell.   600

                    *Recedit paulisp*er.

CAYPHA.   Vn-to my hart thys ys gret admyrac*i*on,
    That Saule ys thus m*er*velously changyd ;
I trow he ys bewytchyd by sum co*n*iurac*i*on,
    Or els the devyll on hym ys auengyd.
    Alas ! to my hart yt ys dessendyd
That he ys thus takyn fro o*ur* relygyon !
How say ye, Anna, to thys co*n*uercyon ?   607

                    1 *Corr. by* F.   2 MS. Con; *corr. by* F.

ANNA.   ffull mervelously, as in my concepcion,
    Thys wnderfull case how yt be-fell,
To se thys chaunce so sodenly don,
    Vn-to my hart yt doth grete yll.
    But for hys falsnes we shall hym spyll ;
By myn assent to deth we wyll hym bryng,
Lest *tha*t more myschef of hym may spryng.   614

CAYPHA.   Ye say very trew, we my3t yt all rewe !
    But shortly in thys we must haue aduysement,
ffor thus a-gayns vs he may nott contynew, —
    Perauentur than of Cesar we may be shent.
    ANNA.   Nay, I had leuer in fyer he were brent
Than of Cesar we shuld haue dysp[l]easure [1]
ffor sych a rebell and subtyle fals treator.   621

CAYPHA.   We wyll command the gates to be kept aboute
    And the walles suerly on euery stede,
That he may not eskape no-where ow3te ;
    For dye he shall, I ensuer yow indede.
    ANNA.   Thys traytour rebellyous, evyll mut he spede,
That doth *th*is vnhappynes a-gayns all !
Now euery costodyer kepe well hys wall !   628

SERUUS.   The gatys be shytt, he can not eskape ; [2]
    Euery place ys kepte well & sure,
That in no wyse he may, tyll he be take,
    Gett owt of *th*e cyte, by ony coniecture.
    Vpon *tha*t caytyf & fals traytour
Loke ye be auengyd w*ith* deth mortall,
And iudge hym as ye lyst to what end he shall.   635

           [They go out ; an angel appears to Saulus.]

ANGELUS.   Holy Saule, I gyf yow monycyon,
    The princes of Iues entende, sertayn,
To put yow to deth, but by Goddes provysyon

    [1] *Corr.* by F.   [2] F. note skape.

He wyll ye shall lyue lenger, and optayn,
And after thy deth *tho*u shalt rayng
Above in heuyn, w*ith* owr Lord*es* grace.
Co*n*uay yowr-self shortly in-to a-nother place. 642

SAULUS.   That Lord*es* pleasur eu*er* mut be down
Both in heuyn & in hell, as hys wyll ys !
In a beryng-baskett or a lepe, a-non
I shall me co[*n*]uay [1] w*ith* help ot the dyscyplys,
For eu*er*y gate ys shett & kept w*ith* multytud of pe-
pull[ys] ;
But I trust in owr Lord, that ys my soco*u*r,
To resyst ther malyce & cruell furo*u*r. 649

CO*N*CLUSYO[N].

[EPILOGUE.] [2]

POETA.   Thus leve we Saule w*ith*-in *th*e cyte,
The gat*es* kep by co*m*mandme*n*t of Caypha & Anna ;
But the dyscyplys in the ny3t ou*er* the wall, truly,
As the Bybull sayeth : *dim*[*i*]*seru*n*t* [1] *eu*m *su*m*mitte*ntes [3]
*i*n *sporta ;*
And Saule after that, in Ierusalem, vera,
Ioyned hym-self & ther accompenyed
W*ith* *th*e dyscyplys, wher *th*ei were vnfayned. 656

Thys lytyll pagent thus co*n*clud we
As we can, lackyng lytturall scyens ;
Besechyng yow all, of hye & low degre,
Owr sympylnes to hold excusyd & lycens,
That of Retoryk haue no*n* intellygens ;
Co*m*myttyng yow all to owr Lord Ihesus,
To whoys lawd ye syng : *Exultet celu*m *laudibus !* 663

ffinis co[n]*uercio*n*is* [1] *Sancti Pauli.*

---

[1] *Corr. by* F.   [2] *Supplied by* F.   [3] F. su*m*mitte*n*s.

THE PLAY OF THE SACRAMENT.

The basis of the text is the edition by Whitley Stokes, *Publications of the Philological Society*, 1860–61, collated with the MS. in the Library of Trinity College, Dublin. The MS. is assigned to the end of the fifteenth century. In the footnotes, S. indicates the readings of Stokes's edition, which represents the MS. unless the contrary is expressly stated; H. indicates the emendations of Holthausen, *Englische Studien*, XVI, 150 f., and *Anglia*, XV, 198 ff.

[THE BANES OF THE PLAY.]

PRIMUS VEXILLATOR.   Now *th*e Father & *th*e Sune & *th*e
   Holy Goste,
  That all *th*is wyde worlde hat[h] [1] wrowg[h]t, [1]
Save all thes semely, [2] bothe leste & moste,
  And bry*n*[g]e [1] yow to *th*e blysse *tha*t he hath yow to
   bowght!
  We be ful purposed w*ith* hart & w*ith* thowght
Off our*e* mater to tell *th*e entent, —
  Off *th*e marvell*is tha*t wer wondurfely wrowght
Off *th*e holi & bleyssed Sacrament.   8

SECUNDUS.   Sid[s]eyns, & yt lyke yow to here *th*e purpoos
   of *th*is play,
  That [ys] [1] re-presentyd now in yower syght
Whych in Aragon was doon, [3] *th*e sothe to saye,
  In Eraclea, that famous cyte, aryght, —
  Ther-in wo*n*neth a m*er*chante off mekyll myght,
Syr Arystorye was called hys name,
  Kend full fere w*ith* mani a wyght,
Full fer in *th*e worlde sprong hys fame.   16

  [1] *Corr. by* S.   [2] S. femely.   [3] S.; MS. doon.

PRIMUS.   A-non to hym [1] ther ca*m* a Jewe,
    Wi*th* grete rychesse for the nonys,
And won*n*eth i*n* *th*e cyte of Surrey, — *th*is [2] full trewe, —
    Yn wyche [3] had gret ple*n*te off p*r*ecyous stonys.   20

Off *th*is Cristen me*r*chante he freyned [4] sore,
    Wane he wolde haue had hys entente.
Twenti pownd [5] and me*r*chandyse mor
    He p*r*oferyd for *th*e holy Sacrament.   24

SECUNDUS.   But *th*e Christen mercha*n*nte theroff sed nay,
    Be-cause hys profer was of so lityll valewe ;
An hundder pownd [6] but he wolde pay,
    No lenger theron he shuld pursewe.   28

But mor off ther purpos they gun*n*e [7] speke,
    The holi Sacramente for to bye ;
And all for [that] *th*e[i] wolde [8] be wreke,
    A gret sume off gold be-gune down ley.   32

PRIMUS.   Thys Crysten me*r*chante co*n*sentyd, *th*e sothe' to
        sey,
    And in *th*e nyght affte*r* made hym delyue*r*ance.[9]
Thes Jewes all grete joye made they,
    But off thys betyde a stranger chanc*e* :   36

They grevid our Lord gretly on grownd,
    And put hym to a new*e* [10] passyon ;

---

    [1] MS. hyn; *corr. by* S.   [2] S. *supplies* [ys].
    [3] S. *supplies* [he], *but the final* -e *of* wyche *contains* he. *In* MS. *at the
beginning of this line the first four words of the next line were written by
mistake and then crossed out.*
    [4] MS. freynend; *corr. by* S.
    [5] MS. xxti li; S. xxti pownd.
    [6] MS. An c li; S. An c pownd.
    [7] S. gune; MS. gune.
    [8] MS. woldr; S. *composed a new line:* And all on the sauyowr of the
world to be wreke; *the corrections above are by* H.
    [9] MS.; S. deliue*r*ance.
    [10] *The word in* MS. *is said to look like* nell*e*, *but cf.* 723.

W*ith* daggers gouen hym many a greuyos wou*n*d ;
 Nayled hym to a pyller ; w*ith* pynsons plukked hym
  dou*n*e.   40

SECUNDUS. And sythe thay toke *tha*t blysed Brede so
  sow*n*de
And in a cawdron they ded hym boyle,[1]
In a clothe full just they yt wou*n*de,
 And so they ded hym sethe in oyle ;   44

And than thay putt hym to a new to*r*mentry,
 In an hoote ouyn[2] speryd hym fast.
There he appyred w*ith* wou*n*d*is* blody ;
 The ovyn refe a-sondre & all tobrast.
  PRIMUS. Thus in ou*e*r lawe they wer made stedfast ;
The holy Sacreme*n*t sheuyd them grette faueur ;
 In contrycyon th[e]yr hertis wer cast,
And went & shewyd ther lyues to a co*n*fesour. 52

Thus be maracle off *th*e Kyng of hevyn
 And by myght & power govyn to *th*e p*r*est*is* mowthe
In an howshold wer con[v]*er*tyd[3] i-wys elevyn.[4]
 At Rome *thi*s[5] myracle ys knowen well kowthe.
  SECUNDUS. Thys marycle at Rome was p*r*esented, for
  sothe,
Yn the yere of ou*e*r[6] Lord a M¹cccclxi[7]
 That *th*e Jewes *tha*t[8] holy Sacrament dyd w*ith*[9]
In the forest seyd of Aragon.   60

Be-low thus God at a tyme showyd hym there,
 Thorwhe hys m*er*cy & hys mekyll myght ;
Vnto the Jewes he gan[10] appere
 That *th*ei shuld nat lesse hys hevenly lyght.

---

[1] MS. boylde; *corr. by* S.
[2] MS. hoote ob ouyn; *corr. by* S.
[3] *Corr. by* S.
[4] S. I wyll wys xi.
[5] MS. *apparently* yˢ yˢ ; *corr. by* S.
[6] S. you*r*.
[7] S. M¹cccc.c.lxi.
[8] S. wᵗ.
[9] H. *suggested the addition of* nothe ; *but later* 627 *made him doubtful.*
[10] MS. gayn ; S. [did a-]gayn.

PRIMUS.   So therfor, frend*is*, w*ith* all your myght
Vnto youer gostly father shewe your synne ;
    Beth in no wanhope daye nor nyght.
No man*er* off dowght*is* *tha*t Lord put in ;   68

ffor *tha*t *th*e dowgtht*is* *th*e Jewys than in stode, —
    As ye shall se pleyd, both more & lesse, —
Was yff *th*e Sacrament wer flesshe & blode ;
    Therfor they put yt to suche dystresse.
    SECUNDUS.   And yt place yow, thys gaderyng *tha*t
        here ys,
At Croxston on Monday yt shall be sen ;
    To see [1] the conclusyon of *th*is lytell p*ro*cesse
Hertely welcu*m* shall yow bene.   76

Now Jh*e*su yow sawe from [2] trey [3] & tene,
    To [4] send vs hys hyh*e* ioyes of hevyne,
There myght ys w*ith*outon mynd [5] to mene !
    Now, mynstrell, blow vp w*ith* a mery stevyn !   80

           Explicit.

Here aft*er* foloweth *th*e Play of *th*e Conversyon of S*er* Jonathas *th*e Jewe by Myracle of *th*e Blyssed Sac*ra*ment.

ARISTORIUS MERCATOR.[6]   Now Cryst, *tha*t ys ou*er* Creatour,
        from shame he cure vs ;
    He [7] maynteyn vs w*ith* myrth *tha*t meve vpon *th*e mold ;
Vnto hys endlesse joye myghtly he restore vs,
    All tho *tha*t in hys [8] name in peas well them hold ;

---

[1] H. *wishes to read* say.
[2] MS. fron; *corr. by* S.
[3] S. treyn; *corr. by* H.
[4] *Qy.* And.
[5] *Qy.* end, *or* mynn.
[6] *A list of* dramatis personae *is given at the end of the play,* p. 276.
[7] MS. be; *corr. by* S.
[8] S. thys.

For of a merchante most myght therof my tale ys told,
In Eraclea ys no*n* suche, woso[1] wyll vnder-stond,
    For off all Aragon I am most myghty of sylu*er* & of
      gold, —
ffor, & yt wer a cou*n*tre to by, now wold I nat wond.   8

Syr Arystory is my name,
    A m*er*chante myghty of a roy*a*ll araye ;
fful wyde in *th*is worlde spryngyth my fame,
    Fer*e* kend & knowen, *th*e sothe for to saye.
    In all man*er* of lond*is*, wi*th*out ony naye,
My m*er*chandyse renneth, *th*e sothe for to tell ;
    In Gene & in Jenyse & in Genewaye,
In Surrey[2] & in Saby & in Saleru*n* I sell ;   16

In Antyoche & in Almayn moch ys my myght,
    In Braban & in Brytayn I am full bold,
In Calabre & in Coleyn *ther* rynge[3] I full ryght,
    In Dordrede & in De*n*mark [I] be *th*e chyffe cold,[4]
    In Alysander I haue abu*n*daw[n]se[5] in the wyde world,
In France & in Farre fresshe be my flower[is],[5]
    In Gyldre & in Galys haue I bowght & sold,
In Hamborowh*e* & in Holond moch*e* m*er*chantdyse ys owr*is* ;   24

In Jerusalem & in Jherico a-mo*n*g the Jewes jentle,
    Amo[n]g[5] tho Caldeys & Cattlyng*is* kend ys my komyng ;
In Raynes[6] & in Rome to Seynt Petyrs temple
    I am knowen certenly for bying & sellyng ;   28

In Mayn & in Melan full mery haue I be ;
    Owt of Naveru*n* to Naples moch good ys *tha*t I bryng ;
In Pondere & in Portyngale moche ys my gle ;
    In Spayne & in Spruce moche ys my spedyng ;
    In Lombardy & in Lachborn, there ledde ys my lykyng ;

---

[1] S. w[h]oso.   [2] MS. surgery; S. surry.   [3] S. *suggests* reygne.
[4] H. *reads* I haue be the chyffe told; told *is probably right.*
[5] S.   [6] H. *reads* Raymes.

In Taryfe & in Turkey, there told ys my tale ;
　　And in *th*e dukedo*m* of Oryon moche have I in weldyng :
And thus thorowght all *th*is world sett ys my sale.　　　　36

No ma*n* in thys world may weld more rychesse;
　　All I thank God of hys grace, for he yt [1] me sent ;
And as a lord*is* pere thus lyve I in worthynesse.
　　My curat waytheth [2] vpon me to knowe myn intent,
　　And me*n* at my weldyng, & all ys me lent
My well for to worke in thys worlde so wyde.[3]
　　Me dare they nat dysplese by no condescent,[4]
And who-so doth, he ys nat able to a-byde.　　　　44

PRESBYTER.　No ma*n* shall you tary ne t[r]owble [5] thys tyde,
　　But eve*r*y ma*n* delygently shall do yow plesance ;
And I vnto my connyng to *th*e best shall hem guyde
　　Vnto [6] God*is* plesyng to se*r*ue yow to utterance ; [7]
ffor ye be worthy & notable in substance of good,
　　Off me*r*chant*is* of Aragon ye have no pere, —
And ther-of thank God *tha*t dyed on *th*e roode,
　　That was your maker*e* & hath yow dere.　　　　52

ARISTORIUS.　For soth, syr pryst, yower talkyng ys good ;
　　And therfor affter your talkyng I wyll atteyn
To wourshyppe my God that dyed on *th*e roode,
　　Neue*r* [8] whyll *tha*t I lyve ageyn *tha*t wyll I seyn.
　　But, Petyr Powle, my clark, I praye the goo wele pleyn
Thorowght all Eraclea,[9] that thow ne wonde,[9]
　　And wytte yff ony me*r*chante be come to *th*is reyn
Of Surrey or of Sabe or of Shelys-down.　　　　60

CLERICUS.　At youe*r* wyll for to walke I wyl nat say nay,
　　Smertly to go serche at *th*e water*is* syde ;

---

　　　1 S. y^t.　　　　　　　　　4 MS. condestent; *corr. by* S.
　　　2 H. *corrects to* wayteth.　　5 S.
　　　3 *In* S. *misprinted* wydc.　　6 *Qy.* Vnder.
　　　7 S. attruēance; H. *proposes* accrueance.
　　　8 MS.; S. Ever, *but, as* H. *points out,* Neuer *is right.*
　　9-9 H. *proposes* both vp and down, *cf.* l. 66.

Yff ony pleasant bargyn be to your paye,
 As swyftly as I ca*n* I shall hym to yow guyde.
 Now wyll I walke by thes pathes wyde,
And seke the haven both vp and down
 To wette yf ony unkowth [1] shyppes therin do ryde,
Of Surrey or of Saby [or] [2] of Shelys-down.   68

  Now shall the mer*chantis man with-drawe hym and* the *Jewe Jonathas shall*
  make hys lest. [3]

JONATHAS. Now, almighty Machomet, marke [4] in *th*i mageste,
 Whose [5] lawes tendrely I have to fulfyll,
After my dethe bryng me to thy hyh*e* see,
 My sowle for to save yff yt be thy wyll ;
 For myn entent ys for to fulfyll
As my gloryus God the to honer. [6]
 To do agen thy entent, yt shuld gr[e]ue me yll
Or agen thyn lawe for to reporte ;   76

For I tha*n*ke the hayly *tha*t hast me sent
 Gold, [7] sylu*er* & *pre*syous stonys,
And abu*n*ddance of spyc*is tho*u hast me lent,
 A[s] [2] I shall reherse before yow onys :
 I have amatyst*is* ryche for *th*e nonys
And baryll*is* that be bryght of ble,
 And saphyre semely I may show yow attonys
And crystalys clere for to se ;   84

I have dyamant*is* dere-wourthy to [8] dresse,
 And emerawd*is*, ryche I trow they be,
Onyx and achat*is* [9] both more & lesse,
 Topa3yons, smaragd*is* of grete degre,
 Perlys precyous grete plente ;

---

[1] MS. on knowth ; *corr. by* S.   [2] S.
[3] H. *reads* best; *I can suggest nothing better than* bost (= boast).
[4] *Qy.* moste.   [5] S. whoses ; *see Notes.*
[6] H. *points out that* honer *does not rhyme with* reporte ; *possibly* beste
should be added after honer, *and* resiste *substituted for* reporte ; *for rhyme,*
cf. l. 142.   [7] S. *prints* godd, *but emends to* gold *in his Glossary.*
[8] MS. *appears to have* do *before* to.   [9] MS. Machat*is ; corr. by* S.

Of rubes ryche I have grete renown ;
 Crepawd*is* & calcedonyes semely to se,
A[nd] [1] curyous carbu*n*clys here ye fynd mown ;   92

Spyc*is* I hawe both grete & smale
 In my shyppes, the sothe for to saye,
Gyngere, lycoresse and ca*n*nyngalle,
 And fyg*is* fatte to plese yow to paye,
Peper and saffyro*n* & spyc*is* smale,
 And dat*is* wole dulcett for to dresse,
Almu*n*dis and reys, full eu*er*y male,
 And reysones both more & lesse ;   100

Clowys, greynis [2] & gynger grene,
 Mace, mastyk that myght ys,
Synymone, suger, as yow may [3] sene,
 Long [4] peper and Indas lycorys,
 Oreng*is* a[nd] [1] apples of grete apryce,
Pungarnet*is* [5] & many other spyc*is* —
 To tell yow all I have now, i-wys,[6] —
And moche other m*er*chandyse of e[v]*er*y [1] sondry spycis. 108

Jew Jonathas thys ys my name,[7]
 Jazon & Jazdon *th*ei waytyn on my wyll*e*,
Masfat & Malchus they do the same,
 As ye may knowe, yt ys bothe rycht & skyll*e*.
 I telle yow all*e*, bi dal and by hyll*e*,
In Eraclea ys noon so moche of myght.
 Werfor ye owe tenderli to tende me tyll*e*,
For I a*m* chefe m*er*chant*e* of Jewes, I telle yow be ryght. 116

But, Jazon & Jazdon, a mater wolld*e* [8] I mene, —
 Mer-velously [9] yt ys ment in mynde, —

   [1] S.   [4] S. leng.
   [2] MS. grenyis; *corr. by* S. [5] MS.; S. pumgarnet*is*.
   [3] S. may*n*.   [6] S. I wyse.
   [7] MS. Jew Jonathas ys my ys name; *corr. by* S.
   [8] MS. wolld*is*; *corr. by* S.
   [9] H.; S. *retains reading of* MS., mer velensly.

*Th*e beleve of thes *Cryst*en me*n* ys false, as I wene,
 For *th*e[i] beleve on a cake, — me thynk yt ys onkynd, —
 And all*e* they seye how *th*e prest dothe yt bynd,
And be *th*e myght of hys word make yt[1] flessh & blode, —
 And thus be a conceyte *th*e[i][2] wolde make vs blynd, —
And how *tha*t yt shuld be he *tha*t deyed upon *th*e rode. **124**

JASON. Yea, yea, master, a strawe for talis !
 That ma not falle[3] in my beleve ;
But myt[4] we yt gete onys w*ith*in our pales,
 I trowe we shuld sone aff*ter* putt yt in a preve.[5]
  JASDON. Now, be Machomete so myghty, *tha*t ye doon of[6] meue
I wold I wyste how *tha*t we myght yt gete ;
 I swer[7] be my grete god, & ellys mote I nat cheue
But wyghtly the[r]on[2] wold I be wreke. **132**

MASPHAT. Yea, I dare sey feythfulli *tha*t ther feyth [ys fals :][8]
 That was neu*er* he that on Caluery was kyld,
Or *in* bred for to be blode yt ys ontrewe als ;[9]
 But yet w*ith* ther wyles *th*ei wold we were wyld.
  MALCUS. Yea, I am myghty Malchus, *tha*t boldly am byld ;
That brede for to bete byggly am I bent.
 Onys out of ther hand*is* & yt myght be exyled,
To helpe castyn yt in care wold I consent. **140**

JO*N*AT[H]AS.[2] Well, syrse, than kype cu*n*sel, I cu*m*mande yow all,
 And no word of all thys be wyst.
But let us walke to see Arystories hall*e*,

  1 S. y^e.   4 H. *corrects the spelling to* myght.
  2 S.   5 S.; MS. praye. 7 S. seuer. 9 S. als[o].
  3 H.; S. manot sale. 6 S. of[t]. 8 S. [ys so].

And affter-ward more cou*n*sell*e* amo*n*g vs shall [1] caste.
W*it*h hym to bey & to sel I am of powere prest ;
A bargyn w*it*h hym to make I wyll assaye ;
    ffor gold & syluer I am nothyng agast
But *tha*t we shall get *tha*t cake to ower paye.   148

*Her shall s*er *Ysodyr, the prest, speke w*it*h [2] s*er *Arystori, seyng on thys
wyse to hym ; & Jonathas goo don [3] of his stage.*

PRESBITER.   Syr, be your leue, I may [no] [4] le*n*gere dwell ;
    Yt ys fer paste none, yt ys tyme to go to cherche,
There to saye myn evy*n*song, forsothe as I yow tell,
    And syth come [5] home ageyne, as I a*m* wont to werche. 152

ARISTORIUS.   Sir Isydor, I praye yow, walke at yowr wyll*e*,
    ffor to serfe God yt ys well done ;
And syt[h] [6] com*e* agen & ye shall suppe your fyll*e*,
And walke tha*n* to your [7] cha*m*ber, as ye ar wont to doon. 156

*Her shall the m*ar*chan*ti*s man [8] mete w*it*h the Jewes.*

JONAT[H]AS. [6]   A ! Petr*e* Powle, good daye & wele i-mett ! [9]
    Wer ys thy [10] master, as I the pray ?
CLERICUS.   Lon[g] [6] from hym haue I not lett
    Syt[h] [6] I cam fro*m* hym, *th*e sothe for to saye.
Wat tidyng w*it*h yow, s*er*, I yow praye,
Afft*er* my master *tha*t ye doo fraye*n* ?
    Haue ye ony bargen *tha*t wer to hys paye ?
Let me haue knowlech ; I shall wete hym to seyn.   164

JHONATHAS.   I haue bargenes royall*e* & ry[c]h [6]
    ffor a marchant*e* w*it*h to bye and sell ;
In all thys lond is ther non lyke
    Off abu*n*danc*e* of good, as I will tell.   168

[1] S. *inserts* [be].	[6] S.
[2] S. out.	[7] S. yōr.
[3] H. *corrects the spelling to* down.	[8] MS. marchant men ; *corr. by* S.
[4] S. [nat].	[9] MS. I mett ; S. imett.
[5] MS. coñe ; *corr. by* S.	[10] S. they.

Her shall the *clerk goon to* se*r Aristori, saluting him thus :*

CLERICUS. All hayll, master, & wel mot yow be ! [1]
  Now tydyng*e* can I yow tell :
*Th*e grettest marchant*e* i*n* all Surre
  Ys come w*ith* yow to bey & sell,
    This tale ryght well he me told.[2]
  Sir Jonat[h]as [3] ys hys nam,
  A marchant of ryght gret fame ;
  He wolld*e* sell yow, w*ith*-out blame,
    P[l]ente [3] of clothe of golde.   **177**

ARISTORIUS. Petre Powle, I can *th*e thanke !
  I prey *th*e rychely araye myn hall*e*
As owyth for a marchant of *th*e banke ;
  Lete non defawte be fownd at all*e*.
    CLERICUS. Sekyrly, mast*er*, no m[o]re [3] ther shall.
Styffly about I thynke to stere,
  Hasteli [4] to hange yo*ur* p*ar*lowr w*ith* pall,
As longeth for a lordis pere.   **185**

Here shall the *Jewe* me*r*chant*e &º his* me*n* come to the *Crist*e*n* me*r*chante.

JONATHAS. All haylle, syr Aristorye, semele to se,
  The myghtyest me*r*chante off Arigon !
Off yower welfare fayn wet wold we,
  And to bargeyn w*ith* you *th*is day am [5] I bou*n*.   **189**

ARISTORIUS. Sir Jonathas, ye be well*e*cu*m* vnto myn hall*e* !
  I pray yow come vp & sit bi me,
And tell*e* me wat good ye haue to sell*e*,
  And yf ony bargeyn [6] mad may be.   **193**

JONATHAS. I haue clothe of gold, p*r*ecyous stons & spyc*e*
            plente.
  Wyth yow a bargen wold I make ; —

---

[1] S. *for* MS. yowbe.
[2] MS. this t l [?] ryght nell heme tell; *corr. by* S. *Perhaps the fourth
word should be* now; *cf.* p. 240, l. 38.   [4] H.; S. hasterli.
[3] S.   [5] S.; MS. an.
[6] S. bargeny ; bargen ymade *seems unlikely.*

I wold bartre wyth yow in pryvyte
　　On lytelle thyng,[1] ye wylle me yt take
　　　Prevely in this stownd
　　And I wolle sure yow be thys lyght,
　　Neuer dystrie yow daye nor nyght,
　　But be sworn to yow full ryght
　　　And geve yow twenti pownde.[2]　　　　　202

ARISTORIUS.　Sir Jonathas, sey me for my sake,
　　What maner of marchandis ys yt[3] ye mene?
JONATHAS.　Yowr God, that ys full mytheti, in a cake,
　　And thys good anoon shall yow seen.
　　[ARISTORIUS.][4]　Nay, in feyth, that shall not bene.
I wollnot for an hundder[5] pownd
　　To stond in fere my Lord to tene
And for so lytelle a walew in conscyence[6] to stond bownd.　210

JONATHAS.　Sir, the entent ys if I myght knowe or vnder-
　　　　take
　　Yf that he were God alle-myght ;
Off all my mys I woll amende make
　　And doon hym wourshepe bothe day & nyght.　　214

ARISTORIUS.　Jonathas, trowth I shall the tell :
　　I stond in gret dowght to do that dede,
To yow that bere all[7] for to sell
　　I fere me that I shuld stond in drede ;
　　ffor, & I vnto the chyrche yede,
And preste or clerke myght me aspye,
　　To the bysshope thei wolde go telle that dede
And apeche me of eresye.[8]　　　　　　　　222

JONATHAS.　Sir, as for that, good shyffte may ye make,
　　And, for a vaylle, to walkyn on a nyght

---

[1] H. inserts yf.
[2] MS. xx^{ti} li.; S. xx^{ti} pownd.
[3] S. yt.
[4] S.
[5] H. reads hunderd.
[6] S.; MS. constyene.
[7] Qy. bereall = beryl.
[8] S. tresyē; H. apostasye, but cf. l. 777.

Wan prest & clerk to rest ben take ;
>Than shall ye be spyde of no wyght.
>>ARISTORIUS.   Now sey me, Jonathas, be this lyght !
Wat payment *the*rfor wollde yow me make ?
>>JONATHAS.   Forty pownd,[1] & pay yt fulryght,
Evyn for *tha*t Lorde[2] sake.   230

>>ARISTORIUS.   Nay, nay, Jonathas, there-agen ;
>I w[o]ld[3] not for an hunder[4] pownd.
>>JONATHAS.   Sir, hir ys [yo]wer[3] askyng toolde pleyn,
>I shall yt tell in this stownd.   234

>>>*[Counts out the money.]*

Here is an hunder pownd,[5] neyther mor nor lesse,
>Of dokett*is* good, I dar well saye ;
Tell yt er yow from me passe.
>>Me thynketh yt a royall*e* araye !   238

But fyrst, I pray yow, tell me thys :
>Off thys thyng whan shall*e* I hafe delyu*er*ance ?
>>ARISTORI.   To-morowe be-tymes ; I shallnot myse ;
>>This nyght therfor I shall*e* make p*ur*veance.   242

Syr Isodyr he ys now at chyrch,
>There seyng hys evynsong,
As yt ys[6] worshepe for to werche ;
>He shall sone cu*m* home, he wyll nat be long,
>>Hys soper for to eate ;
>And when*e* he ys buskyd to hys bedde,
Ryght sone [t]here-after he[7] shalbe spedd. —
No speche among yow ther be spredd ;
>>To kepe yo*ur* toung*is* ye nott lett.   251

>>JONATHAS.   Syr, almyghty Machomyght be *with* yow !
>And I shall*e* cum agayn ryght sone.

---

1 MS. xl li.; S. xl pownd.   4 S. has C.
2 H. *reads* lordes.   5 MS. has C. li.; S. has C. pownd.
3 S.   6 S. As yt hys; H. As yt [ys] hys.   7 H. ye.

ARYSTORIUS.   Jonathas, ye wott what I haue sayd, & how
    I shall*e* warke [1] for that we haue to donn.   255

Here goeth the *Jewys away &* the *preste com*myth *home.*

PRESBITER.   Syr, almyghty God mott be yow*er* gyde
    And glad yow where-soo ye rest !
ARISTORIUS.   Syr, ye be welcom home thys tyde !
    Now, Peter, gett vs wyne of the best.   259

CLERICUS.   Syr, here ys a drawte of Romney Red,
    Ther ys no better in Aragon,
And a lofe of lyght bred, —
    Yt ys holesom, as sayeth *th*e fesycyon.   263

ARYSTORIUS.   Drynke of,[2] s*er* Isoder, & be of good chere !
    Thys Romney ys good to goo w*ith* to reste ;
Ther ys no precyouser fer nor nere,
    For all*e* wykkyd metys yt wyll*e* degest.   267

PRESBITER.   Syr, thys wyne ys good at a taste,
    And ther-of haue I drunke ryght well*e*.
To bed to gone thus haue I cast
    Euyn strayt after thys mery mele.   271

Now, s*er*, I pray to God send yow good nyght,[3]
    ffor to my chamber now wyll*e* I gonne.
ARISTORIUS.   S*er*, w*ith* yow be God almyght,[4]
    And sheld yow euer from yowr fone !   275

[*Exit the priest.*]   *Here shall Aristorius call hys clarke to hys* presens.

Howe, Peter ! In the ys all my trust,
    In especyall*e* to kepe my consell*e* :

[1] S. walke.
[2] H. *reads* therof, *as in* 269; *but* of *is* off.
[3] S. rest; *emend. by* H.
[4] S. *reads* almyght[est], *and says:* " *The scribe had added a* y *and ex-punged it imperfectly.*" *This seems to justify* H. *in retaining the* MS. *reading.*

ffor a lytylle waye walkyn I must.
  I wylle not be long ; trust as I the telle.   279

[He goes toward the church.]

Now *pr*euely wylle I *per*sew my pace,
  My bargayn thys nyght for to fulfylle.
S*er* Isoder shalle nott know of thys case,
  For he hath oftyn sacred, as yt ys skylle.
  The chyrche key ys at my wylle ;
Ther ys no-thyng*e that* me shalle tary,
  I wylle nott abyde by dale nor hylle
Tylle yt be wrowght, by Saynt Mary !   287

Here shal he enter the *chyrche &* take th*e Hoost.*

Ah ! now haue I alle my*n* entent ;
  Vnto Jonathas now wylle I fare ;
To fulle*fy*lle my bargayn haue I ment,
  For *tha*t mony wylle amend my fare,
   As thynketh me.

[Exit from church.]

But now wylle I passe by thes pathes playne ;
To mete w*ith* Jonathas I wold fayne.
Ah ! yonder he com*m*yth in certayne ;
  Me thynkyth I hym see !   296

Welcom, Jonathas, gentylle & trew,
  ffor welle & tr[e]wly [1] *tho*u kepyst thyn howre ;
Here ys *th*e Host, sacred newe.
  Now wylle I home to halle & bowre.   300

JONATHAS. And I shall kepe thys trusty treasure
  As I wold doo my gold and fee.
Now in thys clothe I shalle the couer,
  That no wyght shalle the see.   304

[1] S.

Here shall Arystory goo hys waye & Jonathas & hys seruauntis shall goo
to the tabyll thus sayng:

JONATHAS. Now, Jason & Jasdon, ye [1] be Jewys jentyll*e*,
   Masfat & Malchus, that myghty arn in mynd,
Thys m*e*rchant from the Crysten temple
   Hath*e* gett vs thys bred that [2] make vs thus blynd.
   Now, Jason, as jentyll*e* as eu*e*r was the lynde,
Into the forsayd p*a*rlowr pr*e*uely take thy pase ;
   Sprede a clothe on the tabyll *that* ye shall*e* *th*ere fynd,
And we shall*e* folow after to carpe of thys case.   312

*Now the Jewys goo*n *& lay the Ost on the tabyll, sayng:*

JONATHAS. Syr*is*, I praye yow all*e*, harkyn to my sawe !
   Thes Crysten men carpyn of a m*e*rvelows [3] case ;
They say *that th*is ys Ih*e*su *tha*t was attaynted in ow*e*r lawe
   *And tha*t thys ys he *tha*t crwcyfyed was.   316

On thes wordys ther*e* law growndyd hath he
   That he sayd on Sherethursday at hys soper :
He brake the brede & sayd *Accipite*,
   And gave hys dyscyplys them for to chere ;
   And mor*e* he sayd to them there,
Whyle they were all*e* together & sum,
   Syttyng at the table soo clere,
Comedite, [*hoc est*] *corpus meum*.   324

And thys powre he gaue Pet*e*r to pr*o*clame,
   And how the same shuld be suffycyent to all*e* pr*e*chors ;
The bysshoppys & curat*is* saye the same,
   And soo, as I vnderstond, do all*e* hys pr*o*genytors.   328

JASON. Yea, su*m* men in *tha*t law reherse a-nother :
   They say of a maydyn borne was hee,
And how Joachyms dowght*e*r shuld be hys mother,
   And how Gabrell*e* apperyd & sayd *Aue* ;

----

[1] *Qy.* y^t.   [2] S. *inserts* wold.   [3] MS.; S. m*e*rvelous.

And wi*th tha*t worde she [1] shuld conceyuyd be,
*And tha*t in hyr shuld lyght the Holy Gost, —
Ageyns ow*e*r law thys ys false heresy, —
A nd yett they saye he ys of mygh*tis* most.   336

JASDON.   They saye *tha*t Ih*e*su to be ow*e*r kyng*e*,
      But I wene he bowght yt [2] full*e* dere.
But they make a royall*e* aray of hys vprysy*n*g ;
      And that in eu*e*ry place ys p*re*chyd farre & nere,
      And how he to hys dyscyples agayn dyd appere,
To Thomas and to Mary Mawdelen,
      And syth how he styed by hys own powr*e* ; [8]
And thys, ye know well, ys heresy full*e* playn.   344

MASPHAT.   Yea, & also they say he sent them wytt & wys-
         dom
      ffor to vnderstond eu*e*ry langwage ;
When *th*e Holy Gost to them came, [4]
      They faryd as dronk men of pyment*e* or v*e*rnage ;
      And sythen how *tha*t he lykenyd hym-self a lord of
         p*a*rage,
On hys fatherys ryght hond he hym sett.
      They hold hym wyser *th*an eu*e*r was Syble sage,
And strenger than Alexander, *tha*t all*e th*e worde [5] ded
         gett.   352

MALCHUS.   Yea, yet they say as fals, I dare laye my hedde,
      How they that be ded shall com agayn to Judgement,
And ow*e*r dredfull*e* Judge shalbe thys same brede,
      And how lyfe eu*er*lastyng them shuld be lent.
      And thus they hold, all at on*e* [6] consent,
Be-cause that Phylyppe sayd for a lytyll*e* glosse —
      To turne vs from owr beleve ys ther entent, —
ffor that he sayd *judecare viuos & mortuos.*   360

---

1 H. *wishes to read* he.   4 *So* MS.; S. [dyd] come.
2 S. y^t.   5 S. wor[l]de ; *but* worde *is a common spelling.*
8 H. *corrects the spelling to* power.   6 MS.; S. on.

JONATHAS.   Now, ser*is*, ye haue rehersyd the substance of
    ther [1] lawe.
    But thys bred I wold myght be put in a p*re*fe
Whether *th*is be he that in Bosra of vs had awe.
    Ther staynyd were hys clothys, *th*is may we belefe ;
    Thys may we know, ther*e* had he grefe,
For ow*e*r old bookys veryfy thus, —
    Thereon he was jugett to be hangyd as a thefe, —
Tinctis [2] [*de*] *Bosra vestibus.*   368

JASON.   Yff *tha*t thys be he that on Caluery was mad red,
    Onto my mynd, I shall*e* kenne yow a conceyt good :
Surely w*ith* ow*e*r daggars we shall*e* ses on [3] thys bredde,
    And so w*ith* clowt*is* we shall know yf [4] he haue eny
        blood.
    JASDON.   Now, by Machomyth so myghty, *tha*t meuyth
        in my mode !
Thys ys mast*e*rly ment, thys matter thus to meue ;
    And w*ith* ow*e*r strokys we shall*e* fray hym as he was on
        the rode,
That he was on don w*ith* grett repreue.   376

MASPHAT.   Yea, I pray yow, smyte ye in the myddys of
    *th*e cake,
    And so shall*e* we smyte *ther*on woundys fyve ;
We wyll*e* not spare to wyrke yt wrake
    To prove in thys brede yf *ther* be eny lyfe.   380

MALCHUS.   Yea, goo we to, than, & take ow*e*r [5] space,
    And looke owr daggar*is* be sharpe & kene ;
And when eche man a stroke smytte hase,
    In *th*e mydyll*e* p*ar*t ther*e*-of ow*e*r master shall*e* bene.
    JONATHAS.   When ye haue all*e* smytyn, my stroke
        shalbe sene ;

---

[1] MS. o[r] ; *corr. by* S.   [4] MS. ys. ; *corr. by* S.
[2] S. Tinctio ; *corr. by* H.   [5] MS. yow[r] ; *emend. by* S.
[3] S. seson ; *cf.* 390.

W*ith th*is same dagger that ys so styf & strong
   In *th*e myddys of thys prynt I thynke for to prene ;
On lashe I shall*e* hym*e* lende or yt be long.   388

*Here shall*e the *iiij Jewys pryk* ther *dagger*is *in iiij* qua[r]*ters,*[1] thus *sayng:*

JASON.   Haue at yt ! Haue at yt, w*ith* all*e* my myght !
   Thys syde I hope for to sese !
JASDON.   *And* I shall w*ith* thys blade so bryght
   Thys other syde freshely a-feze !
   MASPHAT.   *And* I yow plyght I shall*e* hym not please,
For w*ith* thys punche I shall*e* hym pryke.
   MALCHUS.   *And* w*ith* thys angus [2] I shall*e* hym not ease,
A-nother buffett shall*e* he lykke.   396

JONATHAS.   Now am I bold w*ith* batayle hym to bleyke,
   *Thi*s mydle part all*e* for to prene ;
A stowte stroke also for to stryke, —
   In *th*e myddys yt shalbe sene !   400

Here the Ost *must blede.*

Ah ! owt ! owt ! harrow ! what deuyll*e* ys thys ?
   Of thys wyrk I am in were ;
Yt bledyth as yt were woode, i-wys ;
   But yf ye helpe, I shall dyspayre.   404

JASON.   A fyre ! a fyre ! & that in hast !
   Anoon a cawdron full*e* of oyle !
JASDON.   And I shalle helpe yt wer in cast,
   All *th*e iij howr*is* fo[r] [1] to boyle !   408

[*Malchus goes to get the oil.*]

MASPHAT.   Yea, [3] here is a furneys stowte & strong,
And a cawdron therin dothe hong !
Malcus, wher art thow so long,
   To helpe thys dede were dyght ?

[1] S.

[2] Kittredge *suggests* dagger ; H. anguish.

[3] *An attempt seems to have been made to cancel the* a *of* yea *in* MS.

MALCUS.   Loo, here ys iiij galons off oyle clere !
Haue doon*e* [1] fast ! blowe up *th*e fere !
Syr, bryng that ylke cake nere,
     Ma*n*ly, w*ith* all yowre mygthe.   416

JONATHAS.   And I shall bryng *tha*t ylke cak[e] [2]
And throw yt in, I undertake.
Out ! out ! yt werketh me wrake !
     I may not awoyd yt owt of my hond !
I wylle goo drenche me i*n* a lake, —
And i*n* woodnesse I gynne to wake ! [3]
     I rene, I lepe, ou*er th*is lond !   423

          *Her he renneth wood, wi*t*h the Ost in hys hond.*

JASON.   Renne, felawes, renne, [4] for Cokk*is* peyn !
Fast [5] we had ow*er* mayst*er* agene !

              [*They catch Jonathas.*]

Hold p*re*stly [6] on thys pleyn [7]
     A nd faste bynd hyme to a poste.
JASDON.   Here is an hamer & naylys iij, I s[e]ye. [2]
Lyffte vp hys armys, felawe[s], on hey,
Whyll*e* I dryue *th*es nayles, I yow praye,
     W*ith* strong strok*is* fast.   431 [8]

MASPHAT. [9]   Now set on, felouse, w*ith* mayne & myght,
And pluke hys armes awey in hyght ! [10]
Wat ! I se [11] he twycche, felovse, a-ryght !
     Alas, balys breweth ryght badde !

---

[1] MS. ; S. doon.   [2] S.   [3] H. *proposes* rake.
[4] MS. reme ; *corr. by* S.   [5] H. *inserts* that.
[6] S. p*re*stly [?], *but* MS. *is fairly clear.*
[7] S. feleyn [?] ; MS. *has* pleyn *with an elaborate curl and stroke over*
n ; H. *proposes* sely sweyn.
[8] *The line numbering in* S. *is wrong from here on ; six lines are twice
numbered as five.*
[9] MS. Malspas ; *corr. by* S.   [10] S. fyght ; *possibly* sight *was intended.*
[11] S. *reads* yse, *and suggests* yfe.

Here shalle thay pluke the *arme, & the hand shalle fang*[1] *stylle with the Sacrament.*

MALCHUS.[2]   Alas, alas, what deuyll ys thys?
Now hat[h][3] he but oon hand, i-wyse !
ffor sothe, mayst*er*, ryght woo me is
    *Tha*t ye *th*is harme hawe hadde.   439

JONATHAS.   Ther ys no more ; I must enduer !
    Now hastely to ow*er* cha*m*ber lete us go[n],
Tyll*e* I may get me su*m* recuer ;
    And ther-for [I] charge yow euery-choon
    That yt be consell*e* that we haue doon.   444

[They go out.]
*Here shall*e the *lechys ma*n *come into* the *place sayng :*

COLLE.   Aha ! here ys a fayer felawshyppe,
Thewh*e* I be nat shapyn,[4] [yn] I lyst to sleppe.
I haue a mast*er* I wolld he had *th*e pyppe,
    I tell yow i*n* consel.
He ys a ma*n* off all*e* syence,
But off thryfte — I may w*ith* yow dyspe*n*ce !
He syttyth[5] w*ith* su*m* tapstere in *th*e spence ;
    Hys hoode there wyll he sell*e*.   452

Mayster Brendyche of Braban,
I tell*e* yow he ys *tha*t same ma*n*,
Called *th*e most famous phesy[cy]an[3]
    *Tha*t eu*er* sawe vryne.
He seeth as wele at noone as at nyght,
And su*m*tyme by a candelleyt
Can gyff a judgyment[6] aryght
    As he *tha*t hathe noon[7] eyn.   460.

---

[1] MS. sang ; *emend. by* S. ; *his proposal of* hang (*in Glossary*) *can derive no support from* " a-fingred *for* ahungered."
[2] *Wanting in* MS. ; S. *gives* [Malchas].   [3] S.
[4] S. Sh[ ]pyn ; *the reading adopted was suggested by* Dr. F. N. Robinson.
[5] MS. sytthyt ; *corr. by* S.
[6] MS. Judyyment ; *corr. by* S.
[7] MS. nood, *which* S. *thinks may mean* use [of].

He ys all-so a boone-setter, —
I knowe no man go *th*e better ;
In euery tau*er*ne he ys detter,
 Yt ys a good tokenyng.
But eu*er* I wonder he ys so long ;
I fere ther gooth sum-thyng a-wrong,
For he hath dysa[rv]yde[1] to be hong, —
 God se*n*d neu*er* warse tydyng !   468

He had a lady late in cure ;
I wot be *th*is she ys full sure ;
There shall*e* neuer *Cryst*en creatur*e*
 Here hyr tell no tale.
And I stode here tyll*e* mydnyght,
I cowde not declare a-ryght
My masteris cu*n*yng in-syght
 *Tha*t he hat[h][2] in good ale.   476

But[3] what deuyll ayleth[4] hym so long to tare?
A seekma*n* myght soone myscary.
Now all*e* *th*e deuyllys of hell hym wari ! —
 God g[ra]nte[2] me my boon !
I trowe best, we mak a crye :
Yf any ma*n* can hym[5] aspye,
Led hym to *th*e pyller[ye].[2]
 In fayth, yt shall be don.   484

  Here shalle he stond vp & make proclamacion, seyng thys:

COLLE. Yff therbe eyther ma*n* or woma*n*
That sawe Mast*er* Bru*n*dyche of Braban,
Or owyht of hym tel can,
 Shall wele be quit hys mede ;[6]
He hath a cut berd & a flatte noose,
A therde-bare gowne & a rent hoose ;
He spekyt[h][2] neuer good mater*e* nor p*ur*poose ; —
 To *th*e pyllere ye hym led[e].[2]   492

---

[1] H.   [3] S. By.   [5] MS. I; *emend. by* S.
[2] S.   [4] S. dyleth.   [6] MS. me*n*; *corr. by* S.

[*The master has entered during the proclamation.*]

MASTER BRUNDYCHE.   What, thu boye, what janglest here?

COLL.   A ! master, master, but to your reue*r*ence !
I wend neuer to a seen yowr goodly chere,
    Ye tared hens so long.

MASTER BRUNDYCHE.   What hast thow sayd in my absense?

COLL.   Nothyng, master, but to yowr reue*r*ence,
I haue told all *th*is audiense,
    And some lyes among.   500

But, mast*er*, I pray yow, how dothe yowr pa[c]yent [1]
That ye had last vnder yowr medycament*e*?

MASTER BRUNDYCHE.   I warant she neu*er* fele a-noyment. [2]

    COLL.   Why, ys she in hyr graue?

MASTER BRUNDYCHE.   I haue gyven hyr a drynke made full
      well
Wyth scamoly and *with* oxennell, [3]
Letwyce, sawge and pympernelle.

    COLL.   Nay, than she ys full*e* saue.   508

ffor, now ye ar cu*m*, I dare well*e* saye
Betwyn Douyr & Calyce *th*e ryght wey
Dwellth non so cu*n*nyng, be my fey,
    In my judgyment.

MASTER BRUNDYCHE.   Cu*n*nyng?   Yea, yea ; & *with* prat-
      tise
I haue sauid many a manys lyfe.

COLLE.   On wydowes, maydese and wy[v]se [1]
    Yowr connyng yow haue nyh*e* spent.   516

MASTER BRUNDYCHE.   Were ys bowgtt *with* [4] drynk*e* profyt-
      able.

COLL.   Here, mast*er*, mast*er*, ware how ye tugg !

  [1] S.

  [2] S. *gives* MS. *as* a noynment ; *my collation shows* a noyntment.

  [3] S. *emends to* oxymell.

  [4] S. *emends to* browghtt *tha*t, *but, as the stanza (or rather, fragment)
is unintelligible to me, I give the readings of* MS.

The devylle, I trowe, with-in shrugge,
    For yt gooth rebylle-rable.   520

MASTER BRUNDYCHE.   Here ys a grete congregacyon,
And alle benot hole, without negacyon.
I wold haue certyfycacyon ;
Stond vp & make a proclamacion.
Haue do faste,[1] and mak no pausa[c]yon,[2]
But wyghtly mak a declaracion
    To alle people that helpe w[o]lde [2] haue.   527

Sic interim [3] proclamacionem faciet.

COLL.   All manar off men that haue any syknes,
To Master Brentberecly loke that yow re-dresse.
What dysease or syknesse that euer ye haue,
He wyll neuer leue yow tylle ye be in yow[r] [2] graue.
Who hat[h] [2] the canker, the collyke, or the laxe,
The tercyan, the quartane, or the brynny[n]g [2] axs, —
ffor wormys, for gnawyng, gryndy[n]g[2] in the wombe or in
        the boldyro, —
Alle maner red eyne, bleryd eyn, & the myegrym also,
For hedache, bonache, & therto the tothache, —
The colt-euyll,[4] & the brostyn men he wyll undertak,
All tho that [haue] [2] the poose, the sneke, or the tyseke, —
Thowh [5] a man w[e]re [2] ryght heyle, he cowd soone make
        hym seke.
Inquyre to the Colkote, for ther ys hys loggyng,
A lytylle be-syde Babwelle Mylle, yf ye wyll haue und[er]-
        stondyng.[2]   541

MASTER BRUNDYCHE.   Now, yff therbe ether man or woman
That nedethe helpe of a phesyscion — [6]
COLL.   Mary, master, that I tell can,
    And ye wyll vnderstond.

---

[1] S. dofaste; *corr. by* H.   [2] S.
[3] S. *gives this reading with a query; there is no comment in my collation.*
[4] S. Coltugll [?] ; *emend. by* New Eng. Dict.
[5] MS.; S. Thowgh.   [6] MS.; S. phesyscian.

MASTER BRUNDYCHE.   Knoest any abut *th*is plase?
COLL.   Ye, *tha*t I do, master, so haue [I] [1] grase ;
Here ys a Jewe, hyght Jonathas,
    Hath lost hys ryght hond.   **549**

MASTER BRUNDYCHE.   ffast to hym I wold inquere.
COLL.   ffor God, mast*er*, *th*e gate ys here.[2]
MASTER BRUNDYCHE.   Than to hym I wyll*e* go nere.

        [Approaches the Jews.]
    My master, wele mot yow be !
JONATHAS.   What doost here, felawe? what woldest thu
      hanne?
MASTER BRUNDYCHE.   Syr, yf yow nede ony surgeon or
      physycyan,
Off yow[r] [3] dyse[se] [3] help yow welle I cane,
    What hurt*is* or hermes [4] so-eu*er* they be.   **557**

JONATHAS.   Syr, thu art ontawght to come in thus [on-]henly [5]
Or to pere in my presence thus malep*er*tly.
Voydeth [6] from my syght, & *tha*t wyghtly,
    ffor ye be mysse-a-vysed.
COLL.   Syr, *th*e hurt of yowr hand ys knowen full*e* ryfe,
And my mast*er* haue [7] sauyd many a manes lyfe.
JONATHAS.   I trowe ye be cum to make sum stryfe.
    Hens fast, lest *tha*t ye be chastysed.   **565**

COLL.   Syr, ye know well*e* yt can nott mysse,
    Men that be masters of scyens be p*ro*fytable.
In a pott yf yt please yow to pysse,
    He can tell*e* yf yow be curable.
    [JONATHAS.] [8]   Avoyde, fealows, I loue not yow*er* bable !

---

  [1] S. [yow]; H. *suggests* so haue [I] **grase**, *or* saue yowr **grase**.
  [2] S. *for* MS. hyre.
  [3] S.
  [4] S. *for* MS. hermet.
  [5] S.; H. *retains* henly *regarding it as* héanlíce.
  [6] S. *for* MS. voydoth.
  [7] H. *reads* hath.   [8] *Supp. by* S.

Brushe them hens bothe, & that anon !
Gyff them ther reward *that* they were gone !   572

*Here shall*e the *iiij Jewys bett a-way* the *leche &c hys man.*

JONATHAS.   Now haue don, felawys, & that anon,
 For dowte of drede what after befall*e* !
I am nere masyd, my wytt*e* ys gon ;
 Therfor of helpe I pray yow all*e*.   576

And take yowr pynsonys *that* ar so sure,
 And pluck owt the naylys won & won ;
Also in a clothe ye yt cure
 And throw yt in *the* cawdron, & *that* anon.   580

*Here shall*e *Jason pluck owt the naylys &c shake* the *hond in-to* the *cawdron.*

JASON.   And I shall*e* rape me redely anon
 To plucke owt the naylys that stond so fast,
And bear thys bred & also thys bone
 And in-to the cawdron I wyll*e* yt cast.   584

JASDON.   And I shall*e* wit*h* thys dagger so stowte
 Putt yt down that yt myght plawe,
And steare the clothe rounde abowte
 That no-thyng ther-of shalbe rawe.   588

MASPHAT.   And I shall*e* manly, wit*h* all*e* my myght,
 Make the fyre to blase & brenne,
And sett ther-vnder suche a lyght
 That yt shall*e* make yt ryght thynne.

*Here shall*e the *cawdron b[o]yle,*[1] *apperyng to be as blood.*

MALCHAS.   Owt ! & harow ! what deuyll*e* ys here-in ?
All*e* thys oyle waxyth redde as blood,
 And owt of the cawdron yt begyn*n*yth to rinn.[2]
I am so aferd I am nere woode.   596

   [1] S.   [2] MS. run *or* rnn ; *corr. by* S.

Here shalle Jason & hys compeny goo to ser Jonathas sayng :

JASON.   Ah ! master, mast*er*, what there ys w*ith* yow,
　　I can not see owr werke wyll avayle ;
I beseche yow avance yow now
　　Sum-whatt w*ith* yowr counsayle.　　　　　　　　　　600

JONATHAS.   The best counsayle that I now wott,
　　That [1] I can deme, farre & nere,
[Ys] [2] to make an ovyn as redd hott
　　As eu*er* yt can be made w*ith* fere ;
And when ye see yt soo hott appere,
　　Then throw yt in-to the ovyn fast, —
Sone shall*e* he stanche hys bledyng chere, —
When ye haue done, stoppe yt, — be not agast !　　　608

JASDON.　Be my fayth, yt shalbe wrowgh[t],
　　And that anon, in gret hast.
Bryng on fyryng, ser*is* ; here [3] ye nowght ?
　　To hete thys ovyn be nott agast !　　　　　　　　612

MASPHAT.   Here ys straw & thornys kene ;
　　Com*e* [4] on, Malchas, & bryng on fyre,
ffor that shall hete yt well*e*, I wene ;

Here thei kyndylle the fyre.

　　Blow on fast, that done yt were !
　　MALCHAS.　Ah, how ! thys fyre gynnyth to brenne clere !
Thys ovyn ryght hotte I thynk to make.
　　Now, Jason, to the cawdron [5] *tha*t ye stere
And fast fetche hether that ylke cake !　　　　　　　620

*Here shalle Jason goo to the cawdron & take owt the Ost wi*th *hys pynsonys
　　& cast yt in-to the ovyn.*

JASON.　I shall*e* w*ith* thes pynsonys, w*ith*-owt dowt,
　　Shake thys cake owt of thys clothe,

---

[1] MS. ys that ; S. [and] that ; *cf. next note.*
[2] *Supplied by* S. ; *but the scribe merely wrote it in the wrong line.*
[3] S. *emends to* fere ; *but, as* H. *points out,* MS. *is correct.*
[4] S. couer ; *corr. by* Kittredge.　　　[5] S. *inserts* [see].

And to the ovyn I shall yt rowte
    And stoppe hym there, thow he be loth.
    Thys cake I haue cawght here, in good sothe, —
The hand ys soden, the fleshe from *th*e bonys, —
    Now in-to the ovyn I wyll ther-w*ith*.
Stoppe yt, Jasdon, for the nonys !   628

JASDON.   I stoppe thys ovyn, wythowtyn dowte,
    W*ith* clay I clome yt vppe ryght fast,
That non heat shall cum [1] owte.
    I trow there shall*e* he hete & drye in hast !   632

      Here the ovyn must ryve asunder, &° blede owt at the cranys, &° an image
      appere owt with woundis bledyng.

MASPHAT.   Owt ! owt ! here is a grete wonder !
    Thys ovyn b[l]edyth owt on eu*er*y syde !
MALCHAS.   Yea, *th*e ovyn on peacys gynnyth to ryve
      asundre ;
    Thys ys a mer velows case thys tyde !   636

      *Here shall*e *the image speke to the Juys sayng thus :*

JHESUS.   *O mirabiles Judei, attendite et videte*
Si est dolor similis [2] *dolor meus !*   638

Oh ye merveylows Jewys,
    Why ar ye to yow*er* kyng onkynd,
And [3] so bytterly bowt yow to my blysse ?
    Why fare ye thus fule w*ith* yowr frende ?
    Why peyne yow me & straytly me pynde,[4]
And I yow*er* loue so derely haue bowght ?
    Why are ye so vnstedfast in yo*u*r mynde ?
Why wrath ye me ? I greve yow nowght.   646

Why wyll*e* ye nott beleue that I haue tawght,
    And forsake yo*u*r fowle neclygence,
And kepe my com*m*andement*is* in yow*er* thowght,
    And vnto my godhed to take credence ?   650

[1] S. *inserts* ther.   [3] H. *inserts* I.
[2] *Probably a careless mistake for* sicut.   [4] H. *wishes to read* bynde.

Why blaspheme yow me? Why do ye thus?
　　Why put yow me to a newe tormentry,
And I dyed for yow on the crosse?
　　Why consyder not yow what I dyd crye?
　　Whylle that I was *with* yow, ye ded me velanye.
Why remember ye nott my bitter chaunce,
How yow*er* kynne dyd me awance
ffor claymyng of myn enherytaunce?
I shew yow the streytnesse of my greuance,
　　And all*e* to meue yow to my mercy.　　　　　　660

JONATHAS.　*Tu es protector vite mee; a quo trepidabo?*
　　O thu, Lord, whyche art my defendowr,
　　ffor dred of the I trymble & quake.
Of thy gret m*er*cy lett vs receyue [1] *th*e showre ;
　　And mekely I aske m*er*cy, ame*n*dys to make.　　665

　　　　*Here shall they knele down all*e *on ther kneys, sayng :*

JASON.　Ah! Lord, w*ith* sorow & care & grete wepyng
Alle we felawys lett vs saye thus,
W*ith* condolent harte & grete sorowyng :
　　Lacrimis nostris conscienciam nostram baptizemus !　　669

JASDON.　Oh thow blyssyd Lord of mykyll*e* myght,
　　Of thy gret m*er*cy, thow hast shewyd vs *th*e path,
Lord, owt of grevous slepe & owt of dyrknes to lyght,
　　Ne grauis sompnus irruat.　　　　　　　　　　673

MASPHAT.　Oh Lord, I was very cursyd, for I wold know
　　　　*th*i crede.
　　I can no men[d]ys [2] make, but crye to the thus :
O gracyows [3] Lorde, forgyfe me my mysdede !
　　W*ith* lamentable hart : *miserere mei, Deus !*　　677

MALCHAS.　Lord, I haue offendyd the in many a sundry
　　　　vyse,
　　That styckyth at my hart as hard as a core.

　　　[1] MS.; S. receue.　　　[2] S.　　　[3] MS.; S. gracyous.

Lord, by *th*e water of contryc[i]on lett me aryse :
　　Asparges me, Domine, ysopo, et mundabor.　　　　681

JHESUS.　All ye that desyryn my seruant*is* for to be
　　And to fulfyll*e th*e precept*is* of my lawys,
The intent of my co*m*mandeme*n*t knowe ye :
　　Ite et ostendite vos sacerdotibus meis.
　　To all yow *that* desyre in eny wyse
To aske me*r*cy, to grau*n*t yt redy I am.
　　Remember & lett yow*er* wytt*is* suffyce,
Et tunc non auertam a vobis faciem meam.　　　　689

[1] Jonathas, on thyn hand thow art but lame,
　　And *thi*s [2] thorow thyn own cruelnesse.
ffor thyn hurt [3] *tho*u mayest *th*i-selfe blame,
　　Thow woldyst preve thy powr me to oppresse ;
　　But now I consydre thy necesse ;
Thow wasshest thyn hart w*ith* grete [4] contryc[i]on ;
　　Go to the cawdron, — *th*i care shalbe the lesse, —
And towche thyn hand to thy saluac[i]on.　　　　697

　　　Here shall ser *Jonathas put hys hand in-to* the *cawdron, and yt shalbe*
　　　hole agayn ; & then say as fo[lo]wyth : [5]

JONATHAS.　Oh thow my Lord God & Sauyow*er*, osanna !
　　Thow Kyng of Jewys & of Jerusalem!
O thow myghty, strong Lyon of Iuda,[6]
　　Blyssyd be the tyme *tha*t *tho*u were [7] in Bedlem !
　　Oh *tho*u myghty, strong, gloryows & gracyows Oyle-
　　　streme,
Thow myghty Conquerrowr of infernall*e* tene,
　　I am quyt of moche combrance thorowgh thy meane,
That eu*er* blyssyd mott *tho*u bene !　　　　705

Alas *tha*t eu*er* I dyd agaynst thy wyll*e*,
　　In my wytt to be soo wood

---

[1] *Before* Jonathas, S. *has* . . , *the meaning of which is not explained.*
[2] MS. ys; S. [thys] ys.　　　　[5] S.
[3] MS.; S. hart.　　　　[6] MS.; S. Jwda.
[4] MS.; S. gret.　　　　[7] *Qy. insert* born.

That I with [1] ongoodly wyrk shuld soo gryll !
   A3ens my mysgouernaunce thow gladdyst me with good :
   I was soo prowde to prove the on the roode,
And thou haste sent me lyghtyng that late was lame ;
   To bete the & boyle the I was myghty in moode,
And now thou hast put me from duresse and dysfame.   **713**

But, Lord, I take my leve at thy hygh presens
   And put me in thy myghty mercy.
The bysshoppe wyll I goo fetche to se ower offens,
   And onto hym shew ower lyfe, how that we be gylty.   **717**

Here shall the master Jew goo [2] to the byshopp, & hys men knele styll.

JONATHAS.   Hayle, father of grace !   I knele vpon my knee
   Hertely besechyng yow & interely
A swemfulle syght alle for to see
   In my howse apperyng verely :
   The holy Sacrament, [3] the whyche we haue done tor-
      mentry
And ther we haue putt hym to a newe passyon,
   A chyld apperyng with wondys blody :
A swemfulle syght yt ys to looke vpon.   **725**

EPISCOPUS.   Oh Jhesu, Lord, fulle of goodnesse !
   With the wylle I walke with alle my myght.
Now, alle my pepulle, with me ye dresse
   ffor to goe see that swymfulle syght.   **729**

Now, alle ye peple that here are,
   I commande yow, euery man,
On yower feet for to goo, bare,
   In the devoutest wyse that ye can.   **733**

Here shalle the bysshope enter into the Jewys howse & say :

O Jhesu fili Dei,
   How thys paynfulle passyon rancheth myn hart !
Lord, I crye to the, *miserere mei,*

---

[1] MS. So; *corr. by* S.   [2] MS.; S. go.   [3] S. *inserts* [to].

ffrom thys rufulle syght *tho*u wylt reu*er*te.
 Lord, we all*e with* sorowys smert
ffor thys vnlefull*e* work we lyue in langow*er* ;
 Now, good Lord, in thy grace let vs be gertt,[1]
And of thy sou*er*eyn marcy send vs thy socow*er* ;   741

And for thy holy grace forgyfe vs ow*er* errowr.
 Now lett thy pete spryng & sprede ;
Thowgh we haue be vnrygh[t]full*e*,[2] forgyf vs o*ur* rygore,
 And of ow*er* lamentable hart*is*, good Lord, take
  hed[e].[2]   745

   *Here shall*e the im[a]ge[2] *change agayn on-to brede.*

Oh thu largyfluent Lord, most of l*y*ghtnesse,
 On-to owr prayers thow hast applyed ;
Thu hast receyued them *with* grett swettnesse,
 ffor all*e* ow*er* dredfull*e* dedys *tho*u hast not vs denyed.
 ffull*e* mykyll*e* owte thy name for to be magnyfyed
W*ith* ma*n*suete myrth and gret swettnes,
 And as o*ur* gracyows God for to be gloryfyed,
ffor thu shewyst vs gret gladnes.   753

Now wyll*e* I take thys holy Sacrament
 W*ith* humble hart & gret devoc[i]on,
And all*e* we wyll*e* gon *with* on consent
 And bear yt to chyrche *with* sole[m]pne[2] p*r*ocessyon ;
 Now folow me, all*e* & sume !
And all*e* tho that bene here, both more & lesse,
 Thys holy song, *O sacrum*[3] *Dominum,*
Lett vs syng all *with* grett swetnesse.   761

  *Here shall*e the *pryst,* ser *Isoder, aske hys m*aster *what* this *menyth.*

[PRESBITER.][2] S*er* Arystory, I pray yow, what menyth all*e*
  thys ?
  Sum myracle, I hope, ys wrowght be Godd*is* myght ;

---

[1] MS. grett ; *corr. by* S. [2] S. [3] MS. scacrum ; *corr. by* S.

The bysshope co*m*myth [in][1] processyon w*ith* a gret meny
    of Jewys ;
  I hope sum myracle ys shewyd to hys syght.
  To chyrche in hast wyll*e* I run*n*e full ryght,
ffor thether, me thynk, he begynnyth to take hys pace.
  The Sacrame*n*t so semly is borne in syght,
  I hope that God hath shewyd of hys grace.   769

ARYSTORIUS. To tell yow the trowth I wyll*e* nott lett :
  Alas *tha*t eu*er* thys dede was dyght !
An onlefull*e* bargayn [I][2] began for to beat ;
  I sold yon same Jewys ow*er* Lord full*e* ryght
  For couytyse of good as a cursyd wyght.
Woo the whyle that bargayn I dyd eu*er* make !
  But yow be my defensour in owr dyocesans syght,
  ffor an heretyke I feare he wyll*e* me take.   777

PRESBITER. ffor sothe, nothyng wellavysed was yo*ur* wytt,—
  Wondrely was yt wrowght of a man of dyscresc[i]on
In suche p*er*ayle yo*ur* solle for to putt ;
  But I wyll*e* labor for yo*ur* absolucyon.   781

Lett vs hye vs fast that we were hens,
  And beseche hym of hys benygne g*ra*ce
That he wyll*e* shew vs hys benyvolens
  To make a-mendys [3] for yow*er* trespas.   785

Here shall the m*er*chant *&* hys *p*rest go *to* the *chyrche &* the *bysshop shall*e
entre[4] the *chyrche & lay* the *Os*[*t*][1] *u*[*p*]*on*[1] the *auter, sayng thus :*

[EPISCOPUS.] *Estote fortes in bello et pugnate cum*[5] *antico*
    serpente,
Et accipite regnum eternum, et cetera.

My chyldern, be ye [6] strong in batayll*e* gostly
  For to fyght agayn the fell serpent,
That nyght and day ys eu*er* besy ;
  To dystroy owr sollys ys hys intent.

---

   [1] S.   [3] S. a menyn.   [5] MS. co; *corr. by* S
   [2] H.   [4] MS.; S. enter.   [6] MS. ye be; *corr. by* S.

Look ye be not slow nor neclygent
To arme yow in the vertues seuyn ;
   Of synnys forgetyn [1] take good avysement
And knowlege them to yowr confessor full*e* euyn ;   795

ffor that s*er*pent, the deuyll*e*, ys full*e* strong
   Meruelows myscheves [2] for man to mene,
But that the Passyon of Cryst ys meynt vs among,
   And that ys in dyspyte of hys infernall*e* tene.
   Beseche ow*er* Lord & Sauyow*er* so kene
To put doun that s*er*pent, cu*m*berer of man,
   To w*ith*draw hys furyous froward doctryn by-dene,
ffulfyllyd of *th*e fend callyd Leuyathan.   803

Gyff lawrell*e* to that Lord of myght
   That he may bryng vs to the joyous fruyc[i]on
ffrom [8] vs to put the fend to flyght,
   That neu*er* he dystroy vs by hys temptac[i]on.   807

PRESBITER.   My ffather vnder God, I knele vnto yow*er* kne,
   In yowr myhty mys*er*icord to tak vs in reme*m*brance ;
As ye be materyall to owr degre,
   We put vs in yow*er* moderat ordynance,
   Yff yt lyke yow*er* hyghnes to here ow*er* greuau*n*ce ;
We haue offenddyd sorowfully in a syn mortall*e*,
   Wherfor we fere vs owr Lord wyll*e* take vengaunce
ffor owr synnes both grete and small*e*.   815

EPISCOPUS.   And in fatherhed, that longyth to my dygnyte,
   Vn-to yow*er* grefe I wyll*e* gyf credens.
Say what ye wyll*e*, in *th*e name of the Trynyte,
   Agayn[s]t [4] God yf ye haue wroght eny inco*n*uenyence.   819

ARISTORIUS.   Holy ffather, I knele to yow vnder benedycite.
   I haue offendyd in the syn of couytys ;
I sold o*ur* Lordys body for lucre of mony
   And delyu*er*yd to the wyckyd w*ith* cursyd advyce.

---

1 MS. fog. . tyn ; S. forgottyn.   8 MS. fform ; *corr. by* S.
2 S. myschevos.   4 S.

And for that p*re*sumpc[i]on gretly I agryse
That I p*re*sumed to go to the auter
There to handyll*e* *th*e holy sacryfyce, —
I were worthy to be putt in breny*ng* fyre.　　　　827

But, gracyous lord, I can no more
But put me to Goddys mercy & to yow*er* grace.
My cursyd werkys for to restore,
I aske penaunce now in thys place.　　　　831

EPISCOPUS.　Now for thys offence that *th*ou hast donne
A3ens the Kyng of hevyn & Emperow*er* of hell*e*,
Eu*er* whyll*e* *th*ou lyuest good dedys for to done
And neu*er*-more for to bye nor sell*e* ;
Chastys thy body as I shall the tell*e*,
W*ith* fastyng & prayng & other good wyrk,
To w*ith*stond the temtacyon of fend*is* of hell ;
And to call*e* to God for grace looke *th*ou neu*er* be irke.　　　839

Also, *th*ou preste, for thy neclygens,
That thou were no wyser on thyn office,
Thou art worthy inpresu[n]ment [1] for thyn offence ;
But beware eu*er* herafter & be mor wyse.　　　843

And all*e* yow creaturys [2] & curatys [3] that here be,
Off thys dede yow may take example
How that yo*ur* pyxys lockyd ye shuld see
And be ware of the key of Goddys temple.　　　847

JONATHAS.　And I aske crystendom w*ith* great devoc[i]on,
W*ith* repentant hart in all degrees.
I aske for vs all a gen*er*all*e* absoluc[i]on,

Here the *Juys must knele al down.*

ffor that we knele all vpon ow*er* knees ;　　　851
ffor we haue greuyd ow*er* Lord on grovnd
And put hym to a new paynfull*e* passion,

[1] S.　　　[2] *Qy.* vicarys ; *or* prechorys, *cf. above*, l. 326.
[3] S. *proposes* curatys wyth creaturys.

W*ith* daggars styckyd hym w*ith* greuos wo[u]nd*e*,[1]
  New naylyd hym to a post, & w*ith* pynsonys pluckyd
    hy*m* down.   855

JASON.   And syth we toke that blyssyd Bred so sownd
  And in a cawdron we dyd hym boyle,
In a clothe full*e* just we hym wou*n*de
  And so dyd we seth hym in oyle.   859

JASDON.   And for that we myght not[2] oue*r*com hym w*ith*
    tormentry,
  In an hott ovyn we speryd hym fast.
Ther he apperyd with wo[u]nd*is* all bloody ;
  The ovyn rave asunder & all to-brast.   863

MASPHAT.   In hys law to make vs stedfast,
  There spake he to vs woord*is* of grete favor ;
In contrycyon owr hart*is* he cast
  And bad take vs to a confessor.   867

MALCHUS.   And therfor all we w*ith* on consent
  Knele onto yow*er* hygh soue*r*eynte ;
ffor to be crystenyd ys ow*er* intent,
  Now all ow*er* dedys to yow shewyd haue we.   871

  Here shall the *bysshoppe crysten* the *Jewys with gret solempnyte.*

EPISCOPUS.   Now the Holy Gost at thys tyme mot yow
    blysse[3]
  As ye knele all*e* now in hys name,
And w*ith* the water of baptyme I shall*e* yow blysse[3]
  To saue yow all*e* from the fendis blame.
  Now, that fendys powr*e* for to make lame,
In *th*e name of *th*e Fath*er*, *th*e Son & *th*e Holy Gost,
  To saue yow from the deuyllys flame,
I crysten yow all*e*, both lest & most.   879

----

  [1] S.
  [2] S. *omits* not; *but, as* H. *points out, it is correct.*
  [3] H. *proposes* lysse *for one* blysse.

S*er* JONATHAS.   Now owr father & byshoppe *tha*t we well*e*
        know,
    We thank yow interly, both lest & most.
Now ar we bownd to kepe Crystis lawe
    And to s*er*ue *th*e Father, *th*e Son & *th*e Holy Gost.
    Now wyll*e* we walke by contre & cost,
Owr wyckyd lyuy*n*g for to restore ;
    And trust in God, of myght*is* most,
Neuer [1] to offend as we have don before.[2]   887

Now we take ow*er* lea[v]e [3] at lesse & more, —
    Forward on ow*er* vyage we wyll*e* vs dresse ;
God send yow all as good welfare
    As hart can thynke or towng expresse.   891

ARYSTORIUS.   In-to my contre now wyll*e* I fare
    For to amende myn wyckyd lyfe,
And to kep[e] [8] *th*e people owt of care
    I wyll teache thys lesson to man & wyf*e*.   895

Now take I my leave in thys place, —
    I wyll*e* go walke, my penau*n*ce to fullfyll*e* ;
Now, God, a3ens whom I haue done thys trespas,
    Graunt me forgyfnesse [yf] [8] yt be thy wyll*e* !   899

PRESBITER.   ffor joy of thys me thynke my hart do wepe,
    That yow haue gyuyn yow all*e* Cryst*is* s*er*uaunt*is* to be,
Hym for to s*er*ue w*it*h hart full*e* meke, —
    God, full*e* of pacyens & humylyte, —   903

And the conu*er*sac[i]on of all*e* thes fayre men,
    W*it*h hart*is* stedfastly knett in on,
Godd*is* lawys to kepe & hym to serue by-dene,
    As faythfull*e* Crystyanys eu*er*more for to gon*n*e.   907

EPISCOPUS.   God omnypotent euermore looke ye s*er*ue
    W*it*h deuoc[i]on & prayre whyll*e* *tha*t ye may ;

---

[1] MS. neuere[r]; *corr. by* S.   [2] MS. befer; *corr. by* S.   [8] S.

Dowt yt not he wyll*e* yow p*r*es*er*ue
    ffor eche good prayer *tha*t ye sey to hys pay ;
    And therfor in eu*er*y dew tyme loke ye nat delay
ffor to s*er*ue the Holy Trynyte,
    And also Mary, that swete may ;
And kepe yow in p*er*fyte loue & charyte.   915

Cryst*is* commandement*is* x there bee ;
    Kepe well*e* them ; doo¹ as I yow tell*e*.
Almyght God shall*e* yow please in eu*er*y degre,
    And so shall*e* ye saue yow*er* sollys from hell*e* ;
    ffor there ys payn & sorow cruell*e*,
And in heuyn ther ys both joy & blysse,
    More then eny towng can tell,
There angellys syng w*ith* grett swetnesse ; —   923

To the whyche blysse he bryng vs
    Whoys name ys callyd Jh*es*us,
And in wyrshyppe of thys name gloryows
    To syng to hys honor *Te Deum laudamus.*   927

FFINIS.

Thus endyth the Play of the Blyssyd Sacrament, whyche myracle was don in the forest of Aragon, in the famous cite Eraclea, the yere of ow*er* Lord God. M¹cccc.lxi., to whom be honow*er*, Amen !

The namys & n*u*mber of the players :

Jh[es]us.²
Episcopus.
Aristorius, christianus mercator.
[Isoder, presbiter.]
Clericus.
Jonathas, Judeus i^mus.

Jason, Judeus ij^us.
Jasdon, Judeus iij^us.
Masphat, Judeus iiij^us
Malchus, Judeus v^tus.
Magister phisicus.
Coll*e*, seruus.

IX may play yt at ease.
R. C.

¹ H. *proposes* too.   ² S.

PART III.

ROBIN HOOD PLAYS.

The first is printed from a copy made for Professor Child by Henry Bradshaw, Esq. The original, formerly among Sir John Fenn's papers and now the property of Dr. W. Aldis Wright, " is evidently," says Dr. Wright, " the last leaf, or rather half leaf, of a folio MS. For this reason it is clear that the memoranda [acknowledgments of payments] on the blank page are later in date than the writing of the ballad [*i.e.*, play]." This would date the play before 1475. Besides the copy by Bradshaw, I have used a collation made by Dr. Wright. The play was first correctly printed in Child's " English and Scottish Popular Ballads," III, 90 f.

The second and third are really two plays, though printed as one in both the old editions : Copland's (about 1550) and White's of 1634. They are printed separately in Child's " English and Scottish Popular Ballads," III, 127 f., 114 f., Boston [1888]. In the footnotes, Co. indicates the readings of Copland as given in Ritson's " Robin Hood," 1795, II, 199 ff. ; R. indicates Ritson's edition ; W. indicates the variants of White's edition as given by Child.

I.

[ROBIN HOOD AND THE KNIGHT.]

[Enter a Knight to the Sheriff.]

[KNYGHT.]   Syr Sheryffe, for thy sake
Robyn Hode wull Y take.
  [SHERIFF.]   I wyll the gyffe golde and fee ;
  This be-heste *tho*u holde me !

[The Knight goes to Robyn Hode.]

  [KNYGHT.]   Robyn Hode, fayre [1] and fre,   5
Vndre this lynde shote we !
  [ROBYN.]   With the shote Y wyll,
Alle thy lustes to full-fyll.
                [They shoot.]

  [KNYGHT.]   Have at the pryke !
  [ROBYN.]   And Y cleue the styke.   10

1 Wright, ffayre.

[KNYGHT.]   Late vs caste the stone.

[ROBYN.]   I graunte well, be Seynt John !

[They cast the stone ; Robyn is again successful.]

[KNYGHT.]   Late vs caste the exaltre.

[ROBYN.]   Have a foote be-fore the !

[Then they wrestle.]

Syr knyght, ye haue a falle.   15

[KNYGHT.]   And I the, Robyn, qwyte shall :

Owte on the ! I blowe myn horne.

[ROBYN.]   Hit ware better be vnborne.

Lat vs fyght at outtraunce.

[KNYGHT.]   He that fleth, God gyfe hym myschaunce !   20

[Robyn slays the Knight.]

[ROBYN.]   Now I haue the maystry here.

Off I smyte this sory swyre ;

This knyghtys clothis wolle I were,

And in my hode his hede woll bere.

*[He disguises himself. Meantime the Sheriff has attacked Robyn Hode's
men and a fierce battle is in progress. Robyn meets a man coming
from the scene of the battle.]*

[ROBYN.]   Welle mete, felowe myn !   25

What herst *tho*u of gode Robyn ?

[MAN.]   Robyn Hode and his menye

W*ith* the Sheryff takyn be.

[ROBYN.]   Sette on foote, w*ith* gode wyll,

And the Sheryffe wull we kyll.   30

[They come in sight of the battle.]

[ROBYN.]   Be-holde wele ffrere Tuke,

Howe he dothe his bowe pluke.

[On the battle-field the Sheryff speaks.]

[SHERYFF.]   ȝeld yow, syrs, to the Sheryff[e],

Or elles shall yo*u*r bowes clyffe !

[ONE OF ROBYN'S MEN.]   Now we be bownden alle in
          same;   35

Frere [T]uke,[1] *th*is is no game.

   [SHERYFF.]   Co[m]e[1] *tho*u forth, *tho*u fals outlawe :
*Tho*u shall b[e][1] hangyde and ydrawe !

   [FRERE TUKE.]   Now, allas ! what shall we doo ?
We [m]oste[1] to the prysone goo.   40

   [SHERYFF.]   Opy[n][1] the yatis faste anon,
An[d][1] [d]oo[2] theis[3] thevys ynne gon.

    [*The part of the play in which Robyn follows his men and finally releases
    them is missing.*]

II.

[ROBIN HOOD AND THE FRIAR.]

ROBYN HODE.   Now stand ye forth, my mery men all,
And harke what I shall say ;
Of an adventure I shal you tell,
The which befell this other day.
As I went by the hygh-way,   5
With a stout frere I met,
And a quarter-staffe in his hande ;
Lyghtely to me he lept,
And styll he bade me stande.
There were strypes two or three,   10
But I cannot tell who had the worse,
But well I wote the horeson lept within me,
And fro me he[4] toke my purse.
Is there any of my mery men all
That to that[5] frere wyll go,   15
And bryng hym to me forth-withall,
Whether he wyll or no?

   LYTELL JOHN.   Yes, mayster, I make God avowe,
To that frere wyll I go,
And bring him to you,   20
Whether he wyl or no.

---

[1] MS. *damaged.*

[2] Bradshaw, [d]oo; Wright *reads* [la]te, *and says,* "*There are traces
of* te."   [3] Bradshaw, theis ; Wright, thois.

[4] W. *omits* he.   [5] W. the.

[Exeunt omnes; enter Fryer Tucke, with three dogs.]

FRYER TUCKE.   *Deus hic! Deus hic!*   God be here !
Is not this a holy worde for [1] a frere ?
God save all this company !
But am not I a jolly fryer ?   25
For I can shote both farre and nere,
And handle the sworde and buckler,
And this quarter-staffe also.
If I mete with a gentylman or yeman,
I am not afrayde to loke hym upon,   30
Nor [2] boldly with him to carpe ;
If he speake any wordes to me,
He shall have strypes two or thre
That shal make his body smarte.
But, maisters,[3] to shew you the matter   35
Wherfore and why I am come hither,
In fayth, I wyll not spare :
I am come to seke a good yeman,
In Bernisdale men sai is his habitacion,
His name is Robyn Hode ;   40
And if that [4] he be better man than I,
His servaunt wyll I be, and serve him truely ;
But if that I be better [5] man than he,
By my truth, my knave shall he be
And leade these dogges all three.   45

[Robyn enters and seizes him by the throat.]

ROBYN HODE.   Yelde the, fryer in thy long cote !
FRYER TUCKE.   I beshrew thy hart, knave, thou hurtest
    my throt[e].
ROBYN HODE.   I trowe, fryer, thou beginnest to dote !
Who made the so malapert and so bolde
To come into this forest here,   50
Amonge my falowe-dere ?

    1 W. word of.   4 W. *omits* that.
    2 W. not.   5 W. be a better.
    3 Co. W. maister; *corr. by* R.

FRYER.   Go louse the, ragged knave !
If thou make mani wordes, I will geve the on the eare,
Though I be but a poore fryer.
To seke Robyn Hode I am com here,   55
And to him my hart to breke.
 ROBYN HODE.   Thou lousy frer, what wouldest thou with
  hym?
He never loved fryer, nor none of freiers kyn.
 FRYER.   Avaunt, ye [1] ragged knave,
Or ye shall have on the skynne !   60
 ROBYN HODE.   Of all the men in the [2] morning thou art
  the worst ;
To mete with the I have no lust,
For he that meteth a frere or a fox in the morning,
To spede ill [3] that day he standeth in jeoperdy :
Therfore I had lever [4] mete with the devil of hell — [5]   65
Fryer, I tell the as I thinke —
Then mete with a fryer or a fox
In a mornyng or I drynk.
 FRYER.   Avaunt, thou ragged knave ! this is but a mock ;
If thou [6] make mani words, thou [6] shal have a knock.   70
 ROBYN HODE.   Harke, frere, what I say here :
Over this water thou shalt me bere,
The brydge is borne away.
 FRYER.   To say naye I wyll not ;
To let the of thine oth it were great pitie and sin ;   75
But up on a fryers backe, and have even in !
 ROBYN HODE.   Nay, have over !

     [Gets on the Fryer's back.]

FRYER.   Now am I, frere, within, and thou, Robin, without,
To lay the here I have no great doubt.

   1 W. *omits* ye.   4 W. rather.
   2 W. a.   5 W. *omits* of hell.
   3 Co. ell.   6 Co. you; W. y^u; y^u shalt.

[*Throws him into the stream.*]

Now am I, frere, without, and thou, Robyn, within ![1]   80
Lye ther, knave !   Chose whether thou wilte sinke [2] or swym.
  ROBYN HODE.   Why, thou lowsy frere ! what hast thou
    done ? [3]
  FRYER.   Mary, set a knave over the shone.
  ROBYN HODE.   Therfore thou shalt abye.

[*Runs at the Fryer.*]

  FRYER.   Why, wylt thou fyght a plucke?   85
  ROBYN HODE.   And God send me good lucke !
  FRYER.   Than have a stroke for Fryer Tucke !

[*They fight.*]

  ROBYN HODE.   Holde thy hande, frere, and here me speke !
  FRYER.   Say on, ragged knave,
Me semeth ye begyn to swete.   90
  ROBYN HODE.   In this forest I have a hounde,
I wyl not give him for an hundreth pound ;
Geve me leve my horne to blowe,
That my hounde may knowe.
  FRYER.   Blowe on, ragged knave, without any doubte,   95
Untyll bothe thyne eyes starte out.

[*Robyn blows ; his men enter.*]

Here be [4] a sorte of ragged knaves come in,
Clothed all in Kendale grene,
And to the they take their way nowe.
  ROBYN HODE.   Peradventure they do so.   100
  FRYER.   I gave the leve to blowe at thy wyll,
Now give me leve to whistell my fyll.
  ROBYN HODE.   Whystell, frere, evyl mote [5] thou fare !
Untyll bothe thyne eyes stare. [6]

---

[1] Co. W. R. Now art thou, Robyn, without, and I, frere, within ; *corr.*
by Child.
  [2] W. choose either sinke.
  [3] Co. donee.

[4] W. is.
[5] might.
[6] Co. starte.

[The Fryer whistles ; his men enter.]

FRYER.   Now, Cut and Bause !   105
Breng forth the clubbes and staves,
And downe with those ragged knaves !

[They fight.]

ROBYN HODE.   How sayest thou, frere ? wylt thou be my
      man,
To do me the best servyse thou can ?
Thou shalt have both golde and fee ;   110
And also here is a lady free,
I wyll geve her unto the,
And her chapplayn I the make
To serve her for my sake.   114
      FRYER.   Go home, ye knaves, and lay crabbes in the fyre, 119
For my lady and I wil daunce in the myre,
For veri pure joye.[1]   120

III.

[ROBIN HOOD AND THE POTTER.]

ROBYN HODE.   Lysten to [me],[2] my mery men all,   121
And harke what I shall say ;
Of an adventure I shall you tell
That befell this other daye.
With a proude potter I met,   125
And a rose-garlande on his head,
The floures of it shone marvaylous freshe ;
This seven yere and more he hath used this waye,
Yet was he never so curteyse a potter
As one peny passage to paye.   130
Is there any of my mery men all
That dare be so bolde
To make the potter paie passage,
Either silver or golde ?

[1] *These two lines as one in* R. *and* W.   *I have omitted four lines of the*
Friar's *speech, before* l. 119.   [2] *Supplied by* R.; W. *omits* to, also.

LYTELL JOHN.   Not I, master, for twenty pound redy tolde, 135
For there is not among us al one
That dare medle with that potter, man for man.
I felt his handes not long agone,
But I had lever have ben here by the ;
Therfore I knowe what he is.   140
Mete him when ye wil, or mete him whan ye shal,
He is as propre a man as ever you medled [1] withal.
    ROBYN HODE.   I will lai with the, Litel John, twenti pound
            so read,
If I wyth that potter mete,
I wil make him pay passage, maugre his head.   145
    LETTEL JOHN.   I consente therto, so eate I bread !
If he pay passage, maugre his head,
Twenti pound shall ye have of me for your mede.

[Exeunt all but Robyn.   Enter the Potter's Boy, Jacke.]

JACKE.   Out, alas, that ever I sawe this daye !
For I am clene out of my waye   150
From Notyngham towne ;
If I hye me not the faster,
Or I come there the market [2] wel be done.
    ROBYN HODE.   Let me se, are the [3] pottes hole and
            sounde ?
    JACKE. Yea, meister, but they will not breake the ground. 155
    ROBYN HODE.   I wil them breke, for the cuckold thi
            maisters sake ;
And if they will [4] breake the grounde,
Thou shalt have thre pence for a pound.

[Dashes the pots to the ground.]

JACKE.   Out, alas ! what have ye done?
If my maister come, he will breke your crown.   160

---

[1] Co. medle.
[2] Co. maryet.
[3] W. thy.
[4] Co., R. will not.

[*Enter the Potter.*]

THE POTTER. Why, thou horeson, art thou here yet?
Thou shouldest have bene at market.

JACKE. I met with Robin Hode, a good yeman;
He hath broken my pottes,
And called you kuckolde by your name. 165

THE POTTER. Thou mayst be a gentylman, so God me save,
But thou semest a noughty knave.
Thou callest me cuckolde by my name,
And I swere by God and Saynt John,
Wyfe had I never none: 170
This cannot I denye.
But if thou be a good felowe,
I wil sel mi horse, mi harneis, pottes and paniers to,
Thou shalt have the one halfe, and I will have the other.
If thou be not so content, 175
Thou shalt have strypes, if thou were my brother.

ROBYN HODE. Harke, potter, what I shall say:
This seven yere and more thou hast used this way,
Yet were thou never so curteous to me
As one penny passage to paye. 180

THE POTTER. Why should I paye passage to thee?

ROBYN HOODE. For I am Robyn Hode, chiefe governoure
Under the grene-woode tree.

THE POTTER. This seven yere have I used this way up and
downe,
Yet payed I passage to no man, 185
Nor now I wyl not beginne, to [1] do the worst thou can.

ROBYN HODE. Passage shalt thou pai here under the
grene-wode tre,
Or els thou shalt leve a wedde [2] with me.

THE POTTER. If thou be a good felowe, as men do the call,
Lay awaye thy bowe, 190
And take thy sword and buckeler in thy hande,
And se what shall befall.

---

[1] W. *omits* to; R. *reads* so.   [2] Co. wedded; W. wed; *corr. by* R.

ROBIN HODE.   Lyttle John, where art thou?

LYTTEL [JOHN].[1]   Here, mayster, I make God avowe.

I tolde you, mayster, so God me save,   195

That you [2] shoulde fynde the potter a knave.

Holde your buckeler faste in your hande,

And I wyll styfly by your stande,

Ready for to fyghte ;

Be the knave never so stoute,   200

I shall rappe him on the snoute,

And put hym to flyghte.

                          The rest is wanting.

[1] *Supplied by* R.   [2] Co. your.

ST. GEORGE PLAYS.

The first is printed from *Notes and Queries*, Fifth Series, II, 503-505, to which it was communicated by the Rev. Frederick George Lee. Mr. Lee says: "The text was taken down by myself from the lips of one of the performers in 1853. I first saw it acted in the Hall of the old Vicarage House at Thame, in the year 1839. ... The man from whom I took [it] down had performed at Brill in the year 1807, and his father had done the same at Thame Park in the previous century. Nothing whatsoever has been altered or added by myself [except **stage** directions]."

The second is printed from W. Kelly's "Notices of Leicester," London, 1865, pp. 53-56. It was performed near Lutterworth, at Christmas, 1863.

I.

[OXFORDSHIRE ST. GEORGE PLAY.]

Dramatis Personae.

OLD FATHER CHRISTMAS.	GIANT BLUNDERBORE.
ST. GEORGE OF ENGLAND.	OLD DR. BALL.
KING ALFRED.	LITTLE JACK.
KING ALFRED'S QUEEN.	THE OLD DRAGON.
KING WILLIAM.	THE MERRY ANDREW.
OLD KING COLE (*with a wooden leg*).	MORRIS-MEN.

All the mummers come in singing and walk round the place in a circle, and then stand on one side.

Enter [1] KING ALFRED *and his* QUEEN, *arm in arm.*

I am King Alfred, and this here is my bride.
I 've a crown on my pate and a sword by my side.

Stands apart.

---

[1] *In such plays* enter *means "advance from the circle of players."*

Enter KING COLE.

I am King Cole, and I carry my stump.
Hurrah for King Charles ! down with old Noll's Rump !

Stands apart.

Enter KING WILLIAM.

I am King William of blessed me-mo-ry,   5
Who came and pulled down the high gallows tree,
And brought us all peace and pros-pe-ri-ty.

Stands apart.

Enter GIANT BLUNDERBORE.

I am Giant Blunderbore, fee, fi, fum,
Ready to fight ye all, — so I says, " Come " ;

Enter LITTLE JACK.

And this here is my little man Jack —   10
A thump on his rump and a whack on his back !

Strikes him twice.

I 'll fight King Alfred, I 'll fight King Cole,
I 'm ready to fight any mortal soul ;
So here I, Blunderbore, takes my stand,
With this little devil, Jack, at my right hand,   15
Ready to fight for mortal life.   Fee, fi, fum !

The GIANT *and* LITTLE JACK *stand apart.*

Enter ST. GEORGE.

I am St. George of Merry Eng-land,
Bring in the morres-men, bring in our band.

MORRES-MEN *come forward and dance to a tune from fife and drum.*
The dance being ended, ST. GEORGE *continues :*

These are our tricks, Ho ! men, ho !
These are our sticks, — whack men so !   20

Strikes THE DRAGON, *who roars, and comes forward.*

THE DRAGON *speaks.*

Stand on head, stand on feet !
Meat, meat, meat for to eat !

Tries to bite KING ALFRED.

I am the Dragon, here are my jaws ;
I am the Dragon, here are my claws.
Meat, meat, meat for to eat !   25
Stand on my head, stand on my feet !

Turns a summersault and stands aside.

All sing, several times repeated :

Ho ! ho ! ho !
Whack men so !

*The drum and fife sound. They all fight, and after general disorder,
fall down.*

Enter OLD DR. BALL.

I am the Doctor, and I cure all ills,
Only gullup my portions,[1] and swallow my pills ;   30
I can cure the itch, the stitch, the pox, the palsy and the gout,
All pains within and all pains without.
Up from the floor, Giant Blunderbore !

Gives him a pill, and he rises at once.

Get up, King ; get up, Bride ;
Get up, Fool, and stand aside.   35

Gives them each a pill, and they rise.

Get up, King Cole, and tell the gentlefolks all
There never was a doctor like Mr. Doctor Ball.
Get up, St. George, old England's knight,

Gives him a pill.

You have wounded the Dragon and finished the fight.

All stand aside but THE DRAGON, *who lies in convulsions on the floor.*

Now kill the Dragon and poison old Nick ;   40
At Yule-tyde, both o' ye, cut your stick !

THE DOCTOR *forces a large pill down* THE DRAGON'S *throat, who thereupon roars, and dies in convulsions.*

Then enter FATHER CHRISTMAS.

I am Father Christmas ! hold, men, hold !
Be there loaf in your locker, and sheep in your fold,
A fire on the hearth, and good luck for your lot,
Money in your pocket, and a pudding in the pot !   45

[1] Lee *suggests* potions, *which is right.*

He sings :

    Hold, men, hold !
    Put up your sticks,
    End all your tricks ;
    Hold, men, hold !

Chorus (all sing, while one goes round with a hat for gifts).

    Hold, men, hold !   50
    We are very cold,
    Inside and outside,
    We are very cold.
    If you don't give us silver,
    Then give us gold   55
From the money in your pockets —

Some of the performers show signs of fighting again.

    Hold, men, hold !

Song and chorus.

God A'mighty bless your hearth and fold,
Shut out the wolf, and keep out the cold!
You gev' us silver, keep you the gold,   60
For 't is money in your pocket. — Hold, men, hold !

Repeat in chorus.

God A'mighty bless, &c.

                            Exeunt omnes.

II.

LUTTERWORTH CHRISTMAS PLAY.

Dramatis Personae.

KING OF ENGLAND; *in robes, wearing the crown.*
PRINCE GEORGE, HIS SON; *in robes, with sword by his side.*
CAPTAIN SLASHER; *in military costume, with sword and pistol.*
TURKISH CHAMPION; *ditto.*   BEELZEBUB.
A NOBLE DOCTOR.   A CLOWN.

Enter CAPTAIN SLASHER.

[CAPT. S.]   I beg your pardon for being so bold,
I enter your house, the weather 's so cold.

Room, a room ! brave gallants give us room to sport,
For in this house we do resort,
Resort, resort for many a day. 5
Step in, the King of England,
And boldly clear the way !

Enter KING OF ENGLAND.

[KING OF E.] I am the King of England that boldly does
    appear ;
I come to seek my only son, — my only son is here.

Enter PRINCE GEORGE.

[PRINCE G.] I am Prince George, a worthy knight ; 10
I 'll spend my blood for England's right,
England's right I will maintain,
I 'll fight for old England once again.

Enter TURKISH KNIGHT.

[TURK. KN.] I am the Turkish Champion,
From Turkey's land I come ; 15
I come to fight the King of England
And all his noble men.

CAPTAIN SLASHER.

[CAPT. S.] In comes Captain Slasher,
Captain Slasher is my name ;
With sword and pistol by my side 20
I hope to win the game.

KING OF E. I am the King of England,
As you may plainly see ;
These are my soldiers standing by me.
They stand by me your life to end, 25
On them doth my life depend.
    PRINCE G. I am Prince George, the champion bold,
And with my sword I won three crowns of gold ;
I slew the fiery dragon and brought him to the slaughter
And won the King of Egypt's only daughter. 30
    TURK. KN. As I was going by St. Francis' School.

I heard a lady cry, " A fool ! a fool ! "
" A fool ! " was every word ;
That man 's a fool,
Who wears a wooden sword.   35
   PRINCE G.   A wooden sword? you dirty dog !
My sword is made of the best of metal free.
If you would like to taste of it,
I 'll give it unto thee.
Stand off, stand off, you dirty dog !   40
Or by my sword you 'll die ;
I 'll cut you down the middle
And make your blood to fly.

    They fight; PRINCE GEORGE *falls, mortally wounded.*

   KING OF E.   Oh horrible ! terrible ! what hast thou done ?
Thou hast ruined me, ruined me,   45
By killing of my only son !
Oh, is there ever a noble doctor to be found,
To cure this English champion
Of his deep and deadly wound ?

    Enter NOBLE DOCTOR.

   [DOCTOR.]   Oh yes, there is a noble doctor to be found,   50
To cure this English champion
Of his deep and deadly wound.
   KING OF E.   And pray what is your practice ?
   DOCTOR.   I boast not of my practice, neither do I study
     in the practice of physic.   55
   KING OF E.   What can you cure ?
   DOCTOR.   All sorts of diseases,
Whatever you pleases :
I can cure the itch, the pitch,
The phthisic, the palsy, and the gout ;   60
And if the devil 's in the man,
I can fetch him out.
My wisdom lies in my wig.
I torture not my patients with excations
Such as pills, boluses, solutions, and embrocations ;   65

But by the word of command
I can make this mighty prince to stand.
 KING. What is your fee?
 DOCTOR. Ten pounds, is true.
 KING. Proceed, noble doctor ;   70
You shall have your due.
 DOCTOR. Arise, arise ! most noble prince, arise,
And no more dormant lay ;
And with thy sword
Make all thy foes obey.   75

The PRINCE arises.

 PRINCE G. My head is made of iron,
My body is made of steel,
My legs are made of crooked bones,
To force you all to yield.

Enter BEELZEBUB.

 BEEL. In comes I, old Beelzebub ;   80
Over my shoulder I carry my club,
And in my hand a frying-pan,
Pleased to get all the money I can.

Enter CLOWN.

 CLOWN. In comes I, who 's never been yet,
With my great head and little wit :   85
My head is great, my wit is small,
I 'll do my best to please you all.

Song by all.

And now we are done and must be gone,
 No longer will we stay here ;
But if you please, before we go,   90
 We 'll taste your Christmas beer.

Exeunt omnes.

[THE REVESBY SWORD PLAY.]

Printed from *The Folk-Lore Journal*, VII, 338–53, where it is published by
T. F. Ordish. In the footnotes, O. indicates this edition. I have made no unindicated alteration except in capitals, punctuation, and the abbreviation of the
names of the speakers. Although the play contains, as Ordish points out,
many different elements, I have indicated in the title chosen for it only its
most prominent feature.

OCTOBER YE 20, 1779.

The Morrice Dancers (named in Dramatis Personæ) acted
their merry dancing, &c., at Revesby, in their ribbon dresses, &c.,
and two men from Kirtley, without any particular dresses, sung
the song of Landlord and Tenant.[1]

John Ironmonger *acted the* LANDLORD, *and*
John Clarkson " " TENANT.

Dramatis Personæ.

Men.

THE FOOL	John Johnson.
PICKLE HERRING . . .	Richd. Johnson.
BLUE BREECHES . . .	Henry Johnson.
PEPPER BREECHES . .	John Tomlinson.
GINGER BREECHES . .	Chas. Hodgson.
MR. ALLSPICE . . .	Thos. Harness.

Women.

CICELY	John Fisher.
FIDLER, *or* MR. MUSICK MAN,	John Johnson, jun[r].

[1] *This song is omitted here because it has nothing to do with the play
and is a not very interesting specimen of the* débat, *examples of which will
be given in* vol. III. [See Publisher's Note].

THE PLOW BOYS, or MORRIS DANCERS.

Enter FOOL.

You gentle Lords of honour,
 Of high and low, I say,
We all desire your favour
 For to see our pleasant play.   4

Our play it is the best, kind sirs,
 That you would like to know;
And we will do our best, sirs,
 And think it well bestowd.   8

Tho' some of us be little,
 And some of a middle sort,
We all desire your favour
 To see our pleasant sport.   12

You must not look on our actions,
 Our wits they are all to seek,
So I pray take no exceptions
 At what I am a-going to speak.   16

We are come over the mire and moss ;
We dance an Hobby Horse ;
A Dragon you shall see,
And a wild Worm for to flee.
Still we are all brave, jovial boys
And takes delight in Christmas toys.   22

We are come both for bread and beer,
And hope for better cheer
And something out of your purse, sir,
Which I hope you will be never the worse, sir. ·
Still we are all brave, jovial boys
And takes delight in Christmas toys.   28

Come now, Mr. Musick Man, play me my delight.

FIDLER.   What is that, old father?   30

FOOL.   Ah! boy, times is hard!   I love to have money in
both pockets.

FID.   You shall have it, old father.

FOOL.   Let me see it.

THE FOOL *then calls in his five sons: first* PICKLE HERRING, *then* BLUE
BRITCHES, *then* GINGER BRITCHES, PEPPER BRITCHES, *and last calls out:*

Come now, you Mr. Allspice!   35

*They foot it once round the room, and the man that is to ride the Hobby
Horse goes out, and the rest sing the following song:*

Come in, come in, thou Hobby Horse,
And bring thy old fool at thy arse!
Sing tanter[a]day, sing tanter[a]day,
Sing heigh down, down, with a derry down a!   39

Then THE FOOL *and the Horse fights about the room, whilst the following
song is singing by the rest:*

Come in, come in, thou bonny wild Worm!
For thou hast ta'en many a lucky turn.
Sing tanteraday, sing tanteraday,
Sing heigh down, down, with a derry down!   43

*The wild Worm is only sprung three or four times, as the man walks
round the room, and then goes out, and the Horse and* THE FOOL *fights
again, whilst the following song is sung:*

Come in, come in, thou Dragon stout,
And take thy compass round about!
Sing tanteraday, sing tanteraday,
Sing heigh down, down, with a derry down!   47

Now you shall see a full fair fight
Between our old Fool and his right.
Sing tanteraday, sing tanteraday,
Sing heigh down, down, with a derry down!   51

Now our scrimage is almost done;
Then you shall see more sport soon.

Sing tanteraday, sing tanteraday,
Sing heigh down, down, with a derry down !   55

FOOL.   Up well hart,[1] and up well hind !
Let every man then to his own kind.
Sing tanteraday, sing tanteraday,
Sing heigh down, down, with a derry down !   59

Come, follow me, merry men all !
Tho' we have made bold for to call,
It is only once by the year
That we are so merry here.
Still we are all brave, jovial boys,
And takes delight in Christmas toys.   65

Then they all foot it round the room and follows THE FOOL *out.   They
all re-enter, and lock their swords to make the glass,* THE FOOL *running
about the room.*

PICKLE HERRING.   What is the matter now, father?

FOOL.   Why, I tell the[e] what, Pickle Herring.   As a I was
a-looking round about me through my wooden spectacles
made of a great, huge, little tiney bit of leather, placed
right behind me, even before me, I thought I saw a feat   70
thing —

P. H.   You thought you saw a feat thing?   What might this
feat thing be, think you, father?

FOOL.   How can I tell, boy, except I see it again?

P. H.   Would you know it if you see it again?   75

FOOL.   I cannot tell thee, boy.   Let me get it looked at.

PICKLE HERRING, *holding up the glass, says:*

[P. H.]   Is this it, father?

THE FOOL, *looking round, says:*

[FOOL.]   Why, I protest, Pickle Herring, the very same
thing !   But what might thou call this very pretty thing?

P. H.   What might you call it?   You are older than I am.   80

FOOL.   How can that be, boy, when I was born before you?

P. H.   That is the reason that makes you older.

----

[1] O. hark.

FOOL.   Well, what dost thou call this very pretty thing?

P. H.   Why, I call it a fine large looking-glass.

FOOL.   Let me see what I can see in this fine large looking-   85
glass.   Here's a hole through it, I see.   I see, and I
see !

P. H.   You see and you see? and what do you see?

FOOL.   Marry, e'en a fool, just like the[e] !

P. H.   It is only your own face in the glass.   90

FOOL.   Why, a fool may be mistain sometimes, Pickle Herring.   But what might this fine large looking-glass cost
the[e]?

P. H.   That fine large looking-glass cost me a guinea.

FOOL.   A guinea, boy?   Why, I could have bought as good   95
a one at my own door for three half-pence.

P. H.   Why, fools and cuckolds has always the best luck !

FOOL.   That is as much to say thy father is one.

P. H.   Why, you pass for one !

THE FOOL, *keeping the glass all the while in his hands, says:*

FOOL.   Why was thou such a ninnie, boy, to go to ware a 100
guinea to look for thy beauty where it never was?   But
I will shew thee, boy, how foolish thou hast wared a
deal of good money.

Then THE FOOL *flings the glass upon the floor, jumps upon it ; then the
dancers every one drawing out his own sword, and* THE FOOL *dancing
about the room,* PICKLE HERRING *takes him by the collar and says :*

P. H.   Father, father, you are so merrylly disposed this
good time there is no talking to you !   Here is very bad 105
news.

FOOL.   Very good news?   I am glad to hear it ; I do not
hear good news every day.

P. H.   It is very bad news !

FOOL.   Why, what is the matter now, boy?   110

P. H.   We have all concluded to cut off your head.

FOOL.   Be mercyfull to me, a sinner !   If you should do as
you have said, there is no such thing.   I would not lose
my son Pickle Herring for fifty pounds.

P. H.   It is your son Pickle Herring that must lose you.   It 115
is your head we desire to take off.

FOOL.   My head?   I never had my head taken off in all my
life !

P. H.   You both must and shall.

FOOL.   Hold, hold, boy ! thou seem'st to be in good ear- 120
nest ; but I 'll tell thee where I 'll be buryed.

P. H.   Why, where will you be buried but in the churchyard,
where other people are buried?

FOOL.   Churchyard?   I never was buried there in all my
life !   125

P. H.   Why, where will you be buried?

FOOL.   Ah ! boy, I am often dry ; I will be buried in Mr.
Mirfin's ale-celler.

P. H.   It is such a place as I never heard talk off in all my
life.   130

FOOL.   No, nor nobody else, boy.

P. H.   What is your fancy to be buried there?

FOOL.   Ah ! boy, I am oftens dry, and, when they come to
fill the quart, I 'll drink it off, and they will wonder what
is the matter.   135

P. H.   How can you do so when you will be dead?   We shall
take your head from your body, and you will be dead.

FOOL.   If I must die, I will dye with my face to the light, for
all you !

Then THE FOOL, *kneeling down, with the swords round his neck, says:*

FOOL.   Now, gentlemen, you see how ungratefull my chil- 140
dren is grown !   When I had them all at home, small,
about as big as I am, I put them out to good learning :
I put them to Coxcomb Colledge, and then to the University of Loggerheads ; and I took them home again
this good time of Christmas, and I examin'd them all 145
one by one, all together [1] for shortness.   And now they
are grown so proud and so presumptious they are a-going
to kill their old father for his little means.   So I must
dye for all this?

[1] O. altogether.

P. H.   You must dye, father.   150

FOOL.   And I will die for all the tother.   But I have a little
   something, I will give it amongst you as far as it goes,
   and then I shall dye quietly.

P. H.   I hope you will.

FOOL.   So, to my first son, Pickle Herring, — [1]   155
     I 'll give him the roaned nag,
     And that will make the rogue brag.
  And to my second son, —
     I 'll give him the brindled cow.
  And to my third son, —   160
     I 'll give him the sanded sow ;
     And hope I shall please you all enow.
  And to my fourth son, —
     I 'll give him the great ruff dog,
     For he always lives like a hog.   165
  And to my fifth son, —
     I 'll give him the ram,
     And I 'll dye like a lamb.

  Then they draw their swords, and THE FOOL *falls on the floor, and the
   dancers walk once round* THE FOOL ; *and* PICKLE HERRING *stamps with
   his foot and* THE FOOL *rises on his knees again ; and* PICKLE HERRING
   says :*

P. H.   How now, father ?

FOOL.   How now, then, boy ?   I have another squeak for   170
   my life ?

P. H.   You have a many.

  Then, the dancers puting their swords round THE FOOL'S *neck again,*

FOOL.   So I must dye ?

P. H.   You must dye, father.

FOOL.   Hold ! I have yet a little something more to leave   175
   amongst you, and then I hope I shall dye quietly.   So
   to my first son, Pickle Herring, —
     I 'll give him my cap and my coat, —
     A very good sute, boy.

    [1] *Lines* 156–185 *as prose in* O.

And to my second son, —   180
      I 'll give him my purse and apparel,
      But be sure, boys, you do not quarrel.

      As to my other three,
      My executors they shall be.

Then, PICKLE HERRING *puting his hand to his sword,*

FOOL.   Hold, hold, boy ! Now I submit my soul to God. 185
P. H.   A very good thought, old father !
FOOL.   Mareham churchyard, I hope, shall have my bones.

Then the dancers walk round THE FOOL *with their swords in their
hands, and* PICKLE HERRING *stamps with his foot and says :*

[P. H.]   Heigh, old father !
FOOL.   Why, boy, since I have been out of this troublesome
    world I have heard so much musick of fiddles playing 190
    and bells ringing that I have a great fancy to go away
    singing. So, prithee, Pickle Herring, let me have one
    of thy best songs.
P. H.   You shall have it, old father.
FOOL.   Let me see it.   195

They sing.

Good people all, I pray you now behold,
Our old Fool's bracelet is not made of gold,
But it is made of iron and good steel,
And unto death we 'll make this old Fool yield.   199

FOOL.   I pray, forbear, my children small ;
For, as I am lost as parent to you all,
O, let me live a while your sport for to advance,
That I may rise again and with you have a dance.   203

THE SONS *sing.*

Now, old father, that you know our will,
That for your estate we do your body kill,
Soon after death the bell for you shall toll,
And wish the Lord he may receive your soul.   207

Then THE FOOL *falls down, and the dancers, with their swords in their hands, sings the following song :*

Good people all, you see what we have done :
We have cut down our father like the [1] evening sun,
And here he lies all in his purple gore,
And we are afraid he never will dance more.   211

FOOL rises from the floor and says :

[FOOL.]   No, no, my children ! by chance you are all mistaen !
For here I find myself, I am not slain ;
But I will rise, your sport then to advance,
And with you all, brave boys, I 'll have a dance.   215

Then the Foreman and CICELY *dances down and the other two couple
stand their ground. After a short dance called "Jack, the brisk young
Drummer," they all go out but* THE FOOL, FIDLER, *and* CICELY.

FOOL.   Hear you, do you please to hear the sport of a fool?
CICELY.   A fool? for why?
FOOL.   Because I can neither leap, skip, nor dance, but cut
   a caper thus high.   [*He capers.*]   Sound, music !   I must
   be gon ; the Lord of Pool draws nigh.   220

Enter PICKLE HERRING.

P. H.   I am the Lord of Pool,
   And here begins my measure,[2]
And after me a fool,
   To dance a while for pleasure
In Cupid's school.   225

FOOL.   A fool, a fool, a fool,
   A fool I heard thou say,[2]
   But more the other way,
For here I have a tool
   Will make a maid to play,
Although in Cupid's school.
   Come all away !   232

---

[1] O. ye.
[2] O. *has these two lines as one.*

Enter BLUE BRITCHES.

BLUE B.   I am the Knight of Lee,
   And here I have a dagger,
Offended not to be.
   Come in, thou needy beggar,
And follow me !   237

Enter GINGER BRITCHES.

GINGER B.   Behold, behold, behold
   A man of poor estate !
Not one penny to infold !   240

Enter PEPPER BRITCHES.

PEPPER B.   My money is out at use, or else I would.

Enter MR. ALLSPICE.

ALLSPICE.   With a hack, a hack, a hack,
   See how I will skip and dance
   For joys that we have found !
Let each man take his chance,   245
   And we will all dance around.

*Then they dance the sword dance which is called " Nelly's Gig " ; then
they run under their swords, which is called " Runing Battle " ; then
three dancers dances with three swords, and the Foreman jumping
over the swords ; then* THE FOOL *goes up to* CICELY.

FOOL.   Here comes I that never come yet,
   Since last time, lovy !
I have a great head but little wit.
Tho' my head be great and my wits be small,   250
I can play the fool for a while as well as [the] best of ye all.
¹ My name is noble Anthony ;
I am as meloncholly as a mantle-tree.
I am come to show you a little sport and activity,
   And soon, too !   255
Make room for noble Anthony
And all his good company !
Drive out all these proud rogues, and let my lady and I have
   a parl !   [*Exeunt all but* FOOL *and* CICELY.]

¹ *Lines 253–266 as prose in* O.

CICELY.   O, ye clown ! what makes you drive out my men
 so soon? 261

  FOOL.   O, pardon, madam, pardon ! and I
  Will never offend you more.
  I will make your men come in as fast
   As ever they did before. 265

  CICELY.   I pray you at my sight,
   And drive it not till night,[1]
  That I may see them dance once more
   So lovely in my sight.[1] 269

  FOOL.   A-faith, madam, and so I will !
   I will play the man [1]
  And make them come in
   As fast as ever I can. —[1] 273

  But hold, gip ! Mrs. Clagars,
   How do you sell geese ? [1]
  CICELY.   Go, look, Mister Midgecock !
   Twelve pence apiece. [1] 277

  FOOL.   Oh, the pretty pardon !
  CICELY.   A gip for a frown !
  FOOL.   An ale-wife for an apparitor !
  CICELY.   A rope for a clown !
  FOOL.   Why, all the devise in the country
   Cannot pull this down ![1] 283

I am a valiant knight just come from the seas :[2]
 You do know me, do you?
I can kill you ten thousand, tho' they be but fleas.
I can kill you a man for an ounce of mustard,
Or I can kill you ten thousand for a good custard.
 I have an old sheep skin,
 And I lap it well in, 290
Sword and buckler by my side, all ready for to fight !

---

 [1] *As one line in* O.   [2] *Two lines in* O.

Come forth, you whores and gluttons all ! for, had it not been
   in this country, I should not have shewen my valour
   amongst you.   But sound, music ! for I must be gone.   294

[Exit Fool.]

Enter Pickle Herring.

P. H.   In first and formost do I come,
    All for to lead this race,
Seeking the country far and near
    So fair a lady to embrace.   298

So fair a lady did I never see,
    So comely in my sight,
Drest in her gaudy gold
    And silver shining bright.   302

She has fingers long, and rings
    Of honor of beaten gold :
    My masters all, behold !
It is now for some pretty dancing time,
And we will foot it fine.   307

Blue B.   I am a youth of jollitree ;
Where is there one like unto me ?
My hair is bush'd very thick ;
My body is like an hasel stick ;   311

My legs they quaver like an eel ;
My arms become my body weel ;
My fingers they are long and small :
Am not I a jolly youth, proper and tall ?   315

Therefore, Mister Musick Man,
    Whatsoever may be my chance,
It is for my ladie's love and mine,
    Strike up the morris dance.   316

Then they foot it once round.

Ginger B.   I am a jolly young man of flesh, blood and bone ;
Give eare, my masters all, each one !   321

And especially you, my lady dear,
    I hope you like me well.
Of all the gallants here
    It is I that doth so well.   325

Therefore, Mister Musick Man,
    Whatsoever may be my chance,
It is for my ladie's love and mine,
    Strike up the morris dance.   329

                     Then they foot it round.

PEPPER B.   I am my father's eldest son,
    And heir of all his land,
And in a short time, I hope,
    It will fall into my hands.   333

I was brought up at Lindsey Court
    All the days of my life.
Here stands a fair lady,
    I wish she was my wife.   337

I love her at my heart,
    And from her I will never start.
Therefore, Mr. Musick Man, play up my part.
FOOL (*rushing in*).   And mine, too !   341

    Enter ALLSPICE, *and they foot it round.* PICKLE HERRING, *suter to*
    CICELY, *takes her by the hand, and walks about the room.*

P. H.   Sweet Ciss, if thou wilt be my love,
    A thousand pounds I will give thee.
CICELY.   No, you 're too old, sir, and I am too young,
    And alas ! old man, that must not be.   345

P. H.   I 'll buy the[e] a gown of violet blue,
    A petticoat imbroidered to thy knee ;
Likewise my love to thee shall be true.
    CICELY.   But alas ! old man, that must not be.   349

P. H.   Thou shalt walk at thy pleasure, love, all the day,
    If at night thou wilt but come home to me ;

And in my house bear all the sway.
    CICELY.   Your children they 'll find fault with me.   **353**

P. H.   I 'll turn my children out of doors.
    CICELY.   And so, I fear, you will do me.
P. H.   Nay, then, sweet Ciss, ne'er trust me more,
    For I never loved lass before like the[e]. [1]   **357**

Enter FOOL.

FOOL.   No, nor behind, neither.
Well met, sweet Cis, well over-ta'en !
    CICELY.   You are kindly wellcome, sir, to me.
FOOL.   I 'll wipe my eyes, and I 'll look again !
    Methinks, sweet Cis, I now the[e] see !   **362**

CICELY.   Raf, what has thou to pleasure me?
    FOOL.   Why, this, my dear, I will give the[e],
And all I have it shall be thine.
    CICELY.   Kind sir, I thank you heartilly.   **366**

P. H. (*to* THE FOOL).   Stand back, stand back, thou silly old
       swain !
    This girl shall go with none but me.
FOOL.   I will not !
P. H.   Stand back, stand back, or I 'll cleave thy brain !

Then PICKLE HERRING *goes up to* CIS, *and says:*

    O, now, sweet Cis, I am come to thee !   **371**

CICELY.   You are as wellcome as the rest,
    Wherein you brag so lustilly.
FOOL.   For a thousand pounds she loves me best !
    I can see by the twinkling of her ee.   **375**

P. H.   I have store of gold, whereon I boast ;
    Likewise my sword, love, shall fight for the[e];
When all is done, love, I 'll scour the coast,
    And bring in gold for thee and me.   **379**

    [1] O. like the before ; *emend. by* Kittredge.

CICELY.   Your gold may gain as good as I,
　　But by no means it shall tempt me ;
For youthfull years and frozen age
　　Cannot in any wise agree.   383

　　　　　Then BLUE BRITCHES *goes up to her, and says:*

[BLUE B.]   Sweet mistress, be advised by me :
　　Do not let this old man be denyed,
But love him for his gold in store ;
　　Himself may serve for a cloak, beside.   387

CICELY.   Yes, sir, but you are not in the right.
　　Stand back and do not council me !
For I love a lad that will make me laugh
　　In a secret place, to pleasure me.
FOOL.   Good wench !   392

PICKLE HERRING.   Love, I have a beard as white as milk.
　　CICELY.   Ne'er better for that, thou silly old man !
P. H.   Besides, my skin, love, is soft as silk.
　　FOOL.   And thy face shines like a dripping pan.   396

P. H.   Rafe, what has thou to pleasure her ?
　　FOOL.   Why a great deal more, boy, than there's in
　　　　the[e].
P. H.   Nay then, old rogue, I thee defye.
　　CICELY.   I pray, dear friends, fall not out for me !   400

P. H.   Once I could skip, leap, dance, and sing ;
　　Why will you not give place to me ?
FOOL.   Nay, then, old rogue, I thee defye ;
　　For thy nose stands like a Maypole tree.   404

　　　　Then goes up GINGER BRITCHES [1] *to* CISLEY *and says:*

[GINGER B.]   Sweet mistress, mind what this man doth say,
　　For he speaks nothing but the truth :
Look on the soldier, now I pray ;
　　See, is not he a handsome youth?   408

　　　　　　　　[1] O. Breeches.

CICELY.   Sir, I am engaged to one I love,
    And ever constant I will be,
There is nothing that I prize above.
        P. H.   For a thousand pounds, she 's gone from me !
FOOL.   Thou may lay two !   413

CICELY (*to* PICKLE HERRING).   Old father, for your reverend
        years,
    Stand you the next man unto me ;
Then he that doth the weapon bear ;
    For I will have the hind man of the three !   417

FOOL (*to* PICKLE HERRING).   Old father, a fig for your old gold !
    The soldier, he shall bear no sway !
But you shall see, and so shall we,
    'T is I that carries the lass away !   421

Then the dancers takes hold of their swords, and foots it round the room ;
then every man makes his obeisance to the master of the house, and the
whole concludes.

FINIS.

PART IV.

[MANKIND.]

For the opportunity to print this specimen of the " Macro Moralities " I am indebted to the courtesy of Dr. Furnivall, who allowed me to have a copy made from his copy of the original MS. The original MS., now the property of J. H. Gurney, Esq., was written apparently in the reign of Edward IV (cf. l. 684), a few miles east or northeast of Cambridge (cf. ll. 499 ff.), and was once the property of a monk named Hyngham (cf. verse at end of play). I have disregarded the flourishes of *n*, *ll*, *r*, etc.

[*Dramatis Personae.*

MANKYNDE.	MERCY.
NEW GYSE.	NOW-A-DAYS.
NOUGHT.	MYSCHEFF.

TITYVILLUS.]

[Enter Mercy.]

MERCY.   The very fownder & begynn*er* of ow*er* fyrst crea-
  *ci*on,
  A-monge ws synfull wrechys he oweth to be magnyfyede,
*Tha*t for ow*er* dysobedyenc[e] he hade non indygnac*i*on
  To sende hys own son to be torn & crucyfyede ;
  Ow*er* obsequyouse s*er*uyce to hym xulde be aplyede ;
Wher*e* he was Lorde of all & made all thy*n*ge of nought,
  For *th*e synfull synner to late [1] hym revyuyde
And [2] for hys redempcyon sett hys own son at nought.   8

*Tha*t may be seyde & veryfyede : Mankynde was der*e* bought;
  By *th*e pytouse deth of Ih*e*su he hade hys remedye ;
He was p*ur*gyde of hys defawte, *th*at wrechydly hade
    wrought,
  By hys gloryus Passyon, *th*at blyssyde lauatorye.

---

[1] MS. lade.   [2] Qy. *omit* And, *and insert* he *before* sett.

O souerence, I be-seche you yower condycyons to
   rectyfye
Ande with humylite & reuerence to haue a remocyon
   To this blyssyde prynce that ower nature doth gloryfye,
*Tha*t ye may be partycypable of hys retribucyon.   16

I haue be the very mene for yower restytucyon ;
   Mercy ys my name, that mornyth for yower offence.
Dyverte not yower-sylffe in tyme of temtacyon,
      That ye may be acceptable to Gode at yower goynge
      hence.
      The grett Mercy of Gode, that ys of most preemmy-
      nence,
Be medyacyon[1] of Ower Lady, that ys euer habundante[2]
      To the synfull creature that wyll repent hys ne[g]ly-
      gence, —
I prey Gode, at yower most nede *tha*t Mercy be yower de-
      fendawnte !   24

In goode werkys I a-wyse yow, souerence, to be perseuer-
   ante,
      To puryfye yower sowlys that thei be not corupte ;
For yower gostly enmy wyll make hys a-vaunte,[3]
      Yower goode condycions yf he may interupte.
      O ȝe souerens that sytt, & ȝe brothern that stonde ryghte
      wppe,
Pryke not yower felycytes in thynges transytorye !
      Be-holde not the erthe, but lyfte yower ey wppe !
Se how the hede the members dayly do magnyfye !   32

Who ys the hede, forsoth, I xall yow certyfye :
   I mene ower Sauyower, that was lykynnyde to a lambe ;
Ande hys sayntes be the members, that dayly he doth satysfye
      With the precyose reuer that runnyth from hys wombe ;
      Ther ys non such foode be water ner by lande,
So precyouse, so gloryouse, so redefull to ower entent,

---

[1] MS. medytacyon.   [2] MS. habundance.   [3] MS. a-vaunce.

For yt hath dyssoluyde Ma*n*kynde from *th*e bitter bonde
Of *th*e mortall enmye, [the] venymouse ¹ s*er*pente ;   40

From *th*e wyche Gode pres*er*ue yow all at *th*e last Iugeme*n*t,
      For sekyrly *ther* xall be a streat ² examynacyon ;
The corn xall be sauyde, *th*e chaffe xall be brente :
      I be-sech yow hertyly, haue *th*is premedytacyon*e*.   44

[*Enter Myscheffe.*]

Mys.   I be-seche yow hertyly, leue yow*er* calc[ul]acyon !
Leue yow*er* chaffe, leue yow*er* corn, leue yow*er* dalyacyon !
Yow*er* wytt ys lytyll, yow*er* hede ys mekyll, ye ar*e* full of
      predycacyon !
      But, s*er*, I prey *th*is questyon to claryfye :
Dryff-draff, mysse-masche,
Sume was corn & sume was chaffe,
My dame seyde my name was Raffe,
      On-shett yow*er* loke & take an halpenye !   52

Mercy.   Why com*e* ʒe hethyr, bro*th*er ? ʒe we*re* not dysyryde.
Mys.   For a wynt*er* corn-threscher, s*er*, I haue hyryde ;
Ande ʒe sayde *th*e corn xulde be sauyde & *th*e chaffe xulde
      be fyryde,⁸
      Ande he pr*o*uyth nay, as yt schewth be *th*is werse :
*Corn s*eru*it bredib*us, *chaffe horsib*us, *straw fyrybusq*ue.
Thys ys as moche to say, to yow*er* leude wndyrstondynge,
As, *th*e corn xall s*er*ue to brede at *th*e nexte bakynge ;
      Chaff horsibus &° reliquid,
The chaff to horse xall be goode pr*o*duce ;
Whe*n* a ma*n* ys for-colde, *th*e straw may be brent,
And so forth, &c.   63

Mercy.   A-voyde, goode bro*th*er ! ʒe ben culpable
To interupte thus my talkyng*e* delectable.
Mys.   Ser, I haue no*th*er horse nor ⁴ sadyll,
      Therfor I may not ryde.

¹ MS. vemynouse.   ⁸ MS. feryrde.
² MS. sterat.   ⁴ MS. for.

MERCY.   Hye yow forthe on fote, brother, in Godes name!
MYS.   I say, ser, I am cumme hedyr to make yow game.
зet bade зe me not go out in the deullys name,
     Ande I wyll a-byde.   71

MERCY.[1]   Ande how, mynstrellys! pley the comyn trace.
     Ley on with thi bowys[2] tyll his bely breste.   73

NOUGHT.   I put case I breke my neke;[3] how than?
NEW.   I gyff no[4] force, by Sent Tanne!
NOW.   Leppe[5] a-bout lyuely! thou art a wyght man;
     Let ws be mery wyll we be here!
NOUGHT.   Xall I breke my neke to show yow sporte?
NOW.   Therfor euer beware of thi reporte!
NOUGHT.   I be-schrew ye all! her ys a schrewde sorte;
     Haue ther at them, with a mery chere!   81

Her thei daunce. Mercy sayth:

MERCY.   Do wey! dowey! this reuell, sers, do wey!
NOW.   Do wey! goode Adam, do wey!
Thys ys no parte of thin pley.
     NOUGHT.   зys, mary, I prey yow! for I loue not this
          rewelynge.
Euer forth, goode fader, I yow prey;
Be a lytyll зe may assay.
A-non of with yower clothes yf зe wyll pray.
     Go to, for I haue hade a praty scottlynge.   89

MERCY.   Nay, brother, I wyll not daunce.[6]
NEW.   Yf зe wyll, ser, my brother wyll make yow to prawnce.

---

[1] *These lines begin a new leaf in the MS. They seem highly inappro-priate in the mouth of Mercy, cf. especially l. 73. Moreover, it is clear from ll. 98, 111 that the entrance of New Gyse, Nowadays, and Nought was immediately preceded by Mercy's use of the words forming their names. I therefore suppose that at least one leaf of MS. (containing their entrance) has been lost at this point, and suggest that the command to the minstrels be assigned to New Gyse.*   [2] *MS.* bollys.

[3] *MS.* reke.   [4] *MS.* us.   [5] *MS.* Leffe.

[6] *MS.* dauunce; *but it often has the* au-*contraction for* a.

Now. W*ith* all my herte, s*er*, yf I may yow a-va*u*nce ;
  ȝe may assay be a lytyll*e* trace.
NOUGHT. ȝe, s*er*, wyll ȝe do well?
Trace not w*ith th*em, be my cownsell ;
For I haue tracyed su*m*what to fell,[1] —
  I tell [yow] yt ys a narow space.   97

But, s*er*, I trow, of ws thre I herde you speke.
NEW. Crys*tes* curse haue ȝe [2] *th*er-for, for I was in slepe !
Now. A[nd] I hade *th*e cuppe [3] in my honde redy to goo to
        met.
  Therfor, s*er*, curtly grett yow well.
MERCY. Few word*es*! few & well sett !
NEW. S*er*, yt ys *th*e new gyse & *th*e new iett :
Many word*es* & schortely sett, —
  Thys ys *th*e new gyse, eu*er*y dele.   105

MERCY. Lady, helpe ! How wrechys delyte in *th*er synn-
        full [4] weys !
Now. Say no[ugh]t ageyn *th*e new gyse now-a-days.
*Tho*u xall fynde ws sch[r]ewys at all assays ;
  Be war*e*, ȝe may son lyke a bofett !
MERCY. He was well occupyede *tha*t browte yow hether ! [5]
NOUGHT. I harde yow call New Gyse, Now-a-days, Nought,
        — all *th*es thre to-gether.
Yf ȝe sey *tha*t I lye, I xall make yow to slyther ;
  So take yow her*e* a trefett !   113

MERCY. Say me yower namys ; I know yow not.
NEW. New Gyse I !
[Now.]   Now-a-days [I] !

---

[1] MS. fylde fell. Kittredge *suggests that* fylde *was written by mistake, and that the copyist then, observing that* fylde *neither rhymed nor made sense, added the right word but neglected to erase* fylde.

[2] MS. hade; *corr. by* Kittredge, *who thinks the scribe may have caught up* hade *from the following line. I had conjectured* had he.

[3] MS. *has* redy *here as well as later in the line.*

[4] MS. *has three strokes each for* nn *and* u.

[5] MS. brethern : *possibly we ought to read* brether.

[NOUGHT.]   I Nought!

MERCY.   Be Jhesu Cryst, that me dere bowte,
    ȝe be-tray many men!

NEW.   Be-tray? Nay, nay, ser, nay, nay!
We make them both fresch & gay.
But of yower name, ser, I yow prey,
    That we may yow ken!   121

MERCY.   Mercy ys my name & my¹ denomynacyon!
I conseyue ȝe haue but a lytyll fors² in my commenycacyon.

NEW.   Ey, ey, yower body ys full of Englysch Laten!³

NOW.   I prey yow hertyly, worschypfull clerke —   125

I haue etun a dysch full of curdes,
Ande I haue schetun yower mowth fulle of turdes;
Now opyn yower sachell with Late[n]⁴ wordes,
    And sey me this in clerycall maner!
Also I haue a wyf, her name ys Rackell;
Betwyx her & me was a gret batell,
Ande fayne of yow I wolde her[e] tell
    Who was the most master.   133

NOUGHT.   Thy wyf, Rachell, I dare ley xxᵗⁱ lyse!

NOW.   Who spake to the, foll? Thou art not wyse!
Go & do that⁵ longyth to thin offyce:
    Osculare fundamentum!

NOUGHT.   Lo, master! lo,⁶ here ys a pardon bely mett,⁷—
Yt ys grawntyde of Pope Pokett:
Yf ȝe wyll putt yower nose in hys wyffes sokett,
    ȝe xall haue xlᵗʸ days of pardon.   141

---

¹ By written over in MS.   ² MS. looks like fans.
³ A note in the margin says, Haue this Englysch made in Laytin:
        I am a-ferde yt wyll brest;
        "I rausch," quod the baeger on-to me,
        When I stall a leg a motun,
        Ye are a stronge cunnynge clerke.
        I trey, &c.

⁴ MS. late; corr. by Kittredge.   ⁶ MS. to.
⁵ MS. doyt.   ⁷ MS. melt; qy. be lymett.

MERCY. Thys ydyll¹ language ȝe xall repent !
Out of *th*is place I wolde ȝe went.
NEW. Goo we hens² all thre w*ith* on assent ;
 My fadyr ys yrke of ow*er* eloquence,
*Th*er-for I wyll no lenger tary.
Gode brynge yow, mast*er*, & blyssyde Mary
To *th*e nu*m*ber of *th*e demonycall frayry !   148

 . . . . ³

NOW. Eu*er* wynde ! eu*er* reyn !
Thow I cu*m*me new a-geyn.
*Th*e deull put out both you*re* eyen !
 Felouse, go we hens tyght !
NOUGHT. Go we hens, a deull wey !
Her ys *th*e dor*e*, her ys *th*e wey !
Farwell, ientyll Iaffrey,
 I prey Gode gyf yow goode-nyght !   156

       Exiant.

MERCY. Thankyde be Gode, we haue a fayer dylyu*er*ance
 Of *th*es iij onthryfty gest*es*.
They know full lytyll what ys *th*er ordyna*n*ce ;
 I preve by reson *th*ei be wers *then* best*es* : 160

A best doth aft*er* hys naturall instytucyon ;
 ȝe may co*n*seyue by ther dysporte & be-hauo*ur*,
*Th*er ioy ande delyte ys in derysyon
 Of [t]her owyn Cryste to his dyshon*ur*. 164

Thys co*n*dycyon of leuyng, yt ys preiudycyall ;
 Be war*e th*er-of, yt ys wers *than* ony felony or treson.
How may yt be excusyde be-for *th*e Iustycė of all,
 Whe*n* for eu*er*y ydyll⁴ worde ws⁵ must yelde a reson? 168

¹ MS. yeyll, *cf.* l. 168.
² MS. haue; *corr. by* Kittredge.
³ *There is no indication in* MS. *of the loss of this line.*
⁴ MS. yeyll, *cf.* l. 142.
⁵ *Perhaps this should be amended to* we; *but, as the construction* us
must *is common, I retain the* MS. *reading.*

They haue grett ca[u]se *th*er-for ; *th*e[i] wyll take no thought;
    But how *than* whe*n* *th*e angell of hewyn xall blow *th*e
        tru*m*pe
Ande sey to *th*e transgressers *that* wykydly hath wrought :
    " Cu*m* forth on-to yow*er* Iuge & ȝelde yow*er* a-cownte "?   172

The*n* xall I, Mercy, be-gyn sor to wepe ;
    No*th*er comfort nor cownsell *th*er xall no*n* be hade,
But such as *th*ei haue sowyn, such xall *th*ei repe ;
    *Th*ei be wanton now, but *then* xall *th*ei be sade.   176

The goode new gyse now-a-days I wyll not dysalow ;
    I dyscomende *th*e vycyouse gyse, I prey haue me excusyde,
I nede not to speke of yt, yow*er* reson wyll tell it yow,
    Take *that*[1] ys to be takyn & leue *that*[1] ys to be
        refusyde !   180

               [Enter Mankynde.]

MANK.   Of *th*e erth & of *th*e gler[2] we haue ow*er* pr*o*pagacyon,
    By *th*e pr*o*uydens of Gode *th*us be we deryvatt,
To whos mercy I recome*n*de *th*is holl co*n*grygacyon ;
    I hope on-to hys blysse ye be all predestynatt !
    Eu*er*y ma*n* for hys degre, I trust, xall be p*ar*tycypatt,
Yf we wyll mortyfye ow*er* carnall co*n*dycyon
    And ow*er* volu*n*tarye dysyres, *that* eu*er* be perverto*n*nat,
To renu*n*ce *th*es & yelde ws wnd*er* God*es* pr*o*vycyon.   188

My name ys Mankynde : I haue my composycyon
    Of a body & of a soull, of co*n*dycyon co*n*trarye ;
Betwyx *th*e tweyn ys a grett dyvisyon ;
    He *tha*t xulde be as soiette,[3] now he hath *th*e victory.
    Thys ys to me a lame*n*table story,
To se my flesch of my soull to haue gou*er*nance :
    Wher *th*e goode-wyff ys mast*er* *th*e goode-ma*n* may be
        sory.   195

   •   •   •   •   •   •   •   •   •   •

---

[1] MS. yt.
[2] MS. cler; *emend. by* Kittredge; *but possibly* cley.
[3] MS. seietle; Collier, H. E. D. P., II, 213 *has* sojecte.

Alasse ! what was thy fortune & *th*i chaunce [1]
   To be assocyat w*ith* my flesch, *that* stynkynge dunge-
      hyll !

.   .   .   .

      .   .   .   .

   Lady, helpe ! Sou*er*ens, yt doth my soull myche yll
To se *th*e flesch prosp*er*ouse & *th*e soull trodyn wnd*er* fote.
   I xall go to yondyr man, & assay hym I wyll ;
I trust of gostly solace he wyll be my bote.   201

[Goes to Mercy.]

All heyll, semely father ! ȝe be welcom to *th*is house !
   Of *th*e very wysda*u*m ȝe haue p*ar*tycypacyon.
My body w*ith* my soull ys eu*er* querulose ;
   I pray yow for sent charyte of yow*er* supportacyon.   205

I be-seche yow hertyly of yow*er* gostly comforte ;
   I am onstedfast in lywyng ; my name ys Mankynde ;
My gostly enmy, *th*e deull, wyll haue a grett dysporte,
   In synnfull [2] gydynge yf he may see me ende.
   MERCY.   Cryst sende yow goode comforte ! ȝe be wel-
      cu*m*, my frende !
Stonde wppe on yow*er* fete ; I prey yow aryse.
   My name ys Mercy ; ȝe be to me full hende.
To eschew vyce I wyll yow avyse.   213

MANK.   O Mercy, of all grace & v*er*tue ȝe are *th*e well !
   I haue herd*e* tell of ryght worschypfull clerk*es*,
ȝe be approxymatt to Gode & ner*e* of hys co*n*sell,
   He hat[h] instytut you aboue all hys werk*es*.   217

---

[1] *Marginal note in* MS. :

     I may both syth & sobbe, *th*is ys a pituose reme*m*brence
     & in my soull*e* sosotyll in thy s*u*bstance.

This may be a part of the three lines necessary to restore the versifica-
tion. I have indicated by dots the places where, in my opinion, the lines
are missing.

[2] MS. *has three strokes each for* nn *and* u.

O ! yow*er* louely work*es* to my soull ar*e* swetere *th*en hony !
    MERCY.   The temtacyon of *th*e flesch ʒe must resyst
    lyke a ma*n*,
For *th*er ys euer a batell betwyx *th*e soull & *th*e body :
    *Vita ho*min*is est milicia su*p*er terram.*   221

Oppresse yow*er* gostly enmy & be Cryst*es* own knyght ;
    Be neu*er* a cowarde ageyn yow*er* adu*er*sary.
If ʒe wyll be crownyde, ʒe must ned*es* fyght.
    Intende well & Gode wyll be yow adiutory.   225

Reme*m*b*re*, my frende, *th*e tyme of co*n*tynuance, —
    So helpe me Gode, yt ys but a chery-tyme !
Spende yt well ; s*er*ue Gode w*ith* hertes affyance ;
    Dystempur not yow*er* brayn w*ith* goode ale nor w*ith* wyn; 229

' Mesur*e* ys tresur*e*,' Y for-byde yow not *th*e vse ;
    Mesure yow*er*-sylf, eu*er* be-ware of excesse ;[1]
*Th*e sup*er*fluouse gyse I wyll *th*at ʒe refuse ;
    Whe*n* natur ys suffysyde, a-non *th*at ʒe sese !   233

Yf a ma*n* haue an hors & kepe hym not to hye,
    He may the*n* reull hym at hys own desyer*e* ;
Yf he be fede ou*er*-well, he wyll dysobey
    Ande, in happe, cast his mast*er* in *th*e myre.   237

NEW.   ʒe say trew, s*er* ; ʒe ar*e* no faytour !
I haue fede my wyff so well tyll sche ys my mast*er* ;
I haue a grett wonde on my hede ; lo ! & *th*eron leyth a
    playst*er*
    Ande a-no*th*er *th*er I pysse [2] my peson.
Ande my wyff were yow*er* hors, sche wolde yow all to-sāne. [3]
ʒe fede yow*er* hors in mesur ; ʒe ar a wyse man !
I trow [4] & ʒe wer*e* *th*e kyng*es* palfrey-ma*n*,[5]
    A' goode horses [6] xulde be geson.[7]   245

---

[1] *These two lines as one in* MS.   [2] MS. pyose.
[3] *This appears to be the reading of the* MS; *qy.* to-lam.
[4] MS. It row.   [5] MS. ma*r*e (?).
[6] MS. A goode horse ; *emend. by* Kittredge.   [7] MS. gesum*m*a.

MANK. Wher spekys *th*is felow ? Wyll he not com*e* ner*e* ?
 MERCY. All to son*e*, my brother, I fer*e* me, for yow.
He was her*e* ryght now, by hym *tha*t bowte me dere !
 W*ith* o*th*er of hys felouse, — *th*ei kan moche sorow !   249

They wyll be her*e* ryght son*e* if I owt dep*a*rte.
 Thynke on my doctryne ; *tha*t xall be yow*er* defence ;
Lerne wyll I am her*e*, sett my word*es* in herte ;
 W*ith*-in a schorte space I must ned*es* hens.   253

Now. *Th*e sonner, *th*e leu*er*, & *th*at be ewyn a-non !
I trow [1] yow*er* name ys do-lytyll, ʒe be so longe fro hom !
If ʒe wolde go hens, we xall cum eu*er*ychon,
 Me thynk a full goode sorte.[2]
ʒe haue leu*e*,[3] I dare well say ;
To [t]hem ʒe wyll, go forth yow*er* wey ;
Me*n* haue lytyll deynte of yow*er* pley,
 Be-cause ʒe make no sporte.   261

NOUGHT. Yow*er* potage xall be for-colde, s*er* ; whe*n* wyll
   ʒe go dyn*e* ?
I haue sen*e* a ma*n* lost xx^ti noblys in as lytyll tyme, —
ʒet yt was not I, be Sent Gis, certeyn,[4]
 For I was neu*er* worth a pottfull a' wort*es* sythyn I wos
  born*e* !
My name ys Nought, I loue well to make mery ;
I haue be seche [5] w*ith* the [6] comyn tapster of Bury ;
I pleyde so longe *th*e foll *tha*t I am ewyn very wery,
 ʒyt xall I be *th*er ageyn to-morne ![7]   269

MERCY. I haue moche car*e* for yow, my own frende ;
 Yow*er* enmys wyll be her*e* anon, *th*ei made *th*er avau*n*te.[8]
Thynke well in yow*er* hert yow*er* name ys Ma*n*kynde ;

---

1 MS. It row.
2 MS. Mo *th*e a goode sorte ; *emend. by* Kittredge.
3 MS. leu*er*.
4 *This word is illegible in* MS. ; *the last four letters look like* ntyn.
5 MS. seche*n*.   7 MS. to morow.
6 MS. ʒe.   8 MS. avau*n*ce.

Be not wnkynde to Gode, I prey yow ; be hys seruante.
    Be stedefast in condycyon ; se ȝe be not varyant ;
Lose not thorow foly that ys bowte so dere.
    God wyll proue yow sone ; ande, yf that ȝe be constant,
Of hys blysse perpetuall ȝe xall be partener.   277

ȝe may not haue yower intent at yower fyrst dysyer ; —
    Se the grett pacyence of Iob in [1] tribulacyon :
Lyke as the smyth trieth ern in the feer,
    So was he lede by Godes vysytacyon.   281

He was of yower nature & of yower fraylyte ; [2]
    Folow the steppys of hym, my own swete son, [3]
Ande sey, as he seyde, in yower trobyll & aduersyte :
Dominus dedit, Dominus abstulit, sicut placuit; sit nomen
        Domini benedictum.   285

More-ouer, in specyall I gyue yow in charge,
    Be-war of Newgyse, Now-a-days & Nought, —
Nyse in ther a-ray, in language thei be large ;
    To peruerte yower [4] condycyons all ther menys xall be
        sowte.   289

Gode son, intyrmyse [5] yower-sylff not in ther cumpeny ;
    Thei harde not a masse thi[s] twelmonyth, I dare well
        say ;
Gyff them non audyence, thei wyll tell yow many a lye ;
    Do truly yower laboure & kepe [6] yower haly-day ;
    Be-ware of Tytivillus, for he lesyth no [7] wey,
That goth in-vysybull & wyll not be sen ;
    He wyll ronde in yower ere & cast a nett be-for
        yower ey. [8]
He ys worst of them all, Gode let hym neuer then !   297

---

[1] MS. &; *corr. by* Kittredge.   [2] MS. frayylyte.
[3] *Beside this line another hand has written* ita factum est.
[4] MS. *ther.*
[5] *Over this another hand has written* intromytt not.
[6] MS. kefe.   [7] MS. us.   [8] MS. eyn.

Yff ȝe dysples Gode, aske mercy a-non ;
    Ellys Myscheff wyll be redy to brace yow in hys brydyll.
Kysse me now, my dere darlynge, Gode sche[l]de yow from
      yower fon ! [1]
    Do truly yower labure & be neuer ydyll.   301

The blyssynge of Gode be with yow & with all yower [2] wor-
    schypfull men !
MANK.   Amen ! for sent charyte, Amen !   303

Now, blyssyde be Ihesu, my soull ys well sacyatt
    With the mellyfluouse doctryne of this worschypfull man !
The rebellyn of my flesch, now yt ys superatt,
    Thankyd [3] be Gode of the connynge that I kan ! [4]   307

Her wyll I sytt & tytyll in this papyr
    The incomparable astat of my promycyon !
Worschypfull souerence, I haue wretyn here
    The gloryuse remembrance of my nobyll condycyon.   311

To haue remo[r]s & memory of my-sylff, thus wretyn yt ys,
    To defende me from all superstycyous charmys :
Memento, homo, quod cinis es et [in] cinere[m] reuerteris ;
    Lo ! I ber on my bryst the bagge of myn armys !   315

        [Enter New Gyse at the back of the stage.]

NEW.   The wether ys colde, Gode send ws goode ferys !
Cum sancto sanctus eris, & cum peruerso [5] peruerteris,
Ecce quam [6] bonum & quam [6] iocundum, [7] quod the deull to
    the frerys,
    Habitare fratres in uno. [8]
MANK.   Ther a felow speke ; with hym I wyll not mell.
Thys erth with my spade I xall assay to delffe ;

---

[1] MS. son ; corr. by Kittredge.   [4] MS. commynge that I kam.
[2] Qy. omit, or read yow.   [5] MS. peruerse.
[3] MS. Thankynge.   [6] MS. quiam.   [7] MS. Iocundie.
    [8] MS. vino, perhaps intentionally ; but vnion, which is very near the
MS. form, would rhyme with fusyon.

To eschew ydullnes [1] I do *tha*t myn own selffe ;
   I prey Gode sende [2] hys fusyon !   323

                [*Enter Now-a-days, Nought.*]

Now.   Make rom, s*er*s, for we haue be longe !
We wyll cu*m* gyf yow a Crystemes songe.
NOUGHT.   Now I prey all *th*e yemandry *tha*t ys her*e*
To synge w*it*h ws w*it*h a mery cher*e* :   [*He sings.*]   327

   Yt ys wretyn w*it*h a coll !   Yt ys wretyn w*it*h a cole ! [3]

             Cantant omnes :

Holyke ! holyke ! holyke ! holyke ! holyke ! holyke !   336

NEW.   Ey, Mankynde, Gode spede yow w*it*h yow*er* spade ! [4]
I xall tell yow of a maryage ;
I wolde yow*er* mowth & hys ars *tha*t *th*is [5] made
   Wer maryede iu*n*ctly together !
MANK.   Hey yow hens, felouse, w*it*h bredynge !
Leue yow*er* derysyon & yow*er* iapyng*e* !
I must ned*es* labur*e*, yt ys my lyvynge.
   Now.   What, s*er* ! we cam*e* but late [6] hethyr.   344

Xall all *th*is corn grow here
*Tha*t ʒe xall haue *th*e nexte ʒer ?
Yf yt be so, corn hade nede be der*e*,
   Ellys ʒe xall haue a por*e* lyffe.
NOUGHT.   A-lasse, goode fader*e*, *th*is labor fretyth yow to
     *th*e bon*e* ;
But for yow*er* croppe I take grett mone,
ʒe xall neu*er* spende yt a-lonne,
   I xall assay to geett yow a wyffe.   352

How many acres suppose ʒe her*e*, by estymacyon ?
NEW.   Ey ! how ʒe t*ur*ne *th*e erth wppe & down !

---

[1] MS. yeullnes.   [2] MS. *tha*t *before* hys.
  [3] NEW. *and* NOW. *reply with the same line ; each of the four lines of the vulgar song is similarly treated.*   [4] MS. space.
  [5] MS. ys. *corr. by* Kittredge.   [6] MS. eat ; *corr. by* Kittredge.

I haue be in my days in many goode town,
   3ett saw I neu*er* such a-no*th*er tyllynge !
MANK. Why stonde 3e ydyll? Yt ys pety *tha*t 3e wer*e*
   born !
Now. We xall bargen w*ith* yow & no*ther* moke nor scorne :
Take a goode carte in herwest & lode yt w*ith* yow*er* corne,
   Ande what xall we gyf yow for *th*e levynge?   360

NOUGHT. He ys a goode, starke laburer, he wolde fayn do
      well,
He hath mett w*ith th*e goode ma*n* Mercy in a schroude sell ;
For all *th*is he may haue many a hu*n*gry mele.
   3yt well 3e se, he ys polytyke :
Her*e* xall be goode corn, he may not mysse yt ;
Yf he wyll haue reyn, he may ou*er*-pysse yt ;
Ande [1] yf he wyll haue compost,[2] he may ou*er*-blysse yt
   A lytyll w*ith* hys ers lyke.   368

MANK. Go & do yow*er* labu*r* — Gode lett yow neu*er* the !
Or w*ith* my spade I xall yow dynge, by *th*e Holy Tr*i*nyte !
Haue 3e non other ma*n* to moke but eu*er* me ?
   3e wolle haue me of yow*er* sett !
Hye yow forth lyvely, for hens I wyll yow dryffe !

                     [He beats them with his spade.]
NEW. Alas, my iewell*es* ! [3] I xall be schent of my wyff.
Now. A-lasse ! & I am lyke neu*er* for to thryue,
   I haue such a buffett !   376

MANK. Hens, I say, Newgyse, Now-a-days & Nowte !
Yt was seyde be-forn, all *th*e menys xulde [4] be sought
To p*er*uerte my condycions & brynge me to nought.
   Hens, thevys, 3e haue made many a lesynge !
NOUGHT. Marryde I was for colde, but now am I warme !
3e ar*e* ewyll avysyde, s*er*, for 3e haue don*e* harme.
By Cokkys body sakyrde, I haue such a peyn in my arme
   I may not chonge a ma*n* a ferthynge !   384

---

1 MS. Arde.   3 MS. Iewell*er*.
2 MS. compasse; *corr. by* Kittredge.   4 MS. x*a*ll.

MANK.   Now I thanke Gode, knelynge on my kne :
B[l]yssyde be hys name, he ys of hye degre !
By *th*is spade,[1] of hys grace *th*at he hath sente me,
    Thre [2] of myn enmys I haue putt to flyght ;
3yt *th*is instrument, sou*er*ens, ys not made to defende.
Dauide seyth : *Nec in hasta,*[3] *nec in gladio saluat D*omi*nus.*[4]
NOUGHT.   No, mary, I be-schrew yow, Yt ys *in spadib*us !
Therfor Crystes curse cu*m* on yow*er hedybus,*
    To sende yow lesse myght !   393

                              Exiant.

MANK.   I p*r*omytt yow, *th*es felouse wyll no-mor*e* cum her*e* ;
For su*m*me of *th*em, certe*n*ly, wer*e* su*m*me-what to rer*e* !
My fadyr, Mercy, a-vysyde me to be of a goode cher*e*
    And agayn my enmys ma*n*ly for to fyght.   397

I xall co*n*vycte [5] *th*em, I hope, eu*er*ychon ;
3et I say a-mysse, I do yt not a-lon ;
W*ith th*e helpe of *th*e grace of Gode I re[s]yst my fon
    Ande *th*er malycyuse herte.
W*ith* my spade I wyll dep*ar*te, my worschypfull [6] soue*r*ence,
Ande lyue eu*er* w*ith* labur*e* to corecte my insolence.
I xall go fett [7] corn for my londe ; I prey yow of pacyence,
    Ryght son*e* I xall reverte.   405

                   [Exit : enter Myscheff.]

[MYS.]   Alas ! alasse, *that* eu*er* I was wrought !
Alasse *th*e whyll ! I [am] wers *th*e[n] nought !
Sythyn I was her*e*, by hym *th*at me bought,
    I am utterly on-don !
I, Myscheff, was her*e* at *th*e begy*n*nynge of *th*e game
And arguyde w*ith* Mercy, Gode gyff hym schame !
He hath taught Mankynde, wyll I haue be vane,
    To fyght ma*n*ly a-geyn hys fon ;   413

---

[1] MS. By *th*e fesyde ; *corr. by* Kittredge.
[2] MS. iij.   [5] MS. co*n*vytte.
[3] MS. hastu.   [6] MS. worschyppull.
[4] MS. o͞ns.   [7] MS. sett.

For w*ith* hys spade, *tha*t was hys wepyn,
New Gyse, Now-a-days, Nought, hath all to-betyn.
I haue grett pyte to se *th*em wepyn.
    Wyll ȝe lyst?   I her*e th*em crye !

        [*Enter New Gyse, Now-a-days, Nought.*]

A-lasse ! a-lasse ! cu*m* hether, I xall be yow*er* borow !
A-lac ! a-lac ! ven! ven! cu*m* hether*e*, w*ith* sorowe !
Pesse, fayer babys ! ȝe xall haue a nappyll to-morow !
    Why grete ȝe so? why?   421

NEW. A-lasse, mast*er* ! a-lasse my p*ri*vyte !
MYS. A ! wher? A-lake ! fayer babe, ba me !
A-byde to son*e*, I xall yt se.
    NOW. Her*e*, her*e* ! se my hede, goode mast*er* !
MYS. Lady, helpe ! Sely darlynge, ven, ven!
I xall helpe *th*e of *th*i peyn ;
I xall smytt of *th*i hede & sett yt on agayn.
    NOUGHT. By Ow*er* Lady, s*er*, a fay*er* playst*er* !   429

Wyll ȝe of w*ith* hys hede ? Yt ys a schreude charme !
As for me I haue non harme ! —
I wer*e* loth to for-bere myn arme ;
    Ȝe pley, *in no*m*in*e P*atri*s, choppe !
NEW. Ȝe xall not choppe my iewellys, & I may !
NOW. Ȝe, Cristes[1] crose ![2] wyll ȝe smyght my hede a-wey?
Ther wer on anon ![3] Oute ! ȝe xall not assay !
    I myght well be callyde a foppe !   437

MYS. I kan choppe yt of & make yt a-gayn.
NEW. I hade a schreude recu*m*be*n*tib*us*,[4] but I fele no peyn.
NOW. Ande my hede ys all saue & holl agayn.
    Now, towchynge *th*e mater of Ma*n*kynde,
Lett ws haue an interreccyon sythen ȝe be cu*m* hether*e*.
    Yt wer*e* goode to haue an ende.   443

---

1 MS. Craftes.
2 *For* cross, *or, perhaps,* curse, *cf.* l. 802
3 MS. wher on & on ; *corr. by* Kittredge.
4 MS. recu*m*te*n*tib*us*.

Mys.   How, how ! A mynstrell !   Know ȝe ony ou[gh]t ?
Nought.   I kan pype in a Walsyngham [1] wystyll, I,
   Nought, Nought.
Mys.   Blow a-pase ! *Tho*u xall bryng*e* hym in w*ith* a flewte.[2]

    [Tytivullus shouts outside.]

 Tyt.   I com w*ith* my legg*es* vnd*er* me !
Mys.   How ! Newgyse, Now-a-days, herke or I goo :
Whe*n* ow*er* hed*es* wer*e* to-gether*e* I spake of *Si dedero.*[3]
New.   Ȝe,[4] go *th*i wey, we xall ga*ther* mony on-to.
  Ellys *th*er [5] xall no-man hym se.   451

Now gostly to ow*er* p*ur*pos, worschypfull soue*r*ence :
We intende to gather mony, yf yt plesse yow*er* n*e*clygence,
For a ma*n* w*ith* a hede *tha*t of grett om*n*ipotens —
  Now.   Kepe yow*er* tayll, in goodnes I prey yow, good
    bro*ther* !
He ys a worschypfull [6] ma*n*, s*er*s, sauyng*e* yow*er* reu*er*ens ;
He louyth no grot*es* nor pens or[7] to-pens,
Gyf ws rede reyallys yf ȝe wyll se hys abhomynabull p*r*esens.
  New.   Not so ! Ȝe *tha*t mow not pay *th*e ton, pay *th*e
    to*th*er.   459

At *th*e goode-ma*n* of *th*is house fyrst we wyll assay.
Gode blysse yow, mast*er* ! Ȝe say as yll, ȝet ȝe wyll not sey
  nay.
Lett ws go by & by, & do *th*em pay.
  Ȝe pay all a-lyke, well must ȝe far*e* !
Nought.   I sey, New Gyse, Now-a-days ! *Est*is *vos pecu-*
  *niat*us *?*
I haue cryede a fayer wyll, I beschrew yow*er* patus !
Now.   *Ita uere, magister ;* cum*m*e forth now yow*er* gatus !
  He ys a goodly ma*n*, s*er*s ; make space & be-war*e* ! 467

_____

[1] MS. *has the contraction for* au. [5] MS. *thei.*
[2] *Qy.* flowte.   [6] MS. worschyppull.
[3] MS. Tidedere; *corr. by* Kittredge. [7] MS. of.
[4] MS. Ȝo.

[*Enter Titivillus, arrayed like a devil and with a net in his hand.*]

TIT.   *Ego* s*u*m *dominantium*[1] *dominus*, & my name ys
   Titivillus !

Ʒe *tha*t haue goode hors, to yow I sey *caueat*is ;
Her*e* ys an abyll felyschyppe to tryse hym out at yow*er* gat*es*.
   Ego probo sic : S*er* New Gys, lende me a peny !   471

Loquitur ad Newgyse.

NEW.   I haue a grett purse, s*er*, but I haue no monay ;
By *th*e masse, I fayll ij farthyng*es* of an halpeny.

   Ʒyt hade I ten pownd [2] *th*is nyght *tha*t wos.

TIT.   What ys in *th*i purse ? *th*ou art a stout felow.[3]

Loquitur ad Now-a-days.

NOW.   *Th*e deull haue [the] qwyll, I am a clen ientyllma*n* !
I prey Gode, I be neu*er* wers storyde *the*n I am.

   Yt xall be otherwyse, I hope, or *th*is nyght passe.   478

TYT.   Herke now, I say *th*ou hast many a peny.

Loquitur ad Nought.

NOUGHT.   *No*[*n*] *nobis*, *d*omin*e*, *non nobis*, by sent Deny !
*Th*e deull may da*u*nce in my purse for ony peny, —

   Yt ys as clen as a byrd*es* ars.   482

TIT.   Now I sey Ʒet a-geyn *caueat*is ;
Here ys an abyll felyschyppe to tryse he*m* of yow*er* gat*es*.   484

Now, I say, New Gyse, Now-a-days & Nought,
Go & serche *th*e contre, anon *th*at [yt] be sowƷte,
Su*m*me her*e*, su*m*me *th*er, — what yf Ʒe may cache owƷte ! — 487

Yf Ʒe fayll of hors, take what Ʒe may ellys.

NEW.   The*n* speke to Ma*n*kynde for *th*e recu*m*bentib*us* of
   my iewellys.

NOW.   Reme*m*bre my brokyn hede, in the worschyppe of *th*e
   v voli ellys ! [4]

---

[1] MS. dūancum.   [3] *Qy.* man.
[2] MS. x^li.   [4] *Qy.* the vij (*or* xx) devellys.

Nought.   3e, goode s*er*, tye sytica[1] in my erme !
Tit.   I know full well what Mankynde dyde to yow,
Myschyff hat[h] informyde of all *th*e mater*e* thorow ;
I xall venge yow*er* quarell, I make Gode a-vow.
      Forth & espye wer*e* 3e may do harme.   495

Take w[ith yow] Fyde[2] yf 3e wyll haue ony mo.
I say, New Gyse ! wether art *tho*u avysyde to go?   497

New.   Fyrst I xall begyn at M[aster] Hu*n*tyngton of
         Sanston ;[3]
Fro thens I xall go to Wyll*a*m[4] Thuolay of Hanston ;
Ande so forthe to Pycharde of Tru*m*pyngton :
      I wyll kepe me to *th*es thre.[5]
Now.   I xall goo to Wyllyh*a*m[4] Baker*e* of Walton ;[6]
To Rycherde Bo*l*lma*n* of Gayton ;
I xall spar*e* Mast*er* Woode of Fullburn,
      He ys a *noli me tangere !*   505

Nought.   I xall goo to Wyllyam Patryke of Massyngh*a*m ;[4]
I xall spar*e* Mast*er* Alyngton of Botysam
Ande Hamonde of Soffeham.[4]
Felous, cu*m* forth, & go we hens to-gethyr,
      For drede of *in man*u*s tuas*, qweke ![7]
New.   Syth we xall go, lett ws se[8] well ware & wether ;
Yf we may be take, we com no-more hethyr ;
      Lett ws con[9] well ow*er* neke-verse *th*at we haue not a
         cheke.[10]   513

Tit.   Goo yow*er* wey, a deull wey, go yow*er* wey, all !
I blysse yow w*ith* my lyfte hond ; foull yow be-fall !
Com a-geyn, I werne, as son*e* as I yow call,
      A[nde] brynge yow*er* a-vantage in-to *th*is place.

---

[1] *Qy. th*e syatica (= sciatica).   [4] MS. *has the contraction for* au.
[2] MS. Iake w . . . Fyde.   [5] MS. iij.
[3] MS. sansten.   [6] MS. Waltom.
[7] *The stanza-structure can be restored by interchanging* ll. 509, 510.
[8] MS. be.   [9] MS. com.   [10] MS. choke.

To speke w*it*h Ma*n*kynde I wyll tary her*e th*is tyde,
Ande assay hys goode p*ur*pose for to sett a-syde.
*Th*e goode man, Mercy, xall no lenger be [be] hys syde ;
    I xall make hym to dawnce a-no*th*er trace !   521

Eu*er* I go invysybull, yt ys my rett,
Ande be-for hys ey *th*us I wyll hange my nett
To blench hys syght ; I hope to haue hys fote wett.
    To yrke hym of hys lab*ur* I xall make a frame.
Thys borde xall be ¹ hyde wnd*er th*e erth preuely ;
Hys spade xall ent*er*, I hope, on-redyly ; ²
Be *then* he hath a-wayde,³ he xall be uery angry
    Ande lose hys pacyens, peyn of schame.   529

I xall menge hys corne w*it*h draw & w*it*h durnell,
Yt xall not be lyke to sow ⁴ nor to sell.
Yondyr he co*m*myth, I prey of cownsell ;
    He xall wene grace wer*e* wane.⁵   533

        [Enter Mankynde.]

MANK. Now, Gode, of hys mercy, sende ws of hys sonde !
I haue brought seed her to sow w*it*h my londe ;
I wyll ron dylew*er*, *tha*t ⁶ here yt xall stonde.
    *In n*om*in*e Patris &* Filii ⁷ &* Spir[i]*t*us S*an*cti, now I
      wyll be-gyn.⁸
Thys londe ys so harde, yt makyth wn-lusty & yrke,
I xall sow my corn at wynt*er* & lett Gode werke.
A-lasse, my corn ys lost ! Her*e* ys a foull werke.
    I se well, by tyllynge lytyll xall I wyn.   541

Her*e* I gyf wppe my spade for now & for eu*er* ;

      *Her*e *Titivillus goth out wi*t*h* the *spade.*

To occupye my body, I wyll not putt me in deuer.⁹
I wyll her*e* my ewynsonge her*e* or I dysseu*er* ;

---

¹ MS. he.   ² MS. ou*er* redyly.
³ *Unintelligible ; read, perhaps,* assayde.   ⁴ MS. sew.
⁵ *A later hand has added what looks like* Cruis.   ⁶ MS. yt.
⁷ MS. filius.   ⁸ MS. le-fyn.
⁹ MS. eeuer.

Thys place I assyng*e* as my kyrke.
Her in my kerke I knell on my kneys.
*Pater nost*er, *qui es in celis.*

[*Enter Tytyvillus.*]

Tyt. I promes yow I haue no lede on my helys,
    I am her*e* a-geyn to make *th*is felow yrke.   549

I-wyst, pesse !   I xall go to hys er*e* & tytyll *th*er-in.

[*Goes to Mankynde.*]

A schorte preyer*e* thyrlyth [1] hewyn ; of *th*i preyer*e* blyn ;
*Tho*u art holyer *then* eu*er* was ony of *th*i kyn ;
    A-ryse & avent *the*, nature compellys.   553

Mank. I wyll in-to *th*i[s] ȝerde, sou*er*ens, & cum a-geyn
        son*e* ;
For drede of *th*e colyke & eke of *th*e stone
I wyll go do *that* [2] ned*es* must be don.
    My bedes [3] xall be her*e* for who-su*m*me-eu*er* wyll cu*m*me. 557

                Exiat.

Tit. Mankynde was besy in hys prayer*e*, ȝet I dyde [4] hym
        aryse ;
He is co*n*veyde, be Cryst ! from hys devyn s*er*uyce.
Whether ys he, trow ȝe ?   I-wysse, I am wond*er* wyse :
    I have sent hym forth to schyte lesynges.
Yff ȝe haue ony sylu*er*, in happe pur*e* brasse,
Take a lytyll pow[d]er of Parysch & cast ou*er* hys face,
Ande ewyn in *th*e howll-flyght let hym passe, —
    Titivillus kan lerne yow many praty thyng*es* !   565

I trow Ma*n*kynde wyll cu*m* a-geyn son,
Or ellys, I fer me, ewynsonge wyll be don.
Hys bed*es* xall be trysyde a-syde, & *th*at a-non.
    Ȝe xall [se] a goode sport [5] yf ȝe wyll a-byde.
Mankynde cu*m*myth a-geyn, well far*e* he !

    [1] MS. thyr lyth.   [3] MS. ledes.   [5] MS. spert.
    [2] MS. yt.   [4] MS. eyde.

I xall answere hym *ad omnia quare.*
Ther xall be set a-broche a clerycall mater ;
 I hope of hys purpose to sett hym a-syde.   573

     [*Enter Mankynde.*]

MANK. Ewynsonge hath be in *th*e saynge, I trow, a fayer
  wyll ;
I am yrke of yt, yt ys to longe be on myle.
Do wey ; I wyll no-more so oft on *th*e chyrche-style ; [1]
  Be as be may, I xall do a-no*th*er.
Of labure & preyer I am nere yrke of both ;
I wyll no-more of yt, thowgh [2] Mercy be wroth.
My hede ys uery heuy, I tell yow for soth,
  I xall slepe [3] full my bely & he were my bro*th*er ! 581

TIT. Ande euer ȝe dyde, for me kepe now yower sylence !
Not a werde, I charge yow, peyn of xl pens !
A praty [4] game xall be schowde [5] yow or ȝe go hens.
  ȝe may here hym snore, he ys sade on [6] slepe.
I-wyst, pesse ! *Th*e deull ys dede ! I xall go ronde in hys
  ere :
Alasse, Mankynde, alasse ! Mercy stown [7] a mere ;
He ys runn a-way fro hys master, *th*er wot no man where ;
  More-ouer he stale both a hors & a nete.   589

But ȝet I herde say he brake hys neke as he rode [8] in
  Fraunce ;
But I thynke he rydyth ouer *th*e galous [9] to lern for to
  daunce,
By-cause of hys theft. *Th*at ys hys gouernance ;
  Trust no-more on hym, he ys a marryde man.
Mekyll sorow wi*th* *th*i spade be-forn *th*ou hast wrought ;
A-ryse & aske mércy of Newgyse, Now-a-days, & Nought.

---

[1] *Lines 576–579 are added in a note at botton of page in* MS.
[2] MS. then ; *corr. by* Kittredge. [6] MS. & ; *corr. by* Kittredge.
[3] MS. skope.   [7] *That is,* has stolen.
[4] MS. pauty.   [8] MS. reke ab herode ; *corr. by* Kittredge.
[5] MS. schende.   [9] MS. galouf.

*Th*ei cu*m* ; a-vyse *th*e for *th*e best ; lett *th*er goode wyll be
   sought ;
And *th*i own wyff brechell¹ & take *th*e a lemma*n*.   597

For-well, eu*er*ychon, for I haue don my game,
For I haue brought Mankynde to myscheff & to schame.   599

[Exit Tityvillus.]

MANK.   Whope! who! M*er*cy hath brokyn hys neke-kycher,
   a vows,
Or he hangyth by *th*e neke hye wppe on *th*e gallouse.
A-dew, fayer mastere !   I wyll hast me to *th*e ale-house,
   Ande speke w*ith* Newgyse, Now-a-d*ays* & Nought,
A[nde] geett me a lemma*n* w*ith* a smattrynge face.

[Enter New Gyse.]

NEW.   Make space ! for Cokk*es* body sakyrde, make space !
A ha ! well ! on ! ron !   Gode gyff hym ewyll grace !
   We wer*e* ner*e* Sent Patrykes wey, by hym *tha*t me
   bought !   607

I was twychyde by *th*e neke, *th*e game was be-gu*n*ne ;
A grace was, *th*e halt*er* brast a-sondre — *ecce signu*m ! —
The halff ys a-bowte my neke.   We hade a rere rune!
   Be-war*e* ! quod *th*e goode-wyff, whe*n* sche smot of her*e*
   husbond*es* hede, beware !
Myscheff ys a co*n*victe for he coude hys neke-verse ;
My body gaff a swynge whe*n* I hynge wppon *th*e casse.²
A-lasse ! he wyll hange such a lyghtly ma*n* & a fers
   For stelynge of an horse, I prey Gode gyf hym car*e* !   615

Do wey *th*is halt*er* !   What deull doth Ma*n*kynde her*e*, w*ith*
   sorow !
A-lasse, how my neke³ ys sore, I make⁴ a-vowe !
MANK.   ȝe be welcom, Newgyse !   S*er*, what cher*e* w*ith*
   yow ?
   NEW.   Well, s*er*, I haue no cause to morn.

¹ *Qy.* brethell.   ² *So* MS.   ³ MS. nekes.   ⁴ MS. made.

MANK. What was *th*er abowte yow*er* neke, so Gode yow
    a-mende ?

NEW. In feyth, Sent Andrys holy bende ;

I haue a lytyll dyshes as yt plesse Gode to sende,

    W*ith* a ru*nn*ynge rynge-worme.   623

[Enter Now-a-days.]

NOW. Stonde a rom, I prey *th*e, bro*th*er myn !

I haue laburyde all *th*is nyght ; we*n* xall we go dyn ?

A chyrche her be-syde xall pay for ale, brede & wyn ;

    Lo ! her*e* ys stoffe wyll s*er*ue.

NEW. Now, by *th*e holy Mary, *th*ou art bett*er* marchande
    *th*a*n* I !

[Enter Nought.]

NOUGHT. A-vante, knavys ! lett me go by !

    I kan not gret & I xulde sterue !   630

[Enter Myscheff.]

MYS. Her*e* cu*m*myth a ma*n* of armys ; why stonde ye so
    styll ?

Of murd*er* & ma*n*slawt*er* I haue my bely-fyll.

NOW. What, Myscheff, haue ye ben*e* in presun, & yt be
    yow*er* wyll ?

    Me sĕmyth ʒe haue sco[w]ryde a payer of fetters.

MYS. I was chenyde by *th*e armys, — lo ! I haue *th*em her*e* ;

The chenys I brast a-sundyr & kyllyde *th*e iayler*e*,

ʒe, ande hys fayer wyff halsyde in a corner*e*.

    A ! how swetly I kyssyde *tha*t [1] swete mowth of hers ! 638

Whe*n* I hade do, I was myn owyn bottler,

I brought a-wey w*ith* me both dysch & dubler*e*.

Her*e* ys a-now for me ; be of goode cher*e*.

    ʒet well fare *th*e new chesance !

MANK. I aske m*er*cy of New Gyse, Now-a-days, &
    Nought.

Onys w*ith* my spade I reme*m*ber that I faught ;

---

[1] MS. *the*.

I wyll make yow a-mend*es* yf I hurt yow ought,
    Or dyde ony grev*au*nce.   646

NEW.   What a deull lykyth ye to be of *th*is dysposycyon?
MANK.   I drempt Mercy was hange, *th*is was my vysyon,
Ande *tha*t to yow iij I xulde haue recors & remocyon.
    Now I prey yow hertyly of yow*er* goode wyll ;
I crye yow mercy of all *tha*t I dyde a-mysse.
NOW. [*Aside*] I sey, New Gys, Nought ! Tytivillus made
    all *th*is ;
As sekyr as Gode ys in hewyn, so yt ys.
    NOUGHT.   Stonde wppe on yow*er* feet ! Why stonde
    ȝe so styll?   654

NEW.   Mast*er* Myscheff, we wyll yow exort
Mankynde name in yow*er* bok for to report.
MYS.   I wyll not so ; I wyll sett a corte ;
    A[nde] do yt *in* [1] *forma iurys*, desarde !

Now-a-days mak proclamacyon.

NOW.   Oy yt ! Oy yȝt ! Oyet !
All man*er* of me*n* & comu*n* women,
To *th*e cort of Myschyff other*e* cu*m* or sen ;
Mankynde xall retorn, he ys on*e* of ow*er* me*n* !
    MYS.   Nought, cu*m* forth ! *th*ou xall be stewerde.   663

NEW.   Mast*er* Myscheff, hys syde gown may be solde ; [2]
He may haue a iakett [3] *th*er-of & mony tolde.
MANK.   I wyll do for *th*e best, so I haue no colde.
    Holde, I prey yow, & take yt w*ith* yow,
Ande let me haue yt a-geyn in ony [4] wyse.

Nought scri[bit].

NEW.   I p*ro*mytt yow a fresch iakett aft*er* *th*e new gyse.
MANK.   Go & do *tha*t longyth to yow*er* offyce
    A[nde] spare *tha*t ȝe mow ! [5]   671
                                  [*Exit New Gyse* ?]

---

[1] MS. se.	[3] MS. rakett.	[5] MS. may.
[2] MS. tolde.	[4] MS. mony *for* in ony.	

NOUGHT.   Holde, Master Myscheff, & rede *th*is !
MYS.   Here ys *blottybus in blottis*
*Blottoru*m *blottib*us *ist*is.
 Be-schrew yow*er* erys, a [1] fayer hande !
NOW.   Ʒe, yt ys a goode rennynge fyst ; [2]
Such an hande may not be myst !
NOUGHT.   I xulde haue don bett*er*, hade I wyst.
 MYS.   Take hede, sers, yt stonde you on hande !   679

Garici tota [3] *generalis,*
In a place *th*er goode ale ys,
Anno regni regitalis
 *Edwa*r*di millatene,* [4]
On Ʒestern-day in Feuerer*e*, *th*e Ʒere passyth [5] fully,
Do [6] Nought hath wrytyn, — here ys ow*er* Tulli, —
Anno regni regis nulli.   686

NOW.   What how, Newgyse !   *Tho*u makyst moche [taryyng].
*Tha*t iakett xall not be worth a ferthynge.

    [Enter New Gyse].

NEW.   Out of my wey, s*er*s, for drede of fyghtynge !
 Lo ! here ys a feet tayll, lyght to leppe a-bowte !
NOUGHT.   Yt ys not schapyn worth a morsell of brede ;
Ther ys to moche cloth, yt weys as ony lede ;
I xall goo & me*n*de yt, ellys I wyll lose my hede.
 Make space, s*er*s ; lett me go owte. *[Exit.]* 694

MYS.   Mankynde, cu*m* hether, God sende yow *th*e gowte !
Ʒe xall goo [to] all *th*e goode felouse in *th*e cu*n*tre a-boute,
On-to *th*e goode-wyff whe*n* *th*e goode-ma*n* ys owte ;
 " I wyll," say Ʒe !

 1 MS. &.   2 MS. syft.
 3 *A stroke over* o.
 4 *An* m *written above* n ; *the first part of the word may be* nulla.
 5 *Qy.* passyd.
 6 *Qy.* Lo ; *or, as* Kittredge *suggests,* So.

MANK.[1]   I wyll, s*er*.

NEW.   Ther*e* arn but sex dedly synnys ; lechery ys non,

As yt may be verefyede be ws brethellys eu*er*ychon.

ȝe xall goo robbe, stell & kyll, as fast as ye may gon ;

  " I wyll," say ȝe !

MANK.[1]   I wyll, s*er*.   702

NOW.   On Sundays, on *th*e morow, erly be-tyme,

ȝe xall w*ith* ws to *th*e all-house, erly to go dyn*e* ;

And forber [2] masse & matens, ow*er*s & prime ;

  " I wyll," say ȝe !

MANK.[1]   I wyll, s*er*.

MYS.   ȝe must haue be yow*er* syde a longe *da pace*m,

As trew-me*n* ryde be *th*e wey, for to on-brace *th*em ;

Take *th*e monay, kytt *th*er throt*es*, tans ou*er* face *th*em ; [3]

  " I wyll," say ȝe !

MANK.[4]   I wyll, s*er*.   710

[Enter Nought.]

NOUGHT.   Here ys a ioly iakett ; how say ȝe?

NEW.   It ys a goode iake[tt] of s[er]u[i]ce for a ma*n*nys
          body.

Hay, doo y*e* ! hay, whoppe, whoo ! go yow*er* wey lyghtly ;

  ȝe are well made for to ren !

MYS.   Tydyng*es* ! tydyng*es* ! I haue a-spyede on !

Hens w*ith* yow*er* stuff, fast we wer*e* gon !

I be-schrew *th*e last xall com to hys hom !

  [ALL.]   Ame*n* ! [5]   718

[Enter Mercy.]

MERCY.   What, how, Mankynde ! fle [6] *th*at felyschyppe, I
          yow prey.

MANK.   I xall speke w*ith* [the] a-no*th*er tyme, — to-morn
          or *th*e next day ;

---

[1] MS. *has only* M.   [2] MS. A for bef.

[3] *Read* trus ! (*or, perhaps,* thus) overpass them !

[4] MS. Ma.   [5] MS. Ame*n* dica*n*t om*n*es.

[6] MS. sle ; *corr. by* Kittredge.

We xall goo forth to-gether to kepe my faders ȝer-day.

A tapster ! a tapster ! stow, stall, stow !

MYS. A myscheff go with here, I haue a foull fall !

Hens a-wey fro me, or I xall be-schyte yow all !

NEW. What how, ostler ! hostler ! lende ws a foot-ball.

Whoppe, whow ! a-now, a-now, a-now ! 726

MERCY. My mynde ys dyspersyde, my body trymmelyth as

the aspen leffe ;

The terys xuld trekyll down by my chekys, were not

yower reuerence ;

Yt were to me solace — the cruell vysytacyon of deth.

With-out rude behaver I kan [not] expresse this incon-

venyens ;

Wepynge, sythynge & sobbynge were my suffycyens ;

All naturall nutriment to me as caren ys odybull ;

My inwarde aff[l]ixyon yeldyth me tedyouse wn-to

yower presens ;

I kan not bere yt ewynly, Mankynde ys so flexibull. 734

Man on-kynde, wher-euer thou be ! for all this world was

not apprehensyble

To dyscharge thin orygynall offence, thraldaum & captyuyte,

Tyll Godes own welbylouyde son was obedient & passyble, —

Euery droppe of his bloode wos schede to purge thin

iniquite.

I dyscomende & dysalow this oftyn mutabylyte ! [1]

To euery creature thou art dyspectuose & odyble.

Why art thou so on-curtess, so inconsyderatt ? A-lasse,

who is me !

As the fane that turnyth with the wynde, so thou art con-

uertyble. 742

In trust ys treson, this [2] promes ys not credyble ;

Thys [3] peruersyose ingratytude I can not rehers ;

To go ouer all the holy corte of hewyn, thou art despectyble,

[1] MS. imutabylyte.   [2] Qy. thi.   [3] Qy. thy.

As a nobyll ve*r*syfyer makyth mencyon in *th*is verse :
" *Lex* et *natura*, Christus et omni*a* [1] *iura*
     Damna*n*t *in-gratu*m ; *luget*ur *eu*m *for*e *natu*m."   748

O goode Lady & Mo*th*er of Mercy, haue pety & compasyon
     Of *th*e wrechydnes of Mankynde, *tha*t ys so wanton &
        so frayll !
Lett mercy excede iustice ; der*e* Mo*th*er, a[d]mytt this supply-
        cacyon, —
     Equyte [2] to be leyde ou*er*, pety [3] & mercy to prevayll !   752

To sensuall lyvynge ys rep*r*ouable, *tha*t ys now-a-days,
     As be *th*e comprehence of *th*is mat*er* yt may be specy-
        fyede.
New Gyse, Now-a-days, Nought, w*ith th*er allectuose ways
     They haue p*er*vertyde Mankynde, my swet sun, I haue
        well espyede.   756

A ! w*ith th*es cursyde caytyfs,[4] and I may, he xall not long
     indur !
     I, Mercy, hys father gostly, wyll p*r*ocede forth & do my
        propyrte.
Lady, helpe ! *Th*is man*er* of lyvynge ys a detestabull
        plesure ;
     *Vanitas vanitatu*m, all ys but vanyte !   760

Mercy xall neu*er* be· convicte of hys onc*ur*tes co*n*dycyon ;
W*ith* wepynge terys, be ny3te & be day, I wyll goo & neu*er*
     sease ;
Xall I not fynde hym ? Yes, I hope. Now Gode be my
     protecyon !
     My predylecte son, wher be ye ? Mankynde, *vbi es?*   764

Mys.   My prepotent father, whe*n* 3e sowpe, sowpe owt yow*er*
     messe.
3e ar*e* all to-glosyede [5] in yow*er* termys, 3e make many a lesse.

---

[1] MS. sit o͞lat ; *corr. by* Kittredge.   [2] MS. O quyte.
[3] MS. pe*r*ty ; *corr. by* Kittredge.   [4] MS. cayftys.   [5] MS. gloryede.

Wyll ȝe here? he cryeth ouer Mankynde *vbi es!*
NEW. Hic, hyc, hic, hic, hic, hic, hic, hic ![1]
That ys to say, her*e*, her*e*, her*e*, ny[2] dede in the cryke.
Yf ȝe wyll haue hym, goo & syke, syke, syke!
    Syke not ouer-long*e*, for losyng*e* of yower mynde!   771

Now. Yf ȝe wyll haue Mankynde, how, domine, domine,
    domine!
ȝe must speke to *th*e schryue for a *cape corpus,*[3]
Ellys ȝe must be fayn to retorn w*ith non est inve*ntus.
    How sey ȝe, s*er?* My bolte ys schotte.
NOUGHT. I am doynge of my nedyng*es*; be-war*e* how ȝe
    schott!
Fy, fy, fy! I haue fowll a-rayde my fote!
Be wyse for schottyng*e* w*ith* yow*er* takyllys, for, Gode wott,
    My fote ys fowly ouer-schott.   779

MYS. A p*ar*lement! a p*ar*leme*n*t! Cu*m* forth, Nought,
    be hynde!
A cownsell be-lyue! I am a-ferde Mercy wyll hym fynde.
How sey ȝe? & what sey ȝe? How xall we do w*ith* Man-
    kynde?
    NEW. Tysche, a flyes weyng*e*! Wyll ȝe do well?
He wenyth M*er*cy wer*e* honge for stelyng*e* of a mer*e*;
Myscheff, go sey to hym *that* Mercy sekyth eu*er*y-were,—
He wyll honge hym-selff, I wndyrtake, for fer*e*.
    MYS. I assent *th*er-to; yt ys wyttyly seyde & well.   787

Now. I! Wyppe yt in *th*i cote, a-non yt wer don!
Now, Sent Gabryell*es* modyr saue *th*e clowtes[4] of *th*i schon!
All *th*e bokys in *th*e worlde, yf *th*ei hade be wndon,
    Cowde[5] not a cownselde ws bett.
                                    Hic exit Myscheff.[6]

1 *A line rhyming with* 771 *is needed to complete the stanza.*
2 MS. my; *corr. by* Kittredge.
3 MS. cepe coppus, *which may be intentional.*
4 MS. clo*th*es.
5 MS. Howde.
6 *Apparently he returns immediately with Mankynde.*

MYS.   How, Mankynde ! cu*m* & speke w*ith* Mercy !   He ys
          her*e* fast by.

MANK.   A roppe ! a rope ! a rope ! I am not worthy.

MYS.   A-non, a-non, a-non ! I haue yt her*e* redy ;
       W*ith* a tre also *that* I haue gett.   795

Holde *th*e tre, Now-a-days !   Nought, take hede & be wyse !

NEW.   Lo ! Mankynde, do as I do ; *th*is ys *th*e[1] new
          gyse.

Gyff *th*e roppe iust to *th*y[2] neke, *th*is ys myn a-vyse.

       MYS.   Helpe *th*i-sylff, Nought ; lo ! Mercy ys her*e*.

He skaryth ws .w*ith* a balef,[3] we may no lenger*e* tarye.

NEW.   Qweke, qweke, qweke ! A-lass, my thrott ! I be-
          schrew yow, mary !

A ! mercy, Cryst*es* coppyde curse go w*ith* yow, — and Sent
          Dauy !

       A-lasse, my wesant ȝe wer su*m*-what to nere !   803

                                                           Exiant.

MERCY.   A-ryse, my precyose, redempt son !   Ȝe be to me
            full der*e*.

       He ys[4] so tymerouse, me semyth hys vytall spryt doth
          expy[re]

MANK.   Alasse ! I haue be so bestyally dysposyde, I dar*e*
            not a-per*e*.

       To se yow*er* solacyose[5] face I am not worthy to
          dysyer.   807

MERCY.   Yow*er* crymynose compley*n*t wondyth my hert as a
            lance.

       Dyspose yow*er*-sylff mekly to aske mercy, & I wyll
          assent.

Ȝelde me nethyr golde nor tresur*e*, but yow*er* hu*m*byll obey-
          syance,

       The volu*n*tary subieccyon of yow*er* hert, & I am co*n*tent. 811

---

[1] MS. *th*i.	[4] MS. He ys ys.
[2] MS. pye.	[5] MS. solycyose.
[3] MS. bales.	

[1] MANK.   What !   Aske me*r*cy ȝet onys a-geyn?   Alas yt
were a wyld [2] petysyon ! [3]
   Ewyr to offend & eu*er* to aske me*r*cy, *tha*t ys a puerilite.
Yt ys so abhomi*n*abyll to rehers my wekit [4] transgresion,
   I am not worthy to haue me*r*cy; be no possibilite.   815

MERCY.   O Ma*n*kend, my singler solas, *th*is is a lamentabyll
excuse.
   The dolorus fer*es* [5] of my hert, how *th*ei begyn to a-
mownte !
O blyssed Ih*e*su, help *th*ou *th*is synfull synner to reduce : [6]
   *Ira hec ℧ mutaes dexire excelsi veint Impios et non su*nt.[7] 819

A-ryse & aske me*r*cy, Ma*n*kend, & be associat to me !
   Thy deth schall be my hewynesse !   Alas, tys pety yt
schuld be *th*us !
Thy obstinacy wyll exclude [the] fro *th*e glori*us* per[p]etuite.
   ȝet, for my lofe ope [8] thy lyppys & sey *miserere mei,*
Deus !   823

MANK.   The egall Iustyse of God wyll not pe*r*mytte sych a
synfull wrech
   To be reuyu[y]d & restoryd a-geyn ; yt were impossibyll.
MERCY.   The Iustice of God wyll as I wyll, as hym-sylfe
doth pre-cyse : [9]
   N*olo* [10] *morte*m *peccator*is, *inquit,*[11] yff he wyll [be]
reducyble.   827

---

1 *The copyist remarks that the page beginning here seems to be in a dif-*
ferent hand from what precedes.   The remark probably applies to the
whole remaining part of the play; certainly from here on the spelling is
very different.

  2 *I take this to be* vild (= vile.)   3 MS. pety syn.

  4 MS. *appears to have* werut, *but is almost illegible.*

  5 MS. ser*es*.

  6 MS. redeme ; *corr. by* Kittredge, *cf.* l. 827.

  7 *So* MS. ; *see Notes, vol. III.*   8 MS. ofe.

  9 Precyse *does not rhyme*; *qy.* preche *or, as* Kittredge *suggests,* precysely
teche.

  10 MS. Mole.   11 MS. *apparently* inquis.

MANK.   *Than*, mercy, good Mercy !   What ys a man wyth-
    owt Mercy?
      Lytyll ys our parte of paradyse where Mercy ne were.
Good Mercy, excuse the ineuetabyll obieccion of my gostly
    enmy ;
      The prowerbe seyth, the trewth tryith the sylfe.   Alas, I
      haue mech care !   831

MERCY.   God wyll not make ʒow preuy on-to [1] hys last iuge-
    ment :
      Iustyce & Equite xall be fortyfyid, I wyll not denye ;
Trowthe [2] may not so cruelly procede in hys streyt argument [3]
    But that Mercy schall rewle the mater with-owte con-
    trouersaye.   835

Ryse [4] now & go with me in thys deambulatorye.
    Inclyne yowur capacite, my doctrine ys conuenient. [5]
Synne not in hope of Mercy ; That ys a cryme notorie ! [6]
    To truste ouermoche in a prince yt ys not expedient,   839

In hope when ʒe syn [7] to haue mercy; be-ware of that awen-
    ture ;
    The [8] good Lord seyd to the lecherus woman of Cha-
    nane, —
The holy gospell ys the awtorite, as we rede in Scrypture, —
    " Vade et *iam amplius* [9] *noli peccare*."   843

Cryst preseruyt this synfull woman takyn in a-wowtry,
    He seyde to here theis wordes : " Go & syn no-more."

        [1] MS. peruyon to.
        [2] MS. Growthe.
        [3] MS. *apparently* acgmmes; *corr. by* Kittredge.
        [4] MS. Byse.
        [5] MS. My doctrine ys conuenient Inclyne yowur capacite.
        [6] MS. notaries.
        [7] MS. ʒe thynke *after* syn; *corr. by* Kittredge.
        [8] MS. Then.
        [9] MS. ism amperhees.

So to yow : Go & syn no-more ; be-ware of weyn -co*n*fide*n*s
    of Mercy ;
  Offend not a p*r*ince on trust of hys fauo*ur*, as I [1] seyd
    before.   847

Yf ʒe fele yo*ur*-sylfe trappyd in *th*e snare of yo*ur* gostly
    enmy,
  Aske mercy a-non ; be-ware of *th*e co*n*tynuance ;
Whyll a wond ys fresch yt is p*r*owyd curabyll be surgery,
    *Tha*t, yf yt procede ouyrlong*e*, yt ys cawse of gret grev-
    anc*e*.[2]   851

MANK.   To aske m*e*rcy & to haue, — *th*is ys a lyberall pos-
    sescion !
  Schall *th*is expedyci*us* [3] petycion euer be a-lowyd, as ʒe
    haue in-syght ?
MERCY.   In *th*is presente lyfe m*e*rcy ys plente tyll deth
    makyth hys dywysion ;
  But wha*n* ʒe be go, *vs*que *ad minimu*m *qu*a*drantem* [4] ʒe
    scha[ll] rekyn *th*is ryght.   855

Aske m*e*rcy & haue, whyll *th*e body w*ith* *th*e sow[l]e hath
    hys annexio*n* ;
  Yf ʒe tarye tyll yo*ur* dysesse, ʒe may hap of yo*ur* desyre
    to mysse ;
Be repe*n*tant here, trust not *th*e ow*er* of deth ; thynke on *th*is
    lessu*n* :
Ecce [5] *nu*n*c tem*p*us acceptabile*,[6] *ecce nu*nc *dies salut*is !   859

All *th*e wertu in the wor[l]d yf ʒe myght comprehend,
  Yo*ur* meryt*es* were not premyabyll to *th*e blys a-boue,
Not to *th*e holest [7] ioy of heuyn of yo*ur* proper efforte to
    ascend ;
  W*ith* Mercy ʒe may, — I tell yow no fabyll, Scrypture
    doth prove.[8]   863

[1] MS. he.	[5] MS. Este.
[2] MS. grewang*e*.	[6] MS. aūcptabile.
[3] MS. expedici*es*.	[7] *Qy*. loliest *or* lest.
[4] MS. q*u*adrūte[m].	[8] MS. prewe.

MANK.   O Me*r*cy, my solati*us* [1] solas & synguler recreatory,
  My p*r*edilecte specyall, ʒe are worthy to haue my lowe ;
For, wyth-owte deserte & menys supplicatorie,
  ʒe be-co*m* pacient to my inexcusabyll [2] reproue.   867

A ! yt siremyth [3] my brest to thynk how on-wysely I haue
    wroght !
  Tytiuilly, *that* goth invisibele, hyng*e* hys nett be-fore m*y*
    eye,
And, by hys fantasticall visionys sedulously [4] sowght,
  He [5] Newgyse, Now-a-days, Nought causyd me to obey.   871

MERCY.   Ma*n*kend, ʒe were obliuyous of my doctrine mary-
    torye ;
  I seyd be-fore, Titiuilly wold a-say yow a bronte. [6]
Be-ware fro hens-forth of hys fablys delusory,
  The prowerbe seyth : *Iacula perfectum non ledunt.* [7]   875

ʒe haue iij adu*er*sarys, — he ys mast*er* of [t]hem all, —
  That ys to sey, the dewell, *th*e world, [8] *th*e flesch ; & [I]
    *th*e tell
That [9] Newg*yse*, Now-a-days & Nought, *th*e world we may
    [t]hem call ;
  And propy[r]lly Titiuilly syngnyf[ie]th the fend of helle ; 879

The flesch, — *th*at ys *th*e vnclene co*n*cupisens of ʒo*ur* body;
  These be yo*ur* iij gostly enmys in whom ʒe haue put yo*ur*
    co*n*fidens ;
*Th*ei browt yow to Myscheffe to co*n*clude ʒo*ur* temperull glory,
  As yt hath be schewyd *th*is worschypfyll [10] audiens.   883

---

[1] MS. suati*us* ; *corr. by* Kittredge, *cf.* l. 807.

[2] MS. inexousobyll ; inexorable *may be better.*

[3] Kittredge *suggests* sore nyeth (= noieth) ; streinyth *would be closer to* MS.

[4] MS. sedeculy.   [5] MS. Be.

[6] *After* bronte *is apparently an* a.

[7] MS. p*er*fectumm*us* ledict*ur* ; *corr. by* Kittredge.

[8] MS. would.   [9] MS. The.

[10] MS. worschyppyll.

Reme*m*byr how redy I was to help ʒow ; fro sweche I was
        not dangerous ;
Wherfore, good sunne, absteyne fro syn eu*er*-more aft*er* th*is*.
ʒe may both saue & spyll yow*er* sowle, *tha*t ys so p*r*ecyvs
    Libere velle, libere velle,[1] God may not deny, i-wys.   887

Beware of Titiuilly w*ith* hys net & of all hys enmys [2] wyll,
    Of ʒo*ur* synfull delectacion *tha*t grewyth ʒo*ur* gostly
    s*u*bstans.
ʒo*ur* body ys yo*ur* enmy, let hym not haue hys wyll.
    T*a*ke yo*ur* lewe whan ʒe wyll, God send ʒow good p*er*-
    seue*r*ans ! [3]   891

[MANK.]   Syth I schall dep*a*rte, blyse me, fad*er* her *th*en I go.
    God send ws all plente of hys gret m*er*cy !
MERCY.   Dominus [4] *custodi*[*a*]*t te ab omni malo* [5]
    *In nom*ine Pat*ris* [*et*] *Filii* [6] et *Spir*it*us* Sancti. *Amen!* 895
                                   *Hic exit Ma*n*kende.*

Wyrschep[f]yll sofereyns, I haue do my p*r*opirte ;
    Mankynd· ys deliu*er*yd by my sune*r*all [7] patrocynye.
God prese*r*ue hym fro all wyckyd captiuite
    And se*n*d hym grace hys sensuall condicion to mortifye ! 899

Now, for hys lowe *tha*t for vs receyuyd hys humanite,
    Serche [8] yo*ur* condicyo*n*s w*ith* dew exami*n*acio*n* !
Thynke & remembyr *th*e world ys but a wanite,
    As yt ys p*r*owyd daly by diu*er*se mutacyon.   903

Ma*n*kend ys wrechyd, he hath sufficyent prowe ;
    There-fore God [kepe] ʒow all, *p*er *sua*m *mi*sericordi*am*,
*Tha*t ye may be pleser*es* [9] w*ith* *th*e angell[es] abowe,
    And hawe to ʒo*ur* porcyon *vita*m *eterna*m. *Amen !*   907

---

[1] MS. Libere welle leibere welle ; *corr. by* Kittredge.
[2] *Possibly* enuius.   [6] MS. filiis.
[3] MS. p*er*seue*r*nas.   [7] Kittredge *suggests* special.
[4] MS. D*o*mine.   [8] MS. Serge.
[5] MS. mali.   [9] *Perhaps* partakers.

FYNIS.

C . . ūber ſi q¹ cūi . . cōstu forte queret*ur*
h . y . gh*a*m q*uod* omtche dices sup ōīa costa.[1]

[1] *This is almost entirely effaced.   At the end of* Mind, Will and Understanding, *the same lines occur in this form:*

> O liber, siquis cui cōstās q*ue*retur,
> Hyngh*a*m q*uod* monacho dices sup*er omn*ia cōsti.

Query:

> O liber, si quidem cui constes forte queretur,
> Hyngham quod monacho dices super omnia constas.

(Kittredge.)

MUNDUS ET INFANS.

Printed from the Roxburghe Club reprint (London, 1817). A collation with the original, in the Library of Trinity College, Dublin, shows only two errors in this reprint. The editions of Collier (Coll.) and Hazlitt (Haz.), in Dodsley's "Old Plays," are quoted in the footnotes only for important variants and emendations. Punctuation, capitals, and division into stanzas are mine; other deviations from the Roxburghe reprint (R.) are indicated as they occur.

[*Dramatis Personae.*

MUNDUS, *also called* THE WORLDE.
INFANS, *also called* WANTON, LUST AND LYKYNGE, MANHODE, SHAME, *and* AGE.

      CONSCYENCE.   FOLYE.   PERSEUERAUNCE.]

Here begynneth a propre newe Interlude of the worlde and the chylde / otherwyse called [Mundus & Infans][1] & it sheweth of the estate of Chyldehode and Manhode.[2]

[*Mundus, seated on his throne.*]

MUNDUS.   Syrs, seace of your sawes, what-so befall,
    And loke ye bow bonerly to my byddynge,
For I am ruler of realmes, I warne you all,
    And ouer all fodys [3] I am kynge, —

For I am kynge and well knowen in these realmes rounde.
    I haue also paleys [4] ypyght ;

4

[1] *These brackets are in* R.
[2] *Beneath this title* R. *has a wood-cut representing a crowned king seated on a throne and holding as symbols of his power a sceptre and a ball surmounted by a cross. Above the cut is his name, Mundus.*
[3] Coll. *suggests* folys.
[4] *A word, perhaps* princely, *has fallen out.*

I haue stedes in stable stalworthe and stronge,
    Also stretes and strondes full strongely ydyght ;   8

For all the Worlde [1] wyde, I wote well, is my name ;
    All rychesse, redely, it renneth in me,
All pleasure worldely, both myrthe and game.
    My-selfe semely in sale I sende with you to be,   12

For I am the Worlde, I warne you all,
    Prynce of powere and of plente.
He that cometh not whan I do hym call,
    I shall hym smyte with pouerte,   16

For pouerte I parte in many a place
    To them that wyll not obedyent be.
I am a kynge in euery case ;
Me thynketh I am a [2] god of grace,   20

The floure of vertu foloweth me.
    Lo ! here I sette semely in se !
I commaunde you all obedyent be,
    And with fre wyll ye folowe me.   24

              [*Enter Infans.*]

INFANS.   Cryst, our kynge, graunte you clerly to know *the*
    case !
    To meue of this mater that is in my mynde,
Clerely [to] declare it Cryst graunte me grace !   27
   .   .   .   .[3]
Now, semely syrs, beholde on me
    How mankynde doth begynne :
I am a chylde, as you may se,
    Goten in game and in grete synne.   31

Fourty [4] wekes my moder me founde,
    Flesshe and blode my fode was tho ;

---

[1] R. storlde.
[2] R. *omits* a; *original has* it, *so also* Coll., Haz.
[3] *A line out?*   [4] R. xl.

Whan I was rype from her to founde,
    In peryll of dethe we stode bothe two.   35

Now [1] to seke dethe I must begyn,
    For to passe that strayte passage ;
For body and soule that shall than twynne
    And make a partynge of that maryage.   39

Fourty wekes I was frely fedde
    Within my moders wombe ; [2]
Full oft of dethe she was adred
    Whan that I sholde parte her from.   43

Now in to the Worlde she hathe me sent,
    Poore and naked as ye may se ;
I am not worthely wrapped nor went,
    But powerly prycked in pouerte.   47

Now in to the Worlde wyll I wende,
    Some comforte of hym for to craue.
                        [Goes to Mundus.]
All hayle, comely crowned kynge !
    God, that all made, you se and saue !   51

MUND.[3] Welcome, fayre chylde ! What is thy name?
INF.   I wote not, syr, withouten blame ;
But ofte tyme my moder, in her game,
    Called me Dalyaunce.
MUND.   Dalyaunce, my swete chylde?
It is a name that is ryght wylde,
For, whan thou waxest olde,
    It is a name of no substaunce.   59

But, my fayre chylde, what woldest thou haue?
INF.   Syr, of some comforte I you craue,
Mete and clothe my lyfe to saue ;
    And I your true seruaunt shall be.

---

[1] R. Oow.   [2] R. possessyon.
[3] *Here and below* R. *spells the speakers' names in full.*

MUND. Now, fayre chylde, I graunte the thyne askynge ;
I wyll the fynde whyle thou art yinge,
So thou wylte be obedyent to my byddynge.
    These garmentes gaye I gyue to the ;   67

And also I gyue to the a name
And clepe the Wanton, in euery game,
Tyll xiiij yere be come and gone, —
    And than come agayne to me.
WANTON. Gramercy, Worlde, for myne araye !
For now I purpose me to playe.
MUNDUS. Fare-well, fayre chylde, and haue good-daye !
    All rychelesnesse is kynde for the.   75

WANTON. A ha ! Wanton is my name !
I can many a quaynte game :
Lo, my toppe I dryue in same, —
    Se, it torneth rounde !
I can with my scorge-stycke
My felowe vpon the heed hytte,
And wyghtly from hym make a skyppe,
    And blere on hym my tonge.   83

If brother or syster do me chyde,
I wyll scratche and also byte ;
I can crye and also kyke
    And mocke them all be rewe.
If fader or moder wyll me smyte,
I wyll wrynge with my lyppe
And lyghtly from hym make a skyppe
    And call my dame shrewe.   91

A ha ! a newe game haue I founde !
Se this gynne, it renneth rounde ;
And here another haue I founde ;
    And yet mo can I fynde.
I can mowe on a man ;
And make a lesynge well I can,

And mayntayne it ryght well than, —
    This connynge came me of kynde. 99

Ye, syrs, I can well gelde a snayle ;
And catche a cowe by the tayle,[1] —
    This is a fayre connynge ;
I can daunce and also skyppe ;
I can playe at the chery-pytte ;
And I can wystell you a fytte,
    Syres, in a wylowe[2] ryne. 106

Ye, syrs, and euery daye
Whan I to scole shall take the waye,
Some good mannes gardyn I wyll assaye,
    Perys and plommes to plucke.
I can spye a sparowes nest.
I wyll not go to[3] scole but whan me lest,
For there begynneth a sory fest
    Whan the mayster sholde lyfte my docke. 114

But, syrs, whan I was seuen yere of age,
I was sent to the Worlde to take wage,
And this seuen yere I haue ben his page
    And kept his commaundement.
Now I wyll wende to the Worlde, *that* worthy emperou[r].

[He approaches Mundus.]

Hayle, lorde of grete honour !
This vij yere I haue serued you in hall *and* in boure
    With all my trewe entent. 122

MUND. Now, welcome, Wanton, my derlynge dere !
A newe name I shall gyue the here :
Loue, Lust, Lykynge, in-fere, —
    These thy names they shall be, —
All game and gle and gladnes,
All loue-longynge in lewdnes.

---

[1] *Line missing?*   [2] R. whylowe.   [3] R. fo.

This seuen yere forsake all sadnes,
   And than come agayne to me.   130

LUST-AND-LYKYNG.   A ha! now Lust and Lykyng is my
      name !
   I am as fresshe as flourys in Maye ;
I am semely shapen in same,
   And proudely apperelde in garmentes gaye ;   134

My lokes ben full louely to a ladyes eye,
   And in loue-longynge my harte is sore sette ;
Myght I fynde a fode that were fayre and fre,
   To lye in hell tell domysdaye for loue [1] I wolde not let,
      My loue for to wynne.
   All game and gle,
   All myrthe and melodye,
   All reuell and ribaudye,[2]
      And of bost wyll I neuer blynne.   143

But, syrs, I am now [3] xix wynter olde ;
I-wys, I waxe wonder bolde.
Now I wyll go to the Worlde,
   A heygher seyence to assaye.
For the Worlde wyll me auaunce,
I wyll kepe his gouernaunce ;
For he is a kynge in all substaunce,
   His plesynge wyll I praye.[4]   151

          [*He approaches Mundus.*]

All hayle, mayster, full of myght !
I haue you serued bothe day and nyght ;
Now I come [5] as I you behyght, —
   One and twenty wynter is comen and gone.
MUND.   Now, welcome, Loue, Lust and Lykynge !
For thou hast ben obedyent to my byddynge,

    [1] R. foue; Kittredge *suggests the omission of* for loue.
    [2] R. ryotte ; Kittredge *suggests :* All ryotte and reuellrye.
    [3] *So in original ;* R. now am ; Coll., Haz. now I am.
    [4] *The order of* ll. 150, 151 *is reversed in* R.
    [5] R. comen.

I encreace the in all thynge
    And myghtly I make the a man.   159

Manhode myghty shall be thy name ;
Bere the prest in euery game,
And wayte well that thou suffre no shame
    Neyther for londe nor for rente.
Yf ony man wolde wayte the with blame,
    Withstonde hym with thy hole entent ;
Full sharpely thou bete hym to shame
    With doughtynesse of dente ! [1]   167

For of one thynge, Manhode, I warne the :
I am moost of bounte,
For seuen kynges sewen me,
    Bothe by daye and nyght ;
One of them is the kynge of Pryde ;
The kynge of Enuy, doughty in dede ;
The kynge of Wrathe, that boldely wyll abyde,
    For mykyll is his myght ;   175

The kynge of Couetous [2] is the fourt[h]e ;
The fyfte kynge he hyght Slouthe ;
The kynge of Glotony hath no iolyte
    There pouerte is pyght ;
Lechery is the seuenth kynge,
All men in hym haue grete delytynge,
Therfore worshyp hym aboue all thynge,
    Manhode, with all thy myght.   183

MANH. Yes, syr kynge, without lesynge
    It shall be wrought !
Had I knowynge of the fyrst kynge, [3]
    Well ioyen I mought.   187

[1] R. dede.

[2] *The author evidently pronounced this* Covetyse (*cf.* ll. 412, 441) ; *but,
as this spelling occurs many times and* Couetys *only once, it seems best to
retain the spelling of the text.*

[3] *After* kynge, R. *repeats* without lesynge *from* l. 184.

MUND. The fyrste kynge hyght Pryde.

MANH. A, lorde ! with hym fayne wolde I byde.

MUND. Ye, but woldest thou serue hym truely in euery tyde?

    MANH. Ye, syr ; and therto my trouthe I plyght.

That I shall truely Pryde present

I swere by Saynt Thomas of Kent ;

To serue hym truely is myn entent,

    With mayne and all my myght. 195

MUND. Now, Manhode, I wyll araye the newe

In robes ryall, ryght of good hewe ;

And I praye the pryncypally be trewe ;

    And here I dubbe the a knyght, —

And haunte alwaye to chyualry !

I gyue the grace and also beaute,

Gold and syluer, gret plente,

    Of the wronge to make the ryght. 203

MANH. Gramercy, Worlde and emperour !

Gramercy, Worlde and gouernoure !

Gramercy, comforte in all coloure ![1]

    And now I take my leue ; fare-well !

MUND. Farewell, Manhode, my gentyll knyght !

Fare-well, my sone, semely in syght !

I gyue the a swerde [2] *and* also strength and myght,

    In batayle boldly to bere the well. 211

MANH. Now I am dubbed a knyght hende,

    Wonder wide shall waxe my fame !

To seke aduentures now wyll I wende,

    To please the Worlde in gle and game. 215

MUND. Lo, syrs, I am a prynce, peryllous [3] yprovyde,[4]

    I-preuyd full peryllous [3] and pethely i-pyght,

As a lorde in eche londe I am belouyd ;

    Myne eyen do shyne as lanterne bryght ; 219

[1] *Possibly for* doloure, *but perhaps correct as it stands.*
[2] R. aswerde.   [4] R. yprobyde.
[3] *Probably* pereles, *see Notes.*

I am a creature comely, out of care ;
    Emperours and kynges they knele to my kne ;
Euery man is a-ferde whan I do on hym stare,
    For all mery medell-erthe maketh mencyon of me ;   223

Yet all is my [1] hande-werke, both by downe *and* by dale,
    Bothe the see and the lande [2] and foules that fly ;
And I were ones moued, I tell you in tale,
    There durst no [3] sterre stere, that stondeth in the sky,   227

For I am lorde and leder so in that londe,
    All boweth to my byddynge bonerly aboute ;
Who *that* styreth w*ith* ony stryfe or wayteth me with
               wro*n*ge,
    I shall myghtly make hym to stamer *and* stowpe,
        For I am rychest in myne araye,
    I haue knyghtes and toures,
    I haue ladyes bryghtest in bourys.
    Now wyll I fare on these flourys ;
        Lordynges, haue good-daye !   *[Exit.]*   236

MANH.   Peas, now peas, ye felowes all aboute !
    Peas now, and herken to my sawes !
For I am lorde bothe stalworthy and stoute ;
    All londes are ledde by my lawes.   240

Baron was there neuer borne that so well hym bare,
    A better ne a bolde[r] nor a bryghter of ble ;
For I haue myght *and* mayne ouer countrees fare,
    And Manhode myghty am I namyd in euery cou*n*tre ;   244

For Salerne and Samers and Ynde the loys,[4]
    Caleys, Kente, *and* Cornewayle I haue conquered clene,
Pycardye and Pountes and gentyll Artoys,
    Florence, Flaunders and Frau*n*ce, *and* also Gascoyne, —
    All I haue conquered as a knyght.

[1] R. is at my.
[2] *Perhaps* Bothe the see and the sande, *the common alliterative phrase.*
[3] R. do ; *corr. by* Collier.   [4] Haz. *reads* Andaluse.

There is no emperour so kene
That dare me lyghtly tene,
For lyues and lymmes I lene,
    So mykyll is my myght ;   253

For I haue boldely blode full dyspyteously spylde,[1]
  There many hath lefte fyngers *and* fete, both heed *and*
    face.
I haue done harme on hedes *and* knyghtes haue I kyld ;
  And many a lady for my loue hath sayd ' alas.'   257

Brygaunt ernys [2] I haue beten to backe *and* to bonys,
  And beten also many a grome to grounde ;
Brestplates I haue beten as Steuen was *with* stonys ;
  So fell a fyghter in felde [3] was there neuer yfounde.
    To me no man is makyde ;
  For Manhode myghty, that is my name,
  Many a lorde haue I do lame ;
  Wonder wyde walketh my fame,
    And many a kynges crowne haue I crakyd.   266

I am worthy and wyght, wytty and wyse,
I am ryall arayde to reuen vnder the ryse,
I am proudely aparelde in purpure and byse,
  As golde I glyster in gere ;
I am styffe, stronge, stalworthe and stoute,
I am the ryallest redely that renneth in this route,
There is no knyght so grysly that I drede nor dout,
  For I am so doughtly dyght ther may no dint me dere.[4] 274

And *the* kynge of Pryde, full prest, w*ith* all his proude p*r*esens,
And *the* kynge of Lechery louely his letters hath me sent,
And *the* kynge of Wrathe full wordely, w*ith* all his entent,
  They wyll me mayntayne w*ith* mayne *and* all theyr
    myght ; [5]

1 R. pyteously dyspylde.
2 R. Brygaunt Ernys; Coll. Brygaunt Ermys; Haz. Brigand harness.
3 R. in a felde.
4 *Qy. after* dyght, *read* no dint may me dere.
5 *Qy.* with mayne & with myght.

The kynge of Couetous, and the kynge of Glotony,
The kynge of Slouthe, and the kynge of Enuy,
All those sende me theyr leuery.
  Where is now so worthy a wyght? —
     A wyght?
Ye, as a wyght wytty,
Here in this sete sytte I ;
For no loues lette I
  Here for to sytte.   287

    [Enter Conscyence.]

CONSC. Cryst, as he is crowned kynge,
  Saue all this comely company,
And graunte you all his dere blessynge,
  That bonerly bought you on the roode-tree !   291

Now praye you prestly on euery [1] syde
  To God omnypotent
To set our enemy sharpely on-syde, —
  That is, the deuyll and his couent, —   295

And all men to haue a clere knowynge
  Of heuen blysse, that hye toure.
Me thynke it is a nessarye [2] thynge
  For yonge and olde, both ryche and pore,   299

Poore Conscyence for to knowe ;
  For Conscyence clere it is my name.
Conscyence counseyleth both hye and lowe,
  And Conscyence comenly bereth grete blame, —
      Blame?
  Ye, and oftentymes set in shame.
  Wherfore I rede you men, bothe in ernest *and* in game,
Conscyence that ye knowe.   307

For I knowe all the mysterys of man,
They be as symple as they can ;

---

[1] R. enery.   [2] *Probably intentional.*

And in euery company where I come
　　Conscyence is out cast.
All the worlde dothe Conscyence hate ;
Mankynde and Conscyence ben at debate,
For yf mankynde myght Conscyence take
　　My body wolde they brast, —
　　　　　　　　　　Brast? [1]
Ye, and warke me moche wo.
MANHODE.　Say, how felowe! who gaue the leue this way
　　　　to go?
What! wenest thou I dare not come the to?
　　Say, thou harlot! whyder in hast?　　　　　　　　320

CONSC.　What! let me go, syr ; I knowe you nought !
MANHODE.　No, bychyde brothell?　Thou shalt be taught!
For I am a knyght, and I were sought ;
　　The Worlde hath auaunced me,
CONSC.　Why, good syr knyght, what is your name?
MANH.　Manhode, myghty in myrthe and in game ;
All powere of Pryde haue I tane ;
　　I am as gentyll as iay on tre.　　　　　　　　328

CONSC.　Syr, thoughe the Worlde haue you to manhode
　　　　brought,
To mayntayne maner[s] ye were neuer taught :
No ; Conscyence clere ye knowe ryght nought,
　　And this longeth to a knyght.
MANH.　Conscyence! what the deuyll, man, is he?
CONSC.　Syr a techer of the spyrytualete.
MANH.　Spyrytualyte! what the deuyll may that be?
　　CONSC.　Syr, all that be leders in-to lyght.　　　　336

MANH.　Lyght?　Ye, but herke, felowe, yet!　Lyght fayne
　　　　wolde I se.
CONSC.　Wyll ye so, syr knyght?　Than do after me.
MANH.　Ye, and it to Prydes pleasynge be,
　　I wyll take thy techynge.

[1] *In* R. *this word is in the following line.*

CONSC. Nay, syr ; beware of Pryde, and you do well, —
For pryde Lucyfer fell in-to hell ;
Tyll domysday ther shall he dwell,
  Withouten ony out-comynge :   344

For pride, syr, is but a vayne glorye.
MANH. Peas, thou brothell, and lette those wordes be !
For the Worlde and Pryde hath auaunced me ;
  To me men lewte full lowe.
CONSC. And to beware of pryde, syr, I wolde you counsayll ;[1]
And thynke on Kynge Robert of Cysell,
How he for pryde in grete pouerte fell
  For he wolde not Conscyence knowe.   352

MANH. Ye, Conscyence, go forthe thy waye,
For I loue Pryde and wyll go gaye ;
All thy techynge is not worthe a straye,
  For Pryde I clepe my kynge.
CONSC. Syr, there is no kynge but God alone,
That bodely bought vs with payne and passyon
Bycause of mannes soule redempcyon, —
  In Scrypture thus we fynde.   360

MANH. Saye, Conscyence, syth *thou* woldest haue Pryde
  fro me,
What sayest thou by the kynge of Lechery ?
With all mankynde he must be,
  And with hym I loue to lende.[2]
CONSC. Nay, Manhode, that may not be ;
From Lechery fast you fle,
For in combraunce it wyll brynge the
  And all that to hym wyll wende.[3]   368

MANH. Saye, Conscyence, of the kynge of Slouthe !
He hath behyght me mykell trouthe ;
And I may not forsake hym for ruthe,
  For with hym I thynke to rest.

[1] R. counsayll you.   [2] R. lynge.   [3] R. lynde.

CONSC.   Manhode, in Scrypture thus we fynde,
That Slouthe is a traytour to heuen kynge ;
Syr knyght, yf you wyll kepe your kynde, [1]
    Frome [2] Slouthe clene you cast.   376

MANH.   Say, Conscyence, [of] the kynge of Glotonye !
He sayth he wyll not for-sake me ;
And I purpose his saruaunt to be,
    With mayne and all my myght.
CONSC.   Thynke, Manhode, on substaunce,
And put out Glotonye for combraunce,
And kepe with you Good-Gouernaunce,
    For this longeth to a knyght.   384

MANH.   What ! Conscyence, frome all my maysters *thou*
    woldest haue me ;
But I wyll neuer forsake Enuy,
For he is kynge of company,
    Bothe with more and lasse.
CONSC.   Nay, Manhode, that may not be ;
And ye wyll cherysshe Enuy,
God wyll not well pleased be
    To comforte you in that case.   392

MANH.   Ey, ey ! from fyue kynges thou hast counseyled me ;
But from the kynge of Wrathe I wyll neuer fle,
For he is in euery dede doughty,
    For hym dare no man rowte.
CONSC.   Nay, Manhode, beware of Wrathe,
For it is but superfluyte that cometh and goeth ;
Ye, and all men his company hateth,
    For ofte they stonde in doubte.   400

MANH.   Fye on the, fals, flatterynge frere !
Thou shalte rewe the tyme that thou came here ;
The deuyll mote set the on a fyre,
    That euer I with the mete !

    [1] R. **kynge**; *corr. by* Collier.   [2] R. **Rrome**.

For thou counseylest me from all gladnes
And wolde me set vnto all sadnes,
But, or thou brynge me in this madnes,
    The deuyll breke thy necke!   408

But, syr frere, — euyll mote thou thye! —
Frome vi kynges thou hast conseyled me ;
But that daye shall thou neuer se
    To counsayll me frome Couetous,[1]
CONSC.   No, syr, I wyll not you from Couetous brynge,
For Couetous I clepe a kynge :
Syr, Couetous in good doynge
    Is good in all wyse.   416

But, syr kynght, wyll ye do after me,
And Couetous your kynge shall be ?
MANH.   Ye, syr, my trouthe I plyght to the
    That I wyll warke at thy wyll.
CONSC.   Manhode, wyll ye by this worde stande?
MANH.   Ye, Conscyence, here my hande!
I wyll neuer from it fonge,[2]
    Neyther loude ne styll.   424

CONSC.   Manhode, ye must loue God aboue all thynge ;
His name in ydelnes ye may not mynge ;
Kepe your holy daye from worldly doynge ;
    Your fader and moder worshyppe aye ;
Coueyte ye to sle no man ;
Ne do no lechery with no woman ;
Your neyboures good take not be no waye ;[3]
    And all false-wytnesse ye must denaye ;   432

Neyther ye must not couete no mannes wyfe,
Nor no good that hym be-lythe, —
This couetys shall kepe you out of stryfe :
    These ben the commaundementes ten.
Manhode,[4] and ye these commaundementes kepe,

---

[1] *See note on* l. 176.   [3] *Qy.* take not than.
[2] *Qy.* wande.   [4] R. Mankynde.

Heuen blysse I you behete,
For Crystes commaundementes [ben] all [1] full swete
    And full necessary to all men.   440

MANH.   What! Conscyence, is this thy Couetous? [2]
CONSC.   Ye, Manhode, in all wyse!
And coueyte to Crystes seruyse,
    Bothe to matyns and to masse!
Ye must, Manhode, with all your myght
Mayntayne Holy Chyrches ryght,
For this longeth to a knyght,
    Playnly in euery place.   448

MANH.   What! Conscyence, sholde I leue all game and gle?
CONSC.   Nay, Manhode, so mote I thye ;
All myrthe in measure is good for the,
    But, syr, measure is in all thynge.
MANH.   Measure, Conscyence? what thynge may measure
    be?
CONSC.   Syr, kepe you in charyte,
And from all euyll company
    For doubte of foly doynge.   456

MANH.   Folye? what thynge callest thou folye?
CONSC.   Syr, it is Pryde, Wrathe, and Enuy,
Slouthe, Couetous and Glotonye, —
    Lechery the seuente is :
These seuen synnes I call folye.
    MANH.   What, thou lyest! [3]   To this
Seuen the Worlde delyuered me,
And sayd they were kynges of grete beaute
    And most of mayne and myghtes ;   465

But yet I pray the, syr, tell me :
May I not go arayde honestly?

----

[1] Haz. *emends* all *to* are.   [2] *See note on* l. 176.
[3] *The stanza is abnormal, it can be reduced to the usual form by
omitting,* What, thou lyest.

CONSC. Yes, Manhode, hardely,
    In all maner of degre.
MANH. But I must haue sportynge of playe.
CONSC. Sykerly, Manhode, I say not naye,
But good gouernaunce kepe both nyght and daye,
    And mayntayne mekenes and all mercy.   473

MANH. All mercy, Conscyence? what may that be?
CONSC. Syr all dyscrecyon that God gaue the.
MANH. Dyscressyon I knowe not, so mote I the!
CONSC. Syr, it is all the wyttes that God hath you sende.[1]   477

MANH. A, Conscyence, Conscyence! now I knowe and se
    Thy cunnynge is moche more than myne;
But yet I pray the, syr, tell me:
    What is moost necessary for man in euery tyme?   481

CONSC. Syr, in euery tyme beware of folye, —
    Folye is full of false flaterynge;
In what occupacyon that euer ye be,
    Alwaye, or ye begyn, thynke on the endynge,
        For blame.
    Nowe fare-well, Manhode; I must wende.
    MANH. Now fare-well, Conscyence, myne owne frende!
    CONSC. I pray you, Manhode, have God in mynde
        And beware of Folye and Shame.   490

MANH. Yes, yes! Ye, come wynde and rayne,
God let hym neuer come here agayne!
Now he is forwarde,[2] I am ryght fayne,
    For in faythe, syr, he had nere counsayled me all amys. 494

                                    [*Exit Conscyence.*]

A, a! now I haue be-thought me! Yf I shall heuyn wyn,
Conscyence techynge I must begyn,
And clene forsake the kynges of synne,
    That the Worlde me taught,

---

[1] *Qy.* hath sent the.   [2] Kittredge *suggests* frowarde.

And Conscyence seruaunt wyll I be,
And beleue, as he hath taught me,
Upon one God and persones thre
    That made all thynge of nought.   502

For Conscyence clere I clepe my kynge
And [me] his knyght in good doynge,
For, ryght of reason as I fynde,
    Conscyence techynge trewe is.[1]
The Worlde is full of boost,
And sayth he is of myghtes moost;
All his techynge is not worthe a toost,[2]
    For Conscyence he dothe refuse.   510

But yet wyll I hym not forsake,
For mankynde he doth mery make.
Thoughe the Worlde and Conscyence be at debate,
    Yet the Worlde wyll I not despyse;
For bothe in chyrche and in chepynge
And in other places beynge,
The Worlde fyndeth me all thynge
    And dothe me grete seruyse.   518

Now here full prest
I thynke to rest![3]
Now myrthe is best!   521

               [*Enter Folye.*]

FOLYE.   What, hey how, care awaye!
My name is Folye! Am I[4] not gaye?
Is here ony man that wyll saye naye!
    That renneth in this route!
A, syr, God gyue you good eue!
MANH.   Stonde vtter, felowe! Where doest *tho*u thy cur-
      tesy preue?
FOLYE.   What! I do but clawe myne ars, syr, be your leue.
    I praye you, syr, ryue me this cloute.   529

---

[1] R. is trewe.   [3] R. to ro rest.
[2] R. coost; *corr. by* Kittredge. [4] R. I am.

MANH. What, stonde out, thou sayned [1] shrewe!

FOLYE. By my [2] faythe, syr, there the cocke crewe,
For I take recorde of this rewe
    My thedome is nere past.

MANH. Now, trewely, it may well be so.

FOLYE. By God, syr, yet haue I felowes mo,
For in euery countre where I go
    Some man his thryfte hath lost.   537

MANH. But herke, felowe ; art thou ony craftes man ?

FOLYE. Ye, syr, I can bynde a syue and tynke a pan ;
And, therto, a coryous bukler-player I am.
    Aryse, felowe ; wyll thou assaye ?

MANH. Now, truely, syr, I trow thou canst but lytell skyl
    of playe.

FOLYE. Yes, by Cockes bones, that I can !
I wyll neuer fle for no man
    That walketh by the waye.   545

MANH. Felowe, thoughe thou haue kunnynge,
I counsayll the leue thy bostynge,
For here thou may thy felowe fynde,
    Whyder thou wylte at longe or shorte.

FOLYE. Come, loke, and thou darest ; aryse and assaye !

MANH. Ye, syr, but yet Conscyence byddeth me naye.

FOLYE. No, syr, thou darest not, in good faye,
    For truely thou faylest no false herte.   553

MANH. What sayst thou? haue I a false herte?

FOLYE. Ye, syr, in good faye.

MANH. Manhode wyll not that I saye naye !
Defende the, Folye, yf thou [3] maye,
    For, in feythe, I purpose to wete what thou art.   558

[They fight.]

How sayste thou now, Folye ? hast thou not a touche ?

FOLYE. No, ywys, but a lytell on my pouche ;

---

[1] Collier *suggests* fayned.   [2] R. By by.   [3] R. tyou.

On all this meyne I wyll me wouche,
    That stondeth here aboute.
MANH.   And I take recorde on all this rewe
Thou hast two touches, though I saye but fewe.
FOLYE.   Ye, this place is not without a shrewe,
    I do you all out of doute.[1]   566

MANH.   But herke, felowe ; by thy faythe, where was thou
        bore ?
FOLYE.   By my faythe, in Englonde haue I dwelled yore,
And all myne auncetters me before ;
    But, syr, in London is my chefe dwellynge.
MANH.   In London?   Where, yf a man the sought?
FOLYE.   Syr, in Holborne I was forthe brought ;
And with the courtyers I am betaught ;
    To Westmynster I vsed to wende.   574

MANH.   Herke, felowe !   why doost thou to Westminster
        drawe ?
FOLYE.   For I am a seruaunt of the lawe ;
Couetous is myne owne felowe, —
    We twayne plete for the kynge ;
And poore men that come from vplande,
We wyll take theyr mater in hande, —
Be it ryght or be it wronge,
    Theyr thryfte with vs shall wende.   582

MANH.   Now here, felowe !   I praye *the* whyder wendest
        *tho*u tha*n* ?
FOLYE.   By my feyth, syr, into London I ran
To the tauernes to drynke the wyne ;
    And than to the innes I toke the waye,
And there I was not welcome to the osteler,
But I was welcome to the fayre tapester,
And to all the housholde I was ryght dere,
    For I haue dwelled with her [2] many a daye.   590

[1] R. dewe.
[2] *Qy. for* with her, *read* there, *or* with them.

MANH.   Now, I praye *the*, whyder toke *tho*u the waye
          than ? [1]
FOLYE.   In feythe, syr, ouer London-brydge I ran,
And the streyght waye to the stewes I came,
     And toke lodgynge for a nyght ;
And there I founde my brother, Lechery :
There men and women dyde folye,
And every man made of me as worthy
     As thoughe I hadde ben a knyght.   598

MANH.   I praye the yet tell me mo of thyne aduentures.
FOLYE.   In feythe, euen streyght to all the freres,
And with them I dwelled many yeres ;
     And they crowned Folye a kynge.
MANH.   I praye the, felowe, whyder wendest thou tho?
FOLYE.   Syr, all Englande to and fro,
In-to abbeys and in-to nonneryes also ;
     And alwaye Folye dothe felowes fynde.   606

MANH.   Now, herke, felowe ! I praye the, tell me thy name.
FOLYE.   I-wys, I hyght bothe Folye and Shame.
MANH.   A ha ! thou arte he that Conscyence dyd blame,
     Whan he me taught.
I praye the, Folye,[2] go hens and folowe not me.
FOLYE.   Yes, good syr, let me your seruaunt be !
MANH.   Naye, so mote I thye,
     For than a shrewe had I caught !   614

FOLYE.   Why, good syr, what is your name ?
MANH.   Manhode myghty, that bereth no blame.
FOLYE.   By *the* roode, and Manhode mystereth in euery
               game
     Somdele to cherysshe Folye ;
For Folye is felowe with the Worlde,
And gretely beloued with many a lorde,
And yf ye put me out of your warde,
     The Worlde ryght wroth wyll be.   622

---

[1] R. than the waye.   [2] R. folyc.

MANH.   Ye, syr, yet had I leuer the Worlde be wrath
Than lese the cunnynge that Conscyence me gaue.
FOLYE.   A cuckowe for Conscyence, he is but a dawe !
  He can not elles but preche.   626

MANH.   Ye ; I praye the, leue thy lewde claterynge,
For Conscyence is a counseler for a kynge.
FOLYE.   I wolde not gyue a strawe for his techynge,
  He dooth but make men wrothe.   630

But wottest thou what I saye, man ?
  By that ylke trouthe that God me gaue,
Had I that bychyde Conscyence in this place,
  I sholde so bete hym with my staffe
    That all his stownes sholde stynke.
  MANH.   I praye the, Folye, go hens and folowe not me.
  FOLYE.   Yes, syr, so mote I thye,
  Your seruaunt wyll I be ;
    I axe but mete and drynke.   639

MANH.   Peace, man ! I may not haue the for thy name ;
For thou sayst thy name is bothe Folye and Shame.
FOLYE.   Syr, here in this cloute I knyt Shame,
  And clype me but Propre Folye.
MANH.   Ye, Folye, wyll thou be my trewe seruaunt ?
FOYLE.   Ye, syr Manhode ; here my hande !
MANH.   Now let vs drynke at this comnaunt,
  For that is curtesy.   647

  FOLYE.   Mary, mayster, ye shall haue in hast.
[*Aside*] A ha ! syrs, let the catte wynke !
For all ye wote not what I thynke,
I shall drawe hym suche a draught of drynke
  That Conscyence he shall awaye cast.   652

Haue, mayster, and drynke well,
And let vs make reuell, reuell !
For I swere by the chyrche of Saynt Myghell
  I wolde we were at stewes,

For there is nothynge but reuell-route ;
And we were there, I haue [1] no doubte
I sholde be knowen all aboute,
  Where Conscyence they wolde refuse.   **660**

MANH. Peas, Folye, my fayre frende !
For, by Cryste, I wolde not *that* Conscyence sholde me here [2]
   fynde.
FOLYE. Tusshe, mayster, thereof speke no-thynge,
  For Conscyence cometh no tyme here.[2]
MANH. Peace, Folye ; there is no man that knoweth me.
FOLYE. Syr, here my trouthe I plyght to the,
And thou wylte go thyder with me,
  For knowlege haue thou no care.   **668**

MANH. Pease ! but it is hens a grete waye.
FOLYE. Parde, syr, we may be there on a daye.
Ye, and we shall be ryght welcome, I dare well saye,
  In Estchepe for to dyne ;
And than we wyll with Lombardes at passage playe,
And at the Popes Heed swete wyne assaye ;
  We shall be lodged well a-fyne.   **675**

MANH. What sayest thou, Folye ; is this the best ?
FOLYE. Syr, all this is manhode, well thou knowest.
MANH. Now, Foly, go we hens in hast ;
  But fayne wolde I chaunge my name,
For well I wote yf Conscyence mete me in this tyde,
Ryght well I wote he wolde me chyde.
FOLYE. Syr, for fere of you his face he shall hyde :
  I shall clepe you Shame.   **683**

MANH. Now, gramercy, Folye, my felowe in-fere !
Go we hens ; tary no lenger here ;
Tyll we be gone me thynke it seuen yere, —
  I haue golde and good to spende.

   [1] R. had.   [2] *Qy.* there.

FOLYE.   A ha! mayster, that is good chere.

[*Aside*]   And or it be passed halfe a yere,

I shall the shere ryght a lewde frere,

   And hyther agayne the sende.   691

MANH.   Folye, go before and teche me the waye.

FOLYE.   Come after, Shame, I the praye,

And Conscyence clere ye cast awaye.

   [*Aside*]   Lo, syrs, this Folye techeth aye,

For where Conscyence cometh with his cunnynge,

Yet Folye full fetely shall make hym blynde :

Folye before and Shame behynde, —

   Lo, syrs, thus fareth the worlde alwaye!   ·   699

                                           [*Exit Folye.*]

MANH.   [*Sings*] [1]   Now I wyll folowe Folye,

                  For Folye is my man ;

               Ye, Folye is my felowe

                  And hath gyuen me a name :

               Conscyence called me Manhode,

                  Folye calleth me Shame.   705

[*Speaks*]   Folye wyll me lede to London to lerne reuell ;

Ye, and Conscyence is but a flaterynge brothell,

   For euer he is carpynge of care.

The Worlde and Folye counseylleth me to all gladnes ;

Ye, and Conscyence counseylleth me to all sadnes, [2] —

Ye, to moche sadnes myght brynge me in-to madnes.

   And now haue good-daye, syrs; to London to seke

      Folye wyll I fare.   712

                  [*Enter Conscyence.*]

CONSC.   Saye, Manhode, frende, whyder wyll ye go?

MANH.   Nay, syr, in faythe, my name is not so.

Why, frere, what the deuyll hast thou to do

   Whyder I go or abyde?

---

[1] *This is not indicated as a song in* R., *and is printed as three long lines.*

[2] R. sadnts.

Consc. Yes, syr, I will counsell you for the best!
Manh. I wyll none of thy counsell, so haue I rest!
I wyll go whyder me [1] lest,
 For thou canst nought elles but chyde.   720

      [*Exit Manhode.*]

Consc. Lo, syrs, a grete ensample you may se :
 The freylnes of Mankynde,
How oft he falleth in folye
 Throughe temptacyon of the fende ;   724

For, whan the fende and the flesshe be at one assent,
 Than Conscyence clere is clene out cast ;
Men thynke not on the grete iugement
 That the sely soule shall haue at the last ;   728

But wolde God, all men wolde haue in mynde
 Of the grete daye of dome,
How he shall gyue a grete rekenynge
 Of euyll dedes that he hath done.   732

But natheles,[2] syth it is so,
 That Manhode is forthe with Folye wende,
To seche Perseueraunce now wyll I go,
 With the grace of God Omnypotent.   736

His counseylles ben [with God] in-fere ;
Perseueraunce counsell is moost dere ;
Nexte to hym is Conscyence clere
 From synnynge.
Now in-to[3] thys presence, to Cryst I praye
To spede me well in my iournaye !
Fare-well, lordynges, and haue good daye ;
 To seke Perseueraunce wyll I wende.   744

    [*Exit Conscyence ; enter Perseueraunce.*]

[1] R. my.   [2] R. nedeles; Haz. [it is] nedeles.   [3] *Qy.* in.

PERS. Now Cryst, our comely Creature,[1] clerer than crystal
      clene,
    That craftly made euery creature by good recreacyon,
Saue all this company that is gathered here, bydene,
    And set all your soules in-to good saluacyon !   748

Now good God, *that* is moost wysest and welde[2] of wyttes,
    This company counsell, comforte and glad,
And saue all this multytude[3] that semely here syttes !
    Now, good God, for his mercy, that all men made, —   752

Now Mary, Moder, mekest that I mene,
    Shelde all this company from euyll conuersacyon,[4]
And saue you from our enemy, as she is bryght *and* clene,
    And at *the* last day of dome delyuer you fro*m* euerlast-
        ynge dampnac[y]on !   756

Syrs, Perseueraunce is my name ;
    Conscyence [my] borne broder is ;
He sente me hyder mankynde to endoctryne,
That they sholde to no vyces enclyne,
    For ofte mankynde is gouerned amys
        And throughe foly mankynde is set in shame.
    Therfore in this presens to Cryst I praye,
    Or that I hens wende awaye,
    Some good worde that I may saye
        To borowe mannes soul from blame.   766

                [*Enter Manhode*[5] *old and broken.*]

AGE. Alas, alas, that me is wo !
    My lyfe, my lykynge I haue forlorne ;
My rentes, my rychesse, it is all ygo ;
    Alas the daye that I was borne !   770

---

   [1] *This spelling of* Creator *is too common to change.*
   [2] Welde (= weldy) *seems more likely than* welder *or* welle.
   [3] R. symylytude; *apparently a confusion of* semely (= assembly) *and* multitude.
   [4] R. Inuersacyon.
   [5] *Henceforth called* Age.

For I was borne Manhode, moost of myght,
　　Styffe, stronge, both stalworthy and stoute ;
The Worlde full worthely hath made me a knyght,
　　All bowed to my byddynge bonerly aboute ;　　774

Than Conscyence clere, comely and kynde,
　　Mekely he met me in sete there I sate,
He lerned me a lesson of his techynge,
　　And the vij deedly synnes full lothely he dyde hate :　778

Pryde, Wrathe and Enuy and Couetous in kynde,—
　　The Worlde all these synnes delyuered me vntyll,—
Slouthe, Glotony,[1] and Lechery, that is full of false flaterynge, —
　　All these Conscyence reproued both lowde and styll.　782

To Conscyence I helde vp my hande
To kepe Crystes commaundementes,[2]
He warned me of Folye, that traytour, and bade me beware ;
　　And thus he went his waye.
But I haue falsly me forsworne, —
Alas the daye that I was borne !
For body and soule I haue forlorne,
　　I clynge as a clodde in claye.　　790

In London many a daye
At the passage I wolde playe,
I thought to borowe and neuer paye ;[3]
Than was I sought and set in stockes.
In Newgate I laye vnder lockes ;
If I sayd ought, I caught many knockes, —
　　Alas ! where was Manhode tho?
Alas, my lewdenes hath me lost !
Where is my body so proude and prest?
I coughe and rought, my body wyll brest,
　　Age dothe folowe me so.

---

[1] R. couetous, Glotony *being omitted.*
[2] *Qy.* commaunde.　　　[3] *Line out ?*

I stare and stacker as I stonde,
I grone grysly [1] vpon the grounde ;
Alas ! Dethe, why lettest thou me lyue so longe?
    I wander as a wyght in wo
        And care.
    For I haue done yll,
    Now wende I wyll
    My-selfe to spyll,
        I care not whyder nor where !   810

PERS.   Well ymet, syr ! well ymet ! and whyder awaye?
AGE.   Why, good syr, wherby do ye saye?
PERS.   Tell me, syr, I you praye,
    And I with you wyll wende.
AGE.   Why, good syr, what is your name?
PERS.   Forsothe, syr, Perseueraunce, the same.
AGE.   Syr, ye are Conscyence brother that me dyd
        blame,
    I may not with you lende. [2]   818

PERS.   Yes, yes, Manhode, my frende in-fere.
AGE.   Nay, syr, my name is in another maner,
For Folye his owne selfe was here
    And hath clepyd me Shame.
PERS.   Shame ! [3] Nay, Manhode, let hym go,
Folye and his felowes also ;
For they wolde the brynge in-to care and wo,
    And all that wyll folowe his game,   826

AGE.   Ye, game who-so game,
Folye hath gyuen me a name ; [4]
    So where-euer I go
He clypped me Shame.
    Now Manhode is gone, [5]
    Folye hath folowed me so.   832

---

[1] R. glysly.   [4] R. aname.
[2] R. lynge.   [5] *Qy.* go.
[3] R. *has* Shame *in a line by itself.*

Whan I fyrst from my moder cam,
The Worlde made me a man,
And fast in ryches I ran
  Tyll I was dubbed a knyght :
And than I met with Conscyence clere,
And he me set in suche manere
Me thought his techynge was full dere
  Bothe by daye and nyght :   840

And than Folye met me,
And sharpely he beset me,
And from Conscyence he fet me,
  He wolde not fro me go ;
Many a daye he keped me,
And to all folkes he cleped me
  For [1] Shame,
And vnto all synnes he set me.
  Alas, that me is wo !   849

For I haue falsely me forsworne ;
Alas that I was borne !
Body and soule I am but lorne ;
  Me lyketh neyther gle nor game.   853

PERS. Nay, nay, Manhode, saye not so !
Be-ware of Wanhope,[2] for he is a fo.
A newe name I shall gyue you to,
  I clepe you Repentaunce ;
For, and you here repente your synne,
Ye are possyble heuen to wynne,
But with grete contrycyon ye must begynne
  And take you to abstynence.   861

For, thoughe a man had do alone
The deedly synnes euerychone,
And he with contrycyon make his mone
  To Cryst our heuyn kynge,

---

1 R. Fro.; Coll., Haz. *omit.*
2 R. Wanhode ; *corr. by* Kittredge ; Coll., Haz. **Manhode.**

God is also gladde of hym
As of the creature that neuer dyde syn.
AGE.   Now, good syr, how sholde I contrycyon begyn?
  PERS.   Syr, in shryfte of mouthe without varyenge ; 869

And another ensample I shall shewe you to :
Thynke on Peter and Poule and other mo,
Thomas, James, and Johan also,
  And also Mary Maudeleyn ;
For Poule dyde Crystes people grete vylany,
And Peter at the Passyon forsoke Cryst thry,[1]
And Maudelayne lyued longe in lechery,
  And Saynt Thomas byleued not in the Resurreccyon, 877

And yet these to Cryst are derlynges dere,
And now be sayntes in heuen clere ;
And therfore, thoughe ye haue trespased here,
  I hope ye be sory for your synne.
AGE.   Ye, Perseuerance, I you plyght,
I am sory for my synne both daye and nyght;
I wolde fayne lerne with all my myght
  How I sholde heuyn wynne. 885

PERS.   So[2] to wynne heuyn v nessarye thynges there ben
That must be knowen to all mankynde ;
The v wyttes doth begynne,
  Syr, bodely and sprytually.
AGE.   Of the v wyttes I wolde haue knowynge.
PERS.   Forsoth, syr, herynge, seynge, and smellynge,
The remenaunte, tastynge and felynge, —
  These ben the v wyttes bodely. 893

And, syr, other v wyttes ther ben.
AGE.   Syr Perseueraunce, I knowe not them.
PERS.   Now, Repentaunce, I shall you ken, —
  They are the power of the soule :

---

[1] R. thryes.   [2] Haz. *emends to* Sir.

Clere in mynde, — there is one, —
Imagynacyon and all reason,
Understondynge and compassyon, —
 These belonge vnto Perseueraunce. 901

AGE. Gramercy, Perseueraunce, for your trewe techynge !
But, good syr, is there ony more behynde
That is necessary to all mankynde
 Frely for to knowe ?
PERS. Ye, Repentaunce, more there be
That euery man must on byleue, —
The xij artycles of the byleue [1]
 That mankynde must on trowe : 909

The fyrst, that God is in one substaunce,
And also that God is in thre persones,
Begynnynge and endynge without varyaunce,
 And all this worlde made of nought ;
The seconde, that the Sone of God, sykerly,
Toke flesshe and blode of the Vyrgyn Mary
Without touchynge of mannes flessh[l]e [2] companye, —
 This must be in euery mannes thought ; 917

The thyrde, that that same God Sone,
[Was] born of that Holy Vyrgyn,
And she after his byrthe mayden as she was beforne
 And clerer in all kynde ;
Also the fourthe, that same Cryst, God and man,
He suffred payne and passyon
Bycause of mannes soule redempcyon,
 And on a crosse dyde hynge ; 925

The fyfte artycle I shall you tell, —
Than the Spyryte of Godhed went to hell,
And bought out the soules that there dyde dwell,
 By the power of his owne myght ;

---

[1] R. fayth. [2] *Corr. by* Kittredge.

The vi artycle I shall you saye, —
Cryst rose vpon the thyrde daye,
Very God and man withouten naye,
  That all shall deme and dyght ;   933

He sent mannes soule [1] in-to heuen,
Alofte all the aungelles euerychone,
There is the Fader [and] the Sone,
  And sothfast Holy Goost ; [2]
The eyght artycle we must beleue on, —
That same God shall come downe,
And deme mannes soule at the daye of dome,
  And on mercy than must we trust ;   941

The ix artycle, with-outen stryfe, —
Euery man, mayden, and wyfe,
And all the bodyes that euer bare lyfe
  And at the daye of dome body and soule shall pere ; [3]
Truely the x artycle is, —
All they that hath kepyd Goddes seruyce,
They shall be crowned in heuen blysse
  As Crystes seruauntes, to hym full dere ;   949

The xi artycle, the sothe to sayne, —
All they that hath falsely to God guyded [4] them,
They shall be put in-to hell-payne,
  There shall be no synne couerynge ;
Syr, after the xii we must wyrche,
And beleue in all the sacramentes of Holy Chyrche,
That they ben necessary to [5] both last and fyrste,
  To all maner of mankynde.   957

Syr, ye must also here *and* knowe *the* commaundementes x.
Lo, syr, this is your beleue and all men ;
Do after it and ye shall heuen wyn,
  Without doubte, I knowe.

---

[1] R. sonle.   [4] R. gayded.
[2] *These two lines as one in* R. [5] *Qy. omit* to.
[3] *Qy. omit* And *and* body and soule.

AGE. Gramercy, Perseueraunce, for your trewe techynge,
For in the spyryte of my soule wyll I fynde
That it is necessary to all mankynde
    Truely for to knowe.   965

Now, syrs, take all ensample by me,
How I was borne in symple degre ;
The Worlde ryall receyued me
    And dubbed me a knyght ;
Than Conscyence met me ;
So after hym came Folye ;
Folye falsely deceyued me,
    Than Shame my name hyght.   973

PERS. Ye, and now is your name Repentaunce
    Throughe the grace of God Almyght ;
And therfore, withoute ony dystaunce,
    I take my leue of kynge and knyght ;
And I praye to Jhesu whiche [h]as made vs all,
Couer you with his mantell perpetuall !   979
                  Amen !

Here endeth the Interlude of Mundus et *Infans.* *Imprynted
at London in Fletestrete at the sygne of* the *Son*ne *by me wynkyn
de worde. The yere of our Lorde M.CCCCC. and .xxij. The
.xvij. daye of July.*

HYCKESCORNER.

The basis of the text is a collation of the reprint by Hawkins, " The Origin of the English Drama, Oxford, 1773," I, 69-111, with the original edition by Wynkyn de Worde (indicated in the footnotes by W.). Hawkins interchanged *u* and *v*, to conform to modern usage, and in this I have followed him, as the collation made for me does not go into detail on this particular point. In the footnotes I have tried to record all really important variants in both Hawkins (Haw.) and Hazlitt's Dodsley (Haz.), but no note is made of insignificant variations in spelling.

[Dramatis Personae.

HYCKE-SCORNER.	PYTE.
IMAGYNACYON.	CONTEMPLACYON.
FREWYLL.	PERSEVERAUNCE.]

[Enter Pyte alone.]

PYTE.   Now Ih*e*su the gentyll, that bought[1] Adam fro hell,
  Save you all, soveraynes, and solas you sende ;
And, or[2] this mater that I begynne to tell,
  I praye you of audyence tyll I have made an ende ;
For I saye to you my name is Pyte,
  That ever yet hath ben mannes frende.
In the bosome of the Seconde Persone in Trynyte
  I sprange as a plante, mannes mysse to amende.   8

You for to helpe I put to my honde, —
  Recorde I take of Mary that wepte teres of blode ;
I, Pyte, within her herte dyde stonde,
  Whan she sawe her sone on the rode.

[1] *So* W.; Haw. Haz. brought.   [2] Haz. of.

The swerde of sorowe gave that lady [a] wounde,
　　Whan a spere clave her sones herte a-sondre ;
She cryed out and fell to the grounde ;
　　Thoughe she was woo, hyt was lytell wonder.　　　16

This delycate colour,[1] that goodly lady,
　　Full pale and wanne she sawe her sone, all deed,
Splayed on a crosse with the fyve welles of pyte,
　　Of purple velvet poudred with roses reed.
　　Lo ! I, Pyte, thus made your erande to be spede,
Or elles man for-ever sholde have ben forlore ;[2]
　　A mayden so layde hys life to wedde ;
Crowned as a kynge, the thornes prycked hym sore.　　24

Charyte and I of true love ledes the double rayne ;
　　Who-so me loveth dampned never shall be.
Of some vertuous company I wolde be fayne ;
　　For all that wyll to heven nedes must come by me,
　　Chefe porter I am in that hevenly cyte.
And now here wyll I rest me a lytell space,
Tyll hyt please Ihesu of his grace
Some vertuous felyshyp for to sende.　　　32

[Enter Contemplacyon, soliloquizing.]

CONT.　Chryste, that was crystened, crucyfyed and crowned,
　　In his bosum true love was gaged with a spere ;
His vaynes braste and brosed, and to a pyller bounde,
　　With scourges he was lashed, the knottes the skyn tare ;
　　On his necke to Calvary the grete crosse he bare;
His blode ran to the grounde, as Scrypture doth tel,
His burden was so hevy that downe under it he fell.　　39

Lo ! I am kyn to the Lorde which is Goddes Sone ;
　　My name is wryten formest in the boke of lyfe ;

---

[1] Haz. *inserts* had; *qy.* creature; *the original reading may, however, be right, and, as* Kittredge *suggests, possibly* ll. 17 *and* 19 *should change places.*　　[2] W. forlorne; Haz. forlore.

For I am perfyte Contemplacyon,
  And brother to Holy Chyrche, that is our Lordes wyfe. 43

Johan Baptyst, Anthony, and Jherome, with many mo,
  Folowed me here in holte, hethe, and in wyldernes ;
I ever with them went where they dyde go,
  Nyght and daye towarde the waye of ryghtwysenes. 47

I am the chefe lanterne of all holynes,
  Of prelates and preestes I am theyr patron ;
No armure so stronge in no dystresse, —
  Habergyon, helme, ne yet no jeltron. 51

To fyght with Sathan I am [1] the champyon
  That dare abyde and manfully stonde ;
Fendes fle away where they se me come.
  But I wyll shewe you why I came to this londe : 55

For to preche and teche of Goddes soth sawes
Ayenst vyce, that dothe rebell ayenst hym and hys lawes.
  PYTE. God spede, good brother ! Fro whens came you
    now ?
  CONT. Syr, I came frome Perseveraunce to seke you.
  PYTE. Why, syr, knowe you me ?
  CONT. Ye, syr, and have done longe ; your name is Pyte.
  PYTE. Your name fayne wolde I knowe. 62

CONT. In-dede I am called Contemplacyon,
  That useth to lyve solytaryly ;
In wodes and in wyldernesse [2] I walke alone
  Bycause I wolde saye my prayers devoutly.
  I love not with me to have moche company,
But Perseveraunce ofte with me doth mete
  Whan I thynke on thoughtes that is full hevenly, —
Thus he and I togyder full swetely doth slepe. 70

[1] W. ; Haw. Haz. am I.
[2] W. ; Haw. wyldenesse ; Haz. wildness.

PYTE. I thanke God that we be mette togyder.

CONT. Syr, I trust that Perseveraunce shortly wyll come
hyder.

PYTE. Than I thynke to here some good tydynge.

CONT. I warant you, brother, that he is comynge. 74

[Perseveraunce enters, and addresses the audience.]

PERS. The eternal God, that named was Messyas,
He gyve you grace to come to his glorye,
Wher ever¹ is joye, in the celestyall place,
Whan you of Sathan wynneth the vyctorye !
Every man ought to be gladde to have [me] in company,
For I am named good Perseveraunce,
That ever is guyded by vertuous governaunce. 81

I am never varyable, but doth contynue,
Styll goynge upwarde the ladder of grace,
And lode² in me planted is so true,
And fro the poore man I wyll never tourne my face. 85

Whan I go by my-selfe, ofte I do remembre
The grete kyndnes³ that God shewed unto man,
For to be borne in the moneth of Decembre,
Whan the daye waxeth shorte and the nyght longe :
Of his goodnesse that Champyon stronge
Descended downe fro the Fader of Ryghtwysnes,
And rested in Mary, the floure of mekenes. 92

Now to this place hyder come I am
To seke Contemplacyon my kynnesman.

CONT. What, brother Perseveraunce ? Ye be welcome ! 95

PERS. And so be you also, Contemplacyon.

CONT. Loo ! here is our mayster, Pyte.

PERS. Now truly, ye be welcome in-to this countre !

PYTE. I thanke you hertely, syr Perseveraunce.

---

¹ Haz. Wherever.   ² *Qy.* love.   ³ W. knydnes.

PERS. Mayster Pyte, one thynge is com to my remembraunce :
What tythynges here you now ?
PYTE.   Syr, suche as I can I shall shewe you :   102

I have herde many men complayne pyteously ;
They saye they be smyten with the swerde of poverty
    In every place where I do go.
Fewe frendes poverte dooth fynde,
And these ryche men ben unkynde,
    For theyr neyghboures they wyll nought do.
Wydowes dooth curse lordes and gentyll-men,
For they constrayne [1] them to mary with theyr men,
    Ye, wheder they wyll or no.   III

Men mary for good, and that is dampnable,
    Ye, with olde women that is fyfty and beyonde.
The peryll now no man drede wyll, —
    All is not Goddes lawe that is used in londe ;
    Beware wyll they not tyll Deth in his honde
Taketh his swerde and smyteth asonder the lyfe vayne
And with his mortall stroke cleveth the herte atwayne.   118

They trust so in Mercy, the lanterne of bryghtnesse,
That no-thynge do they drede Goddes Ryghtwysnes.[2]
    PERS. O Ihesu, syr, here is a hevy tydynge !
    PYTE. Syr, this is trewe that I do brynge.
    CONT. How am I beloved, Mayster Pyte, where ye come?
    PYTE. In good faythe, people have now small devocyon ;
And as for with you, brother Contemplacyon,   125
There medleth fewe or none.
    CONT. Yes, I trust that prestes love me wele.
    PYTE. But a fewe, i-wys, and some never a dele.[3]
    CONT. Why, syr, without me they maye not lyve clene !
    PYTE. Nay, that is the leest thought [4] that they have of
        fyftene,   130
And that maketh me full hevy.

---

[1] *Misprinted* contrayne *in* Haw.   [3] W. adele.
[2] *Misprinted* ryghtwynes *in* Haw.   [4] W. though ; Haw. Haz. thought.

CONT.   How, trowe you that there be no remedy?

PYTE.   Full harde ; for synne is now so grevous and yll
That I thynke that it be growen to an impossyble.
And yet one thynge maketh me ever mournynge,   135
That prestes lack utterance to showe theyr cunnynge ;
And, al the whyle that clerkes do use so grete synne,
Amonge the lay people loke never for no mendynge.

PERS.   Alas ! that is a hevy case
That so grete synne is used in every place ;
I praye God hyt[1] amende !   141

PYTE.[2]   Now God, that ever hath ben mannes frende,
Some better tydynges soone us sende ;
     For now I must be gone.
Fare-well, good bretherne[3] here,
A grete erande I have elles-where,
     That must nedes be done.
I trust I wyll not longe tary ;
Theder wyll I hye me shortely,
     And come agayne whan I have done.   150

PERS.   Hyder agayne I trust you wyll come ;
Therfore God be with you !

PYTE.[2]   Syr, nedes I must departe now ;
Ihesu me spede this daye !   [Exit.]

PERS.   Now, brother Contemplacyon, let us go our waye.   155

[Exeunt ; enter Frewyll.]

FREWYLL.   Aware, felowes, and stande a-roume !
How saye you, am not I a goodly persoune ?[4]
     I trowe you knowe not suche a geste.
What ! syrres, I tell you, my name is Frewyll ;
I may chose wheder I do good or yll,
     But, for all that, I wyll do as me lyst.   161

---

[1] W. ; Haw. it.   [3] W. ; Haw. brethrene.
[2] *These two speeches are assigned to* Contemplacyon *by* W. Haw. and
Haz., *but see Notes.*   [4] W. personue.

My condycyons ye knowe not, perde ;
I can fyght, chyde and be mery ;
Full soone of my company ye wolde be wery
    And you [1] knewe all !
What ! fyll the cup and make good chere ;
I trowe I have a noble here !
Who lente hyt me ?   By Cryste, a frere ;
    And I gave hym a fall !   169

Where be ye, syr ? be ye at home ?

             [Searching his pockets.]

Kockes passyon, my noble is tourned to a stone !
Where laye I last ?   Beshrewe your herte, Jone !
    Now, by these bones, she hath begyled me !
Let se ! a peny my souper, a pece of flesshe x pence,
My bedde ryght nought : let all this expence —
    Now, by these bones, I have lost an halfpeny !   176

Who laye there ?   My felowe Imagynacyon.
He and I had good communycacyon
    Of syr Johan and Sybbell,   179

How they were spyed in bedde togyder,
And he prayed her ofte to come thyder,
    For to synge lo-le, lo-lowe !
They twayne togyder had good sporte ;
But at the stewes syde I lost a grote,
    I trowe I shall never ythe !   185

My felowe promysed me here to mete ;
But I trowe the horesone be a-slepe
    With a wenche some-where.
How, Imagynacyon ! come hyder !
And you thryve, I lose a feder !
    Beshrowe your herte, appere !   191

        [1] W.; Haw. Haz. ye.

[Enter Imagynacyon.]

IMAG. What, how, how! who called after me?
FREWYLL. Come nere! Ye shall never i-the!
    Where have ye be so longe?   194

IMAG. By God, with me hyt is [1] all wronge,
    I have a payre of sore buttockes ;
All in irons was my songe,
    Even now I satte gyved in a payre of stockes.   198

    FREWYLL. Cockes passyon, and how so?
    IMAG. Syr, I wyll tell you what I have do :   200

I mette with a wenche, and she was fayre,
And of love hertely I dyde praye her,
    And so promysed her monaye.
Syr, she wynked on me and sayd nought,
But by her loke I knewe her thought ;
    Than in-to loves daunce we were brought,
    That we played the pyrdewy.
I wote not what we dyde togyder,
But a knave catchpoll nyghed us nere,
    And so dyde us aspye.   210

A strype he gave me ; I fled my touche ;
And frome my gyrdle he plucked my pouche, —
    By your leve, he lefte me never a peny.
Loo, nought have I but a buckyll,
And [2] yet I can imagen thynges sotyll,
    For to get monaye plenty.
In Westminister Hall every terme I am ;
To me is kynne many a grete gentyll-man ;
    I am knowen in every countre.   219

And I were deed, the lawyers thryfte were lost,
For this wyll I do yf men wolde do cost :

---

1 W.; *misprinted* it *in* Haw.
2 Haw. Ane ; *no note in my collation.*

Prove ryght wronge, and all by reason,
And make men lese bothe hous and londe ;
     For all that they can do in a lytell season.   224

Peche men of treason prevyly I can,
And, whan me lyst, to hange a trewe man.
     If they wyll me monaye tell,
Theves I can helpe out of pryson ;
And into lordes favours I can get me soone,
     And be of theyr prevy counseyll.   230

But, Frewyll, my dere broder,
Sawe you nought [1] of Hyckscorner?
He promysed me to come hyder.
     FREWYLL.   Why, syr, knowest thou hym?
     IMAG.   Ye, ye, man ; he is full nye of my kynne,   235
And in Newgate we dwelled togyder,
For he and I were bothe shakeled in a fetter.
     FREWYLL.   Syr, laye you beneth, or on hye on the soller? [2]
     IMAG.   Nay, ywys, amonge the thyckest of yemen of the
          coller.
     FREWYLL.   By God, than ye were in grete fere !   240
     IMAG.   Syr, had I not be, CC had be thrast in an haltere.
     FREWYLL.   And what lyfe have they there, al that grete
          sorte?
     IMAG.   By God, syr, ones a yere som taw halts of Burporte ;
Ye, at Tyburne there stondeth the grete frame,
And some take a fall that maketh theyr neck lame.   245
     FREWYLL.   Ye, but can they than go no more?
     IMAG.   O no, man ; the wrest is twyste so sore ;
For as soone as they have sayd *in manus tuas* ones,
By God, theyr brethe is stopped at ones.
     FREWYLL.   Why, do they praye in that place there?   250
     IMAG.   Ye, syr ; they stonde in grete fere,
And so fast tangled in that snare,
Hyt falleth to theyr lotte to have the same share.

---

[1] Haz. ; W. not.   [2] W. Haw. Haz. seller.

FREWYLL.   That is a knavisshe syght to se them totter on
     a beme.

IMAG.   Syr, the horesones coude not convaye clene ;   255
For, and they coude have caryed by crafte, as I can,
In processe of yeres eche of them sholde be a gentyll-man.
Yet, as for me, I was never thefe.
If my handes were smyten of, I can stele with my tethe ;
For ye knowe well there is crafte in daubynge.   260
I can loke in a mannes face and pycke his purse ;
And tell newe tydynges that was never trewe, ywys,
For my hood is all lyned with lesynge.

    FREWYLL.   Ye, but wente ye never to Tyburne a pylgrym-
       age ?

    IMAG.   No, ywys, nor none of my lynage ; [1]   265

For we be clerkes all, and can our necke-verse,
And with an oyntment the iuges hande I can grece
That wyll hele sores that be uncurable.

    FREWYLL.   Why, were ye never founde reprovable?   269

IMAG.   Yes, ones I stall a hors in the felde,
    And lepte on hym for to have ryden my waye ;
At the last a bayly me mette and behelde
    And badde me stonde, — than was I in a fraye.   273

He asked wheder with that horse I wolde gon,
And than I tolde hym hyt was myne owne ;
He sayd I hadde stollen hym, and I sayde naye ;
" This is," sayd he, " my brothers hacknaye " ;
For, and I had not scused me without fayle,
By Our Lady, he wolde have lad me strayte to iayle ;
And than I tolde hym the horse was lyke myne,   280
A browne baye, a long mane, and dyde halte behyne, —
Thus I tolde hym that such an-other hors I dyde lacke,
And yet I never sawe hym nor came on his backe.
So I delyvered hym the hors agayne ;
And whan he was gone, than was I fayne ;   285

       [1] W. lygnages ; Haw. lynages ; Haz. lineage.

For, and I had not scused me the better,
I knowe well I sholde have daunsed in a fetter.

    FREWYLL.   And sayd he no more to the but so?

    IMAG.   Yes, he pretended me moche harme to do;
But I tolde hym that mornynge was a grete myste,   290
That what horse hyt was I ne wyste;
Also I sayd that in my heed I had the megryne
That made me dasell so in myne eyen
That I myght not well se:
And thus he departed shortely frome me.   295

    FREWYLL.   Ye, but where is Hycke-scorner now?

    IMAG.   Some of these yonge men hath hydde hym in
Theyr bosomes, I warraunt you,[1]
Let us make a crye, that he may us here!

    FREWYLL.   How, how![2]   Hycke-scorner appere!   300
I trowe thou be hyde in some cornere.

    HYCKE-SCORNER [*without*].   A-le[3] the helme! a-le![3] vere!
      shot of! vere sayle! vera!

    FREWYLL.   Cockes body! herke, he is in[4] a shyppe on
      the see!

             [*Enter Hycke-scorner.*]

    HYCKE.   God spede! God spede! Who called after me?

    IMAG.   What! brother, welcome, by this precyous body!   305
I am gladde that I you se;
Hyt was tolde me that ye were hanged.[5]
But out of what countre come ye?

    HYCKE.   Syr,[6] I have ben in many a countre;
As, in Fraunce, Irlonde, and in Spayne,   310
Portyngale, Sevyll, also in Almayne,
Freslonde, Flaunders, and in Burgoyne,
Calabre, Poyle,[7] and Erragoyne,

---

[1] *These two lines ought perhaps to be printed as one.*
[2] W.; Haw. Haz. How now.
[3] W. Haw. ale; Haz. ale (= heel).
[4] Haw. Haz. *omit* in.
[5] *Qy.* That ye were hanged hyt was told me.
[6] W.; Haw. Haz. Syrs.   [7] Haz. Pugle.

Brytayne, Byske, and also in Gascoyne,
Naples, Grece, and in myddes of Scotlonde,
At Cape [1] Saynt Vyncent, and in the Newe-founde Ilonde ;   316

I have ben in Gene and in Cowe,
Also in the londe of Rumbelowe,
  Thre myle out of hell ;
At Rodes, Constantyne, and in Babylonde,
In Cornewale, and in Northumberlonde,
  Where men sethe russhes in gruell ;   322

Ye, syr, in Caldey, Tartare, and Inde,
And in the Londe of Women, that fewe men dothe fynde :
In all these countres have I be.
  FREWYLL.   Syr, what tydynges here ye now on the see ?   326

HYCKE.   We mette of shyppes a grete nave,
  Full of people that wolde in-to Irlonde,
And they came out of this countre ;
  They wyll never-more come to Englonde.   330

  IMAG.   Whens were the shyppes of them ?   Knowest thou
    none ?
  HYCKE.   Herken, and I wyll shewe you theyr names eche
    one :
Fyrst was the Regent with the Myghell, of Brykylse,
The George, with the Gabryell and the Anne, of Foye,
The Starre of Salte-Asshe, with the Ihesus of Plumoth,   335
Also the Hermytage with the Barbara of Darmouth,
The Nycolas and the Mary Bellouse of Brystowe,
With the Elyn of London and James also.
Grete was the people that was in them,
All true relygyous and holy women :   340
There was Trouthe and his kynnesmen,[2]
With Pacyence, Mekenes, and Humylyte,
And all true maydens wyth theyr vyrgynyte,
Ryall prechers, Sadnes, and Charyte,

----

[1] Haw. Haz. *comma after* Cape (= Cape of Good Hope).
[2] W. Haw. kynnesman ; Haz. kinsmen.

Ryght Conscyence, and Fayth, with Devocyon,   345
And all true monkes that kepe theyr relygyon,[1]
True byers and sellers, and almes-dede [2] doers,
Pyteous people, that be of synne destroyers,
With Just Abstynence and good counseyllers,
Mourners for synne, with Lamentacyon,   350
And good ryche men that helpeth folke out of pryson,
True Wedlocke was there also,
With yonge men that ever in prayer dyde go :
The shyppes were laden with suche unhappy company ;
But at the laste God shope a remedy,   355
For they all in the see were drounde,
And on a quycke-sonde they strake to grounde, —
The see swallowed them everychone,
I wote well alyve there scaped none.
    IMAG.   Lo! now my herte is gladde and mery ;   360
For joye now let us synge " dery, dery ! "
    HYCKE.   Felowes, they shall never more us withstonde,
For I se them all dr[o]wned in the Rase of Irlonde.
    FREWYLL.   Ye, but yet herke, Hycke-scorner :
What company was in your shyppe that came over ?   365
    HYCKE.   Syr, I wyll ayd [3] you to understande ;
There were good felawes above fyve thousande,
And all they ben kynne to us thre ;
There was Falshode, Favell, and Sotylte,[4]
Ye, theves and hores, with other good company,   370
Lyers, bacbyters, and flaterers the whyle,
Braulers, lyers, getters, and chyders,
Walkers by nyght, with grete murderers,
Overthwarte gyle[rs],[5] and joly carders,
Oppressers of people, with many swerers ;   375
There was False Lawe, with Oryble Vengeaunce,

[1] W. Haw. relyon ; Haz. religion.
[2] W. dede ; Haw. dedes ; Haz. deed.
[3] W. Haw. sayd ; *corr. by* Haz.
[4] W. fotylte ; Haw. jolyte ; Haz. jollity.
[5] *Corr. by* Haz.

Froward Obstynacyon, with Myschevous Governaunce,
Wanton wenches, and also mychers,
With many other of the devylles offycers ;
And Haterede, that is so myghty and stronge,   380
Hath made a-vowe for-ever to dwell in Englonde.
 IMAG. But is that true that thou doste shewe now ?
 HYCKE. Syr, every worde as I do tell you.
 FREWYLL. Of whens is your shyppe ? of London ?
 HYCKE. Ye, ywis, frome thens dyde she come ;   385
And she is named the Envy, —
I tell you, a grete vessell and a myghty ;
The owner of her is called Yll Wyll,
Brother to Jacke Poller of Shoters Hyll.
 IMAG. Syr, what offyce in the shyppe bare ye ?
 HYCKE. Mary, I kepte a fayre shoppe of baudrye : 391

I had thre wenches that were full praty,
Jane true, Ann [1] thryftles, and wanton Sybble ;
If ye ryde her a journay, she will make you wery,
 For she is trusty at nede.
If ye wyll hyre her for your pleasure,
I warraunt, tere her shall ye never,
 She is so sure in dede ;
Ryde and you wyll ten tymes a daye,
I warraunt you she wyll never saye naye, —
 My lyfe I dare lay to wedde.   401

IMAG. Now plucke up your hertes, and make good chere,
 These tydynges lyketh me wonder wele.
Now vertu shall drawe arere, arere !
 Herke, felous, a good sporte I can you tell :   405

At the stues we wyll lye to-nyght,
And, by my trouth, yf all go aryght,
I wyll begyle some praty wenche
To gette me monaye at a pynche.
How saye you ? shall we go thyder ?   410

   [1] W. Haw. Haz. and.

Let us kepe company all togyder,
And I wolde that we had Goddes curse
If we some-where do not get a purse !   413

Every man bere his dagger naked in his honde,
And, if we mete a treue man, make hym stonde,
   Or elles that he bere a strype !
If that he struggle and [1] make ony werke,
Lyghtly stryke hym to the herte,
   And throwe hym into Temmes quyte !   419

FREWYLL.   Naye, thre knaves in a lease is good at nale !
   But, thou lubber, Imagynacyon,
     That cukcolde, thy fader, — where is he become?
At Newgate dothe he ly styll at gayle?   423

IMAG.   Avant, horsone ! thou shalt bere me a strype !
   Sayst thou that my moder was a hore ?
FREWYLL.   Naye, syr, but the last nyght
   I sawe syr Johne and she tombled on the flore.   427

IMAG.   Now, by Kockes herte, thou shalte lose an arme !
HYCKE.   Naye, syr, I charge you, do hym no harme.
IMAG.   And thou make to moche, I wyll breke thy heed,
   to !   430
HYCKE.   By Saynt Mary, and I wyst that, I wolde be ago !
IMAG.   Aware ! aware ! the horsone shall aby !
His preest wyll I be, by Cockes body !
HYCKE.   Kepe pease, lest knaves blode be shedde.
FREWYLL.   By God, if his was nought, myn was as
   badde !   435
IMAG.   By Kockes herte, he shall dye on this dager !
HYCKE.   By Our Lady, than wyll ye be straungled in a
   halter.
IMAG.   The horesone shall ete hym as fer as he shall
   wade !
HYCKE.   Beshrewe your herte ! and put up your blade !

---

[1] Haw. ond; *no note in my collation.*

Shethe your whytell! or by Hyz[1] that was never borne 440
I wyll rappe you on the costarde with my horne!
What! wyll ye playe all the knave?

IMAG. By Kockes herte, and thou a buffet shalte have!

[Imagynacyon and Hycke-scorner fight.]

FREWYLL. Lo, syrres, here is a fayre company, God us
     save!
For, yf ony of us thre be mayre of London, 445
I-wys, ywys, I wyll ryde to Rome on my thom!
Alas! a! se! is not this a[2] grete feres?
I wolde they were in a myll-pole above the eres;
And than, I durst warraunt, they wold departe anone.

HYCKE. Helpe! helpe! for the passyon of my soule! 450
He hath made a grete hole in my poule,
That all my wytte is set to the grounde.
Alas, a leche for to helpe my wounde!

IMAG. Naye, ywys, horesone, I wyll bete the or I go!

FREWYLL. Alas, good syr! what have I do? 455

IMAG. Ware! make rome! he shall have a strype, I
     trowe!

[Enter Pyte.]

PYTE. Peas, peas, syrres! I commaunde you!

IMAG. Avaunt, old churle! Whens comest thou?
And thou make to moche, I shall breke thy browe
And sende the home agayne! 460

PYTE. A! good syr, the peas I wolde have kepte fayne;
Myne offyce is to se no man slayne,
And, where they do amyse, to gyve them good counseyl
Synne to forsake, and Goddes lawe them tell.

IMAG. A! syr, I wende thou haddest ben drowned and
     gone!
But I have spyed that there scaped one. 466

HYCKE. Imagynacyon, do by the counseyll of me:
Be a-greed with Frewyll, and let us good felowes be;

---

[1] Haz. *changes to* Jis.   [2] *Qy.* are not these.

And than, as for this chorle, Pyte,
Shall curse the tyme that ever he came to londe!
IMAG.   Brother Frewyll, give me your honde !
And all myne yll wyll I forgyve the.   472

FREWYLL.   Syr, I thanke you hertely.
But what shall we do with this chorle, Pyte?
IMAG.   I wyll go to hym, and pyke a quarell,   475
And make hym a thefe and saye he dyde stele
Of myne forty pounde in a bagge.
FREWYLL.   By God, that tydynges wyll make hym sadde !
And I wyll go fetche a payre of gyves,
For, in good faythe, he shall be sette fast by the heles.   480
HYCKE.   Have ado lyghtly, and be gone,
And let us twayne with hym alone !
FREWYLL.   Now, farewell ; I beshrewe you everychone !
                              [*Exit.*]
HYCKE.   Ho, ho ! Farewell, you shrewe[1], and no mo !   484

IMAG.   Thou lewde felowe, sayst thou that thy name is
          Pite?
Who sente the hyder to controll me?
PYTE.   Good syr, hyt is my properte
For to dyspyse synfull lyvynge.
And unto vertu men to brynge
          If that they wyll do after me.   490

IMAG.   What, syr, art thou so pure holy?
A ! se! this caytyfe wolde be praysed, trowe I.[2]
And you thryve this yere, I wyll lose a peny !
Lo ! syrres, outwarde he bereth a fayre face,
But, and he mette with a wenche in a prevy place,   495
I trowe he wolde shewe her but lytell grace,
By God, ye maye trust me !
HYCKE.   Loo ! wyll ye not se this caytyves menynge?
He wolde destroye us all, and all our kynne !

---

[1] W. Haw. Haz. Frewyll you threwe; *emend. by* Kittredge.
[2] W. Haw. Haz. I trowe.

Yet had I lever se hym hanged by the chynne 500
Rather than that sholde be brought aboute.
And with this dager thou shalte have a cloute,
Without thou wylte [1] lyghtly be gone!

IMAG.   Naye, brother, laye honde on hym soone! 504

For he japed my wyfe and made me cukolde,
And yet the traytour [2] was so bolde
   That he stale forty pounde of myne in monaye.
HYCKE.   By Saynt Mary, than shall he not scape!
We wyll lede hym streyght to Newgate;
   For-ever there shall he lye! 510

[*Enter Frewyll.*]

FREWYLL.   A, se! a, se, syrres, what I have brought!
   A medycyne for a payre of sore shynnes.
At the Kynges Benche, syrres, I have you sought;
   But, I praye you, who shall were these [rynges]? 514

HYCKE.   By God, this felowe that maye not go hence,
   I wyll go gyve hym these hose-rynges;
Now, yfaythe, they be worth forty pence,
   But to his hondes I lacke two bondes.
IMAG.   Holde, horesone, here is an halter!
Bynde hym fast and make hym sure. 520

PYTE.   O men, let Trouth, that is the trewe man,
   Be your guyder, or elles ye be forlore; [3]
Laye no fals wytnes, as nye as ye can,
   On none, for afterwarde ye wyll repent hyt full sore. 524

FREWYLL.   Naye, naye, I care not therfore!
HYCKE.   Ye, whan my soule hangeth on the hedge, cast stones! [4]
For I tell the playnly, by Kockes bones,
Thou shalte be guyded and layd in irons, —
They fared even so.

[1] W. Haw. Haz. *have an unnecessary* be *here.*
[2] Haw. traytove; *not noticed in collation.*
[3] W. Haw. Haz. forlorne.
[4] Haz. hedge-cast, *which is unintelligible to me.*

PYTE.   Awaye,[1] syr ! what have I do?
IMAG.   Well, well ; that thou shalte knowe or thou go.   530
PYTE.   O syrres, I se hyt can not be amended.
You do me wronge, for I have not offended.
Remembre God, that is our heven Kynge,
For he wyll rewarde you after your deservynge,   534

Whan Deth with his mace dooth you areest ;
    We all to hym owe fewte[2] and servyce.
Fro the ladder of lyfe downe he wyll the threste ;
    Than maystershyp may not helpe nor grete offyce.   538

FREWYLL.   What! Dethe, and he were here, he sholde syt
        by the !
Trowest thou that he be able to stryve with us thre?
Nay, nay, nay !
IMAG.   Well, felawes, now let us go our waye,
For at[3] Shoters Hyll we have a game to playe.   542
HYCKE.   In good fayth, I wyll tary no lenger[4] space.
FREWYLL.   Beshrewe hym for me that is last out of this
        place !

    [*Exeunt Imagynacyon, Frewyll and Hycke-scorner.*]

PYTE.   Lo, lordes, they may curs the tyme they were borne
For the wedes that over-groweth the corne ;
They troubled me gyltelesse, and wote not why ;
For Goddes love, yet wyll I suffre pacyently.   548

We all may say weleaway
For synne that is now-adaye ;[5]
Loo, vertue is vanysshed for ever and aye :[6]
    Worse was hyt never !

1 Haz. *changes* Awaye *to* Well-a-way.
2 Haz. *prints* fea'ty.
3 W. Haz.; Haw. a.
4 W. lender; Haw. Haz. lenger.
5 *These two lines as one in* W. Haw. Haz.
6 W. Haz.; Haw. ever daye.

We have plente of grete othes
And clothe ynoughe in our clothes,
But charyte many men lothes :
    Worse was hyt never !
Alas ! now is lechery called love, indede,
And murdure named manhode in every nede ;
Extorsyon is called lawe, so God me [1] spede :
    Worse was hyt never !   560

Youth walketh by nyght with swerdes and knyves,
And, ever amonge, true men leseth theyr lyves ;
Lyke heretykes we occupy other mennes wyves
    Now-a-dayes in Englonde.
Baudes be the dystryers of many yonge women,
And full lewde counseyll they gyve unto them ;
How you do mary, beware, you yonge men,
    The wyse never taryeth to longe.   568

There be many grete scorners,
But for synne there be fewe mourners ;
We have but fewe true lovers
    In no place now-a-dayes.
There be many goodly gylte knyves ; [2]
And, I trowe,[3] as well [4] apparaylled wyves,
Yet many of them be unthryfty of theyr lyves
    And all set in pryde to go gaye.   576

Mayers on synne dooth no correccyon,
Gentyll-men [5] bereth trouthe adowne,
Avoutry is suffred in every towne,
    Amendyment is there none.
And Goddes commaundementes we breke them all x ;
Devocyon is gone many dayes syn ;
Let us amende us, we trewe Crysten men,
    Or Deth make you grone !   584

[1] W. Haz.; Haw. we.   [3] W.; Haw. Haz. knowe.
[2] W. knyues; Haw. Haz. knaves.   [4] W.; Haw. Haz. many.
[5] W. Haw. With gentyll men; Haz. *changes* With *to* While.

Courtyers go gaye and take lytell wages,
And many with harlottes at the taverne hauntes,
They be yemen of the wrethe that be shakled in gyves,
    On themselves they have no pyte.
God punyssheth full sore with grete sekenesse,
As pockes, pestylence, purple[s] and axes ;
Some dyeth sodeynly that deth full peryllous ;
    Yet was there never so grete poverte.   592

There be some sermones made by noble doctoures,
But truly the fende dothe stoppe mennes eres ;
For God nor good man some people not feres :
    Worse was hyt never !
All trouth is not best sayd,
And our prechers now-adayes be halfe afrayde.
Whan we do amende, God wolde be well apayde :
    Worse was hyt never !   600

          [Enter Contemplacyon and Perseveraunce.]

CONT.   What, mayster Pyte ; how is hyt with you ?
PERS.   Syr, we be sory to se you in this case now.
PYTE.   Bretherne,[1] here were thre peryllous men,
Frewyll, Hycke-scorner and Imagynacyon ;
They sayd I was a thefe and layd felony upon me,   605
And bound me in irons as ye maye se.
CONT.   Where be the traytours become nowe ?
PYTE.   In goode faythe, I can not shewe you.
PERS.   Brother, let us unbynde hym of his bondes.
CONT.   Unlose the fete and [2] the hondes.   610

          [They release Pyte.]

PYTE.   I thanke you for your grete kyndnes
That you two shewe in this dystresse ;
For they were men without ony mercy,
That delyteth all in myschefe and tyranny.
    PERS.   I thynke they wyll come hyder agayne,   615
Frewyll and Imagynacyon, bothe twayne ;

    [1] Haw. Brethrene.   [2] *Qy. insert* I.

Them wyll I exorte to vertuous lyvynge
And unto vertu them to brynge
By the helpe of you, Contemplacyon.
    CONT.   Do my counseyll, brother Pyte :   620

Go you and seke them throughe the countre,
In vyllage, towne, bourghe and cyte,
    Throughe-out all the realme of Englonde ;
Whan you them mete, lyghtly them arest
And in pryson put them faste,
    Bynde them sure in irons stronge,
For they be so faste [1] and sotyle
That they wyll you begyle
    And do true men wronge.   629

PERS.   Brother Pyte, do as he hath sayd ;
    In every quarter loke you aspye,
And let good watche for them be layde
    In all the haast that thou can, and that pryvely ;
For, and they come hyder, they shall not scape
For all the crafte that they can make.   635

PYTE.   Well, than wyll I hye me as fast as I maye
    And travayle throughe every countre ;
Good watche shall be layde in every waye
    That they stele not into sentwary.   639

Now fare-wele, bretherne ; and praye for me,
For I must go hens, in-dede.
    PERS.   Now God be your good spede ! [2]
    CONT.   And ever you defende, whan you have nede !
    PYTE.   Now, bretherne [3] bothe, I thanke you.   [Exit.] 644

                  [Enter Frewyll.]

FREWYLL.   Make you rome for a gentylman, syrs, and pease!
Duegarde,[4] seygnours, tout le preasse !

----

[1] Qy. false.   [3] Haw. brethrene.
[2] W. spende.   [4] Haz. prints Dieu garde.

And of your jangelynge yf ye wyll sease
  I wyll tell you where I have be.[1]
Syrres, I was at the taverne and dronke wyne ;
Methought I sawe a pece that was lyke myne,
And, syr[res], all my fyngers were arayed with lyme,
  So I convayed [2] a cuppe manerly.   652

And yet, ywys, I played all the fole ;
For there was a scoler of myne own scole,
  And, syr[res], the horesone aspyed me.
Than was I rested and brought in pryson ;
For woo than I wyste not what to have done,
  And all bycause I lacked monaye.
But a frende in courte is worth a peny in purs ;
For Imagynacyon, myne owne felowe, i-wys,
  He dyde helpe me out full craftely :   661

Syrres, he walked thrughe Holborne
Thre houres after the sonne was downe,
And walked up towarde Saynte Gyles in the Felde ;
He hoved styll, and there behelde,   665
But there he coude not spede of his praye ;
And strayght to Ludgate he toke the waye, —
Ye wote well that potycaryes wake [3] very late, —
He came to a dore, and pryvely spake
To a prentes for a peny-worth of uforbyum,   670
And also for a half-peny-worth of alom plomme ;
This good servaunte served hym shortely,
And sayd, " Is there ought elles that you wolde bye ? "
Than he asked for a mouthfull of quycke brymstone ;
And, doune in-to the seller whan the servant was gone, 675
Asyde as he kest his eye,
A grete bagge of monaye dyde he spye,
Therin was an hondred pounde.
He trussed hym to his fete and yede his waye rounde ;
He was lodged at Newgate at the Swanne,   680

---

[1] W. Haw. Haz. bene.   [3] W. Haw. Haz. walke.
[2] Haw ; W. conuayued.

And every man toke hym for a gentyll-man ;
So on the morowe he delyvered me
Out of Newgate by this polyce ;
And now wyll I daunce an[d] make ryall chere !
But I wolde Imagynacyon were here,   685
For he is pereles at nede.
Labour to hym, syrres, yf ye wyl your maters spede.
Now wyll I synge and lustely sprynge !
But whan my feters on my leges dyde rynge,
I was not gladde, perde ! but now : Hey, trolly, lolly !   690
Let us se who can descaunt on this same.
To laughe and gete monaye,[1] hyt were a good[2] game !
What ! whome have we here ?
A preest, a douctoure, or else a frere !   694

What, mayster doctour Dotypoll,
Can not you preche well in a blacke boll,
     Or dispute ony dyvynyte?
If ye be cunnynge I wyll put hyt in a prefe :
Good syr, why do men ete mustarde with befe?
     My[3] questyon can you assoyle me?   700

PERS.   Peas, man ! thou talkest lewdly ;
And of thy lyvynge, I reed, amende the !
FREWYLL.   Avaunt, catyfe ! dost thou thou me?
     I am come of good kynne, I tell the :
My moder was a lady of the stewes blode borne,
And, knyght of the halter, my fader ware an horne ;
Therfore I take hyt in full grete scorne
     That thou sholdest thus cheke me.   708

CONT.   Abyde, felowe ; thou ca[n]st[4] lytell curtesye !
     Thou shalte be charmed or thou hens pase,
For thou troubled Pyte and layd on hym felony.
     Where is Imagynacyon, thy felawe that was?   712

---

1 W. Haw. manaye; Haz. money.   3 W. Haw. Haz. By.
2 *Misprinted* goed *in* W.   4 W. Haw. cast ; Haz. hast.

FREWYLL.   I defye you bothe ! Wyll you arest me ?

PERS.   Naye, naye, thy grete wordes maye not helpe the.

Fro us thou shalte not escape.   715

FREWYLL.   Make rome, syrres, that I maye breke his pate !

I wyll not be taken for them bothe.

CONT.   Thou shalt abyde, whether thou be leve or lothe !

[Seizes him.]

Therfore, good sone, lysten unto me,

And marke these wordes that I do tell the :   720

Thou hast folowed thyne one wyll many a daye

    And lyved in synne without amendement ;

Therfore in thy conceyte assaye

    To axe God mercy, and kepe his commaundement ;

Than on the he wyll have pyte

And brynge the to heven, that ioyfull cyte.   726

FREWYLL.   What, horesone, wyll ye have me now a fole?

    Naye, yet had I lever be captayne of Calays ;

For, and I sholde do after your scole

    To lerne to pater to¹ make me pevyss[h]e,

    Yet had I lever loke with a face full thevysshe :

And therfore prate no lenger here

Leest my knaves fyste hytte you under the yere !   733

What, ye dawes, wolde ye reed me

For to lese ² my pleasure in youth and jolyte,

To basse and kysse my swete trully mully,

    As Jane, Cate, Besse, and Sybble, [to] ?

I wolde that hell were full of suche prymmes !

Than wolde I renne thyder on my pynnes

    As fast as I myght go.   740

PERS.   Why, syr, wylte ³ thou not love vertu

And forsake thy synne for the love of God Almyghty ?   742

---

¹ *Qy.* wolde.   ³ *Misprinted* whylte *in* Haw.
² W. Haw. lesese.

FREWYLL.   What, God Almyghty?   By Goddes fast at Salys-
      bury, —
    And I trowe Eester-day fell on Whytsonday that yere, —
There were v score save an hondred in my company,
    And at Pety Judas we made ryall chere.
There we had good ale of Myghelmas bruyng,
There heven-hye lepynge and spryngynge ;   748

And thus dyde I
Lepe out of Burdeaus unto Caunterbury,
    Almost ten myle bytwene !   751

  CONT.   Frewyll, forsake all this worlde wylfully here
And change by-tyme !   Thou oughtest to stonde in fere,
For Fortune wyll tourne her whele to[1] swyfte,
That clene fro thy welthe she wyll the lyfte.   755
    FREWYLL.   What, lift me ?   Who ?   And Imagynacyon
        were here now,
I-wys, with his fyst he wolde all to-cloute you.
Hens, horesone[s], tary no lenger here,
For by Saynt Pyntell the apostell I swere
That I wyll dryve you bothe home, —   760
And yet I was never wonte to fyght alone ;
Alas, that I had not one to bolde me !
Than you sholde se me playe the man shamfully.
Alas, hyt wolde do me good to fyghte !
How saye you, lordes, shall I smyte ?   765
Have amonge you, by this lyght !
Hens, horesones ! and home at ones !
Or with my wepen I shall breke your bones !
Avaunt, you knave[s], walke, by my counseyll !
  PERS.   Sone, remembre the grete paynes of hell ;   770
They are so horryble that no tonge can tell ;
Beware lest thou thyder do go !
   FREWYLL.   Naye, by Saynt Mary, I hope, not so !
I wyll not go to the devyll whyle I have my lyberte ;

1 W. Haw. to; Haz. so.

He shall take the laboure to fet me and he wyl have me !   775
For he that wyll go to hell by his wyll voluntary,[1]
The devyll and the worlewynde go wyth hym !
I wyll you never fro thens tydynges brynge ;
Go you before and shewe me the waye,
And as to folowe you I wyll not saye naye,   780
For, by Goddes body, and you be in ones,
By the masse, I wyll shytte the dore at ones,
And than be ye taken in a pytfall !

 CONT. Now, Ihesus soone defende us frome that hole !
For *Qui est in inferno, nulla est redemptio :*   785
Holy Job spake these wordes full longe ago.

  FREWYLL. Nay, I have done and you lade [2] out Latyn
    with scopes ![3]
But therewith can you cloute me a payre of botes ?
By Our Lady, ye sholde have some werke of me ;
I wolde have them well underlayd and easely,   790

For I use alwaye to go one [4] the one syde.
And trowe ye how? By God, in the stockes I sate tyde [5]
  I trowe a thre wekes, and more a lytell stounde ;
And there I laboured sore daye by daye,
And so I tred my shone inwarde, in good faye.

  Lo, therefore, methynke, you must soule them rounde !   796

If you have ony newe botes, a payre I wolde by ;
But I thynke your pryce be to hye.
Syr, ones at Newgate I bought a payre of sterrups,[6]
A myghty payre and a stronge ;   800
A hole yere I ware them so longe,
But they came not fully to my knee,
And to cloute them hyt cost not me a peny.
Even now, and ye go thyder, ye shall fynde a grete hepe ;
And you speke in my name, ye shall have good chepe.   805

---

[1] W.; Haw. Haz. voluntarily.	[4] Haz., *of course*, on.
[2] Haz. laid.	[5] W. Haw. tyd(e) ; Haz. till.
[3] W.; Haw. Haz. scope.	[6] W.; Haw. sterrup.

PERS.   Syr, we came never there, ne never shall do.

FREWYLL.   Mary, I was taken in a trap there, and tyde
  by the to,

That I halted a grete whyle and myght not go.

I wolde ye bothe sate as fast there ;   809

Than sholde ye daunce as a bere,

  And all by gangelynge of your chaynes.

CONT.   Why, syr, were ye there ?

  FREWYLL.   Ye, and that is sene by my braynes ; 813

For, or I came there, I was as wyse as a woodcock,

And, I thanke God, as wytte as a haddocke.

Yet I trust to recover, as other dose ;

For, and I had ones as moche wytte as a gose,

I sholde be marchaunt of the banke.

Of golde than I sholde have many a franke ;

For yf I myȝt make iii good vyages to Shoters Hyl, 820

And have wynde and weder at my wyll,

Than wolde I never travell the see more.

But hyt is harde to kepe the shyppe fro the shore,

And yf hyt happe to ryse a storme ;

Than throwen in a rase,[1] and so aboute borne, 825

On rockes or brachis for to ronne,

Elles to stryke grounde at Tyborne, —

That were a myschevous case !

For that rocke of Tyborne is so peryllous a place

Yonge galauntes dare not venture into Kente, 830

But whan theyr monaye is gone and spente,

With theyr longe botes[2] they rowe on the baye, —

And ony man-of-warre lye by the waye,

They must take a bote and throwe the helme a-le ;[3]

And full harde hyt is to scape that grete jeopardye, 835

For at Saynt Thomas of Watrynge and they stryke a sayle,

Than must they ryde in the haven of hempe[4] without fayle.

---

[1] Haz. raft.   [2] Haz. *prints* boots.

[3] W. Haw. Haz. ale ; *in spite of the rhyme,* Haz. *explains it as* heel.

[4] Haz. hemp ; W. Haw. hepe.

And were not these two jeopordous place in-dede,
Ther is many a marchaunt that thyder wolde spede.
But yet we have a sure canell[1] at Westmynster,　　　840
A thousande shyppes of theves therin may ryde sure ;
For yf they may have ankerholde and grete spendynge,
They may lyve as mery as ony kynge.

　　PERS.　Good[2] wote, syr, there is a pyteous lyvynge !
Than ye drede not the grete mayster above?　　　845
Sone, forsake thy mysse for his love,
And than mayst thou come to the blisse also.

　　FREWYLL.　Why, what wolde you that I sholde do?
　　CONT.　For to go towarde heven.[3]
　　FREWYLL.　Mary, and you wyll me thyder brynge,[4]
I wolde do after you.

　　PERS.　I praye you remembre my wordes now :　　　852

Frewyll, bethynke the that thou shalte dye,
　　And of the houre thou art[5] uncertayne,
Yet by thy lyfe thou mayst fynde a remedy ;
　　For, and thou dye in synne, all laboure is in vayne, —
　　Than shall thy soule be styll in payne,
Loste and dampned for evermore,
　　Helpe is past, thoughe thou wolde fayne,
Than thou wylte curse the tyme that thou were bore.　　　860

　　FREWYLL.　Syr, yf ye wyll undertake that I saved shall
　　　　be,
I wyll do all the penaunce that you wyll sette me.
　　CONT.　If that thou for thy synnes be sory,
Our Lorde wyll forgyve them the.[6]　　　864

FREWYLL.　Now of all my synnes I axe God mercy ;
　　Here I forsake synne and trust to amende ;
I beseche Ihesu, that is moost myghty,
　　To forgyve all that I have offende.　　　868

---

[1] Haz., *of course*, channel.
[2] Haz. *prints* God.
[3] *Qy.* Towarde heven for to go.
[4] *Qy.* me brynge therto.
[5] Haz.; W. Haw. are, *which is possible*.
[6] W. Haw. Haz. the them.

PERS. Our Lorde now wyll shewe the his mercy ;
    A new name thou nede none have,
For all that wyll to heven hye,
By his owne frewyll he must forsake folye, —
    Than is he sure and save.   873

CONT. Holde here a newe garment,
    And here-after lyve devoutly,
And for thy synnes do ever repente, —
    Sorowe for thy synnes is very remedy.
    And, Frewyll, ever to Vertue applye ;
Also to Sadnes gyve ye attendaunce,
Let hym never out of remembraunce.
FREWYLL. I wyll never frome you, syr Perseveraunce ;   881

With you wyll I abyde bothe daye and nyght,
    Of mynde never to be varyable,
And Goddes commandementes to kepe them ryght
    In deed and worde, and ever full stable.
    PERS. Than heven thou shalte have, without fable,
But loke that thou be stedfaste,
And let thy mynde with good wyll laste !   888

[Enter Imagynacyon.]

IMAG. Huffe ! huffe ! huffe ! who sent after me ?
I am Imagynacyon, full of jolyte ;
    Lorde, that my herte is lyght !
Whan shall I perysshe ? I trowe, never !
By Cryst, I recke not a feder !
    Even now I was dubbed a knyght.   894

Where ? At Tyburne. Of the coller.
And of the stewes I am made controller,
    Of all the houses of lechery ;
There shall no man playe doccy there,
At the Bell, Hertes Horne, ne elles-where,
    Without they have leve of me.   900

But, syrres, wote ye why I am come hyder?
By Our Lady, to gyder[1] good company togyder.
Sawe ye no[ugh]t of my felawe, Frewyll?
I am aferde lest he be serchynge on a hyll ;
By God, than one of us is begyled !   905
What felawe is this that in this cote is fyled?
Kockes deth ! whome have we here?
What ! Frewyll, myn owne fere?
Arte thou out of thy mynde?

    FREWYLL.   God graunte the waye to heven I maye fynde, 910
For I forsake thy company.
    IMAG.   Goddes armes ! my company? and why?
    FREWYLL.   For thou lyvest to synfully.
    IMAG.   Alas ! tell me how hyt is with the !
    FREWYLL.   Forsake thy synne for the love of me.   915
    IMAG.   Kockes herte ! arte thou waxed made?
    FREWYLL.   Whan I thynke on my synne, it makes me ful
       sade.
    IMAG.   Goddes woundes ! who gave the that counsell?
    FREWYLL.   Perseveraunce and Contemplacyon, I the tell.
    IMAG.   A vengeaunce on them ! I wolde they were in hell! 920
    FREWYLL.   Amende, Imagynacyon, and mercy crye !
    IMAG.   By Goddes sydes, I hadde lever be hanged
       on hye!
Naye, that wolde I not do ; I hadde lever dye.
By Goddes passyon, and I hadde a longe knyfe,
I wolde bereve these two horesones of theyr lyfe !   925
How, how ![2] twenty pounde[3] for a dagger !
    CONT.   Peas, peas, good sone, and speke softer !
And amende or Deth drawe his draught,
For on the he wyll stele full softe, —
He gyveth never no man warnynge,
And ever to the he is comynge :
Therfore remember the well.   932

        [1] W. Haw. togyder; Haz. to gather.
        [2] Haz. *modernizes to* how, *not* ho.
        [3] W.; Haw. Haz. pounds.

IMAG.   A ! horesone, if I were jayler of hell,
 I-wys, some sorowe sholde thou fele ;
For to the devyll I wolde the sell,
 Than sholde ye have many a sory mele.   936

I wolde never gyve you mete ne drynke ;
Ye sholde faste, horesones, tyll ye dyde stynke
 Even as a roten dogge,—ye, by Saynt Tyburne of
  Kent !
PERS.   Imagynacyon, thynke what God dyd for the :
On Good Frydaye he hanged on a tre,
 And all his precyous blode spent ;[1]   942

A spere dyde ryve his herte a-sonder ;
The gates he brake up with a clappe of thunder,
And Adam and Eve there delyvered he.   945
 IMAG.   What devyll, what is that to me ?
By Goddes fast, I was ten yere in Newgate,
And many more felawes with me sate,
Yet he never came there to helpe me ne my company.
 CONT.   Yes, he holpe the, or thou haddest not ben here
  now.
 IMAG.   By the masse, I can not sewe[2] you ; 951

For he and I never dranke togyder,
 Yet I knowe many an ale-stake ;
Neyther at the stues, I wyste[3] hym never come[4] thyder.
 Gooth he arrayed in whyte or in blacke ? 955

For, and he out of pryson hadde holpe me,
I knowe well ones I sholde hym se ;
I praye you, what gowne wereth he ?[5]
 PERS.   Syr, he halpe you out by his myght.

[1] W. Haw. Haz. And spent all his precyous blode.
[2] W. Haw. Haz. shewe.
[3] Haz. i-wis.
[4] W.; Haw. Haz. he never came.
[5] W. Haw. Haz. What gowne wereth he, I praye you ?

IMAG.   I can not tell you, by this lyght !   960
But me thought that I laye there to longe ;
And the horesone fetters were so stronge
That hadde almost brought my necke out of joynt.
PERS.   Amende, and thou shalt knowe hym, sone,[1]
That delyvered the out of pryson ;   965
And, yf thou wylt forsake thy mysse,
Surely thou shalt come to the blysse
And be inherytoure of heven.   968

IMAG.   What, syr, above the mone ?
Naye, by the masse ; then sholde I fall soone !
      Yet I kepe not to clymme so hye ;
But to clymme for a byrdes neste,
There is none bytwene eest and weste
      That dare therto ventre better than I !   974

But to ventre to heven — what and my fete slyppe ?
I knowe well than I sholde breke my necke,
And, by God, than hadde I the worse syde !
Yet had I lever be by the nose tyde
In a wenches ars somewhere
Rather than I wolde stande in that grete fere,   980
For to go up to heven.   Naye, I praye you lette be.
FREWYLL.   Imagynacyon, wylte thou do by the counseyll
      of me ?
IMAG.   Ye, syr, by my trouthe, what-somever it be.
FREWYLL.   Amende yet, for my sake ;
Hyt is better be-tyme than to late !
How saye you, wyll you Goddes hestes fulfyll ?
IMAG.   I wyll do, syr, even as you wyll.   987

But, I praye you, let me have a newe cote
Whan I have nede, and in my purse a grote
      Than wyll I dwell with you styll.

---

[1] W. Haw. Haz. Amende, sone, and thou shalt knowe hym.

FREWYLL. Beware, for whan thou arte buryed in the
     grounde,
Fewe frendes for the wyll be founde :
     Remembre this styll !   993

IMAG. No-thynge drede I so sore as deth ;
     Therefore to amende I thynke hyt be tyme.
Synne have I used all the dayes of my breth,
     With pleasure, lechery and mysusynge,   997

And spent amys my v wyttes ; therfore I am sory.
Here of all my synnes I axe God mercy.
    PERS. Holde ! here is a better clothynge for the.   1000
And loke that thou forsake thy foly ;
Be stedfast, loke that thou fall never.
    IMAG. Now, here I forsake my synne for-ever.
    FREWYLL. Syr, wayte thou now on Perseveraunce,
For thy name shall be called Good Remembraunce ;   1005
And I wyll dwell with Contemplacyon,
And folowe hym where-ever he become.
    CONT. Well, are ye so bothe agrede ?
    IMAG. Ye, syr, so God me spede !   1009

PERS. Syr, ye shall wete on me soone,
     And be Goddes servaunt daye and nyght ;
And in every place where ye become
     Gyve good counseyle to every wyght ;   1013

And men axe your name, tell you Remembraunce,
     That Goddes lawe kepeth truly every daye,
And loke that ye forget not Repentaunce ;
     Than to heven ye shall go the nexte waye,   1017

Where ye shall se in the hevenly quere
     The blessyd company of sayntes so holy,
That lyved devou[t]ly whyle they were here :
     Unto the whiche blysse I beseche God Almyghty

To brynge there your soules that here be present
 And unto vertuous lyvynge that ye maye applye,·
Truly for to kepe his commaundemente.[1]   1024

Of all our myrthes here we make an ending ;[2]
Unto the blysse of heven Ihesu your soules brynge ! 1026

AMEN.

Enprynted
by me *Wynkyn de
Worde.*

[1] Haz. commandments.   [2] W. Haw. Haz. ende.

THE PLAY OF WYT AND SCIENCE.

By JHON REDFORD.

Printed from the edition by J. O. Halliwell (Shakespeare Society, 1848). In the footnotes, H. indicates this edition. The MS., formerly the property of B. H. Bright, Esq., is now in the British Museum. The play is incomplete at the beginning; a reconstruction of the plot of the missing part will be found in vol. III of this book.[1a]

[*Dramatis Personae.*

WYT.	STUDY.
SCIENCE.	DYLYGENCE.
REASON.	INSTRUCCION.
EXPERYENCE.	TEDIOUSNES.
CONFYDENCE.	IDELLNES.
HONEST RECREACION,	SHAME.

CUMFORT, QUYCKNES, STRENGTH.
FAME, RYCHES, FAVOR, WOORSHYP.]

. . . .

REASON.   Then in remembrance of Reson hold yee
A glas of Reson, wherein beholde yee
Youre-sealfe to youre-selfe.   Namely when ye
Cum neere my dowghter, Science, then see
That all thynges be cleane and trycke abowte ye,   5
Least of sum sloogyshnes she myght dowte ye.
Thys glas of Reason shall show ye all ;
Whyle ye have that, ye have me, and shall.
Get ye foorth, now ! Instruccion, fare-well !
INSTR.[1]   Syr, God keepe ye !

Heere all go out save Resone.

1 H. *gives the name of each speaker in full.*

1a See Publisher's Note.

REASON.   And ye all from parell !   10
If anye man now marvell that I
Woolde bestowe my dowghter thus baselye,
Of truth I, Reson, am of thys mynde :
Where partyes together be enclynde
By gyftes of graces to love ech other,   15
There let them joyne the tone wyth the toother.
Thys Wyt such gyftes of graces hath in hym
That makth my dowghter to wysh to wyn hym :
Yoong, paynefull, tractable and capax, —
Thes be Wytes gyftes whych Science doth axe.   20
And as for her, as soone as Wyt sees her,
For all the world he woold not then leese her.
Wherfore, syns they both be so meete matches
To love ech other, strawe for the patches
Of worldly mucke !   Syence hath inowghe   25
For them both to lyve.   Yf Wyt be throwhe
Stryken in love, as he synes hath showde,
I dowte not my dowghter well bestowde.
Thende of hys jornay wyll aprove all.
Yf Wyt hold owte, no more proofe can fall ;   30
And that the better hold out he[1] may,
To refresh my soone, Wyt, now by the way
Sum solas for hym I wyll provyde.
An honest woman dwellth here besyde
Whose name is cald Honest Recreacion ;   35
As men report, for Wytes consolacion
She hath no peere ; yf Wyt were halfe deade,
She cowld revyve hym, — thus is yt sed.
Wherfore, yf monye or love can hyre her,
To hye after Wyt I wyll desyre her.   40

          [Exit Reason.]   *Confydence cumth in with a pycture of Wyt.*

     [CONF.]   Ah ! syr, what tyme of day yst, who can tell ?
The day ys not far past, I wot well,
For I have gone fast and yet I see

                    [1] H. ye.

I am far from where as I wold be.
Well, I have day inowgh yet, I spye ;   45
Wherfore, or I pas hens, now must I
See thys same token heere, a playne case,
What Wyt hath sent to my ladyes grace.

[Examines his packet.]

Now wyll ye see a goodly pycture
Of Wyt hymsealfe, hys owne image sure, —   50
Face, bodye, armes, legges, both lym and joynt, —
As lyke hym as can be, in every poynt ;
Yt lakth but lyfe.   Well I can hym thanke,
Thys token in-deede shall make sum cranke ;
For, what wyth thys pycture so well faverde,   55
And what wyth those sweete woordes so well saverd
Dystyllyng from the mowth of Confydence, —
Shall not thys apese the hart of Science ?
Yes ; I thanke God I am of that nature
Able to compas thys matter sure,   60
As ye shall see now, who lyst to marke yt,
How neately and feately I shall warke yt.

[Exit Confydence.] Wyt cumth in without Instruccion, with Study, &c.

[WYT.]   Now, syrs, cum on ; whyche is the way now,
Thys way or that way ?   Studye, how say you?

[Study considers.]

Speake, Dylygence, whyle he hath bethowghte hym.   65
    DYL.   That way, belyke ; most usage hath wrowht hym.
    STUD.   Ye, hold your pesse !   Best we here now stay
For Instruccion ; I lyke not that waye.
    WYT.   Instruccion, Studye ? I weene we have lost hym.

Instruccion cumth in.

[INSTR.]   Indeade, full gently abowte ye have tost hym !   70
What mene you, Wyt, styll to delyghte
Runnynge before thus, styll owt of syghte,
And therby out of your way now quyghte?

What doo ye here excepte ye woold fyghte?
Cum back agayne, Wyt, for I must choose ye   75
An esyer way then thys, or ells loose ye.
 Wyt. What ayleth thys way? Parell here is none.
 Instr. But as much as your lyfe standth upon ;
Youre enmye, man, lyeth heere before ye, —
Tedyousnes, to brayne or to gore ye!   80
 Wyt. Tedyousnes? Doth that tyrant rest
In my way now? Lord, how am I blest
That occacion so nere me sturres
For my dere hartes sake to wynne my spurres !
Ser, woold ye fere me with that fowle theeafe,   85
Wyth whome to mete my desyre is cheafe?
 Instr. And what woold ye doo, — you havyng nowghte
For your defence? for thowgh ye have cawghte
Garmentes of Science upon your backe,
Yet wepons of Science ye do lak.   90
 Wyt. What wepons of Science shuld I have?
 Instr. Such as all lovers of ther looves crave, —
A token from Ladye Science wherbye
Hope of her favor may spryng, and therbye
Comforte, whych is the weapon dowteles   95
That must serve youe agaynst Tedyousnes.
 Wyt. Yf hope or comfort may be my weapen,
Then never with Tedyousnes mee threten ;
For, as for hope, of my deere hartes faver —
And therby comforte — inowghe I gather.   100
 Instr. Wyt, here me ! Tyll I see Confydence
Have browght sum token from Ladye Science,
That I may feele that she favorth you,
Ye pas not thys way, I tell you trew.
 Wyt. Whych way than?
 Instr.   A playner way, I told ye,   105
Out of danger from youre foe to hold ye.
 Wyt. Instruccion, here me ! Or my swete hart
Shall here that Wyt from that wreche shall start
One foote, thys bodye and all shall cracke !

Foorth I wyll, sure, what-ever I lacke ! 110
   DYL.   Yf ye lacke weapon, syr, here is one.
   WYT.   Well sayde, Dylygence, thowe art alone !
How say ye, syr ; is not here weapon?
   INSTR.   Wyth that weapon your enmy never threton,
For wythowt the returne of Confydence 115
Ye may be slayne, sure, for all Dylygence.
   DYL.   God, syr ! and Dylygence, I tell you playne,
Wyll play the man or my master be slayne !
   INSTR.   Ye ; but what! sayth Studye no wurde to thys?
   WYT.   No, syr ; ye knowe Studyes ofyce is 120
Meete for the chamber, not for the feeld.
But tell me, Studye, wylt thow now yeld?
   STUD.   My hed akth sore ; I wold wee returne !
   WYT.   Thy hed ake now? I wold it were burne !
Cum on ; walkyng may hap to ese the. 125
   INSTR.   And wyll ye be gone, then, wythout mee ?
   WYT.   Ye, by my fayth ; except ye hy ye after,
Reson shall know yee are but an hafter.

Exceat Wyt, Study and Dylygence.

   INSTR.   Well, go your way ! Whan your father, Reson,
Heerth how ye obay me at thys season, 130
I thynke he wyll thynke hys dowghter now
May mary another man for you.
When wytes stand so in ther owne conceite,
Best let them go, tyll pryde at hys heyghte
Turne and cast them downe hedlong agayne, 135
As ye shall see provyd by thys Wyt playne.
Yf Reson hap not to cum the rather,
Hys owne dystruccion he wyll sure gather;
Wherefore to Reson wyll I now get me,
Levyng that charge whereabowt he set mee. 140

Exceat Instruccion. Tedyousnes cumth in with a vyser over hys hed.

   [TEDY.]   Oh the body of me !
      What kaytyves be those

That wyll not once flee
    From Tediousnes nose,
But thus dysese me   145
    Out of my nest,
When I shoold ese mee
    Thys body to rest!
That Wyt, that vylayne,
    That wrech, — a shame take hym! —   150
Yt is he playne
    That thus bold doth make hym,
Wythowt my lycence
    To stalke by my doore
To that drab, Syence,   155
    To wed that whore!
But I defye her;[1]
    And for that drabes sake,
Or Wyt cum ny her,
    The knaves hed shall ake;   160
Thes bones, this mall,
    Shall bete hym to dust
Or that drab shall
    Once quench that knaves lust!
But, hah! mee thynkes   165
    I am not halfe lustye;
Thes jo[y]ntes, thes lynkes,
    Be ruffe and halfe rustye;
I must go shake them,
Supple to make them!   170
Stand back, ye wrechys!
Beware the fechys
Of Tediousnes,
Thes kaytyves to bles!
Make roome, I say!   175
Rownd evry way,
Thys way, that way!
What cares [2] what way?

---

[1] H. here.   [2] *Qy.* What care I *or* Who cares.

Before me, behynd me,
Rownd abowt wynd me!   180
Now I begyn
To swete in my skin;
Now am I nemble
To make them tremble.
Pash hed! pash brayne!   185
The knaves are slayne,
All that I hyt!
Where art thow, Wyt?
Thow art but deade!
Of goth thy hed   190
A' the fyrst blow!
Ho, ho! ho, ho!

Wyt spekyth at the doore.

[WYT.]   Studye!
STUD.   Here, syr!
WYT.   How, doth thy hed ake?
STUD.   Ye, God wot, syr, much payne I do take!
WYT.   Dylygens!
DYL.   Here, syr, here!
WYT.   How dost thow?   195
Doth thy stomak serve the to fyght now?
    DYL.   Ye, syr, wyth yonder wrech, — a vengans on
            hym!
That thretneth you thus.   Set evyn upon hym!
    STUD.   Upon hym, Dylygence? Better nay![1]
    DYL.   Better nay, Studye? Why shoold we fray?[2]   200
    STUD.   For I am wery; my hed akth sore.
    DYL.   Why, folysh Studye, thow shalt doo no more
But ayde my master wyth thy presens.
    WYT.   No more shalt thow nether, Dylygence.
Ayde me wyth your presence, both you twayne,   205
And for my love myselfe shall take payne!

[1] *Lines* 199–201 *erased in* MS.
[2] Kittredge *suggests that* fray *may be a misreading of* stay.

STUD.   Syr, we be redye to ayde you so.
WYT.   I axe no more, Studye.   Cum then, goe!

Tedyiousnes rysyth up.

[TEDY.]   Why, art thow cum?
WYT.   Ye, wrech, to thy payne!
TEDI.   Then have at the!
WYT.   Have at the, agayne!   210

Here Wyt fallyth downe and dyeth.

TEDI.   Lye thow there! Now have at ye, kaytyves!
Do ye fle, ifayth? A! horeson theves!
By Mahowndes bones, had the wreches taryd,
Ther neckes wythowt hedes they showld have caryd!
Ye, by Mahowndes nose, myght I have patted them,   215
In twenty gobbetes I showld have squatted them,
To teche the knaves to cum neere the snowte
Of Tediousnes! Walke furder abowte
I trow now they wyll.   And as for thee,
Thow wylt no-more now troble mee.   220
Yet, lest the knave be not safe inowghe,
The horeson shall bere me another kuffe.   [*Strikes him.*]

Now ly styll, kaytyv, and take thy rest,
Whyle I take myne in myne owne nest.   224

Exceat Tedy[ousnes].

*Here cumth in Honest Recreacion, Cumfort, Quycknes, and Strenght,
and go and knele abowt Wyt; and at the last verce reysyth hym up upon
hys feete, and so make an end.*

[*While they kneel, they sing this song:*] [1]

Gyve place, gyve place to Honest Recreacion;
Gyve place, we say, now for thy consolacion.   226

When travelles grete in matters thycke
Have duld your wyttes and made them sycke,

----

[1] *The song inserted here occurs in* MS. *among the songs that follow
the play.   It clearly belongs here, however, as it has the superscription:*
" The fyrst song in the play of Science."

What medson than your wyttes to quycke?
Yf ye wyll know, the best phisycke
 Is to geve place to Honest Recreacion ;
 Gyve place, we say, now for thy consolacion!   232

Where is that Wyt that we seeke than?
Alas, he lyeth here pale and wan!
Helpe hym at once now, yf we can.
O Wyt, how doest thow? Looke up, man !
 O Wyt, geve place to Honest Recreacion ;
 Gyve place, we say, now for thy consolacion !   238

After place gyvyn, let eare obay ;
Gyve an eare, O Wyt, now we the pray ;
Gyve eare to that we syng and say ;
Gyve an eare, and healp wyll cum strayghteway ;
 Gyve an eare to Honest Recreacion ;
 Gyve an ere, now, for thy consolacion !   244

After eare gyvyn, now gyve an eye !
Behold thy freendes abowte the lye :
Recreacion I, and Comfort I,
Quicknes am I, and Strength herebye.
 Gyve an eye to Honest Recreacion ;
 Gyve an eye, now, for thy consolacion !   250

After eye gyvyn, an hand gyve ye !
Gyve an hand, O Wyt, feele that ye see ;
Recreacion feele, feele Comfort fre,
Feele Quicknes here, feale Strength to the !
 Gyve an hand to Honest Recreacion ;
 Gyve an hand, now, for thy consolacion !   256

Upon his feete woold God he were !
To rayse hym now we neede not fere.
Stay you hys handes, whyle we hym[1] bere ;
Now all at once upryght him rere !

[1] H. here.

O Wyt, gyve place to Honest Recreation ;
Gyve place, we say, now for thy consolacion !   262

And than Honest Recreacion sayth as folowyth : [1]

HON. REC.   Now, Wyt, how do ye ?   Wyll ye be lustye ?
WYT.   The lustier for you needes be must I.
HON. REC.   Be ye all hole yet after your fall ?
WYT.   As ever I was, thankes to you all.

Reson cummth in, and sayth as folowyth :

[RESON.] Ye myght thanke Reson that sent them to ye ;
But syns the[y] have [do] that the[y] shoold do ye,
Send them home, soonne, and get ye forwarde.

WYT.   Oh father Reson, I have had an hard   270
Chance synce ye saw me !

RESON.[2]   I wot well that.
The more to blame ye,[3] when ye wold not
Obay Instruccion, as Reson wyld ye.
What marvell thowgh Tedyousness had kyld ye ?
But let pas now, synce ye ar well agayne.   275
Set forward agayne Syence to attayne !

WYT.   Good father Reson, be not to hastye ;
In honest cumpany no tyme wast I.
I shall to youre dowghter all at leyser.

RESON.   Ye, Wyt, is that the grete love ye rayse her ?   280
I say, yf ye love my dowghter Science,
Get ye foorth at once, and get ye hence.

Al go out save Honest.[4]
Here Comfort, Quiknes and Strength go out.

---

[1] *In* H. *this and the stage direction preceding the song form a single
sentence. For the sake of clearness, I have broken the sentence and inserted the song between the parts.*

[2] MS. Reson cumth in ; *corr. by* H.

[3] H. *says :* " *This sentence is repeated in the* MS. *by mistake, but part
of the previous line seems to be wanting* " ; *but I see no reason for the latter
statement.*

[4] H. *adds* [RECREACION]. *But it should seem that the scribe began to
write :* Al go out save Honest Recreacion, Reason and Wyt, *but halfway
through the sentence decided upon another form of expressing the same
fact, and then neglected to erase what he had written.*

WYT. Nay, by Saynt George, they go not all yet!

RESON. No? wyll ye dysobey Reson, Wyt?

WYT. Father Reson, I pray ye content ye, 285
For we parte not yet.

RESON. Well, Wyt, I went ye
Had bene no such man as now I see.
Fare-well! *Exceat.*

HON. REC. He ys angry.

WYT. Ye, let hym be!
I doo not passe!
Cum now, a basse! 290

HON. REC. Nay, syr, as for bassys,
From hence none passys
But as in gage
Of mary-age.

WYT. Mary, evyn so. 295
A bargayne, lo!

HON. REC. What, wythout lycence
Of Ladye Science? 298

WYT. Shall I tell you trothe?
I never lovde her.

HON. REC. The common voyce goth
That mariage ye movd her. 302

WYT. Promyse hath she none.
Yf we shalbe wone,
Wythout mo wurdes grawnt!

HON. REC. What, upon this soodayne?
Then myghte ye playne
Byd me avawnt! 308

Nay, let me see
In honeste
What ye can doo
To wyn Recreacion ;
Upon that probacion
I grawnt therto. 314

WYT.   Small be my dooinges,
But apt to all thynges
    I am, I trust.
HON. REC.   Can ye dawnce than?
WYT.   Evyn as I can,
    Prove me ye must.   320

HON. REC.   Then for a whyle
Ye must excyle
    This garment cumbryng.[1]
WYT.   In-deede, as ye say,
This cumbrus aray
    Woold make Wyt slumbryng.   326

HON. REC.   Yt is gay geere
Of Science cleere, —
    Yt seemth her aray.
WYT.   Whose-ever it were,
Yt lythe now there!   *[Takes off his gown.]*
    HON. REC.   Go to, my men, play!   332

Here [the minstrels play and Honest Recreacion and Wyt] dawnce,[2]
and in the mene-whyle Idellnes cumth in and sytth downe, and when the
galyard is doone, Wyt sayth as folowyth, and so falyth downe in Idellnes
lap.

WYT.   Sweete hart, gramercys!
HON. REC.   Why, whether now?   Have ye doone, synce?
WYT.   Ye, in fayth, with wery bones ye have possest me ;
Among thes damselles now wyll I rest me.
HON. REC.   What, there?
WYT.   Ye, here ; I wylbe so bold.
IDLE.   Ye, and wellcum, by hym that God sold !
HON. REC.   Yt ys an harlot, may ye not see?
IDLE.   As honest a woman as ye be !   340
HON. REC.   Her name is Idlenes.   Wyt, what mene you?
IDLE.   Nay, what meane you to scolde thus, you quene,
    you?

---

[1] H. cum bryng; *but cf.* l. 325.
[2] H. *Here they dawnce.*

WYT.   Ther, go to !   Lo ! now for the best game !
Whille I take my ese, youre toonges now frame !
  HON. REC.   Ye, Wyt ; by youre fayth, is that youre
        facion ?   345
Wyll ye leave me, Honest Recreacion,
For that common strumpet, Idellnes,
The verye roote of all vyciousnes ?
  WYT.   She sayth she is as honest as ye.
Declare yourselves both now as ye be !   350
  HON. REC.   What woolde ye more for my declaracion
Then evyn my name, Honest Recreacion ?
And what wold ye more her to expres
Then evyn her name, to, Idlenes —
Dystruccion of all that wyth her tarye ?   355
Wherfore cum away, Wyt ; she wyll mar ye !
  IDEL.   Wyll I mar hym, drabb, thow calat, thow !
When thow hast mard hym all-redye now ?
Cawlyst thow thysealfe Honest Recreacion,
Ordryng a poore man after thys facion,   360
To lame hym thus and make his lymmes fayle
Evyn wyth the swyngyng there of thy tayle ?
The dyvyll set fyre one the ! for now must I,
Idlenes, hele hym agayne, I spye.
I must now lull hym, rock hym, and frame hym   365
To hys lust agayne, where thow dydst lame hym.
Am I the roote, sayst thow, of· vyciousnes ?
Nay ; thow art roote of all vyce dowteles !
Thow art occacion, lo ! of more evyll
Then I, poore gerle, — nay, more then the dyvyll !   370
The dyvyll and hys dam can not devyse
More devlyshnes then by the doth ryse.
Under the name of Honest Recreacion,
She, lo ! bryngth in her abhominacion !
Mark her dawnsyng, her maskyng, and mummyng —   375
Where more concupyscence then ther cummyng ?
Her cardyng, her dycyng, dayly and nyghtlye —
Where fynd ye more falcehod then there ?   Not lyghtly.

Wyth lyeng and sweryng by no póppetes,
But teryng God in a thowsand gobbetes.   380
As for her syngyng, pypyng and fydlyng,
What unthryftynes therin is twydlyng !
Serche the tavernes and ye shall here cleere
Such bawdry as bestes wold spue to heere.
And yet thys is kald Honest Recreacion,   385
And I, poore Idlenes, abhomynacion !
But whych is wurst of us twayne, now judg, Wyt.
　　Wyt.　Byrladye, not thow, wench, I judge yet.
　　Hon. Rec.　No?　Ys youre judgment such then that ye
Can neyther perseve [1] that best, how she   390
Goth abowte to dyceve you, nor yet
Remembre how I savyd youre lyfe, Wyt?
Thynke you her meete wyth mee to compare
By whome so manye wytes curyd are?
When wyll she doo such an act as I dyd,   395
Savynge your lyfe when I you revyved?
And as I savyd you, so save I all
That in lyke jeoperdy chance to fall.
When Tediousnes to grownd hath smytten them,
Honest Recreacion up doth quyken them   400
Wyth such honest pastymes, sportes or games
As unto myne honest nature frames,
And not, as she sayth, with pastymes suche
As be abusyd lytell or muche, —
For where honest pastymes be abusyd,   405
Honest Recreacion is refused ;
Honest Recreacion is present never
But where honest pastymes be well usyd ever.
But in-deede Idlenes, she is cawse
Of all such abuses ; she, lo ! drawes   410
Her sort to abuse myne honest games,
And therby full falsly my name defames.
Under the name of Honest Recreacion
She bryngth in all her abhomynacion,

---

[1] MS. peseve ; *corr. by* H.

Dystroyng all wytes that her imbrace,   415
As youre-selfe shall see wythin short space.
She wyll bryng you to shamefull end, Wyt,
Except the sooner from her ye flyt.
Wherefore cum away, Wyt, out of her pawse!
Hence, drabb! let hym go out of thy clawse!   420
   IDLE.   Wyll ye get ye hence? or, by the mace,
Thes clawes shall clawe you by youre drabbes face!
   HON. REC.   Ye shall not neade; syns Wyt lyethe as wone
That neyther heerth nor seeth, I am gone.   *Exceat.*
   IDLE.   Ye, so? fare-well! And well fare thow, toonge!   425
Of a short pele this pele was well roong, —
To ryng her hence, and hym fast asleepe
As full of sloth as the knave can kreepe!
How, Wyt! awake! How doth my babye?
Neque vox neque sensus, byr Ladye!   430
A meete man for Idlenes, no dowte.
Hark my pygg, how the knave dooth rowte!
Well, whyle he sleepth in Idlenes lappe,
Idlenes marke on hym shall I clappe.
Sum say that Idlenes can not warke;   435
But those that so say, now let them marke!
I trowe they shall see that Idlenes
Can set hersealfe abowt sum busynes;
Or, at the lest, ye shall see her tryde,
Nother idle nor well ocupyde.   440

         [*She marks Wyt.*]

Lo! syr, yet ye lak another toye!
Wher is my whystell to call my boye?

     Here she whystleth, and Ingnorance cumth in.

   [INGN.]   I cum! I cum!
   IDLE.   Coomme on, ye foole!
All thys day or ye can cum to scoole?
   INGN.   Um! mother wyll not let me cum.   445
   IDLE.   I woold thy mother had kyst thy bum!

She wyll never let the thryve, I trow.
Cum on, goose!   Now, lo! men shall know
That Idlenes can do sumwhat, ye,
And play the scoolemystres, to, yf neade bee.   450
Mark what doctryne by Idlenes cummes!
Say thy lesson,[1] foole.

INGN.   Upon my thummes?

IDEL.   Ye, upon thy thummes ; ys not there thy name?

INGN.   Yeas.

IDLE.   Go to, than ; spell me that same.   454
Where was thou borne?

INGN.   Chwas i-bore in Ingland, mother sed.

IDLE.   In Ingland?

INGN.   Yea.

IDLE.   And whats [2] half Ingland?
Heeres ing ; and heeres land.   Whats tys?

INGN.   Whats tys?

IDEL.   Whats tys? horeson, whats tys?
Heeres ing ; and heeres land.   Whats tys?   459

INGN.   Tys my thum.

IDEL.   Thy thum?   Yng, horeson, ing, ing!

INGN.   Yng, yng, yng, yng.

IDEL.   Foorth !   Shall I bete thy narse, now?

INGN.   Um-m-m —

IDEL.   Shall I not bete thy narse, now?

INGN.   Um-um-um —

IDEL.   Say "no," foole, say "no."

INGN.   Noo, noo, noo, noo, noo!   465

IDEL.   Go to, put together : yng!

INGN.   Yng.

IDEL.   No!

INGN.   Noo.

IDEL.   Forth now!   What sayth the dog?

[1] *It will aid the reader to follow this exemplification of the syllabic method if he bears in mind from the start that the name of Ignorance is pronounced Ing-no-ran-s-y.*

[2] H. *prints* what's *here only.*

INGN.   Dog barke.
IDLE.   Dog barke ?   Dog ran, horeson, dog ran !
INGN.   Dog ran, horson, dog ran, dog ran.
IDEL.   Put together : ing !
INGN.   Yng.
IDEL.   No !
INGN.   Noo.
IDEL.   Ran !
INGN.   Ran.   470
IDLE.   Foorth now ; what seyth the goose ?
INGN.   Lag ! lag !
IDLE.   Hys, horson, hys !
ING[N].   Hys, hys-s-s-s-s.
IDLE.   Go to, put together : yng.
INGN.   Ing.
IDLE.   No.
INGN.   Noo.
IDLE.   Ran.
INGN.   Ran.
IDLE.   Hys.
ING[N].   Hys-s-s-s-s-s-s.
IDLE.   No[w], who is a good boy ?
INGN.   I, I, I, I, I, I.   475
IDLE.   Go to, put together : ing.
INGN.   Ing.
IDLE.   No.
INGN.   Noo.
IDEL.   Ran.
INGN.   Ran.
IDEL.   His.
INGN.   Hys-s-s-s-s.
IDEL.   I.
INGN.   I.
IDEL.   Ing-no-ran-his-I.
INGN.   Ing-no-ran-hys-s-s-s.
IDLE.   I.
INGN.   I.

IDEL.	**Ing.**	
INGN.	Ing.	
IDEL.	Foorth !	
INGN.	Hys-s-s-s.	480
IDEL.	Ye, no, horeson, no.	
INGN.	Noo, noo, noo, noo.	
IDLE.	Ing-no.	
INGN.	Ing-noo.	
IDLE.	Forth now !	
INGN.	Hys-s-s-s-s.	
IDEL.	Yet agayne ; ran, horeson, ran, ran.	
INGN.	Ran, horson, ran, ran.	
IDLE.	Ran, say !	
INGN.	Ran-say.	
IDLE.	Ran, horson !	
INGN.	Ran, horson.	
IDLE.	Ran.	
INGN.	Ran.	485
IDLE.	Ing-no-ran.	
INGN.	Ing-no-ran.	
IDEL.	Foorth, now ! What sayd the goose ?	
INGN.	Dog barke.	
IDLE.	Dog barke? Hys, horson, hys-s-s-s-s-s,	
INGN.	Hys-s-s-s-s-s-s.	
[1] IDLE.	I ; Ing-no-ran-hys-I.	490
INGN.	Ing-no-ran-hys-I-s-s-s.	
IDLE.	I.	
INGN.	I.	
IDLE.	How sayst, now, foole ? Is not there thy name ?	
INGN.	Yea.	
IDLE.	Well than ; can me that same !	

What hast thow lernd ?

[1] H. *has:* IDLE   I.
     INGN.   Ing-no-ran-hys-I.
           Ing-no-ran-hys-I-s-s-s.
and says that the whole speech assigned to INGN. " *should possibly be given
to* IDLE., *but the* MS. *is apparently carelessly written in this place.*"

INGN.   Ich can not tell.

IDLE.   " Ich can not tell "? thou sayst evyn very well,   495
For, yf thow cowldst tell, then had not I well
Towght the thy lesson which must be tawghte, —
To tell all when thow canst tell ryghte noght.

INGN.   Ich can my lesson.

IDLE.   Ye ; and therfore
Shalt have a new cote, by God I swore !   500

INGN.   A new cote?

IDLE.   Ye, a new cote by-and-by.
Of wyth thys old cote ; " a new cote " crye !

INGN.   A new cote, a new cote, a new cote !

IDLE.   ¹ Pease, horson foole !
Wylt thow wake hym now?   Unbuttun thy cote, foole !
Canst thow do nothyng?

INGN.   I note how choold be.¹   505

IDLE.   " I note how choold be "?   A foole betyde the !
So wysly hyt spekyth ; cum on now ; whan ?
Put bak thyne arme, foole !

                    [*Takes off Ingnorance's coat.*]

INGN.   Put backe?

IDLE.   So, lo! now let me see how thys geere
Wyll trym this jentle-man that lyeth heere, —   510
Ah ! God save hyt, so sweetly hyt doth sleepe ! —
Whyle on your back thys gay cote can creepe,
As feete as can be for this one arme.

                    [*Puts Wyt's gown on Ingnorance.*]

INGN.   Oh ! cham a-cold.

IDLE.   Hold, foole ! keepe the warme,
And cum hyther ; hold this hed here ; softe now, for wakyng ! 515
Ye shall see wone here browght in such takynge
That he shall soone scantlye knowe hymsealfe.
Heere is a cote as fyt for this elfe
As it had bene made evyn for thys bodye.

                    [*Puts Ingnorance's coat on Wyt.*]

¹⁻¹ *As three lines in* H., *ending,* now, nothyng, be.

So! It begynth to looke lyke a noddye! 520

INGN. Um-m-m-m —

IDLE. What aylest now, foole?

INGN. New cote is gone!

IDLE. And why is it gone?

INGN. 'Twool not byde on.

IDLE. "'Twool not byde on"? 'Twoold if it cowlde!

But marvell it were that byde it shoold, —

Sciens garment on Ingnorance bak! — 525

But now lets se, syr; what do ye lak?

Nothyng but evin to bukell heere this throte,

So well this Wyt becumthe a fooles cote!

INGN. He is I now!

IDLE. Ye; how lykste hym now?

Is he not a foole as well as thow? 530

INGN. Yeas.

IDLE. Well, than, won foole keepe another!

Geve me this, and take thow that brother.

INGN. Um-m —

IDLE. Pyke the home, go!

INGN. Chyll go tell my moother! [*Exit.*]

IDLE. Yea, doo!

But yet to take my leve of my deere, lo! 535

Wyth a skyp or twayne, heere lo! and heer lo!

And heere agayne! and now this heele

To bles his weake brayne! Now are ye weele,

By vertu of Idellnes blessyng toole,

Cunjurd from Wyt unto a starke foole! 540

[*Exit Idlenes.*]

Confydence cumth in with a swoord by his syde; and sayth as folowyth:

[CONF.] I seake and seake, as won on no grownde

Can rest, but lyke a masterles hownde

Wandryng all abowt seakyng his master.

Alas! jentle Wyt, I feare the fasster

That [1] my tru servyce clevth unto thee, 545

[1] H. Thy; *perhaps it would be better to read* Thys.

The slacker thy mynd cleevth unto mee!
I have doone thye message in such sorte
That I not onlye, for thy comfort,
To vanquishe thyne enmy have browght heere
A swoord of comfort from thy love deere,   550
But also, furder, I have so enclynd her
That upon my wurdes she hath assynd her
In her owne parson half-way to meete thee,
And hytherward she came for to greete thee.
And sure, except she be turned agayne,   555
Hyther wyll she cum or be long, playne,
To seake to meate the heere in this cost.
But now, alas! thy-selfe thow hast lost,
Or, at the least, thow wylt not be fownd.
Alas! jentle Wyt, how doost thow woonde   560
Thy trusty and tru servant, Confydence,
To lease my credence to Ladye Science!
Thow lesyst me, to; for yf I can not
Fynd the shortly, lenger lyve I ma not,
But shortly get me evyn into a corner   565
And dye for sorowe throwhe such a scorner!   *Exceat.*

Here the[y] cum in with vyols.

FAME.   Cum syrs, let us not dysdayne to do
That the World hath apoynted us too.
FAVOR.   Syns to serve Science the World hath sent us,
As the World wylth us, let us content us.   570
RYCHES.   Content us we may, synce we be assynde
To the fayrest lady that lyvth, in my mynde!
WOORSHYP.   Then let us not stay here muet and mum,
But tast we thes instrumentes tyll she cum.   574

Here the[y] syng " Exceedynge Mesure." [1]

Exceedyng mesure, wyth paynes continewall,
     Langueshyng in absens, alas! what shall I doe,
Infortunate wretch, devoyde of joyes all,

---

[1] *In* MS. *this song immediately follows* " The fyrst song in the play of
Science," *and is headed* " The ij song."

Syghes upon syghes redoublyng my woe,
  And teares downe fallyng fro myne eyes toe?
Bewty wyth truth so doth me constrayne
Ever to serve where I may not attayne!   581

Truth byndyth me ever to be true,
  How-so-that fortune faverth my chance.
Duryng my lyfe none other but you
  Of my tru hart shall have the governance!
  O good swete hart, have you remembrance
Now of your owne, whych for no smart
Exyle shall yow fro my tru hart!   588

  [*While they sing, Experyence and Science enter.*]

EXPER.   Dowghter, what meanyth that ye dyd not syng?
SCIENCE.   Oh mother, for heere remaynth a thynge!
Freendes, we thanke you for thes your plesures,
Takyn on us as chance to us measures.
  WOORSHYPPE.   Ladye, thes our plesures, and parsons too,
Ar sente to you, you servyce to doo.
  FAME.   Ladye Science, to set foorth your name   595
The World, to wayte on you, hath sent me, — Fame.
  FAVOR.   Ladye Science, for your vertues most plentye
The World, to cherysh you, Favor hath sent ye.
  RYCHES.   Lady Science, for youre benefytes knowne
The World, to mayntayne you, Ryches hath thrown.   600
  WOORSHYP.   And as the World hath sent you thes three,
So he sendth mee, — Woorshypp, — to avawnce your degre.
  SCIENCE.   I thank the World; but cheefly God be praysed,
That in the World such love to Science hath raysed!
But yet, to tell you playne, ye iiij ar suche   605
As Science lookth for lytell nor muche ;
For beyng, as I am, a lone wooman,
Neede of your servyce I nether have nor can.
But, thankyng the World and you for your payn,
I send ye to the World evyn now agayne.   610
  WOORSHYPPE.   Why, ladye, set ye no more store by
    mee, —

Woorshypp? Ye set nowght by yourselfe, I se!

FAME. She setthe nowght by Fame; wherby I spye her,
She carethe not what the World sayth by her.

FAVOR. She setthe nowght by Favor; wherby I trye her, 615
She caryth not what the World sayth or dooth by her.

RYCHES. She setth nowght by Ryches; whych dooth showe
She careth not for the World. Cum, let us goe!

[*The four go out.*]

SCIENCE. In-deede, smalle cawse gevyn to care for the
    Worldes favering,
Seeyng the wyttes of [the] Worlde be so waveryng. 620
    EXPER. What is the matter, dowghter, that ye
Be so sad? Open your mynd to mee.
    SCIENCE. My marvell is no les, my good moother,
Then my greefe is greate, to see — of all other —
The prowde scorne of Wyt, soone to Dame Nature, 625
Who sent me a pycture of hys stature,
Wyth all the shape of hymselfe there openyng, —
Hys amorous love therby betokenyng,
Borne toward me in abundant facion;
And also, furder, to make ryght relacion 630
Of this hys love he put in commyshion
Such a messenger as no suspicion
Cowld growe in mee of hym, — Confydence.
    EXPER. Um!
    SYENCE. Who, I ensure ye, wyth such vehemence
And faythfull behavoure in hys movynge 635
Set foorth the pyth of hys masters lovynge
That no lyvyng creature cowld conjecte
But that pure love dyd that Wyt dyrect.
    EXPER. So?
    SCIENCE. Now, this beinge synce the space
Of three tymes sendyng from place to place 640
Betwene Wyt and hys man, I here no more
Nether of Wyt, nor his love so sore.

How thynk you by thys, my nowne deere mother ?

EXPER.   Dowghter, in this I can thynke none oother
But that it is true — thys proverbe old: 645
Hastye love is soone hot and soone cold!
Take hede, dowghter, how you put youre trust
To lyght lovers, to hot at the furst!
For had this love of Wyt bene growndyd
And on a sure fowndashyon fowndyd,   650
Lytell voyde tyme wold have bene betwene ye
But that this Wyt wolde have sent or seene ye.

SCIENCE.   I thynke so.

EXPER.   Ye ; thynke ye so or no,
Youre mother, Experience, proofe shall showe
That Wyt hath set hys love — I dare say   655
And make ye warrantyse — another way.

Wyt cumth before.

[WYT.]   But your warrantyse warrant no trothe !
Fayre ladye, I praye you be not wrothe
Tyll you here more ; for, deere Ladye Science,
Had your lover, Wyt, — ye, or Confydence,   660
Hys man, — bene in helth all this tyme spent,
Long or this tyme Wyt had cumme or sent ;
But the trothe is they have bene both sykke,
Wyt and hys man, ye and wyth paynes thycke
Bothe stayde by the way, so that your lover   665
Could neyther cum [1] nor send by none other.
Wherefore, blame not hym, but chance of syknes.

SCIENCE.   Who is this ?

EXPER.   Ingnorance, or his lykenes.

SCIENCE.   What, the common foole ?

EXPER.   Yt is much lyke hym.

SCIENCE.   By my soothe, his toong servth him now trym ! 670
What sayst thow, Ingnorance ? Speak agayn !

WYT.   Nay, ladye, I am not Ingnorance, playne,
But I am your owne deere lover, Wytt,

[1] MS. cumne ; *corr. by* H.

That hath long lovd you, and lovth you yet ;
Wherefore, I pray the now, my nowne swetyng,   675
Let me have a kys at this our meetyng.

    SCIENCE.   Ye, so ye shall anone, but not yet.
Ah, syr, this foole here hath got sum wyt !
Fall you to kyssyng, syr, now-a-dayes?
Your mother shall charme you ; go your wayes !   680

    WYT.   What nedth all this, my love of long growne?
Wyll ye be so strang to me, your owne?
Youre aquayntance to me was thowht esye ;
But now your woordes make my harte all quesye,
Youre dartes at me so strangely be shott.   685

    SCIENCE.   Heere ye what termes this foole here hath got?

    WYT.   Well, I perseve my foolyshnes now ;
Indeede, ladyes no dasterdes alowe ;
I wylbe bolde wyth my nowne darlyng !
Cum now, a bas, my nowne proper sparlyng !   690

    SCIENCE.   What wylt thow, arrand foole?

    WYT.   Nay, by the mas,
I wyll have a bas or I hence pas !

    SCIENCE.   What wylt thow, arrande foole? Hence, foole,
        I say !

    WYT.   What ! nothyng but foole and foole all this day?
By the mas, madam, ye can no good.   695

    SCIENCE.   Art a-sweryng, to? Now, by my hood,
Youre foolyshe knaves breeche vj strypes shall bere !

    WYT.   Ye, Godes bones! foole and knave to? be ye there?
By the mas, call me foole once agayne,
And thow shalt sure call a blo or twayne.[1]   700

    EXPER.   Cum away, dowghter, the foole is mad.

    WYT.   Nay, nor yet nether hence ye shall gad!
We wyll gre better, or ye pas hence.
I praye the now, good swete Ladye Science,
All this strange maner now hyde and cover,   705
And play the goodfelowe wyth thy lover !

   1 H. *says that the scribe here began to write the preceding speech of*
Science, but erased it.

SCIENCE.   What goodfelowshyppe wold ye of me,
Whome ye knowe not, nether yet I knowe ye?
   WYT.   Know ye not me?
   SCIENCE.   No ; how shoold I know ye?
   WYT.   Dooth not my pycture my parson shoow ye?   710
   SCIENCE.   Your pycture?
   WYT.   Ye, my picture, ladye,
That ye spake of.   Who sent it but I?
   SCIENCE.   Yf that be youre pycture, then shall we
Soone se how you and your pycture agree.
Lo, here! the pycture that I named is this.   715
   WYT.   Ye, mary, myne owne lykenes this is.
You havyng this, ladye, and so lothe
To knowe me, whych this so playne showthe?
   SCIENCE.   Why, you are nothyng lyke, in myne eie.
   WYT.   No?   How say ye?   [*To Experience.*]
   EXPER.   As she sayth, so say I.   720
   WYT.   By the mas, than are ye both starke blynde!
What dyference betwene this and this can ye fynd?
   EXPER.   Marye, this is fayer, plesant and goodlye,
And ye are fowle, dysplesant and uglye.
   WYT.   Mary, avawnt, thow fowle ugly whoore!   725
   SCIENCE.   So! lo! now I perseve ye more and more.
   WYT.   What! perseve you me as ye wold make me,
A naturall foole?
   SCIENCE.   Nay, ye mystake me ;
I take ye for no foole naturall,
But I take ye thus, — shall I tell all?   730
   WYT.   Ye, marye, tell me youre mynd, I pray ye,
Wherto I shall trust.   No more delay ye.
   SCIENCE.   I take ye for no naturall foole,
Browght up among the innocentes scoole,
But for a nawgty vycious foole,   735
Browght up wyth Idellnes in her scoole.
Of all arrogant fooles thow art one!
   WYT.   Ye, Goges bodye!
   EXPER.   Cum, let us be gone!
                    [*The two go out.*]

Wyt.   My swerd! is yt gone?   A vengeance on them!
Be they gone, to, and ther hedes upon them?   740
But, prowde quenes, the dyvyll go wyth you both!
Not one poynt of curtesye in them gothe.
A man is well at ease by sute to payne him
For such a drab, that so doth dysdayne hym!
So mokte, so lowted, so made a sot,   745
Never was I erst, synce I was begot!
Am I so fowle as those drabes wold make me?
Where is my glas that Reson dyd take me?
Now shall this glas of Reson soone trye me
As fayre as those drabes that so doth belye me.   750
Hah!   Goges sowle! what have we here? a dyvyll?
This glas, I se well, hath bene kept evyll.
Goges sowle! a foole, a foole, by the mas!
What a very vengeance aylth this glas?
Other this glas is shamefully spotted,   755
Or els am I to shamefully blotted!
Nay, by Goges armes, I am so, no dowte!
How loke ther facis heere rownd abowte?
All fayre and cleere they, evrychone;
And I, by the mas, a foole alone,   760
Deckt, by Goges bones, lyke a very asse!
Ingnorance cote, hoode, eares, — ye, by the masse,
Kokescome and all; I lack but a bable!
And as for this face, [it] is abhominable,
As black as the devyll!   God, for his passion!   765
Where have I bene rayde affter this fassyon?
This same is Idlenes, — a shame take her!
This same is her wurke, — the devill in hell rake her!
The whoore hath shamd me for-ever, I trow! —
I trow?   Nay verely, I knowe!   770
Now it is so, the stark foole I playe
Before all people; now see it I maye.
Evrye man I se lawhe me to scorne;
Alas, alas, that ever I was borne!

Yt was not for nowght, now well I se,   775
That those too ladyes dysdayned me.
Alas ! Ladye Science, of all oother —
How have I rayled on her and her moother !
Alas ! that lady I have now lost
Whome all the world lovth and honoryth most !   780
Alas ! from Reson had I not varyd,
Ladye Science or this I had maryd ;
And those fower gyftes which the World gave her
I had woon, to, had I kept her favor ;
Where now, in-stede of that lady bryght   785
Wyth all those gallantes seene in my syght, —
Favor, Ryches, ye, Worshyp and Fame, —
I have woone Hatred, Beggry and Open Shame.

Shame cumth in wyth a whyppe.   [*Reason follows him.*]

WYT.   Out upon the, Shame ! what doost thowe heere ?
RESON.   Mary, I, Reason, bad hym heere appeere.   790
Upon hym, Shame, wyth stryppes inow smitten,
While I reherce his fawtes herein wrytten :
Fyrst, he hath broken his promyse formerly
Made to me, Reson, my dowghter to marye ;
Nexte, he hath broken his promyse promisyd   795
To obay Instruccion, and him dyspised ;
Thurdlye, my dowghter Science to reprove,
Upon Idlenes he hath set his love ;
Forthlye, he hath folowed Idellnes scoole
Tyll she hath made him a verye stark foole ;   800
Lastlye, offendyng both God and man,
Sweryng grete othes as any man can,
He hath abused himselfe, to the grete shame [1]
Of all his kynred and los of his good name.
Wherfore, spare him not, Shame ; bete him well there !   805
He hath deservyd more then he can beare.

[1] H. greteshame.

Wyt knelith downe.

[WYT.]   Oh father Reson, be good unto me!
Alas, thes strypes of Shame will[1] undo me!
RESON.   Be still a while, Shame! Wyt, what sayst thow?
WYT.   Oh syr, forgeve me, I beseech you!   810
RESON.   Yf I forgeve the thy ponyshment,
Wylt thow than folow thy fyrst entent
And promyse made, my dowghter to marye?
WYT.   Oh syr, I am not woorthy to carye
The dust out where your dowghter shoold syt.   815
RESON.   I wot well that; but yf I admyt
The, unwoorthy, agayne to her wooer,
Wylt thow then folow thy sewte unto her?
WYT.   Ye, syr, I promyse you, while lyfe enduryth.
RESON.   Cum neere, masters; heere is wone ensuryth   820

Here cumth Instruccion, Studye and Diligens in.

In woordes to becum an honest man!
Take him, Instruccion; do what ye can.
INSTR.   What, to the purpose he went before?
RESON.   Ye, to my dowghter prove him once more.
Take him, and trym hym in new aparell,   825
And geve that to Shame there to his farewell.
INSTR.   Cum on your way, Wyt; be of good cheere;
After stormy clowdes cumth wether clere!

Instrucion, Study, Wyt and Dyligens go out.

RESON.   Who lyst to marke now this chance heere doon,
May se what Wyt is wythout Reson.   830
What was this Wyt better then an asse
Being from Reson strayde, as he was?
But let pas now, synce he is well poonyshyd,
And thereby, I trust, meetely well monyshyd.
Ye, and I lyke him never the wurs, I,   835
Thowgh Shame hath handled hym shamefullye;
For, lyke as, yf Wyt had prowdly bent hym

1 *Written over* wold *in* MS.

To resyst Shame, to make Shame absent hym,
I wold have thowght than that Wyt had bene —
As the sayeng is, and daylye seene —   840
Past Shame once, and past all amendment:
So, contra[r]ye, syns he dyd relent
To Shame, when Shame ponysht him evyn yll,
I have, I say, good hope in him styll.
I thynke, as I thowght, — yf joyne thei can, —   845
My dowghter wel bestowd on this man.
But all the dowte now is to thynke how
My dowghter takth this ; for I may tell yow,
I thynk she knew this Wyt evyn as weele
As she seemd heere to know him no deele,   850
For lak of knoledge in Science there is none ;
Wherfore, she knew him, and therupon
His mysbehavor perchance evyn strykyng
Her hart agaynst him, she — now myslykyng,
As women oft-tymes wylbe hard-hartyd —   855
Wilbe the stranger to be revertyd.
This must I helpe ; Reson must now walke,
On Wytes part wyth my Science to talke.
A neere way to her know I, wherebye
My soonnes cummyng prevent now must I.   860
Perchance I may bryng my dowghter hyther ;
Yf so, I dowght not to joyne them together.

Exceat Reson. Confydence cumth in.

[CONF.]   I thanke God, yet at last I have fownd hym ;
I was afrayde sum myschance had drownd him,
My master, Wyt, wyth whome I have spoken,   865
Ye, and deliverd token for token,
And have anoother to Science agayne, —
A hart of gold, syngnifyeng playne
That Science hath wun Wytes hart for-ever,
Whereby, I trust, by my good endever   870
To that good ladye, so sweete and so sortly,
A maryage betwene them ye shall see shortlye.

Confydens exceat. Instruccion cumth in wyth Wyt, Study and Dylygence.

[INSTR.]   Lo ! syr, now ye be entryd agayne
Toward that passage where dooth remayne
Tedyousnes, your mortall enmy ;   875
Now may ye choose whether ye wyll trye
Your handes agayne on that tyrant stowte,
Or els walkyng a lytell abowte.
  WYT.   Nay ; for Godes pashion, syr, let me meete him !
Ye se I am able now for to greete him.   880
This sword of cumfort, sent fro my love,
Upon her enmy needes must I proove !
  INSTR.   Then foorth there ; and turne on your ryght hand
Up that mownt before ye shall see stand.
But heere ye !   Yf your enmye chance to ryse,   885
Folowe my cowncell in anye wyse ;
Let Studye and Dyligence flee ther towche, —
The stroke of Tediousnes, — and then cowche
Themselves, as I told ye, — ye wot how.
  WYT.   Ye, syr, for that how, marke the proofe now !   890
  INSTR.   To mark it, indeede, here wyll I abyde,
To see what chance of them wyll betyde ;
For heere cumth the pyth, lo ! of this iornaye,
That mowntayne before which they must assaye
Is cald in Laten *Mons Pernassus*,   895
Which mowntayne, as old auctors dyscus,
Who attaynth ones to sleepe on that mownt,
Ladye Science his owne he may cownt.
But, or he cum there, ye shall see fowght
A fyght with no les polycye wrowght   900
Then strenghth, I trow, if that may be praysed.
  TEDI.   Oh ! ho ! ho !
  INSTR.   Hark !
  TEDI. [*entering*]   Out, ye kaytyves !
  INSTR.   The feend is raysyd !
  TEDI.   Out, ye vilaynes ! be ye cum agayne ?
Have at ye, wretches !

WYT. Fle, syrs, ye twayne!

TEDI. Thei fle not far hens! 905

DYLI. Turne agayne, Studye!

STUDYE. Now, Dylygence!

INSTR. Well sayde! Hold fast now!

STUDYE. He fleeth!

DYLI. Then folowe!

INSTR. Wyth his owne weapon now wurke him sorow!
Wyt lyth at reseyte!

TEDI. (*dyeth*) Oh! ho! ho!

INSTR. Hark! he dyeth!
Where strength lakth, policye ssupplieth. 910

*Heere Wyt cumth in and bryngth in the hed upon his swoorde, and sayth
as folowyth:*

WYT. I can ye thanke, syrs; this was well doone!

STUDYE. Nay, yours is the deede!

DYLI. To you is the thank![1]

INSTR. I can ye thank, all; this was well doone!

WYT. How say ye, man? Is this feelde well woonne?

Confydence cumth running in.

[CONF.] Ye, by my fayth, so sayth ycur deere hart. 915

WYT. Why where is she, that here now thow art?

CONF. Upon yonder mowntayne, on hye,
She saw ye strike that hed from the bodye;
Wherby ye have woonne her, bodye and all;
In token whereof reseve heere ye shall 920
A gowne of knoledge, wherin you must
Reseve her here strayght.

WYT. But sayst thow just?

[CONF.][2] So just I say that, except ye hye ye,
Or ye be redye, she wylbe by ye.

WYT. Holde! Present unto her this hed heere, 925
And gyve me warning when she cumth nere.

[Exit Confydence.]

[1] *Qy. insert* alone *after* thank. [2] *Supplied by* H.

Instruccion, wyll ye helpe to devyse
To trim this geere now in the best wyse?

    INSTR.   Geve me that gowne, and cum wyth me, all!

    DYLI.   Oh, how this gere to the purpose dooth fall!   **930**

Confidens cumth running in.

    [CONF.]   How, master, master! Where be ye now?

    WYT.   Here, Confydence; what tydynges bryngst thow?

    CONF.   My ladye at hand heere dooth abyde ye;

Byd her wellcum! What, do ye hide ye?   **934**

Here Wyt, Instruccion, Studye, and Diligence syng " Wellcum, my nowne," and Syence, Experience, Reson and Confidence cum in at L[eft], and answer evre second verse: [1]

                Wellcum, myne owne!

                Wellcum, myne owne!   **936**

WYT *and his Cumpanye.*   O ladye deere,

                Be ye so neere

                  To be knowne?

                My hart yow cheere

                Your voyce to here;

                  Wellcum, myne owne!   **942**

SCIENCE *and hir Cumpanye.*   As ye rejoyse

                To here my voyce

                  Fro me thus blowne,

                So in my choyce

                I show my voyce

                  To be your owne.   **948**

WYT *and his Cumpanye.*   Then drawe we neere

                To see and heere

                  My love long growne!

                Where is my deere?

                Here I apeere

                  To see myne owne.   **954**

---

[1] *Here as before I have removed the song from the latter part of the volume and inserted it in the middle of the stage direction. The song is headed:* " The thyrd Song."

SCIENCE *and hir Cumpanye.* To se and try
         Your love truly
          Till deth be flowne,
         Lo! here am I,
         That ye may spie
          I am your owne.   960

WYT *and his Cumpanye.* Then let us meete,
         My love so sweete,
          Halfe-way heere throwne !

SIENS *and hir Cumpanye.* I wyll not sleete
         My love to greete.
          Wellcum, myne owne ! 966

WYT *and his Cumpanye.* Wellcum, myne owne!
ALL *sing :*   Wellcum, myne owne ! 968

 And when the song is doone, Reson sendyth Instruccion, Studye, and Dyli-
 gence, and Confidens out ; and then, standyng in the myddell of the place,
 Wyt sayth as folowyth :

WYT. Wellcum, myne owne, wyth all my hole harte,
Whych shalbe your owne till deth us depart !
I trust, ladye, this knot evyn syns knyt.
 SCIENCE. I trust the same ; for syns ye have smitt
Downe my grete enmye, Tedyousnes,
Ye have woon me for-ever, dowghtles, —
Althowgh ye have woon a clogg wyth-all !   975
 WYT. A clogg, sweete hart ? what ?
 SCIENCE.   Such as doth fall
To all men that joyne themselves in mariage, —
In kepyng ther wyves ; a carefull cariage !
 WYT. Careful ? Nay, ladye, that care shall imploye
No clogg, but a key of my most joye.   980
To kepe you, swete hart, as shall be fyt,
Shalbe no care, but most joy to Wyt !
 SCIENCE. Well, yet I say, — marke well what I saye ! —
My presence brynghth you a clogg, no naye,
Not in the kepynge of me onelye,   985
But in the use of Science cheeflye ;

For I, Science, am, in this degree,
As all, or most part, of woomen bee :
Yf ye use me well, in a good sorte,
Then shall I be youre joy and comfort; 990
But yf ye use me not well, then dowt me,
For, sure, ye were better then wythout me !
   Wyt.   Why, ladye, thinke you me such a wyt,
As being avansyd by you, and yet
Wold mysuse ye?   Nay, yf ye dowt that, 995
Heere is wone lovth thee more then sumwhat, —
Yf Wyt mysuse ye at any season,
Correct me then your owne father, Reson.
   Reson.   Ho, dowghter, can ye desyre any more?
What neede thes dowtes?   Avoyde them therfore ! 1000
   Exper.   Byrlakyn, syr, but, under your favor,
This dowgt our dowghter doth well to gather
For a good warnyng now at begynnynge
What Wyt in the end shall looke for in wynning,
Whych shalbe this, syr : yf Science here, 1005
Whych is Godes gyft, be usyd meere
Unto Godes honor, and profyt both
Of you and your neybowre, whych goth
In her, of kynd, to do good to all, —
This seene to, Experience, I, shall 1010
Set you forth, Wyt, by her to imploye
Doble encrece to your doble joye ;
But yf you use her contrarywyse
To her good nature, and so devyse
To evyll effectes to wrest and to wry her, 1015
Ye, and cast her of and set nowght by her,
Be sure I, Experience, shall than
Declare you so before God and man
That thys talent from you shalbe taken
And you ponysht for your gayne forsaken. 1020
   Wyt.   " Once warne[d], half-armd," folk say, namely whan
Experience shall warne a man, than
Tyme to take heede.   Mother Experience,

Towchyng youre dowghter, my deere hart, Siens,
As I am sertayne that to abuse her   1025
I brede myne owne sorow, and well to use her
I encrece my joy, and so to make yt
Godes grace is redye yf I wyll take yt:
Then, but ye cownt me no wyt at all,
Let never thes dowtes into your hed fall;   1030
But, as yourself, Experience, cleryng
All dowtes at lenght, so, tyll tyme aperyng,
Trust ye wyth me in God; and, swete hart,
Whyle your father, Reson, takth wyth parte,
To reseve Godes grace as God shall send it,   1035
Dowte ye not our joy, tyll lyves [1] end yt!
  SCIENCE.   Well, than, for the end of all dowtes past
And to that end whiche ye spake of last,
Among our weddyng matters heere rendryng,
Thend of our lyves wold be in remembryng;   1040
Which remembrance, Wyt, shall sure defend ye
From the mysuse of Science and send ye [2]
The gayne my mother to mynd did call,
Joy wythout end, — that wysh I to all!   1044

RESON.   Well sayd! and as ye, dowghter, wyshe it,
     That joy to all folke in generall,
So wysh I, Reson, the same; but yet
     Fyrst in this lyfe wysh I here to fall
        To our most noble Kyng and Quene in especiall,
To ther honorable Cowncell, and then to all the rest,
Such joy as long may rejoyse them all best!   1051

All say Amen.

*Heere cumth in fowre wyth violes and syng, " Remembre me," [3] and at
the last quere all make cur[t]sye, and so goe forth syngyng.*

  *Thus endyth the Play of Wyt and Science, made by Master
Jhon Redford.*

  [1] *Qy. insert* end (*noun*).   [2] H. you.   [3] *This song is not given in* MS.

A PREATY INTERLUDE

CALLED, NICE WANTON.

———

Wherein ye may see
    Three braunc[h]es of an yll tree:
The mother and her chyldren three,
    Twoo naught, and one godlye.

Early sharpe that wyll be thorne;
    Soone yll that wyll be naught;
To be naught, better vnborne;
    Better vnfed than naughtely taught.

Ut magnum magnos, pueros puerilia [1] decent.[2]

———

Personages.

THE MESSENGER.

BARNABAS.	INIQUITIE.
ISMAEL.	BAILY ERRAND.[3]
DALILA.	XANTIPE.
EULALIA.	WORLDLY SHAME.

DANIEL, THE IUDGE.

Anno Domini,
M.D.LX.

[1] K. puerllia.
[2] K. deocus; *emend. by* Kittredge; Haz. *prints* doctus, *with no note.*
[3] *This and* INIQUITE *on the same line in* K.

Printed from the copy in the British Museum. Whether Hazlitt, in his edition of Dodsley's "Old Plays," printed from this copy or from that belonging to the Duke of Devonshire, I do not know. If he printed from the latter, the variations between his reading of the original and that of my copyist may perhaps be accounted for; but if so, both copies have been trimmed too close. In some instances I have omitted to point out that Hazlitt has silently corrected spellings and restored dropped letters; but I believe I have neglected nothing important in his text or his notes. His edition is indicated by Haz.; the old edition by K. In K. the names of the speakers are always spelled in full; the abbreviations are mine.

This play was licensed to the printer, John Kyng, in 1560; but the last stanza shows that it was written before the death of Edward VI.

[NICE WANTON.]

The Prologue.

The Messenger. The prudent prince, Salomon, doth say,
"He that spareth the rod, the chyld doth hate";
He wold youth shuld be kept in awe alwaye
By correction in tyme at reasonable rate,   4

To be taught to fear God and theyr parents obey,
To get learning and qualities, thereby to maintain
An honest quiet lyfe, correspondent alway
To Gods law and the kynges ; for it is certayne   8

If chyldren be noseled in idlenes and yll
And brought vp therin, it is hard to restrayne
And draw them from naturall wont euyll,
As here in thys interlude ye shall se playne   12

By two chyldren brought vp wantonly in play,
Whom *th*e mother doth excuse whe*n* she should chastise :
They delyte in daliaunce and mischief alway ;
At last they ende theyr lyues in miserable wyse.   16

The mother, perswaded by Worldly Shame
That she was the cause of theyr wretched lyfe,
So pensife, so sorowfull for theyr death she became,
That in despaire she would slea her-self with a knife.   20

Then her sonne, Barnabas, — by interpretacyon,
The sonne of comfort, — her yll[1] purpose do[2] stay,

---

[1] K. all ; Haz. ill.
[2] Haz. do[th] ; *perhaps a mistake for* to.

By the Scriptures he geueth her godly consolation ;
    And so concludeth.   All these partes wyll we [1] playe.   24
                                           [*Exit.*]

Barnabas commeth.

BARN.   My mayster in my lesson yester-day
    Dyd recite this text of Ecclesiasticus :
" Man is prone to euil fro*m* hys youth," did he say ;
    Which sentence may wel be verified in vs, —   28

My-selfe, my brother, and sister Dalila,
    Whom our parentes to theyr cost to scoole do fynde.
I tary for them here ; time passeth away,
    I loose my learnyng ; they ever loyter behynde.   32

If I go before, they do me threate
    To complayne to my mother ; she for theyr sake,
Being her tender tidlynges, wyll me beate.
    Lorde, in thys perplexitye, what way shall I take ?   36

What wyl become of them ?   Grace God them sende
To apply their learnyng and theyr maners amend !

Ismael & Dalila come in syngyng :

    Here we comen ! and here we louen ! [2]
    And here we will abide, abyde ay ! [3]   40

BARN.   Fye, brother, fye ! *and* specyally you, sister Dalila !
Sobrenes becommeth maydes alway.
    DAL.   What, ye dolt ! Ye be euer in one songe !
    ISM.   Yea, sir, it shall cost you blowes ere it be longe !
    BARN.   Be ye not ashamed the treauandes to play,   45
Losing your time *and* learning, *and* that euery day?
Lernyng bringeth knowledge of God *and* honest liuing to get.
    DAL.   Yea, mary, I warrant you, Master Hodypeke !
    BARN.   Learne a-pace, syster, and after to spyn and sowe,
And other honest huswifely poyntes to knowe.   50

---

[1] K. me ; Haz. we.   [2] Haz. lonen.   [3] Haz. abide-a.

Ism.   Spyn, quod ha?   Yea, by *the* masse, *and* w*ith* youre
    heles vp-wynd,
For a good mouse-hunt is cat after kynd.[1]
    Barn.   " Lewd spekyng corrupteth good maners," S. Paule
    doeth sai.
Come, let vs go, if ye wil to scole thys day.
I shal be shent for taryng so longe.   55

Barnabas goeth oute.

Ism.   Go, get the hence, thy mouth full of horse-donge!
Now, prety syster, what sport shall we deuyse?
Thus paltyng to scole, I thynke vs vnwyse ;
In sommer dye for thryst, in wynter for colde,
And styl to liue in feare of a churle, — who would?
    Dal.   Not I, by the masse!   I had rather he hanged were
Then I would syt quakyng like a mome for feare.   62

I am sonne-burned in sommer, in winter the colde
    Maketh my limmes grosse and my beauty decay.
If I should vse it as they would I should,
    I should neuer be fayre woman, I dare say.   66

Ism.   No, syster, no! but I can tell
    Where we shal haue good chiere,
Lusty companyons two or three,
    At good wyne, ale and biere.   70

    Dal.   Oh good brother, let vs go ;
I wyl neuer go more to[2] scoole.
Shall I neuer knowe
What pastyme meaneth?
Yes, I wyll not be suche a foole.
    Ism.   Haue with the, Dalila!   76

---

[1] Haz. *prints* after Saint Kind, *and says* "Old copy, Kynge"; *my
copyist gives the reading of the old edition as,* after kyng.
[2] K. *repeats* to; Haz. *prints* to-to.

[They sing :]

　　　Fare-well our scoole!
　　　Away with boke and all!

[T]hey caste [aw]aye their [bo]kes.[1]

　　　I wyll set my heart
　　　On a mery pynne,
　　　What-euer shall be-fall!　　　　　　　　　　81

[They go out singing.　Enter Eulalia.]

EUL.　Lorde, what folly is in youth!
　　Howe vnhappy be chyldren now-a-dayes!
And, the more pitye, to say the truth,
　　　Theyr parentes mainteyn them in euyll wayes,
　　　Which is a great cause that the world decayes,
For chyldren brought vp in ydlenes and play
Unthrifty and desobedient continue alway.　　　　88

A neyghbour of myne hath chyldren here-by,
　　　Ydle, desobedyent, proude, wanton and nyce.
As they come by, they do shrewed turnes daily ;
　　　Their parentes so to suffer them, surely be not wise.
　　　They laugh me to scorne when I tel them mine aduise ;
I wil speake to their elders *and* warne them neighborly.
Neuer in better tyme! — their mother is here-by.　　95

[Enter Xantippe.]

[EUL.]　God saue you, gossyp!　I am very fayne
　　That you chaunce now to come thys way ;
I longe to talke with you a word or twayne,
　　　I pray you take it frendly that I shall say.
　　　Ismael, your sonne, and your daughter, Dalila,
Do me shrewde turnes, dayly more and more,
Chide and beat my chylren, — it greueth me sore.　　102

They sweare, curse *and* scold, as they go by *th*e way,
　　Giuyng other yll ensample to do the same,

　　1 *The letters in brackets were cut off by the binder.*

To Gods displeasure, and theyr hurt an-other day.
    Chastyce them for it, or els ye be to blame! 106

XANT. Tusshe! tusshe! If ye haue no more than that to
    saye,
Ye maye holde your tonge and get ye awaye.
Alas! poore soules, they sit a' scoole all day
In feare of a churle; *and* yf a lytle they play, 110
He beateth them lyke a deuyl. When they come home,
Your mestresship would haue me lay on.
If I should beate them so oft as men complayne,
By *the* masse! w*ith*-in this month I shuld make the*m* lame. 114

EUL. Be not offended, I pray you; I must say more:
    Your sonne is suspect lyght-fyngered to be;
Your daughter hath nyce trickes three or foure;
    See to it in tyme, leaste worse ye do see.
    He that spareth the rod, hateth the chyld truely;
Yet Salomon sobre correction doth meane,
Not to beate and bounce them to make them lame. 121

XANT. God thanke you, mestres, I am well at ease!
[*Aside*] Such a foole to teache me, preachyng as she please!
Dame, ye belye them deadly; I know playne,
Because they go handsomly, ye disdayne.
    EUL. Then on the other as well would I complayne;
But your other sonne is good, and no thank to you!
These wyl ye make naught, by swete Iesu! 128

XANT. Eulalia,[1] my chyldren naught? Ye lye!
By your malyce they shal not set a flye.[2]
I haue but one mome, in comparison of hys brother, —
Him the foole prayseth, and despiseth the other.
    EUL. Well, Xantippe, better in time then to late!
Seing ye take it so, here my leaue I take.   *Exit.* 134

---

[1] K. Eupliade; Haz. *gives* Gupliade *as reading of* K. *and prints* Gup
liar.   [2] K. ffye.

XANT.   Mary, good leaue haue ye, the gret God be w*ith*
you!
My chyldren or I be curst, I thinke ;
They be complayned on where-euer they go,
That for theyr pleasure they might drynke ;
Nay, by thys the poor soules be come fro*m* scole [1] wery,
I will go get them meate to make them mery. [2]   [*Exit.*]   140

Iniquitie, Ismael, and Dalila come in together, [singing :]

INIQ.   Lo ! lo ! here I bryng her. [3]
ISM.   What is she, nowe ye haue her?
DAL.   I, [4] lusty mynyon louer? [5]
INIQ.   For no golde wyll I gyue her.
All together.   Welcome my hony ay.   145

Here he speaketh :

INIQ.   Oh my heart !
Thys wenche can synge
And play her parte.
DAL.   I am yours (and you mine), [6] with all my heart.   149

INIQ.   By the masse, it is well songe !
Were ye not sory ye were a mayd so longe?
DAL.   Fye, Maister Iniquitie ! fye ! I am a mayd yet.
ISM.   No, sister, no ; your maidenhead is sicke.
INIQ.   That knaue, your brother, wyl be a blabbe styl.
I-wisse, Dalila, ye can say as muche by him, if ye wil !   155
DAL.   By him, quod ha? He hath whores two or
three.
But iche tell your minion Doll, by Gogs body, —
It skylleth not, she doth holde you as muche.
ISM.   Ye lye falsly, she wyll play me no suche touche.
DAL.   Not she ! Yes, to do your heart good !   160
I could tell you who putteth a bone in your hood.

---

[1] K. foules be come frō ferle.
[2] K. mercy.
[3] K. brynger; Haz. bring a.
[4] Haz. A.
[5] Haz. *reads* loner.
[6] *This is perhaps spoken aside.*

Ism. Peace, whore ! or ye beare me a boxe¹ on theare.²

Dal. Here is mine eare, knaue, stryke and thou dare !

[He strikes her.]

[Dal. *(to Iniq.)*] To suffer him thus ye be no man!

If ye wyl not reuenge me, I wyl fynd one! 165

To set so litle by me ye were not wont.

Well, it is no matter ! Though ye do, *ceteri nolunt.*³

Iniq. Peace, Dalila ! Speake ye Laten, poore foole?

Dal. No, no, but a prouerbe I learned at scoole.

Ism. Yea, syster, you went to scole til ye were past grace. 170

Dal. Yea, so dydst thou, by thy knaues face !

Iniq. Well, no more a-do ; let all thys go.

We kinsfolke must be frendes ; it must be so.

Come on ! come on ! come on !

Here they be that wyll do vs al good. 175

He casteth dice on the bord.

Ism. If ye vse it long, your hear wil grow throught⁴ your [hood].⁵

Iniq. Come on, knaue, with Christes curse !

I must haue some of the mony

Thou hast pickt out of thy fathers purse.

Dal. He, by the masse, if he can get his purse 180

Now and then, he maketh it by halfe the worse.

Ism. I defie you both, whore and knaue !

Iniq. What, ye pryncockes, begin ye to raue?

Come on !

Dal. Mayster Iniquitie, by your leaue,

I wyll play a crowne or two here by your sleue. 185

Ism. Then be ye seruaunt to a worshypful mon ;

Mayster Iniquitie, — a right name, by Saint John !

---

¹ *In* K. *the* x *of this word is broken and looks like* r ; Haz. *of course prints* box.

² K. *has* an theare (= on the ear) ; Haz. *reads* on there.

³ *As two lines in* K. *and* Haz.

⁴ Haz. through.

⁵ *Supplied by* Haz. *who, however, does not mention that it is missing in* K.

DAL.   What can ye say by Mayster Iniquitie?
I loue hym and his name most hertely.
    INIQ.   God a mercy, Dalila, good lucke, I warrant the!   190

            [H]e kisseth [h]er.

I wil shryue you both by-and-by.
    ISM.   Come on, but fyrst let vs haue a songe.
    DAL.   I am content, so that it be not longe.   193

        Iniquitie and Dalila singe:

    INIQ.   Golde lockes,
She must haue knockes,
    Or els I do her wronge.
    DAL.   When ye haue your wyl,
Ye were best lye styll,
    The winter nightes be longe.   199

    INIQ.   When I ne may
An-other assay,
    I wyl take it for no wronge.
    DAL.   Then, by the roode,
A bone in your hoode
    I shall put ere it be longe.   205

    ISM.   She macheth you, sira!
    INIQ.   By Gogs bloud, she is the best whore in England!
    DAL.   It is knauishly praysed, gyue me your hand.
    INIQ.   I woud thou haddes suche an-other.[2]
    ISM.   By the masse, rather then xl pound, brother.   210
    INIQ.   Here, sirs, come on ; seuen!

        They set him.
              A-leauen at all!
    ISM.   Do ye nycke vs? be-knaue your noly![8]
    INIQ.   Ten myne!
    ISM.   Syxe[4] myne!
                Casteth d[ice].[1]

[1] *Cut away in* K.
[2] K. *in other.*
[8] Noll (=noddle) *would give a sort of rhyme to* all.
[4] *In* K. *the* x *is broken.*

Haue at it, and it were for all my fathers kyne!
It is lost, by His woundes! and ten to one! 215
  INIQ. Take the dice, Dalila; cast on!
  DAL. Come on; fyve!

She casteth, and they set.[1]

        Thryue at fayrest!
  ISM. Gup, whore! and I at rest.   *He loseth.*
Bi Gogs bloud, I wene God *and* the deuyl be agenst me!
  INIQ. If thone forsake the, thother wyll take the. 220
  ISM. Then is he a good felow; I would not passe,
So that I myght beare a rule in hell, by the masse,
To tosse fierbrandes at these penyfathers pates.
I would be porter and receiue them at the gates.
In boyling lead *and* brimston I wold sethe the*m* ech-one. 225
The knaues haue al *th*e mony, good felows haue none!
  DAL. Play, brother; haue ye lost all your money now?
  ISM. Yea, I thanke that knaue and suche a whore as y*o*w!
Tis no matter;[2] I wyll haue money, or I wyll swete.
By Gogs bloud, I wyll robbe the next I mete! 230
Yea, and it be my father!

He goeth out.

  INIQ. Thou boy! by the masse, ye wyl clyme the ladder!
Ah, sira, I loue a wenche that can be wylye:
She perceyued my mind with a twinke of myne eie.
If we two play booty[3] on any man, 235
We wyll make him as bare as Iob anone.
Wel, Dalila, let se what ye haue won!
  DAL. Sir, I had x shillinges when I begon,
And here is all, euery fart[h]yng.

They tell i[t].[4]

  INIQ. Ye lye lyke a whoore! ye haue won a pound. 240
  DAL. Then the deuyll stryke me to the grounde!

---

[1] K. fet.   [3] K. booby; Haz. boody, *without note.*
[2] K. marter.   [4] Haz. *omits* it; *the* t *is missing in* K.

INIQ.   I will fele your pocket, by your leaue, mestres!
DAL.   A-way knaue ; not mine, by the masse!
INIQ.   Yes, bi God, and geue you this to boot!   244

He geueth her a box.

DAL.   Out, horeson knaue, I beshrew thy hert-root!
Wilt thou rob me and beat[1] me, to?
INIQ.   In the way of correction, but a blowe or twoo.
DAL.   Correct thy dogges! thou shalt not beate me !
I wyl make your knaues flesshe cut, I warrant the.
Ye thynke I haue no frendes?   Yes, I haue in store   250
A good felow or two, — perc[h]aunce more.
Yea, by the masse, they shall boxe[2] you for this geare !
A knaue I found the ; a knaue I leaue the here!

She goeth oute.

INIQ.   Gup, whore !   Do ye heare this iade?
Louing when [she][3] is pleased ;   255
When she is angry, thus shrewd.
Thief brother, syster whore, —
      Two graffes of an yll tree!
I wyl tary no longer here ;
      Fare-well, God be with ye !   260

He goeth out.

[*A long interval.*]

Dalila commeth in ragged, her face hid or disfigured, halting on a staffe.

DAL.   Alas, wretched wretche that I am !
      Most miserable caitife that euer was borne!
Full of payne and sorow, croked and lame,[4]
      Stuft with diseases, in this world forlorne !   264

My senowes be shronken, my flesh eaten w*ith* pocks,
      My bones ful of ache[s] and great payne ;

----

[1] K. breat.   [3] *Supplied by* Haz. *without note.*
[2] *The* x *is broken in* K.   [4] K. lome ; H. lorn.

My head is bald, that bare yelowe lockes;
　　Croked I crepe to the earth agayne; 268

Mine eie-sight [1] is dimme; my hands tremble *and* shake;
　　My stomake abhorreth all kynd of meate;
For lacke of clothes great colde I take;
　　When appetite [2] serueth I can get no meate; 272

Where I was fayre and amiable of face,
　　Now am I foule and horrible to se:
Al this I haue [3] deserued for lacke of grace,
　　Iustly for my sinnes God doth plague me. 276

My parentes did tidle me, — they were to blame, —
　　In-steade of correction, in yll did me maintain.
I fell to [4] naught, and shall dye with shame!
　　Yet all thys is not halfe of my greife and payne: 280

The worme of my conscience, *tha*t shall neuer dye,
　　Accuseth me dayly more and more.
So oft haue I sinned wilfully
　　That I feare to be damned for-euermore. 284

[Enter Barnabas.]

BARN.　What wofull wight art thou, tell me,
　　That here most greuously doest lament?
Confesse the truth, and I wil comfort the
　　By the word of God Omnipotent.
　　Although your tyme ye haue mispent,
Repent and amend while ye haue space,
And God wyll restore you to health [5] and grace. 291

DAL.　To tell you who I am, I dare not for shame;
　　But my filthy liuing hath brought me in this case.
Full oft for my wantonnes you dyd me blame,
　　Yet to take your councel I had not the grace. 295

[1] K. sigth.　　　　[3] K. I haue I.　　　　[5] K. heatlh.
[2] K. appetide.　　[4] K. no; *corr. by* Haz.

To be restored to health, alas, it is past,
  Disease hath brought me into suche decay!
Helpe me with your almose while my lyfe doth laste,
  That, like a wretche as I am, I may go my way.
    BARN.   Shewe me your name, sister, I you pray,
And I wil helpe you now at your nede:
Both body and soule wyl I fede.   302

    DAL.   You[1] haue named me already, if I durst be so bold.
  Your[1] sister Dalila, that wreche I am.
My wanton, nice toyes ye knew of olde, —
  Alas, brother, they haue brought me to thys shame!   306

When you went to scole, my brother *and* I wold play,
  Sweare, chide and scolde[2] with man and woman;
To do shrewde turnes our delyte was alwaye;
  Yet were we tidled, and you beaten now *and* than.   310

Thus our parentes let vs do what we woulde,
  And you, by correction, they kept[3] vnder awe;
When we grewe bigge, we were sturdye and bolde,
  By father and mother we set not a strawe.   314

Small matter for me, I am past!
  But your brother and mine is in great[4] ieoperdy,
In daunger to come to shame at the last,
  He frameth hys liuyng so wyckedly.   318

    BARN.   Well, siker,[5] I euer feared ye would be nought,
  Your lewde behauiours sore greue[d][6] my hart.
To trayn you to goodnes al meanes haue I sought,
  But in vaine; yet wyl I play a brotherly part,   322

For the[7] soul is more precyous, most derely bought
  With the bloud of Christe dying therfore,

---

[1] Haz. *says that* K. *interchanges* You *and* Your; *my copyist wrote* **Your**
for You, *but scratched out* r.   [2] K. scodle.
  [3] K. kepthe; *possibly for* kept the, *which* Haz. *prints without note.*
  [4] K. gread.   [5] Haz. *changes to* sister.
  [6] *Corr. by* Haz.   [7] K. For ye the; Haz. *no note.*

To saue it fyrst a meane must be sought
    At Gods hand by Chryste, mannes onely Sauior.   326

Consider, Dalila, Goddes fatherly godnes,
    Which for your good hath brought you in thys case,
Scourged you with hys rod, of pure loue doubtles,
    That ones knowing your-self, ye might cal for grace.   330

Ye seme to repent, but I doubt what[h]er[1]
    For your sinnes or for the misery ye be in.
Earnestly repent for your synne rather,
    For these plagues be but the reward of sinne.   334

But so repent that ye sinne no more,
    And then beleue with stedfast faith
That God wyll forgeue you for-euermore
    For Chrystes sake, as the Scripture sayth.   338

As for your bodye, if it be curable,
    I wyll cause to be healed, or[2] duryng your life
I wyl clothe you and fede[3] you as I am able.
    Come, sister, go with me; ye haue nede of relief.   342

Thei goo.

The iuge [Daniel], Iniquitie, Bayly [Errand] come in; t[he] iudge sitteth down.[4]

DANIEL.   As a iudge of the countrey here am I come,
    Sent by the Kynges Maiestye iustyce to do,
Chiefly to procede in iudgement of a felon;
    I tary for the verdite of the quest ere I go.
    Go, baily; know whether they be all a-greed or no;
If they be so, byd them come a-way,
And bring their prisoner; I wold hear what they say.   349

[1] K. whater; Haz. whether.
[2] Haz. *wrongly changes to* and.
[3] K. fete; H. feed, *with no note.*
[4] Haz. *gives this after* l. 347 *in this form:* Iniquity, Baily errand, comes in; the judge sitteth down. *In* K. *it is in the margin opposite* ll. 344–347; *the words in brackets were cut away.*

[BAILY.]   I go, my lord, I go, to soone for one,
He is lyke to play a cast wil breake his necke-bone.
I beseche your lor[d]shyp be good to hym ;
The man is come of good kynne.

He tellet[*h*][1] *hym in hy*[*s*][1] *eare, that*[2] *a*[*ll*][1] *may heare.*[3]

If your lordshyp would be so good to me
As for my sake to set hym free,   355
I could haue xx pound [4] in a purse ;
Yea, and your lordshyp a right faire horse,
Well worth ten pound.
        DAN.[5]   Get the a-way, thou hell-hound !
If ye were well examined and tried,   360
Perchaunce a false knaue ye would be spyed.

*Iniquitye goeth oute ; th*e *iudge sp*[*e*]*keth*[1] *styll.*

Brybes, saith Salomon, blind *th*e wise mans sight,[6]
That he can not se to geue iudgement right.
Should I be a bribar? Nay ; he shall haue the law,
As I owe to God and the kyng obedience and awe.   365

        They bring Ismael in, bound lyke a prysoner. [*The jury comes also.*
        Iniquitie whispers to Ismael.]

INIQ.   Ye be tyed fayre ynough for runnyng away ;
If ye do not after me, ye wyll be hanged, I dare say.
If thou tell no tales, but holde thy toungue,
I wyl set the at lybertye ere it be longe,
Though thou be iudged to dye anon.   370
        [IU]DGE.[1]   Come on, sirs, I pray you, come on.
Be you all agreed in one?

        *One of the*m *speketh for* the *quest.*

[JUROR.]   Yea, my lord, euery-chone.   373

---

[1] *Cut away.*   [4] K. pount.
[2] K. the.   [5] K. Daniel th[e] iudge.
[3] Haz. He telleth him in his ear the rest may not hear, *which cannot
have stood in the British Museum copy, as may be seen by arranging in
lines.*   [6] K. light ; Haz. sight.

[Iu]DGE.[1] Where Ismael was indited[2] by xij men
    Of felony, burglary and murdre,
As thinditement declareth how, where, and when, —
    Ye heard it read to you lately, in ordre, —
You, with the rest, — I trust, all true men, —
Be charged vpon your othes to gyue verdyte directly
Whether Ismael therof be gilty or not gilty.   380

[On]e for the [qu]est.[3]

[Juror.][4] Gilty, my lord, and most gilty.
[I]NIQ.[5] [*to Ismael*] Wilt thou hange, horeson noddy?[6]
[I]UDGE. [*to Ismael*] The Lorde haue mercy vpon the!
[I]NIQ. [*to Ismael*] Tusshe, holde thy tonge, and I warrant
    the!   384

[I]UDGE. [*to Ismael*] Thou shalt go to the place thou camst
    fro,
    Tyl to-morow ix of the clocke there to remain;
To the place of execution then shalt thou go,
    There be hanged to death; and after, again,
    Being dead, for ensample to be hanged in a chain.
Take hym away, and se it be done,
At your perill, that may fall thereupon!   391

[I]SM. Though I be iudged to dye, I require respite,
For the kings aduantage in[7] thinges I can recite.

[I]NIQ. A-way with him, he wyll speake but of spyte.

[I]UDGE. Well, we will heare you say what you can;   395

1 *Cut away.*
2 K. intided; *corr. by* Haz.
8 Haz. rest; *letters cut away.*
4 *The assignment of the speeches here is confused in* K.; *One for the* quest *is opposite* l. 381; Iniquitie *opp.* 382, Iudge *opp.* 383, Iniquitie *opp.* 384, *and* Iudge *opp.* 385. Haz. *assigns* 381–383 *as I do, but assigns all after to the Judge, and transposes* 384 *and* 385. *My assignment merely supposes that, like the first, all the names were put one line too high.*
5 *The first letter of the next ten speakers is cut away.*
6 Haz. Wilt thou hang, my lord, [this] whoreson noddy; K. *has* my Lord, *but I regard it as an intrusion from the preceding line.*
7 Haz. *emends to* some.

But se that ye wrongfully accuse no man.

    [I]SM.   I wyll be-lye no man, but thys I may say:
Here standeth he that brought me to thys waye.

    [I]NIQ.   My lorde, he lyeth like a dampned knaue;
The feare of death doth make hym raue.   400

    [I]SM.   His naughtye company and playe at dice
Dyd me first to stealyng entice;
He was w*ith* me at roberies, I say it to his face;
Yet can I say more in tyme and place.[1]

    INIQ. [*aside*]   Thou hast said to much, I beshrew thi hor-
        sons face!—   405
Hange him, my lord, out of the way;
The thief careth not what he doth say.

    [*Aside*]   Let me be hangman, I wil teache [2] him a sleight;
For feare of talkyng I wil strangle him streight.—
Tary here that lyst, for I wyl go.   410

He would go.

    IUDG[E].[3]   No, no, my frend, not so!
I thought alwayes ye should not be good,
And now it wil proue, I se, by the rood!
Take him and lay him in yrons stronge.
We wil talke with you more ere it be longe.   415

They ta[ke] him in a h[al]ter; he fig[h]teth with the[m].[3]

    INIQ.   He that layeth handes on me in this place,
Iche lay my brawlyng-yron on his face!
By Gogs bloud, I defye thy worst!
If thou shouldest hange me, I were a-curst.
I haue bene at as low an ebbe as this,   420
And quyckely a-loft again, by Gisse!
I haue mo frendes then ye thynke I haue;
I am entertained of all men lyke no slaue.
Yea, within this moneth, I may say to you,
I wyl be your seruaunt, and your maister, to,—   425

---

    [1] K. space.   [2] K. teathe.
    [3] *The letters in brackets are cut away.*

Ye, crepe into your brest!   Wyl ye haue it so?

   IUDGE.   A-way with them both! leade them away!

At his death, tell me what he doth say;

For then, be-lyke, he wyll not lye.

   INIQ.   I care not for you both; no, not a fly!   430

They lead them out.

   IUDGE.   If no man haue here more matter to say,

I must go hence some other way.

                               He goeth out.

       [Enter Worldly Shame.]

   WORLDLY SHAME.   Hah ha! though I come in rudely, be

      not agast!

I must worke a feate in al the hast.

I haue caught two byrdes: I wyll set for the dame;   435

If I catche her in my clutche, I wyl her tame!

Of all thys while know ye not my name?

I am right worshipfull Maister Wor[l]dly Shame.

The matter that I come now about

Is euen thys, I put you out of dought: 440

There is one [1] Xantippe, a curst shrew, —

I thynke al the world doth her knowe, —

Suche a iade she is and so curst a quene

She would out-scold the deuils dame, I wene.

Sirs, thys fine woman had babes three: 445

Twayne the derest darlinges that might be, —

Ismael and faire Dalila, these two;

With the loute Barnabas I haue nothyng to do.

Al was good that these tidlynges do might, —

Sweare, lye, steale, scolde, or fight,   450

Carde, [2] dyce, kysse, clippe, and so furth:

All this our Mammy would take in good worth.

Now, sir[s], Dalila, my daughter, is dead of *th*e pockes,

And my son hanged [3] in chaynes and waueth his locks.

---

    [1] K. none; *corr. by* Haz.   [3] Haz. *emends to* hangeth.

    [2] K. Cardes.

These newes wil I tel her, and the matter so frame   455
That she shal be thyne owne, Mayster Worldly Shame.
Hah ha ha!

Xantippe commeth in.

   Peace, peace! she commeth hereby.
I spoke no word of her, no, not I!   458

Oh Mestres Xantippe, I can tell you newes:[1]
  The fayre wenche, your dere daughter Dalila,
Is dead of the pockes, taken at the stewes;
  And thy sonne Ismael, that preaty boy,
Whom, I dare say, you loued very well,
Is hanged in chaynes, euer[y][2] man can tell.   464

Euery man saith thy daughter was a strong whore,
  And thy sonne a strong thief *and* a murderer, to;
It must nedes greue you wonderous sore[3]
  That they died so shamefully, both two.
Men wyl taunt you and mock you, for they say now
The cause of their death was euen verye you.   470

XANT.   I the cause of their death!

She wold sowne.

WORLDLY SHAME.   Will ye sowne? the deuyl stop thy
    breath!   472

Thou shalt die, I trow, with more shame;
  I wyl get me hence out of the way;
If the whore should dye, men would me blame, —
  That I killed her, knaues should say.   *Exit.*   476

XANT.   Alas, alas, and weale-away!
  I may curse the time that I was borne!
Neuer woman had suche fortune, I dare say;
  Alas, two of my chyldren be forlorne!   480

[1] K. nedes; *corr. by* Haz., *who gives reading of* K. *as* neder.
[2] *Corr. by* Haz.   [3] K. sors.

My faire daughter Dalila is dead of the pockes;
    My dere sonne Ismael hanged vp in chaynes, —
Alas, the wynd waueth his yelow lockes!
    It sleaeth my heart and breaketh my braynes!   484

Why should God punish and plague me so sore,
    To se my children dye so shamefully?
I wil neuer eate bread in this world more;
    With this knife wyl I sley my-self by-*and*-by!   488

            She wold stick herselfe with a knife.

               [Enter Barnabas.]

BARN.   Beware what ye do! fye, mother, fye!
    Wyl ye spyl your-selfe for your own offence,
And seme for-euer to exclude Gods mercy?
    God doth punysh you for your negligence;
    Wherfore take his correction with pacience
And thanke him hertely that, of his godnes,
He bringeth you in knowledge of your trespas.   495

For when my brother *and* sister were of yonge age,
    You saw they were geuen to ydlenes and play,
Would apply no learnyng but liue in outrage,
    And men complayned on them euery day;
    Ye winked at theyr faultes and tidled them alway;
By maintenaunce they grew to mischief and yll;
So, at last, Gods iustice did them both spill.   502

In that God preserued[1] me, small thanke to you!
    If God had not geuen me speciall grace
To auoyd euil and do good, — this is true —
    I had liued and dyed in as wretched case
    As they did, for I had both suffraunce and space;
But it is an olde prouerbe,[2] — you haue herd it, I think, —
That God wyl haue se, shall not wynke.   509

Yet in this we may al take comfort:
    They toke great repentaunce, I heard say;

---

[1] K. preseruerued.   [2] K. prouerke.

And, as for my sister, I am able to report
 She lamented for her sinnes to her dy[i]ng-day.
 To repent and beleue I exhorted[1] her alway.
Before her death she beleued that God, of his mercy,
For Christes sake, would saue her eternally.   516

If you do euen so, ye nede not despaire,
 For God will frely remitte your sinnes all.
Christe hath payed the raunsom; why shuld ye fear?
 To beleue this and do well, to God for grace call;
 All worldly cares let passe and fall;
And thus comfort my father, I pray you hertely!
I haue a lytle to say, I wyl come by-and-by.   523

    Xantippe goeth out.

Right gentle audience, by thys interlude ye may se
 How daungerous it is for the frailtye of youth,
Without good gouernaunce, to lyue at libertye.
 Suche chaunces as these oft happen, of truth;
 Many miscary, it is the more ruth,
By negligence of their elders *and* not taking payne
In tyme good learnyng *and* qualities to attayne.   530

Therfore exhort I[2] al parentes to be diligent
 In bringing vp their children, yea,[3] to be circumspect;
Least they fall to euill, be not negligent,
 But chastice them before they be sore infect;
 Accept their well-doing, in yll them reiect.
A yonge plant ye may platte *and* bowe as ye wyll;
Where it groweth strong, there wyll it abyde styll: 537

Euen so by chyldren, — in theyr tender age
 Ye may worke them like waxe[4] to your own entent;
But if ye suffer them longe to liue in outrage,
 They wil be sturdy and stiffe, and will not relent.
 O ye chyldren, let your tyme be well spent;

---

[1] K. exorthed; *the x broken.*   [3] Haz. *emends to* aye.
[2] K. exhortyng; *corr. by Haz.*   [4] *The x is broken.*

Applye your learnyng and your elders obey:
It wil be your profit an-other day.   544

He knele[th]¹ downe.

Now for the Quenes² Royal Maiestie let vs pray,
    That God, in whose handes is *the* hert of al quenes,²
Maye endue Her² Highnes w*ith* godly puissance alwaye,
    That Her² Grace may long raign and prosper in al things,
    In Gods word *and* iustice may giue light to al quenes.²
Let vs pray for the Honorable Councel *and* Nobilitie,
That they may alwayes cou*n*sel in wisdo*m* w*ith* tra*n*quility.
God saue the Quene, the Realme, and Cominaltie!   552

He mak[eth]¹ curtesy an[d]¹ goeth out.

FINIS.

T. R.

———

A Song.

[He]re fyng⁸
[ech a]s anfwea-
[rin]g other,
[tha]t alwaies   It is good to be mery.
[the] iii⁵ ftaffe   But who can be⁴ mery?
[the]y fing⁶ to·   He that hath a pure conscience,
[ge]ther.⁷   He may well be mery.   4

¹ *Cut away by binder.*
² *It is clear from the rhymes that this play was originally composed for production before a king.*   ³ K. refyng.   ⁴ K. cam me.
⁵ *Perhaps this should be* iiii, *but I take the last two lines to be meant by the third stave.*   ⁶ K. yfing.
⁷ *I supply letters cut off by the binder. The alignment is that given by my copyist;* Haz. *prints some of the words in italics, and so aligns the edges as to give a different idea of the amount missing; thus:*

                    resyng,
                    answer-
            ing   other
                t always
                        staff
            ,   *ysing to*
            other.

Who hath a pure conscience? tel me!
No man, of him-self, I ensure the.
Then must it folow of necessitie
  That no man can be mery.   8

Puritie it-selfe may purenes geue;
You must aske it of God in true beleue.
Then wyl he geue it, and none repreue;
  And so we may be mery.   12

What is the practice of a conscience pure?
To loue and feare God, and other allure;
And, for his sake, to helpe hys neighbour, —
  Then may he well be mery.   16

What shall he haue that can and wil do this?
After this life euerlasting blisse:
Yet not by desert, but by gyft, y-wisse.
  There God make vs all mery!   20

FINIS.

Imprinted at London, in Paules
Churche yearde at the Sygne of
the Swane by John Kyng.

PART V.

THE FOURE PP.

Printed from the first edition (by Wyllyam Myddylton, London, n. d. [before 1547]). In the footnotes M. indicates this edition ; A. indicates the third edition (by John Allde, London, 1569); Coll. indicates the edition by Collier, in Dodsley's "Old Plays" (London, 1825). For the readings of A. I have had to rely upon Collier, who, it must be admitted, is inaccurate. I have not pointed out the numerous instances in which his text differs from mine in final *e*'s. Hazlitt's edition seems, so far as the textual notes are concerned, mainly a reprint of Collier's ; I have usually disregarded it.

The playe called the foure PP.

A newe and a very mery enterlude of

A PALMER.
A PARDONER.
A POTYCARY.
A PEDLER.

Made by John Heewood.

[Enter Palmer.]

PALMER. Nowe God be here, who kepeth this place!
　Now, by my fayth, I crye you mercy ;
Of reason I must sew for grace,
　My rewdnes sheweth me no[w] [1] so homely.
Wherof your pardon axt and wonne,
　I sew you, [2] as curtesy doth me bynde,
To tell thys whiche shalbe begonne
　In order as may come beste in mynde. [3]

8

[1] A. not ; Coll. *rejects* no.
[2] A. sue now.
[3] M. myndy.

I am a palmer, as ye [1] se,
Whiche of my lyfe much part hath [2] spent
In many a fayre and farre [3] countre,
As pylgrymes do of good intent.   12
At Hierusalem [4] haue I bene
Before Chrystes blessed sepulture;
The Mount of Caluery haue I [5] sene,
A holy place, ye may be sure;   16
To Iosophat and Olyuete
On fote, God wote, I wente ryght bare, —
Many a salt tere dyde I swete
Before thys carkes coulde [6] come there;   20
Yet haue I bene at Rome also,
And gone the stacions all arow,
Saynt Peters Shryne and many mo
Then, yf I tolde, all ye do know, —   24
Except that there be any suche
That hath ben there and diligently
Hath taken hede and marked muche,
Then can they speke as muche as I.   28
Then at the Rodes also I was;
And rounde about to Amyas;
At Saynt Toncomber; and Saynt Tronion;
At Saynt Bothulph; and Saynt Anne of Buckston;
On the Hylles of Armony, where I see [7] Noes arke;   33
With holy Iob; and Saynt George in Suthwarke;
At Waltam; and at Walsyngam;
And at the good Rood of Dagnam;
At Saynt Cornelys; at Saynt Iames in Gales;
And at Saynt Wynefrydes Well in Walles;   38
At Our Lady of Boston; at Saynt Edmundes-byry;
And streyght to Saynt Patrykes Purgatory;
At Rydybone; and at the Blood of Hayles,

---

[1] A. you, *so regularly.*   [5] A. I have.
[2] Coll. A. have.   [6] A. would.
[3] A. far and faire.   [7] A. saw.
[4] A. Jerusalem.

Where pylgrymes paynes ryght muche auayles ;
At Saynt Dauys ; and at Saynt Denis ;   43
At Saynt Mathew ; and Saynt Marke in Venis ;
At Mayster Iohan Shorne ; at Canterbury ;
The Graet God of Katewade ; at Kynge Henry ; [1]
At Saynt Sauyours ; at Our Lady of Southwell ;
At Crome ; at Wylsdome ; and at Muswell ;   48
At Saynt Rycharde ; and at Saynt Roke ;
And at Our Lady that standeth in the Oke :
To these with other many one
Deuoutly haue I prayed and gone,
Prayeng to them to pray for me   53
Unto the Blessed Trynyte ;
By whose prayers and my dayly payne
I truste the soner to obtay[n]e [2]
For my saluacyon grace and mercy,
For be ye sure I thynke surely [3]   58
Who seketh sayntes for Crystes sake —
And namely suche as payne do take
On fote to punyshe their [4] frayle body —
Shall therby meryte more hyely
Then by any-thynge done by man.   63

[The Pardoner has entered while the Palmer is speaking.]

PARDONER.   And when ye haue gone as farre as ye can,
For all your labour and gostely entente
Yet welcome [5] home as wyse as ye wente!
    PALMER.   Why, sir, dyspyse ye pylgrymage?
    PARDONER.   Nay, for [6] God, syr, then dyd I rage!   68
I thynke ye ryght well occupyed
To seke these sayntes on euery syde.
Also your payne [7] I nat disp.rayse it,

---

[1] A. Herry.   [5] A. Ye will come.
[2] *Corr. by* Coll. *from* A.   [6] Coll. A. fore.
[3] A. assuredly ; *here and in several other instances* Coll. *calls* A. *the
second ed. ;* Haz. *usually follows him.*   [7] A. paynes.
[4] *So* Coll. *from* A ; M. *has* thy, *perhaps for* thys.

But yet I discomende your wit,
And, or [1] we go, euen so shall ye,   73
If ye in this wyl answere me:
I pray you, shew what the cause is
Ye wente al these pylgrymages.

    PALMER.   Forsoth this lyfe I dyd begyn
To rydde the bondage of my syn,   78
For whiche these sayntes rehersed or this
I haue both sought and sene, i-wys,
Besechynge them to be [2] recorde
Of all my payne vnto the Lorde,
That gyueth all remyssyon   83
Upon eche mans contricyon;
And by theyr good mediacyon,
Upon myne [3] humble submyssion,
I trust to haue in very dede
For my soule helth the better spede.   88

    PARDONAR.   Nowe is your owne confessyon lyckely
To make your-selfe [4] a fole quyckely,
For I perceyue ye wolde obtayne
No nother [5] thynge for all your payne
But onely grace your soule to saue.   93
Nowe marke in this what wyt ye haue
To seke so farre, and helpe so nye:
Euen here at home is remedy,
For at your dore my-selfe doth dwell,
Who coulde haue saued your soule as well   98
As all your wyde wandrynge shall do,
Though ye wente thryes to Iericho.
Nowe, syns ye myght haue spedde at home,
What haue ye wone by ronnyng [6] at Rome?

    PALMER.   If this be true that ye haue moued,   103
Then is my wyt in-dede reproued;
But let vs here fyrste what ye are.

---

[1] A. ere; *so regularly.*   [3] A. my.   [5] Coll. A. other.
[2] Coll. bear, *no note.*   [4] A. you.
[6] *So my copyist;* Coll. *gives* ronnying *as reading of this edition.*

PARDONAR. Truly I am a pardoner.

PALMER. Truely a pardoner, — that may be true;

But a true pardoner doth nat ensew!   108

Ryght selde is it sene or neuer

That treuth and pardoners dwell together;

For, be your pardons neuer so great,

Yet them to enlarge ye wyll nat let

With suche lyes that oftymes, Cryste wot,   113

Ye seme to haue that ye haue nat.

Wherfore I went my-selfe to the selfe thynge

In euery place, and, without faynynge,

Had as muche pardon there assuredly

As ye can promyse me here doutefully.   118

Howe-be-it I thynke ye do but scoffe;[1]

But yf ye hadde all the pardon ye speke[2] of,

And no whyt of pardon graunted

In any place where I haue haunted,

Yet of my labour I nothynge repent.   123

God hathe respect how eche tyme is spent,

And, as in his knowledge all is regarded,

So by his goodnes all is rewarded.

PARDONAR. By the[3] fyrste parte of this laste tale

It semeth you come late[4] from the ale;   128

For reason on your syde so farre doth fayle

That ye leue [re]sonyng[5] and begyn to rayle;

Wherin ye forget your owne parte clerely,

For ye be as vntrue as I;

And in one poynte ye are beyonde me,   133

For ye may lye by aucthoryte, —

And all that hath[6] wandred so farre

That no man can be theyr controller.

And, where ye esteme your labour so muche,

I say yet agayne my pardons be[7] suche   138

---

[1] Coll. *gives* scofte *as reading of* M.; *my copyist wrote* scofte, *but changed the* t *to* f.

[2] *So* Coll. *from* A.; M. *has* kepe.

[3] A. this.

[4] Coll. A. ye came of late.

[5] *Corr. by* Coll. *from* A.

[6] Coll. A. have.

[7] Coll. A. are; *so usually.*

That, yf there were a thousande soules on a hepe,
I wolde brynge them all to heuen as good chepe
As ye haue brought your-selfe on pylgrymage
In the leste quarter of your vyage,
Which is [1] farre a thys side heuen, by God!   143
There your labour and pardon is od,
With smale cost and without any payne
These pardons bryngeth [2] them to heuen playne :
Geue me but a peny or two pens,
And as sone as the soule departeth hens,   148
In halfe an hour, or thre quarters at moste,
The soule is in heuen with the Holy Ghost.

[The Potycary has entered during the last speech.]

POTYCARY.   Sende ye any soules to heuen by water?
PARDONER.   If we dyd,[3] syr, what is the mater?
POTYCARY.   By God, I haue a drye soule shulde thyther! 153
I praye you let our soules go to heuen togyther.
So bysy you twayne be in soules helth,
May nat a potycary come in by stelth?
Yes, that I [4] wyll, by Saynt Antony!
And, by the leue of thys company,   158
Proue ye false knaues bothe, or we goo,
In parte of your sayenges, as thys, lo : [5]
Thou by thy trauayle thynkest heuen to gete ;
And thou by pardons and relyques countest no lete
To sende thyne owne soule to heuen sure,   163
And all other whome thou lyste to procure :
If I toke an accyon, then were they blanke ;
For lyke theues the knaues rob[6] away my thanke.
All soules in heuen hauynge relefe,
Shall they thanke your craftes? nay, thanke myn chefe!   168
No soule, ye knowe, entreth heuen gate
Tyll from the bodye he be separate ;

[1] Coll *gives reading of this ed. as* as.
[2] Coll. A. bring.
[3] Coll. A. doo.
[4] A. we.
[5] *So* Coll., *without note ;* M. *has* so.
[6] A. they rob.

And whome haue ye knowen dye ho[ne]stlye [1]
Without helpe of the potycary?
Nay, all that commeth to our handlynge, —   173
Except ye happe to come to hangynge :
That way, perchaunce, ye shall nat myster
To go to heuen without a glyster!
But, be ye sure, I wolde be wo
If [2] ye shulde chaunce [3] to begyle me so.   178
As good to lye with me a-nyght
As hange abrode in the mone lyght !
There is no choyse to fle my hande
But, as I sayd, into the bande.
Syns of our soules the multitude   183
I sende to heuen, when all is vewed,
Who shulde but I then all-togyther
Haue thanke of all theyr commynge thyther?

    PARDONER.   If ye kylde a thousande in an houre
      space,
When come they to heuen, dyenge from state of grace? [4]   188
    POTYCARY.   If a thousande pardons about your [5] neckes
      were teyd,
When come they to heuen yf they neuer dyed?
    PALMER.   Longe lyfe after good workes in-dede
Doth hynder mannes receyt of mede,
And deth before one dewty done   193
May make vs thynke we dye to sone ;
Yet better tary a thynge, then haue it,
Then go to sone and vaynly craue it.
    PARDONER.   The longer ye dwell in communicacion,
The lesse shall you lyke thys ymagynacyon ;   198
For ye may perceyue euen at the fyrst chop
Your tale is trapt in such a stop
That, at the leste, ye seme worse then we.
    POTYCARY.   By the masse, I holde vs nought all thre!

---

[1] *Corr. by* Coll. *from* A.   [4] Coll. A. dyenge out of grace.
[2] A. That.   [5] *Qy.* their.
[3] M. chaunge ; Coll. chaunce, *without note.*

[*The Pedler has entered in time to hear the last speech.*]

PEDLER.   By Our Lady, then haue I gone wronge ;   203
And yet to be here I thought longe!

POTYCARY.   Brother, ye haue gone wronge no w[h]yt
I prayse your fortune and your wyt,
That can dyrecte you so discretely
To plante you in this company :   208
Thou [a] [1] palmer, and thou a pardoner,
I a potycary.

PEDLER.   And I a pedler.

POTYCARY.   Nowe on my fayth full well watched! [2]
Were [3] the deuyll were we foure hatched?

PEDLER.   That maketh no mater, syns we be matched.   213
I coulde be mery yf that I catchyd
Some money for parte of the ware in my packe.

POTYCARY.   What the deuyll hast thou there at thy backe?

PEDLER.   Why, dost thou nat knowe that every pedler [4]
In euery tryfull [5] must be a medler?   218
Specyally in womens tryflynges, —
Those vse we chefe [6] aboue all thynges.
Whiche thynges to se yf ye be disposed,
Beholde what ware here is disclosed.
Thys gere sheweth it-selfe in suche bewte   223
That eche man thynketh [7] it sayth : come, bye me!
Loke, were [8] your-selfe can lyke to be chooser,
Your-selfe shall make pryce though I be looser !
Is here [9] nothynge for my father Palmer?
Haue ye nat a wanton in a corner   228
For [10] your walkyng to holy places?
By Cryste, I haue herde of as straunge cases!
Who lyueth in loue or loue wolde wynne,
Euen at this packe he must begynne,

---

[1] *Inserted by* Coll., *without note.*

[2] *Qy.* matched.

[3] Coll. Where, *without note.*

[4] M. pedled ; *corr. silently by* Coll.

[5] Coll. A. In all kind of trifles.

[6] Coll. A. cheefly.

[7] A. thinks.

[8] Coll. where, *without note.*

[9] A. there.

[10] Coll. For all, *without note.*

Where [1] is ryght many a proper token,   233
Of whiche by name parte shall be spoken:
Gloues, pynnes, combes, glasses vnspottyd,
Pomanders, hookes, and lasses knotted,[2]
Broches, rynges, and all maner bedes,
Lace,[3] rounde and flat, for womens hedes,   238
Nedyls, threde, thymbell[s],[4] shers, and all suche knackes, —
Where louers be, no suche thynges lackes, —
Sypers, swathbondes, rybandes, and sleue-laces,
Gyrdyls, knyues, purses, and pyncases.

    POTYCARY.   Do women bye theyr pyncases of you?   243
    PEDLER.   Ye, that they do, I make God a-vow!
    POTYCARY.   So mot I thryue, then for my parte,
I be-shrewe thy knaues nakyd herte
For makynge my wyfeys pyncase so wyde!
The pynnes fall out, they can nat abyde.   248
Great pynnes must she haue, one or other;
Yf she lese one, she wyll fynde an-other, —
Wherin I fynde cause to complayne, —
New pynnes to her pleasure and my payne!

    PARDONER.   Syr, ye seme well sene in womens causes: 253
I praye you, tell me what causeth this,
That women, after theyr arysynge,[5]
Be so longe in theyr apparelynge?

    PEDLER.   Forsoth, women haue many lettes,
And they be masked[6] in many nettes:[7]   258
As, frontlettes, fyllettes, par[t]lettes [8] and barcelettes;
And then theyr bonettes, and theyr poynettes.
By these lettes and nettes the lette is suche
That spede is small whan haste is muche.

    POTYCARY.   An-other cause why they come nat forwarde, 263

---

[1] Coll. A. Wherin.   [3] Coll. A. Laces.
[2] A. unknotted.   [4] A. *has the plural.*   [5] A. uprising.
[6] *So* Coll., *without note; the word now looks like* maiked.
[7] *So* Coll., *without note; the word now looks like* frettes, *but the line is at the top of the page and the upper half of long letters has been trimmed away.*   [8] Coll. partlettes, *without note.*

Whiche maketh them dayly to drawe backwarde,
And yet[1] is a thynge they can nat forbere :
The trymmynge and pynnynge vp theyr gere,
Specyally theyr fydlyng with the tayle-pyn,—
And when they wolde haue it prycke[2] in,   268
If it chaunce to double in the clothe
Then be they[3] wode and swereth[4] an othe.
Tyll it stande ryght, they wyll nat forsake it.
Thus, though it may nat, yet wolde they make it.
But be ye sure they do but defarre it,   273
For, when they wolde make it, ofte tymes marre it.
But prycke them and pynne them as myche[5] as ye wyll,
And yet wyll they loke for pynnynge styll ;
So that I durste holde you a ioynt[6]
Ye shall neuer haue them at a full[7] poynt.   278

  PEDLER.   Let womens maters passe, and marke myne!
What-euer theyr poyntes be, these poyntes be fyne.
Wherfore, yf ye be wyllynge to bye,
Ley downe money ! come of quyckely!

  PALMER.   Nay, by my trouth, we be lyke fryers :   283
We are but beggers, we be no byers.

  PARDONER.   Syr, ye maye showe your ware for your
        mynde,
But I thynke ye shall no profyte fynde.

  PEDLER.   Well, though thys iourney[8] acquyte no coste,
Yet thynke I nat my labour loste ;   288
For, by the fayth of my body,
I lyke full well thys company.
Up shall this packe, for it is playne
I came not hyther al for gayne.
Who may nat play one day in a weke,   293

---

[1] A. it.   [3] A. they be.
[2] Coll. A. prickt.   [4] Coll. A. swere.

[5] M. nyche; A. nie; Coll. *suggested* much *as the meaning;* Haz. *emends
to* nice.

[6] M. toynt; Coll. with you a joynt, *without note.*

[7] Coll. A. ful(l) ; M. fall, *which is possible.*

[8] M. your ney; Coll. journey, *without note.*

May thynke hys thryfte is farre to seke!
Deuyse what pastyme ye thynke beste,
And make ye sure to fynde me prest.

POTYCARY.   Why, be ye so vnyuersall
That you can do what-so-euer ye shall?   298

PEDLER.   Syr, yf ye lyste to appose [1] me,
What I can do then shall ye se.

POTYCARY.   Then tell me thys: be ye perfyt in drynkynge?

PEDLER.   Perfyt in drynkynge as may be wysht by thynk-
yng!

POTYCARY.   Then after your drynkyng how fall ye to
wynkyng?   303

PEDLER.   Syr, after drynkynge, whyle the shot is
tynkynge,
Some hedes be swynking,[2] but myne wyl be synkynge,
And vpon drynkynge myne eyse wyll be pynkynge,
For wynkynge to drynkynge is alway lynkynge.

POTYCARY.   Then drynke and slepe ye can well do.   308
But, yf ye were desyred therto,
I pray you, tell me, can you synge?

PEDLER.   Syr, I haue some syght in syngynge.

POTYCARY.   But is your brest any-thynge swete?

PEDLER.   What-euer my breste be, my voyce is mete.   313

POTYCARY.   That answer sheweth you a ryght syngynge
man.
Now what is your wyll, good father, than?

PALMER.   What helpeth wyll where is no skyll?

PARDONER.   And what helpeth skyll where is no wyll?[3]

POTYCARY.   For wyll or skyll, what helpeth it   318
Where frowarde knaues be lackynge wyt?[4]
Leue of thys curyosytie;
And who that lyste, synge after me!

---

1 Coll. oppose, *without note.*
2 A.; Coll. M. swymmyng.
3 Coll. A. wil; M. wyt; *see next note.*
4 Coll. A. wit; M. wyll; *see preceding note.*

Here they synge.[1]

PEDLER.　Thys lyketh me well, so mot I the!

PARDONER.　So helpe me God, it lyketh nat me!　　323
Where company is met and well agreed,
Good pastyme doth ryght well in-dede;
But who can syt[2] in dalyaunce
Men syt[3] in suche a variaunce
As we were set or ye came in?　　328
Whiche stryfe thys man dyd fyrst begynne,
Allegynge that suche men as vse
For loue of God, and nat[4] refuse,
On fot to goo from place to place
A pylgrymage, callynge for grace,　　333
Shall in that payne with penitence
Obtayne discharge of conscyence, —
Comparynge that lyfe for the beste
Enduccyon to our endles reste.
Upon these wordes our mater grewe;　　338
For, yf he coulde auow them true,
As good to be a gardener
As for to be a pardoner.
But, when I harde hym so farre wyde,
I then aproched and replyed,　　343
Sayenge this: that this[5] indulgence,
Hauyng the forsayd penitence,
Dyschargeth man of all offence
With muche more profyt then this pretence.
I aske but two pens at the moste, —　　348
I-wys, this is nat very great coste, —
And from[6] all payne, without dyspayre, —
My soule for his, — kepe euen his chayre,[7]
And when he dyeth he may be sure
To come to heuen, euen at pleasure.　　353

[1] *The song is not given.*　　[2] *Qy.* fet.　　[3] *Qy.* set.
[4] M. nat and; Coll. A. and not.
[5] A. his, *which would be very appropriate in* l. 347.
[6] A. for.　　[7] A. for to keep even in his chair.

And more then heuen he can[1] nat get,
How farre so-euer he lyste to iet.
Then is hys payne more then hys wit
To wa[l]ke[2] to heuen, syns he may syt !
Syr, as we were in this contencion,   358
In came thys daw with hys inuencyon,
Reuelynge vs, hym-selfe auauntynge,
That all the soules to heuen assendynge
Are most bounde to the potycary,
Bycause he helpeth most men to dye;   363
Before whiche deth he sayeth, in-dede,
No soule in heuen can haue hys mede.

  PEDLER.   Why, do potycaries kyll men?

  POTYCARY.   By God, men say so now and then !

  PEDLER.   And I thought ye wolde nat haue myst   368
To make men[3] lyue as longe as ye lyste.

  POTYCARY.   As longe as we lyste? nay, longe[4] as they
    can !

  PEDLER.   So myght we lyue without you than.

  POTYCARY.   Ye, but yet it is[5] necessary
For to haue a potycary;   373
For when ye fele your conscyens redy,
I can sende you to heuen[6] quyckly.
Wherfore, concernynge our mater here,
Aboue these twayne I am best, clere;
And, yf ye[7] lyste to take me so,   378
I am content you and no mo
Shall be our iudge as in thys case,
Whiche of vs thre shall take the best place.

  PEDLER.   I neyther wyll iudge the beste nor worste;
For, be ye bleste or be ye curste,   383
Ye know it is no whyt my sleyght[8]
To be a iudge in maters of weyght.

---

[1] A. may.
[2] M. wake; Coll. A. walke.
[3] Coll. them, *without note.*
[4] Coll. as longe, *without note.*
[5] A. but it is very.
[6] A. *inserts* very.
[7] *So* Coll. A.; M. he.
[8] M. fleyght; *corr. silently by* Coll.

It behoueth no pedlers not proctours
To take on them iudgemente as doctours.
But, yf your myndes be onely set   388
To worke for soule helthe, ye be well met;
For eche of you somwhat doth showe
That soules towarde heuen by you do growe;
Then, yf ye can so well agree
To contynue togyther all thre   393
And all you thre obey on[1] wyll,
Then all your myndes ye may fulfyll:
As, yf ye came all to one man
Who shulde goo[2] pylgrymage more then he can,
[*To Palmer*]   In that ye, palmer, as debite,   398
May clerely dyscharge[3] hym, parde;
[*To Pardoner*]   And for all other syns, ones had contryssyon,
Your pardons geueth hym full remyssyon;
[*To Potycary*]   And then ye, mayster potycary,
May sende hym to heuen by-and-by.   403
    POTYCARY.   Yf he taste this boxe nye aboute the
        pryme,
By the masse, he is in heuen or euensonge tyme!
My craft is suche that I can ryght well
Sende my fryndes to heuen and my-selfe to hell.
But, syrs, marke this man, for he is wyse   408
How[4] coulde deuyse suche a deuyce;
For yf we thre may be as one,
Then be we[5] lordes euerychone, —
Betwene vs all coulde nat be myste
To saue the soules of whome we lyste.   413
But, for good order, at a worde,
Twayne of vs must wayte on the thyrde;
And vnto that I do agree,
For bothe you twayne shall wayt on me.

---

[1] Coll. *silently corrects to* one.   [2] A. *inserts* on.
[3] M. dyscharde : *so* Coll., *without note.*
[4] Coll. *gives reading of* M. *as* Howe, *and corrects the spelling to* who.
[5] A. were we as.

PARDONER.   What chaunce is this that suche an elfe[1]   418
Commaund two knaues, besyde hym-selfe?
Nay, nay, my frende, that wyll nat be;
I am to good to wayt on the!
   PALMER.   By Our Lady, and I wolde be loth
To wayt on the better on[2] you both!   423
   PEDLER.   Yet be ye sewer, for all thys dout,
Thys waytynge must be brought about.
Men can nat prosper, wylfully ledde;
All thynge decayeth[3] where is no hedde.
Wherfore, doutlesse, marke what I say: 428
To one of you thre twayne must obey;
And, synnes ye can nat agree in voyce
Who shall be hed, there is no choyse
But to deuyse some maner thynge
Wherin ye all be lyke connynge;   433
And in the same who can do beste,
The other twayne to make them preste
In euery thynge of hys entente
Holly[4] to be at commaundement.
And now haue I founde one mastry   438
That ye can do in-dyfferently,
And is nother sellynge nor byenge,
But euyn only very lyenge;
And all ye thre can lye as well
As can the falsest deuyll in hell.   443
And, though afore ye harde me grudge
In greater maters to be your iudge,
Yet in lyeng I can some skyll,
And, yf I shall be iudge, I wyll;
And, be ye sure, without flatery,   448

---

[1] *Both* M. *and* A. *assign* ll. 418, 419 *to the Potycary, and have* 419:
Commaunded two knaues be, besyde hym selfe; *the present text appeared
in the first edition of Dodsley;* Collier *thinks* M. A. *may be correct.*
  [2] Coll. *silently changes to* of.
  [3] M. decayed; Coll. A. decay.
  [4] *For some occult reason* Coll. *changes this to* Holy.

Where my consciens fyndeth the mastrye,
Ther shall my iudgement strayt be founde,
Though I myght wynne a thousande pounde.

    PALMER.   Syr, for lyeng, though I can do it,
Yet am I loth for to goo to it.   453

    PEDLER. [*to Palmer*] Ye haue nat[1] cause to feare to be
        bolde,[2]
For ye may be here[3] vncontrolled.

[*To Pardoner*]   And ye in this haue good auauntage,
For lyeng is your comen vsage.

[*To Potycary*]   And you in lyenge be well spedde,   458
For all your craft doth stande in falshed.
Ye nede nat care who shall begyn,
For eche of you may hope to wyn.
Now speke, all thre, euyn as ye fynde:
Be ye agreed to folowe my mynde?   463

    PALMER.   Ye, by my trouth, I am content.

    PARDONER.   Now, in good fayth, and I assente.

    POTYCARY.   If I denyed, I were a nody,
For all is myne, by Goddes body!

Here the Potycary hoppeth.

    PALMER.   Here were a hopper to hop for the rynge!   468
But, syr,[4] thys gere goth nat by hoppynge.

    POTYCARY.   Syr, in this hopynge I wyll hop so well
That my tonge shall hop as well as[5] my hele;
Upon whiche hoppynge I hope, and nat doute it,
To hope[6] so that ye shall hope[6] without it.[7]   473

    PALMER.   Syr, I wyll neyther boste ne brawll,[8]
But take suche fortune as may fall;
And, yf ye wynne this maystry,
I wyll obaye you quietly.

---

[1] Coll. A. no.

[2] A. beholde.

[3] Coll. *gives reading of* M. *as* may here, *and that of* A. *as* may lie; *he prints* may here lie.

[4] A. sirs.

[5] M. aswell as; Coll. A. better than.

[6] Coll. A. hop.

[7] M. *omits* it.

[8] M. drawll; *corr. silently by* Coll.

And sure I thynke that quietnesse 478
In any man is great rychesse,
In any maner company,
To rule or [1] be ruled indifferently.
    PARDONER. By that bost thou semest a begger in-dede.
What can thy quyetnesse helpe vs at nede? 483
Yf we shulde starue, thou hast nat, I thynke,
One peny to bye vs one potte of drynke.
Nay, yf rychesse mygh[t]e [2] rule the roste,
Beholde what cause I haue to boste!
Lo, here be [3] pardons halfe a dosyn! 488
For gostely ryches they haue no cosyn;
And, more-ouer, to me they brynge
Sufficient succour for my lyuynge.
And here be [3] relykes of suche a kynde
As in this worlde no man can [4] fynde. 493
Knele downe, all thre, and, when ye leue kyssynge,
Who lyste to offer shall haue my blyssynge!
Frendes, here shall ye se euyn anone
Of All-Hallows the blessyd iaw-bone, —
Kys it hardely, with good deuocion! 498
    POTYCARY. This kysse shall brynge vs muche promo-
        cyon. —
Fogh! by Saynt Sauyour, I neuer kyst a wars!
Ye were as good kysse All-Hallows ars!
For, by All-Halows, me thynketh
That All-Halows breth stynkith. 503
    PALMER. Ye iudge All-Halows breth vnknowen;
Yf any breth stynke, it is your owne.
    POTYCARY. I knowe myne owne breth from All-Halows,
Or els it were tyme to kysse the galows.
    PARDONER. Nay, syrs, beholde, here may ye se 508
The great-toe of the Trinite:
Who to thys toe any money voweth,
And ones may role it in his moueth,

---

[1] A. *inserts* to.   [3] A. are.
[2] M. myghe; *corr. silently by* Coll.   [4] A. may.

All hys lyfe after, I vndertake,
He shall be ryd of[1] the toth-ake.   513
    POTYCARY.   I praye you torne that relyke aboute !
Other[2] the Trinite had the goute,
Or elles, bycause it is iii toes in one,
God made it muche as[3] thre toes alone.
    PARDONER.[4]   Well, lette that passe, and loke vpon
        thys ; —   518
Here is a relyke that doth nat mys
To helpe the leste as well[5] as the moste :
This is a buttocke-bone of Pentecoste.
    POTYCARY.   By Chryste, and yet, for all your boste,
Thys relyke hath be-shyten the roste !   523
    PARDONER.   Marke well thys relyke, — here is a whipper !
My friendes[6] vnfayned, here[7] is a slypper
Of one of the Seuen Slepers, be sure.
Doutlesse thys kys shall do you great pleasure,
For all these two dayes it shall so ease you   528
That none other sauours shall displease you.
    POTYCARY.   All these two dayes ! nay, all thys[8] two yere !
For all the sauours that may come here
Can be no worse ; for, at a worde,
One of the Seuen Slepers tróde in a torde.   533
    PEDLER.   Syr, me thynketh your deuocion is but smal.
    PARDONER.   Small ? mary, me thynketh he hath none at
        all !
    POTYCARY.   What the deuyll care I what ye thynke ?
Shall I prayse relykes when they stynke ?
    PARDONER.   Here is an eye-toth of the Great Turke :   538
Whose eyes be ones sette on thys pece of worke
May happely lese parte of his eye-syght,
But nat all[9] tyll he be blynde out-ryght.

---

[1] Coll. A. shall never be vext with.
[2] Coll. A. either.
[3] Coll. A. as much(e) as.
[4] M. Potycary.
[5] M. aswell.
[6] A. freend.
[7] A. this.
[8] Coll. A. these.
[9] Coll. *omits* all, *without note.*

POTYCARY.   What-so-euer any other man seeth,
I haue no deuocion [1] to [2] Turkes teeth ;   543
For, all-though I neuer sawe a greter,
Yet me thynketh I haue sene many better.
   PARDONER.   Here is a box full of humble-bees
That stonge Eue as she sat on her knees
Tastynge the frute to her forbydden :   548
Who kysseth the bees within this hydden
Shall haue as muche pardon, of ryght,
As for any relyke he kyst thys nyght.
   PALMER.   Syr, I wyll kysse them, with all my herte.
   POTYCARY.   Kysse them agayne, and take my parte,   553
For I am nat worthy, — nay, lette be,
Those bees that stonge Eue shall nat stynge me !
   PARDONER.   Good frendes, I haue ye[s]t[e] here in [3] thys glas,
Whiche on the drynke at the weddynge was
Of Adam and Eue vndoutedly ;   558
If ye honor this relyke deuoutly,
All-though ye thurste no whyt the lesse,
Yet shall ye drynke the more doutlesse, —
After whiche drynkynge ye shall be as mete
To stande on your hede as on your fete.   563
   POTYCARY.   Ye, mary, now I can [4] ye [5] thanke ;
In presents of thys the reste be blanke.
Wolde God this relyke had come rather !
Kysse that relyke well, good father !
Suche is the payne that ye palmers take   568
To kysse the pardon-bowle for the drynke sake.
O holy yeste, that loketh full sowr and stale,
For Goddes body helpe me to a cuppe of ale !
The more I be-holde [6] the, the more I thurste ;
The oftener I kysse the, more lyke to burste !   573
But syns I kysse the so deuoutely,
Hyre me, and helpe me with drynke till I dye !

---

[1] M. devacion; Coll. devocyon, *without note.*
[2] Coll. A. unto.   [4] Coll. A. con.   [6] A. see.
[3] A. *omits* here.   [5] Coll. you, *without note.*

What, so muche prayenge and so lytell spede?

PARDONER.   Ye, for God knoweth whan it is nede
To sende folkes drynke; but, by Saynt Antony,   578
I wene he hath sent you to muche all-redy.

POTYCARY.   If I haue neuer the more for the,
Then be the relykes no ryches to me,
Nor to thy-selfe, excepte they be
More benefycyall then I can se.   583
Rycher is one boxe of [t]his[1] tryacle
Then all thy relykes that do no myrakell.
If thou haddest prayed but halfe so muche to me
As I haue prayed to thy relykes and the,
Nothynge concernynge myne occupacion   588
But streyght shulde haue wrought in[2] operacyon.
And, as in value, I pas you an ace.
Here[3] lyeth muche rychesse in lytell space, —
I haue a boxe of rebarb here,
Whiche is as deynty as it is dere.   593
So[4] helpe me God and hollydam,
Of this I wolde nat geue a dram[5]
To the beste frende I haue in Englandes grounde
Though he wolde geue me xx pounde;
For, though the stomake do it abhor,   598
It pourget[h] you clene from the color,
And maketh your stomake sore to walter,
That ye shall neuer come to the halter.

PEDLER.   Then is that medycyn a souerayn thynge
To preserue a man from hangynge.   603

POTYCARY.   If ye wyll taste but thys crome that ye se,
If euer ye be hanged, neuer truste me!

---

[1] M. his; Coll. this, *without note.*

[2] Coll A. one.

[3] Coll. So here, *without note, cf.* l. 594.

[4] *In* Coll. So *is marked as "addition," upon which* Collier *himself remarks that his predecessors are mistaken, as the word is found in both
the old copies; of course, it is really* l. 591 *to which* so *was added (in con-
sequence of failure to understand the construction).*

[5] M. deam; *corr. silently by* Coll.

Here haue I diapompholicus, —
A speciall oyntement, as doctours discuse, —
For a fistela or a [1] canker   608
Thys oyntement is euen shot-anker,
For this medecyn [2] helpeth one and other,
Or bryngeth them in case that they nede no other.
Here is [3] syrapus de Byzansis, —
A lytell thynge is i-nough of this,   613
For euen the weyght of one scryppull [4]
Shall [5] make you stronge as [6] a cryppull.
Here be [7] other: as, diosfialios,
Diagalanga, and sticados,
Blanka manna, diospoliticon,   618
Mercury sublyme, and metridaticon,
Pelitory,[8] and arsefetita,
Cassy, and colloquintita.
These be [9] the thynges that breke all stryfe
Betwene mannes sycknes and his lyfe;   623
From all payne these shall you deleuer,
And set you euen at reste for-euer.
Here is a medecyn — no mo lyke the same! —
Whiche comenly is called thus by name:
Alikakabus or alkakengy, —   628
A goodly thynge for dogges that be [10] mangy.
Suche be these medycynes that I can
Helpe a dogge as well as a man.
Nat one thynge here partycularly
But worketh vniuersally,   633
For it doth me as muche good when I sell it
As all the byers that taste it or smell it.
Now, syns my medecyns be so specyall,
And in [11] operacion so generall,

---

[1] Coll. or for a, *without note.*
[2] A. oyntment.
[3] Coll. is a, *without note.*
[4] Coll. scryppall.
[5] A. Wil.
[6] Coll. as stronge as, *without note.*
[7] Coll. are, *without note.*
[8] Coll. Pellitory, *without note.*
[9] A. are.   [10] A. are.
[11] Coll. in one, *without note.*

And redy to worke when-so-euer they shall,   638
So that in ryches I am principall,
If any rewarde may entreat ye,
I besech your mashyp [1] be good to [2] me,
And ye shall haue a boxe of marmelade
So fyne that ye may dyg it with a spade.   643
    PEDLER.   Syr, I thanke you, but your rewarde
Is nat the thynge that I regarde;
I muste and wyll be indifferent:
Wherfore procede in your intente.
    POTYCARY.   Nowe, yf I wyst thys wysh no synne,   648
I wolde to God I myght begynne!
    PARDONER.   I am content that thou lye fyrste.
    PALMER.   Euen so am I; and [3] say thy worste!
Now let vs here of all thy lyes
The greatest lye thou mayst deuyse,   653
And in the fewyst wordes thou can.
    POTYCARY.   Forsoth, ye be [4] an honest man.
    PALMER.[5]   There sayde ye muche, but yet no lye.
    PARDONER.   Now lye ye bothe, by Our Lady!
Thou lyest in bost of hys honestie,   658
And he hath lyed in affyrmynge the.
    POTYCARY.   Yf we both lye and ye say true,
Then of these lyes your parte adew!
And yf ye wyn, make none auaunt;
For ye [6] are sure of one yll seruaunte.   663
[To Palmer]   Ye [6] may perceyue by the wordes he gaue
He taketh your mashyp but for a knaue. —
But who tolde true [7] or lyed in-dede,
That wyll I knowe or [8] we procede:
Syr, after that I fyrste began   668
To prayse you for an honest man,

---

[1] Coll. masshyp.   [3] Coll. A. now.
[2] A. unto.   [4] A. you are.
  [5] Coll., *followed by* Haz., *silently transfers this speech to the Pedler; but*
ll. 669–674 *confirm* M.   [7] Coll. A. truthe.
  [6] Coll. you, *without note.*   [8] A. ere.

When ye affyrmed it for no lye, — [1]
Now, by our [2] fayth, speke euen truely, —
Thought ye your affyrmacion true?

PALMER. Ye, mary, I ! [3] for I wolde ye knewe   673
I thynke my-selfe an honest man.

POTYCARY. What thought ye in the contrary than?

PARDONER. In that I sayde the contrary,
I thynke from trouth I dyd nat vary.

POTYCARY. And what of my wordes?

PARDONER.   I thought ye lyed.   678

POTYCARY. And so thought I, by God that dyed !
Nowe haue you twayne eche for hym-selfe layde
That none [4] hath lyed ou[gh]t [5] but both truesayd ;
And of vs twayne none hath denyed,
But both affyrmed, that I haue lyed :   683
Now syns [ye] both your [6] trouth confes,
And that we both my lye so witnes
That twayne of vs thre in one agree, — [7]
And that the lyer the wynner must be, —
Who coulde prouyde suche euydens   688
As I haue done in this pretens?
Me thynketh this mater sufficient
To cause you to gyue iudgement
And to giue me the mastrye,
For ye perceyue these knaues can nat lye.   693

PALMER. Though nother [8] of vs as yet had lyed,
Yet what we can do is yntryed ;
For yet [9] we haue deuysed nothynge,

---

1 Collier's *note is confused, but I infer that* A. *has* for to lye.
2 Coll. A. your; *but* our *is possible.*
3 Coll. *omits* I, *without note.*   4 A. one.
5 M. out, *which is silently omitted by* Coll.
6 Coll. A. ye the.
7 Coll. A. (*apparently through failure to follow the* argument):

> How that I lyed, doo bear witnes.
> That twain of us may soon agree,

8 Coll. A. neyther.   9 Coll. For as yet, *without note.*

But answered you and geuen [1] hyrynge.

PEDLER.   Therfore I haue deuysed one waye   698
Wherby all thre your myndes may saye :
For eche of you one tale shall tell,
And whiche of you telleth most meruell
And most vnlyke [2] to be true,
Shall most preuayle, what-euer ensew.   703

POTYCARY.   If ye be set in [3] mervalynge,
Then shall ye here a meruaylouse thynge,
And though, in-dede, all be nat true,
Yet suer the most parte shall be new.
I dyd a cure no lenger [4] a-go   708
But [5] *Anno Domini millesimo*
On a woman yonge and so fayre
That neuer haue I sene a gayre.
God saue all women from [6] that lyknes !
This wanton had the fallen-syknes, —   713
Whiche by dissent came lynyally,
For her mother had it naturally ;
Wherfore, this woman to recure
It was more harde ye may be sure.
But, though I boste my crafte is suche   718
That in suche thynges I can do muche,
How ofte she fell were muche to reporte ;
But her hed so gydy and her helys so shorte
That, with the twynglynge of an eye,
Downe wolde she falle euyn by-and-by.   723
But, or [7] she wolde aryse agayne,
I shewed muche practyse muche to my payne ;
For the tallest man within this towne
Shulde [8] nat with ease haue broken her sowne. [9]
All-though for lyfe I dyd nat doute her,   728
Yet dyd I take more payne [10] about her

[1] Coll. geven you, *without note.*
[2] Coll. A. unlikest.
[3] Coll. on, *without note.*
[4] Coll. longer, *without note.*
[5] Coll. But in, *without note.*
[6] Coll. A. of.
[7] A. ere.
[8] Coll. A. Could.
[9] Coll. swowne, *without note.*
[10] Coll. A. paines.

Then I wolde take with my owne syster.
Syr, at the last I gaue her a glyster, —
I thrust a tampyon[1] in her tewell
And bad her kepe it for a iewell.

But I knewe[2] it so heuy[3] to cary   733
That I was sure[4] it wolde nat tary ;
For where gonpouder is ones fyerd
The tampyon[5] wyll no lenger be hyerd, —

Whiche was well sene in tyme of thys chaunce,   738
For, when I had charged this ordynaunce,
Sodeynly as it had thonderd,
Euen at a clap losed her bumberd.

Now marke, for here begynneth the reuell :
This tampion[6] flew x longe myle leuell.   743
To a fayre castell of lyme and stone, —
For strength I knowe nat suche a one, —
Whiche stode vpon an[7] hyll full hye
At fote wherof a ryuer ranne bye,
So depe, tyll chaunce had it forbyden,   748
Well myght the Regent there haue ryden.

But when this tampyon[8] on this castell lyght,[9]
It put the castels[10] so farre[11] to flyght
That downe they came eche vpon other,
No stone lefte standynge, by Goddes Mother !   753
But rolled downe so faste the hyll
In suche a nomber and so dyd fyll
From botom to bryme, from shore to shore,
Thys forsayd ryuer, so depe before,
That who lyste nowe to walke therto,   758
May wade it ouer and wet no shoo.
So was thys castell layd wyde open
That euery man myght se the token.

---

[1] M. Coll. thampyon.
[2] Coll. inserts there from A.
[3] Coll. it was to heevy, without note.
[4] Coll. sure was.
[5] Coll. Thampyon, without note.
[6] M. tampton ; Coll. thampion, without note.
[7] Coll. a, without note.
[8] Coll. thampyon, without note.
[9] Coll. A. at this castle did lyght.
[10] Coll. castel, without note.
[11] Qy. read stones for so farre.

But — in a good houre maye these wordes [1] be spoken! —
After the tampyon on the walles was wroken,　　　　763
And pece by pece in peces broken,
And she delyuered, with suche violens,
Of all her inconueniens,
I left her in good helth and luste;
And so she doth contynew, I truste!　　　　768
　　PEDLER.　Syr, in your cure I can nothynge tell,
But to our [2] purpose ye haue sayd well.
　　PARDONER.　Well, syr, then marke what I can say:
I haue ben a pardoner many a day,
And done greater [3] cures gostely　　　　773
Then euer he dyd bodely, —
Namely thys one whiche ye shall here,
Of one departed within thys seuen yere, —
A frende of myne, and lykewyse I
To her agayne was as frendly, —　　　　778
Who fell so syke so sodeynly
That dede she was euen by-and-by,
And neuer spake with preste nor clerke,
Nor had no whyt of thys holy warke.
For I was thens, it coulde nat be;　　　　783
Yet harde I say she asked for me.
But when I bethought me howe thys chaunced,
And that I haue to heuen auaunced
So many soules to me but straungers
And coude nat kepe my frende from daungers,　　　　788
But she to dy so daungerously,
For her soule helth especyally, —
That was the thynge that greued me soo
That nothynge coulde release my woo
Tyll I had tryed euen out of hande　　　　793
In what estate her soule dyd stande;
For whiche tryall, shorte tale to make,

---

[1] *It is impossible to tell from the note in* Coll. *whether* A. *has* **this wordes** *or* this word, — *apparently the former.*

[2] Coll. A. your.　　　　　　　[3] A. more.

I toke thys iourney for her sake, —
Geue eare, for here begynneth the story, —
From hens I went to purgatory,   798
And toke with me thys gere in my fyste,
Wherby I may do there what I lyste.
I knocked and was let in quyckly,
But, Lorde, how lowe the soules made curtesy!
And I to euery soule agayne   803
Dyd gyue a beck them to retayne,
And axed them thys question than :
Yf that the soule of suche a woman
Dyd late amonge them there appere.
Wherto they sayd she came nat here.   808
Then ferd I muche it was nat well ;
Alas, thought I, she is in hell!
For with her lyfe I was so acqueynted
That sure I thought she was nat saynted.
With thys it chaunced¹ me to snese ;   813
"Christe helpe!" quoth a soule that ley for his fees.
"Those wordes," quoth I, "thou shalt nat lees!"
Then with these pardons of all degrees
I payed hys tole, and set hym so quyght
That strayt to heuen he toke his flyght.   818
And I from thens to hell that nyght,
To help this woman yf I myght,
Nat as who sayth by authorite,
But by the waye of entreate.
And fyrst [to]² the deuyll that kept the gate   823
I came, and spake after this rate :
"All hayle, syr deuyll!" and made lowe curtesy.
"Welcome!" quoth he thys³ smillyngly.
He knew me well ; and I at laste
Remembred hym syns longe tyme paste,   828
For, as good happe wolde haue it chaunce,

---

¹ *Misprinted* channced *in* M.
² Coll. *inserts* to, *without note.*
³ Coll. A. thus.

Thys deuyll and I were of olde acqueyntaunce,
For oft in the play of Corpus Cristi
He had played the deuyll at Couentry.
By his acqueyntaunce and my behauoure   833
He shewed to me ryght frendly fauoure.
And, to make my returne the shorter,
I sayd to this deuyll : " Good mayster porter,
For all olde loue, yf it lye in your power,
Helpe me to speke with my lorde and your."   838
" Be sure," quoth he, " no tongue can tell
What tyme thou coudest haue come so well,
For [1] thys daye Lucyfer fell, —
Whiche is our festyuall in hell.
Nothynge vnreasonable craued thys day   843
That shall in hell haue any nay.
But yet be-ware thou come nat in
Tyll tyme thou may [2] thy pasporte wyn ;
Wherfore stande styll, and I wyll wyt
If I can get thy saue-condyt."   848
He taryed nat, but shortely gat it,
Under seale and the deuyls hande at it,
In ample wyse, as ye shall here, —
Thus it began : " Lucyfere,
By the power of God chyefe deuyll of hell,   853
To all the deuyls that there do dwell,
And euery of them, we sende gretynge,
Under streyght [3] charge and commaundynge,
That they aydynge and assystent be
To suche a pardoner, — and named [4] me, —   858
So that he may at lybertie
Passe saue without hys [5] ieopardy
Tyll that he be from vs extyncte
And clerely out of helles precincte ;
And, hys pardons to kepe sauegarde,[6]   863

1 Coll. A. For as on.   4 M. maned, *silently corr. by* Coll.
2 A. maist.   5 Coll. A. any.
3 M. streygyt ; *corr. silently by* Coll. 6 Coll. in savegarde, *without note.*

We wyll they lye in the porters warde.
Geuyn in the fornes of our palys,
In our hye courte of maters of malys,
Suche a day and yere of our reyne."
" God saue the deuyll!" quoth I, " for, for playne,[1]   868
I truste thys wrytynge to be sure."
" Then put thy truste," quoth he, " in euer,[2]
Syns thou art sure to take no harme."
Thys deuyll and I walket arme in arme
So farre tyll he had brought me thyther   873
Where all the deuyls of hell togyther
Stode in a-ray in suche apparell
As for that day there metely fell :
Theyr hornes well gylt, theyr clowes full clene,
Theyr taylles well kempt, and, as I wene,   878
With sothery butter theyr bodyes anoynted, —
I neuer sawe deuyls so well appoynted.
The mayster deuyll sat in his iacket,
And all the soules were playnge at racket.
None other rackettes they hadde in hande   883
Saue euery soule a good fyre-brande ;
Wherwith they played so pretely
That Lucyfer laughed merely,
And all the resedew of the fendes [3]
Dyd laugh full well togytther [4] lyke frendes.   888
But of my frende I sawe no whyt,
Nor durst nat axe for her as yet.
Anone all this rout was brought in silens,
And I by an vsher brought in presens.
Then to Lucyfer low as I coude [5]   893
I knelyd ; which he so well alowde

1 Coll. *follows* A. *in reading* quoth I amain, *and gives reading of* M. *as*
quoth I for playne.

2 A. cure, *possibly a misprint of* eure (= ure), *but perhaps a substitute*
for it.

3 M. frendes ; *corr. by* Coll., *from* A.

4 Coll. A. thereat ful wel.

5 Coll. A. : in presens Of Lucyfer : then lowe, as well as I could.

That thus he beckte and, by Saynt Antony,
He smyled on me well-fauoredly,
Bendynge hys browes, as brode as barne-durres,
Shakynge hys eares, as ruged as burres,   898
Rolynge hys yes, as rounde as two bushels,
Flastynge¹ the fyre out of his nose-thryls,
Gnashynge hys teeth so vaynglorousely
That me thought tyme to fall to flatery.
Wherwith I tolde, as I shall tell :   903
" O plesant pycture! O prince of hell,
Feurred² in fashyon abominable !
And syns that is inestimable
For me to prayse the worthyly,
I leue of prays, vnworthy³   908
To geue the prays, besechynge the
To heare my sewte and then to be
So good to graunt the thynge I craue ;
And, to be shorte, thys wolde I haue, —
The soule of one whiche hyther is flytted   913
Deliuered⁴ hens and to me remitted.
And in thys doynge, though al be nat quyt,
Yet some⁵ parte I shall⁶ deserue it ;
As thus, — I am a pardoner
And ouer soules as a controller,   918
Thorough-out the erth my power doth stande,
Where many a soule lyeth on my hande,
That spede in maters as I vse them,
As I receyue them or refuse them ;
Wherby, what tyme thy pleasure is,   923
Ye shall requyre⁷ any part of thys, —
The leste deuyll here that can come thyther

---

¹ *Qy*. Fnastynge, *or* Flashynge.   ⁴ A. Deliver.
² Coll. Feutred, *without note*.   ⁵ Coll. Yet in some, *without note*.
³ Coll. as unworthy, *without note*.   ⁶ A. wil.
⁷ M. I shall requyre ; Coll., I shall requyte, *with a note implying that his text contains* Ye, *but that he himself prefers* I. *He has no textual note on* requyte. *Any part of this seems to support my emendation rather than* Collier's.

Shall chose a soule and brynge hym hyther."

" Nowe,"[1] quoth the deuyll, " we are well pleased.

What is hys name thou woldest haue eased?" 928

" Nay," quoth I, " be it good or euyll,

My comynge is for a she-deuyll."

" What calste her? " quoth he, " thou horson ! "[2]

" Forsoth," quoth I, " Margery Coorson."

" Now, by our honour," sayd Lucyfer, 933

" No deuyll in hell shall witholde her ;

And yf thou woldest haue twenty mo,

Were[3] nat for iustyce, they shulde goo,

For all we[4] deuyls within thys den

Haue more to do with two women 938

Then with all the charge we haue besyde.

Wherfore, yf thou our frende wyll be tryed,

Aply thy pardons to women so

That vnto vs there come no mo."

To do my beste I promysed by othe ; 943

Whiche I haue kepte, for, as the fayth goth,

At these dayes[5] to heuen I do procure

Ten women to one man, be sure.

Then of Lucyfer my leue I toke,

And streyght vnto the mayster coke ; 948

I was hadde into the kechyn,

For Margaryes[6] offyce was ther-in.

All thynge[7] handled there discretely, —

For euery soule bereth offyce metely, —

Whiche[8] myght be sene to se her syt, 953

So bysely turnynge of the spyt ;

For many a spyt here hath she turned,

And many a good spyt hath she burned,

And many a spyt full hot[9] hath tosted[10]

---

[1] Coll A. Ho, ho.

[2] M. horyson ; Coll. A. whoorson.

[3] Coll. Wert, *without note.*

[4] A. the.

[5] M. thys dayes ; Coll. A. this day.

[6] Coll. Margerie's, *without note.*

[7] Coll. thyngs, *without note.*

[8] *Misprinted* woiche *in* Coll.

[9] M. Coll. hoth.

[10] Coll. rosted, *without note.*

Before the meat coulde be halfe rosted;   958
And, or [1] the meate were halfe rosted in-dede,
I toke her then fro the spyt for [2] spede.
But when she sawe thys brought to pas,
To tell the ioy wherin she was,
And of all the deuyls, for ioy how they   963
Dyd rore at her delyuery,
And how the cheynes in hell dyd rynge,
And how all the soules therin dyd synge,
And how we were brought to the gate,
And how we toke our leue therat, —   968
Be suer lacke of tyme sufferyth nat
To reherse the xx parte of that;
Wherfore, thys tale to conclude breuely,
Thys woman thanked me chyefly
That she was ryd of thys endles deth;   973
And so we departed on New-Market Heth.
And yf that any man do mynde her,
Who lyste to seke her there shall he fynde her!
    PEDLER.   Syr, ye haue sought her wonders [3] well,
And, where ye founde her, as ye tell,   978
To here the chaunce ye founde [4] in hell,
I fynde ye were in great parell.[5]
    PALMER.   His tale is all muche parellous,[6]
But parte is muche more meruaylous;
As where he sayde the deuyls complayne   983
That women put them to suche payne
By [7] theyr condicions so croked and crabbed,
Frowardly fashonde, so waywarde and wrabbed,[8]
So farre in deuision, and sturrynge suche stryfe,
That all the deuyls be wery of theyr lyfe.   988

---

[1] A. ere.
[2] Coll. with, *without note.*
[3] Coll. A. wunderous.
[4] Coll. A. had.
[5] Coll. A. peril.
[6] Coll. A. perilous.
[7] Coll. Be, *without note, though he entirely changes the construction of the passage.*
[8] *There is no occasion to correct the spelling to* rabid.

This [1] in effect he tolde for [2] trueth;
Wherby muche maruell [3] to me ensueth,
That women in hell suche shrewes can be
And here so gentyll, as farre as I se.
Yet haue I sene many a myle 993
And many a woman in the whyle, —
Nat one good cytye, towne, nor borough
In Cristendom but I haue ben th[o]rough, —
And this I wolde ye shulde vnderstande:
I haue sene women v hundred thousande 998

. . . .

And oft with them haue longe tyme taryed,[4]
Yet in all places where I haue ben,
Of all the women that I haue sene,
I neuer sawe nor knewe, in my consyens, 1003
Any one woman out of paciens.

POTYCARY.   By the masse, there is a great lye! [5]
PARDONER.   I neuer harde a greater, by Our Lady!
PEDLER.   A greater? nay, knowe ye any so great?
PALMER.   Syr, whether that I lose or get, 1008
For my parte iudgement shall be prayed.
PARDONER.   And I desyer as he hath sayd.
POTYCARY.   Procede, and ye shall be obeyed.
PEDLER.   Then shall nat iudgement be delayd:
Of all these thre, yf eche mannes tale 1013
In Poules [6] Churche-yarde were set on sale
In some mannes hande that hath the sleyghte,
He shulde sure sell these tales by weyght;
For, as they wey, so be they worth.
But whiche weyth beste, — to that now forth! 1018
Syr, all the tale that ye dyd tell
I bere in mynde; and yours as well;

---

1 A. thus.   2 A. of.
3 *Misprinted* muruell *in* M.
4 M. maryed (*or* matyed); Coll. A. taried; *a line has, as* Collier *suggests,*
probably been lost, — *perhaps:* Wives and widows, maids and married.
5 M. greatlye, *corr. silently by* Coll.   6 Coll. Poole's, *without note.*

And, as ye sawe the mater metely,
So lyed ye bothe well and discretely.
Yet were your lyes with the lest, truste me;   1023
[*To Potycary*]   For, yf ye had sayd ye had made fle
Ten tampyons out of ten womens tayles
Ten tymes ten myle to ten castels or iayles[1]
And fyll[2] ten ryuers ten tymes so depe
As ten of that whiche your castell stones dyde kepe,[3]—   1028
[*To Pardoner*]   Or yf ye ten tymes had bodely
Fet ten soules out of purgatory,
And ten tymes so many out of hell, —
Yet, by these ten bonnes, I could ryght well
Ten tymes sonner all that haue beleued   1033
Then the tenth parte of that he hath meued.

   POTYCARY.   Two knaues before i lacketh ii knaues of
     fyue;
Then one, and then one, and bothe knaues a-lyue;
Then two, and then two, and thre at a cast;
Thou knaue, and thou knaue, and thou knaue, at laste!   1038
Nay, knaue, yf ye try me by nomber,
I wyll as knauyshly you accomber.
Your mynde is all on your pryuy tythe,
For all in ten me thynketh your wit lythe.
Now ten tymes I beseche Hym that hye syttes   1043
Thy wyfes x commaundementes may serch thy v wittes;
Then ten of my tordes in ten of thy teth,
And ten of[4] thy nose, whiche euery man seth,
And twenty tymes ten this wyshe I wolde, —
That thou haddest ben hanged at ten yere olde,   1048
For thou goest about to make me a slaue, —
I wyll thou knowe yf I am a gentylman,[5] knaue!
And here is an other shall take my parte.

   PARDONER.   Nay, fyrste I be-shrew your knaues herte
Or I take parte in your knauery!   1053

---

[1] M. tayles; Coll. jayles, *without note.*   [4] Coll. on, *without note.*
[2] Coll. fild, *without note.*   [5] A. gentle.
[3] *These two words are cut off at the top.*

I wyll speke fayre, by Our¹ Lady!
Syr, I beseche your mashyp to be
As good as ye can² be to me.

    PEDLER.   I wolde be glade to do you good
And hym also, be he neuer so wood;   1058
But dout you nat I wyll now do
The thynge my consciens ledeth me to.
Both your tales I take farre impossyble³
Yet take I his fa[r]ther⁴ incredyble.
Nat only the thynge it-selfe alloweth it,   1063
But also the boldenes therof auoweth it,
I knowe nat where your tale to trye,⁵
Nor yours but in hell or purgatorye;
But hys boldnes hath faced a lye
That may be tryed euyn in thys companye: 1068
As, yf ye lyste, to take thys order, —
Amonge the women in thys border,
Take thre of the yongest and thre of the oldest,
Thre of the hotest and thre of the coldest,
Thre of the wysest and thre of the shrewdest,   1073
Thre of the chastest and thre of the lewdest,⁶
Thre of the lowest and thre of the hyest,
Thre of the farthest and thre of the nyest,
Thre of the fayrest and thre of the maddest,
Thre of the fowlest and thre of the saddest, —   1078
And when all these threes be had a-sonder,
Of eche thre two iustly by nomber
Shall be founde shrewes, excepte thys fall,
That ye hap to fynde them shrewes all.
Hym-selfe for trouth all this doth knowe,   1083
And oft hath tryed some of thys rowe;
And yet he swereth by his consciens
He neuer saw woman breke paciens.⁷

¹ Coll. A.; M. one.   ⁵ M. crye; *corr. silently by* Coll.
² A. you may.   ⁶ *This line supp. by* Coll. *from* A.
³ Coll. unpossyble, *without note.* ⁷ Coll. patiens, *without note.*
⁴ *Corr. by* Coll., *without note.*

Wherfore, consydered with true entente
Hys lye to be so euident,   1088
And to appere so euydently
That both you affyrmed it a ly,
And that my consciens so depely
So depe hath sought thys thynge to try,
And tryed it with mynde indyfferent,   1093
Thus I awarde, by way of iudgement,
Of all the lyes ye all haue spent
Hys lye to be most excellent.

    PALMER.   Syr, though ye [1] were bounde of equyte
To do as ye haue done to me,   1098
Yet do I thanke you of your payne,
And wyll requyte some parte agayne.

    PARDONER.   Mary, syr, ye can no les do
But thanke hym as muche as it cometh to;
And so wyll I do for my parte: 1103
Now a vengeaunce on thy knaues harte!
I neuer knewe pedler a iudge before
Nor neuer wyll truste pedlynge-knaue more!

    [He sees the Potycary curtesying about the Palmer.]

What doest thou there, thou horson nody?

    POTYCARY.   By the masse, lerne to make curtesy!   1108
Curtesy before, and curtesy behynde hym,
And then on eche syde, the deuyll blynde hym!
Nay, when I [2] haue it perfytly,
Ye shall haue the deuyll and all of curtesy!
But it is nat sone lerned, brother, [3]   1113
One knaue to make curtesy to another;
Yet, when I am angry, that is the worste,
I shall call my mayster knaue at the fyrste.

    PALMER.   Then wolde some mayster perhappes clowt ye,
But as for me ye nede nat doute ye;   1118
For I had leuer [4] be without ye

---

  [1] M. we; *corr. silently by* Coll.   [3] Coll. A. gentle brother.
  [2] Coll. A. ye.   [4] A. rather.

Then haue suche besynesse aboute ye.

PARDONER.   So helpe me God, so were ye better!
What shulde a begger be a ietter?
It were no whyt your honestie   1123
To haue vs twayne iet after ye.

POTYCARY.   Syr, be ye sure he telleth you true;
Yf we shulde wayte, thys wolde ensew:
It wolde be sayd, truste me at a worde,
Two knaues made [1] curtesy to a [2] thyrde.   1128

PEDLER.   Now, by my trouth, to speke my mynde, —
Syns, they be so loth to be assyned,[3]
To let them lose I thynke it beste,
And so shall ye lyue beste [4] in rest.

PALMER.   Syr, I am nat on them so fonde   1133
To compell them to kepe theyr bonde;
And, syns ye lyste nat to wayte on me,
I clerely of waytynge dyscharge ye.

PARDONER.   Mary, syr, I hertely thanke you.

POTYCARY.   And I lyke-wyse, I make God auowe.[5]   1138

PEDLER.   Now be ye all euyn as ye begoon;
No man hath loste nor no man hath woon.
Yet in the debate wherwith ye began,
By waye of aduyse I wyll speke as I can:
[To Palmer]   I do perceyue that pylgrymage   1143
Is chyefe [6] the thynge ye haue in vsage;
Wherto, in effecte, for loue of Chryst
Ye haue, or shulde haue, bene entyst;
And who so doth with suche entent,
Doth well declare hys tyme well spent;   1148
[To Pardoner]   And so do ye in your pretence,
If ye procure thus [7] indulgence
Unto your neyghbours charytably
For loue of them in God onely. —

---

[1] A. make.   [2] Coll. the, *without note.*
[3] Steevens *suggests* affyned, *but, as* Collier *points out,* assyned *is correct.*
[4] Coll. A. the better.   [6] A. cheefest.
[5] Coll. A. And likewise I, to God I vow.   [7] A. this.

All thys may be ryght well applyed 1153
To shew [1] you both well occupyed;
For, though ye walke nat bothe one waye,
Yet, walkynge thus, thys dare I saye:
That bothe your walkes come to one [2] ende.
And so for all that do pretende, 1158
By ayde of Goddes grace, to ensewe
Any maner kynde of vertue:
As, some great almyse for to gyue,
Some in wyllfull pouertie to lyue,
Some to make hye-wayes and suche other [3] warkes, 1163
And some to mayntayne prestes and clarkes
To synge and praye for soule[s] departed, —
These, with all other vertues well marked,
All-though they be of sondry kyndes,
Yet be they nat vsed with sondry myndes; 1168
But, as God only doth all those moue,
So euery man, onely for his loue,
With loue and dred obediently
Worketh in these vertues vnyformely.
Thus euery vertue, yf we lyste to scan, 1173
Is pleasaunt to God and thankfull to man;
And who that by grace of the Holy Goste
To any one vertue is moued moste, —
That man, by that grace, that one apply,
And therin serue God most plentyfully! [4] 1178
Yet nat that one so farre wyde to wreste,
So lykynge the same to myslyke the reste;
For who so wresteth hys worke is in vayne.
And euen in that case I perceyue you twayne, —
Lykynge your vertue in suche wyse 1183
That eche others vertue you do dyspyse.
Who walketh thys way for God wolde fynde hym,
The farther they seke hym, the farther behynde hym.
One kynde of vertue to dyspyse another

---

[1] M. shewell; *corr. by* Coll. *from* A.   [3] Coll. A. lyke.
[2] A. on.   [4] A. plenteously.

Is lyke as the syster myght hange the brother. 1188
  POTYCARY.   For fere lest suche parels to me myght fall,
I thanke God I vse no vertue at all!
  PEDLER.   That is of all the very worste waye;
For more harde it is, as I haue harde saye,
To begynne vertue where none is pretendyd 1193
Then, where it is begonne, the abuse to be mended.
How-be-it, ye be[1] nat all to begynne;
One syne of vertue ye are entred in:
As thys, I suppose ye dyd saye true,
In that ye sayd ye vse no vertue; 1198
In the whiche wordes I dare well reporte,
Ye are well be-loued[2] of all thys sorte,
By your raylynge here openly
At pardons and relyques so leudly.
  POTYCARY.   In that I thynke my faute nat great, 1203
For all that he hath I knowe conterfete.[3]
  PEDLER.   For his and all other that ye knowe fayned
Ye be nother[4] counceled nor constrayned
To any suche thynge in any suche case
To gyue any reuerence in any suche place; 1208
But where ye dout the truthe, nat knowynge,
Beleuynge the beste, good may be growynge, —
In iudgynge the beste, no harme at the leste,
In iudgynge the worste, no good at the beste.
But beste in these thynges it semeth to me 1213
To take[5] no iudgement vpon ye;
But, as the Churche doth iudge or take them,
So do ye receyue or forsake them;
And so, be sure,[6] ye can nat erre,
But may be a frutfull folower. 1218
  POTYCARY.   Go ye before and, as I am true man,
I wyll folow as faste as I can.

---

1 A. are.
2 Kittredge *suggests* beleued.
3 Coll. counterfete, *without note.*
4 Coll. A. not.
5 M. Coll. make.
6 Coll. be you sure, *without note.*

PARDONER.　And so wyll I, for he hath sayd so well,
Reason[1] wolde we shulde folowe hys counsell.　　　　1222

PALMER.　Then to our reason God gyue vs his grace,
　　That we may folowe with fayth so fermely
His commaundementes, that we may purchace
　　Hys loue, and so consequently
　　　To byleue hys Churche faste and faythfully;
So that we may, accordynge to his promyse,
Be kepte out of errour in any wyse.　　　　1229

And all that hath scapet [2] vs here by neglygence,
　　We clerely reuoke and forsake it.
To passe the tyme in thys without offence,
　　Was the cause why the maker dyd make it;
　　And so we humbly beseche you take [3] it;
Besechynge Our Lorde to prosper you all
In the fayth of hys Churche Vniuersall !　　　　1236

[1] *Smudged over in* M.　　　[2] A. escapte.　　　[3] Coll. you to take.

FINIS.

Imprynted at London in Fletestrete at the
sygne of the George by Wyllyam
Myddylton.·.

PART VI.

KYNGE JOHAN.

By JOHN BALE.

Printed from the edition by J. P. Collier (Camden Society, 1838). Punctuation, capitals, and arrangement of lines are, as usual, mine ; all other changes are indicated in the footnotes. The statements in regard to the readings of the MS. are, of course, derived from Collier's introduction and notes. Several additions to the play in Bale's own hand are pointed out as they occur, but it must be added that he seems to have corrected the whole play, cf. p. 530, n. 1. For an account of the play, see vol. III. of this book.[1a]

[*Dramatis Personae.*

KYNGE JOHAN.	PRYVAT WELTH.
YNGLOND.	DISSIMULACYON.
CLARGY.	RAYMUNDUS.
SEDYCYON.	SYMON OF SWYNSETT.
CYVYLE ORDER.	USURPYD POWER.
STEVYN LANGTON.	THE POPE.
COMMYNALTE.	INTERPRETOUR.
NOBYLYTE.	TREASON.
CARDYNALL PANDULPHUS.	VERYTE.
IMPERYALL MAJESTYE.]	

[*Enter Kynge Johan alone.*]

K. JOHAN.[1] To declare the powres and their force to
          enlarge,
     The Scripture of God doth flow in most abowndaunce ;
And of sophysters the cauteles to dyscharge,
     Bothe Peter and Pawle makyth plenteosse utterauns ;
     How that all pepell shuld shew there trew alegyauns

---

[1] *I have not followed* C. *in the abbreviation of the names of speakers.*

[1a] See Publisher's Note.

To ther lawfull kyng, Christ Jesu dothe consent,
 Whych to the hygh powres was ever obedyent.   7

To shew what I am, I thynke yt convenyent:
 Johan, Kyng of Ynglond, the cronyclys doth me call.
My granfather was an emp[er]owr excelent,
 My father a kyng by successyon lyneall,
 A kyng my brother, lyke as to hym ded fall,
Rychard Curdelyon they callyd hym in Fraunce,
Whych had over enymyes most fortynable chaunce.   14

By the wyll of God and his hygh ordynaunce,
 In Yerlond and Walys, in Angoye and Normandye,
In Ynglond also, I have had the governaunce;
 I have worne the crowne and wrowght vyctoryouslye,
 And now do purpose by practyse and by stodye
To reforme the lawes and sett men in good order,
That trew justyce may be had in every border.   21

     [Enter] Ynglond vidua.

[YNGL.] Than I trust yowr Grace wyll waye a poore
    wedowes cause,
Ungodly usyd, as ye shall know in short clause.
 K. JOHAN. Yea, that I wyll swere, yf yt be trew and just.
 YNGL. Lyke as yt beryth trewth, so lett yt be dyscust.   25
 K. JOHAN. Than, gentyll wydowe, tell me what the
    mater ys.
 YNGL. Alas, yowr clargy hath done very sore amys
In mysusyng me ageynst all ryght and justyce,
And for my more greffe therto they other intyce.
 K. JOHAN. Whom do they intyce for to do the injurye?   30
 YNGL. Soch as hath enterd by false hypocrysye,
Moch worse frutes havyng than hathe the thornes unplesaunt,
For they are the trees that God dyd never plant,
And, as Christ dothe saye, blynd leaders of the blynd.
 K. JOHAN. Tell me whom thou menyst, to satysfy my
    mynd.   35

YNGL.   Suche lubbers as hath dysgysed heads in their
       hoodes,
Whych in ydelnes do lyve by other menns goodes, —
Monkes, chanons and nones, in dyvers coloure and shappe,
Bothe whyght, blacke and pyed, God send ther increase yll
       happe!
K. JOHAN.   Lete me know thy name or I go ferther with
       the.   40
YNGL.   Ynglond, syr, Ynglond my name is ; ye may trust me.
K. JOHAN.   I mervell ryght sore how thow commyst
       chaungyd thus.

[Enter] Sedwsyon.

[SED.]   What, yow ij alone ? I wyll tell tales, by Jesus!
And saye that I se yow fall here to bycherye.
K. JOHAN.   Avoyd, lewde person, for thy wordes are un-
       godlye.   45
SED.   I crye you mercy, sur, pray yow be not angrye ;
Be me fayth and trowth, I came hyther to be merye.
K. JOHAN.   Thou canst with thy myrth in no wysse
       dyscontent me,
So that thow powder yt with wysdome and honeste.
SED.   I am no spycer, by the messe! ye may beleve me.   50
K. JOHAN.   I speke of no spyce, but of cyvyle honeste.
SED.   Ye spake of powder, by the Holy Trynyte!
K. JOHAN.   Not as thow takyst yt, of a grosse capasyte,
But as Seynt Pawle meanyth unto the Collossyans[1] playne :
" So seasyne yowr speche, that yt be withowt disdayne."   55
Now, Ynglond, to the : go thow forth with thy tale,
And showe the cawse why thow lokyst so wan and pale.
YNGL.   I told yow before the faulte was in the clergye
That I, a wedow, apere to yow so barelye.
SED.   Ye are a Wylly Wat, and wander here full warelye !   60
K. JOHAN.   Why in the clargye? do me to understande!
YNGL.   For they take from me my cattell, howse and land,
My wods and pasturs, with other commodyteys,

               [1] C. Collessyans.

Lyke as Christ ded saye to the wyckyd Pharyseys :
" Pore wydowys howsys ye grosse up by long prayers," —   65
In syde cotys wandryng lyke most dysgysed players.

    SED.   They are well at ese that hath soch soth-sayers !

    K. JOHAN.   They are thy chylderne, thou owghtest to say
        then[1] good.

    YNGL.   Nay, bastardes they are, unnaturall, by the rood !
Sens ther begynnyng they ware never good to me.   70
The wyld bore of Rome, — God let hym never to thee ! —
Lyke pygges they folow in fantysyes, dreames and lyes,
And ever are fed with hys vyle cerymonyes.

    SED.   Nay, sumtyme they eate bothe flawnes and pygyn-
        pyes.

    K. JOHAN.   By the bore of Rome, I trow, thou menyst
        the Pope.   75

    YNGL.   I mene non other but hym, God geve hym a rope !

    K. JOHAN.   And why dost thow thus compare hym to a
        swyne?

    YNGL.   For that he and hys to such bestlynes inclyne ;
They forsake Gods word, whych is most puer and cleane,
And unto the lawys of synfull men they leane ;   80
Lyke as the vyle swyne the most vyle metes dessyer
And hath gret plesure to walowe them-selvys in myre,
So hath this wyld bore with his Church Unyversall,
His sowe with hyr pygys, and monstres[2] bestyall,
Dylyght in mennys draffe and covytus lucre all ;   85
Yea, *aper de sylva* the prophet dyd hym call.

    SED.   Hold yowr peace, ye whore, or ellys, by masse, I
        trowe,
I shall cawse the Pope to curse the as blacke as a crowe.

    K. JOHAN.   What art thow, felow, that seme so braggyng
        bolde?

    SED.   I am Sedycyon, that with the Pope wyll hold   90
So long as I have a hole within my breche.

    YNGL.   Command this felow to avoyd, I you beseche,
For dowghtles he hath done me great injury.

---

    [1] *Qy.* them.   [2] C. monstros.

K. JOHAN. A-voyd, lewd felow, or thou shalt rewe yt
truly!

SED. I wyll not a-waye for that same wedred wytche; 95
She shall rather kysse where-as it doth not ytche.
Quodcunque ligaveris, I trow, wyll playe soch a parte,
That I shall abyde in Ynglond, magry yowr harte.
Tushe, the Pope ableth me to subdewe bothe kyng and
keyser.

K. JOHAN. Off that thow and I wyll common more at
leyser. 100

YNGL. Trwly of the devyll they are that do ony thyng
To the subdewyng of any Christen kyng;
For, be he good or bade, he is of Godes apoyntyng;
The good for the good, the badde ys for yll doyng.

K. JOHAN. Of that we shall talke here-after: say forth
thy mynd now, 105
And show me how thou art thus be-cum a wedowe.

YNGL. Thes vyle popych swyne hath clene exyled my
hosband.

K. JOHAN. Who ys thy husbond? Tel me,[1] good gentyll
Ynglond.

YNGL. For soth, God hym-selfe, the spowse of every sort
That seke hym in fayth to the sowlys helth and comfort. 110

SED. He is scant honest that so many wyfes wyll have.

K. JOHAN. I˙saye, hold yowr peace, and stand asyde lyke
a knave!
Ys God exylyd owt of this regyon? Tell me.

YNGL. Yea, that he is, ser, yt is the much more pete.

K. JOHAN. How commyth yt to passe that he is thus
abusyd? 115

YNGL. Ye know he abydyth not where his word ys re-
fusyd;
For God is his word, lyke as Seynt John dothe tell
In the begynnyng of his moste blyssyd gospell.
The Popys pyggys may not abyd this word to be hard,
Nor knowyn of pepyll, or had in anye regard: 120

---

[1] C. telme.

Ther eyes are so sore they may not abyd the lyght,
And that bred so hard ther gald gummes may yt not byght.
I, knowyng yowr Grace to have here the governance
By the gyft of God, do knowlege my allegeance,
Desyeryng yowr Grace to waye suche injuryes   125
As I daylye suffer by thes same subtyll spyes,
And lett me have ryght, as ye are a ryghtfull kyng
Apoyntyd of God to have such mater in doyng;
For God wyllyth yow to helpe the pore wydowes cause,
As he by Esaye protesteth in this same clause: 130
Querite judicium, subvenite oppresso,
Judicate pupillo, defendite viduam:
Seke ryght to poore,[1] to the weake and fat[h]erlesse,
Defende the wydowe whan she is in dystresse.
    SED.   I tell ye, the woman ys in great hevynes.   135
    K. JOHAN.   I may not in nowyse leve thi ryght undyscuste,
For God hath sett me by his apoyntment just
To further thy cause, to mayntayne thi ryght,
And therfor I wyll supporte the daye and nyght;
So long as my symple lyffe shall here indewer   140
I wyll se the haue no wrong, be fast and swer.
I wyll fyrst of all call my nobylyte,
Dwkis, erlyes and lords, yche one in ther degre;
Next them the clargy, or fathers spirituall,
Archebysshopes, bysshoppes, abbottes, and pryers all;   145
Than the great juges and lawers every-chone,
So opyny[n]g to them thi cause and petyfull mone,
By the meanys wherof I shall their myndes vnderstande.
Yf they helpe the not, my-selfe wyll take yt in hande,
And sett such a waye as shall be to thi comforte.   150
    YNGL.   Than, for an answere I wyll shortly ageyne resort.
    K. JOHAN.   Do, Ynglond, hardly, and thow shalt have
        remedy.
    YNGL.   God reward yowr Grace, I beseche hym hartely,
And send yow longe dayes to governe this realme in peace!

---

[1] C. *suggests* procure, *but remarks that* Bale *did not make the change,*
although he inserted a *in* weake *in the same line.*

K. JOHAN. Gramercy, Ynglond! and send the plentyus
    increse!   155

Go owt Ynglond, and drese for Clargy.

SED. Of bablyng-matters, I trow, yt is tyme to cease.

K. JOHAN. Why dost thow call them bablyng-maters?
    Tell me.

SED. For they are not worth the shakyng of a per-tre[1]
Whan the peres are gone; they are but dyble-dable.
I marvell ye can abyd suche byble-bable.   160

K. JOHAN. Thow semyst to be a man of symple dys-
    crescyon.

SED. Alas, that ye are not a pryst to here confessyon!

K. JOHAN. Why for confessyon? Lett me know thi fan-
    tasye.

SED. Becawse that ye are a man so full of mercye,
Namely to women, that wepe with a hevy harte   165
Whan they in the churche hath lett but a lytyl farte.

K. JOHAN. I perseyve well now thow speakyst all this in
    mockage,
Becawse I take parte with Englandes ryghtfull herytage.
Say thu what thow wylt, her maters shall not peryshe.

SED. Yt is joye of hym that women so can cheryshe.   170

K. JOHAN. God hathe me ordeynned in this same princely
    estate,
For that I shuld helpe such as be desolate.

SED. Yt is as great pyte to se a woman wepe
As yt is to se a sely dodman crepe,
Or, as ye wold say, a sely goose go barefote.   175

K. JOHAN. Thou semyste by thy wordes to have no more
    wytt than a coote.
I mervell thou arte to Englond so unnaturall,
Beyng her owne chyld: thou art worse than a best brutall.

SED. I am not her chyld! I defye hyr, by the messe!
I her sone, quoth he? I had rather she were hedlesse.   180
Thowgh I sumtyme be in Englond for my pastaunce,

---

[1] C. pertre.

Yet was I neyther borne here, in Spayne, nor in Fraunce,
But under the Pope in the holy cyte of Rome,
And there wyll I dwell unto the daye of dome.

K. JOHAN.　But what is thy name?　Tell me yett onys
　　　　agayne.　　　　　　　　　　　　　　　185

SED.　As I sayd afore, I am Sedycyon playne:
In euery relygyon and munkysh secte I rayne,
Havyng yow prynces in scorne, hate and dysdayne.

K. JOHAN.　I pray the, good frynd, tell me what ys thy
　　　　facyon.

SED.　Serche and ye shall fynd in euery congregacyon　190·
That long to the Pope, for they are to me full swer,
And wyll be so long as they last and endwer.

K. JOHAN.　Yff thow be a cloysterer, tell of what order
　　　　thow art.

SED.　In euery estate of the clargye I playe a part:
Sumtyme I can be a monke in a long syd cowle;　　　195
Sumtyme I can be a none and loke lyke an owle;
Sumtyme a chanon in a syrples fayer and whyght;
A chapterhowse monke sumtyme I apere in syght;
I am ower Syre John sumtyme, with a new-shaven crowne;
Sumtyme the person, and swepe the stretes with a syd gowne; 200
Sumtyme the bysshoppe with a myter and a cope;
A graye fryer sumtyme with cutt shoes and a rope;
Sumtyme I can playe the whyght monke, sumtyme the fryer,
The purgatory prist, and euery mans wyffe desyer.
This cumpany hath provyded for me morttmayne,　　　205
For that I myght ever among ther sort remayne.
Yea, to go farder, sumtyme I am a cardynall;
Yea, sumtyme a pope and than am I lord over all,
Bothe in hevyn and erthe and also in purgatory,
And do weare iij crownes whan I am in my glorye.　　　210

K. JOHAN.　But what doeste thow here in England?　Tell
　　　　me shortlye.

SED.　I hold upp the Pope, as in other places many,
For his ambassador I am contynwally,
In Sycell, in Naples, in Venys and Ytalye,

In Pole, Spruse, and Berne, in Denmarke and Lumbardye,   215
In Aragon, in Spayne, in Fraunce and in Germanye,
In Ynglond, in Scotlond, and in other regyons elles;
For his holy cawse I mayntayne traytors and rebelles,
That no prince can have his peples obedyence
Except yt doth stond with the Popes prehemynence.   220

 K. JOHAN. Gett the hence, thow knave, and moste pre-
  sumptuows wreche,
Or, as I am trew kyng, thow shalt an halter streche!
We wyll thow know yt, owr power ys of God,
And therfore we wyll so execute the rod
That no lewde pryst shall be able to mayneteyne the.   225
I se now they be at to mych lyberte;
We wyll short ther hornys, yf God send tyme and space!

 SED. Than I in Englond am lyke to have no place?
 K. JOHAN. No, that thow arte not, and therfor avoyd
  apace!
 SED. By the holy masse, I must lawgh to here yowr
  Grace!   230
Ye suppose and thynke that ye cowd me subdewe;
Ye shall never fynd yowr supposycyon trewe,
Thowgh ye wer as strong as Hector and Diomedes,
Or as valyant as ever was Achylles.
Ye are well content that bysshoppes contynew styll?   235

 K. JOHAN. We are so, in-dede, yf they ther dewte fullfyll.
 SED. Nay than, good inowgh! Yowr awtoryte and power
Shall passe as they wyll; they have sawce bothe swet and
  sower.
 K. JOHAN. What menyst thow by that? shew me thy
  intente this hower.
 SED. They are Godes vycars, they can both save and
  lose.   240
 K. JOHAN. Ah, thy meening ys that they maye a prynce
  depose.
 SED. By the rood, they may, and that wyll appere by yow!
 K. JOHAN. Be the helpe of God, we shall se to that well
  inow.

SED. Nay, ye can not, thowgh ye had Argus eyes,
In abbeyes they haue so many suttyll spyes;   245
For ones in the yere they have secret vysytacyons,
And yf ony prynce reforme ther ungodly facyons,
Than ij of the monkes must forthe to Rome by-and-by
With secrett letters to avenge ther injury.
For a thowsand pownd they shrynke not in soch matter,   250
And yet for the tyme the prynce to his face they flater.
I am ever-more ther gyde and ther advocate.

K. JOHAN. Than with the bysshoppes and monkes thu
    art checke-mate?

SED. I dwell among them and am one of ther sorte.

K. JOHAN. For thy sake they shall of me have but small
    comforte.   255
Loke, wher I fynd the, that place wyll I put downe.

SED. What yf ye do chance to fynd me in euery towne
Where-as is fownded any sect monastycall?

K. JOHAN. I pray God I synke yf I dystroye them not all!

SED. Well, yf ye so do, yett know I where to dwell.   260

K. JOHAN. Thow art not skoymose thy fantasy for to tell.

SED. Gesse! At a venture ye may chance the marke to
    hytt.

K. JOHAN. Thy falssed to shew, no man than thy selfe
    more fytt.

SED. Mary, in confessyon under-nethe *benedicite*.

K. JOHAN. Nay, tell yt agayne, that I may understond the. 265

SED. I say I can dwell, whan all other placys fayle me,
In ere-confessyon undernethe *benedicite;*
And whan I am there, the pryst may not bewray me.

K. JOHAN. Why, wyll ere-confesshon soch a secret traytor
    be?

SED. Whan all other fayle, he is so sure as stele.   270
Offend Holy Churche, and I warrant ye shall yt fele;
For by confessyon the Holy Father knoweth
Throw-owt all Christendom what to his Holynes growyth.

K. JOHAN. Oh, where ys Nobylyte, that he myght knowe
    thys falshed?

SED. Nay, he is becum a mayntener of owr godhed.   275
I know that he wyll do Holy Chyrche no wronge,
For I am his gostly father and techear amonge.
He belevyth nothyng but as Holy Chyrch doth tell.

    K. JOHAN. Why, geveth he no credence to Cristes holy
        gospell?

    SED. No, ser, by the messe, but he callyth them here-
        tyckes   280
That preche the gospell, and sedycyows scysmatyckes,
He tache them, vex them, from prison to prison he turne them,
He indygth them, juge them, and, in conclusyon, he burne
them.

    K. JOHAN. We rewe to here this of owr nobylyte.
But in this be-halfe what seyst of the spretuallte?   285

    SED. Of this I am swer to them to be no stranger,
And spesyally, whan ther honor ys in dawnger.

    K. JOHAN. We trust owr lawers have no such wyckyd
        myndes.

    SED. Yes, they many tymys are my most secrett fryndes.
With faythfull prechers they can play leger-demayne,   290
And with falcʒe colores procure them to be slayne.

    K. JOHAN. I perseyve this worlde is full of iniquite.
As God wold have yt, here cummyth Nobylyte.

    SED. Doth he so in-dede? By Owr Lord, than wyll I
        hence!

    K. JOHAN. Thow saydest thu woldyst dwell where he
        kepyth resydence.   295

    SED. Yea, but fyrst of all I must chaunge myn apparell
Unto a bysshoppe, to maynetayene with my quarell,
To a monke or pryst, or to sum holy fryer;
I shuld never elles accomplych my dysyre.

    K. JOHAN. Why, art thow goyng? Naye, brother, thow
        shalte not hence.   300

    SED. I wold not be sene as I am for fortye pence.
Whan I am relygyouse, I wyll returne agayne.

    K. JOHAN. Thow shalt tary here, or I must put the to
        payne.

SED. I have a great mynd to be a lecherous man —
A wengonce take yt! I wold saye, a relygyous man. 305
I wyll go and cum so fast as evyr I can.

    K. JOHAN. Tush, dally not with me! I saye thow shalt
        abyde.

    SED. Wene yow to hold me that I shall not slyppe asyde?

    K. JOHAN. Make no more prattyng, for I saye thu shalt
        abyde.

    SED. Stoppe not my passage, I must over see at the next
        tyde! 310

    K. JOHAN. I will ordeyne so, I trowe, thow shalt not over.

    SED. Tush, tush, I am sewer of redy passage at Dover.

    K. JOHAN. The devyll go with hym! The unthryftye
        knave is gone.

Her go owt Sedwsion and drese for Syvyll Order. [*Enter Nobelyte.*]

    NOB. Troble not yowr-sylfe with no such dyssolute per-
        sone;

For ye knowe full well very lyttell honeste 315
Ys gote at ther handes in every commynnalte.

    K. JOHAN. This is but dallyaunce; ye do not speke as ye
        thynke.

    NOB. By my trowthe, I do, or elles I wold I shuld synke!

    K. JOHAN. Than must I marvell at yow of all men
        lyvynge.

    NOB. Why mervell at me? tell me yowr very menyng. 320

    K. JOHAN. For no man levynge is in more famylyerite
With that wycked wrech, yf it be trew that he told me.

    NOB. What wrech speke ye of? For Jesus love, inty-
        mate!

    K. JOHAN. ‘ Of that presumtous wrech that was with me
        here of late,

Whom yow wyllyd not to vexe my-selfe with-all. 325

    NOB. I know hym not, I, by the waye that my sowll to
        shall!

    K. JOHAN. Make yt not so strange, for ye know hym wyll
        inow.

NOB. Beleve me yff ye wyll! I know hym not, I assuer
    yow.

K. JOHAN. Ware ye never yett aquantyd with Sedission?

NOB. Syns I was a chyld, both hym and his condycyon   330
I ever hated for his iniquite.

[Enter Clargy.]

K. JOHAN. A clere tokyn that is of trew nobelyte;
But I pray to God we fynde yt not other-wyse.
Yt was never well syns the clargy wrowght by practyse,
And left the Scripture for mens ymagynacyons,   335
Dyvydyng them-selvys in so many congrygacyons
Of monkes, chanons and fryers, of dyvers colors and facyons.

THE CLARGY. I do trust yowr Grace wyll be as lovyng
    now
As yowr predysessowrs have bene to us before yow.

K. JOHAN. I wyll, suer, wey my love with yowr be-havers: 340
Lyke as ye deserve, so wyll I bere yow favers.
Clargy, marke yt well, I have more to yow to say
Than, as the sayeng is, the prest dyd speke a Sonday.

CLARGY. Ye wyll do us no wrong, I hope, nor injurye.

K. JOHAN. No, I wyll do you ryght in seyng yow do
    yowr dewtye.   345
We know the cawtelles of yowr sotyll companye.

CLARGY. Yf ye do us wrong, we shall seke remedy.

K. JOHAN. Yea, that is the cast of all yowr company.
Whan kynges correcte yow for yowr actes most ungodly,
To the Pope, syttyng in the chayer of pestoolens,   350
Ye ronne to remayne in yowr concupysens.
Thus sett ye at nowght all princely prehemynens,
Subdewyng the order of dew obedyens.
But with-in a whyle I shall so abate yowr pryde
That to yowr Pope ye shall noyther runne nor ryde,   355
But ye shall be glad to seke to me, yowr prynce,
For all such maters as shall be with-in this provynce,
Lyke as God wyllyth yow by his Scripture evydente.

NOB. To the Church, I trust, ye wyll be obedyent.

K. JOHAN.   No mater to yow whether I be so or no.   360
NOB.   Yes, mary, is yt, for I am sworne therunto.
I toke a great othe whan I was dubbyd a knyght
Ever to defend the Holy Churches ryght.
     CLARGY.   Yea, and in her quarell ye owght onto deth to
         fyght.
     K. JOHAN.   Lyke backes, in the darke ye always take
         yowr flyght,   365
Flytteryng in fanseys, and ever abhorre the lyght.
I rew yt in hart that yow, Nobelyte,
Shuld thus bynd yowr-selfe to the grett captyvyte
Of blody Babulon, the grownd and mother of whordom,
The Romych Churche I meane, more vyle than ever was
         Sodom,   370
And, to say the trewth, a mete spowse for the fynd.

           [*Enter Syvyll Order.*]

     CLARGY.   Yowr Grace is fare gonne; God send yow a
         better mynd!
     K. JOHAN.   Hold yowr peace, I say! ye are a lytyll to
         fatte;
In a whyle, I hope, ye shall be lener sumwhatte!
We shall loke to yow and to Sivyll Order also;   375
Ye walke not so secrett but we know wher-a-bowght ye goo.
     S. ORDER.   Why, yowr Grace hath no cawse with me to
         be dysplesyd.
     K. JOHAN.   All thyngs consyderyd, we have small cause
         to be plesyd.
     S. ORDER.   I besech yowr Grace to graunt me a word or
         too.
     K. JOHAN.   Speke on yowr pleasure, and yowr hole mynd
         also.   380

     S. ORDER.   Ye know very well, to set all thynges in order
         I have moche ado, and many thynges passe fro me,
For yowr common-welth, and that in euery border
         For offyces, for londes, for lawe and for lyberte,
         And for transgressors I appoynt the penalte;

That cytes and townes maye stand in quiotose peace,
That all theft and murder, with other vyce, maye seace.   387

Yff I have chaunsed, for want of cyrcumspeccyon,
    To passe the lymytes of ryght and equite,
I submyte my-selfe unto yowr Graces correccyon,
    Desyryng pardon of yowr benygnyte.
    I wot I maye fall throwgh my fragylyte;
Therfore I praye yow tell me what the mater ys,
And amends shall be where-as I have done amyse.   394

    K. JOHAN.   Aganste amendement no resonnable man can
        be.
    NOB.   That sentence rysyth owt of an hygh charyte.
    K. JOHAN.   Now that ye are here assembled all to-gether,
Amongeste other thynges ye shall fyrst of all consyder
That my dysplesure rebounyth [1] on-to yow all.
    CLARGY.   To yow non of us ys prejudycyall.   400
    K. JOHAN.   I shall prove yt. Yes! how have ye usyd
        Englond?
    NOB.   But as yt becommyth us, so fare as I understond.
    K. JOHAN.   Yes! the pore woman compląyneth her gre-
        vosly,
And not with-owt a cawse, for she hath great injurye.
I must se to yt, — ther ys no remedy, —   405
For it ys a charge gevyn me from God All-myghtye.
How saye ye, Clargye? Apperyth it not so to yow?
    CLARGY.   Yf it lykyth yowr Grace, all we know that well
        ynow.
    K. JOHAN.   Than yow, Nobelyte, wyll affyrme yt, I am
        suer.
    NOB.   Ye, that I wyll, sur, so long as my lyfe endure.   410
    K. JOHAN.   And yow, Cyvyll Order, I thynke wyll graunte
        the same!
    S. ORDER.   Ondowghted, sir; yea, elles ware yt to me gret
        shame.

---

[1] C. rebonnyth; Kittredge *suggests* redounyth, *but* rebounyth *is possible.*

K. JOHAN.   Than for Englondes cawse I wyll be sume-
   what playne.
Yt is yow, Clargy, that hathe her in dysdayne :
With yowr Latyne howrs, serymonyes, and popetly playes, 415
In her more and more Gods holy worde decayes ;
And them to maynteyn, unresonable ys the spoyle
Of her londs, her goods, and of her pore chylders toyle.
Rekyn fyrst yowr tythis, yowr devocyons and yowr offrynges,
Mortuaryes, pardons, bequests and other thynges, 420
Besydes that ye cache for halowed belles and purgatorye,
For juelles, for relyckes, confessyon and cowrts of baudrye,
For legacyes, trentalls, with Scalacely messys,
Wherby ye have made the people very assys ;
And over all this ye have browght in a rabyll 425
Of Latyne mummers and sects desseyvabyll,
Evyn to dewore her and eat her upp attonnys.
  CLARGY.   Yow wold have no Churche, I wene, by thes
    sacred bones!
  K. JOHAN.   Yes, I wold have a Churche, not of dysgysyd
    shavelynges,
But of faythfull hartes and charytable doynges ; 430
For whan Christes Chyrch was in her hyeste glory,
She knew neyther thes sectes nor their ipocrysy.
  CLARGY.   Yes, I wyll prove yt by David substancyally :
Astitit Regina a dextris tuis in vestitu
Deaurato, circumdata varietate : 435
A quene, sayth Davyd, on thy ryght hand, Lord, I se
Apparrellyd with golde and compassyd with dyversyte.
  K. JOHAN.   What ys yowr meanyng by that same Scrip-
    ture?   Tell me.
  CLARGY.   This quene ys the Chyrch, which thorow all
    Cristen regions
Ys beawtyfull, dectyd [1] with many holy relygyons : 440
Munks, chanons and fryers, most excellent dyvynis,
As Grandy Montensers and other Benedictyns,
Primostratensers, Bernards and Gylbertynys,

    [1] Kittredge *suggests* deccyd.

Jacobytes, Mynors, Whyght Carmes and Augustynis,
Sanbenets, Cluniackes, with holy Carthusyans,   445
Heremytes and ancors, with most myghty Rodyans,
Crucifers, Lucifers, Brigettis, Ambrosyanes,
Stellifers, Ensifers, with Purgatoryanes,
Sophyanes, Indianes and Camaldulensers,
Clarynes and Columbynes, Templers, Newe Ninivytes,   450
Rufyanes, Tercyanes, Lorytes and Lazarytes,
Hungaryes, Teutonykes, Hospitelers, Honofrynes,
Basyles and Bonhams, Solanons and Celestynes,
Paulynes, Hieronymytes, and Monkes of Josaphathes Valleye,
Fulygynes, Flamynes, with Bretherne of the Black Alleye,   455
Donates and Dimysynes, with Canons of S. Marke,
Vestals and monyals, a worlde to heare them barke,
Abbotts and doctors, with bysshoppes and cardynales,
Archedecons and pristes, as to ther fortune falles.

S. ORDER.   Me thynkyth yowr fyrst text stondeth nothyng
        with yowr reson,   460
For in Davydes tyme wer no such sects of relygyon.

K. JOHAN.   Davyd meanyth vertuys by the same diversyte,
As in the sayd psalme yt is evydent to se,
And not munkysh sects ; but it is ever yowr cast
For yowr advauncement the Scripturs for to wrast.   465

CLARGY.   Of owr Holy Father in this I take my grownd,
Which hathe awtoryte the Scripturs to expond.

K. JOHAN.   Nay, he presumyth the Scripturs to confownd.
Nowther thow nor the Pope shall do pore Englond wronge,
I beyng governor and kyng her peple amonge.   470
Whyle yow for lucre sett forth yowr popysh lawys
Yowr-selvys to advaunce, ye wold make us pycke strawes.
Nay, ipocryts, nay !   We wyll not be scornyd soo
Of a sort of knavys ; we shall loke yow otherwyse too !

NOB.   Sur, yowr sprytes are movyd, I persayve by yowr
        langage.   475

K. JOHAN.   I wonder that yow for such veyne popych bag-
        gage
Can suffyr Englond to be impoveryshyd

And mad a begger; yow are very yll advysyd.

 Nob. I marvell grettly that ye say thus to me.

 K. Johan. For dowghtles ye do not as becummyth

  Nobelyte;   480

Ye spare nouther lands nor goods, but all ye geve

To thes cormerants; yt wold any good man greve

To se yowr madnes, as I wold God shuld save me!

 Nob. Sur, I suppose yt good to bylde a perpetuite

For me and my frendes to be prayed for evermore. 485

 K. Johan. Tush, yt is madnes all to dyspayre in God so

  sore,

And to thynke Christs deth to be unsufficient!

 Nob. Sur, that I have don was of a good intent.

 K. Johan. The intente ys nowght whych hath no sewer

  grounde.

 Clargy. Yff yow continue, ye wyll Holy Chyrch con-

  funde.   490

 K. Johan. Nay, no Holy Chyrch, nor feythfull congre-

  gacyon,

But an hepe of adders of Antechrists generacyon.

 S. Order. Yt pyttyth me moche that ye are to them so

  harde.

 K. Johan. Yt petyeth me more that ye them so mych

  regarde.

They dystroye mennys sowlls with damnable supersticyon, 495

And decaye all realmys by meyntenaunce of sedycyon.

Ye wold wonder to know what profe I have of this.

 Nob. Well, amenment shalbe wher anythyng is amysse;

For, undowtted, God doth open soche thyngs to prynces

As to none other men in the Crystyen provynces, 500

And therfor we wyll not in this with yowr Grace contend.

 S. Order. No, but with Gods grace we shall owr myse-

  dedes amend.

 Clargy. For all such forfets as yowr pryncely Mageste

For yowr owne person or realme can prove by me

I submytte my-selfe to yow, bothe body and goods. 505

               Knele.

K. JOHAN.   We pety yow now, consyderyng yowr repent-
   ante modes,
And owr gracyous pardone we grawnte yow upon amendment.
   CLARGY.   God preserve yowr Grace and Mageste excelent!
K. JOHAN.   Aryse, Clargy, aryse, and ever be obedyent,
And, as God commandeth yow, take us for yowr governer.   510
   CLARGY.   By the grace of God, the Pope shall be my ruler!
K. JOHAN.   What saye ye, Clargy? who ys yowr governer?
   CLARGY.   Ha! ded I stomble?   I sayd my prynce ys my
   ruler.
K. JOHAN.   I pray to owr Lord this obedyence maye in-
   dewre.
   CLARGY.   I wyll not breke yt, ye may be fast and suer.   515
K. JOHAN.   Than cum hether all thre; ye shall know more
   of my mynde.
   CLARGY.   Owr kyng to obeye, the Scriptur doth us bynde.
K. JOHAN.   Ye shall fyrst be sworne to God and to the
   Crowne
To be trew and juste in every cetye and towne;
And this to performe set hand and kysse the bocke!   520
   S. ORDER.   With the wyffe of Loth we wyll not backe-
   ward locke,
Nor turne from owr oth, but ever obeye yowr Grace.
K. JOHAN.   Than wyll I gyve yow yowr chargys her in
   place,
And accepte yow all to be of owr hyghe councell.
   ALL THREE.   To be faythfull, than, ye us more streytly
   compell.   525
K. JOHAN.   For the love of God, loke to the state of
   Englond!
Leate non enemy holde her in myserable bond;
Se yow defend her as yt becummyth Nobilite;
Se yow instructe [1] her acordyng to yowr degre;
Fournysh her yow with a cyvyle honeste: 530
Thus shall she florysh in honor and grett plente.
With godly wysdom yowr matters so conveye

1 C. instrutte.

That the commynnalte the powers maye obeye,
And ever be ware of that false thefe Sedycyon,
Whych poysenneth all realmes and bryng them to perdycyon. 535
 Nob. Sur, for soche wrecches we wyll be so circumspecte
That neyther ther falsed nor gylle shall us infecte.
 Clargy. I warrant yow, sur, no, and that shall well apere.
 S. Order. We wyll so provyde, yff anye of them cum
  here
To dysturbe the realme, they shall be full glad to fle. 540
 K. Johan. Well, yowr promyse includeth no small dyffy-
  culte ;
But I put the case that this false thefe Sedycyon
Shuld cum to yow thre and call hym-selfe Relygyon,
Myght he not under the pretence of holynes
Cawse yow to consent to myche ungodlynes? 545
 Nob. He shall never be able to do yt, veryly.
 K. Johan. God graunt ye be not deceyvyd by hypocresye!
I say no more, I ; in shepes aparell sum walke
And seme relygeyose that deceyvably can calke.
Be ware of soche hypocrites as the kyngdom of hevyn fro man 550
Do hyde for a-wantage, for they deceyve now and than.
Well, I leve yow here ; yche man consyder his dewtye !
 Nob. With Gods leve, no faute shall be in this companye !
 K. Johan. Cum, Cyvyle Order, ye shall go hence with
  me.
 S. Order. At your commandmente ! I wyll gladlye
  wayte upon ye. 555

 Here Kyng Johan and Sivile Order go owt, and Syvile Order drese hym
 for Sedwsyon.

 Nob. Me thynke the kyng is a man of a wonderfull wytt.
 Clargy. Naye, saye that he, is of a vengeable craftye
  wytt,
Than shall ye be sure the trewth of the thyng to hytt.
Hard ye not how he of the Holy Church dyd rayle?
His extreme thretynyngs shall lytyll hym avayle : 560
I wyll worke soch wayes that he shall of his purpose fayle.
 Nob. Yt is meet a prince to saye sumwhat for his plesure.

CLARGY. Yea, but yt is to moch to rayle so withowt
mesure.

NOB. Well, lett every man speke lyke as he hathe a cawse.

CLARGY. Why, do ye say so? Yt is tyme for me, than,
to pawse. 565

NOB. This wyll I saye, sur, that he ys so noble a prynce
As this day raygneth in ony Cristyen provynce.

CLARGY. Mary, yt apereth well by that he wonne in
Fraunce!

NOB. Well, he lost not there so moche by martyall
chaunce

But he gate moche more in Scotland, Ireland and Wales. 570

CLARGY. Yea, God sped us well, Crystmes songes are
mery tales!

NOB. Ye dysdayne soche mater as ye know full evydent.
Are not both Ireland and Wales to hym obedyent?
Yes, he holdyth them bothe in pessable possessyon,
And—by-cause I wyll not from yowr tall make degressyon,— 775
For his lond in Fraunce he gyveth but lytell forsse,
Havyng to Englond all his love and remorse;
And Angoye he gave to Artur his nevy in chaunge.

CLARGY. Our changes are soche that an abbeye turneth
to a graunge.

We are so handled we have scarce eyther horse or male. 580

NOB. He that dothe hate me the worse wyll tell my tale![1]
Yt is yowr fassyon soche kyngs to dyscommend
As yowr abuses reforme or reprehend.
You pristes are the cawse that chronycles doth defame
So many prynces, and men of notable name, 585
For yow take upon yow to wryght them evermore;
And therfore Kyng Johan ys lyke to rewe yt sore,
Whan ye wryte his tyme, for vexyng of the Clargy.

CLARGY. I mervell ye take his parte so ernestlye.

NOB. Yt be-comyth Nobelyte his prynces fame to preserve. 590

CLARGY. Yf he contynew, we are lyke in a whyle to starve:

1 C. *suggests that this line belongs to Clergy.*

He demaundeth of us the tenth parte of owr lyvyng.

NOB.   I thynke yt is then for sum nessessary thyng.

CLARGY.   Mary, to recover that he hath lost in Fraunce,

As Normandy dewkedom, and his land beyond Orleaunce.   595

NOB.   And thynke ye not that a mater nessesary?

CLARGY.   No, sur, by my trowth, he takyng yt of the
   Clergy.

NOB.   Ye cowde be content that he shuld take yt of us.

CLARGY.   Yea, so that he wold spare the Clargy, by swet
   Jesus !

This takyng of us myght sone growe to a custom,   600

And than Holy Churche myght so be browght to thraldom,

Whych hath ben ever from temporall prynces free,

As towchyng trybute or other captyvyte.

NOB.   He that defendeth yow owght to have parte of yowr
   goodes.

CLARGY.   He hath the prayers of all them that hathe
   hoodes.   605

NOB.   Why, ys that inowgh to helpe hym in his warre?

CLARGY.   The Churche he may not of lyberte debarre.

NOB.   Ded not Crist hym-selfe pay trybutt unto Ceser?

Yf he payd trybute, so owght his holy vycar.

CLARGY.   To here ye reson so ondyscretlye, I wonder.   610

Ye must consyder that Crist that tyme was under,

But his vycar now ys above the prynces all ;

Therfor be ware ye do not to herysy fall.

Ye owght to beleve as Holy Chyrche doth teche yow,

And not to reason in soche hygh maters now.   615

NOB.   I am vnlernyd ; my wytts are sone confowndyd.

CLARGY.   Than leve soch maters to men more depely
   growndyd.

NOB.   But how wyll ye do for the othe that ye have take?

CLARGY.   The keyes of the Church can all soche maters
   of-shake.

NOB.   What call ye those keyes? I pray yow hartly, tell
   me!   620

CLARGY.   Owr Holy Fathers power and hys hygh autoryte.

Nob. Well, I can no more say; ye are to well lernyd
    for me.
My bysynes ys soche that here now I must leve ye.
    Clargy. I must hence also so fast as ever maye be,
To sewe vn-to Rome for the Churches lyberte.   625

Go owt Nobylyte and Clargy. Here Sedycyon cummyth in.

Sed. Haue in onys a-geyne, in spyght of all my enymyes!
For they cannot dryve me from all mennys companyes;
And, thowgh yt were so that all men wold forsake me,
Yet dowght I yt not but sume good women wold take me.
I loke for felowys that here shuld make sum sporte: 630
I mervell yt is so longe ere they hether resorte.
By the messe, I wene the knaves are in the bryers,
Or ells they are fallen into sum order of fryers!
Naye, shall I gesse ryght? they are gon into the stues;
I holde ye my necke, anon we shall here newes.   635

[He hears Dyssymulacyon] seyng the Leteny.[1]

Lyst, for Gods passyon! I trow her cummeth sum hoggherd
Callyng for his pygges. Such a noyse I neuer herd!

Here cum Dyssymulacyon syngyng of the letany.

Dys. (*syng*) *Sancte Dominice, ora pro nobis!*
Sed. (*syng*) Sancte pyld monache, I be-shrow *vobis!*
Dys. (*syng*) *Sancte Francisse, ora pro nobis!*   640
Sed. Here ye not? Cocks sowle, what meaneth this ypo-
    crite knaue?
Dys. *Pater noster*, I pray God bryng hym sone to his
    grave,
Qui es in celis, with an vengeable *sanctificetur*,
Or elles Holy Chyrche shall neuer thryve, by Saynt Peter!
    Sed. Tell me, good felowe, makyste thu this prayer for
    me?   645
    Dys. Ye are as ferce as thowgh ye had broke yowr nose
    at the buttre.

---

[1] C. *has only* Seyng the leteny.

I medyll not with the, but here to good sayntes I praye
Agenst soch enmyes as wyll Holy Chyrche decaye.

Here syng this:

A Johanne Rege iniquo, libera nos, Domine!

SED.   Leve, I saye! or, by messe, I wyll make yow
     grone!   650

DYS.   Yff thow be jentyll, I pray the leate me alone,
For with-in a whyle my devocyon wyll be gone.

SED.   And wherfor dost thou praye here so bytterly,
Momblyng thy pater noster and chauntyng the letany?

DYS.   For that Holy Chyrch myght save hyr patrymonye, 655
And to haue of Kyng Johan a tryumphant vyctorye.

SED.   And why of Kyng Johan? doth he vexe yow so
     sore?

DYS.   Both chyrchys and abbeys he oppressyth more and
     more
And take of the clergye, yt is onresonable to tell.

SED.   Owte with the Popys bulles than, and cursse hym
     downe to hell!   660

DYS.   Tushe! man, we haue done so, but all wyll not helpe:
He regardyth no more the Pope than he dothe a whelpe.

SED.   Well, lett hym alone; for that wyll I geve hym a
     scelpe.
But what arte thu callyd of thyn owne munkych nacyon?

DYS.   Kepe yt in counsell: Dane Davy Dyssymulacyon. 665

SED.   What, Dyssymulacyon? Coks sowle, myn old aquen-
     tence!

Par me faye, mon amye, je [suis] [1] *tote ad voutre plesaunce.*

DYS.   Gramercyes, good frend, with all my very hert!
I trust we shall talke more frely or we deperte.

SED.   Why, vylayn horson, knowyst not thi cosyn Sedy-
     cyon?   670

DYS.   I have ever loved both the and thy condycyon.

SED.   Thow must nedes, I trowe, for we cum of ij breth-
     erne;

[1] *Supplied by* C.

Yf thu remember, owr fathers were on mans chylderne,—
Thow comyst of Falsed and I of Prevy Treason.

DYS. Than Infydelyte owr granfather ys by reason. 675

SED. Mary, that ys trewe, and his begynner Antycrist,
The great Pope of Rome, or fyrst veyne popysh prist.

DYS. Now welcum, cosyn, by the waye that my sowle
shall to !

SED. Gramercy, cosyn, by the holy bysshope Benno!
Thow kepyst thi old wont, thow art styll an abbe-man. 680

DYS. To hold all thynges vp I play my part now and than.

SED. Why, what manere of offyce hast thu with-in the
abbey?

DYS. Of all relygyons I kepe the chyrch-dore keye.

SED. Than of a lykelyhod thow art ther generall porter?

DYS. Nay, of munks and chanons I am the suttyll sorter. 685
Whyle sum talke with Besse, the resydewe kepe sylence ;
Thowgh we playe the knavys, we must shew a good pretence ;
Where-so-ever sum eate, a serten kepe the froyter ;[1]
Where-so-ever sum slepe, sum must nedes kepe the dorter.
Dedyst·thu never know the maner of owr senyes? 690

SED. I was never with them aqueynted, by seynt Denyes.

DYS. Than never knewyst thu the knavery of owr menyes.
Yf I shuld tell all, I cowd saye more than that.

SED. Now, of good felowshyppe, I beseche the shew me
what.

DYS. The profytable lucre cummyth ever in by me. 695

SED. But by what meane? tell me, I hartely pray the.

DYS. To wynne the peple, I appoynt yche man his place :
Sum to syng Latyn, and sum to ducke at grace ;
Sum to go mummyng, and sum to beare the crosse ;
Sum to stowpe downeward as the[r] heades ware stopt with
mosse ; 700
Sum rede the epystle and gospell at hygh masse ;
Sum syng at the lectorne with long eares lyke an asse ;
The pawment of the chyrche the aunchent faders tredes,
Sum-tyme with a portas, sumtyme with a payre of bedes.

---

[1] *Qy*. freyter.

And this exedyngly drawt peple to devoycyone,　　　705
Specyally whan they do se so good relygeone.
Than have we imagys of Seynt Spryte and Seynt Savyer;
Moche is the sekynge of them to gett ther faver;
Yong whomen berfote, and olde men seke them brecheles.
The myracles wrought there I can in no wyse expresse.　　710
We lacke neyther golde nor sylwer, gyrdles nor rynges,
Candelles nor taperes, nor other customyd offerynges.
Thowgh I seme a shepe, I can play the suttle fox;
I can make Latten to bryng this gere to the boxe.
Tushe! Latten is alone to bryng soche mater to passe,　　715
There ys no Englyche that can soche slyghtes compasse;
And therfor we wyll no servyce to be songe,
Gospell nor pystell, but all in Latten tonge.
Of owr suttell dryftes many more poyntes are behynde;
Yf I tolde you all, we shuld never have an ende.　　720
　　　SED.　*In nomine Patris*, of all that ever I hard
Thow art alone yet of soche a dremyng bussard!
　　　DYS.　Nay, dowst thu not se how I in my colours jette?
To blynd the peple I have yet a farther fette:
This is for Bernard, and this is for Benet,　　725
This is for Gylbard, and this is for Jhenet,
For Frauncys this is, and this is for Domynyke,
For Awsten and Elen, and this is for Seynt Partryk.
We haue many rewlles, but never one we kepe;
Whan we syng full lowde our harts be fast aslepe.　　730
We resemble sayntes in gray, whyte, blacke, and blewe,
Yet vnto prynces not one of owr nomber trewe, —
And that shall Kyng Johan prove shortly, by the rode!
　　　SED.　But in the meane-tyme yowr-selves gett lytyll good;
Yowr abbeys go downe, I heresaye, every-where.　　735
　　　　DYS.　Yea, frynd Sedysyon, but thow must se to that
　　　　　　gere.
　　　　SED.　Than must I have helpe, by swete Saynt Benetts
　　　　　　cuppe!
　　　　DYS.　Thow shalt have a chylde of myn owne bryngyng
　　　　　　uppe.

SED. Of thy bryngyng uppe? Coks sowle, what knave
    is that?

DYS. Mary, Pryvat Welth ; now hayve I tolde the what. 740
I made hym a monke and a perfytt cloysterer,
And in the abbeye he began fyrst celerer,
Than pryor, than abbote of a thowsand pownd land, no wors,
Now he is a bysshoppe and rydeth with an hondryd hors,
And, as I here say, he is lyke to be a Cardynall. 745

SED. Ys he so in-dede? By the masse, than have att all!

DYS. Nay, fyrst Pryvat Welth shall bryng in Usurpyd
    Power
With hys autoryte, and than the gam ys ower.

SED. Tush, Usurpyd Power dothe faver me of all men,
For in his trobles I ease his hart now and then. 750
Whan prynces rebell agenste hys autoryte,
I make ther commons agenst them for to be.
Twenty M^d men are but a mornyng breckefast
To be slayne for hym, he takyng his repast.

DYS. Thow hast, I persayve, a very suttyll cast. 755

SED. I am for the Pope, as for the shyppe the mast.

DYS. Than helpe, Sedycyon, I may styll in Englond be!
Kyng John hath thretned that I shall ouer see.

SED. Well, yf thow wylte of me have remedy this ower,
Go seche Pryvat Welth and also Usurpyd Power. 760

DYS. I can bryng but one, be Mary, Jesus mother!

SED. Bryng thow in the one, and let hym bryng in the
    other.

Here cum in Usurpyd Power and Private Welth, syngyng on after another.

Usurpyd Power syng this :

Super flumina Babilonis suspendimus organa nostra.

Private Welth syng this :

Quomodo cantabimus canticum bonum in terra aliena ?

SED. By the mas, me thynke they are syngyng of *placebo !*

DYS. Peace, for with my spectables *vadam et videbo !*
Coks sowll, yt is they! At the last I have smellyd them owt.

Her go and bryng them.

SED.   Thow mayst be a sowe, yf thou hast so good a snowt. 768

Surs, marke well this gere, for now yt begynnyth to worke :
    False Dyssymulacion doth bryng in Privat Welth ;
And Usurpyd Power, which is more ferce than a Turke,
    Cummeth in by hym to decaye all spyrytuall helth ;
    Than I by them bothe, as clere experyence telth ;
We iiij by owr crafts Kyng Johan wyll so subdwe,
That for iij C yers all Englond shall yt rewe.   775

    DYS.   Of the clergy, frynds, report lyke as ye se,
That ther Privat Welth cummyth ever in by me.
    SED.   But by whom commyst thu?   By the messe, evyn
      by the devyll,
For the grownd thow art of the Cristen peplys evyll !
    DYS.   And what are yow, ser?   I pray yow say good by
      me.   780
    SED.   By my trowth, I cum by the and thy affynyte.
    DYS.   Feche thow in thy felow so fast as ever thow can.
    PR. WELTH.   I trow thow shalt se me now playe the
      praty man.
Of me, Privat Welth, cam fyrst Usurpyd Power :
Ye may perseyve yt in pagent here this hower.   785
    SED.   Now welcum, felowys, by all thes bonys and naylys !
    US. POWER.   Among companyons good felyshyp never
      faylys.
    SED.   Nay, Usurpid Power, thu must go backe ageyne,
For I must also put the to a lytyll payne.
    US. POWER.   Why, fellaue Sedysyon, what wylt thu have
      me do?   790
    SED.   To bare me on thi backe and bryng me in also,
That yt may be sayde that, fyrst, Dyssymulacion
Browght in Privat Welth to every Cristen nacion,
And that Privat Welth browght in Usurpid Power,
And he Sedycyon, in cytye, towne and tower ;   795
That sum man may know the feche of all owr sorte.
    US. POWER.   Cum on thy wayes than, that thou mayst
      make the fort.

Dys. Nay, Usurped Power, we shall bare hym all thre,
Thy-selfe, he and I, yf ye wyll be rewlyd by me,
For ther is non of us but in hym hath a stroke. 800
   Pr. Welth. The horson knave wayeth and yt were a
    croked oke.

Here they shall bare hym in, and Sedycyon saythe :

Sed. Yea, thus it shuld be, mary, now thu art [1] alofte!
I wyll be-shyte yow all yf ye sett me not downe softe.
In my opynyon, by swete Saynt Antony,
Here is now gatheryd a full honest company : 805
Here is nowther Awsten, Ambrose, Hierom nor Gregory,
But here is a sorte of companyons moch more mery.
They of the Chirch than were fower holy doctors,
We of the Chirch now are the iiij generall proctors.
Here ys, fyrst of all, good father Dyssymulacion, 810
The fyrst begynner of this same congregacion ;
Here is Privat Welthe, which hath the Chyrch infecte
With all abusyons, and brought yt to a synfull secte ;
Here ys Usurpid Power that all kyngs doth subdwe
With such autoryte as is neyther good ner trewe ; 815
And I last of all am evyn, sance pere, Sedycyon.
   Us. Power. Under hevyn ys not a more knave in con-
    dycyon.
Wher-as thu dost cum, that commonwelth cannot thryve.
By owr Lord, I marvell that thou art yet alyve.
   Pr. Welth. Wher herbes are pluckte upp, the wedes
    many tymes remayne. 820
   Dys. No man can utter an evydence more playn.
   Sed. Yea, ye thynke so, yow? Now Gods blyssyng
    breke yowr heade !
I can do but lawgh to here yow, by thys breade !
I am so mery that we are mett, by Saynt John,
I fele not the ground that I do go uppon. 825
For the love of God, lett us have sum mery songe.

   [1] C. *suggests* I am ; Kittredge *suggests assigning the line to Dyssymu-*
lacion.

Us. POWER. Begyne thy-self than, and we shall lepe in
    amonge.   *Here syng.*

SED. I wold ever dwell here, to have such mery sporte.

PR. WELTH. Thow mayst have yt, man, yf thow wylt
    hether resorte,

For the Holy Father ys as good a felowe as we.   830

DYS. The Holy Father? Why, pray the, whych is he?

PR. WELTH. Usurped Power here, which, thowgh he
    apparaunt be

In this apparell, yet hathe he autoryte

Bothe in hevyn and erth, in purgatory and in hell.

Us. POWER. Marke well his saynges, for a trew tale he
    doth tell.   835

SED. What, Usurpid Power? Cocks sowle, ye are owr
    Pope?

Where is yowr thre crounnys, yowr crosse keys, and your
    cope?

What meanyth this mater? Me thynke ye walke astraye.

Us. POWER. Thow knowest I must have sum dalyaunce
    and playe,

For I am a man lyke as an-other ys;   840

Sumtyme I must hunt, sumtyme I must Alyson kys.

I am bold of yow, I take ye for no straungers;

We are as spirituall, I dowght in yow no daungers.

DYS. I owght to conseder yowr Holy Father-hode,

From my fyrst infancy ye have ben to me so good.   845

For Godes sake, wytsave to geve me yowr blyssing here

A pena et culpa, that I may stand this day clere.
                                    Knele.

SED. From makyng cuckoldes? mary, that were no mery
    chere !

DYS. *A pena et culpa* : I trow thow canst not here.

SED. Yea, with a cuckoldes wyff ye have dronke dobyll
    bere.   850

DYS. I pray the, Sedycyon, my pacyens no more stere.

A pena et culpa I desire to be clere,

And than all the devylles of hell I wold not fere.

Us. POWER.   But tell me one thyng : dost thu not preche
  the gospell?

DYS.   No, I promyse yow, I defye yt to the devyll of hell. 855

Us. POWER.   Yf I knewe thow dydest, thu shuldest have
  non absolucyon.

DYS.   Yf I do, abjure me or put me to execucyon.

PR. WELTH.   I dare say he brekyth no popyshe constytucyon.

Us. POWER.   Soche men are worthy to have owr contry-
  bucyon.

I assoyle the here, behynde and also beforne!   860

Now art thu as clere as that daye thow wert borne.

Ryse, Dyssymulacion, and stond uppe lyke a bold knyght ;

Dowght not of my power, thowgh my aparell be lyght!

 SED.   A man, be the masse, can not know yow from a
  knave,

Ye loke so lyke hym, as I wold God shuld me save !   865

 PR. WELTH.   Thow art very lewde owr father so to
  deprave.

Thowgh he for his plesure soche lyght apparell have,

Yt is now sommer and the heate ys withowt mesure,

And among us he may go lyght at his owne plesure.

Felow Sedycyon, thowgh thu dost mocke and scoffe,   870

We have other materes than this to be commyned of.

Frynd Dyssymulacion, why dost thu not thy massage,

And show owt of Englond the causse of thi farre passage?

Tush, blemysh not, whoreson, for I shall ever assyst the.

 SED.   The knave ys whyght-leveryd, by the Holy Trynyte ! 875

 Us. POWER.   Why so, Privat Welth, what ys the mater?
  Tell me.

 PR. WELTH.   Dyssymulacion ys a massanger for the
  Clargy ;

I must speke for hym, there ys no remedy.

The Clargy of Ynglond, which ys yowr specyall frynde,

And of a long tyme hath borne yow very good mynde,   880

Fyllyng yowr coffers with many a thowsande pownde,

Yf ye sett not to hand, he ys lyke to fall to the grownde.

I do promyse yow truly his hart ys in his hose;
Kyng Johan so usyth hym that he reconnyth all to lose.
    Us. POWER.   Tell, Dyssymulacion, why art thow so
            asshamed   885
To shewe thy massage?   Thow art moche to be blamed.
Late me se those wrytyngs; tush! man, I pray the cum nere.
    Dys.   Yowr Horryble Holynes putth me in wonderfull fere.
    Us. POWER.   Tush! lett me se them, I pray the hartely.

Here Dissimulacyon shall delever the wrytynges to Usurpyd Power.

I perseyve yt well, thow wylt lose no ceremony.   890
    SED.   Yet is he no lesse than a false knave veryly.
I wold thow haddyst kyst hys ars, for that is holy.
    Pr. WELTH.   How dost thow prove me that his arse ys
          holy now?
    SED.   For yt hath an hole, evyn fytt for the nose of yow.
    Pr. WELTH.   Yowr parte ys not elles but for to playe
          the knave,   895
And so ye must styll contynew to yowr grave.
    Us. POWER.   I saye, leve yowr gawdes, and attend to me
          this hower.
The bysshoppes writeth here to me, Usurped Power,
Desyryng assystence of myne auctoryte
To save and support the Chyrches lyberte.   900
They report Kyng Johan to them to be very harde,
And to have the Church in no pryce nor regarde.
In his parliament he demaundeth of the Clargy
For his warres the tent of the Chyrches patrymony.
    Pr. WELTH.   Ye wyll not consent to that, I trow, by
          Saynt Mary!   905
    SED.   No; drawe to yow styll, but lett none from yow
          cary!
    Us. POWER.   Ye know yt is cleane agenst owr holy
          decrees
That princes shuld thus contempne owr lybertees.
He taketh uppon hym to reforme the tythes and offrynges,
And intermedleth with other spyrytuall thynges.   910

PR. WELTH.　Ye must sequester hym, or elles that wyll
　　　mare all.

Us. POWER.　Naye, besydes all this, before juges temporall
He conventeth clarkes of cawses crymynall.

PR. WELTH.　Yf ye se not to that, the Churche wyll haue
　　　a fall.

SED.　By the masse, than pristes are lyke to have a pange; 915
For treson, murder and thefte they are lyke to hange!
By Cocks sowle, than I am lyke to walke for treasone,
Yf I be taken; loke to yt therfore in seasone!

PR. WELTH.　Mary, God forbyd that ever yowr holy
　　　anoynted
For tresone or thefte shuld be hanged, racked or joynted,　920
Lyke the rascall sorte of the prophane layete.

Us. POWER.　Naye, I shall otherwyse loke to yt, ye may
　　　trust me.
Before hym-selfe also the bysshopps he doth convent,
To the derogacyon of ther dygnyte excelent,
And wyll suffer non to the court of Rome to appele.　　925

DYS.　No; he contemnyth yowr autoryte and seale,
And sayth in his lond he wyll be lord and kyng,
No prist so hardy to enterpryse any-thyng.
For the whych of late with hym ware at veryaunce
Fower of the bysshopps, and, in maner, at defyaunce,　930
Wyllyam of London, and Eustace bysshope of Hely,
Water of Wynchester, and Gylys of Hartford, trewly.
Be yowr autoryte they have hym excommunycate.

Us. POWER.　Than have they done well; for he is a
　　　reprobate;
To that I admytt he ys alwayes contrary:　　　　935
I made this fellow here the arche-bysshope of Canterbery,
And he wyll agree therto in no condycion.

PR. WELTH.　Than hath he knowlege that his name ys
　　　Sedycyon.

DYS.　Dowtles he hath so, and that drownnyth his opynyon.

Us. POWER.　Why do ye not saye his name ys Stevyn
　　　Langton?　　　　　　　　　　　　　940

DYS. Tush! we haue done so, but that helpyth not the
mater;
The bysshope of Norwych for that cawse doth hym flater.
Us. POWER. Styke thow to yt fast, we have onys ad-
mytted the.
SED. I wyll not one jote from my admyssyon fle;
The best of them all shall know that I am he.
Naye, in suche maters lett men be ware of me. 946

Us. POWER. The monkes of Canterbery ded more at my
request
Than they wold at his concernyng that eleccyon.
They chase Sedycyon, as yt is now manyfest,
In spytt of his harte; than he for ther rebellyon
Exyled them all, and toke ther hole possessyon
In-to his owne hands, them sendyng over see
Ther lyvyngs to seke in extreme poverte. 953

This custum also he hath, as it is told me :
Whan prelates depart, — yea, bysshope, abbott, or
curate, —
He entreth theyr lands with-owt my lyberte,
Takyng the profyghts tyll the nexte be consecrate,
Instytute, stallyd, inducte or intronyzate,
And of the Pyed Monkes he entendeth to take a dyme.
All wyll be marryd yf I loke not to yt in tyme. 960

DYS. Yt is takyn, ser; the some ys unresonnable,
A nynne thowsand marke; to lyve they are not able.
His suggesteon was to subdew the Yrysh men.
PR. WELTH. Yea that same peple doth ease the Church,
now and then;
For that enterpryse they wold be lokyd uppon. 965
Us. POWER. They gett no mony, but they shall have
clene remyssion,
For those Yrysh men are ever good to the Church;
Whan kynges dysobeye yt, than they begynne to worch.
PR. WELTH. And all that they do ys for indulgence and
pardon.

SED. By the messe, and that is not worth a rottyn wardon! 970

Us. POWER. What care we for that? to them yt is venyson.

PR. WELTH. Than lett them haue yt, a Gods dere
benyson!

Us. POWER. Now, how shall we do for this same wycked
kyng?

SED. Suspend hym and curse hym, both with yowr word
and wrytyng.

Yf that wyll not helpe,[1] than interdyght his lond   975

With extreme cruellnes; and yf that wyll not stond,

Cawse other prynces to revenge the Churchys wronge,

Yt wyll profytte yow to sett them aworke amonge.

For clene remyssyon, one kyng wyll subdew a-nother,

Yea, the chyld sumtyme wyll sle both father and mother.   980

Us. POWER. This cownsell ys good; I wyll now folow yt
playne.

Tary thow styll here tyll we returne agayne.

*Here go owt Usurpid Power and Privat Welth and Sedycyon: Usurpyd
Power shall drese for the Pope; Privat Welth for a Cardynall; and
Sedycyon for a Monke. The Cardynall shall bryng in the crose, and
Stevyn Launton the booke, bell, and candell.*

DYS. This Usurpid Power, whych now is gon from hence,
For the Holy Church wyll make such ordynance

That all men shall be under his obedyens,

Yea, kyngs wyll be glad to geve hym their alegyance,

And than shall we pristes lyve here withowt dysturbans;

As Godes owne vyker anon ye shall se hym sytt,

His flocke to avaunse by his most polytyke wytt.   989

He shall make prelates, both byshopp and cardynall,[2]

Doctours and prebendes with furdewhodes and syde
gownes;

He wyll also create the orders monastycall,

Monkes, chanons, and fryers with graye coates and shaven
crownes,

---

[1] C. holpe.

[2] *Lines 990-1010 are an insertion in* Bale's *hand.*

And buylde them places to corrupt cyties and townes ;
The dead sayntes shall shewe both visyons and myracles ;
With ymages and rellyckes he shall wurke sterracles.   996

He wyll make mattens, houres, masse and evensonge,
    To drowne the Scriptures for doubte of heresye ;
He wyll sende pardons to save mennys sowles amonge,
    Latyne devocyons with the holye rosarye ;
      He wyll apoynt fastynges, and plucke downe matri-
        monye ;
Holy water and bredde shall dryve awaye the devyll ;
Blessynges with blacke bedes wyll helpe in every evyll.   1003

Kynge Johan of Englande, bycause he hath rebelled
    Agaynst Holy Churche, usynge it wurse than a stable,
To gyve up his crowne shall shortly be compelled,
    And the Albygeanes, lyke heretykes detestable,
      Shall be brent bycause agaynst our father they babble.
Through Domynyckes preachynge an xviij thousande are
      slayne,
To teache them how they shall Holye Churche disdayne.   1010

All this to performe he wyll cawse a generall cowncell
    Of all Cristendom to the church of Laternense.
His intent shall be for to supprese the gospell,
    Yet wyll he glose yt with a very good pretens,
    To subdwe the Turkes by a Cristen vyolens.
Under this coloure he shall grownd ther many thynges,
Which wyll at the last be Cristen mennys undoynges.   1017

The Popys power shall be abowe the powers all,
    And eare-confessyon a matere nessessary ;
Ceremonys wyll be the ryghtes ecclesyastycall ;
    He shall sett up there both pardowns and purgatory ;
    The gospell prechyng wyll be an heresy.
Be this provyssyon, and be soch other kyndes,
We shall be full suere allwaye to have owr myndes.   1024

[*Enter Usurped Power as the Pope with Privat Welth as a Cardinal and
    Sedycyon as a Monk.*]

POPE. Ah, ye are a blabbe! I perseyve ye wyll tell all;
I lefte ye not here to be so lyberall.

DYS. *Mea culpa, mea culpa, gravissima mea culpa!*
Geve me yowr blyssyng *pro Deo et sancta Maria!*

Knele and knoke on the bryst.

POPE. Thou hast my blyssyng. Aryse now, and stond
a-syde.

DYS. My skyn ys so thyke, yt wyll not throw glyde. 1030

POPE. Late us goo abowght owr other materes now.

Say this all thre:

[ALL.] We wayte her upon the greate holynes of yow.

POPE. For as moch as Kyng Johan doth Holy Church
so handle,
Here I do curse hym wyth crosse, boke, bell and candle:
Lyke as this same roode turneth now from me his face, 1035
So God I requyre to sequester hym of his grace;
As this boke doth speare by my worke mannuall,
I wyll God to close uppe from hym his benefyttes all;
As this burnyng flame goth from this candle in syght,
I wyll God to put hym from his eternall lyght; 1040
I take hym from Crist, and, after the sownd of this bell,
Both body and sowle I geve hym to the devyll of hell;
I take from hym baptym, with the other sacramentes
And sufferages of the Churche, bothe amber-dayes and lentes;
Here I take from hym bothe penonce and confessyon, 1045
Masse of the v wondes, with sensyng and processyon;
Here I take from hym holy water and holy brede,
And never wyll them to stande hym in any sted.
This thyng to publyshe I constytute yow thre,
Gevyng yow my power and my full autoryte. 1050

Say this all thre:

[ALL.] With the grace of God, we shall performe yt than.

POPE. Than gett yow foreward so fast as ever ye can
Uppon a bone vyage; yet late us syng meryly.

SED. Than begyne the song, and we shall folow gladly.

Here they shall syng.[1]

1 *The song is not given.*

POPE.   To colour this thyng thow shalte be callyd Pan-
    dulphus ;   1055
Thow Stevyn Langton ; thy name shall be Raymundus.
Fyrst, thou, Pandolphus, shall opynly hym suspend
With boke, bell and candle ; yff he wyll not so amend,
Interdycte his lande, and the churches all up-speare.
   PR. WELTH.   I have my massage ; to do yt I wyll not
    feare.   1060

Here go owt and drese for Nobylyte.

POPE.   And thow, Stevyn Langton, cummand the byssh-
    oppes all
So many to curse as are to hym benefycyall,
Dwkes, erles and lords, wherby they may forsake hym.
   SED.   Sur, I wyll do yt, and that, I trow, shall shake hym.
   POPE.   Raymundus, go thow forth to the Crysten princes
    all :   1065
Byd them in my name that they uppon hym fall
Bothe with fyre and sword, that the Churche may hym con-
    quarre.
   DYS.   Yowr plesur I wyll no longar tyme defarre.
   POPE. Saye this to them also : Pope Innocent the Thred
Remyssyon of synnes to so many men hath granted   1070
As wyll do ther best to slee hym yf they may.
   DYS.   Sur, yt shall be don with-owt ony lenger delay.
   POPE.   In the meane season I shall soch gere avaunce,
As wyll be to us a perpetuall furderaunce :
Fyrst, eare-confessyon, than pardons, than purgatory,   1075
Sayntes-worchyppyng than, than sekyng of ymagery,
Than Laten servyce, with the cerymonyes many,
Wherby owr bysshoppes and abbottes shall gett mony.
I wyll make a law to burne all herytykes,
And kyngs to depose whan they are sysmatykes.   1080
I wyll all-so reyse up the fower beggyng orders,
That they may preche lyes in all the Cristen borders.
For this and other, I wyll call a generall cownsell
To ratyfye them in lyke strength with the gospell.   1084

THE INTERPRETOUR.[1]

In thys present acte we have to yow declared,
    As in a myrrour, the begynnynge of Kynge Johan,
How he was of God a magistrate appoynted
    To the governaunce of thys same noble regyon,
    To see mayntayned the true faythe and relygyon;
But Satan the Devyll, whych that tyme was at large,
Had so great a swaye that he coulde it not discharge.   1091

Upon a good zele he attempted very farre
    For welthe of thys realme to provyde reformacyon
In the Churche therof, but they ded hym debarre
    Of that good purpose; for, by excommunycacyon,
    The space of vij yeares they interdyct thy[s] nacyon.
These bloudsuppers thus, of crueltie and spyght,
Subdued thys good kynge for executynge ryght.   1098

In the second acte thys wyll apeare more playne,
    Wherin Pandulphus shall hym excommunycate
Within thys hys lande, and depose hym from hys reigne.
    All other princes they shall move hym to hate,
    And to persecute after most cruell rate.
They wyll hym poyson in their malygnyte,
And cause yll report of hym alwayes to be.   1105

This noble Kynge Johan, as a faythfull Moyses,
    Withstode proude Pharo for hys poore Israel,
Myndynge to brynge yt owt of the lande of darkenesse,
    But the Egyptyanes did agaynst hym so rebell
    That hys poore people ded styll in the desart dwell,
Tyll that duke Josue, whych was our late Kynge Henrye,
Clerely brought us in-to the lande of mylke and honye.   1112

As a strong David, at the voyce of Verytie,
    Great Golye, the Pope, he strake downe with hys slynge,
Restorynge agayne to a Christen lybertie

---

[1] *Lines* 1085-1119 *are an insertion in* Bale's *hand.*

Hys lande and people, lyke a most vyctoryouse kynge;
To hir first bewtye intendynge the Churche to brynge,
From ceremonyes dead to the lyvynge wurde of the Lorde.
Thys the seconde acte wyll plenteously recorde.　　　　1119

Finit Actus Primus.

[*Incipit Actus Secundus.*]

Here the Pope[1] *go owt, and Sedycyon*[2] *and Nobylyte cum in and say:*

NOB.　It petyeth my hart to se the controvercye
That now-a-dayes reygnethe betwyn the kyng and the clargy.
All Cantorbery monks are now the realme exyled,
The prysts and bysshopps contyneally[3] revyled,
The Cystean monkes are in soche perplexyte
That owt of Englond they reken all to flee.　　　　1125
I lament the chaunce, as I wold God shuld me save.

 SED.　Yt is gracyously sayd; Godes blyssyng myght ye
  have!
Blyssyd is that man that wyll graunte or condyssend
To helpe relygyon, or Holy Churche defend.

 NOB.　For ther mayntenance I have gevyn londes full
  fayer,　　　　1130
I have dysheryted many a laufull ayer.

 SED.　Well, yt is yowr owne good; God shall reward
  yow for ytt,
And in hevyn full hyghe for soch good workes shall ye
  sytt.

 NOB.　Yowr habyte showyth ye to be a man of relygeon.

 SED.　I am no worse, sur; my name is Good Perfectyon. 1135

 NOB.　I am the more glad to be aquented with ye.

 SED.　Ye show yowr-selfe here lyke a noble-man, as ye
  be.
I perseyve ryght well yowr name ys Nobelyte.

 NOB.　Yowr servont and Umfrey! of trewthe, father, I
  am he.

---

[1] *Apparently the* Pope *went out after* l. 1084.

[2] MS. Dyssymulatyon; *corr. by* C.

[3] C. contymeally.

SED. From Innocent, the Pope, I am cum from Rome
    evyn now.   1140

A thowsand tymes, I wene, he commendyth hym unto yow,
And sent yow clene remyssyon to take the Chyrches parte.

    NOB. I thanke his Holynes, I shall do yt with all my harte.

Yf ye wold take paynes for heryng my confessyon,
I wold owt of hand resayve this cleane remyssyon.   1145

    SED. Mary, with all my hart, I wyll be full glad to do ytt.

    NOB. Put on yowr stolle then, and, I pray yow in Godes
        name, sytt.

Here sett downe, and Nobelyte shall say benedycyte.

    NOB. *Benedicite.*

    SED.   *D*[o]*m*[i]*n*[u]*s: In nomine Domini
        Pape, amen!*

Say forth yowr mynd, in Godes name.

    NOB. I have synnyd a-gaynst God; I knowlege my-
        selfe to blame: 1150

In the vij dedly synnys I have offendyd sore;
Godes ten commandyments I have brokyn ever-more;
My v boddyly wytes I have ongodly kepte;
The workes of charyte in maner I have owt-slepte.

    SED. I trust ye beleve as Holy Chyrch doth teache ye,   1155

And from the new lernyng ye are wyllyng for to fle.

    NOB. From the new lernyng! mary, God of hevyn save
        me!

I never lovyd yt of a chyld, so mote I the!

    SED. Ye can say yowr crede, and yowr Laten Ave Mary?

    NOB. Yea, and dyrge also, with sevyn psalmes and letteny. 1160

    SED. Do ye not beleve in purgatory and holy bred?

    NOB. Yes, and that good prayers shall stand my soule in
        stede.

    SED. Well than, good enowgh; I warant my soulle for
        yowr!

    NOB. Than execute on me the Holy Fatheres power.

    SED. Naye, whyll I have yow here underneth *benedicite*,

In the Popes behalfe I must move other thynges to ye.

NOB.   In the name of God, saye here what ye wyll to
    me.   1167

SED.   Ye know that Kyng Johan ys a very wycked man,
    And to Holy Chyrch a contynuall adversary.
The Pope wyllyth yow to do the best ye canne
    To his subduyng for his cruell tyranny;
    And for that purpose this privylege gracyously
Of clene remyssyon he hath sent yow this tyme,
Clene to relesse yow of all yowr synne and cryme.   1174

    NOB.   Yt is clene agenst the nature of Nobelyte
To subdew his kyng with-owt Godes autoryte;
For his princely estate and power ys of God.
I wold gladly do ytt, but I fere his ryghtfull rode.
    SED.   Godes holy vycare gave me his whole autoryte:
Loo! yt is here, man; beleve yt, I beseche the,   1180
Or elles thow wylte faulle in danger of damnacyon.
    NOB.   Than I submyt me to the Chyrches reformacyon.
    SED.   I assoyle the here from the kynges obedyence
By the auctoryte of the Popys Magnifycence:
Auctoritate Roma in pontyficis ego absolvo te   1185
[*Aside*] From all possessyons gevyn to the spiritualte,
In nomine Domini Pape, amen!
Kepe all thynges secrett, I pray yow hartely.   *Go owt Nobelyte.*

    NOB.   Yes, that I wyll, sur, and cum agayne hether
    shortly.

    Here enter Clargy and Cyvyll Order [1] *together, and Sedysyon shall go up
    and down a praty whyle.*

    CLARGY.   Ys not yowr Fatherhod Archbysshope of Can-
    terbery?   1190
    SED.   I am Stevyn Langton.   Why make ye here inquyry?

                             Knele and say both:
[CLARGY AND C. ORDER.]   Ye are ryght welcum to this
    same regyon trewly.

    [1] *I shall mark the speeches of* CIVIL ORDER *with* S. ORDER *or* C.
ORDER *according as MS. has* Syvyll *or* Cyvyll.

SED. Stond up, I pray yow. I trow, thu art the Clargy.

CLARGY. I am the same, sur; and this is Cyvyle Order.

SED. Yf a man myght axe yow, what make yow in this
border? 1195

CLARGY. I herd tell yester-daye ye were cum in-to the
land;

I thowght for to se yow, sum newes to understand.

SED. In fayth thow art welcum; ys Cyvyll Order thy
frynd?

CLARGY. He is a good man, and beryth the Chyrch good
mynd.

C. ORDER. Ryght sory I am of the great controvarsy 1200

Betwyn hym and the kyng, yf I myght yt remedy.

SED. Well, Cyvyll Order, for thy good wyll gramercy!

That mater wyll be of an other facyon shortly.

Fyrst, to begyne with, we shall interdyte the lond.

C. ORDER. Mary, God forbyde we shuld be in soche
bond! 1205

But who shall do yt, I pray yow hartyly?

SED. Pandulphus and I; we have yt in owr legacy.

He went to the kyng for that cawse yester-daye,

And I wyll folow so fast as ever I maye.

Lo, here ys the bull of myn auctoryte! 1210

CLARGY. I pray God to save the Popes Holy Maieste.

SED. Sytt downe on yowr kneys, and ye shall have
absolucion

A pena et culpa, with a thowsand dayes of pardon.

Here ys fyrst a bone of the Blyssyd Trynyte;

A dram of the tord of swete Seynt Barnabe; 1215

Here ys a fedder of good Seynt Myhelles wyng;

A toth of Seynt Twyde; a pece of Davyds harpe-stryng;

The good blood of Haylys; and Owr Blyssyd Ladys mylke;

A lowse of Seynt Frauncis in this same crymsen sylke;

A scabbe of Seynt Job; a nayle of Adams too; 1220

A maggot of Moyses; with a fart of Saynt Fandigo;

Here is a fygge-leafe and a grape of Noes vyneyearde;

A bede of Saynt Blythe; with the bracelet of a berewarde;

The devyll that was hatcht in Maistre Johan Shornes bote,
That the tree of Jesse did plucke up by the roote;   1225
Here ys the lachett of swett Seynt Thomas shewe;
A rybbe of Seynt Rabart; with the huckyll-bone of a Jewe;
Here ys a joynt of Darvell Gathyron;
Besydes other bonys and relyckes many one.
In nomine Domini Pape, amen!   1230
Aryse now lyke men, and stande uppon yowr fete,
For here ye have caught an holy and a blyssyd hete.
Ye are now as clene as that day ye were borne,
And lyke to have increase of chylderne, catell and corne.

    C. ORDER.   Chyldryn he can have non, for he ys not of
            that loade.   1235
    SED.   Tushe, thowgh he hath non at home, he may have
            sume abroade!

Now, Clargy, my frynd, this must thow do for the Pope,
And for Holy Chyrch: thow must mennys conscyence grope,
And as thow felyst them, so cause them for to wurke:
Leat them show Kyng Johan no more faver than a Turke;   1240
Every-wher sture them to make an insurreccyon.[1]

    CLARGY.   All that shall I do; and, to provoke them more,
This interdyccyon I wyll lament very sore
In all my prechyngs, and saye throwgh his occasyon
All we are under the danger of dampnacyon.   1245
And this wyll move peple to helpe to put hym downe,
Or elles compell hym to geve up septur and crowne.
Yea, and that wyll make those kynges that shall succede
Of the Holy Chyrche to stond evermore in drede.
And, by-sydes all this, the chyrch-dores I wyll up-seale,   1250
And closse up the bells that they ryng never a pele;
I wyll spere up the chalyce, crysmatory, crosse, and all,
That masse they shall have non, baptym nor beryall,
And thys, I know well, wyll make the peple madde.

    SED.   Mary, that yt wyll; soche sauce he never had.   1255

---

[1] *There is nothing to indicate that a line rhyming with this has been lost, and it seems better to suppose that the line never had a mate than to emend* insurreccyon *to* uproar.

And what wylte thow do for Holy Chyrche, Cyvyll Order?

 S. ORDER. For the Clargyes sake, I wyll in every border
Provoke the gret men to take the commonys parte.
With cautyllys of the lawe I wyll so tyckle ther hart,
They shall thynke all good that they shall passe upon,   1260
And so shall we cum to ower full intent anon;
For yf the Church thryve, than do we lawers thryve,
And yf they decay, ower welth ys not alyve.
Therfore we must helpe yowr state, masters, to uphold,
Or elles owr profyttes wyll cache a wynter colde.   1265
I never knew lawer whych had ony crafty lernyng
That ever escapte yow with-owt a plentyows levyng;
Therfore we may not leve Holy Chyrchys quarell,
But ever helpe yt, for ther fall ys owr parell.

 SED. Gods blyssyng have ye! this gere than wyll worke,
  I trust.   1270

 S. ORDER. Or elles sum of us are lyke to lye in the dust.

 SED. Let us all avoyde; be the messe, the kyng cummyth here!

 CLARGY. I wold hyde my-selfe for a tyme, yf I wyst
  where.

 S. ORDER. Gow we hence apace, for I have spyed a
  corner.   1274

     Here go owt all, and Kyng Johan cummyth in.

K. JOHAN. For non other cawse God hath kyngs con-
  stytute
  And gevyn them the sword but forto correct all vyce.
I have attempted this thyng to execute
  Uppon transgressers accordyng unto justyce;
  And be-cawse I wyll not be parcyall in myn offyce
For theft and murder to persones spirytuall,
I have ageynst me the pristes and the bysshoppes all.   1281

A lyke dysplesure in my fathers tyme ded fall,
  Forty yeres ago, for ponyshment of a clarke;
No cunsell myght them to reformacyon call,
  In ther openyon they were so stordy and starke,
  But ageynst ther prynce to the Pope they dyd so barke

That here in Ynglond in every cyte and towne
Excommunycacyons as thonder-bolts cam downe.   1288

For this ther captayn had a ster-apared crowne,
   And dyed upon yt with-owt the kynges consent.
Than interdiccyons were sent from the Popes Renowne,
    Whych never left hym tyll he was penytent,
    And fully agreed unto the Popes apoyntment,
In Ynglond to stand with the Chyrches lyberte,
And suffer the pristes to Rome for appeles to flee.   1295

They bownd hym also to helpe Jerusalem cyte
    With ij hundrid men the space of a yere and more,
And thre yere after to maynteyne battell free
    Ageynst the Sarazens whych vext the Spanyards sore.
    Synce my fathers tyme I have borne them groge ther-
      fore,
Consyderyng the pryde and the capcyose dysdayne
That they have to kyngs whych oughte over them to rayne.   1302

       Privat Welth cum in lyke a Cardynall.

God save you, sur Kyng, in yowr pryncly mageste!
    K. JOHAN.   Frynd, ye be welcum; what is yowr plesure
      with me?
    PR. WELTH.   From the Holy Father, Pope Innocent the
      Thred,
As a massanger I am to yow dyrectyd,
To reforme the peace betwyn Holy Chyrch and yow,
And in his behalfe I avertyce yow here now
Of the Chyrchys goods to make full restytucyon,
And to accepte also the Popes holy [1] constytucyon   1310
For Stevyn Langton, archebysshop of Canturbery,
And so admytt hym to his state and primacy;
The monkes exilyd ye shall restore agayne
To ther placys and londes, and nothyng of thers retayne.
Owr Holy Fatheres mynde ys that ye shall agayne restore   1315
All that ye have ravyshyd from Holy Chyrche with the more.

              [1] C. hely.

K. JOHAN.   I reken yowr father wyll never be so harde
But he wyll my cawse as well as theres regarde.
I have done nothyng but that I may do well,
And as for ther taxe I have for me the gospell.   1320
    PR. WELTH.   Tushe, gospell or no, ye must make a
        recompens!
    K. JOHAN.   Yowr father is sharpe and very quycke in
        sentence,
Yf he wayeth the word of God no more than so;
But I shall tell yow in this what Y shall do:
I am well content to receyve the monkes agayne   1325
Upon amendement; but as for Stevyn Langton, playne,
He shall not cum here, for I know his dysposycyon,
He is moche inclyned to sturdynesse and sedycyon.
There shall no man rewle in the lond where I am kyng
With-owt my consent, for no mannys plesure lyvyng.   1330
Never-the-lesse, yet, upon a newe behaver,
At the Popys request here-after I may hym faver,
And graunt hym to have sum other benyfyce.
    PR. WELTH.   By thys I perseyve ye bare hym groge and
        malyce.
Well, thys wyll I say by-cause ye are so blunte: 1335
A prelate to dyscharge, Holy Chyrche was never wont,
But her custome ys to mynyster ponyshment
To kynges and princes beyng dyssobedyent.
    K. JOHAN.   Avant, pevysh prist!   What! dost thow
        thretten me?
I defye the worst both of thi Pope and the!   1340
The power of princys ys gevyn from God above,
And, as sayth Salomon, ther harts the Lord doth move;
God spekyth in ther lyppes whan they geve jugement;
The lawys that they make are by the Lordes appoyntment.
Christ wylled not his[1] the princes to correcte,   1345
But to ther precepptes rether to be subjecte.
The offyce of yow ys not to bere the sword,
But to geve cownsell accordyng to Gods word.

    [1] *One would be inclined to insert* apostles *but for* l. 1349.

He never tawght his to weare nowther sword ne sallett,
But to preche abrode with-owt staffe, scrypp or walett;   1350
Yet are ye becum soche myghty lordes this hower
That ye are able to subdewe all princes power.
I can not perseyve but ye are becum Belles prystes,
Lyvyng by ydolls, yea, the very Antychrysts.

  PR. WELTH. Ye have sayd yowr mynd, now wyll I say
    myn also.   1355

Here I cursse yow for the wrongs that ye have do
Unto Holy Churche, with crosse, bocke, bell and candell;
And, by-sydes all thys, I must yow other-wyse handell:
Of contumacy the Pope hath yow convyt;
From this day forward yowr lond stond interdytt.   1360
The bysshope of Norwyche and the bysshope of Wyn-
   chester,
Hath full autoryte to spred it in Ynglond here;
The bysshope of Salysbery and the bysshope of Rochester
Shall execute yt in Scotland every-where;
The bysshope of Landaffe, Seynt Assys and Seynt Davy   1365
In Walles and in Erlond shall puplyshe yt openly;
Throwgh-owt all Crystyndom the bysshopps shall suspend
All soche as to yow any mayntenance pretend;
And I cursse all them that geve to yow ther harte,
Dewks, erlls and lordes, so many as take yowr parte;   1370
And I assoyle yowr peple from yowr obedyence,
That they shall owe yow noyther fewte [1] nor reverence;
By the Popys awctoryte I charge them yow to fyght
As with a tyrant agenst Holy Chyrchys ryght;
And by the Popes auctoryte I geve them absolucyon   1375
A pena et culpa, and also clene remyssyon.

  SED. (extra locum) Alarum! Alarum! tro ro ro ro ro! tro
    ro ro ro ro! tro ro ro ro ro!
Thomp, thomp, thomp! downe, downe, downe! to go, to go,
   to go!
  K. JOHAN. What a noyse is thys that without the dore
    is made?

      [1] C. sewte.

PR. WELTH.   Suche enmyes are up as wyll your realme
    invade.   1380
K. JOHAN.   Ye cowde do no more and ye cam from the
    devyll of hell
Than ye go abowt here to worke by yowr wyckyd cownsell!
Ys this the charyte of that ye call the Churche?
God graunt Cristen men not after yowr wayes to worche!
I sett not by yowr curssys the shakyng of a rod,   1385
For I know they are of the devyll and not of God.
Yowr curssys we have that we never yet demaundyd,
But we can not have that God hath yow commandyd.
PR. WELTH.   What ye mene by that I wold ye shuld
    opynly tell.
K. JOHAN.   Why, know ye it not? the prechyng of the
    gospell.   1390
Take to ye yowr traysh, yowr ryngyng, syn[g]y[n]g, pypyng,
So that we may have the Scryptures openyng ;
But that we can not have, yt stondyth not with yowr avan-
    tage.
PR. WELTH.   Ahe! now I tell [1] yow, for this heretycall
    langage,
I thynke noyther yow nor ony of yowres, iwys, —   1395
We wyll so provyd, — shall ware the crowne after this.

                Go owt and drese for Nobylyte.

K. JOHAN.   Yt becum not the, Godes secret workes to
    deme.
Gett the hence, or elles we shall teche the to blaspheme !
Oh Lord, how wycked ys that same generacyon
That never wyll cum to a godly reformacyon!   1400
The prystes report me to be a wyckyd tyrant,
Be-cause I correct ther actes and lyfe unplesant.
Of thy prince, sayth God, thow shalt report non yll,
But thy-selfe applye his plesur to fulfyll.
The byrdes of the ayer shall speke to ther gret shame,   1405
As sayth Ecclesyastes, that wyll a prince dyffame.
The powers are of God, — I wot Powle hath soch sentence, —

            [1] C. fell.

He that resyst them, agenst God maketh resystence.
Mary and Joseph at Cyryns[1] appoyntment
In the descripcyon to Cesar were obedyent.   1410
Crist ded paye trybute for hymselfe and Peter, to,
For a lawe prescrybyng the same unto pristes also.
To prophane princes he obeyed unto dethe;
So ded John Baptyst so longe as he had brethe.
Peter, John and Powle, with the other apostles all,   1415
Ded never withstand the powers imperyall.

[Enter Syvyll Order.]

Prystes are so wycked they wyll obeye no power,
But seke to subdewe ther prynces day and hower,
As they wold do me; but I shall make them smart,
Yf that Nobelyte and Law wyll take my parte.   1420
   S. ORDER. Dowghtles we can not tyll ye be reconsylyd
Unto Holy Chyrche, for ye are a man defylyd.
      K. JOHAN. How am I defylyd? Tel me,[2] good gentyll
        mate!
      S. ORDER. By the Popes hye power ye are excomynycate.
      K. JOHAN. By the word of God, I pray the, what power
        hath he?   1425
      S. ORDER. I spake not with hym, and therfore I cannot
        tell ye.
      K. JOHAN. With whom spake ye not? late me know
        yowr intent.
      S. ORDER. Mary, not with God sens the latter weeke of
        Lent.
[Enter Clargy.]

      K. JOHAN. Oh mercyfull God, what an unwyse clawse ys
        this,
Of hym that shuld se that nothyng ware amys!   1430
That sentence or curse that Scriptur doth not dyrect
In my opynyon shall be of non effecte.
     CLARGY. Ys that yowr beleve? Mary, God save me
       from yow!

---

      [1] C. Cyryus.   [2] C. telme.

K. JOHAN. Prove yt by Scriptur, and than wyll I yt
    alowe.
But this know I well, whan Baalam gave the curse   1435
Uppon Godes peple they ware never a whyt the worse.
    CLARGY. I passe not on the Scriptur; that is i-now
    for me
Whyche the Holy Father approvyth by his auctoryte.
    K. JOHAN. Now, alas, alas! what wreched peple ye are
And how ygnorant, yowr owne wordes doth declare.   1440
Woo ys that peple whych hath so wycked techeres!
    CLARGY. Naye, wo ys that peple that hathe so cruell
    rewlars!
Owr Holy Father, I trow, cowd do no lesse,
Consyderyng the factes of yowr owtragyosnes.

[Enter Nobelyte.]

NOB. Com awaye, for shame, and make no more ado!   1445
Ye are in gret danger for commynyng with hym so;
He is accursyd, I mervell ye do not waye yt.
    CLARGY. I here by his wordes that he wyll not obeye yt.
    NOB. Whether he wyll or no, I wyll not with hym
    talke
Tell he be assoyllyd. Com on, my frynds, wyll ye walke?   1450
    K. JOHAN. Oh, this is no tokyn of trew Nobelyte,
To flee from yowr kyng in his extremyte.
    NOB. I shall dyssyer yow as now to pardone me;
I had moche rather do agaynst God, veryly,
Than to Holy Chyrche to do any injurye.   1455
    K. JOHAN. What blyndnes is this? On this peple, Lord,
    have mercy!
Ye speke of defylyng, but ye are corrupted all
With pestylent doctryne or leven pharesyacall.
Good and [1] faythfull Susan sayd that yt was moche better
To fall in daunger of men than do the gretter,   1460
As, to leve [2] Godes lawe, whych ys his word most pure.

---

[1] C. to; amend. by Kittredge.
[2] C. love.

CLARGY.   Ye have nothyng, *th*ow[gh],[1] to allege to us but
    Scripture :
Ye shall fare the worse for that, ye may be sure.
    K. JOHAN.   What shulde I allege elles, thu wycked
        Pharyse?
To yowr false lernyng no faythfull man wyll agree.   1465
Dothe not the Lord say, *nunc, reges, intelligite :* [2]
The kyngs of the erthe that worldly cawses juge,
Seke to the Scriptur, late that be yowr refuge?
    S. ORDER.   Have ye nothyng elles but this? than God
        be with ye!
    K. JOHAN.   One questyon more yet ere ye departe from
        me   1470
I wyll fyrst demaund of yow, Nobelyte :
Why leve ye yowr prince and cleave to the Pope so sore?
    NOB.   For I toke an othe to defend the Chyrche ever-
        more.
    K. JOHAN.   Clergy, I am sure than yowr quarell ys not
        small.
    CLARGY.   I am professyd to the ryghtes ecclesyastycall.   1475
    K. JOHAN.   And yow, Cyvyle Order, oweth her sum
        offyce of dewtye.
    S. ORDER.   I am hyr feed man; who shuld defend her
        but I?
    K. JOHAN.   Of all thre partyes yt is spoken resonably :
Ye may not obeye becawse of the othe ye mad ;
Yowr strong professyon maketh yow of that same trad ;   1480
Yowr fee provokyth yow to do as thes men do ; —
Grett thyngs to cawse men from God to the devyll to go!
Yowr othe is growndyd fyrst uppon folyshenes ;
And yowr professyon uppon moche pevyshenes ;
Yowr fee, last of all, ryseth owt of covetusnes ; —   1485
And thes are the cawses of yowr rebellyosnes !
    CLARGY.   Cum, Cyvill Order, lett us departe from hence !
    K. JOHAN.   Than are ye at a poynt for yowr obedyence?
    S. ORDER.   We wyll in no wysse be partakers of yowr yll.

        [1] C. yow.   [2] C. intellege.

Here go owt Clargy and dresse for Ynglond, and Cyvyll Order for Commynalte.

K. JOHAN. As ye have bene ever, so ye wyll contynew
  styll.   1490
Thowgh they be gone, tarye yow with me a-whyle;
The presence of a prynce to yow shuld never be vyle.
 NOB. Sur, nothyng grevyth me but yowr excomynycacion.
 K. JOHAN. That ys but a fantasy in yowr ymagynacyon.
The Lord refuse not soch as hath his great cursse,   1495
But call them to grace, and faver them never the worsse.
Saynt Pawle wyllyth you, whan ye are among soch sort,
Not to abhore them, but geve them words of comfort.
Why shuld ye than flee from me yowr lawfull kyng,
For plesure of soch as owght to do no suche thyng?   1500
The Chyrches abusyons, as holy Seynt Powle do saye,
By the princes power owght for to be takyn awaye:
" He baryth not the sword withowt a cawse," sayth he.
In this neyther bysshope nor spirituall man is free;
Offendyng the lawe they are under the powers all.   1505
 NOB. How wyll ye prove me that the fathers sprytuall
Were under the princes ever contynewally?
 K. JOHAN. By the actes of kynges I wyll prove yt by-
  and-by:
David and Salomon the pristes ded constitute,
Commandyng the offyces that they shuld execute;   1510
Josaphat, the kyng, the mynysters ded appoynt,
So ded kyng Ezechias, whom God hymselfe ded anoynt;
Dyverse of the princes for the pristes ded make decrees,
Lyke as yt is pleyn in the fyrst of Machabees.
Owr prists are rysyn throwgh lyberte of kyngs   1515
By ryches to pryd and other unlawfull doynges;
And that is the cawse that they so oft dysobeye.
 NOB. Good Lord, what a craft have you thes thynges
  to convaye!
 K. JOHAN. Now, alas, that the false pretence of super-
  stycyon
Shuld cawse yow to be a mayntener of Sedycyon!   1520

Sum thynkyth Nobelyte in natur to consyst
Or in parentage; ther thowght is but a myst;[1]
Wher habundance is of vertu, faith and grace,
With knowlage of the Lord, Nobelyte is ther in place,
And not wher-as is[2] the wylfull contempte of thyngs   1525
Pertaynyng to God in the obedyence of kynges.
Beware ye synke not with Dathan and Abiron
For dysobeyng the power and domynyon.

    Nob. Nay, byd me be aware I do not synke with yow
        here;
Beyng acurssyd, of trowth, ye put me in fere.   1530
    K. Johan. Why, are ye gone hence and wyll ye no
        longar tarrye?
    Nob. No-wher as yow are in place, by swete Seynt Marye!

    Here Nobelyte go owt and dresse for the Cardynall. Here enter Yng-
    lond and Commynalte.

    K. Johan. Blessed Lord of Heaven, what is the wretch-
        ednesse
Of thys wycked worlde! An evyll of all evyls, doubtlesse!
Perceyve ye not here how the Clergye hath rejecte   1535
Their true allegeaunce, to maynteyne the popysh secte?
See ye not how lyghte the lawyers sett the poure,
Whanne God commandyth them to obeye yche daye and
    howre?
Nobylyte also, whych ought hys prynce to assyste,
Is vanyshed awaye as it we[re][3] a wynter myste.   1540
All they are from me; I am now left alone,
And,[4] God wote, knowe not to whome to make my mone.
Oh, yet wolde I fayne knowe the mynde of my Commynalte,
Whether he wyll go with them or abyde with me.

    Yngl. He is here at hond, a symple creature as may be. 1545
    K. Johan. Cum hether, my frynde; stand nere! ys thy-
        selfe he?
    Com. Yf it lyke yowr grace, I am yowr pore Commynalte.

---

  [1] C. amyst.   [3] *Corr. by* C.
  [2] C. in; *emend. by* Kittredge. [4] C. Knd.

K. JOHAN.   Thou art poore inowgh; yf that be, good
      God [1] helpe the.

Me thynke thow art blynd; tell me, frynde, canst thu not
      see?

YNGL.   He is blynd in-dede, yt is the more rewth and
      pytte.   1550

K. JOHAN.   How cummyst thow so blynd? I pray the,
      good fellow, tell me.

COM.   For want of knowlage in Christes lyvely veryte.

YNGL.   This spirituall blyndnes bryngeth men owt of
      the waye,

And cause them oft-tymes ther kynges to dyssobaye.

K. JOHAN.   How sayst thow, Commynalte? wylt not thu
      take my parte?   1555

COM.   To that I cowd be contented with all my hart;

But, alas, in me are two great impedymentes!

K. JOHAN.   I pray the, shew me what are those impedy-
      mentes.

COM.   The fyrst is blyndnes, wherby I myght take with
      the Pope

Soner than with yow; for, alas! I can but grope,   1560

And ye know full well ther are many nowghty gydes.

The nexte is poverte, whych cleve so hard to my sydes

And ponych me so sore that my power ys lytyll or non.

K. JOHAN.   In Godes name, tell me! how cummyth thi
      substance gone?

COM.   By pristes, channons, and monkes, which do but
      fyll ther bely   1565

With my swett and labour for ther popych purgatory.

YNGL.   Yowr Grace promysed me that I shuld have
      remedy

In that same mater whan I was last here, trewly.

K. JOHAN.   Dowghtles I ded so, but, alas, yt wyll not be!

In hart I lament this great infelycyte.   1570

YNGL.   Late me have my spowse and my londes at lyberte,

And I promyse you my sonne here, your Commynallte,

---

[1] Kittredge *suggests*: yf that be thow, God helpe the.

I wyll make able to do ye dewtyfull servyce.

    K. JOHAN.   I wold I ware able to do to the that offyce;
But alas, I am not! for-why my Nobelyte,   1575
My Lawers, and Clargy hath cowardly forsake me,
And now last of all, to my most anguysh of mynd,
My Commynalte here I fynd both poore and blynde.

    YNGL.   Rest upon this, ser, for my governor ye shall be
So long as ye lyve; God hath so apoynted me.   1580
His owtward blyndnes ys but a sygnyficacion
Of blyndnes in sowle for lacke of informacyon
In the word of God, which is the orygynall grownd
Of dyssobedyence, which all realmes doth confund.
Yf yowr Grace wold cawse Godes word to be tawght
       syncerly,   1585
And subdew those pristes that wyll not preche yt trewly,
The peple shuld know to ther prynce ther lawfull dewty;
But, yf ye permytt contynuance of ypocresye
In monkes, chanons and pristes, and mynysters of the
       clargy,
Yowr realme shall never be with-owt moch traytery.   1590

    K. JOHAN.   All that I perseyve, and therfore I kepe owt
       fryers,
Lest they shuld bryng the moch farder into the bryers.
They have mad labur to inhabytt this same regyon;
They shall for my tyme not enter into domynyon.
We have to many of soch vayne lowghtes all-redy;   1595
I beshrew ther harts, they have made you ij full nedy!

    Here enter Pandulphus, the Cardynall, and sayth:

    PAND.   What, Commynalte, ys this the counaunt[1] kepyng?
Thow toldyst me thu woldest take hym no more for thi kyng.

    COM.   *Peccavi, mea culpa!* I submyt me to yowr
       Holynes.

    PAND.   Gett the hence than shortly, and go abowt thi
       besynes!   1600
Wayet on thy capttaynes, Nobelyte and the Clargy,

                     1 C. connaunt.

With Cyvyll Order, and the other company;
Blow owt yowr tromppettes and sett forth manfully;
The Frenche kyng, Phelype, by sea doth hether apply
With the power of Fraunce to subdew this herytyke.   1605
 K. JOHAN.   I defy both hym and the, lewde scysmatyke!
Why wylt thu forsake thy prince or thi prince leve the?
 COM.   I must nedes obbay whan Holy Chirch com-
  mandyth me.

Go owt Commynalte.

 YNGL.   Yf thow leve thy kyng, take me never for thy
  mother.
 PAND.   Tush, care not thu for that, I shall provyd the
  another!   1610
Yt ware fytter for yow to be in another place.
 YNGL.   Yt shall becum me to wayte upon his Grace,
And do hym servyce where-as he ys resydente,
For I was gevyn hym of the Lord Omnypotente.
 PAND.[1]   Thow mayst not abyde here, for-whye we have
  hym curssyd.   1615
 YNGL.   I be-shrow yowr hartes, so have ye me onpursed!
Yf he be acurssed, than are we a mete cuppell,
For I am interdyct; no salve that sore can suppell.
 PAND.   I say, gett the hence, and make me no more
  pratyng.
 YNGL.   I wyll not a-waye from myn owne lawfull kyng,   1620
Appoynted of God, tyll deth shall us departe.
 PAND.   Wyll ye not, in-dede?   Well than, ye are lyke to
  smarte.
 YNGL.   I smarte all-redy throw yowr most suttell practyse,
And am clene ondone by yowr false merchandyce,
Yowr pardons, yowr bulles, yowr purgatory-pyckepurse,   1625
Yowr Lent-fastes, yowr schryftes, that I pray God geve yow
  his cursse!
 PAND.   Thu shalt smart better or we have done with the,
For we have this howr great navyes upon the see

---

[1] *This and the next two speeches of Pandulphus are in* C. *assigned to*
C., *which must be intended as an abbreviation of* Cardynall.

In every quarter, with this Loller here to fyght,
And to conquarre hym for the Holy Chyrchis ryght : 1630
We have on the northe Alexander, the kyng of Scotts,
With an armye of men that for their townnes cast lottes ;
On the sowthe syde we have the French kyng with his power,
Which wyll sle and burne tyll he cum to London Tower ;
In the west parts we have Kyng Alphonso with the Spanyards, 1635
With sheppes full of gonepowder now cummyng hether to-
    wards ;
And on the est syde we have Esterlynges, Danes and Nor-
    ways,
With soch power landynge as can be resystyd nowayes.

> K. JOHAN. All that is not true that yow have here
>   expressed.[1]
> PAND. By the masse, so true as I have now confessed ! 1640
> K. JOHAN. And what do ye meane by such an hurly-
>   burlye?
> PAND. For the Churches ryght to subdue ye ma[n]fullye.[2]
> SED. To all that wyll fyght I proclame a Jubyle

Of cleane remyssyon, thys tyrant here to slee.
Destroye hys people, burne up both cytie and towne, 1645
That the Pope of Rome maye have hys scepture and
    crowne !
In the Churches cawse to dye, thys daye be bolde ;
Your sowles shall to heaven ere your fleshe and bones be
    colde !

> K. JOHAN. Most mercyfull God, as my trust is in the,

So comforte me now in this extremyte ! 1650
As thow helpyst [3] David in his most hevynes,
So helpe me this hour, of thy grace, mercye and goodnes !

> PAND. This owtward remorse that ye show here evydent

Ys a grett lykelyhod and token of amendment.
How say ye, Kyng Johan, can ye fynd now in yowr hart 1655
To obaye Holy Chyrch and geve ower yowr froward part?

---

[1] *Lines 1639-1648 are an insertion in* Bale's *hand.*
[2] *Corr. by* C.
[3] *Read* helpedst, *or* holpyst.

K. JOHAN. Were yt so possyble to hold thes enmyes
    backe,
That my swete Ynglond perysh not in this sheppewracke?[1]
    PAND. "Possyble," quoth he? yea, they shuld go bake
    in-dede,
And ther gret armyse to some other quarters leade,   1660
Or elles they have not so many good blyssyngs now,
But as many cursyngs they shall have, I make God avowe.
I promyse yow, sur, ye shall have specyall faver
Yf ye wyll submyt yowr-sylfe to Holy Chyrch here.
    K. JOHAN. I trust than ye wyll graunt some delyber-
    acyon   1665
To have an answere of thys your protestacyon.
    SED. Tush, gyve upp the crowne, and make no more
    a-do!
    K. JOHAN. Your spirytuall charyte wyll be better to me
    than so.
The crowne of a realme is a matter of great wayght;
In gyvynge it upp we maye not be to slayght.   1670
    SED. I saye, gyve it up; let us have no more a-do.
    PAND. Yea, and in our warres we wyll no farder go.
    K. JOHAN. Ye wyll gyve me leave to talke first with my
    Clergye?
    SED. With them ye nede not; they are at a poynt
    alreadye.
    K. JOHAN. Than with my lawers, to heare what they
    wyll tell.   1675
    SED. Ye shall ever have them as the Clergye gyve them
    counsell.
    K. JOHAN. Then wyll I commen with my Nobylyte.
    SED. We have hym so jugled he wyll not to yow agree.

---

[1] *Besides the insertions noted above, the* MS. *contains three additions in* Bale's *hand, marked with the reference-letters A, B, C.* Collier *says that only for that marked A is the place of insertion indicated. This insertion he made, but without stating precisely where; it is, however, certain that the inserted passage begins between* l. 1658 *and* l. 1683; *for reasons for thinking that it begins with* l. 1665 *and ends with* l. 1727, *see Notes.*

K. JOHAN. Yet shall I be content to do as he counsell
  me.

PAND. Than be not to longe from hence, I wyll advyse
  ye.   [*Exeunt Kynge Johan and Ynglond.*] 1680

SED. Is not thys a sport? By the messe, it is, I trowe!
What welthe and pleasure wyll now to owr kyngedom growe!
Englande is our owne, whych is the most plesaunte grounde
In all the rounde worlde! Now may we realmes confounde.
Our Holye Father maye now lyve at hys pleasure,   1685
And have habundaunce of wenches, wynes and treasure.
He is now able to kepe downe Christe and his gospell,
True fayth to exyle, and all vertues to expell.
Now shall we ruffle it in velvetts, gold and sylke,
With shaven crownes, syde gownes, and rochettes whyte as
  mylke.   1690
By the messe, Pandulphus, now may we synge *cantate,*
And crowe *confitebor* with a joyfull *jubilate!*
Holde me, or els for laughynge I must burste.

PAND. Holde thy peace, whorson ; I wene thu art accurst!
Kepe a sadde countenaunce, a very vengeaunce take the! 1695

SED. I can not do it, by the messe, and thu shuldest
  hange me.
If Solon were here, I recken that he woulde laugh
Whych never laught yet ; yea, lyke a whelpe he would waugh.
Ha, ha, ha! "Laugh," quoth he? yea, laugh and laugh
  agayne :
We had never cause to laugh more free, I am playne.   1700

PAND. I pray the, no more, for here come the kynge
  agayne!   [*Enter Kynge Johan and Ynglond.*]

K. JOHAN. If I shoulde not graunt, here woulde be a
  wondrefull spoyle,[1]
Every-where the enemyes woulde ruffle and turmoyle ;
The losse of [the] people stycketh most unto my harte.

ENGL. Do as ye thynke best, yche waye is to my smarte. 1705

---

[1] Lines 1702–1705 *are the second of the additions mentioned,* p. 583, n. 1.
That they belong here is certain ; they end in MS. *with a repetition of the
first half of* l. 1706: PAND. Are ye at a poynt.

PAND.   Are ye[1] at a poynt wherto ye intende to stande?

SED.   Yea, hardely, sir : gyve up the crowne of Englande.

K. JOHAN.   I have cast in my mynde the great displeas-
ures of warre,

The daungers, the losses, the decayes both nere and farre;

The burnynge of townes, the throwynge downe of buyld-
ynges,   1710

Destructyon of corne and cattell, with other thynges;

Defylynge of maydes, and shedynge of Christen blood,

With suche lyke outrages, neythar honest, true nor good :

These thynges consydered, I am compelled thys houre

To resigne up here both crowne and regall poure.   1715

ENGL.   For the love of God, yet take some better advyse-
ment.

SED.   Holde your tunge, ye whore, or, by the messe, ye
shall repent!

Downe on yowr marry-bones, and make no more a-do.

ENGL.   If ye love me sir, for Gods sake, do never so!

K. JOHAN.   O Englande, Englande! showe now thyselfe
a mother,   1720

Thy people wyll els be slayne here without nomber.

As God shall judge me, I do not thys of cowardnesse,

But of compassyon in thys extreme heavynesse.

Shall my people shedde their bloude in suche habundaunce?

Naye, I shall rather gyve upp my whole governaunce.   1725

SED.   Come of apace, than, and make an ende of it
shortly!

ENGL.   The most pytiefull chaunce that hath bene
hytherto, surely.

K. JOHAN.   Here I submyt me to Pope Innocent the
Thred,

Dyssyering mercy of hys Holy Fatherhed.[2]

PAND.   Geve up the crowne than, yt shalbe the better
for ye;   1730

He wyll unto yow the more favorable be.

---

[1] C. Ye are; *but cf.* p. 584, n. 1.

[2] *See below,* p. 587, n. 1.

Here the Kyng delevyr the crowne to the Cardynall.

K. JOHAN.   To hym I resygne here the septer and the
    crowne
Of Ynglond and Yrelond with the power and renowne,
And put me wholly to his mercyfull ordynance.
    PAND.   I may say this day the Chyrch hath a full gret
        chaunce.   1735
This v dayes I wyll kepe this crowne in myn owne hande,
In the Popes behalfe upseasyng Ynglond and Yerlond.
In the meane season ye shall make an oblygacyon
For yow and yowr ayers in this synyficacyon :
To resayve yowr crowne of the Pope for-ever-more   1740
In maner of fefarme ; and, for a tokyn therfore,
Ye shall every yere paye hym a thowsand marke
With the Peter-pens, and not agenst yt barke.
Ye shall also geve to the bysshoppe of Cantorbery
A thre thowsand marke for his gret injury.   1745
To the Chyrch besydes, for the great scathe ye have done,
Forty thowsand marke ye shall delyver sone.
    K. JOHAN.   Ser, the taxe that I had of the hole realme
        of Ynglond
Amownted to no more but unto xxx^ti thowsand ;
Why shuld I then paye so moche unto the clargy?   1750
    PAND.   Ye shall geve yt them ; ther is no remedy.
    K. JOHAN.   Shall they pay no tribute yf the realme stond
        in rerage?
    PAND.   Sir, they shall pay none ; we wyll have no soch
        bondage.
    K. JOHAN.   The Pope had at once thre hundred thowsand
        marke.
    PAND.   What is that to you?   Ah, styll ye wyll be
        starke?   1755
Ye shall pay yt, sur ; ther is no remedy.
    K. JOHAN.   Yt shall be performed as ye wyll have yt,
        trewly.
    ENGL.   So noble a realme to stande tributarye, alas,
To the devylls vycar! suche fortune never was !

SED. Out with thys harlot! Cocks sowle, she hath lete a
    fart! 1760

ENGL. Lyke a wretche thu lyest. Thy report is lyke as
    thu art.

PAND. Ye shall suffer the monks and chanons to make
    reentry

In-to ther abbayes and to dwell ther peaceably;

Ye shall se also to my great labur and charge;

For other thyngs elles we shall commen more at large. 1765

K. JOHAN. Ser, in every poynt I shall fulfyll yowr plesur.

PAND. Than plye yt apace, and lett us have the tresur.

YNGL. . . . .

. . . .

. . . . offended.[1]

SED. ·And I am full gladde ye are so welle amended. 1770

Unto Holy Churche ye are now an obedyent chylde,

Where ye were afore with heresye muche defyelde.

ENGL. Sir, yonder is a clarke whych is condempned for
    treason.

The shryves woulde fayne knowe what to do with hym thys
    season.

K. JOHAN. Come hyther, fellawe. What! me thynke
    thu art a pryste! 1775

[Enter Treason.]

TREASON. He hath ofter gessed that of the truthe have
    myste!

K. JOHAN. A pryste and a traytour? how, maye that
    wele agree?

TREASON. Yes, yes, wele ynough, underneth *benedicite.*

Myself hath played it, and therfore I knowe it the better.

Amonge craftye coyners[2] there hath not bene a gretter. 1780

---

1 *From here to the end is the third addition (cf.* p. 583, n. 1). *It seems
likely that* Bale *cancelled the original ending of the play and replaced
it with these lines, which, perhaps, should also replace* ll. 1729–1768, *thus:*
Dyssyring mercy of that I have offended, *etc.* Collier *does not state whether*
l. 1768 *comes at the end of a leaf of the* MS. *or not.*
  2 C. cloyners.

K. JOHAN.   Tell some of thy feates; thu mayest the
    better escape.

SED.   Hem! not to bolde yet; for a mowse the catte
    wyll gape.

TREASON.   Twenty thousande traytour[s] I have made
    in my tyme,

Undre *benedicite*, betwyn hygh masse and pryme.

I have made Nobylyte to be obedyent   1785

To the Church of Rome, whych most kynges maye repent.

I have so convayed that neyther priest nor lawer

Wyll obeye Gods wurde, nor yet the gospell faver.

In the place of Christe I have sett up supersticyons:

For preachynges, ceremonyes; for Gods wurde, mennys tra-
    dicyons.   1790

Come·to the temple and there Christe hath no place,

Moyses and the paganes doth utterly hym deface.

ENGL.   Marke wele, sir; tell what we have of Moyses.

TREASON.   All your ceremonyes, your copes and your
    sensers, doubtlesse,

Your fyers, your waters, your oyles, your aulters, your ashes, 1795

Your candlestyckes, your cruettes, your salte, with suche
    lyke trashes;

Ye lacke but the bloude of a goate, or els a calfe.

ENGL.   Lete us heare sumwhat also in the paganes be-
    halfe.

TREASON.   Of the paganes ye have your gylded ymages
    all,

In your necessytees upon them for to call,   1800

With crowchynges, with kyssynges, and settynge up of
    lyghtes,

Bearynge them in processyon, and fastynges upon their
    nyghtes;

Some for the tothe-ake, some for the pestylence and
    poxe;

With ymages of waxe to brynge moneye to the boxe.

ENGL.   What have they of Christe in the Churche?   I
    praye the tell.   1805

TREASON. Marry, nothynge at all, but the epystle and
the gospell,
And that is in Latyne, that no man shoulde it knowe.
SED. Peace, noughty whoreson, peace! Thu playest the
knave, I trowe.
K. JOHAN. Has thu knowne suche wayes, and sought
no reformacyon?
[TREASON.][1] It is the lyvynge of my whole congregacyon. 1810
If supersticyons and ceremonyes from us fall,
Farwele monke and chanon, priest, fryer, byshopp, and all!
My conveyaunce is suche that we haue both moneye and
ware.
SED. Our occupacyon thu wylt marre, God gyve the care!
ENGL. Very fewe of ye wyll Peters offyce take. 1815
TREASON. Yes, the more part of us our Maistre hath
forsake.
ENGL. I meane for preachynge, -- I pray God thu be
curste!
TREASON. No, no, with Judas we love wele to be purste.
We selle owr Maker so sone as we have hym made,
And, as for preachynge, we meddle not with that trade, 1820
Least Annas, Cayphas and the lawers shulde us blame,
Callyng us to reckenynge for preachynge in that name.
K. JOHAN. But tell to me, person, whie wert thu cast in
preson?
[TREASON.][1] For no great matter; but a lyttle petye
treason:
For conjurynge, calkynge, and coynynge of newe grotes, 1825
For clippynge of nobles, with suche lyke pratye motes.
ENGL. Thys is hygh treason, and hath bene evermor.
K. JOHAN. It is suche treason as he shall sure hange for.
TREASON. I have holy orders; by the messe, I defye
your wurst!
Ye can not towche me but ye must be accurst. 1830
K. JOHAN. We wyll not towche the, the halter shall do
yt alone;

1 Supplied by C.

Curse the rope therfor whan thu begynnest to grone.

   TREASON. And sett ye no more by the holy ordre of
      prestehode?

Ye wyll prove your-selfe an heretyke, by the rode!

   K. JOHAN. Come hyther, Englande, and here what I
      saye to the!   1835

   ENGL. I am all readye to do as ye commaunde me.

   K. JOHAN. For so much as he hath falsefyed our coyne,

As he is worthie, lete hym with an halter joyne.

Thu shalt hange no priest, nor yet none honest man,

But a traytour, a thefe, and one that lyttle good can.   1840

   PAND. What, yet agaynst the Churche? Gett me boke,
      belle and candle!

As I am true priest, I shall ye yett better handle!

Ye neyther regarde hys crowne nor anoynted fyngers,

The offyce of a priest, nor the grace that therin lyngers.

   SED. Sir, pacyent yourselfe, and all thynge shall be well. 1845

Fygh, man, to the Churche that ye shulde be styll a rebell!

   ENGL. I accompt hym no priest that worke such hay-
      nouse treason.

   SED. It is a worlde to heare a folysh woman reason!

   PAND. After thys maner ye used Peter Pomfrete,

A good symple man, and, as they saye, a profete.   1850

   K. JOHAN. Sir, I did prove hym a very supersticyouse
      wretche,

And blasphemouse lyar; therfor did the lawe hym upstretche.

He prophecyed first I shulde reigne but xiiij years,

Makynge the people to beleve he coulde bynde bears;

And I have reigned a seventene yeares, and more.   1855

And anon after he grudged at me very sore,

And sayde I shulde be exyled out of my realme

Before the Ascencyon, whych was turned to a fantastycall
      dreame,

Saynge he woulde hange if hys prophecye were not true.

Thus hys owne decaye hys folyshnesse did brue.   1860

   PAND. Ye shuld not hange hym whych is a frynde to
      the Churche.

K. JOHAN.   Alac that ye shoulde counte them fryndes of
     the Churche
That agaynst all truthe so hypocritycally lurche!
An yll Churche is it that hath such fryndes, in-dede!
   ENGL.   Of Maister Morres suche an-other fable we reade,   1865
That in Morgans fyelde the sowle of a knyght made verses,
Apearynge unto hym, and thys one he rehearses:
Destruat hoc regnum Rex regum duplici plaga, —
Whych is true as God spake with the ape at Praga.
The sowles departed from thys heavye mortall payne   1870
To the handes of God, returneth never agayne.
A marvelouse thynge that ye thus delyght in lyes!
   SED.   Thys queane doth not els but mocke the blessed
     storyes.
That Peter angred ye, whan he called ye a devyll incarnate.
   K. JOHAN.   He is now full sure, no more so uncomely to
     prate.   1875
Well, as for thys man, because that he is a priste
I gyve hym to ye; do with hym what ye lyste!
   PAND.   In the Popes behalfe I wyll sumwhat take upon
     me:
Here I delyver hym to the Churches lyberte,
In spyght of your hart; make of it what ye lyste!   1880
   K. JOHAN.   I am pleased, I saye, because he ys pryste.
   PAND.   Whether ye be or no, it shall not greatly force.
Lete me see those cheanes; go thy waye and have remorce!
   TREASON.   God save your lordeshyppes; I trust I shall
     amende,
And do no more so, or els, sir, God defende!   1885
   SED.   I shall make the, I trowe, to kepe thy benefyce.
By the Marye messe, the knave wyll never be wyse!
   ENGL.   Lyke lorde, lyke chaplayne; neyther barrell bet-
     ter herynge.
   SED.   Styll she must trattle; that tunge is alwayes
     sterynge.
A wurde or two, sir, I must tell yow in your eare.   1890
   PAND.   Of some advauntage I woulde very gladly heare.

SED.   Releace not Englande of the generall interdictyon
Tyll the kynge hath graunted the dowrye and the pencyon
Of Julyane, the wyfe of Kynge Richard Cour de Lyon.
Ye knowe very well she beareth the Churche good mynde;   1895
Tush, we must have all, manne, that she shall leave be-
          hynde!
As the saynge is, he fyndeth that surely bynde.
It were but folye suche louce endes for to lose;
The lande and the monye wyll make well for our purpose.
Tush, laye yokes upon hym, more then he is able to beare;   1900
Of Holy Churche so he wyll stande ever in feare;
Suche a shrewe as he it is good to kepe undre awe.

     ENGL.   Woo is that persone whych is undreneth your
          lawe!
Ye may see, good people, what these same merchantes are;
Their secrete knaveryes their open factes declare.   1905

     SED.   Holde thy peace, callet! God gyve the sorowe
          and care!

     PAND.   Ere I releace yow of the interdyctyon heare,
In the whych yowr realme contynued hath thys seven yeare,
Ye shall make Julyane, your syster-in-lawe, thys bande:
To gyve her the thirde part of Englande and of Irelande.   1910

     K. JOHAN.   All the worlde knoweth, sir, I owe her no
          suche dewtye.

     PAND.   Ye shall gyve it to hir; there is no remedye.
Wyll ye styll withstande our Holy Fathers precepte?

     SED.   In peyne of dampnacyon, hys commaundement
          must be kepte.

     K. JOHAN.   Oh, ye undo me, consyderynge my great
          paymentes!   1915

     ENGL.   Sir, disconfort not, for God hath sent debate-
          mentes;
Yowr mercyfull Maker hath shewed upon ye hys powere,
From thys heavye yoke delyverynge yow thys howre:
The woman is dead, — suche newes are hyther brought.

     K. JOHAN.   For me a synnar thys myracle hath God
          wrought;   1920

In most hygh paryls he ever me preserved,
And in thys daunger he hath not from me swerved.

In genua procumbens Deum adorat, dicens:

As David sayth, Lorde, thu dost not leave thy servaunt
That wyll trust in the and in thy blessyd covenaunt.
 SED. A vengeaunce take it! By the messe, it is un-
   happye   1925
She is dead so sone! Now is it past remedye.
So must we lose all, now that she is clerely gone.
If that praye had bene ours, oh, it had bene alone!
The chaunce beynge suche, by my trouth, even lete it go:
No grote no pater noster, no penye no *placebo*. 1930
The devyll go with it, seynge it wyll be no better!
 ENGL. Their myndes are all sett upon the fylthie luker.
 PAND. Than here I releace yow of yowr interdictyons
   all,
And strayghtly commaunde yow, upon daungers that may
  fall,
No more to meddle with the Churches reformacyon, 1935
Nor holde men from Rome whan they make appellacyon,
By God and by all the contentes of thys boke.
 K. JOHAN. Agaynst Holy Churche I wyll nomore speake
   nor loke.
 SED. Go, open the churche-dores and let the belles be
   ronge,
And through-out the realme see that *Te Deum* be songe. 1940
Pryck upp your candels before Saynt Loe and Saynt
  Legearde;
Lete Saynt Antonyes hogge be had in some regarde.
If yowr ale be sowre, and yowr breade moulde, certayne
Now wyll they waxe swete, for the Pope hath blest ye
  agayne.
 ENGL. Than within a whyle I trust ye wyll preache the
   gospell.   1945
 SED. That shall I tell the, kepe thu it in secrete coun-
   sell:

It shall neyther come in churche nor yet in chauncell.

> PAND.   Goo your wayes a-pace, and see my pleasure be
> done !

> K. JOHAN.   As ye have commaunded, all shall be per-
> fourmed sone.

[Kynge Johan and England go out.]

> PAND.   By the messe, I laugh to see thys cleane con-
> veyaunce !   1950

He is now full glad, as our pype goeth, to daunce ;

By Cockes sowle, he is now become a good parrysh clarke.·

> SED.   Ha, ha, wylye whoreson, dost that so busyly
> marke ?

I hope in a whyle we wyll make hym so to rave,

That he shall become unto us a commen slave,   1955

And shall do nothynge but as we byd hym do.

If we byd hym slea, I trowe he wyll do so ;

If we byd hym burne suche as beleve in Christe,

He shall not say naye to the byddynge of a priste.

But yet it is harde to trust what he wyll be,   1960

He is so crabbed ; by the Holy Trinyte,

To save all thynges up, I holde best we make hym more
sure,

And gyve hym a sawce that he no longar endure.

Now that I remembre, we shall not leave hym thus.

> PAND.   Whye, what shall we do to hym els, in the name
> of Jesus ?   1965

> SED.   Marry, fatche in Lewes, Kynge Phylyppes sonne
> of Fraunce,

To falle upon hym with his menne and ordynaunce,

With wyldefyer, gunpouder, and suche lyke myrye trickes,

To dryve hym to holde and scarche hym in the quyckes.

I wyll not leave hym tyll I brynge hym to hys yende.   1970

> PAND.   Well, farwele, Sedicyon, do as shall lye in thy
> [mynde].[1]   *[Exit.]*

---

[1] *A blot makes the* MS. *illegible here;* C. *suggests* intende (= intent) ;
but cf. the rhymes in ll. 719, 879, 2238, *etc.*

ssayle, wassayle, in snowe, froste and hayle,
ssayle, wassayle, with partriche and rayle,
ssayle, wassayle, that muche doth avayle,
ssayle, wassayle, that never wyll fayle !   2056

K. JOHAN.   Who is that, Englande?[1]   I praye the stepp
   fourth and see.
ENGL.   He doth seem a-farre some relygyous man to be.

[Enter Dyssymulacyon.]

DYS.   Now Jesus preserve your worthye and excellent
   Grace,
r doubtlesse there is a very angelyck face !   2060
w forsoth and God, I woulde thynke my-self in heaven !
I myght remayne with yow but yeares alevyn,
oulde covete here none other felicyte.
K. JOHAN.   A lovynge persone thu mayest seme for to be.
DYS.   I am as gentle a worme as ever ye see.   2065
K. JOHAN.   But what is thy name, good frynde? I praye
   the, tell me.
DYS.   Simon of Swynsett my very name is per-dee,
m taken of men for monastycall Devocyon;
d here have I brought yow a marvelouse good pocyon,
r I harde ye saye that ye were very drye.   2070
K. JOHAN.   In-dede, I wolde gladlye drynke. I praye
   the come nye.
DYS.   The dayes of your lyfe never felt ye suche a cuppe,
   good and so holsome, if ye woulde drynke it upp ;
passeth malmesaye, capryck, tyre, or ypocras ;
   my faythe, I thynke a better drynke never was.   2075
K. JOHAN.   Begynne, gentle monke; I pray the, drynke
   half to me.
DYS.   If ye dronke all up, it were the better for ye ;
woulde slake your thirst and also quycken your brayne ;
better drynke is not in Portyngale nor Spayne,
erfore suppe it of, and make an ende of it quycklye.   2080

[1] C. Fngland.

SED.   I mervele greatly where Dissymulacyon is.
DYS.   *[without]*   I wyll come anon, if thu tarry tyll I pysse.

[Enter Dyssymulacyon.]

SED.   I beshrewe your hart, where have ye bene so longe?
DYS.   In the gardene, man, the herbes and wedes
   amonge ;   1975
And there have I gote the poyson of toade.
I hope in a whyle to wurke some feate abroade.
   SED.   I was wonte sumtyme of thy prevye counsell to be ;
Am I now-adayes become a straunger to the?
   DYS.   I wyll tell the all, undreneth *benedicite*,   1980
What I mynde to do, in case thu wylte assoyle me.
   SED.   Thu shalt be assoyled by the Most Holy Fathers
   auctoryte.
   DYS.   Shall I so in-dede? by the masse, than now have
   at the!
Benedicite.
   SED.   *In nomine papae, amen !*
   DYS.   Sir, thys is my mynde: I wyll gyve Kynge Johan
   thys poyson,   1985
So makynge hym sure that he shall never have foyson.
And thys must thu saye to colour with the thynge,
That a penye lofe he wolde have brought to a shyllynge.
   SED.   Naye, that is suche a lye as easely wyll be felte.
   DYS.   Tush, man, amonge fooles it never wyll be out-
   smelte !   1990
Though it be a foule[1] lye, set upon it a good face,
And that wyll cause men beleve it in every place.
   SED.   I am sure, than, thu wylt geve it hym in a drynke.
   DYS.   Marry, that I wyll, and the one half with hym
   swynke,
To encourage hym to drynke the botome off.   1995
   SED.   If thu drynke the halfe, thu shalt fynde it no scoff ;

[1] *Above* foule *is written, in* Bale's *hand,* great. C. *says* "*this is by no
means a singular instance in the course of the drama,*" *but he does not
point out the others.*

Of terryble deathe thu wylt stacker in the plashes.

DYS.   Tush, though I dye, man, there wyll ryse more of
       my ashes.

I am sure the monkes wyll praye for me so bytterlye,

That I shall not come in helle nor in purgatorye.   2000

In the Popes Kychyne the scullyons shall not brawle

Nor fyght for my grese. If the priestes woulde for me
       yawle,

And grunt a good pace *placebo* with requiem masse,

Without muche tarryaunce I shulde to paradyse passe,

Where I myght be sure to make good cheare and be myrye,   2005

For I can not awaye with that whoreson purgatorye.

SED.   To kepe the from thens, thu shalt have five monkes
       syngynge

In Swynsett abbeye so longe as the worlde is durynge;

They wyll daylye praye for the sowle of father Symon,

A Cisteane monke whych poysened Kynge John.   2010

DYS.   Whan the worlde is done, what helpe shall I have
       than?

SED.   Than shyft for thy-self so wele as ever thu can.

DYS.   Cockes sowle, he cometh here! Assoyle me that
       I were gone, then.

SED.   *Ego absolvo te in nomine papae, amen!*   2014

[*They go out; enter Kynge Johan and England.*]

K. JOHAN.   No prince in the worlde in suche captivyte
       As I am thys howre, and all for ryghteousnesse.

Agaynst me I have both the lordes and commynalte,
       Byshoppes and lawers, whych in their cruell madnesse
       Hath brought in hyther the Frenche kynges eldest
         sonne, Lewes.

The chaunce unto me is not so dolourrouse

But my lyfe thys daye is muche more tedyouse.   2021

More of compassyon for shedynge of Christen blood
       Than any-thynge els, my sceptre I gave up latelye

To the Pope of Rome, whych hath no tytle good

Of jurisdycyon, but of usurpacyon onlye;

And now to the, Lorde, I woulde resygne

Both my crowne and lyfe, for thyne owne ryg

If it would please the to take my sowle to thy

ENGL.   Sir, discomfort ye not! in the hond
       Jesu,

God wyll never fayle yow, intendynge not els

K. JOHAN.   The anguysh of sprete so pang
       where

That incessantly I thyrst tyll I be there.

ENGL.   Sir, be of good chere, for the Pop
       legate,

Whose name is Gualo, your foes to excommuny

Not only Lewes, whych hath wonne Rochestre,

Wynsore and London, Readynge and Wynche

But so many els as agaynst ye have rebelled,

He hath suspended and openly accursed.

K. JOHAN.   They are all false knaves; all
       be-ware;

They never left me tyll they had me in their sn

Now have they Otto, the emproure, so wele as

And the French kynge, Phylypp, undre their ca

All Christen princes they wyll have in their han

The Pope and his priestes are poyseners of all

All Christen people be-ware of trayterouse prist

For of truthe they are the pernicyouse Antichris

ENGL.   This same Gualo, sir, in your cause do
       barke.

K. JOHAN.   They are all nought, Englande,
       weare that marke.

From thys habytacyon, swete Lorde, delyver me

And preserve thys realme, of thy benygnyte!

[*Dyssymulacyon sings without:*]

DYS.   Wassayle, wassayle out of the mylke pay

Wassayle, wassayle, as whyte as my nayle,

K. JOHAN. Naye, thu shalte drynke half, there is no
remedye.

DYS. Good lucke to ye, than! have at it by-and-bye!

[*Aside*] Halfe wyll I consume, if there be no remedye.

K. JOHAN. God saynt the, good monke, with all my very
harte!

DYS. I have brought ye half; conveye me that for your
parte. 2085

[*Dyssymulacion goes to another part of the stage and says :*]

Where art thu, Sedicyon? by the masse I dye, I dye!
Helpe now at a pynche! Alas, man, cum awaye shortlye!

SED. Come hyther apace, and gett thee to the farmerye;
I have provyded for the, by swete Saynt Powle,
Fyve monkes that shall synge contynually for thy sowle, 2090
That, I warande the, thu shalt not come in helle.

DYS. To sende me to heaven goo rynge the holye belle,
And synge for my sowle a masse of Scala Celi,
That I may clyme up aloft with Enoch and Heli.
I do not doubte it but I shall be a saynt; 2095
Provyde a gyldar myne image for to paynt;
I dye for the Churche with Thomas of Canterberye.
Ye shall fast my vigyll and upon my daye be merye;
No doubt but I shall do myracles in a whyle,
And therfore lete me be shryned in the north yle. 2100

SED. To the, than, wyll offer both crypple, halte and
blynde,
Mad-men and mesels, with such as are woo behynde.

Exeunt.

K. JOHAN. My bodye me vexeth; I doubt much of a tym-
panye.

ENGL. Now, alas, alas! your Grace is betrayed cow-
ardlye!

K. JOHAN. Where became the monke that was here with
me latelye? 2105

ENGL. He is poysened, sir, and lyeth a-dyenge, surelye.

K. JOHAN. It can not be so, for he was here even now.

ENGL. Doubtlesse, sir, it is so true as I have tolde yow;

A false Judas kysse he hath gyven and is gone.
The halte, sore and lame thys pitiefull case wyll mone;   2110
Never prynce was there that made to poore peoples use[s]
So many masendewes, hospytals and spyttle-howses
As your Grace hath done, yet sens the worlde began.

    K. JOHAN. Of priestes and of monkes I am counted a
        wycked man,
For that I never buylte churche nor monasterye,   2115
But my pleasure was to helpe suche as were nedye.

    ENGL. The more grace was yours, for at the daye of
        judgment
Christe wyll rewarde them whych hath done hys com-
        maundement;
There is no promyse for voluntarye wurkes,
No more than there is for sacrifyce of the Turkes.   2120

    K. JOHAN. Doubtlesse I do fele muche grevaunce in my
        bodye.

    ENGL. As the Lorde wele knoweth, for that I am full
        sorye.

    K. JOHAN. There is no malyce to the malyce of the
        clergye!
Well, the Lorde God of heaven on me and them have mer-
        cye!   2124

For doynge justyce they have ever hated me;
    They caused my lande to be excommunycate,
And me to resygne both crowne and princely dygnyte,
    From my obedyence assoylynge every estate;
    And now last of all they have me intoxycate;
I perceyve ryght wele their malyce hath none ende.
I desyre not els but that they maye sone amende.   2131

I have sore hungred and thirsted [1] ryghteousnesse
    For the offyce sake that God hath me appoynted,
But now I perceyve that synne and wyckednesse
    In thys wretched worlde, lyke as Christe prophecyed,
    Have the overhande; in me it is verefyed.

        [1] *Qy. insert* for.

Praye for me, good people, I besych yow hartely,
That the Lorde above on my poore sowle have mercy.   2138

Farwell, noble-men, with the clergye spirytuall,
    Farwell, men-of-lawe, with the whole commynalte.
Your disobedyence I do forgyve yow all,
    And desyre God to perdon your iniquyte.
    Farwell, swete Englande, now last of all to the!
I am ryght sorye I coulde do for the nomore.
Farwell ones agayne, yea, farwell for evermore!   2145

    ENGL.   With the leave of God, I wyll not leave ye thus,
But styll be with ye tyll he do take yow from us,
And than wyll I kepe your bodye for a memoryall.
    K. JOHAN.   Than plye it, Englande, and provyde for my
            buryall;
A wydowes offyce it is to burye the deade.   2150
    ENGL.   Alas, swete maistre, ye waye so heavy as leade.
Oh horryble case, that euer so noble a kynge
Shoulde thus be destroyed and lost for ryghteouse doynge
By a cruell sort of disguysed bloud-souppers,
Unmercyfull murtherers, all dronke in the bloude of marters!
Report what they wyll in their most furyouse madnesse,
Of thys noble kynge muche was the godlynesse.   2157
                                    Exeunt.
            [*Enter Veryte.*]

VERY.   I assure ye, fryndes, lete men wryte what they wyll,
    Kynge Johan was a man both valiaunt and godlye.
What though Polydorus reporteth hym very yll
    At the suggestyons of the malicyouse clergye,
    Thynke yow a Romane with the Romans can not lye?
Yes; therfore, Leylonde, out of thy slumbre awake,
And wytnesse a trewthe for thyne owne contrayes sake!   2164

For hys valiauntnesse many excellent writers make,
    As Sigebertus, Vincentius, and also Nauclerus;
Giraldus and Mathu Parys with hys noble vertues take;
    Yea, Paulus Phrigio, Johan Major, and Hector Boethius.

Nothynge is allowed in hys lyfe of Polydorus,
Whych discommendeth hys ponyshmentes for trayterye,
Advauncynge very sore hygh treason in the clergye.   2171

Of hys godlynesse thus muche report wyll I :
        Gracyouse provysyon for sore, sycke, halte and lame
He made in hys tyme,[1] both in towne and cytie,
        Grauntynge great lyberties for mayntenaunce of the
            same,
        By markettes and fayers in places of notable name ;
Great monymentes are in Yppeswych, Donwych and Berye,
Whych noteth hym to be a man of notable mercye ;   2178

The cytie of London, through his mere graunt and premye,
        Was first privyleged to have both mayer and shryve,
Where before hys tyme it had but baylyves onlye ;
        In hys dayes the Brydge the cytizens ded contryve.
        Though he now be dead, hys noble actes are alyve.
Hys zele is declared, as towchynge Christes religyon,
In that he exyled the Jewes out of thys regyon.   2185

[*Enter Nobylyte, Clergy and Cyvyll Order.*]

NOB.   Whome speake ye of, sir? I besyche ye hartelye.
VERY.   I talke of Kynge Johan, of late your prynce most
            worthye.
NOB.   Sir, he was a man of a very wycked sorte.
VERY.   Ye are muche to blame your prynce so to reporte.
How can ye presume to be called Nobilyte,   2190
Diffamynge a prynce in your malygnyte?
Ecclesiastes sayth : " If thu with an hatefull harte
Misnamest a kynge, thu playest suche a wycked parte
As byrdes of ayer to God wyll represent,
To thy great parell and exceedynge ponnyshment."   2195
Saynt Hierome sayth also that he is of no renowne,
But a vyle traytour, that rebelleth agaynst the Crowne.
    CLERGY.   He speaketh not agaynst the crowne, but the
            man, per-dee !

        ¹ C. *repeats* he made.

VERY.   Oh, where is the sprete whych ought to reigne
  in the?
The crowne of it-selfe without the man is nothynge. 2200
Learne of the Scriptures to have better undrestandynge.
The harte of a kynge is in the handes of the Lorde,
And he directeth it, wyse Salomon to recorde.
They are abhomynable that use hym wyckedlye.
 CLERGY.   He was never good to us, the sanctifyed
  Clergye. 2205
 VERY.   Wyll ye know the cause, before thys worshypfull
  cumpanye?
Your conversacyon and lyves are very ungodlye.
Kynge Salomon sayth: "Who hath a pure mynde,
Therin delyghtynge, shall have a kynge to frynde."
On thys wurde *cleros*, whych signyfieth a lott, 2210
Or a sortynge out into a most godly knott,
Ye do take your name, for that ye are the Lordes
Select, of hys wurde to be the specyall recordes.
As of Saynt Mathias we have a syngular mencyon
That they chose hym owt anon after Christes Ascencyon. 2215
Thus do ye recken; but I feare ye come of *clerus*,
A very noyfull worme, as Aristotle sheweth us,
By whome are destroyed the honycombes of bees,
For poore wydowes ye robbe, as ded the Pharysees.
 C. ORDER.   I promyse yow, it is uncharytably spoken. 2220
 VERY.   Trouthe ingendereth hate; ye shewe therof a
  token.
Ye are suche a man as owght every-where to see
A godly order, but ye loose yche commynalte.
Plato thowght alwayes that no hygher love coulde be
Than a man to peyne hymself for hys own countreye. 2225
David for their sake the proude Philistian slewe,
Aioth mad Eglon hys wyckednesse to rewe,
Esdras from Persye for hys owne countreys sake
Came to Hierusalem their stronge-holdes up to make;
But yow, lyke wretches, cast over both contreye and kynge, —
All manhode shameth to see your unnaturall doynge. 2231

Ye wycked rulers, God doth abhorre ye all!
As Mantuan reporteth in hys Egloges Pastorall,
Ye fede not the shepe, but ever ye pylle the flocke,
And clyppe them so nygh that scarsely ye leve one locke.   2235
Your judgementes are suche that ye call to God in vayne
So longe as ye have yowr prynces in disdayne.
Chrysostome reporteth that nobilyte of fryndes
Avayleth nothynge, except ye have godly myndes.
What profiteth it yow to be called spirytuall,   2240
Whyls yow for lucre from all good vertues fall?
What prayse is it to yow to be called Cyvylyte,
If yow from obedyence and godly order flee?
Anneus Seneca hath thys most provable sentence:
" The gentyll free hart goeth never from obedyence."   2245
    C. ORDER.   Sir, my bretherne and I woulde gladly knowe
        your name.
    VERY.   I am Veritas, that come hyther yow to blame
For castynge awaye of [y]our most lawfull kynge;
Both God and the worlde detesteth your dampnable doynge.
How have ye used Kynge Johan here now of late?   2250
I shame to rehearce the corruptyons of your state.
Ye were never wele tyll ye hym cruelly slayne;
And now, beynge dead, ye have hym styll in disdayne.
Ye have raysed up of hym most shamelesse lyes,
Both by your reportes and by your written storyes.   2255
He that slewe Saul throwgh fearcenesse vyolent
Was slayne sone after at Davids just commaundement,
For-bycause that Saul was anoynted of the Lorde, —
The seconde of Kynges of thys beareth plenteouse recorde.
He was in those dayes estemed wurthie to dye   2260
On a noynted kynge that layed handes violentlye;
Ye are not ashamed to fynde fyve priestes to synge
For that same traytour that slewe your naturall kynge.
A trayterouse knave ye can set upp for a saynte,
And a ryghteouse kynge lyke an odyouse tyrant paynte.   2265
I coulde shewe the place where you most spyghtfullye
Put out your torches upon hys physnomye;

In your glasse wyndowes ye whyppe your naturall kynges.
As I sayde afore, I abhorre to shewe your doynges.
The Turkes, I dare say, are a thowsande tymes better than
    yow. 2270
  NOB. For Gods love, no more! Alas, ye have sayde
    ynough!
  CLERGY. All the worlde doth knowe that we have done
    sore amys.
  C. ORDER. Forgyve it us, so that we never heare more
    of thys.
  VERY. But are ye sorye for thys ungodly wurke?
  NOB. I praye to God else I be dampned lyke a Turke. 2275
  VERY. And make true promyse ye wyll never more do so?
  CLERGY. Sir, never more shall I from true obedyence
    goo.
  VERY. What say you, brother? I must have also your
    sentence.
  C. ORDER. I wyll ever gyve to my prynce due reverence.
  VERY. Well than, I doubt not but the Lorde wyll con-
    descende 2280
To forgyve yow all, so that ye mynde to amende.
Adewe to ye all, for now I must be gone.

[Enter Imperyall Majestye.]

  IMP. MAJ. Abyde, Veryte, ye shall not depart so sone!
Have ye done all thynges as we commanded yow?
  VERY. Yea, most gracyouse prynce, I concluded the
    whole even now. 2285
  IMP. MAJ. And how do they lyke the customs they have
    used
With our predecessours, whome they have so abused,
Specyally Kynge Johan? thynke they they have done well?
  VERY. They repent that ever they folowed sedicyouse
    counsell,
And have made promes they wyll amende all faultes. 2290
  IMP. MAJ. And forsake the Pope with all hys cruell
    assaultes?

VERY. Whie do ye not bowe to Imperyall Majeste?
Knele and axe pardon for yowr great enormyte!

    NOB. Most godly governour, we axe your gracyouse
        pardon,
Promysynge nevermore to maynteyne false Sedicyon.   2295

    CLERGY. Neyther Pryvate Welthe, nor yet Usurped
        Poure
Shall cause me disobeye my prynce from thys same houre;
False Dissymulacyon shall never me begyle;
Where I shall mete hym, I wyll ever hym revyle.

    IMP. MAJ. I perceyve, Veryte, ye have done wele your
        part,   2300
Refowrmynge these men; gramercyes with all my hart!
I praye yow take paynes to call our Commynalte
To true obedyence, as ye are Gods Veryte.

    VERY. I wyll do it, sir; yet shall I have muche a-doo
With your popish prelates; they wyll hunte me to and fro.   2305

    IMP. MAJ. So longe as I lyve, they shall do yow no
        wronge.

    VERY. Than wyll I go preache Gods wurde your com-
        mens amonge.
But first I desyre yow their stubberne factes to remytt.

    IMP. MAJ. I forgyve yow all, and perdon your frowarde
        wytt.

    OMNES UNA. The heavenly Governour rewarde your
        goodnesse for it!   2310

    VERY. For Gods sake obeye, lyke as doth yow befall,
For in hys owne realme a kynge is judge over all
By Gods appoyntment, and none maye hym judge agayne
But the Lorde hymself; in thys the Scripture is playne.
He that condempneth a kynge, condempneth God, without
        dought;   2315
He that harmeth a kynge, to harme God goeth abought;
He that a prynce resisteth, doth dampne Gods ordynaunce,
And resisteth God in withdrawynge hys affyaunce.
All subjectes offendynge are undre the kynges judgement;
A kynge is reserved to the Lorde Omnypotent.   2320

He is a mynyster immedyate undre God,
Of hys ryghteousnesse to execute the rod.
I charge yow, therfore, as God hath charge[1] me,
To gyve to your kynge hys due supremyte,
And exyle the Pope thys realme for-evermore.   2325
    OMNES UNA. We shall gladly doo accordynge to your
        loore.
    VERY. Your Grace is content I shewe your people the
        same?
    IMP. MAJ. Yea, gentle Veryte, shewe them their dewtye,
        in Gods name.
To confyrme the tale that Veryte had now
The seconde of Kynges is evydent to yow: 2330

The younge man that brought the crowne and bracelett
    Of Saul to David, saynge that he had hym slayne,
David commaunded, as though he had done the forfett,
    Strayght-waye to be slayne; Gods sprete ded hym
        constrayne
    To shewe what it is a kynges bloude to distayne.
So ded he those two that in the fyelde hym mett,
And unto hym brought the heade of Isboset.   2337

Consydre that Christe was undre the obedyence
    Of worldly prynces so longe as he was here,
And alwayes used them with a lowly reverence,
    Payinge them tribute, all his true servauntes to stere
    To obeye them, love them, and have them in reverent
        feare.
Dampnacyon it is to hym that an ordre breake
Appoynted of God, lyke as the Apostle speake.   2344

No man is exempt from thys, Gods ordynaunce,
    Bishopp, monke, chanon, priest, cardynall nor pope;
All they by Gods lawe to kynges owe their allegeaunce.
    Thys wyll be wele knowne in thys same realme, I hope.
    Of Verytees wurdes the syncere meanynge I grope:

---

[1] *Perhaps* charged, *but see* Notes.

He sayth that a kynge is of God immedyatlye;
Than shall never pope rule more in thys monarchie.   2351

    CLERGY.   If it be your pleasure we wyll exyle hym
        cleane,
That he in thys realme shall nevermore be seane,
And your Grace shall be the supreme head of the Churche;
To brynge thys to passe, ye shall see how we wyll wurche.   2355
    IMP. MAJ.   Here is a nyce tale!   He sayth, if it be my
        pleasure,
He wyll do thys acte to the Popes most hygh displeasure;
As who sayth, I woulde for pleasure of my persone,
And not for Gods truthe, have suche an enterpryse done.
Full wysely convayed! the crowe wyll not chaunge her
        hewe.   2360
It is marvele to me and ever ye be trewe.
I wyll the auctoryte of Gods holy wurde to do it,
And it not to aryse of your vayne, slypper wytt.
That Scripture doth not, is but a lyght fantasye.
    CLERGY.   Both Daniel and Paule calleth hym Gods
        adversarye,   2365
And therfore ye ought as a devyll hym to expell.
    IMP. MAJ.   Knewe ye thys afore, and woulde it never
        tell?
Ye shoulde repent it, had we not now forgyven ye!
Nobylyte, what say yow?   Wyll ye to thys agree?
    NOB.   I can no lesse, sir, for he is wurse than the Turke, 2370
Whych none other wayes but by tyrannye doth wurke.
Thys bloudy bocher with hys pernycyouse bayte
Oppresse Christen princes by frawde, crafte and dissayte,
Tyll he compell them to kysse hys pestylent fete,
Lyke a levyathan syttynge in Moyses sete.   2375
I thynke we can do unto God no sacrifyce
That is more accept, nor more agreynge to justyce,
Than to slea that beaste and slauterman of the devyll,
That Babylon boore, whych hath done so muche evyll.
    IMP. MAJ.   It is a clere sygne of a true Nobilyte,   2380

To the wurde of God whan your conscyence doth agree;
For, as Christe ded saye to Peter, *Caro et sanguis*
Non revelavit tibi, sed Pater meus celestis:
Ye have not thys gyfte of carnall generacion,
Nor of noble bloude, but by Gods owne demonstracyon.　　2385
Of yow, Cyvyle Order, one sentence woulde I heare.

 C. ORDER.　I rewe it that ever any harte I ded hym
  beare.

I thynke he hath spronge out of the bottomlesse pytt,
And in mennys conscyence in the stede of God doth sytt,
Blowynge fourth a swarme of grassopers and flyes,　　2390
Monkes, fryers and priestes, that all truthe putrifyes.
Of the Christen faythe playe now the true defendar,
Exyle thys monster and ravenous devourar,
With hys venym wormes, hys adders, whelpes and snakes,
Hys cuculled vermyne, that unto all myschiefe wakes!　　2395

 IMP. MAJ.　Than, in thys purpose ye are all of one
  mynde?

 CLERGY.　We detest the Pope, and abhorre hym to the
  fynde.

 IMP. MAJ.　And ye are wele content to disobeye hys
  pryde?

 NOB.　Yea, and his lowsye lawes and decrees to sett
  asyde.

 IMP. MAJ.　Than must ye be sworne to take me for your
  heade.　　2400

 C. ORDER.　We wyll obeye yow as our governour in Gods
  steade.

 IMP. MAJ.　Now that ye are sworne unto me your pryncypall,

I charge ye to regarde the wurde of God over all,
And in that alone to rule, to speake and to judge,
As ye wyll have me your socour and refuge.　　2405

 CLERGY.　If ye wyll make sure, ye must exyle Sedicyon,
False Dyssymulacyon, with all vayne superstycyon,
And put Private Welthe out of the monasteryes;
Than Usurped Power maye goo a-birdynge for flyes.

IMP. MAJ. Take yow it in hande, and do your true dily-
 gence, 2410
Iche man for hys part; ye shall wante no assystence.
 CLERGY. I promyse yow here to exyle Usurped Powre,
And yowr supremyte to defende yche daye and howre.
 NOB. I promyse also out of the monasteryes
To put Private Welthe, and detect hys mysteryes. 2415
 C. ORDER. False Dissymulacyon I wyll hange up in
 Smythfylde,
With suche supersticion as your people hath begylde.
 IMP. MAJ. Than I trust we are at a very good conclu-
 syon,
Vertu to have place, and vyce to have confusyon.
Take Veryte with ye for every acte ye doo, 2420
So shall ye be sure not out of the waye to goo.

Sedicyon intrat.

 SED. [*sings*] Pepe! I see ye! I am glad I have spyed ye![1]
 NOB. There is Sedicyon; stand yow asyde a-whyle,
Ye shall see how we shall catche hym by a wyle.
 SED. No noyse amonge ye? Where is the mery chere 2425
That was wont to be, with quaffynge of double bere?
The worlde is not yet as some men woulde it have.
I have bene abroade, and I thynke I have playde the knave.
 C. ORDER. Thu canst do none other, except thu change
 thy wunte.
 SED. What myschiefe ayle ye that ye are to me so
 blunte? 2430
I have sene the daye ye have favoured me, Perfectyon.
 CLERGY. Thy-selfe is not he, thu art of an other com-
 plectyon.
Sir, thys is the thiefe that first subdued Kynge John,
Vexynge other prynces that sens have ruled thys regyon,
And now he doth prate he hath played the knave, 2435
That the worlde is not yet as some men woulde it have.
It woulde be knowne, sir, what he hath done of late.

 [1] *The music is printed in* C.

IMP. MAJ. What is thy name, frynde? To us here inty-
mate.

SED. A sayntwary! a sayntwary! for Gods dere passion,
a sayntwarye!

Is there none wyll holde me, and I have made so manye? 2440

IMP. MAJ. Tell me what thy name is. Thu playest the
knave, I trowe.

SED. I am wyndelesse, good man, I have muche peyne
to blowe.

IMP. MAJ. I saye, tell thy name, or the racke shall the
constrayne.

SED. Holy Perfectyon my godmother called me playne.

NOB. It is Sedicyon, God gyve hym a very myschiefe! 2445

C. ORDER. Under heaven is not a more detestable thiefe.

SED. By the messe, ye lye! I see wele ye do not knowe
me.

IMP. MAJ. Ah, brother, art thu cum? I am ryght glad
we have the.

SED. By bodye, bloude, bones, and sowle, I am not he!

CLERGY. If swearynge myghte helpe, he woulde do
we[le] [1] ynough. 2450

IMP. MAJ. He scape not our handes so lyghtly, I warande yow.

CLERGY. Thys is that thiefe, sir, that all Christendome
hath troubled,

And the Pope of Rome agaynst all kynges maynteyned.

NOB. Now that ye have hym, no more but hange hym
uppe!

C. ORDER. If ye so be content, it shall be done ere I
suppe. 2455

IMP. MAJ. Loo! the Clergye accuseth the, Nobylyte
condempneth the,

And the Lawe wyll hange the. What sayst now to me?

SED. I woulde I were now at Rome at the sygne of the
Cuppe,

For heavynesse is drye. Alas, must I nedes clymbe uppe?

[1] Corr. by C.

Perdon my lyfe, and I shall tell ye all,   2460
Both that is past and that wyll herafter fall.

    IMP. MAJ. Aryse; I perdon the, so that thu tell the
        trewthe.

    SED. I wyll tell to yow suche treason as ensewthe.

Yet a ghostly father ought not to bewraye confessyon.

    IMP. MAJ. No confessyon is but ought to discover
        treason.   2465

    SED. I thynke it maye kepe all thynge save heresye.

    IMP. MAJ. It maye holde no treason, I tell the verelye,
And therfore tell the whole matter by-and-bye.
Thu saydest now of late that thu haddest played the knave,
And that the worlde was not as some men woulde it have.   2470

    SED. I coulde playe Pasquyll, but I feare to have re-
        buke.

    IMP. MAJ. For utterynge the truthe feare neyther bysh-
        opp nor duke.

    SED. Ye gave injunctyons that Gods wurde myghte be
        taught;
But who observe them?   Full manye a tyme have I laught
To see the conveyaunce that prelates and priestes can fynde.   2475

    IMP. MAJ. And whie do they beare Gods wurde no
        better mynde?

    SED. For, if that were knowne, than woulde the people
        regarde
No heade but their prynce; with the Churche than were it
        harde;
Than shoulde I lacke helpe to maynteyne their estate,
As I attempted in the Northe but now of late,   2480
And sens that same tyme in other places besyde,
Tyll my setters-on were of their purpose wyde.
A vengeaunce take it, it was never well with me
Sens the cummynge hyther of that same Veryte!
Yet do the byshoppes for my sake vexe hym amonge.   2485

    IMP. MAJ. Do they so in-dede? well, they shall not do
        so longe.

    SED. In your parlement commaunde yow what ye wyll,

The Popes ceremonyes shall drowne the gospell styll.
Some of the byshoppes at your injunctyons slepe,
Some laugh and go bye, and some can playe boo-pepe.   2490
Some of them do nought but searche for heretykes,
Whyls their priestes abroade do playe the scysmatykes.
Tell me, in London how manye their othes discharge
Of the curates there ; yet is it muche wurse at large.
If your true subjectes impugne their trecheryes,   2495
They can fatche them in, man, for Sacramentaryes,
Or Anabaptystes ; thus fynde they subtyle shyfte
To proppe up their kyngedome, suche is their wyly dryfte.
Get they false wytnesses, they force not of whens they be,
Be they of Newgate, or be they of the Marshallsee.   2500
Paraventure a thousande are in one byshoppes boke,
And agaynst a daye are readye to the hooke.

    IMP. MAJ.   Are those matters true that thu hast spoken
        here?
    SED.   What can in the worlde more evydent wytnesse
        bere?

First of all consydre the prelates do not preache,   2505
But persecute those that the holy Scriptures teache ;
And marke me thys wele, they never ponnysh for popery,
But the gospell-readers they handle very coursely ;
For on them they laye by hondred poundes of yron,
And wyll suffer none with them ones for to common.   2510
Sytt they never so longe, nothynge by them cometh
        fourthe
To the truthes furtherance that any-thynge ys wourthe.
In some byshoppes howse ye shall not [1] fynde a Testament,
But yche man readye to devoure the innocent.
We lyngar a tyme and loke but for a daye   2515
To sett upp the Pope, if the gospell woulde decaye.

    CLERGY.   Of that he hath tolde hys-selfe is the very
        grounde.
    IMP. MAJ.   Art thu of counsell in this that thu hast
        spoken?

          1 MS. *repeats* shall not.

SED.   Yea, and in more than that, if all secretes myght
          be broken ;

For the Pope I make so muche as ever I maye do.   2520

  IMP. MAJ.   I praye the hartely, tell me why thu doest so.

  SED.   For I perceyve wele the Pope is a jolye fellawe,

A trymme fellawe, a ryche fellawe, yea, and myry fellawe.

  IMP. MAJ.   A jolye fellawe how dost thu prove the Pope?

  SED.   For he hath crosse keyes, with a tryple crowne and
          a cope,   2525

Trymme as a trencher, havynge his shoes of golde,

Ryche in hys ryalte and angelyck to beholde.

  IMP. MAJ.   How dost thu prove hym to be a fellawe
          myrye?

  SED.   He hath pipys and belles, with kyrye, kyrye, kyrye.

Of hym ye maye bye both salt, creame, oyle and waxe,   2530

And after hygh masse ye may learne to beare the paxe.

  IMP. MAJ.   Yea? and nothynge heare of the pystle and
          the gospell?

  SED.   No, sir, by the masse, he wyll gyve no suche
          counsell.

  IMP. MAJ.   Whan thu art abroade, where doest thy
          lodgynge take?

  SED.   Amonge suche people as God ded never make :   2535

Not only cuckoldes, but suche as folow the Popes lawes

In disgysed coates, with balde crownes lyke jacke-dawes.

  IMP. MAJ.   Than every-where thu art the Popes altogyther.

  SED.   Ye had proved it ere thys, if I had not chaunced
          hyther.

I sought to have served yow lyke as I ded Kynge John,   2540

But that Veryte stopte me, the devyll hym poyson !

  NOB.   He is wurthie to dye and there were men nomore !

  C. ORDER.   Hange up the vyle knave, and kepe hym no
          longar in store !

  IMP. MAJ.   Drawe hym to Tyburne ; lete hym be hanged
          and quartered.

  SED.   Whye, of late dayes ye sayde I shoulde not be so
          martyred.   2545

Where is the pardon that ye ded promyse me?

IMP. MAJ. For doynge more harme thu shalt sone par-
doned be.

Have hym fourth, Cyvyle Ordre, and hang hym tyll he be
dead,

And on London Brydge loke ye bestowe hys head.

C. ORDER. I shall see it done and returne to yow
agayne.   2550

SED. I beshrewe your hart for takynge so muche payne!

Some man tell the Pope, I besyche ye with all my harte,

How I am ordered for takynge the Churches parte,

That I maye be put in the holye letanye

With Thomas Beckett, for I thynke I am as wurthye.   2555

Praye to me with candels, for I am a saynt alreadye.

O blessed Saynt Partryck, I see the, I, verylye!   [Exeunt.]

IMP. MAJ. I see by thys wretche there hath bene muche
faulte in ye ;

Shewe your-selves herafter more sober and wyse to be.   2559

Kynge Johan ye subdued, for that he ponnyshed treason,

    Rape, theft and murther in the holye spirytualte ;

But Thomas Beckett ye exalted without reason,

    Because that he dyed for the Churches wanton lyberte,

    That the priestes myght do all kyndes of inyquyte,

And be unponnyshed.   Marke now the judgement

Of your ydle braynes, and, for Gods love, repent!   2566

NOB. As God shall judge me, I repent me of my rude-
nesse.

CLERGY. I am ashamed of my most vayne folyshenesse.   2568

NOB. I consydre now that God hath for sedicyon

    Sent ponnyshmentes great : examples we have in Brute,

In Catilyne, in Cassius and fayer Absolon,

    Whome of their purpose God alwayes destytute,

    And terryble plages on them ded execute

For their rebellyon.   And therfore I wyll be ware,

Least his great vengeaunce trappe me in suche lyke snare.   2575

CLERGY.   I pondre also that sens the tyme of Adam
    The Lorde evermore the governours preserved :
Examples we fynde in Noe and in Abraham,
    In Moyses and David, from whome God never swerved.
    I wyll therfor obeye least he be with me displeased.
Homerus doth saye that God putteth fourth hys shyelde
The prynce to defende whan he is in the fyelde.   2582

C. ORDER.   Thys also I marke : whan the priestes had
    governaunce
    Over the Hebrues, the sectes ded first aryse
As Pharisees, Sadducees, and Esse[n]es, whych wrought
    muche grevaunce
    Amonge the people by their most devylysh practyse,
    Tyll destructyons the prynces ded devyse,
To the quyetnesse of their faythfull commens all,
As your Grace hath done with the sectes papistycall.   2589

IMP. MAJ.   That poynt hath in tyme fallen in your mem-
    oryes.
    The Anabaptystes, a secte newe rysen of late,
The Scriptures poyseneth with their subtle allegoryes,
    The heades to subdue after a sedicyouse rate.
    The cytie of Mynster was lost through their debate.
They have here begunne their pestilent sedes to sowe,
But we trust in God, to increace they shall not growe.   2596

    CLERGY.   God forbyd they shoulde, for they myght do
        muche harme !
    C. ORDER.   We shall cut them short if they do hyther
        swarme.
    IMP. MAJ.   The adminystracyon of a princes governaunce
Is the gifte of God and hys hygh ordynaunce,   2600
Whome with all your power yow thre ought to support
In the lawes of God to all hys peoples confort :
First yow, the Clergye, in preachynge of Gods worde,
Than yow, Nobilyte, defendynge with the sworde,
Yow, Cyvyle Order, in executynge justyce.   2605

Thus, I trust, we shall seclude all maner of vyce,
And, after we have establyshed our kyngedome
In peace of the Lorde and in hys godly fredome,
We wyll confirme it with wholesom lawes and decrees,
To the full suppressynge of Antichristes vanytees.   2610

Hic omnes rex osculatur.

Farwele to ye all : first to yow, Nobilyte,
Than to yow, Clergye, than to yow, Cyvylyte ;
And above all thynges remembre our injunctyon!

OMNES UNA.   By the helpe of God yche one shall do hys
    functyon.   [*Exit Imperyall Majestye.*]   2614

NOB.   By thys example ye may see with your eyes
    How Antichristes whelpes have noble princes used.
Agayne ye may see how they with prodigyouse lyes
    And craftes uncomely their myschiefes have excused ;
    Both nature, manhode and grace they have abused,
Defylynge the lawe and blyndynge Nobilyte, —
No Christen regyon from their abusyons free.   2621

CLERGY.   Marke wele the dampnable bestowynge of their
    masses,
    With their foundacyons for poysenynge of their kynge.
Their confessyon-driftes all other traytery passes.
    A saynt the[y]¹ can make of the moste knave thys
    daye lyvynge,
    Helpynge their market ; and, to promote the thynge,
He shall do myracles.   But he that blemysh their glorye
Shall be sent to helle without anye remedye.   2628

C. ORDER.   Here was to be seane what ryseth of Sedicyon,
    And howe he doth take hys mayntenaunce and grounde
Of ydle persones, brought upp in supersticyon,
    Whose daylye practyse is always to confounde
    Such as myndeth vertu and to them wyll not be bounde.
Expedyent it is to knowe their pestylent wayes,
Consyderynge they were so busye now of late dayes.   2635

¹ *Corr. by* C.

NOB.   Englande hath a quene, — thankes to the Lorde
    above ! —
  Whych maye be a lyghte to other princes all
For the godly wayes whome she doth dayly move
  To her liege people, through Gods wurde specyall.
  She is that Angell, as Saynt Johan doth hym call,
That with the Lordes seale doth marke out his true ser-
    vauntes,
Pryntynge in their hartes his holy wourdes and covenauntes.   2642

CLERGY.   In Danyels sprete she hath subdued the Papistes,
  With all the ofsprynge of Antichristes generacyon ;
And now of late dayes the sect of Anabaptistes
  She seketh to suppresse for their pestiferouse facyon.
  She vanquysheth also the great abhomynacyon
Of supersticyons, witchecraftes and hydolatrye,
Restorynge Gods honoure to hys first force and bewtye.   2649

C. ORDER.   Praye unto the Lorde that hir Grace may con-
    tynewe
The dayes of Nestor to our sowles consolacyon ;
And that hir ofsprynge may lyve also to subdewe
  The great Antichriste, with hys whole generacyon,
  In Helias sprete to the confort of thys nacyon ;
Also to preserve hir most honourable Counsell,
To the prayse of God and glorye of the gospell ! [1]   2656

  [1] *After this line*, MS. *has* Pretium xx^s, *not in* Bale's *hand, but contemporary.*

Thus endeth the ij playes
of Kynge Johan.

END OF VOL. I.

CATALOGUE OF DOVER BOOKS

Literature, History of Literature

ARISTOTLE'S THEORY OF POETRY AND THE FINE ARTS, edited by S. H. Butcher. The celebrated Butcher translation of this great classic faced, page by page, with the complete Greek text. A 300 page introduction discussing Aristotle's ideas and their influence in the history of thought and literature, and covering art and nature, imitation as an aesthetic form, poetic truth, art and morality, tragedy, comedy, and similar topics. Modern Aristotelian criticism discussed by John Gassner. lxxvi + 421pp. 5⅜ x 8. **T42 Paperbound $2.00**

INTRODUCTIONS TO ENGLISH LITERATURE, edited by B. Dobrée. Goes far beyond ordinary histories, ranging from the 7th century up to 1914 (to the 1940's in some cases.) The first half of each volume is a specific detailed study of historical and economic background of the period and a general survey of poetry and prose, including trends of thought, influences, etc. The second and larger half is devoted to a detailed study of more than 5000 poets, novelists, dramatists; also economists, historians, biographers, religious writers, philosophers, travellers, and scientists of literary stature, with dates, lists of major works and their dates, keypoint critical bibliography, and evaluating comments. The most compendious bibliographic and literary aid within its price range.

Vol. I. THE BEGINNINGS OF ENGLISH LITERATURE TO SKELTON, (1509), W. L. Renwick, H. Orton. 450pp. 5⅛ x 7⅞. **T75 Clothbound $4.50**

Vol. II. THE ENGLISH RENAISSANCE, 1510-1688, V. de Sola Pinto. 381pp. 5⅛ x 7⅞. **T76 Clothbound $4.50**

Vol. III. AUGUSTANS AND ROMANTICS, 1689-1830, H. Dyson, J. Butt. 320pp. 5⅛ x 7⅞. **T77 Clothbound $4.50**

Vol. IV. THE VICTORIANS AND AFTER, 1830-1940's, E. Batho, B. Dobrée. 360pp. 5⅛ x 7⅞. **T78 Clothbound $4.50**

EPIC AND ROMANCE, W. P. Ker. Written by one of the foremost authorities on medieval literature, this is the standard survey of medieval epic and romance. It covers Teutonic epics, Icelandic sagas, Beowulf, French chansons de geste, the Roman de Troie, and many other important works of literature. It is an excellent account for a body of literature whose beauty and value has only recently come to be recognized. Index. xxiv + 398pp. 5⅜ x 8. **T355 Paperbound $2.25**

THE POPULAR BALLAD, F. B. Gummere. Most useful factual introduction; fund of descriptive material; quotes, cites over 260 ballads. Examines, from folkloristic view, structure; choral, ritual elements; meter, diction, fusion; effects of tradition, editors; almost every other aspect of border, riddle, kinship, sea, ribald, supernatural, etc., ballads. Bibliography. 2 indexes. 374pp. 5⅜ x 8. **T548 Paperbound $1.85**

MASTERS OF THE DRAMA, John Gassner. The most comprehensive history of the drama in print, covering drama in every important tradition from the Greeks to the Near East, China, Japan, Medieval Europe, England, Russia, Italy, Spain, Germany, and dozens of other drama producing nations. This unsurpassed reading and reference work encompasses more than 800 dramatists and over 2000 plays, with biographical material, plot summaries, theatre history, etc. "Has no competitors in its field," THEATRE ARTS. "Best of its kind in English," NEW REPUBLIC. Exhaustive 35 page bibliography. 77 photographs and drawings. Deluxe edition with reinforced cloth binding, headbands, stained top. xxii + 890pp. 5⅜ x 8. **T100 Clothbound $6.95**

THE DEVELOPMENT OF DRAMATIC ART, D. C. Stuart. The basic work on the growth of Western drama from primitive beginnings to Eugene O'Neill, covering over 2500 years. Not a mere listing or survey, but a thorough analysis of changes, origins of style, and influences in each period; dramatic conventions, social pressures, choice of material, plot devices, stock situations, etc.; secular and religious works of all nations and epochs. "Generous and thoroughly documented researches," Outlook. "Solid studies of influences and playwrights and periods," London Times. Index. Bibliography. xi + 679pp. 5⅜ x 8. **T693 Paperbound $2.75**

A SOURCE BOOK IN THEATRICAL HISTORY (SOURCES OF THEATRICAL HISTORY), A. M. Nagler. Over 2000 years of actors, directors, designers, critics, and spectators speak for themselves in this potpourri of writings selected from the great and formative periods of western drama. On-the-spot descriptions of masks, costumes, makeup, rehearsals, special effects, acting methods, backstage squabbles, theatres, etc. Contemporary glimpses of Molière rehearsing his company, an exhortation to a Roman audience to buy refreshments and keep quiet, Goethe's rules for actors, Belasco telling of $6500 he spent building a river, Restoration actors being told to avoid "lewd, obscene, or indecent postures," and much more. Each selection has an introduction by Prof. Nagler. This extraordinary, lively collection is ideal as a source of otherwise difficult to obtain material, as well as a fine book for browsing. Over 80 illustrations. 10 diagrams. xxiii + 611pp. 5⅜ x 8. **T515 Paperbound $3.00**

CATALOGUE OF DOVER BOOKS

WORLD DRAMA, B. H. Clark. The dramatic creativity of a score of ages and eras — all in two handy compact volumes. Over ⅓ of this material is unavailable in any other current edition! 46 plays from Ancient Greece, Rome, Medieval Europe, France, Germany, Italy, England, Russia, Scandinavia, India, China, Japan, etc. — including classic authors like Aeschylus, Sophocles, Euripides, Aristophanes, Plautus, Marlowe, Jonson, Farquhar, Goldsmith, Cervantes, Molière, Dumas, Goethe, Schiller, Ibsen, and many others. This creative collection avoids hackneyed material and includes only completely first-rate works which are relatively little known or difficult to obtain. "The most comprehensive collection of important plays from all literature available in English," SAT. REV. OF LITERATURE. Introduction. Reading lists. 2 volumes. 1364pp. 5⅜ x 8.　　　　　　　　　　　　　　　　Vol. 1, T57 Paperbound **$2.50**
Vol. 2, T59 Paperbound **$2.50**

MASTERPIECES OF THE RUSSIAN DRAMA, edited with introduction by G. R. Noyes. This only comprehensive anthology of Russian drama ever published in English offers complete texts, in 1st-rate modern translations, of 12 plays covering 200 years. Vol. 1: "The Young Hopeful," Fonvisin; "Wit Works Woe," Griboyedov; "The Inspector General," Gogol; "A Month in the Country," Turgenev; "The Poor Bride," Ostrovsky; "A Bitter Fate," Pisemsky. Vol. 2: "The Death of Ivan the Terrible," Alexey Tolstoy "The Power of Darkness," Lev Tolstoy; "The Lower Depths," Gorky; "The Cherry Orchard," Chekhov; "Professor Storitsyn," Andreyev; "Mystery Bouffe," Mayakovsky. Bibliography. Total of 902pp. 5⅜ x 8.
Vol. 1 T647 Paperbound **$2.25**
Vol. 2 T648 Paperbound **$2.00**

EUGENE O'NEILL: THE MAN AND HIS PLAYS, B. H. Clark. Introduction to O'Neill's life and work. Clark analyzes each play from the early THE WEB to the recently produced MOON FOR THE MISBEGOTTEN and THE ICEMAN COMETH revealing the environmental and dramatic influences necessary for a complete understanding of these important works. Bibliography. Appendices. Index. ix + 182pp. 5⅜ x 8.　　　　　　　　T379 Paperbound **$1.35**

THE HEART OF THOREAU'S JOURNALS, edited by O. Shepard. The best general selection from Thoreau's voluminous (and rare) journals. This intimate record of thoughts and observations reveals the full Thoreau and his intellectual development more accurately than any of his published works: self-conflict between the scientific observer and the poet, reflections on transcendental philosophy, involvement in the tragedies of neighbors and national causes, etc. New preface, notes, introductions. xii + 228pp. 5⅜ x 8.　　　　T741 Paperbound **$1.50**

H. D. THOREAU: A WRITER'S JOURNAL, edited by L. Stapleton. A unique new selection from the Journals concentrating on Thoreau's growth as a conscious literary artist, the ideals and purposes of his art. Most of the material has never before appeared outside of the complete 14-volume edition. Contains vital insights on Thoreau's projected book on Concord, thoughts on the nature of men and government, indignation with slavery, sources of inspiration, goals in life. Index. xxxiii + 234pp. 5⅜ x 8.　　　　　　　　T678 Paperbound **$1.65**

THE HEART OF EMERSON'S JOURNALS, edited by Bliss Perry. Best of these revealing Journals, originally 10 volumes, presented in a one volume edition. Talks with Channing, Hawthorne, Thoreau, and Bronson Alcott; impressions of Webster, Everett, John Brown, and Lincoln; records of moments of sudden understanding, vision, and solitary ecstasy. "The essays do not reveal the power of Emerson's mind . . . as do these hasty and informal writings," N.Y. Times. Preface by Bliss Perry. Index. xiii + 357pp. 5⅜ x 8.　　T477 Paperbound **$1.85**

FOUNDERS OF THE MIDDLE AGES, E. K. Rand. This is the best non-technical discussion of the transformation of Latin pagan culture into medieval civilization. Covering such figures as Tertullian, Gregory, Jerome, Boethius, Augustine, the Neoplatonists, and many other literary men, educators, classicists, and humanists, this book is a storehouse of information presented clearly and simply for the intelligent non-specialist. "Thoughtful, beautifully written," AMERICAN HISTORICAL REVIEW. "Extraordinarily accurate," Richard McKeon, THE NATION. ix + 365pp. 5⅜ x 8.　　　　　　　　　　　　　　　　T369 Paperbound **$2.00**

PLAY-MAKING: A MANUAL OF CRAFTSMANSHIP, William Archer. With an extensive, new introduction by John Gassner, Yale Univ. The permanently essential requirements of solid play construction are set down in clear, practical language: theme, exposition, foreshadowing, tension, obligatory scene, peripety, dialogue, character, psychology, other topics. This book has been one of the most influential elements in the modern theatre, and almost everything said on the subject since is contained explicitly or implicitly within its covers. Bibliography. Index. xlii + 277pp. 5⅜ x 8.　　　　　　　　　　　　　　　　T651 Paperbound **$1.75**

HAMBURG DRAMATURGY, G. E. Lessing. One of the most brilliant of German playwrights of the eighteenth-century age of criticism analyzes the complex of theory and tradition that constitutes the world of theater. These 104 essays on aesthetic theory helped demolish the regime of French classicism, opening the door to psychological and social realism, romanticism. Subjects include the original functions of tragedy; drama as the rational world; the meaning of pity and fear, and fear as means for purgation and other Aristotelian concepts; genius and creative force; interdependence of poet's language and actor's interpretation; truth and authenticity; etc. A basic and enlightening study for anyone interested in aesthetics and ideas, from the philosopher to the theatergoer. Introduction by Prof. Victor Lange. xxii + 265pp. 4½ x 6⅜.　　　　　　　　　　　　T32 Paperbound **$1.45**

Language Books and Records

GERMAN: HOW TO SPEAK AND WRITE IT. AN INFORMAL CONVERSATIONAL METHOD FOR SELF STUDY, Joseph Rosenberg. Eminently useful for self study because of concentration on elementary stages of learning. Also provides teachers with remarkable variety of aids: 28 full- and double-page sketches with pertinent items numbered and identified in German and English; German proverbs, jokes; grammar, idiom studies; extensive practice exercises. The most interesting introduction to German available, full of amusing illustrations, photographs of cities and landmarks in German-speaking cities, cultural information subtly woven into conversational material. Includes summary of grammar, guide to letter writing, study guide to German literature by Dr. Richard Friedenthal. Index. 400 illustrations. 384pp. 5⅜ x 8½.
T271 Paperbound $2.00

FRENCH: HOW TO SPEAK AND WRITE IT. AN INFORMAL CONVERSATIONAL METHOD FOR SELF STUDY, Joseph Lemaitre. Even the absolute beginner can acquire a solid foundation for further study from this delightful elementary course. Photographs, sketches and drawings, sparkling colloquial conversations on a wide variety of topics (including French culture and custom), French sayings and quips, are some of aids used to demonstrate rather than merely describe the language. Thorough yet surprisingly entertaining approach, excellent for teaching and for self study. Comprehensive analysis of pronunciation, practice exercises and appendices of verb tables, additional vocabulary, other useful material. Index. Appendix. 400 illustrations. 416pp. 5⅜ x 8½.
T268 Paperbound $2.00

DICTIONARY OF SPOKEN SPANISH, Spanish-English, English-Spanish. Compiled from spoken Spanish, emphasizing idiom and colloquial usage in both Castilian and Latin-American. More than 16,000 entries containing over 25,000 idioms—the largest list of idiomatic constructions ever published. Complete sentences given, indexed under single words—language in immediately useable form, for travellers, businessmen, students, etc. 25 page introduction provides rapid survey of sounds, grammar, syntax, with full consideration of irregular verbs. Especially apt in modern treatment of phrases and structure. 17 page glossary gives translations of geographical names, money values, numbers, national holidays, important street signs, useful expressions of high frequency, plus unique 7 page glossary of Spanish and Spanish-American foods and dishes. Originally published as War Department Technical Manual TM 30-900. iv + 513pp. 5⅜ x 8.
T495 Paperbound $1.75

SPEAK MY LANGUAGE: SPANISH FOR YOUNG BEGINNERS, M. Ahlman, Z. Gilbert. Records provide one of the best, and most entertaining, methods of introducing a foreign language to children. Within the framework of a train trip from Portugal to Spain, an English-speaking child is introduced to Spanish by a native companion. (Adapted from a successful radio program of the N. Y. State Educational Department.) Though a continuous story, there are a dozen specific categories of expressions, including greetings, numbers, time, weather, food, clothes, family members, etc. Drill is combined with poetry and contextual use. Authentic background music is heard. An accompanying book enables a reader to follow the records, and includes a vocabulary of over 350 recorded expressions. Two 10″ 33⅓ records, total of 40 minutes. Book. 40 illustrations. 69pp. 5¼ x 10½.
T890 The set $4.95

AN ENGLISH-FRENCH-GERMAN-SPANISH WORD FREQUENCY DICTIONARY, H. S. Eaton. An indispensable language study aid, this is a semantic frequency list of the 6000 most frequently used words in 4 languages—24,000 words in all. The lists, based on concepts rather than words alone, and containing all modern, exact, and idiomatic vocabulary, are arranged side by side to form a unique 4-language dictionary. A simple key indicates the importance of the individual words within each language. Over 200 pages of separate indexes for each language enable you to locate individual words at a glance. Will help language teachers and students, authors of textbooks, grammars, and language tests to compare concepts in the various languages and to concentrate on basic vocabulary, avoiding uncommon and obsolete words. 2 Appendixes. xxi + 441pp. 6½ x 9¼.
T738 Paperbound $2.75

NEW RUSSIAN-ENGLISH AND ENGLISH-RUSSIAN DICTIONARY, M. A. O'Brien. Over 70,000 entries in the new orthography! Many idiomatic uses and colloquialisms which form the basis of actual speech. Irregular verbs, perfective and imperfective aspects, regular and irregular sound changes, and other features. One of the few dictionaries where accent changes within the conjugation of verbs and the declension of nouns are fully indicated. "One of the best," Prof. E. J. Simmons, Cornell. First names, geographical terms, bibliography, etc. 738pp. 4½ x 6¼.
T208 Paperbound $2.00

96 MOST USEFUL PHRASES FOR TOURISTS AND STUDENTS in English, French, Spanish, German, Italian. A handy folder you'll want to carry with you. How to say "Excuse me," "How much is it?", "Write it down, please," etc., in four foreign languages. Copies limited, no more than 1 to a customer. **FREE**

Trubner Colloquial Manuals

These unusual books are members of the famous Trubner series of colloquial manuals. They have been written to provide adults with a sound colloquial knowledge of a foreign language, and are suited for either class use or self-study. Each book is a complete course in itself, with progressive, easy to follow lessons. Phonetics, grammar, and syntax are covered, while hundreds of phrases and idioms, reading texts, exercises, and vocabulary are included. These books are unusual in being neither skimpy nor overdetailed in grammatical matters, and in presenting up-to-date, colloquial, and practical phrase material. Bilingual presentation is stressed, to make thorough self-study easier for the reader.

COLLOQUIAL HINDUSTANI, A. H. Harley, formerly Nizam's Reader in Urdu, U. of London. 30 pages on phonetics and scripts (devanagari & Arabic-Persian) are followed by 29 lessons, including material on English and Arabic-Persian influences. Key to all exercises. Vocabulary. 5 x 7½. 147pp. Clothbound $1.75

COLLOQUIAL PERSIAN, L. P. Elwell-Sutton. Best introduction to modern Persian, with 90 page grammatical section followed by conversations, 35-page vocabulary. 139pp.
Clothbound $2.25

COLLOQUIAL ARABIC, DeLacy O'Leary. Foremost Islamic scholar covers language of Egypt, Syria, Palestine, & Northern Arabia. Extremely clear coverage of complex Arabic verbs & noun plurals; also cultural aspects of language. Vocabulary. xviii + 192pp. 5 x 7½.
Clothbound $2.50

COLLOQUIAL GERMAN, P. F. Doring. Intensive thorough coverage of grammar in easily-followed form. Excellent for brush-up, with hundreds of colloquial phrases. 34 pages of bilingual texts. 224pp. 5 x 7½. Clothbound $2.00

COLLOQUIAL SPANISH, W. R. Patterson. Castilian grammar and colloquial language, loaded with bilingual phrases and colloquialisms. Excellent for review or self-study. 164pp. 5 x 7½.
Clothbound $2.00

COLLOQUIAL FRENCH, W. R. Patterson. 16th revision of this extremely popular manual. Grammar explained with model clarity, and hundreds of useful expressions and phrases; exercises, reading texts, etc. Appendixes of new and useful words and phrases. 223pp. 5 x 7½.
Clothbound $2.00

COLLOQUIAL CZECH, J. Schwarz, former headmaster of Lingua Institute, Prague. Full easily followed coverage of grammar, hundreds of immediately useable phrases, texts. Perhaps the best Czech grammar in print. "An absolutely successful textbook," JOURNAL OF CZECHO-SLOVAK FORCES IN GREAT BRITAIN. 252pp. 5 x 7½. Clothbound $3.00

COLLOQUIAL RUMANIAN, G. Nandris, Professor of University of London. Extremely thorough coverage of phonetics, grammar, syntax; also included 70-page reader, and 70-page vocabulary. Probably the best grammar for this increasingly important language. 340pp. 5 x 7½.
Clothbound $2.75

COLLOQUIAL ITALIAN, A. L. Hayward. Excellent self-study course in grammar, vocabulary, idioms, and reading. Easy progressive lessons will give a good working knowledge of Italian in the shortest possible time. 5 x 7½. Clothbound $1.75

COLLOQUIAL TURKISH, Yusuf Mardin. Very clear, thorough introduction to leading cultural and economic language of Near East. Begins with pronunciation and statement of vowel harmony, then 36 lessons present grammar, graded vocabulary, useful phrases, dialogues, reading, exercises. Key to exercises at rear. Turkish-English vocabulary. All in Roman alphabet. x + 288pp. 4¾ x 7¼. Clothbound $4.00

DUTCH-ENGLISH AND ENGLISH-DUTCH DICTIONARY, F. G. Renier. For travel, literary, scientific or business Dutch, you will find this the most convenient, practical and comprehensive dictionary on the market. More than 60,000 entries, shades of meaning, colloquialisms, idioms, compounds and technical terms. Dutch and English strong and irregular verbs. This is the only dictionary in its size and price range that indicates the gender of nouns. New orthography. xvii + 571pp. 5½ x 6¼. T224 Clothbound $2.75

LEARN DUTCH, F. G. Renier. This book is the most satisfactory and most easily used grammar of modern Dutch. The student is gradually led from simple lessons in pronunciation, through translation from and into Dutch, and finally to a mastery of spoken and written Dutch. Grammatical principles are clearly explained while a useful, practical vocabulary is introduced in easy exercises and readings. It is used and recommended by the Fulbright Committee in the Netherlands. Phonetic appendices. Over 1200 exercises; Dutch-English, English-Dutch vocabularies. 181pp. 4¼ x 7¼. T441 Clothbound $2.25

Orientalia

ORIENTAL RELIGIONS IN ROMAN PAGANISM, F. Cumont. A study of the cultural meeting of east and west in the Early Roman Empire. It covers the most important eastern religions of the time from their first appearance in Rome, 204 B.C., when the Great Mother of the Gods was first brought over from Syria. The ecstatic cults of Syria and Phrygia — Cybele, Attis, Adonis, their orgies and mutilatory rites; the mysteries of Egypt — Serapis, Isis, Osiris, the dualism of Persia, the elevation of cosmic evil to equal stature with the deity, Mithra; worship of Hermes Trismegistus; Ishtar, Astarte; the magic of the ancient Near East, etc. Introduction. 55pp. of notes; extensive bibliography. Index. xxiv + 298pp. 5⅜ x 8.
T321 Paperbound **$2.00**

THE MYSTERIES OF MITHRA, F. Cumont. The definitive coverage of a great ideological struggle between the west and the orient in the first centuries of the Christian era. The origin of Mithraism, a Persian mystery religion, and its association with the Roman army is discussed in detail. Then utilizing fragmentary monuments and texts, in one of the greatest feats of scholarly detection, Dr. Cumont reconstructs the mystery teachings and secret doctrines, the hidden organization and cult of Mithra. Mithraic art is discussed, analyzed, and depicted in 70 illustrations. 239pp. 5⅜ x 8.
T323 Paperbound **$2.00**

CHRISTIAN AND ORIENTAL PHILOSOPHY OF ART, A. K. Coomaraswamy. A unique fusion of philosopher, orientalist, art historian, and linguist, the author discusses such matters as: the true function of aesthetics in art, the importance of symbolism, intellectual and philosophic backgrounds, the role of traditional culture in enriching art, common factors in all great art, the nature of medieval art, the nature of folklore, the beauty of mathematics, and similar topics. 2 illustrations. Bibliography. 148pp. 5⅜ x 8.
T378 Paperbound **$1.50**

TRANSFORMATION OF NATURE IN ART, A. K. Coomaraswamy. Unabridged reissue of a basic work upon Asiatic religious art and philosophy of religion. The theory of religious art in Asia and Medieval Europe (exemplified by Meister Eckhart) is analyzed and developed. Detailed consideration is given to Indian medieval aesthetic manuals, symbolic language in philosophy, the origin and use of images in India, and many other fascinating and little known topics. Glossaries of Sanskrit and Chinese terms. Bibliography. 41pp. of notes. 245pp. 5⅜ x 8.
T368 Paperbound **$1.75**

BUDDHIST LOGIC, F.Th. Stcherbatsky. A study of an important part of Buddhism usually ignored by other books on the subject: the Mahayana buddhistic logic of the school of Dignaga and his followers. First vol. devoted to history of Indian logic with Central Asian continuations, detailed exposition of Dignaga system, including theory of knowledge, the sensible world (causation, perception, ultimate reality) and mental world (judgment, inference, logical fallacies, the syllogism), reality of external world, and negation (law of contradiction, universals, dialectic). Vol. II contains translation of Dharmakirti's Nyayabindu with Dharmamottara's commentary. Appendices cover translations of Tibetan treatises on logic, Hindu attacks on Buddhist logic, etc. The basic work, one of the products of the great St. Petersburg school of Indian studies. Written clearly and with an awareness of Western philosophy and logic; meant for the Asian specialist and for the general reader with only a minimum of background. Vol. I, xii + 559pp. Vol. II, viii + 468pp. 5⅜ x 8½.
T955 Vol. I Paperbound **$2.50**
T956 Vol. II Paperbound **$2.50**
The set **$5.00**

THE TEXTS OF TAOISM. The first inexpensive edition of the complete James Legge translations of the Tao Te King and the writings of Chinese mystic Chuang Tse. Also contains several shorter treatises: the T'ai Shang Tractate of Actions and Their Retributions; the King Kang King, or Classic of Purity; the Yin Fu King, or Classic of the Harmony of the Seen and Unseen; the Yu Shu King, or Classic of the Pivot of Jade; and the Hsia Yung King, or Classic of the Directory for a Day. While there are other translations of the Tao Te King, this is the only translation of Chuang Tse and much of other material. Extensive introduction discusses differences between Taoism, Buddhism, Confucianism; authenticity and arrangement of Tao Te King and writings of Chuang Tse; the meaning of the Tao and basic tenets of Taoism; historical accounts of Lao-tse and followers; other pertinent matters. Clarifying notes incorporated into text. Originally published as Volumes 39, 40 of SACRED BOOKS OF THE EAST series, this has long been recognized as an indispensable collection. Sinologists, philosophers, historians of religion of course be interested and anyone with an elementary course in Oriental religion or philosophy will understand and profit from these writings. Index. Appendix analyzing thought of Chuang Tse. Vol. I, xxiii + 396pp. Vol. II, viii + 340pp. 5⅜ x 8½.
T990 Vol. I Paperbound **$2.25**
T991 Vol. II Paperbound **$2.25**

CATALOGUE OF DOVER BOOKS

EPOCHS OF CHINESE AND JAPANESE ART, Ernest T. Fenollosa. Although this classic of art history was written before the archeological discovery of Shang and Chou civilizations, it is still in many respects the finest detailed study of Chinese and Japanese art available in English. It is very wide in range, covering sculpture, carving, painting, metal work, ceramics, textiles, graphic arts and other areas, and it considers both religious and secular art, including the Japanese woodcut. Its greatest strength, however, lies in its extremely full, detailed, insight-laden discussion of historical and cultural background, and in its analysis of the religious and philosophical implications of art works. It is also a brilliant stylistic achievement, written with enthusiasm and verve, which can be enjoyed and read with profit by both the Orientalist and the general reader who is interested in art. Index. Glossary of proper names. 242 illustrations. Total of 704 pages. 5⅜ x 8½.

T364-5 Two vol. set, paperbound **$5.00**

THE VEDANTA SUTRAS OF BADARAYANA WITH COMMENTARY BY SANKARACHARYA. The definitive translation of the consummation, foremost interpretation of Upanishads. Originally part of SACRED BOOKS OF THE EAST, this two-volume translation includes exhaustive commentary and exegesis by Sankara; 128-page introduction by translator, Prof. Thibaut, that discusses background, scope and purpose of the sutras, value and importance of Sankara's interpretation; copious footnotes providing further explanations. Every serious student of Indian religion or thought, philosophers, historians of religion should read these clear, accurate translations of documents central to development of important thought systems in the East. Unabridged republication of Volumes 34, 38 of the Sacred Books of the East. Translated by George Thibault. General index, index of quotations and of Sanskrit. Vol. I, cxxv + 448pp. Vol. II, iv + 506pp. 5⅜ x 8½.

T994 Vol. I Paperbound **$2.00**
T995 Vol. II Paperbound **$2.00**

THE UPANISHADS. The Max Müller translation of the twelve classical Upanishads available for the first time in an inexpensive format: Chandogya, Kena, Aitareya aranyaka and upanishad, Kaushitaki, Isa, Katha, Mundaka, Taittiriyaka Brhadaranyaka, Svetarasvatara. Prasna — all of the classical Upanishads of the Vedanta school—and the Maitriyana Upanishad. Originally volumes 1, 15 of SACRED BOOKS OF THE EAST series, this is still the most scholarly translation. Prof. Müller, probably most important Sanskritologist of nineteenth century, provided invaluable introduction that acquaints readers with history of Upanishad translations, age and chronology of texts, etc. and a preface that discusses their value to Western readers. Heavily annotated. Stimulating reading for anyone with even only a basic course background in Oriental philosophy, religion, necessary to all Indologists, philosophers, religious historians. Transliteration and pronunciation guide. Vol. I, ciii + 320pp. Vol. II, liii + 350pp.

T992 Vol. I Paperbound **$2.25**
T993 Vol. II Paperbound **$2.25**
The set **$4.50**

Prices subject to change without notice.

Dover publishes books on art, music, philosophy, literature, languages, history, social sciences, psychology, handcrafts, orientalia, puzzles and entertainments, chess, pets and gardens, books explaining science, intermediate and higher mathematics, mathematical physics, engineering, biological sciences, earth sciences, classics of science, etc. Write to:

Dept. catrr.
Dover Publications, Inc.
180 Varick Street, N.Y. 14, N.Y.